International Business:
A Canadian Perspective

International Business: A Canadian Perspective

K. C. Dhawan
Concordia University

Hamid Etemad
McGill University

Richard W. Wright
McGill University

Addison-Wesley Publishers
Don Mills, Ontario • Reading, Massachusetts • Menlo Park, California
Amsterdam • London • Manila • Paris • Sydney • Singapore • Tokyo

Canadian Cataloguing in Publication Data

Main entry under title:

International Business: a Canadian perspective

ISBN 0-201-08582-8

1. Canada - Commerce - Addresses, essays, lectures.
I. Dhawan, K. C., 1937-   II. Etemad, Hamid.
III. Wright, Richard W.

HF3226.5.I57   382'.0971   C81-094658-0

Cover and Book Design:
Blair Kerrigan/Glyphics

ISBN 0-201-08582-8

Printed in Canada

    B C D E F - WC - 86 85 84

Contributors

Talaat Abdel-Malek
University of Saskatchewan

D. M. Astwood
Department of Industry, Trade, and Commerce

Peter M. Banting
McMaster University

Sonja A. Bata
Director, Bata Limited

Carl E. Beigie
President, C. D. Howe Institute

Paul Bishop
University of Western Ontario

Herman P. Bones
Ministry of State for Science and Technology

A. L. Calvet
University of Ottawa

Edward A. Carmichael
The Conference Board of Canada

Harold Crookell
University of Western Ontario

Camille A. Dagenais
Chairman and Chief Executive Officer, The SNC Group

Donald J. Daly
York University

G. H. Dewhirst
Foreign Investment Review Agency

K. C. Dhawan
Concordia University

Economic Council of Canada

Hamid Etemad
McGill University

Export Promotion Review Committee

Nicholas J. Fodor
President, Electrovert Ltd.

Joan Gherson
Foreign Investment Review Agency

Steven Globerman
York University

Ian Graham
Graham Fiber Glass Limited

Gilles Gratton
Editor, L'investisseur étranger

Mel Hurtig
President, Hurtig Publishers Ltd.

J. Peter Killing
University of Western Ontario

V. H. Kirpalani
Concordia University

Ursula Kobel
Canadian Pacific Enterprises Limited

Lawrence Kryzanowski
Concordia University

Isaiah A. Litvak
York University

N. B. Macintosh
Queen's University

Stephen P. Magee
University of Texas at Austin

Christopher J. Maule
Carleton University

Carl H. McMillan
Carleton University

Charles J. McMillan
York University

Herbert E. Meyer

J. Alex Murray
University of Windsor

Bertin Nadeau
President, La Société Nadeau Limitée

Jacques Prefontaine
University of Sherbrooke

Randolph E. Ross
McMaster University

Alan M. Rugman
Dalhousie University

David Rutenberg
Queen's University

Science Council of Canada

Roger Y. W. Tang
University of Calgary

Bert Twaalfhoven
President, N. V. Indivers

Mark Witten
Freelance writer

Richard W. Wright
McGill University

Acknowledgements

It has often been mentioned by Canadian academic faculty that textbooks and cases used in several courses offered by Canadian business administration faculties are of U.S. origin; therefore the usefulness of the foreign texts and cases is limited in scope, particularly when faculty members are trying to develop analytical skills from a Canadian perspective for their students. This limitation is much more accentuated in view of the increasing number of offerings of international business courses at Canadian Universities. Canadian business executives also have complained about lack of Canadian materials for their practical use for international markets.

Given the challenge to Canadianize international business courses offered by Canadian business administration faculties, the authors of this textbook embarked upon a pioneering project in June 1980 to develop text, cases, and related readings with Canadian orientation. To meet this objective, we sought materials from Canadian academics, business executives, and government officials. Enthusiastic response from these sources has culminated in the collection of chapters included in this book; eleven cases from a Canadian viewpoint are included as well.

We are hopeful that Canadian students, faculty, executives, and government officials will find this book a useful addition to the literature of international business. Furthermore, foreign communities interested in Canada, will be able to get an insight into Canadian thinking on the various topics covered in the book.

We take this opportunity to express our gratitude to all the contributors to this book. We also express our thanks to Ms. Susan Regan (of Concordia University) for her assistance in editing the manuscript, Mrs. Eva Cucinelli, and Miss Stella Scalia (of McGill University) for their typing and other assistance in preparing the manuscript.

Finally, we are thankful to our publisher, Addison-Wesley (Canada) Limited, and in particular, Messrs. Frank Burns, Ronald Doleman, and Al Reynolds for their painstaking efforts in bringing out this book and assisting us in Canadianizing our international business course materials.

K. C. Dhawan
Concordia University

Montreal
August 10, 1981

Hamid Etemad
Richard W. Wright
McGill University

Contents

Part IV: Foreign Direct Investment Theory, Impact, and Control

Part V: International Operations Management

Part VI: Cases

I
Introduction

1
Canada in the World Economy

International Dimensions of Canada's Economy

Very few countries are more openly linked to the international economy than Canada. Nearly one-quarter of all the goods that Canadians consume are imported from other countries, and more than 25 per cent of Canada's gross national product (GNP) is exported abroad. Investment flows in and out of Canada also are of enormous importance. Much of Canada's domestic capital investment has been financed by borrowing in foreign capital markets. Foreign-owned companies have made direct investments (involving participation in control and management) to the extent that more than half of Canada's manufacturing capacity is owned by foreigners. At the same time, Canadian-owned companies control over US $11 billion of productive assets in other countries. In addition to their major involvement in international trade and investment flows, Canadian companies are engaged increasingly in a variety of other kinds of international activities, such as the export of capital projects. In this chapter, the nature and significance of Canadian international business patterns are discussed, and comparisons are made with other countries.

International Trade Patterns

The aggregate value of the goods and services exported by free world countries grew from US $281.8 billion in 1970 to over US $1.5 trillion in 1979 (Table 1). Canada's exports in 1979 were worth Can $65.2 billion, less than four per cent of the free world total (Appendix 1 and Table 2).

While Canada's exports may not seem very large in proportion to the world total, they are extremely significant in relation to the size of Canada's domestic economy. As seen in Table 3, exports as a proportion of Canada's GNP grew from 19.6 per cent in 1970 to 25.2 per cent in 1979. Among Canada's major trading partners, only the Netherlands has a greater dependence on exports than Canada.

Similarly, Canada's imports, although smaller than those of many countries in absolute terms, are of vital importance in relation to the size of the domestic economy. As seen in Table 3, imports as a proportion of Canadian GNP rose from only 16.3 per cent in 1970 to 24.1 per cent in 1979, among the highest of the world's major trading countries.

Table 1

Free World Exports

Period	Free World[a] total	Total	Developed Countries United States and Canada	Western Europe	Other	Developing Countries Total	OPEC[b]	Other
	Value in billions of dollars							
1970	281.8	227.6	60.0	138.9	28.7	54.3	17.4	36.9
1975	791.4	587.1	141.7	366.7	78.7	204.2	110.3	93.9
1976	900.8	652.1	155.6	405.2	91.3	248.7	133.8	114.9
1977	1,023.5	740.3	164.8	467.9	107.6	283.3	146.9	136.4
1978	1,185.5	888.3	192.1	566.9	129.3	297.8	143.0	154.8
1979	1,498.1	1,091.2	240.0	707.2	144.0	406.2	209.5	196.7
	Percentage change from preceding year							
1976	13.8	11.1	9.8	10.5	16.0	21.8	21.3	22.4
1977	13.6	13.5	5.9	15.5	17.9	13.9	9.8	18.7
1978	15.8	20.0	16.6	21.2	20.2	5.1	−2.7	13.5
1979	26.4	22.8	24.9	24.7	11.4	36.4	46.5	27.1
1980								

Notes:
(a) Free world includes all countries except Albania, Bulgaria, Czechoslovakia, German Democratic Republic, Hungary, Poland, Romania, USSR, People's Republic of China, North Korea, Vietnam, Outer Mongolia and Cuba.
(b) OPEC includes Algeria, Ecuador, Gabon, Indonesia, Iraq, Iran, Kuwait, Libya, Nigeria, Qatar, Saudi Arabia, United Arab Emirates, and Venezuela.

Source: U.S. Department of Commerce, International Trade Administration, "International Economic Indicators", **VI**, No. 4 (December 1980).

Table 2

Shares of Free World Exports: Selected Countries

Period	United States	France	F.R. Germany	Italy	Nether- lands	United Kingdom	Japan	Canada
	Per cent							
1970	15.4	6.4	12.1	4.7	4.2	7.0	6.9	5.9
1975	13.6	6.7	11.4	4.4	4.4	5.6	7.1	4.3
1976	12.8	6.3	11.3	4.1	4.5	5.2	7.5	4.5
1977	11.8	6.4	11.5	4.4	4.3	5.7	7.9	4.3
1978	12.1	6.7	12.0	4.7	4.2	6.0	8.3	4.1
1979	12.1	6.7	11.5	4.8	4.3	6.1	6.8	3.9

Notes:
1. Free world includes all countries except Albania, Bulgaria, Czechoslovakia, German Democratic Republic, Hungary, Poland, Romania, U.S.S.R., People's Republic of China, North Korea, Vietnam, Outer Mongolia, and Cuba.
2. Shares in export markets for total trade are measured as percentages of total exports from the free world. The percentage shares are based on values in U.S. dollars calculated at current exchange rates.
3. World exports are defined as the sums of exports from fifteen major industrial countries.

Source: U.S. Department of Commerce, International Trade Administration, "International Economic Indicators", **VI**, No. 4 (December 1980).

Table 3

International Trade as a Percentage of GNP: Selected Countries

Period	United States	France	F.R. Germany	Italy	Nether- lands	United Kingdom	Japan	Canada
			Ratio of Exports to GNP					
1970	4.3	12.7	18.4	14.2	37.0	15.8	9.5	19.6
1975	7.0	15.4	21.4	18.2	42.4	19.2	11.1	20.2
1976	6.7	15.9	22.8	20.0	44.1	20.8	11.9	20.1
1977	6.3	16.6	22.7	21.1	40.9	23.3	11.6	21.3
1978	6.6	16.1	22.0	21.4	38.5	22.7	10.0	23.2
1979	7.5	17.1	22.4	22.3	42.8	22.5	10.2	25.2
			Ratio of Imports to GNP					
1970	4.1	13.5	16.1	16.1	42.2	17.8	9.2	16.3
1975	6.3	15.9	17.8	20.1	43.0	23.2	11.5	21.0
1976	7.1	18.4	19.7	23.3	44.4	25.1	11.5	19.6
1977	7.8	18.4	19.5	22.4	43.6	25.8	10.3	20.3
1978	8.1	17.3	18.8	21.5	41.3	24.9	8.2	21.8
1979	8.7	18.8	20.8	24.0	45.8	25.5	10.9	24.1

Note: Ratios of exports and imports to GNP or GDP and production are measured in terms of current prices. Production covers all goods organizing in agriculture, forestry, hunting, fishing, mining, quarrying, and manufacturing — that is, the sum of national accounts industry components on a value added basis excluding transportation, wholesaling, retailing, other services, and government enterprises. The U.S. production series for all goods is comparable to that for other countries.

Source: U.S. Department of Commerce, International Trade Administration, "International Economic Indicators", **VI**, No. 4 (December 1980).

The geographic distribution of Canada's exports and imports is highly concentrated. The United States is overwhelmingly the primary purchaser of Canadian exports, taking 67.9 per cent in 1979 (Table 4). Similarly, the United States supplies 72.4 per cent of the goods and services which Canadians import. The European Economic Community (EEC) as a region is also important in Canada's external trade, although Japan has replaced the United Kingdom as Canada's second largest individual trading partner after the United States (Table 4).

Canada's exports and imports are highly concentrated into certain economic sectors. The exports consist mainly of primary goods such as agricultural products (wheat, beef, etc.) and raw materials (petroleum, metals, timber, etc.). Canadian imports, on the other hand, consist overwhelmingly of manufactured products. Concerns raised by this apparent imbalance between the nature of Canada's exports and imports, and proposals to modify the mix, are discussed at length in this book. A detailed breakdown of the composition of Canadian exports and imports is presented in Appendix II at the end of this chapter.

Table 4

Canada's Export and Import Markets
Export Markets

	U.S.A.	Japan	U.K.	Other EEC[a]	Other
	(% of total Canadian exports)				
1975	65.1	6.4	5.5	7.2	15.8
1976	67.3	6.2	4.9	7.0	14.6
1977	69.8	5.7	4.4	6.2	13.9
1978	70.2	5.8	3.8	5.6	14.6
1979	67.9	6.2	4.0	7.1	14.8

Import Sources

	U.S.A.	Japan	U.K.	Other EEC[a]	Other
	(% of total Canadian imports)				
1975	68.1	3.5	3.5	6.0	18.9
1976	68.8	4.1	3.1	5.3	18.7
1977	70.4	4.2	3.0	5.6	16.8
1978	70.7	4.5	3.2	6.1	15.5
1979	72.4	3.4	3.1	5.8	15.3

(a) European Economic Community

Source: Bank of Montreal, *Business Review* (December 1980), p. 4.

International Investment Patterns
Financial flows in and out of Canada are of major importance to the Canadian economy. International financial flows take two major forms: *indirect* or portfolio investments, which are usually arm's length lending or borrowing transactions *not* involving direct participation in control or management; and foreign *direct* investment (FDI), in which a firm acquires at least partial control and participation in the management of an affiliated firm abroad.

Canada's net international financial indebtedness at the end of 1979 totalled $69 billion, calculated as follows[1]:

Canada's Liabilities to Foreigners $135 billion

(Includes foreign direct investment in Canadian industry and resources, retained earnings of foreign controlled companies in Canada, and foreign investment in Canadian bonds, debentures, bank deposits, stocks, treasury bills, and other capital market securities.)

1. *Financial Times*, (January 26, 1981), p. 22, based on *Canada's Investment Position, 1977*, Statistics Canada Catalogue No. 67-202 (January 1981).

Canadian International Assets $ 66 billion

(Includes investments in foreign businesses, stocks,
bonds, treasury bills, foreign currencies and retained
earnings of Canadian-owned companies operating in
foreign countries.)

Net indebtedness $ 69 billion

Of the various forms of international financial movements, *direct*
investment flows are of particular significance, as they represent
direct control of productive assets in one country by firms located
elsewhere. Canada is unique among the major countries of the world
in the extent of foreign ownership of its domestic economic capacity: $39.8 billion of productive assets in Canada, or some 58 per
cent of Canada's manufacturing capacity, were owned by firms in
other countries as of 1972 (Table 5). About 80 per cent of the
foreign ownership is of U.S. origin, clustered mainly in manufacturing
and natural resources (Appendix III). The complex problems raised
by the high degree of foreign ownership in Canada, and Canadian
approaches toward modifying these patterns, are considered at length
in the chapters that follow.

Table 5

Estimated Foreign-Controlled Shares of Selected Industries in Canada, Mexico, Brazil, Turkey, and India

Industry	Canada (1972) % of Foreign-Owned Assets	Mexico (1970) % of Sales by Foreign-Controlled Enterprises	Brazil (1974)(a) % of Foreign-Owned Assets	Turkey (1974) % of Foreign-Owned Assets	India (1973) % of Output by Foreign-Controlled Firms
Total Manufacturing	**58**	**28**	**29**	**41**	**13**
of which:					
Textiles	n.a.	n.a.	n.a.	74	n.a.
Food	n.a.	n.a.	31	58}	n.a.
Tobacco	n.a.	80	99		n.a.
Paper	53	27	n.a.	56	n.a.
Chemicals	88	67	n.a.	n.a.	33
Rubber	99	84	61	59	52
Electrical Machinery	74	79	61	54	n.a.
Non-Electrical Machinery	n.a.	62	n.a.	43	25
Transport Equipment	58	49	68}	n.a.	
Motor Vehicles	96	n.a.		38	10}

(a) Based on 5,113 non-financial enterprises.
  n.a. = not available or negligible.

Source: Adapted from U.N. Economic and Social Council, 1978, Tables III-59, III-60, and III-61.

The value of direct investments owned abroad by Canadian companies grew from US $3.7 billion in 1967 to US $11.1 billion in 1976 (Table 6 and Appendix IV). As with trade, Canadian foreign direct investments appear small in comparison with the world's total (3.9 per cent). But in relation to its domestic economic base, Canada is among the most prominent investing countries. Several Canadian firms rank among the major multinational companies of the world. The challenges in managing Canadian investments abroad are considered at length in this book.

Table 6

Stock of Direct Investment of Developed Market Economies

	Billions of Dollars			Percentages		
	1967	1971	1976	1967	1971	1976
United States	$56.6	$82.3	$137.2	53.8%	52.3%	47.6%
United Kingdom	17.5	23.7	32.1	16.6	15.0	11.2
West Germany	3.0	7.3	19.9	2.8	4.6	6.9
Japan	1.5	4.4	19.4	1.4	2.8	6.7
Switzerland	5.0	9.5	18.6	4.8	6.0	6.5
France	6.0	7.3	11.9	5.7	4.6	4.1
Canada	3.7	6.5	11.1	3.5	4.1	3.9
Netherlands	2.2	4.0	9.8	2.1	2.5	3.4
Sweden	1.7	2.4	5.0	1.6	1.5	1.7
Belgium-Luxembourg	2.0	2.4	3.6	1.9	1.5	1.2
Italy	2.1	3.0	2.9	2.0	1.9	1.0
Total above	**101.1**	**153.1**	**270.4**	**96.1**	**96.7**	**94.2**
All other (estimate)	4.0	5.1	16.8	3.8	3.2	5.8
Grand total	**105.1**	**158.2**	**287.2**	**100.0**	**100.0**	**100.0**

Source: United Nations, Centre on Transnational Corporations, *Transnational Corporations in World Development Re-examined*, 1978.

Capital Projects Abroad

An increasingly important part of Canada's international business activity is the export of manufactured products through major capital projects abroad, such as the construction of industrial processing plants or the installation of telecommunications systems. These projects involve much more than the mere export of machinery or parts: they require the Canadian firm's participation all the way from the conception of the project through the installation and commissioning of a complete, operational plant or system.

The export of manufactures and services via complete capital projects is assuming major world importance, particularly in the emerging less-developed regions and in the newly rich OPEC countries. Although Canadian exports of manufactures rose from US $9.7 billion in 1970 to US $30.2 billion in 1979 (Table 7), Canada's share has declined to only 3.2 per cent of the free world total (Table 8). As a result, two recent task forces — the Export Promotion Review Committee and the Special Committee of the House of Commons on a National Trading Company — have pointed to capital export projects as the most urgent priority for Canada's international business in the 1980s. The opportunities and problems for Canadian firms in securing such projects are examined in detail in this book.

The Balance of Payments
The cumulative effects of the international movements of goods, services, and financial flows are reflected in a country's balance of payments.

Appendix I gives an overview of Canada's international payments position for a number of years. The trade balance is the net sum of the value of Canada's imports and exports of physical goods (raw materials, semi-finished items, and manufactured products). The service accounts reflect mainly Canadians' purchases and sales of services (travel, transportation, consulting, license royalties, etc.) and of interest and dividend receipts from bonds and stocks which Canadians own abroad or payments on similar securities which foreigners own in Canada. After adjusting for unilateral (one-way) transfers, the current account balance reflects the net sum of the trade and service accounts. The capital accounts reflect the purchase or sale of bonds and stocks abroad by Canadians through direct or portfolio investments, and vice versa; and also official governmental loans and grants (such as foreign aid projects).

An examination of the summary balance of payments statement (Appendix I) reveals some significant trends:

1. Canada has enjoyed a favorable merchandise trade balance since 1970.
2. The current account is generally in deficit, indicating that Canadians are making net service payments abroad, mainly for travel, interest payments on loans from abroad, and royalties and dividends to the parent companies of foreign-owned subsidiaries in Canada.
3. The net movement of long-term capital flows is generally positive, mainly as a result of Canadian borrowing abroad.

The broad patterns of Canada's international balances contrast with those of its major trading partners (Table 9). While Canada generally runs a trade account surplus and a current account deficit, the U.S. balances are often the opposite: trade deficit, and a current account moving from deficit to surplus. The situation of Japan,

Canada's second most important trading partner, appears similar to that of Canada in respect to the major balances. There are, however, important differences in the composition of these balances, such as a predominance of primary goods in Canada's exports versus manufactured goods in Japan's, and also in the much greater extent of foreign ownership in Canada.

Approach of the Book

This book is designed to introduce the reader to contemporary concepts and practices of international business, with particular reference to the opportunities and challenges facing Canadian business managers. It seeks to blend theory and application by looking alternatively at conceptual foundations and at their relevance for effective management decisions. The structure of the book is illustrated in Figure 1.

Part Two of the book introduces the economic concepts of comparative advantage and international trade competitiveness. Canada's advantages are identified, and alternative views on Canadian trade policies are presented. Part Three then examines in depth how Canadian business managers can most effectively meet the challenge of overseas markets. Several successful Canadian executives draw on their experience and offer practical recommendations. Important new marketing developments, such as the use of export consortia and the prospects for a national trading company, are discussed.

Part Four moves from international trade to international direct investment. This comprehensive section examines, in sequence, the theoretical foundations of foreign direct investment in a Canadian context; the patterns both of foreign investment in Canada and of Canadian investment abroad; divergent views on the social and economic consequences of foreign ownership in Canada; and Canada's approach to controlling and modifying the impact of foreign investments.

Part Five returns to the decision processes in managing international business operations. A discussion of international expansion strategies explores emerging new vehicles of international involvement, such as turnkey projects. Other decision areas include research and development policies, rationalization of global production, and managing international finances. A concluding section looks to the future, presenting recommendations to both the public and private sectors for strengthening Canada's international business position in the years ahead.

A detailed content profile of the book is presented in Figure 2. This diagram will aid the reader in relating the conceptual foundations to the applied content of the book and will also help to distinguish between those portions focussing on incoming international business flows and those involving Canadian business abroad.

The material that forms the book is drawn from a variety of contributors, including leading Canadian academics, managers of Canadian companies, and senior government officials. The book thus provides its readers with a unique synthesis of perceptions and experiences with respect to Canadian international business.

Table 7

Exports of Manufactured Goods

Period	United States (a)	France	F.R. Germany	Italy	Nether-lands	United Kingdom[a]	Japan	Canada
	Value in billions of dollars[b]							
1970	29.3	13.5	30.7	11.1	6.8	16.6	18.1	9.7
1975	71.0	39.6	79.6	29.2	19.4	37.0	53.2	16.7
1976	77.2	42.5	90.7	31.3	22.3	39.0	64.6	20.6
1977	80.2	48.7	104.3	38.1	23.9	47.4	77.7	23.1
1978	94.5	58.8	125.2	47.6	27.8	57.6	94.2	27.1
1979	116.7	75.6	150.6	60.1	34.5	70.2	99.1	30.2
	Percentage change from preceding year							
1976	8.9	7.3	13.9	7.2	14.9	5.4	21.4	23.4
1977	3.8	14.6	15.0	21.7	7.2	21.5	20.3	12.1
1978	17.9	20.7	20.0	24.9	16.3	21.5	21.2	17.3
1979	23.4	28.6	20.3	26.3	24.1	21.9	5.2	11.4
1980								

(a) Quarterly data are seasonally adjusted.
(b) Values f.o.b., except U.S., f.a.s.

Note:
Manufactures refer to chemicals, machinery, basic manufactures, and other manufactures except mineral fuel products, processed food, fats, oils, firearms of war, and ammunition. U.K. data are based on Revision 2 of the United Nations Standard International Trade Classification. U.S. data are based on Revision 2 beginning 1977; French, German, Italian, and Dutch data, beginning 1978; and Canadian data, beginning 1979. Japanese data are based on Revisions 1.

Source: U.S. Department of Commerce, International Trade Administration, "International Economic Indicators", VI, No. 4 (December 1980).

Table 8

Canada's Share of World Exports of Manufactures in Selected Years

1960	1965	1970	1972	1974	1976	1978
3.6%	3.5%	4.8%	4.3%	3.4%	3.5%	3.2%

Source: Economic Intelligence Branch, Economic Policy and Analysis, Dept. of Industry, Trade, and Commerce, "Canada's
    Merchandise Trade Performance, 1960-1978" (Unpublished mimeograph report, January 1980, Ottawa) p. 25.

Table 9

Trade and Current Balances of Major OECD Countries and Country Groups

	1977	1978	1979	1980	1981
Trade Balances					
United States	−30.9	−33.8	−29.5	−25$\frac{1}{2}$	−17$\frac{1}{2}$
Canada	2.9	3.6	3.8	5$\frac{1}{2}$	6$\frac{1}{2}$
Japan	17.3	24.6	1.8	0	8
France	−2.8	1.5	−1.4	−12	−11$\frac{1}{2}$
Germany	19.7	25.5	17.7	10$\frac{1}{2}$	17$\frac{1}{2}$
Italy	−0.1	2.9	−1.0	−12	−10
United Kingdom	−3.9	−2.9	−7.2	1$\frac{1}{2}$	2
Seven major countries	2.2	21.5	−15.7	−31$\frac{1}{2}$	−5
Other EEC	−4.9	−5.8	−10.0	−11	−11
Other North Europe	−6.6	0.9	−3.8	−12$\frac{1}{2}$	−10$\frac{1}{2}$
Other OECD	−14.4	−10.5	−12.7	−21	−23
Total OECD	−23.4	6.2	−42.3	−75$\frac{1}{2}$	−49$\frac{1}{2}$
Current Balances					
United States	−14.1	−14.3	−0.8	5$\frac{1}{2}$	19$\frac{3}{4}$
Canada	−4.0	−4.4	−4.4	−3$\frac{1}{2}$	−3
Japan	10.9	16.5	−8.8	−13$\frac{1}{4}$	−6$\frac{3}{4}$
France	−3.0	3.7	1.2	−7$\frac{3}{4}$	−6$\frac{1}{4}$
Germany	4.2	8.7	−5.5	−17$\frac{1}{2}$	−10$\frac{1}{2}$
Italy	2.5	6.2	5.1	−5$\frac{1}{4}$	−2$\frac{1}{4}$
United Kingdom	−0.5	1.2	−3.9	4$\frac{1}{2}$	4$\frac{1}{4}$
Total	−4.1	17.7	−17.1	−36$\frac{1}{2}$	−4$\frac{3}{4}$
Other EEC	−2.1	−4.1	−10.4	−12$\frac{3}{4}$	−12$\frac{1}{4}$
Other North Europe	−6.9	1.3	−3.3	−11$\frac{1}{2}$	−9$\frac{1}{2}$
Other OECD	−11.9	−5.9	−4.6	−12$\frac{1}{2}$	−13$\frac{3}{4}$
Total OECD	−24.9	9.0	−35.5	−73$\frac{1}{2}$	−40

Note: $billion, seasonally adjusted, expressed at annual rates.

Source: OECD, *Economic Outlook*, December 1980.

Figure 1

Structure of International Business: A Canadian Perspective

Figure 2

Content Profile of International Business: A Canadian Perspective

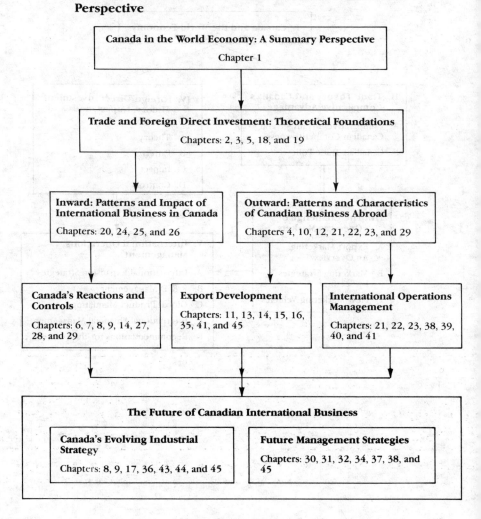

Appendix I

Canadian Balance of International Payments

($ millions)

	1970	1971	1972	1973	1974	1975	1976	1977	1978	1979
Merchandise Trade										
Exports	16.921	17.877	20.129	25.461	32.591	33.511	37.995	44.210	52.511	65.163
Imports	13.669	15.314	18.272	22.726	30.902	33.962	36.607	41.473	49.129	61.178
Trade Balance	3.052	2.563	1.857	2.735	1.639	−451	1.388	2.737	3.382	3.985
Services Balance	−2.099	−2.398	−2.527	−2.971	−3.706	−4.686	−5.760	−7.543	−8.727	−9.624
Net Transfers	153	266	284	344	557	380	530	417	43	620
Current Account Balance	1.106	431	−386	108	−1.460	−4.757	−3.842	−4.299	−5.302	−5.019
Long-term Capital Flows										
Net Direct Investment	590	695	220	60	35	−190	−890	−115	−2.135	−1.120
New Issues of Canadian Securities	1.230	1.191	1.722	1.323	2.423	5.038	9.026	5.916	6.951	5.104
Retirements of Canadian Securities	−552	−845	−603	−738	−626	−851	−931	−937	−1.191	−1.719
Other Long-term Transactions	−261	−377	249	−17	−791	−62	718	−476	14	945
Total Long-term Flows	1.007	664	1.588	628	1.041	3.935	7.923	4.388	3.279	3.210
Short-term Capital Flows[a]	−583	−318	−983	−1.203	443	417	−3.559	−1.510	−1.276	3.509
Allocations of SDRs	133	119	117	—	—	—	—	—	—	219
Net Official Monetary Movements	1.663	896	335	−467	24	−405	522	−1.421	−3.299	1.919

(a) Includes errors and omissions.
Source: Statistics Canada, *Quarterly Estimates of the Canadian Balance of International Payments*, Quarterly. Cat. 67-501.

Appendix II

Merchandise Trade Detail: Exports 1963–1979

Years and quarters	Wheat	Animals and other edible products	Ores and concen- trates	Crude petroleum and natural gas	Other crude materials	Lumber	Wood- pulp	Newsprint
	(Millions of dollars)							
1963....	787	675	703	310	414	452	405	760
1964....	1,024	817	803	360	453	477	461	835
1965....	840	869	863	384	517	490	493	870
1966....	1,051	906	934	430	583	474	520	968
1967....	742	902	1,016	522	571	505	543	955
1968....	684	929	1,262	600	605	656	628	990
1969....	473	992	1,138	702	623	697	754	1,126
1970....	687	1,181	1,522	855	707	664	785	1,111
1971....	833	1,279	1,415	1,038	811	830	798	1,085
1972....	927	1,428	1,397	1,315	848	1,174	830	1,158
1973....	1,221	1,937	2,000	1,833	1,192	1,599	1,082	1,288
1974....	2,065	1,806	2,376	3,914	1,504	1,290	1,889	1,726
1975....	2,023	2,124	2,241	4,144	1,581	973	1,835	1,746
1976....	1,732	2,563	2,512	3,903	1,872	1,649	2,186	2,003
1977....	1,881	2,726	2,730	3,779	2,341	2,387	2,158	2,382
1978....	1,913	3,388	2,403	3,763	2,664	3,229	2,181	2,886
1979....	2,180	4,114	3,889	5,294	3,350	3,911	3,078	3,222

Years and quarters	Fabricated metals	Other fabricated materials	Motor vehicles and parts	Other machinery and equipment	Consumer goods and miscel- laneous	Re- exports	Total
	(Millions of dollars)						
1963....	918	572	88	589	127	182	**6,980**
1964....	1,049	680	177	811	147	209	**8,303**
1965....	1,138	738	356	811	157	242	**8,767**
1966....	1,227	823	1,012	956	195	255	**10,043**
1967....	1,368	858	1,739	1,167	234	298	**11,420**
1968....	1,605	975	2,672	1,340	303	373	**13,624**
1969....	1,499	1,087	3,514	1,595	244	428	**14,871**
1970....	1,996	1,311	3,499	1,666	418	419	**16,820**
1971....	1,678	1,406	4,171	1,660	393	422	**17,818**
1972....	1,716	1,700	4,718	2,014	446	479	**20,150**
1973....	2,084	2,171	5,415	2,455	562	583	**25,421**
1974....	2,760	3,030	5,717	2,868	732	767	**32,442**
1975....	2,475	2,855	6,432	3,399	720	730	**33,328**
1976....	3,015	3,375	8,225	3,670	946	825	**38,475**
1977....	3,543	4,458	10,424	3,975	901	870	**44,554**
1978....	4,682	5,928	12,447	5,234	1,201	923	**52,842**
1979....	5,248	8,907	11,810	7,292	1,900	1,325	**65,518**

(Not seasonally adjusted)

Source: Statistics Canada/Department of Finance, Government of Canada, *Economic Review, A Perspective on the Decade* (April 1980), Ottawa.

Appendix II (Continued)

Merchandise Trade Detail: Imports 1963–1979

Years and quarters	Animals and edible products	Crude petroleum	Other crude materials	Fabricated materials	Motor vehicles and parts	Other machinery and equipment	Other end products and miscellaneous	Total
	(Millions of dollars)							
1963	780	335	563	1,571	669	1,882	759	**6,558**
1964	795	321	640	1,813	818	2,190	911	**7,488**
1965	770	312	694	2,114	1,125	2,573	1,045	**8,833**
1966	805	299	724	2,233	1,581	3,048	1,382	**10,072**
1967	884	356	707	2,310	2,168	3,341	1,106	**10,873**
1968	918	373	754	2,435	3,001	3,477	1,401	**12,358**
1969	1,063	393	692	2,905	3,546	4,031	1,500	**14,130**
1970	1,116	415	757	2,886	3,252	3,991	1,536	**13,952**
1971	1,157	541	781	3,140	4,110	4,328	1,850	**15,617**
1972	1,401	681	859	3,579	4,934	5,184	2,032	**18,669**
1973	1,981	943	1,075	4,282	6,081	6,477	2,487	**23,325**
1974	2,516	2,646	1,426	6,482	7,124	8,414	3,113	**31,722**
1975	2,682	3,302	1,784	5,944	8,236	9,296	3,472	**34,716**
1976	2,871	3,280	1,811	6,211	9,440	9,641	4,240	**37,494**
1977	3,306	3,215	2,101	6,993	11,576	10,584	4,559	**42,332**
1978	3,781	3,471	2,420	8,793	13,256	13,035	5,181	**49,938**
1979	4,235	4,479	3,423	12,059	15,011	17,148	6,324	**62,678**

(Not seasonally adjusted)

Source: Statistics Canada/Department of Finance, Government of Canada, *Economic Review, A Perspective on the Decade* (April 1980), Ottawa.

Appendix III

Book Value of Foreign Direct Investment in Canada, by Area of Ownership and Industry Group

	1965	1966	1967	1968	1969	1970	1971	1972	1973	1974	1975
Owned in:	(Millions of dollars)										
U.S.A.	14,059	15,570	17,000	18,510	19,959	21,403	22,443	23,679	26,113	28,996	32,194
Manufacturing	6,167	6,769	7,437	7,975	8,700	9,231	9,389	10,134	11,079	12,432	13,816
Petroleum and Natural Gas	3,653	4,052	4,290	4,615	4,968	5,290	5,751	6,037	6,746	7,146	7,805
Mining and Smelting	1,875	2,107	2,323	2,669	2,754	2,851	3,057	2,909	3,149	3,397	3,672
Utilities	280	297	316	359	347	366	356	463	469	474	561
Merchandising	696	759	841	964	1,105	1,251	1,397	1,432	1,649	1,861	2,104
Financial	1,043	1,176	1,371	1,479	1,523	1,755	1,857	1,999	2,216	2,669	3,042
Other	345	400	422	449	562	649	626	705	805	1,017	1,194
United Kingdom	2,033	2,046	2,152	2,310	2,426	2,503	2,715	2,821	3,151	3,525	3,717
Manufacturing	836	852	870	874	846	839	847	868	936	1,115	1,213
Petroleum and Natural Gas	488	476	477	471	470	536	597	602	665	728	743
Mining and Smelting	100	111	123	136	154	155	160	162	169	277	281
Utilities	14	14	21	56	56	52	52	53	43	6	4
Merchandising	274	283	304	317	338	298	294	235	252	288	318
Financial	262	248	293	386	487	543	666	787	954	971	1,011
Other	59	62	64	70	75	80	99	114	132	140	147
All other countries	1,264	1,392	1,547	1,714	2,039	2,452	2,760	2,996	3,388	3,580	3,927
Manufacturing	252	269	292	355	496	697	832	977	1,152	1,205	1,268
Petroleum and Natural Gas	459	474	502	557	665	748	779	832	906	960	1,002
Mining and Smelting	42	61	101	126	169	225	271	231	303	358	388
Utilities	7	7	7	8	9	24	37	29	30	32	36
Merchandising	91	90	107	127	117	140	159	174	215	233	246
Financial	389	465	506	495	525	547	604	653	643	670	849
Other	24	26	32	46	58	71	78	100	139	122	138

Source: Foreign Investment Review Agency, "Compendium of Statistics on Foreign Investment", FIRA Papers No. 4, Government of Canada, Ottawa.

Appendix IV

Book Value of Canadian Direct Investment Abroad, by Geographical Area and Industry Group

	1965	1966	1967	1968	1969	1970	1971	1972	1973	1974	1975
Investment in:	(Millions of dollars)										
U.S.A.											
Manufacturing	1,186	1,273	1,358	1,536	1,733	1,870	1,977	2,093	2,133	2,658	3,018
Petroleum and Natural Gas	223	168	168	203	390	453	501	555	722	958	1,155
Mining and Smelting	34	47	36	40	54	51	59	57	222	345	391
Utilities	313	311	316	428	439	469	455	404	427	436	437
Merchandising	109	120	151	138	138	145	140	125	180	179	257
Financial	129	138	115	147	155	190	155	119	132	184	267
Other	47	43	46	54	70	84	91	67	108	139	155
Total	2,041	2,100	2,190	2,546	2,979	3,262	3,399	3,431	3,924	4,909	5,680
United Kingdom											
Manufacturing	423	466	427	459	484	479	504	518	609	669	752
Petroleum and Natural Gas	2	5	6	7	9	11	12	25	33	59	97
Mining and Smelting	1	2	1	2	3	2	2	4	1	-	1
Utilities	10	9	5	7	12	13	10	17	14	26	24
Merchandising	24	28	49	67	50	39	38	33	57	43	38
Financial	13	22	22	23	31	32	13	16	69	71	90
Other	9	9	5	5	6	10	11	17	14	11	17
Total	482	541	515	570	595	586	590	630	797	879	1,019
All other countries											
Manufacturing	501	550	661	749	831	858	964	1,020	1,177	1,360	1,545
Petroleum and Natural Gas	17	18	26	30	29	28	34	53	108	121	185
Mining and Smelting	218	247	287	314	319	325	332	333	398	453	533
Utilities	84	107	110	134	134	743	808	762	826	944	1,025
Merchandising	22	26	62	62	88	94	95	122	139	156	190
Financial	23	30	69	100	127	199	227	238	329	375	397
Other	80	92	110	112	109	93	89	97	112	110	100
Total	945	1,070	1,325	1,501	1,637	2,340	2,549	2,645	3,089	3,519	3,975

Source: Foreign Investment Review Agency, "Compendium of Statistics on Foreign Investment", FIRA Papers, No. 4 (May 1978), Government of Canada, Ottawa.

II
Trade Theory and Canada's Comparative Advantage

Effective management decisions are predicated, directly or indirectly, on economic foundations. The international business manager who understands the underlying economic relationships which lead to the international movement of goods, services, and capital is better equiped to make decisions than the manager lacking such tools. He/she will, firstly, be able to analyse existing patterns of international business more effectively, and to identify potential business opportunities for the future. Secondly, he/she will be better able to anticipate and to deal with such constraints on international operations as governmental regulations and exchange rate changes. Thirdly, the manager who understands the economic rationale underlying public policy and governmental action will be better able to communicate his/her views to the policy makers and, thus, to influence the setting within which the management decisions are being made.

This portion of the book examines the economic foundations of international trade and the governmental policies which affect imports and exports in Canada. In the first section, Magee (Chapter 2) summarizes the theories of comparative advantage which underlie international trade. Daly (Chapter 3) applies these theoretical approaches to a discussion and identification of Canada's international comparative advantages. Finally, Astwood (Chapter 4) discusses the actual record of Canada's manufacturing competitiveness and recent trade record.

The remaining chapters concern Canada's present and future trade policies. Etemad (Chapter 5) discusses the interdependencies between domestic and international economic variables in policy formulation in an open economy such as Canada's. A report of the Economic Council of Canada (Chapter 6) summarizes the origin and development of Canada's current protective trade policies. Kobel (Chapter 7) discusses import policy options in one of the most controversial and protected sectors of Canada's economy, the clothing and textile industry. Beigie (Chapter 8) calls for a move away from protective trade policies in an in-depth study of the political economy of Canada-U.S. free trade arrangements. Meyer (Chapter 9) offers an alternative view of why such arrangements are unlikely.

II
Trade Theory and Canada's Comparative Advantage

A
Comparative Advantage and Canadian Competitiveness

2
Theories of Comparative Advantage

Stephen P. Magee

Dr. Magee is a professor of international business and economics, University of Texas at Austin.

The material in this chapter appeared originally in Stephen Magee, *International Trade*, © 1978, Addison-Wesley Publishing Company, Inc., Chapter 2, pages 17-27, "International Trade in Standardized Products". Reprinted with permission.

After products become older and their production technology becomes known worldwide, costs of production become increasingly important in determining the best production location. It is important that production be located close to the market for new products for a while. With older, standardized products, this dependence of production location on market location weakens. Countries will produce and export products they can produce cheaply and import those they cannot produce cheaply. The various theories of comparative advantage attempt to explain *why* production costs are low in some countries and high in others. Frankly, these theories are not very good at explaining why specific products are produced in specific locations. A large number of international entrepreneurs have done quite well with little or no knowledge of the theory of comparative advantage.

The first theory to be considered is the Ricardo theory of comparative advantage, which assumes a single factor of production, labor, and is based on the labor theory of value developed in the eighteenth and nineteenth centuries. The second theory is the Heckscher-Ohlin model based on two factors of production, usually capital and labor.

The Ricardo Model

The Labor Theory of Value
The labor theory of value states that the value of any product is equal to the value of the labor time required to produce it. For example, if an automobile requires two worker-years worth of labor to construct and a truck requires six worker-years, then the price of a truck will be three times as high as that of a car. We assume that the two worker-years required to produce a car include the amount of time taken to process the materials that go into the automobile.

The Ricardo Theory of Comparative Advantage
Ricardo used this labor theory of value to construct his theory of comparative advantage, which states that a country will produce and export products that use the lowest amount of labor time relative to

foreign countries and import those products that have the highest amount of labor time in production relative to foreign countries. Furthermore, only *relative* amounts of labor time matter.

Table 1

Worker-Years Required for Production
(output per worker-year)

	United States	Canada
1 Car	2 (.5/year)	4 (.25/year)
1 Truck	6 (.17/year)	8 (.125/year)
Price of Truck/Price of Car	3/1	2/1

Consider the production time required to produce one car and one truck in the United States and in Canada (see Table 1). It requires two worker-years to produce a car and six worker-years to produce a truck in the United States. In Canada, it requires four worker-years to construct a car but eight worker-years to construct a truck. According to the labor theory of value, the price of trucks relative to cars will be three to one in the United States, but only two to one in Canada. According to Ricardo's theory, Canada will export trucks since they are relatively less expensive there, while the United States will export cars. Thus Canada produces only trucks for its own consumers and for customers in the United States, while the United States produces only cars, both for its local consumers and for Canadian consumers.

Before international trade was instituted between the United States and Canada, the price of trucks in the United States relative to cars was 3/1, whereas it was only 2/1 in Canada. After international trade opens up, we know that prices will be pushed together in the two markets (ignoring transportation costs). Americans will go to Canada and bid the relative price of trucks above 2/1 while Canadians will sell their trucks in the United States, reducing the U.S. price below 3/1. Eventually, an equilibrium will be reached with the world price of trucks somewhere between 2/1 and 3/1, say, 2.7/1. This result holds in any situation in which the trading partners are both sufficiently large to affect the price in the other market.

In the case of a very small country, such as Luxembourg, trading with a large country, such as the United States, the world price after international trade has opened up may be established at the price existing in the large country before trade started. For example, if we substitute Luxembourg for Canada in Table 1, it is possible that the world price after trade is opened up will still be 3/1. Even though Luxembourg will export trucks to the United States, it may hold such a small percentage of the U.S. market that the U.S. price will not fall noticeably. In this situation of a small country trading with a large one, all of the gains from international trade accrue to the small country. The United States gains little by having an economy only 1/1000th its size trading with it. However, it is a considerable advantage to Luxembourg since it is now able to import cars much more cheaply than it was able to produce them itself. This is a counterargument to the popular belief that large countries gain at the expense of small ones in international trade.

The Myth of Absolute Advantage

A cursory glance at Table 1 would lead one to believe that there would be no advantage for the United States to trade with Canada. The reason is that the United States can produce both cars and trucks using fewer worker-years than is possible in Canada. The United States can produce a car in half the time required in Canada and a truck in only three-quarters the time. However, one of Ricardo's important contributions was to debunk the myth of absolute advantage; that is, the notion that the United States should produce both products and not engage in international trade. This can be shown by examining whether workers in the United States who produce cars could gain by trading those cars for trucks in Canada. A U.S. worker can produce a car in two years. After working twelve years, that worker could take the resulting six cars and purchase two trucks in the U.S. Would there be any gain in taking these six cars to Canada and trading them there for trucks? Clearly there would be, since six cars in Canada can be exchanged for three trucks. Thus, even though U.S. workers are superior in both products, it pays them to specialize in the item in which they have the greatest relative advantage (cars) and trade them in Canada for trucks.

Empirical Evidence for the Ricardo Model

In parentheses in Table 1, we note the number of cars and trucks that can be produced per worker-year in each country. Notice that the ratio of labor productivity (output per worker) in the production of cars relative to trucks is 3/1 in the United States, while it is only 2/1 in Canada. This suggests a direct test of the theory. It should be true that countries will export products in which they have high relative labor productivity and import those products in which they have low relative labor productivity. The results of MacDougall's test of

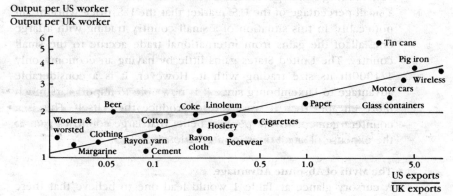

Figure 1

Export Performance Related to Labor Productivity

Output per US worker
Output per UK worker

Source: MacDougall (1951).

this theory[1] are shown in Figure 1. The ratio of labor productivity in the United States to the labor productivity in the United Kingdom is shown on the vertical axis, and the ratio of U.S. exports to U.K. exports, both to third markets, is shown on the horizontal axis. Notice that for goods such as margarine, clothing, and rayon the ratio of U.S. output per worker relative to U.K. output per worker is small. For these items, the ratio of U.S. exports to U.K. exports is also small. However, for tin cans, pig iron, and automobiles, U.S. productivity is high relative to U.K. productivity and so are U.S. exports relative to U.K. exports. Thus it appears that this simple theory of relative advantage has impressive empirical support.

The Heckscher-Ohlin Model

Despite the empirical success of the Ricardo model in explaining trade patterns, it is still unrealistic to believe that a model built on a single factor of production can explain international trade patterns. For this reason, a second model, which is based on two factors of production, has emerged. Each country is assumed to possess the two factors, capital and labor, and each product requires both of them in production. The Heckscher-Ohlin model suggests that countries will export products that use more of the country's abundant

1. D. MacDougall, "British and American Exports: A Study Suggested by the Theory of Comparative Cost". *Economic Journal* **61** (December 1951), pp. 697-724.

factor: Capital-abundant countries will export products that use a lot of capital in their production, that is, *capital-intensive* products, and labor-abundant countries will export *labor-intensive* products.

Assume that cars are more capital intensive in their production than trucks. This might be due to longer production runs on their assembly lines. Assume that it requires three units of capital per worker-year to assemble an automobile compared to only two units of capital per worker-year to assemble a truck. Assume also that the United States has more physical capital per worker than Canada. According to the Heckscher-Ohlin theorem, since the United States is relatively capital abundant, it will export its capital-intensive goods (cars). Canada will do the reverse; since it is relatively well endowed with labor, it will export the labor-intensive good (trucks). In contrast to the Ricardo model, in which each country produced only one good, both countries will produce both goods after free trade is opened. Thus, even though the United States is importing trucks, it will still satisfy some of the U.S. demand by producing trucks. The same is true for car production in Canada.

Before turning to empirical tests of the Heckscher-Ohlin theorem, some discussion of production in the United States and Canada is required. With free international trade, the prices of identical cars will be equated in the United States and Canada; the same will be true for trucks. By the factor of the price equalization theorem, the costs of capital and labor will also be equalized between the two countries because of free trade. When this is the case, within each industry the amounts of capital per worker used in production will be the same in Canada as in the United States. If we observe that 2.5 units of capital per worker are being used in car production in the United States, then 2.5 units of capital per worker will be used in car production in Canada. The same will be true for truck production; if 2.2 units of capital per worker are used in Canada, the same ratio will be used in the United States. If we are to test the Heckscher-Ohlin theorem, we must see if the relative capital intensity of export matches the relative factor abundance of the economy. The first step is to establish whether the export good is more or less capital intensive in production than the import good. It is easy to measure capital intensity for U.S. exports: We simply calculate the dollar value of capital per worker in U.S. industries that produce goods for export. But do we measure capital intensity for U.S. imports in the United States or in Canada? The point just made is that it does not matter whether we measure capital per worker in import-competing production of trucks in the United States or go to Canada and measure units of capital per worker in the production of trucks there.

Empirical Tests of the Heckscher-Ohlin Theorem Based on Capital and Labor

The United States. The most famous tests of the theorem were performed by Leontief in 1953 and 1956 on U.S. data.[2] Because of the presumed physical abundance of capital relative to labor in the United States, the expectation was that the United States would export capital-intensive products and import labor-intensive products. Leontief's studies found that exactly the reverse was true. He found that in 1947, U.S. exports required $14,300 of capital per worker-year, while production that competed with U.S. imports required $18,200 worth of capital per worker-year. Input-output analysis was used to capture direct as well as indirect requirements of capital per worker in order to produce export- and import-competing products. Given our preconception that the United States is capital abundant compared with the rest of the world, this test refutes the ability of the Heckscher-Ohlin model to predict the factor intensity of U.S. trade.

Japan. Given the abundance of labor in Japan relative to other factors, we would expect Japan to export labor-intensive products and import capital-intensive ones. A study by Tatemoto and Ichimura found the reverse: Japan exports capital-intensive goods but imports labor-intensive goods, contrary to the Heckscher-Ohlin predictions. On the other hand, whenever they broke Japanese trade into regions, they found that Japanese exports to the United States were labor intensive relative to the imports from the United States. Vis-à-vis lesser developed countries, Japan's exports were capital intensive and its imports labor intensive. Since 75 per cent of Japan's trade is with developing countries, the paradox for overall trade is explained.[3] Thus, on a more refined basis, the Heckscher-Ohlin theorem appears to hold for Japan.

India. A study by Bharadwaj found that India tends to export labor-intensive goods and import capital-intensive goods. Thus it appears that the Heckscher-Ohlin model applies to India. However, when the bilateral trade of India with the United States was examined, it was found that India exports capital-intensive goods but imports labor-intensive goods.[4] Thus, at a very disaggregated level, the Heckscher-

2. W. W. Leontief, "Domestic Production in Foreign Trade: The American Capital Position Re-examined", *Economia Internazionale* 7 (February 1954), pp. 9-38.
3. S. Ichimura and M. Tatemoto, "Factor Proportions and Foreign Trade: The Case of Japan", *Review of Economics and Statistics* 41 (November 1959), pp. 442-446.
4. R. Bharadwaj, "Factor Proportions and the Structure of Indo-U.S. Trade", *Indian Economic Journal* 10 (October 1962), pp. 105-116.

Ohlin model appears not to hold. Notice that the aggregate-disaggregate Heckscher-Ohlin results for India are exactly the reverse of those for Japan.

East Germany. Stolper and Rosekamp examined East Germany's trade. By comparison with the rest of Eastern Europe, East Germany is capital abundant. Using input-output techniques, these authors found that in fact East Germany exported capital-intensive goods and imported labor-intensive goods from its eastern European bloc trading partners. (They account for three-fourths of East Germany's trade.)[5]

Canada. Wahl found that the capital-labor ratio for Canadian exports exceeded that for the Canadian import-competing production.[6] Most of Canada's trade is with the United States; this is consistent with Leontief's finding for the United States.

What can cause the Heckscher-Ohlin predictions to fail? The results above show a rather mixed pattern in the ability of the theorem to predict trade flows. While there are many factors that can cause the assumptions of a theorem to fail and hence its predictions to be inaccurate, we can cite at least four important considerations.

First, the Heckscher-Ohlin theorem is a *supply-oriented* model. It assumes that the consumer's preference for cars to trucks is the same between economies and that a country's exports can be predicted by the factor intensities of the product and the factor endowments of the countries. However, it is clear that different preferences in two countries can cause the trade pattern to go the other way. Thus, even though the United States might have a comparative production advantage in capital-intensive goods, if U.S. citizens had strong preferences for capital-intensive goods and foreign consumers preferred labor-intensive goods, then the Leontief paradox could be explained. That is, the U.S. comparative production advantage in capital-intensive goods would be more than offset by the desire of Americans to consume them so that capital-intensive goods would be imported into the United States to satisfy total demand. The evidence on this question is quite mixed. Houthakker found that the income elasticities of demand for a wide variety of products are fairly similar

5. W. Stolper and K. W. Rosekamp, "An Input-Output Table for East Germany with Applications to Foreign Trade", *Oxford University: Institute of Economics and Statistics Bulletin* **23** (November 1961), pp. 379-392.
6. D. F. Wahl, "Capital and Labour Requirements for Canada's Foreign Trade," *Canadian Journal of Economics* **27** (August 1961), pp. 349-358.

across countries.[7] Thus it should not be true that low-income countries would have a stronger preference, say, for clothing than the United States. Other evidence is available, however, from Vernon's product cycle. The United States tends to be the first country in the world to consume very sophisticated consumer products, so that it has very strong demands for the types of products in which it has a comparative advantage in production. Thus the question of how tastes affect trade flows is an open one.

Second, any economic condition that can *reverse the pattern of trade* will cause the Heckscher-Ohlin predictions to be reversed. For example, if a labor union ·or any factor of production causes the export industry to pay more for a factor than import-competing industries do, then the export industry will contract. If it contracts far enough, the good that used to be exported may become the importable. Thus, even though the United States may be relatively well endowed with capital, it would have to import capital-intensive goods if labor unions or other distortions in factor markets caused U.S. production of these goods to fall sufficiently.

Third, some products will be capital intensive at very high prices of capital and labor intensive at very low relative prices of capital. This phenomenon is known as a *factor-intensity reversal*. Minhas found that factor reversals occurred in fifteen out of twenty-four industries.[8] Since it might be possible for automobiles to be capital intensive in the United States, but for them to be relatively labor intensive at a different factor price structure in Japan, then it is difficult to tell whether the Heckscher-Ohlin theorem will work. Another assumption of the Heckscher-Ohlin model is that the technology used to combine capital and labor for production in the United States is the same technology available worldwide. If this assumption is also violated, then it is hard to tell whether the model will have much predictive power. Minhas, in fact, found a low correlation between capital and labor ratios in twenty industries in the United States and the same labor-capital ratios in Japan.

Fourth, while *tariffs* do not reverse the pattern of trade, they could generate a result similar to Leontief's. Taxing a good that is imported

7. H. S. Houthakker, "An International Comparison of Household Expenditure Patterns, Commemorating the Centenary of Engel's Law", *Econometrica* **25** (October 1957), pp. 532-551.
8. B. Minhas, "The Homohyphallagic Production Function, Factor-Intensity Reversals, and the Heckscher-Ohlin Theorem", *Journal of Political Economy* **70** (April 1962), pp. 138-156.

cannot make it an exportable. If the tariff becomes prohibitively high, the United States will simply fail to import the good. At the high U.S. price, no U.S. producer would want to sell it abroad at the lower world price. However, if it is true that tariffs are weighted toward discouraging imports of labor-intensive products, then any test of the factor intensities of U.S. trade could be biased. There is evidence showing that effective tariffs tend to be high on low-wage industries. Thus labor-intensive imports are greatly underrepresented in observed U.S. imports because of the high tariff on them.

However, an important consideration is that the simple two factor (capital-labor) model still does not capture all of the factors of production. We turn now to a discussion of the importance of both natural resources and human capital.

Other Factors of Production

Compared with the rest of the world, it appears that the United States is poorly endowed with natural resources relative to other factors. Vanek found that U.S. exports embodied only about half of the natural resources contained in U.S. imports.[9] Thus the United States appears to be importing resources as a scarce factor of production. This observation is consistent with the Heckscher-Ohlin theorem.

A more important consideration is the failure to adjust for human capital. Relative to other countries, the United States has its greatest abundance of human capital in the form of education. A capital good is defined as a durable asset, and education certainly qualifies as a durable asset, albeit intangible. Vernon's product cycle suggests that the United States is exploiting its comparative abundance of skilled labor. Data by Gruber, Mehta, and Vernon showed that U.S. export industries tend to use highly skilled labor.[10] Thus when this consideration is incorporated, it appears that the United States may conform to the theory in exporting skilled labor-intensive products and in importing unskilled labor products. In effect, it is economizing on its scarce factor of imports and exploiting its comparative advantage in skilled labor through its exports.

9. J. Vanek, "The Natural Resource Content of Foreign Trade, 1870-1955, and the Relative Abundance of Natural Resources in the United States", *Review of Economics and Statistics* 41 (May 1959), pp. 146-153.
10. W. Gruber, D. Mehta, and R. Vernon, "The R & D Factor in International Trade and International Investment of the United States Industries", *Journal of Political Economy* 75 (February 1967), pp. 20-37.

Other Theories of Comparative Advantage

Scale Economies

Hufbauer has suggested that large countries will export products requiring relatively large plant sizes, and small countries will specialize in the production of products in which the optimum plant size is small. Although the correlation between the size of an economy and the importance of scale economies in production of exports was high, it was not statistically significant. However, when Hufbauer correlated the GNP per capita with scale economies of exports, he found an extremely strong fit.[11] Thus it appears that the ability of an economy to mass-produce goods is even more closely related to the degree of sophistication of the economy than with the absolute size of its industrial sector. Further evidence of this phenomenon has been reported by Grubel, who found that before European economic integration, European plants tended to have higher costs than U.S. plants because European plants were producing more varieties, styles, and sizes of the same commodity than did the corresponding U.S. plant.[12] Thus it is not just the size of the plant that is important in measuring scale economies; at least as important is the length of run. These runs tended to be long in the United States, but short in Europe.

Demand Similarities

Nearly all of the aforementioned theories have focussed on various characteristics of either production or supply, Linder suggested a demand-based theory of comparative advantage. He speculated that countries tend to produce and export the quality of product demanded by most of the people within its borders, while it imports products that are geared primarily to minorities, either the very rich or the very poor. The empirical implication of this theory is that countries with fairly similar levels of per capita income will tend to trade with each other since they will both produce goods that are appropriate for the income level of the average citizen in their countries.[13]

11. G. C. Hufbauer, "The Impact of National Characteristics and Technology on the Commodity Composition of Trade in Manufactured Goods", ed. R. Vernon, *The Technology Factor in International Trade* (New York: Columbia University Press, 1970), pp. 145-231.
12. Hubert G. Grubel, *International Economics* (Homewood, Illinois: Richard D. Irwin, 1977), Chs. 2, 3, and 4.
13. Staffan B. Linder, *An Essay on Trade and Transformation* (New York: John Wiley & Sons, 1961).

In an empirical test of a number of theories of comparative advantage, Hufbauer (1970) found that a country's imports tend to embody characteristics that are exactly the reverse of its exports. His results provide indirect evidence that countries basically engage in trade in order to compensate for national deficiencies. This is consistent with the orthodox theories of Ricardo, Heckscher-Ohlin, and scale economies. Basically the *compensation approach* suggests that if an economy tends to export highly capital-intensive goods, it will import highly labor-intensive goods; if it exports goods employing large amounts of skilled labor, it will import goods using primarily unskilled labor; if it exports goods utilizing large economies of scale, it will import goods that are not primarily based on economies of scale. This is in contrast with the Linder (1961) theory, which suggests that countries import the same types of goods that they export, namely, those that satisfy the average citizen in the economy.

In this chapter we have explored the classic theory of comparative advantage and empirical tests of it. The basic message is that there are gains to be had from production specialization. The story of Marco Polo provides an example of this principle. He spent more than thirty years in the Far East with his father and uncle collecting information about a civilization which was largely unknown to Europe. He returned to Venice in 1292 but was captured in a naval battle between Venice and Genoa in 1295. His stories of the marvels of the East would not have been preserved had he not spent two years in a jail in Genoa. There he told and retold the stories of his travels. However, Marco Polo did not commit these to paper; rather, they were written by a fellow prisoner, Rusticello. Thus, Marco Polo and Rusticello used the theory of comparative advantage: Marco Polo had the stories, Rusticello had the writing ability, and together they created a best seller.[14]

There are also historical examples of failure to appreciate the theory of comparative advantage. For example, Greenberg (1951) quotes an emperor of China who is reported to have said that China did not need to trade with Europe because "We possess all things".[15]

---

14. E. H. Hart, *Marco Polo* (Norman, Oklahoma: University of Oklahoma Press, 1967).
15. Michael Greenberg, *British Trade and the Opening of China 1800-42* (Cambridge: University Press, 1951).

II
Trade Theory and Canada's Comparative Advantage

A
Comparative Advantage and Canadian Competitiveness

3
Theory and Evidence on Canada's Comparative Advantage

D. J. Daly

Dr. Daly is professor of economics in the Faculty of Administrative Studies, York University. His areas of research and teaching include economic growth, the competitive position of Canadian manufacturing, and the productivity performance of Japanese manufacturing. His practical experience includes twenty years with the federal government and consulting with some of Canada's largest companies.

This chapter was written expressly for this volume.

This chapter will briefly summarize the main theories of comparative advantage that have been developed to explain the composition and structure of international trade, but its primary aim will be to summarize the empirical evidence using those theoretical models. The theory makes clear that comparative advantage involves not only a consideration of one country in isolation, but a comparison of the resources, productivity, and cost positions of several countries. This is especially true for a small country such as Canada. This chapter will emphasize comparisons with the United States, Japan, and the major countries of Northwestern Europe — the countries that dominate both exports and imports in the structure of Canadian trade.[1] It will emphasize the longer-term aspects of the quantities and qualities of the main factors of production, the efficient use of resources within industries, and the longer-term shifts in the allocation of resources between industries. The macro-aspects of stabilization, price inflation, exchange rates, and unemployment will be largely ignored apart from the effects of the present wage and exchange rate position on the competitive position of Canadian manufacturing.

This chapter will emphasize the positive analysis of comparative advantage. A later chapter will emphasize the implications of the results for government policy and industrial strategies in Canada.

Theories of Comparative Advantage Distinguished

Comparative advantage has been a part of the discussion on international trade for more than a century and a half — since initially put forth by David Ricardo in 1817. This topic is an integral part of all

---

1. This chapter and the related one on industrial strategies later in this volume draw on earlier work done with financial support from Energy, Mines and Resources, the Economic Council of Canada, and the Social Sciences and Humanities Research Council of Canada. A fuller presentation of the evidence and related discussion is contained in D. J. Daly, *Canada's Comparative Advantage* (Ottawa: Economic Council of Canada, 1979), Discussion Paper No. 135.

introductory and advanced courses in international trade.[2] Much of the discussion has followed the Ricardian method in the sense that it is primarily deductive, is based on some initially simplifying assumptions about behavior of individual consumers and producers, and frequently assumes unchanged technology. This chapter will follow the broad lines developed in the literature and will use this framework to organize the evidence on Canada, with special emphasis on the contrasts between Canada on the one hand and the United States, Northwestern Europe, and Japan on the other.

Almost all the pure theories of international trade emphasize that trade takes place between countries because, in the absence of trade, differences exist in relative prices between the countries concerned. Trade tends to equalize prices of commodities, although the presence of tariffs and transport costs can limit this. There are important differences in emphasis in the literature on the *reasons* for differences in relative prices.

The modern theory of comparative advantage finds the source of the differences in the relative prices of goods produced in different countries in the inequalities of supplies and prices of the main inputs into the process of production (land, capital, and labor). This stream of theory originates with the Swedish economists Eli Hecksher and Bertil Ohlin; Paul Samuelson, Harry Johnson, and others have since explored many aspects of this framework.[3] Two key assumptions

2. As illustrations of some of the main standard texts and books of readings in international trade covering these topics, see Jagdish Bhagwati, ed., *International Trade: Selected Readings* (Middlesex, England: Penguin, 1969), pp. 77-168; Richard E. Caves and Harry G. Johnson, *Readings in International Economics* (Homewood, Ill.: Richard D. Irwin, 1968), pp. 3-98 and 503-604; Richard E. Caves, *Trade and Economic Structure* (Cambridge: Harvard University Press, 1967), pp. 1-189; Richard E. Caves and Ronald W. Jones, *World Trade and Payments, An Introduction* (Boston: Little, Brown and Company, 1973), pp. 103-226; P. J. Ellsworth and J. Clark Leith, *The International Economy*, Fifth edition (New York: Macmillan, 1975), pp. 8-191; Charles P. Kindleberger, Fourth edition, *International Economics* (Homewood, Ill.: Richard D. Irwin, 1968), pp. 19-69; Franklin R. Root, *International Trade and Investment* (Cincinnati: South-Western, 1973), pp. 55-136; W. M. Scammell, *International Trade and Payments* (Toronto: Macmillan, 1974), pp. 13-133; Jacob Viner, *Studies in the Theory of International Trade* (New York: Harper and Bros., 1937), Ch. 7.

3. Eli Heckscher, "The Effects of Foreign Trade on the Distribution of Income", *Economisk Tidskrift*, 1919, ed. Howard S. Ellis and Lloyd A. Metzler, *Readings in the Theory of International Trade* (Homewood, Ill.: Irwin, 1950), pp. 272-300, and Bertil Ohlin, *Interregional and International Trade*, rev. ed., (Cambridge, Mass.: Harvard University Press, 1967). For additional references and discussion of tests of the two main alternative theories of relative prices, see D. J. Daly, "Uses of International Price and Output Data", ed. D. J. Daly, *International Comparisons of Prices and Output* (New York: Columbia University Press, 1972), esp. pp. 91-123.

traditionally made in this theory are the existence of similar production conditions in different countries, and constant returns to scale. The differing relative use of the various factors of production in different countries and differing relative supplies of factors in the various countries are regarded as crucial in explaining the differing structure of relative prices. International specialization then emerges as a result of specialization by each of the various countries in those industries that involved more intensive use of the factors that were relatively more abundant (and thereby less expensive) in that country.

Central to the earlier alternative theory of the source of differences in relative prices is an emphasis on *differences* in production conditions between industries in different countries. Ricardo initially emphasized the differences in relative labor productivities between countries, and this has continued to be a central part of the Ricardian tradition since, although more recognition is given to other factors and other costs in addition to labor than Ricardo had allowed. In light of the importance of labor income in net national income, and labor cost in relation to value added in individual manufacturing income, the emphasis on the importance of labor productivity makes this approach still relevant, especially when intercountry comparisons of productivity show such dramatically large differences.

Both of these theories of relative price differences in relation to comparative advantage are static and rarely allow for changes in technology or for non-price elements in trade. Recent developments in this area include the role of "availability" as a determinant of international trade, research and development as a source of new technology, the product-cycle hypothesis on the introduction of new products, and the role of the multinational corporation in foreign investment and international trade.[4] Individual countries can differ in their strengths in these fields, and Canada's relative role will be assessed where some evidence is available.

Each of these three approaches to comparative advantage will be examined subsequently. It is recognized, of course, that there are simultaneous interactions present in theory and practice, but these are not approached in this short chapter or in the larger study from which it is drawn.

---

4. Irving B. Kravis, "'Availability' and Other Influences on the Commodity Composition of Trade", *Journal of Political Economy* (April 1956), pp. 143-55; Raymond Vernon, "International Investment and International Trade in the Product Cycle", *Quarterly Journal of Economics* (May 1966), pp. 190-207; H. G. Johnson, *Comparative Cost and Commercial Policy Theory in a Developing World Economy* (Stockholm: Alqvist and Wiksell, 1968); Raymond Vernon, ed., *The Technology Factor in International Trade* (New York: Columbia University Press, 1970).

The summary of the evidence on Canada's comparative advantage will draw on the framework for intercountry comparisons of real income levels and growth experience developed by Edward F. Denison.[5] The conceptual framework permits the distinctions that have been made in trade theory to be summarized in quantitative terms for a number of OECD countries. The OECD countries that have been studied include United States, Canada, Japan, and eight countries in Northwestern Europe (Belgium, Denmark, France, Germany, the Netherlands, Norway, and the United Kingdom). The results for individual countries in Northwestern Europe will not be presented here, but are available in the initial study. Although the framework was initially developed for the economy as a whole (or the non-residential business component of it in more recent studies), it can also be applied at a finer level of disaggregation. Such disaggregation is essential to assess the Ricardian tradition of comparative advantage, which emphasizes the differences in productivity levels for similar industries in different countries.

Canada has one of the highest GNP levels of the OECD countries. By 1979, real GDP per person employed was about 6 per cent below the U.S. level. The unweighted average of six European countries in 1979 was about 35 per cent below the United States on a per employed person basis. (The individual countries were Belgium, France, Germany, Italy, Netherlands, and the United Kingdom, ranging from a low of 53 for Italy and the United Kingdom and a high of 79.4 for France.) The rates of increase in real GDP per employed

---

5. There is an extensive literature on the theoretical issues and applications of economic growth accounting to changes over time and intercountry comparisons. The main studies relating to intercountry comparisons of OECD countries include Edward F. Denison, assisted by Jean-Pierre Poullier, *Why Growth Rates Differ: Postwar Experience in Nine Western Countries* (Washington: Brookings Institution, 1967); D. J. Daly, "Why Growth Rates Differ — A Summary and Appraisal", *Review of Income and Wealth* (March 1968), pp. 75-93; Dorothy Walters, *Canadian Income Levels and Growth: An International Perspective* (Ottawa: Queen's Printer for the Economic Council of Canada, 1968); Edward F. Denison and William K. Chung, *How Japan's Economy Grew So Fast: The Sources of Postwar Expansion* (Washington: The Brookings Institution, 1976). For a discussion of the conceptual framework and some of the areas of controversy see Edward F. Denison, "Classification of Sources of Growth", *Review of Income and Wealth*, Series 18, No. 1, (March 1972), pp. 1-25; D. J. Daly, "Combining Inputs to Secure a Measure of Total Factor Input", *Review of Income and Wealth* (March 1972), pp. 27-53; and Edward F. Denison, Zvi Griliches and Dale W. Jorgenson, "The Measurement of Productivity", *Survey of Current Business* (May 1972). For an application of the same framework to the slower economic growth in United States in the 1970s, see Edward F. Denison, *Accounting for Slower Economic Growth: The United States in the 1970's* (Washington: The Brookings Institution, 1979).

person have been more rapid in Canada and each of the European countries than in the United States since 1950, so the real income differences have narrowed significantly over the last three decades.[6]

Factor Supplies and Prices

In the Heckscher-Ohlin model, the relative supplies of various factors are assumed to vary between countries, as reflected in different relative prices of factors between countries or differences in the elasticities of supply of different factors. Very little attention has been given in the literature as to how to make these distinctions operational in practice. In this chapter, data on international comparisons from the Denison analytical and statistical approach to economic growth will be used. This approach has now been applied to the United States, Canada, eight countries in Europe, and Japan. The material on factor inputs has been standardized between countries on a per person employed basis. The discussion will start off with those factors of production with which Canada is relatively well endowed, and will consider later those factors that currently are relatively scarce in Canada. It is recognized that it would be desirable to have comparisons of prices of factors rather than to rely primarily on physical measures, and these will be introduced in several places. However, these data are less available, and are difficult to explain and interpret when they have been assembled.

Land and Mineral Resources

As one would expect, Canada is clearly better endowed with natural resources than any other region (or individual country within Europe) considered, as shown in Table 1. The quantity of arable land per person employed in Canada is more than twice the U.S. level, and more than forty times the Japanese level. However, these comparisons are only a part of the picture. Climate and rainfall are less favorable than in other countries for a wide range of fruits, vegetables, and livestock and thus Canada is a net importer of a wide range of food products. The availability of land is reflected in radically different types of agriculture. Japan, for example, now grows about as much rice as it consumes by the very intensive use of small

---

6. U.S. Department of Labor, *Comparative Real Gross Domestic Product, Real GDP per Capita and Real GDP per Employed Person, Nine Countries, 1950-1979* (Washington: Bureau of Labor Statistics, September 1980), based on own country price weights.

plots of land. Farm production per worker in Canada was consistently well below that of the United States from 1947 to 1965, and the subsequent narrowing of the gap since then has been insufficient to modify that conclusion.[7] The extent of financial assistance to agriculture has grown during the 1970s[8] and Canada has introduced a number of protectionist policies on agricultural products. Gale Johnson concluded that Canada had a clear comparative advantage in wheat, barley, oats, rape seed, and flaxseed, but a clear disadvantage in manufactured dairy products, sugar, wool, lamb, and mutton.[9]

Table 1

Land Area and Mineral Production Per Person Employed, 1960 and 1970 (Relatives, U.S. = 100)

	Land Area Per Person Employed		Value in $ U.S. of Mineral Production Per Person Employed	
	All Land	Arable Land	Denison List	Expanded List
Canada (1970)	1036	218	181	222
United States	100	100	100	100
Northwestern Europe (1960)	13	20	26	26
Japan (1970)	6.4	5.2	3.7	

Sources: United States and Europe: Denison and Poullier, *Why Growth Rates Differ*, Table 14-2, p. 184; Japan: Denison and Chung, *How Japan's Economy Grew So Fast* (Washington: Brookings Institution, forthcoming), Appendix 0; and D. Walters, *Canadian Income Levels and Growth: An International Perspective* (Ottawa: Queen's Printer, 1968), Table 64, updated to 1970 with sources as described on pp. 233-34.

Mineral production is relatively more important in Canada than in any other country studied. On the basis of the expanded list, mineral

7. L. Auer, *Canadian Agricultural Productivity* (Ottawa: Queen's Printer, 1970), pp. 14, 15, 18, and 63. The constant dollar comparisons are based on 1949 prices, and in that year, prices of some of the main crops and livestock were roughly similar or offsetting. Updating can be done by the agricultural data in *Aggregate Productivity Measures, 1946-1973* (Ottawa: Statistics Canada, 1974) and unpublished worksheets made available by Statistics Canada. Results by Yamada and Ruttan give 160 for the United States and 136 for Canada in 1970, or 85 per cent of the U.S. New Zealand and Australia are both well above North American levels at 186 and 198 respectively.

8. The total tariff and non-tariff protection to agriculture in 1970 was 7.00, while it was 27.50 in wheat and 18.20 in industrial milk. See Economic Council of Canada, *Looking Outward* (Ottawa: Information Canada, 1975), p. 17.

9. Economic Council of Canada, *Looking Outward* (Ottawa: Information Canada, 1975), p. 148.

production in Canada was about 120 per cent higher in 1960 than in the United States, about seven times larger than in Europe, and almost fifty times larger than in Japan (all comparisons valued at U.S. prices).[10] Canadian mineral production was relatively larger in 1970 than it was a decade earlier. Over the post-war period Canada has obtained a larger share of world mineral trade, which in total has not been buoyant in relation to world GNP. However, the quantities of Canadian ore deposits are not outstanding in relation to other countries; and the friction between the federal government and the provinces on mineral rents and the changes in federal mining taxation should caution against complacency. Some work by Frank Anton indicates that output in relation to labor and capital in mining fell during the 1970s.

Business Capital Stocks

Reproducible business capital stocks per person employed are even higher in Canada than in the United States, and the extent of this difference has tended to widen during the 1960s and 1970s. In 1960, for example, the stock of machinery and equipment in manufacturing was only slightly higher on a per person employed basis than in the United States, but by the mid-1970s it was about one-third higher. The stock of structures has been higher in all the major industrial sectors (agriculture, manufacturing, and other enterprises). Some of the reasons for the high levels of the stock of capital per person employed would include the industrial structure in Canada (which contains a somewhat larger share of capital-intensive industries such as mining, smelting, and refining); the heavy overhead costs in transportation and communication associated with a small population thinly spread over a wide geographic expanse; the higher real costs of construction to cope with cold winters (such as costs of insulation, double windows, and the higher costs of having water and sewer lines and building foundations below the frost line); greater seasonality in many industries; favorable tax treatment on depreciation of capital assets; and the availability of a wide range of machinery (frequently embodying the latest technology) from the United States and other countries. The result has been that Canada is the most

10. This procedure uses data on current production of mineral products, weighted by U.S. prices. See D. J. Daly, "Mineral Resources in the Canadian Economy: Macro-Economic Implications", ed. Carl Beigie and Alfred O. Hero, Jr., *Natural Resources in U.S. Canadian Relations*, **1**, *The Evolution of Policies and Issues* (Boulder, Colorado: Westview Press, 1980), pp. 125-165.

capital intensive of the OECD countries, and thus the most capital-intensive country in the world.[11]

Although Canada has very high levels of land and real capital assets per person employed, these do not constitute important shares of net national income. For example, land has amounted to less than five per cent of national income in Canada, United States and most of the countries in Northwestern Europe, and the share has tended to decline over the post-war years in most countries. Furthermore, the individual components allot 17 per cent of the U.S. share of land income to farmland and 10 per cent to mineral lands (with the dominant share to non-agricultural site land). The weight for the capital stock is larger, ranging in the area of 10 to 14 per cent for individual countries.[12] Thus, the relatively small weight for farmland and mineral land contributes only modestly to any income differences from those components to Canadian income levels. The effects of the higher capital stock of non-residential structures and equipment per person employed in Canada have been somewhat greater but still contributed less than one percentage point to the real income differences between Canada and the United States.[13]

Labor input receives a much larger share of net national income than capital and land, with shares ranging from 71 to 82 per cent for the eleven countries studied.[14] Differences in educational levels are one of the more important elements in the composition of employment affecting income differences, and one that changes only slowly as younger persons begin employment with higher educational levels

11. For a fuller discussion of the evidence and a number of related tables see Donald J. Daly, *Canada's Comparative Advantage*, Discussion paper No. 135 (Ottawa: Economic Council of Canada, 1979). The tables draw on earlier work by Ed Denison, Dorothy Walters, Craig West, and James Frank, updated with later data on employment and capital stock from the statistical agencies in the United States and Canada. It is interesting that the high capital stock for Canada shows up in a regression study of the capital intensity for manufactured products (covering 184 product categories) for thirty-six countries. Canada had the second highest regression coefficient for both the stock and flow measure of capital intensity with values of 0.75 and 0.87 (both significant at the 5 per cent level) compared to averages of −0.51 and −0.98 for the stock and flow measures of capital intensity respectively. See Bela Balassa, "The Changing Pattern of Comparative Advantage in Manufactured Goods", *Review of Economics and Statistics* (1979), p. 263.

12. Denison and Poullier, *Why Growth Rates Differ*, pp. 42-43 and p. 183 and Edward F. Denison, *Accounting for United States Economic Growth, 1929-1969* (Washington: Brookings Institution, 1974), p. 52.

13. Dorothy Walters, *Canadian Income Levels and Growth: An International Perspective* (Ottawa: Queen's Printer for the Economic Council of Canada, 1968), p. 170.

14. Denison and Poullier, *Why Growth Rates Differ*, p. 42, Denison and Chung, *How Japan's Economy Grew*, pp. 28-29, and Walters, *Canadian Income Levels*, pp. 28-29.

and older workers with lower educational levels retire. A series of studies has established that levels of education in the Canadian labor force are lower than in the United States, and slightly lower than in Japan. There is much less variation in educational levels in the labor force around the average in Japan than in Canada, and the Canadian educational level is pulled down relative to that in Japan by the larger proportion with only primary school education.[15]

To summarize the differences in factor supplies relating to Canada's comparative advantage, Canada has a comparative advantage in the production of highly natural-resource-intensive commodities, especially those of the non-renewable type. However, Canada continues to have a comparative disadvantage with respect to labor-intensive commodities, particularly university labor.[16]

Intercountry Productivity Differences by Industry

The theorists in the Heckscher-Ohlin-Samuelson tradition emphasize differences in factor supplies and prices as the major influence on comparative advantage between countries. However, Ricardo emphasized differences in labor productivities between industries as the major source of differences in comparative costs and comparative advantage between countries. It is unfortunate that so many theorists in the international trade field have neglected the evidence from a large and growing number of published intercountry comparisons of productivity by industry. A survey of such studies by Irving Kravis shows significant intercountry differences in agriculture, mining, and manufacturing. The differences are even more pronounced within manufacturing if a relatively finer level of disaggregation is prepared. Simon Kuznets found the differences in product per worker were greatest in agriculture, and smallest in service sectors, while manufacturing held an intermediate position.[17]

For Canada, it is important to have some evidence on the relative productivity performance within manufacturing with the same in-

15. See *Canada's Comparative Advantage*, pp. 18-22 for fuller discussion, and D. J. Daly, "Japanese Manufacturing: Recent Productivity and Cost Developments", (Mimeo draft report for the Economic Council of Canada, York University, 1980), pp. 15-20.
16. Similar conclusions have been drawn by Harry Postner in *The Factor Content of Canadian Trade: An Input-Output Analysis* (Ottawa: Information Canada, 1976), pp. 26-31. However, this study did not discuss or allow for changes in production conditions with tariff reductions, a very important omission.
17. Irving Kravis, "A Survey of International Comparisons of Productivity", *Economic Journal* (March 1976), pp. 26-39 and Simon Kuznets, *Economic Growth of Nations* (Cambridge: Harvard University Press, 1971), pp. 208-214.

dustries in the United States. Some data for about thirty-five industries for 1974 are shown in Table 2. In that year output per man-hour
in manufacturing was more than 20 per cent below that of the United
States, with a few industries being higher, but a large number below
U.S. levels. The extent of variation around the mean in this study
was very similar to that encountered in other comparisons between
countries, including an earlier Canada-U.S. study done by E. C. West.
It is an important theme in the Ricardian tradition that the industries
in the upper portion of Table 2 would be areas of Canada's comparative advantage, and Canada would tend to be a net exporter, while
those in the bottom portion would tend to be net importers reflecting Canada's comparative disadvantages in those industries.

Persisting differences of this kind between countries physically
close, with easy flows of information, and considerable foreign ownership poses new questions. It is clear from the work on this topic in
Canada that such differences can only persist for extended periods
with the continued presence of important tariff and non-tariff impediments to trade. Even if the relative factor supplies in the two countries were identical and used in the same proportion in the individual
industries, a less efficient use of resources would put such industries
at a comparative disadvantage. It is also significant that a reduction
in tariffs in both directions (or complete industry free trade as in the
Canada-U.S. automotive agreement) has seen a narrowing in the productivity differences.

It has been an important theme for some decades that the presence of tariff and non-tariff barriers to trade prevent individual firms
from achieving all of the potential benefits of economies of scale.
Canadian plants typically produce a wider range of products than
plants of the same size in the same industry in the United States, and
the length of run of each product variety is inevitably short and high
unit costs result. The resulting high costs limit their scales to the
smaller market behind a tariff wall, and the high costs and U.S. tariffs
preclude them from being competitive even in large population
concentrations that are physically close to the Canadian plants. The
shorter runs and frequent down time required to make adjustments
to production specifications make significant differences to unit
costs. There are also plant sizes that are less than optimum, with
examples in some continuous process plants in chemicals and beer
(where provincial preferences are examples of non-tariff barriers
within the domestic market). However, the plant sizes in a number
of Canadian industries are reasonably close to a minimum efficient
scale, or the effects on costs of being below the minimum efficient
scale are modest.

Table 2

Real Net Output Per Man-Hour by Manufacturing Industry in 1974 (Canadian Output/U.S. Output, in Per cent)

Sawmills, Sash and Door Mills	145
Veneer and Plywood Mills	145
Iron and Steel Mills, Steel Pipe and Tube	120
Woollen Textile Mills	115
Baked Products	108
Motor Vehicles, Parts, and Accessories	103
Fruit and Vegetable Processing	101
Other Knitting Mills	97
Synthetic Textile Mills	95
Soft Drinks	94
Men's Clothing Manufacturers	91
Hosiery Mills	87
Iron Foundries	86
Slaughtering and Meat Processing	85
Household Furniture	74
Non-Ferrous Metal Smelting, etc.	73
Pulp and Paper Mills	73
Cotton Yarn and Cloth Mills	71
Petroleum Refining	70
Fabricated Structural Metals	69
Fish Products	69
Major Appliance Manufacturing	68
Breweries	66
Heating and Air Conditioning	66
Other Paper Converters	65
Paper Bag and Box Manufacturing	62
Truck and Bus Bodies	61
Dairy Products	59
Soap and Cleaning Products	58
Biscuit Manufacturers	58
Paint and Varnish Manufacturing	50
Tobacco Products Manufacturing	49
Confectionary Products	46
Total Sample	**77**

Source: James G. Frank assisted by Ian Ladd and Gene Swimmer, *Assessing Trends in Canada's Competitive Position: The Case of Canada and the United States* (Ottawa: The Conference Board in Canada, 1977), pp. 62-66, based on Canadian price weights.

With the reductions in tariffs under the Kennedy Round and the Canada-U.S. Automotive Agreement, the extent of the productivity difference between Canada and the United States narrowed over the last two decades. Some increased specialization has taken place within individual manufacturing industries, as reflected in an increased ratio of purchased materials to value added within individual industries, and an increased flow of trade in manufactured products

in both directions.[18] Further moves in these directions are expected
during the 1980s as the reductions under the Tokyo Round are
implemented.

Although this chapter emphasizes the real costs of resource supplies and factor productivity on comparative advantage, these forces
operate within an overall macro-environment of wages, prices, and
exchange rates. It is significant that as recently as the late 1960s
hourly average earnings in many Canadian manufacturing industries
were about 20 per cent below the national average in comparable
industries in the United States. However, for almost a decade the
increases in hourly compensation in total manufacturing went up
more rapidly in Canada than in the United States, and similar differentials were apparent in labor costs per unit of manufacturing output
and in the GNP deflators for both countries.[19] The purchasing power
parity doctrine would suggest that such changes in domestic purchasing power between two countries so interdependent would lead
to a fall in the value of the Canadian dollar and this is, of course, what
has happened, with the decline amounting to about 19 per cent
between the calendar year averages for 1976 and 1979. This has
restored the competitive position of Canadian manufacturing considerably. However, when output per man-hour in Canadian manufacturing is about 25 per cent below the United States while total
compensation per hour is above United States levels, labor costs per
unit of output will continue to be higher in Canada after adjustment
for the exchange rate, as it has been for most of the post-war and
inter-war period. These cost differences will continue to be reflected
in a net deficit in trade in manufactured products between the two
countries, in spite of significant increases in the price and volume
measures of a wide range of Canadian exports of manufactured
products. At the 1980 levels of wages and exchange rates between
the two countries, a further reduction in the size of the trade deficit
in manufactured products and higher real incomes for Canadians
could only be achieved and maintained on a longer term basis by
further narrowing of the productivity differences between the two
countries. Some steps by which this could be attained are discussed

18. D. J. Daly and S. Globerman, *Tariff and Science Policies: applications of a model
of nationalism* (Toronto: University of Toronto Press, 1976) pp. 21-30 and 53-61
and D. J. Daly, "Size and Economics of Scale", ed. P. K. Gorecki and W. T.
Stanbury, *Perspectives on the Royal Commission on Corporate Concentration*
(Scarborough: Butterworth for Research and Public Policy, 1979), pp. 87-97 and
the references to further studies cited there.
19. See Table 1 in D. J. Daly, "Weak Links in 'The Weakest Link'", *Canadian Public
Policy* (Summer 1979), p. 310.

in the later related chapter in this volume.

Some Dynamic Aspects of Comparative Advantage

It is recognized that the productivity differences reflected in Table 2 and summarized in the preceding paragraphs reflect the environment within which companies make decisions, and that further changes in the environments will lead to further changes in the extent of specialization in the future, as they have in the past. The existing patterns of comparative advantage are not cast in stone, but past experience suggests that changes take place only slowly and require some openness to change on the part of senior and middle management, and probably also further pressure from international competition.

One element that can influence Canada's comparative advantage in manufacturing and other commodity-producing industries in the years and decades ahead is the availability of new technology and the speed at which such new technology is implemented and adopted in individual plants in Canada. Historically, the major source of new technology, new products, new production processes, and new managerial, organizational, and administrative approaches and procedures has been the major industrialized countries. During the present century, the United States was the major source of many of these new ideas, and they were frequently first implemented there. With the rapid post-war growth of Western Europe and Japan, the technological leadership in a small but growing proportion of industrial products has been shifting from the United States to these other industrialized countries. The major industrialized countries such as the United States, the enlarged European Economic Community, and Japan have populations in total about twenty-five times the Canadian level, and thus, inevitably are major sources of new technology.

Knowledge of such new technology becomes available to other industrialized countries far more rapidly now than three or four decades ago with the improvement in transportation and communication, and the increased range and number of international conferences. The diffusion of technology has also been facilitated by the increased number and size of transnational (or multinational) enterprises, with corporate headquarters in one of the major industrialized countries.[20] The transfer of technology in even high technology products

20. Richard N. Farmer, *Benevolent Aggression: The Necessary Impact of the Advanced Nations on Indigenous Peoples* (New York: David McKay, 1972) explores this in the context of developing countries.

to less-developed countries has been relatively easy, especially if the seller of the technology helps in the training of local staff during an initial transitional period.[21]

Canadian companies, both locally owned and managed and subsidiaries, thus have the option of buying existing technology or producing it domestically. However, the costs of both the initial research and development and the later costs of industrial engineering, testing, start up, and marketing will all be higher on a per unit basis if the costs have to be covered in a small market rather than in the larger markets of the United States, the European Common Market, or Japan. This helps to explain why Canadian R & D expenditures are low in relation to sales and GNP, why so few of the patents taken out in Canada were developed here, and why Canada ranks so low in most measures of R & D and innovative activity.

However, the key question for performance in the market place (as gauged by new technology at low prices to both industrial buyers and consumers) is how quickly new technology is implemented, rather than where it was initially developed. A number of studies have been made of the diffusion of new technological developments in Canada, duplicating previous studies by E. Mansfield. The processes studied related to the use of numerical control machine tools, special presses to speed up the removal of water in the manufacture of paper, and tufting equipment in the making of synthetic carpeting. In each instance, the adoption of the new technology was slower in Canada than in the United States, and slower than in Europe in the case of the special presses to remove water in making paper. Production of new synthetics was also started later in Canada than in some of the larger industrialized countries.[22]

The Canadian tariff moderates the competitive pressure from imports and reduces external pressures to adopt new technology quickly. It is also a factor in the higher development costs on a per unit of output basis in a small market than would be experienced in a larger market. There are also the additional costs of bilingualism (French and English) in marketing and labelling. These influences tend to introduce greater risks and higher costs and reduce the economic

---

21. Jack Baranson, "Technology Transfer: Effects on U.S. Competitiveness and Employment", ed. William G. Dewald, *The Impact of International Trade and Investment on Employment* (Washington: U.S. G.P.O. for U.S. Department of Labor, 1978), pp. 177-207.
22. Daly and Globerman, *Tariff and Science Policies*, pp. 82-105 and G. C. Hufbauer, *Synthetic Materials and the Theory of International Trade* (Cambridge: Harvard University Press, 1966), pp. 86-89. There are some exceptions, of course, such as the fast adoption of the oxygen process in the Canadian steel industry.

incentive to introduce a new product or process into a small market such as Canada.

There is also some evidence that Canadian managers are less open to change than managers in the United States, partly reflecting differences in age, education, social background, and influences in selection and promotion.[23]

Thus, there are a number of reinforcing influences that contribute to both the limited production of new technology within Canada, and the slow adoption of new technology (whether produced at home or abroad) by plants and firms in Canada.

This chapter has presented a summary of the evidence on Canada's comparative advantage in the perspective of theories emphasizing factor supplies, differential productivity levels by industry, and the evidence on the production and adoption of new technology. In a related chapter later in this volume the discussion on Canada's comparative advantage will explore the policy implications, including a discussion of industrial strategies.

23. For fuller discussion of this topic see chapters by D. J. Daly in ed. H. C. Jain, *Contemporary Issues in Canadian Personnel Administration* (Toronto: Prentice Hall of Canada, 1974), pp. 24-28 and 96-105 and D. J. Daly, "Canadian Management: Past Recruitment and Future Training Needs", Mimeo York University, March 1980).

II
Trade Theory and Canada's Comparative Advantage

A
Comparative Advantage and Canadian Competitiveness

4
Canada's Merchandise Trade Record and International Competitiveness in Manufacturing, 1960 to 1979

D. M. Astwood

Mr. Astwood is assistant director, policy analysis section, Department of Industry, Trade, and Commerce. His career includes service with the Manitoba Treasury, federal departments of finance and CCA, and four years of teaching economics at Manitoba and Lakehead Universities. He has participated in a number of major economic studies.

This chapter was written expressly for this volume.

Introduction

The 1960s and 1970s was a period in which Canada's external trade displayed many remarkable developments. At the same time, it was also a period not without problems — notably in the mid-1970s. The main developments in Canada's trade performance over this time period include: (1) a massive increase in the volume and value of exports (and imports) which substantially exceeded the growth in the economy as a whole, (2) a significant shift in the composition of Canada's exports towards manufactured goods, (3) a decline in the share of farm products and of metal ores in exports, (4) a simultaneous increase in both the export orientation of Canadian goods production and the degree of import penetration of Canadian domestic markets, (5) although irregular, signs of improvement in Canada's balance of trade in manufactured goods relative to GNP and exports even though the deficit continued to grow in absolute terms, (6) a rise in the Canadian share of world trade in manufactured goods in volume terms but about the same proportion in value terms in the late 1970s compared to the early 1960s, (7) an improvement over the last two decades in Canada's competitive position with regard to prices and costs in manufacturing when measured in terms of a common currency (for example, the U.S. or Canadian dollar), and (8) a trend toward Canada becoming a relatively low labor cost country, among mature industrial economies.

General Trade Developments

The growth in total world merchandise trade since 1960 has been unprecedented. *Canada fully shared in this expansion*, although the value of Canada's merchandise exports did not rise quite as fast as those of the world at large primarily because of the rapid increases in world oil prices in the mid-1970s. In volume terms, Canada's commodity exports have more than tripled with the increase being identical to that for the world as a whole (see Table 1).

Vigorous growth in the trade of manufactured goods brought about a marked change in the composition of Canada's exports and imports. In constant dollar terms, the export share of manufactured

Table 1

Growth in Merchandise Exports
Canada and World: Selected Periods, 1960 to 1979

	1960-1965	1965-1970	1970-1975	1975-1979	1960-1970	1970-1979	1960-1979
	(compared annual rates in per cent)						
Value[a]							
World	7.8	10.9	22.7	16.9	9.4	20.1	14.3
Canada	8.0	14.7	14.8	14.1	11.3	14.5	12.8
Volume							
World[b]	6.8	8.7	5.6	6.8	7.8	6.1	7.0
Canada	8.6	11.1	1.7	6.8	9.8	4.0	7.0

(a) In U.S. Dollars.
(b) Market economies only.

Note: Based on data from: (1) UNCTAD, 1979 *Handbook of International Trade Statistics* (United Nations, 1979), Tables 1.1, 2.1, and 2.3; (2) United Nations, *Monthly Bulletin of Statistics* (April 1979), Special Table B, May, 1979, Special Table A, and July, 1980, Special Tables B and D; and (3) Statistics Canada.

products as a whole rose from 60 per cent in 1960 to 80 per cent in 1978, and that for inedible end products (finished manufactures) from 8 to 47 per cent.

In current dollar terms, strong increases in mineral prices in the 1970s, particularly for crude petroleum and natural gas, combined with more moderate increases in prices for inedible end products, prevented a rise in the share of total manufactured goods in exports since 1970.

The changes in the commodity composition of Canada's exports were accompanied by a significant alternation in the importance of Canada's export markets. The share of total exports going to the United States increased as a result of the auto pact and increases in exports of crude petroleum (from 53 per cent in 1964 to 68 per cent in 1979). The other major change was the decline in the share of our exports going to the United Kingdom, with Japan becóming our second major single country export market (with 6.2 per cent of our exports in 1979 compared to the U.K.'s 4.0 per cent). The only other region to show a significant change is OPEC where the share of Canada's exports going to these countries has risen from 1 per cent in 1960 to 3 per cent in 1979.

On the other hand, the role of the United States as a source of Canada's imports has not increased markedly, its share standing at 67 per cent in 1960 and just over 72 per cent in 1979. Again, as with exports, the share of the United Kingdom in Canada's imports has declined markedly. In contrast to exports, Japan's import share declined slightly. The other major change has been the rise in the share of the Middle East due to its increased role as a supplier of crude petroleum.

Over the last two decades, Canada has become increasingly trade oriented (Table 2). The increase in export orientation of all goods

Table 2

Import Penetration, Export Orientation and Implicit Self-Sufficiency in Canadian Goods Production[a]: Selected Years, 1966 to 1978[b]

	Import Penetration				Export Orientation				Implicit Self-sufficiency			
	1966	1970	1975	1978	1966	1970	1975	1978	1966	1970	1975	1978
	(per cent)											
All Goods Production	20.4	23.5	28.4	28.8	21.3	27.1	27.5	30.0	101.1	105.0	98.8	101.7
Industrial Sectors:												
Agriculture	8.1	8.9	10.0	10.8	29.4	24.5	30.0	28.0	130.2	120.7	128.5	123.9
Forestry	1.9	1.9	2.6	2.1	4.4	4.1	1.9	1.6	102.6	102.4	99.3	99.5
Fishing and Trapping	2.7	3.8	10.5	8.0	32.6	37.9	36.2	33.4	144.3	155.0	140.3	138.0
Mining	28.3	25.7	49.6	34.6	47.2	52.2	62.9	47.3	135.8	155.6	135.8	124.1
Manufacturing	21.0	25.5	28.8	31.5	18.8	26.2	23.9	30.4R	97.2	101.0	93.6	98.4R

(a) Excluding construction.
(b) 1965 data are available but are not completely consistent with the above. Also, 1979 data are available only for manufacturing — see Table 4.
R:Revised.

Note: *Import penetration* is defined as the ratio of imports less re-exports to the implicit Canadian market which in turn is defined as shipments plus imports less exports. *Export orientation* is defined as the ratio of domestic exports to shipments. *Implicit self-sufficiency* is defined as the ratio of shipments to the implicit Canadian market.

Source: Economic Intelligence Branch, Economic Policy and Analysis, Department of Industry, Trade, and Commerce.

production has been almost entirely due to the manufacturing sector for which export orientation rose from about 17 per cent in 1965 to 30 per cent in 1978. The main impetus came in the 1965-1970 period from the auto pact; however, after falling back a bit in the early 1970s, the export orientation of manufacturing resumed its upward march from 1975 to 1978.

Along with the ever-rising export orientation of Canadian goods production has been ever-increasing import penetration of domestic markets which rose from about 20 per cent in 1965 to 29 per cent in 1978. As with export orientation, manufactured goods have been the main contributors to this increase. For merchandise as a whole, the increase in import penetration was more or less offset by the rise in export orientation, and the implicit ability of Canadian producers in the aggregate to meet domestic requirements changed little over the period with domestic goods production generally greater than domestic requirements. Even in manufacturing, where the increase in import penetration has been the greatest, domestic production has generally been within 2 or 3 per cent of total domestic requirements.

Table 3

Import Penetration for all Goods and Services in the Major Industrial Countries[a]: Selected Years, 1960 to 1979[b]

	1960	1965	1970	1975	1979	Compound Annual Percentage Change 1960 to 1979
	(per cent)					
Belgium	33.6	36.2	42.6	46.0	51.4	2.3
Canada	18.5	19.4	21.2	26.7	31.0	2.8
France	13.2	13.0	15.9	18.0	20.7	2.4
Germany	16.9	17.8	19.4	24.2	26.2	2.3
Italy	14.2	13.8	17.3	21.9	26.0	3.2
Japan	10.6	9.5	9.6	13.7	13.2	1.2
Netherlands	49.6	45.8	48.2	50.5	47.2	−0.3
Sweden	23.4	22.4	24.7	29.5	28.2	1.0
Switzerland	29.5	29.3	33.9	29.4	33.6	0.7
United Kingdom	22.3	20.2	22.8	27.4	28.9	1.4
United States	4.4	4.5	5.5	8.4	11.0	4.9

(a) Based on data from the OECD, *National Accounts of OECD Countries, 1950-1978*, Vol. 1 and the *Quarterly National Accounts Bulletin 1980/II*. Import penetration here refers to imports as a percentage of gross domestic product plus imports less exports as calculated by the OECD.
(b) 1978 for the Netherlands, Sweden, and Switzerland.

Increased import penetration is, of course, hardly a unique Canadian phenomenon. As the data for imports of all goods and services in

Table 3 show, almost all of the major industrial countries have shared Canada's experience to a greater or lesser extent. Granted, in 1979 Canada had one of the highest degrees of import penetration based on this measure (it does fluctuate — in 1977 Canada was *below* average, in 1965 it was above average), but it was not much higher than such major industrial countries as Germany and the United Kingdom and was well below that of Belgium and the Netherlands. Furthermore, the *increase* in import penetration in Canada during the 1960s and 1970s was not greatly different from that of many of these countries.

Trade in Manufactured Goods

Importance of Manufacturing Trade to Canada

It is well known that a high proportion of Canada's economic activity is directed towards satisfying world demand — 29 per cent of Gross National Product was exported in 1979. What is not often appreciated is the dominant influence of the manufacturing sector on our export trade. For the period 1966 to 1979, total exports from the manufacturing sector accounted, on average, for over 70 per cent of Canada's total merchandise exports and about 60 per cent of the exports of all goods and services. In contrast, manufacturing accounted for only 23 per cent of total output in the economy and 20 per cent of employment.

Not only has manufacturing been important to trade, but trade has also been very important to manufacturing. The proportion of manufacturing shipments that are exported rose from 19 per cent in 1966 to 30 per cent in 1979 (Table 4). Nearly one third of the jobs and income generated in the manufacturing sector are now derived from export sales. Furthermore, this growth in export orientation has been widely distributed although some industries are far more export oriented than others.

Of all the major industry groups, transportation equipment showed by far the most rapid increase in export orientation. As a result of the implementation of the auto pact in 1965, export orientation in this industry group rose from about 15 per cent in 1965[1] to almost 69 per cent by 1970. It peaked at 76 per cent in 1978 before falling off in 1979 because of the (temporary) collapse of auto sales. Next to

---

1. The 1965 data are not absolutely comparable with the later data. This is why they are not shown in Table 4. For most individual industries, however, the 1965 data are sound enough to provide the correct order of magnitude.

Table 4

Import Penetration, Export Orientation, and Implicit Self-Sufficiency in Canadian Manufacturing[a]: Selected Years, 1966 to 1979

	Import Penetration				Export Orientation				Implicit Self-sufficiency			
	1966	1970	1975	1979	1966	1970	1975	1979	1966	1970	1975	1979
All Manufacturing	21.0	25.5	28.8	32.6	18.8	26.2	23.9	30.3	97.2	101.0	93.6	96.7
Industry Groups:												
Food & Beverage	6.6	7.0	8.4	10.2	9.6	9.7	8.5	12.3	103.4	103.0	100.2	102.4
Tobacco Products	1.0	1.0	1.6	1.7	0.5	0.6	0.4	0.7	99.4	93.6	98.5	99.0
Rubber & Plastics Products	14.5	16.9	24.7	23.2	4.1	4.9	6.8	11.1	89.1	87.4	80.8	86.4
Leather	14.4	22.4	32.7	33.9	4.4	6.8	6.5	8.0	89.6	83.3	72.0	71.8
Textile	25.2	22.8	25.9	28.9	4.8	5.0	4.8	7.1	78.6	81.2	77.8	76.6
Knitting Mills	11.3	21.4	30.9	30.8	1.8	2.9	1.5	1.6	90.3	80.9	70.1	70.4
Clothing	5.1	6.8	9.9	12.7	2.2	4.8	4.4	5.2	97.0	97.9	94.3	92.2
Wood	8.0	8.4	12.4	13.5	38.9	43.0	33.2	56.5	150.6	160.5	131.0	196.9
Furniture & Fixtures	5.1	5.6	10.4	13.3	2.1	4.8	4.2	9.2	96.9	99.2	93.5	95.5
Paper & Allied	5.5	5.9	10.5	9.7	49.9	52.4	54.4	57.2	188.7	197.5	196.1	210.9
Printing, Publishing & Allied	12.3	14.2	13.6	15.5	1.3	2.0	2.3	3.1	88.9	87.5	88.5	87.2
Primary Metal	23.5	24.6	23.3	34.9	42.2	53.4	38.9	44.5	132.5	161.8	125.5	117.3
Metal Fabricating	11.6	12.6	15.0	15.0	2.7	3.8	5.2	7.5	90.8	90.9	89.7	91.6
Machinery	64.2	65.5	71.8	75.2	33.0	38.2	46.3	53.2	53.5	55.8	52.5	53.0
Transportation Equipment	39.1	67.1	69.3	72.3	31.2	68.6	64.1	67.9	68.6	104.8	85.5	86.5
Electrical Products	21.9	25.3	30.4	40.2	9.2	15.8	13.5	20.5	86.0	89.7	80.4	75.3
Non-metallic Mineral Products	15.3	15.6	15.9	18.5	5.8	7.5	6.7	12.5	89.9	91.2	90.1	93.2
Petroleum & Coal Products	10.8	10.3	4.0	3.2	1.0	2.8	5.7	10.7	90.0	92.3	101.8	108.4
Chemical & Chemical Products	23.0	26.8	28.1	35.0	14.4	16.5	15.4	28.9	90.0	87.7	84.9	91.4
Misc. Manufacturing	46.2	51.5	31.5	54.6	22.4	25.9	17.2	21.7	69.4	65.4	58.6	57.9

(a) Import penetration: the ratio of imports less re-exports to the implicit Canadian market which in turn is defined as shipments plus imports less exports.
Export orientation: the ratio of domestic exports to shipments.
Implicit self-sufficiency: the ratio of shipments to the implicit Canadian market.

Source: Economic Intelligence Branch, Policy Planning, Department of Industry, Trade, and Commerce.

transportation equipment, industrial machinery production displayed the greatest increase in export orientation over the last dozen years or so. Currently, export sales are also crucial to paper and allied products, wood products, and primary metal products, although these industry groups have not had the growth in export orientation experienced by transportation equipment or industrial machinery. Exports are less important, but still significant for chemicals and chemical products, electrical products, non-metallic mineral products, and rubber and plastics products. At the other end of the spectrum, exports are of relatively little significance to manufacturing industries involved in clothing, knitting, tobacco, printing and publishing, and processed petroleum and coal.

With falling trade barriers and ever intensifying competition from the developing countries, world trade in manufactured goods has grown tremendously over the last decade. This has meant not only booming export sales for Canadians, but also a marked increase in the import penetration of Canadian markets for manufactured products. As shown in Table 4, import penetration rose from 21 per cent in 1966 to 33 per cent in 1979. This increase has been quite pervasive, although it does vary from market to market. As with export orientation, the import penetration of the Canadian market for transportation equipment reflects the implementation of the auto pact. In contrast, the Canadian market for industrial machinery has always been heavily dependent on imports (75 per cent in 1979) and the increase over the last dozen years or so was not as great as for transportation equipment. Other markets in which import penetration is both significant and has grown rapidly include electrical products, chemical and chemical products, rubber and plastics, leather, textiles, and knitting.

On balance, the implicit ability of Canadian manufacturers as a whole to meet domestic requirements has changed little over the last thirteen years. As measured by the ratio of domestic shipments to the implicit Canadian market,[2] this implicit self-sufficiency varied somewhat over the period, but in 1979 it was virtually no different from what it has been in 1966 and was slightly below the average for the period, which was 97.5 per cent. The drop in both export orientation and implicit self-sufficiency in 1974 and 1975, which does not show up in import penetration, was a reflection of the less severe recession experienced by Canada than by the major OECD countries. With the relatively larger drop in the incomes of our major trading partners, Canada's exports did not grow nearly as rapidly as imports even though both decelerated sharply in 1975.

Canada in the World Market for Manufactures
As well as manufacturing trade being important to Canada, Canada is

---

2. Defined as shipments plus imports less exports.

important to the world as a supplier of manufactured products. Throughout the period 1960 to 1979, Canada ranked ninth in the world in terms of value as an exporter of manufactures and seventh or eighth in terms of volume (as measured in constant dollars in Table 5). Some smaller countries, such as Belgium, the Netherlands, and Switzerland ranked close to Canada, but, unlike Canada, such countries did not also supply vast quantities of mineral, forest, and agricultural products.

Table 5

Ranking of World's Top Ten Exporters of Manufactured Goods: 1960 and 1979

Rank	Current U.S. $ 1960		1979		Constant (1970) U.S. $[a] 1960		1979	
1.	U.S.A.	13.0	Germany	150.5	U.S.A.	16.1	U.S.A.	52.5
2.	Germany	10.1	U.S.A.	116.6	Germany	11.5	Germany	49.2
3.	U.K.	8.7	Japan	99.0	U.K.	10.6	Japan	39.3
4.	France	5.1	France	75.7	France	5.8	France	27.4
5.	Japan	3.6	U.K.	70.4	Japan	3.7	U.K.	24.4
6.	Bel.-Lux.	3.1	Italy	60.0	Bel.-Lux	3.6	Italy	24.1
7.	Italy[b]	2.7	Bel.-Lux.	42.6	Canada[b]	2.9	CANADA	16.9
8.	U.S.S.R.[b]	2.7	Neth.	34.5	Italy[b]	2.9	Bel.-Lux.	16.1
9.	Canada	2.5	CANADA	30.2	Neth.	2.4	Neth.	12.5
10.	Neth.	2.1	Switz.	24.8	Switz.	2.3	Sweden	7.6

(a) Developed market economies only.
(b) Tied for seventh.

Source: Based on data from: UNCTAD, *1979 Handbook of International Trade Statistics* (United Nations, 1979), Tables 1.1, 2.1, and 2.3; and United Nations, *Monthly Bulletin of Statistics* (September 1980), Special Table C "Manufactured Goods Exports".

The U.N. data for the developed market economies shows that throughout the 1960s and into the early 1970s the distribution of merchandise exports continuously shifted towards manufactured products in both value and volume terms (Table 6). Although the value share dropped in 1973 as the prices of materials outstripped those of manufactured goods, it has since resumed its upward trend as the earlier commodity price increases made their way through the distribution system and into the prices of those manufactured products traded in world markets. In comparison, the volume share of manufactured exports has remained fairly stable since 1974, even dipping slightly in 1978 and 1979.

The substitution of manufactured for non-manufactured exports from 1960 to the present was no doubt partly due to relative price shifts. Although U.N. price data show only a 5.1 per cent drop in

Table 6

Developed Market Economies, Manufacturing Share of Total Merchandise Exports: Selected Years, 1960 to 1979

	1960	1965	1970	1975	1976	1977	1978	1979
Current U.S. $	68.0	70.1	75.2	75.2	75.9	76.4	76.7	74.3
Constant								
(1970) U.S. $	70.0	71.3	75.2	79.2	79.5	80.5	79.3	76.5

Source: See Table 5.

the price of manufactured exports relative to the price of other merchandise exports for the entire period, such data unfortunately exclude tariffs and thus do not adequately reflect the impact of the general tariff reductions that have occurred nor that of the creation and expansion of common trading areas.

Within this more-or-less global picture, the *volume* of Canadian manufactured exports outstripped that of the other developed market economies between 1960 and 1979, with an average annual increase of 9.7 per cent for Canada versus 8.0 per cent for the latter (Table 7). Only in the 1970-75 period did Canadian volume growth lag. In consequence, Canada's trade share in manufactured exports as measured by volume rose from 4.2 per cent in 1960 to 5.7 per cent in 1970, fell back to 4.9 per cent in 1974, and then resumed its upward march (Table 8). The developments over the longer run were at least in part a reflection of the fact that Canadian export prices for manufactured goods did not rise nearly as rapidly as those of the other developed market economies (3.9 versus 6.3 per cent per annum). Canadian prices for manufactured exports thus displayed a decline relative to those of the other developed market economies of almost 2.5 per cent per year.

This relative price decline outweighed Canada's more rapid volume growth so that the value of Canada's manufactured exports grew somewhat more slowly than that of the other developed market economies, at 14.0 per cent per annum versus 14.8 per cent (Table 7). As a result, and in contrast to the volume share, Canada's value share of manufactured exports was down slightly in 1979 compared to 1960 (Table 8)[3].

As with total exports, the U.S. dominates Canada's trade in manufactured goods. Not unexpectedly, the U.S. share of Canada's exports

---

3. Canada's value share changed significantly over the 1960s and 1970s, and some of the major causes are discussed more fully in the following section.

Table 7

Manufactured Exports: Canada and Other Developed Market Economies Average Annual Rate of Growth of Value, Volume, and Price[a]: Selected Periods, 1960 to 1979

	1960-1965	1965-1970	1970-1975	1975-1979	1960-1970	1970-1979	1960-1979
Canada:							
Value	8.6	20.8	11.4	16.0	14.5	13.4	14.0
Volume	9.4	16.3	3.7	9.7	12.8	6.4	9.7
Price	−0.9	3.8	7.4	5.8	1.4	6.7	3.9
Other Developed Market Economies							
Value	9.2	13.0	21.2	16.6	11.1	19.1	14.8
Volume	7.8	10.4	7.3	6.4	9.1	6.9	8.0
Price	1.2	2.4	13.0	9.7	1.8	11.5	6.3

(a) Unit Value

Source: See Table 5.

Table 8

Canada's Share of Manufactured Exports: Selected Years, 1960 to 1979

	Share of World Exports Current U.S. $	Share of Exports from Developed Market Economies	
		Current U.S. $	Constant (1970) U.S. $
	(per cent)		
1960	3.6	4.3	4.2
1965	3.5	4.2	4.5
1970	4.8	5.7	5.7
1975	3.2	3.8	4.9
1976	3.5	4.2	5.0
1977	3.4	4.2	5.2
1978	3.2	3.9	5.5
1979	n.a.	3.8	5.5

n.a.: not available.

Source: See Table 5.

has followed the U.S. business cycle and, in addition, in the latter half of the 1960s was heavily influenced by the developments under the auto pact. It rose sharply from 67.3 per cent in 1965 to 75.1 per cent in 1969, fell off in 1970, and rebounded once again to 72.1 per cent

by 1979[4] (see Table 9). The share of our manufactured exports going
to the United Kingdom steadily dropped and pulled with it the share
going to the EEC. The shares going to the other EEC countries and to
Japan rose somewhat.

Table 9

**Percentage Distribution of Canada's Manufacturing Exports
by Destination: Selected Years, 1967 to 1979**

	1966	1970	1975	1979
OECD	86.2	86.8	85.7	87.9
United States	67.3	68.8	69.6	72.1
Japan	1.5	2.2	2.4	3.6
EEC	13.9	12.6	10.8	9.4
United Kingdom	9.7	7.5	4.9	3.5
Other EEC	4.2	5.1	5.9	5.9
Other OECD	3.5	3.3	2.9	2.8
Rest of World	13.8	13.2	14.3	12.1

Source: Economic Intelligence Branch, Economic Policy and Analysis, Department of Industry, Trade, and
Commerce.

Is Canada Competitive in Manufactured Products?

The international competitiveness of Canadian manufacturers has
often been called into question. Actually the evidence is mixed, and
the view that Canada has not been competitive over the last two
decades is not really supported by the facts.

Prices
Price is probably the single most important quantifiable determinant
of competitive success. Quality, service, and salesmanship certainly
play a role, but if prices are out of line, sales simply will not be made.
Table 10 shows the growth in manufacturing export prices for the
major industrial countries, all developed market economies (roughly
equivalent to the OECD), and for developing economies from 1960 to
1979. The basic data are in U.S. dollars and refer to the U.N. definition
of manufacturing. They are displayed for five-year intervals partly for
convenience and partly because such intervals roughly coincide with
major events such as the implementation and maturing of the auto
pact from 1965 to 1970, the move to a floating exchange rate in

4. Seventy-nine per cent according to the U.N. definition of manufacturing.

1970, the general recovery and recession from 1970 to 1974/75, and the recovery again from 1976 to 1978. Between 1960 and 1979, the only sub-period in which Canadian price increases were out of line was 1965 to 1970. For the 1970s and for the period as a whole, Canada's export price performance was second to none.

Table 10

Manufacturing Export Prices[a], Compound Annual Rates of Change: Selected Countries, 1960 to 1979

	1960-1965	1965-1970	1970-1975	1975-1979	1960-1970	1970-1979	1960-1979
	(per cent)						
Belgium	0.4	2.4	13.1	9.4	1.4	11.4	6.0
Canada	−1.0	3.8	7.4	5.7	1.4	6.7	3.8
France	1.3	1.6	14.4	9.0	1.5	12.0	6.3
Germany, F.R.	1.8	0.9	15.8	10.1	1.3	13.2	6.8
Italy	−0.8	1.9	12.7	8.2	0.6	10.7	5.2
Japan	−1.9	2.7	12.3	9.0	0.4	10.8	5.2
Netherlands	4.6	0.4	14.4	8.8	2.5	11.9	6.8
Sweden	1.0	3.7	15.8	9.2	2.4	12.8	7.2
Switzerland	3.3	2.8	16.8	11.4	3.1	14.4	8.3
United Kingdom	2.0	1.9	11.9	13.3	1.9	12.5	6.8
United States	0.8	3.5	9.7	8.8	2.1	9.3	5.5
All Developed Market Economies	1.3	2.0	13.1	9.4	1.8	11.4	6.2
Developing Economies	2.0	2.9	10.8	11.6	2.5	11.1	6.5

(a) Unit values in U.S. $

Source: See Table 5.

Table 11 provides a comparison of Canada's export price performance with that of the domestic manufactured goods in each of Canada's major foreign markets. Again, when measured in a common currency, Canada's price performance was second to none either in the 1970s or in the period as a whole. As the national currency data suggest, although the recent depreciation of the dollar contributed significantly to that position, even without allowing for depreciation, the increases in Canadian export prices were still about average. However, "about average" is what we would expect *after* allowing for depreciation, not before.

As shown in Table 12, there was virtually no difference between domestic and import prices over the long run. Although producers for the domestic market shared the benefits of a superior cost performance with the exporting industries, it would appear that the

Table 11

Price Performance of Canadian Manufactured Exports and Foreign Domestic Manufactured Goods: Selected Periods, 1960 to 1979

	1960-1965	1965-1970	1970-1975	1975-1979	1960-1970	1970-1979	1960-1979
	(compound annual rates of change in per cent)						
Canadian Manufacturing Export Prices (U.S. $)							
Canadian Definition[a]	-1.1	3.6	9.0	6.3	1.2	7.8	4.3
U.N. Definition	-1.0	3.8	7.4	5.7	1.4	6.7	3.8
Foreign Domestic Manufacturing Prices in National Currencies[b]							
Belgium	0.9	2.1	6.8	3.2	1.5	5.2	3.2
France	3.4	3.5	8.3	7.6	3.5	8.0	5.6
Germany, F. R. of	0.7	1.2	6.3	3.2	0.9	4.9	2.8
Italy	1.8	3.8	13.9	13.9	2.8	13.9	7.9
Japan	0.0	1.9	8.4	3.0	0.9	6.0	3.3
Netherlands	2.4	1.9	6.6	4.3	2.1	5.5	3.7
Sweden	3.1	3.1	9.9	8.5	3.1	9.3	6.0
Switzerland	2.1	1.5	6.3	-0.2	1.8	3.4	2.5
United Kingdom	2.6	3.8	13.4	14.1	3.2	13.7	8.0
United States	0.3	2.7	9.2	7.5	1.5	8.4	4.8
Foreign Domestic Manufacturing Prices in U.S. Dollars[b]							
Belgium	0.9	2.1	13.4	9.2	1.5	11.5	6.1
France	3.5	1.0	14.0	7.8	2.3	11.2	6.4
Germany, F. R. of	1.5	3.1	15.0	11.1	2.3	13.2	6.0
Italy	1.8	3.8	12.8	7.2	2.8	10.3	6.3
Japan	0.0	2.1	12.5	11.3	1.1	12.0	6.1
Netherlands	3.1	1.9	14.5	10.8	2.5	12.8	7.3
Sweden	3.1	3.1	15.0	7.6	3.1	11.6	7.0
Switzerland	2.1	1.5	17.7	11.6	1.8	14.9	7.8
United Kingdom	4.1	-0.8	11.7	12.9	1.6	12.2	6.5
United States	0.3	2.7	9.2	7.5	1.5	8.4	4.8
Weighted Average of Above[c]	0.9	2.3	10.2	8.6	1.6	9.5	5.2

(a) The base-weighted price deflator for inedible end products plus inedible fabricated materials. It should be noted that this is the same series used by the U.S. prior to 1975 but using a different weighting scheme.

(b) For Belgium, France, and Japan, industrial products; for Germany, the price index for industrial products from 1970, the general price index prior to 1970; for Italy, producers' goods; for Sweden, producers' goods from 1970 and the general wholesale price index prior to 1970; for the Netherlands and the United Kingdom, finished goods; for Switzerland, domestic goods; and for the U.S., manufactured goods.

(c) Aggregated using 1970 Canadian trade weights.

Sources: United Nations, *Monthly Bulletin of Statistics*, Table 58, June, 1974, May, 1979 and September, 1980 and special Table C, September 1980. Economic Intelligence Branch, Economic Policy and Analysis, Department of Industry, Trade, and Commerce.

depreciation of the dollar was relatively more important in allowing them to compete, because Canadian export prices increased more slowly than those of their competitors, whereas domestic prices just managed to keep pace. However, it may also have been the case that some domestic products were priced *up to* the import price and hence could have met even stiffer import price competition without as much depreciation as actually occurred. Unfortunately, this proposition cannot be properly tested without detailed profit data which are simply not available.

Table 12

Price Performance of Canadian Imports of Manufactured Goods and Canadian Domestic Manufactured Goods: Selected Periods, 1960 to 1979

	1960-1965	1965-1970	1970-1975	1975-1979	1960-1970	1970-1979	1960-1979
Import Prices	2.7	1.6	7.8	11.2	2.1	9.3	5.5
Manufacturing Prices[a]	1.0	2.6	9.4	9.1	1.8	9.3	5.3

(a) The all-items Industry Selling Price Index (ISPI).

Source: Statistics Canada and the Economic Intelligence Branch, Economic Policy and Analysis, Department of Industry, Trade, and Commerce.

Tariffs

In the period 1960 to 1979, there were two general rounds of tariff reductions. Except perhaps during the initial phase-in, the benefits were more or less evenly distributed among participating countries. It is thus probable that they had little effect on any one country's overall competitive position vis-à-vis other exporters, while exporters' positions were improved relative to domestic producers in the exporters' markets. This suggests that the change in Canada's competitive position as displayed by export prices (Table 10) would not be materially altered by the inclusion of the general tariff changes; whereas that shown in Table 11, with respect to other countries domestic prices, represents an understatement of the improvement in Canada's competitive position. On the other hand, the internal reduction of EEC tariffs from January, 1959 and of EFTA tariffs from January, 1960 had a detrimental effect on Canada's competitive position relative to the European countries but not relative to its major trading partner, the United States. On balance, the improved position shown by export prices is thus something of an overstatement.

Labor Costs and Productivity

Arguments concerning Canada's alleged lack of competitiveness generally involve the productivity of labor and/or the costs of labor. Table 13 shows manufacturing unit labor cost developments over the 1960-1979 period for Canada and our major competitors.[5] In national currencies, the increases in Canadian unit labor costs were relatively moderate and second only to those of the U.S. for the whole period, and the increases in costs were below average over the 1970s. As measured in a common currency (the U.S. dollar in this case), Canada ranked first over the period as a whole, and was a close second to the U.S. during the 1970s.

Table 13 also displays developments in the two major components of unit labor costs, namely, productivity growth (growth in output/ man-hour) and hourly compensation. With regard to countries other than the United States, it is quite clear that Canada's improved competitiveness stems from much lower growth in hourly compensation, because Canada trailed all but the United Kingdom with regard to productivity growth.

For the U.S., the picture is the reverse. In spite of a more rapidly increasing labor force, Canadian productivity has grown more quickly than that of the U.S. The problem is that hourly compensation in Canada grew even more rapidly still and virtually offset the productivity gains.

Although it is important to know whether our competitive position is improving or deteriorating, it is equally important to know where we stand at any given moment. The Conference Board in Canada undertook a study of Canada's competitive position vis-à-vis the U.S. for a selection of industries[6] and found that Canada's labor productivity stood at about 65 per cent of that of the U.S. in 1967, but that the gap had been steadily narrowed to about 80 per cent by 1974. To the extent that these thirty-three industries represent manufacturing in total, that position was eroded somewhat in 1975 when Canadian productivity fell, while that of the U.S. continued to rise. Since 1975 Canadian manufacturing productivity has outstripped that of the U.S. and at least partially recovered Canada's position. No doubt there is still a large productivity gap between the two countries, but it is one which shows every sign of closing.

With regard to labor earnings, the Conference Board study concluded that there was a widespread and persistent narrowing of the

---

5. The IMF's so-called "G-10 plus Switzerland".
6. James G. Frank, *Assessing Trends in Canada's Competitive Position: The Case of Canada and the United States* (The Conference Board in Canada, 1977).

Table 13

Labor Cost Measures in Manufacturing: Compound Annual Rates of Change, Selected Countries, 1960 to 1979[a]

	1960-1965	1965-1970	1970-1975	1975-1979[a]	1960-1970	1970-1979[a]	1960-1979[a]
			(per cent)				
A.							
Unit Labor Costs							
I. U.S. Dollar Basis							
Belgium	4.7	1.5	15.9	8.0	3.1	12.9	7.3
Canada	−3.0	4.0	8.2	2.7	0.4	5.7	2.9
Denmark	4.2	2.6	13.8	9.2	3.4	11.7	7.3
France	3.8	−0.3	16.4	7.6	1.7	12.4	6.6
Germany, F.R.	4.3	5.9	16.4	10.4	5.1	13.7	9.1
Italy	4.9	4.2	15.5	5.9	4.5	11.1	7.6
Japan	4.4	2.0	20.3	7.8	3.2	14.5	8.4
Netherlands	7.0	3.4	17.7	8.3	5.2	14.1	9.1
Sweden	3.3	2.5	15.1	8.8	2.9	12.3	7.2
United Kingdom	2.9	1.2	13.5	11.7	2.1	12.7	7.0
United States	−1.1	4.7	5.5	6.1	1.8	5.8	3.6
II. National Currency Basis							
Belgium	4.6	1.5	9.1	2.6	3.0	6.6	4.6
Canada	−0.9	3.3	7.6	6.4	1.2	7.1	3.9
Denmark	4.3	4.3	7.8	6.9	4.3	7.4	5.7
France	3.8	2.1	10.6	7.4	2.9	9.2	5.8
Germany, F.R.	3.4	4.0	7.5	2.6	3.7	5.3	4.5
Italy	5.0	4.3	16.4	12.5	4.6	14.6	9.3
Japan	4.5	1.8	15.8	−0.2	3.2	8.4	5.6
Netherlands	6.0	3.5	9.5	2.8	4.8	7.0	5.7
Sweden	3.2	2.6	10.1	9.7	2.7	9.9	6.2
United Kingdom	3.0	4.4	15.2	13.0	3.7	14.2	8.6
United States	−1.1	4.7	5.5	6.1	1.8	5.8	3.6
B.							
Output/Man-hour							
Belgium	4.6	8.2	7.6	6.9	6.4	7.3	6.8
Canada	4.5	4.1	3.1	4.0	4.3	3.5	3.9
Denmark	5.4	8.3	6.6	3.7	6.9	5.3	6.1
France	5.2	6.5	4.5	6.0	5.8	5.1	5.5
Germany, F.R.	6.0	5.1	5.4	5.0	5.5	5.2	5.4
Italy	7.7	6.6	4.7	5.3	7.1	5.0	6.1
Japan	8.5	13.1	3.6	7.2	10.8	5.2	8.1
Netherlands	5.4	8.8	6.2	6.3	7.1	6.2	6.7
Sweden	6.7	6.8	4.2	3.2	6.8	3.7	5.3
United Kingdom	3.7	3.5	2.6	1.5	3.6	2.1	2.9
United States	4.3	1.3	2.5	2.3	2.8	3.4	2.6
C.							
Hourly Compensation (National Currencies)							
Belgium	9.5	9.7	17.4	9.6	9.6	14.4	11.7
Canada	3.6	7.6	11.0	10.6	5.6	10.8	8.0
Denmark	9.9	12.9	15.0	10.8	11.4	13.1	12.2
France	9.1	8.7	15.5	13.8	8.9	14.8	11.7
Germany, F.R.	9.6	9.2	13.4	7.8	9.4	10.9	10.1
Italy	13.1	11.1	21.9	18.4	12.1	20.3	15.9
Japan	13.5	15.2	20.0	7.0	14.3	14.0	14.2
Netherlands	11.7	12.7	16.3	9.3	12.2	13.6	12.8
Sweden	10.2	9.6	14.7	13.2	9.9	14.0	11.8
United Kingdom	6.8	8.1	18.3	14.7	7.4	16.7	11.7
United States	3.2	6.1	8.2	8.5	4.6	8.3	6.4

(a) Up to 1978 for Belgium and the Netherlands.

Source: U.S. Department of Labor, Bureau of Labor Statistics.

earnings differential between the two countries, to the point where the majority of Canadian industries were very close to or had exceeded parity in U.S. dollars by 1975. As shown in Table 14, U.S. Department of Labor data on total compensation broadly support one of the conclusions of the Conference Board study (which dealt with earnings, not total compensation) that Canadian manufacturing has largely closed the earnings gap with the U.S. At the same time it also shows Canada's position as the country with the second highest labor compensation in 1960, falling to being the seventh highest by 1979 (and incidentally clearly shows the sharp but short-lived increase in 1976). In addition to the U.S., Belgium, Germany, the Netherlands, and Sweden have become higher cost countries, and France and Italy are rapidly gaining ground. Among the mature industrial countries, Canada is rapidly becoming a relatively low labour cost economy.

Table 14

Estimated Hourly Compensation of Production Workers in Manufacturing in Ten Industrial Countries in U.S. Dollars: Selected Years, 1960 to 1979

Country	1960	1965	1970	1975	1976	1977	1978[a]	1979[b]
Belgium	0.83	1.32	2.08	6.44	6.85	8.16	9.88	11.30
Canada	2.12	2.28	3.60	6.14	7.23	7.48	7.52	7.97
France	0.83	1.24	1.74	4.63	4.84	5.43	6.70	8.17
Germany, F.R.	0.85	1.41	2.35	6.24	6.60	7.77	9.48	11.33
Italy	0.63	1.12	1.76	4.65	4.42	5.13	6.18	7.38
Japan	0.26	0.48	0.99	3.05	3.30	4.03	5.47	5.58
Netherlands	0.68	1.24	2.14	6.57	6.95	8.05	9.77	11.31
Sweden	1.20	1.87	2.93	7.18	8.21	8.85	9.65	11.39
United Kingdom	0.83	1.15	1.48	3.27	3.11	3.31	4.19	5.46
United States	2.66	3.13	4.17	6.36	6.93	7.61	8.33	9.09

(a) Preliminary.
(b) Preliminary, mid-year 1979.

Note: Total hourly compensation includes all direct payments made to the worker (pay for time worked, pay for vacations and other leave, all bonuses and pay in kind *before* payroll deductions of any kind). *It also includes* "fringe benefits" such as employer expenditures for social security, insurance, etc. The information is derived from periodic labor cost surveys prorated for intervening years. Small differences in compensation levels should not be considered significant. Total compensation is computed per hour worked.

World Trade Share

Whether in relation to total world exports or just to those of the developed market economies, Canada's share in current dollars of exports of manufactured goods has been slightly lower of late than it was in the early 1960s as was noted previously (see also Chart 1). It did rise sharply from 1965 to 1968, the same period in which

Chart 1

Canada's Share of the Manufactured Exports of the Developed Market Economies: 1960 to 1978

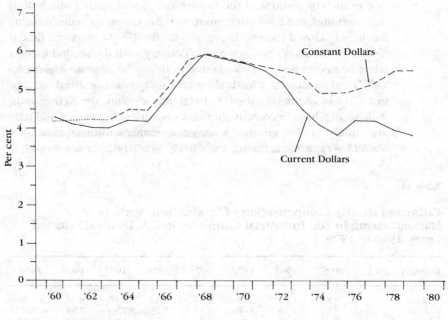

Source: Table 8.

Canada's export prices rose more rapidly than those of our competitors, but then the share declined from 1968 to 1975. In constant dollars, Canada's share has been significantly higher in the last few years than it was at the beginning of the 1960s (Chart 1). Over the same period, the big gainers in relative terms were Japan, Italy, and the smaller developed market economies, and the big share losers were the U.K. and the U.S.A.

The price and cost evidence cited earlier points toward a steady improvement in the competitiveness of Canadian manufacturing over the long haul. In addition, Canada's real trade share is perfectly consistent with this view. Given the price and cost evidence, it has behaved exactly as one might expect. Theory suggests that *if* Canadian producers were becoming *more* competitive over time, we could expect Canadian prices to fall relative to Canada's competitors, and if relative price declined we could expect that the real share of the market would increase.

But what about the value share? First of all, the increase in the shares in the late 1960s was associated with three significant events or circumstances. The Canadian dollar was pegged at 92.5¢ U.S. in May, 1962. After the exchange rate was unpegged in June, 1970, it moved to par in 1971. This suggests that the dollar was undervalued in the later 1960s, the implication being that Canada had a competitive advantage that was the result of this undervalued dollar and not really warranted by underlying economic factors. Also, the auto pact was implemented in 1965, and this gave Canadian manufacturing trade an additional strong upward push which lasted to about 1969/1970. On top of these developments, the increased U.S. involvement in Vietnam in the latter half of the 1960s increased external demand even more, particularly for goods involved in defence-sharing agreements. These three factors, then, contributed to the upswing in Canada's share of world manufacturing trade in the latter half of the 1960s but, of the three, only the effects of the auto pact were in fact sustained.[7]

Although the quantitative impact is not known, both the unpegging of the dollar in 1970, with its subsequent appreciation, and the winding down of U.S. involvement in Vietnam in the early 1970s would tend to lower Canada's trade share towards earlier levels. In addition, there were several factors at work in the early 1970s that also tended to reduce Canada's share. First, with the U.K. joining the European Common Market in 1973, Canada lost its Commonwealth preferences. The effect shows up very clearly in the data for the European Economic Community. Canada's share of U.K. imports dropped off while it remained essentially unchanged for the rest of the community. Second, from 1969 to 1975, sales of overseas cars and trucks in value terms rose almost 60 per cent in the U.S. while domestic sales declined 10 per cent. In consequence, the average share of the U.S. auto market held by overseas imports in the period 1971 to 1975 was almost 50 per cent higher than it had been in the previous five years. This reduced the relative significance of automotive trade in Canada's exports and contributed to the decline in our share of world exports. Third, Canada is the U.S.'s largest trading partner, and the relatively slower growth in the U.S. than in its

---

7. The so-called Kennedy Round of tariff cuts was also being implemented in this period and undoubtedly contributed significantly to world export growth, but there are no a priori reasons for believing that this had any major impact on Canada's trade share. Canada did implement its tariff cuts more rapidly than other countries, but because exports *to* Canada are such a small portion of the world total, this would have only a very marginal effect on Canada's share.

Chart 2

Trade Balance for Manufactured Goods and Inedible End Products: 1960 to 1979

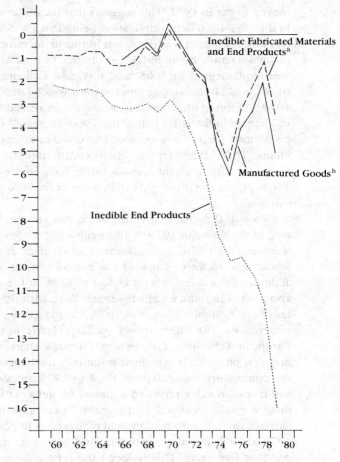

(a) Because of availability, often used as a proxy for all manufactured goods.
(b) As created by ITC on basis of Statistics Canada's Standard Industries Classification (SIC) System.

trading partners in the 1970s had to affect Canada more than it did the U.S.'s other partners.

The Trade Balance
As with the trade shares, trade balances are often employed as indicators of competitiveness even though they too are not direct measures of that competitiveness. In this regard, and with respect to manufacturing, attention is far too often focussed on the absolute size of the deficit in inedible end products as if the absolute size were the relevant measure and as if "inedible end products" were synonymous with "manufacturing".

The trade balances for all manufactured products and for inedible end products are displayed in Chart 2. The latter shows a steady deterioration from 1970 to the present. The balance for manufacturing also shows a sharp deterioration starting in 1970, but from 1975 it improved considerably up to 1978 before falling back again in 1979. However, as would be the case for an individual's debt, in order to evaluate the significance of this deficit it is necessary to relate it to the activity that generates it and to the ability to repay it. In vacuo, the size or change in size of any debt means nothing.

In Chart 3, the trade balances in manufactured goods and end products are shown in relation to GNP. The same balances relative to domestic exports are shown in Charts 4 and 5 respectively. The trade balance for all manufactures relative to either GNP or domestic exports improved (became less negative) from 1965 to 1970 when a small surplus was recorded, deteriorated from 1970 to 1975, and then improved again from 1975 to 1978. The general trend over the period was toward improvement, and even in 1979 the trade deficit relative to GNP was no worse than at the beginning of the 1960s, while relative to exports it was considerably better. For the deficit in inedible end products relative to GNP, the picture is very similar to that for all manufactures except that there is no obvious long-run trend towards improvement.

Relative to domestic exports, as a result of the rapid growth in all inedible end product exports, there was a steady improvement from 1960 to 1970 followed by little change since then. This same general comment also applies to both automotive and non-automotive end products.

In summary, to the extent that the trade balance for manufacturing as a whole does indicate competitiveness or the lack thereof, the data suggest that this is a cyclical phenomenon with an underlying trend of gradual improvement over the period 1960 to 1979. The trade

Chart 3

**Manufactured Goods and Inedible End Products:
Ratio of Trade Balance to GNP 1960 to 1978**

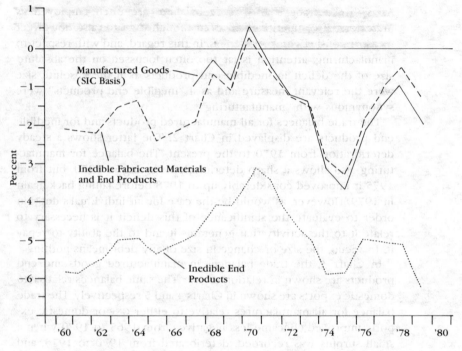

Source: Statistics Canada and the Economic Intelligence Branch, ITC.

balance data thus in fact tend to corroborate the evidence provided
by other indicators.

Challenges and Opportunities Ahead

Although it was not all smooth sailing, the last two decades did see
a remarkable expansion of Canadian trade. In the years ahead there
will continue to be challenges, but at the same time there will also
be many new opportunities. The challenges presented in the 1960
to 1978 period included the brief but alarming period in 1975 and
1976 when a wage explosion in Canada brought costs in manufacturing sharply out of line with other countries; the sluggish investment performance in the 1976-1978 period which is likely to prove

detrimental to our productivity performance in the immediate future; the growing competition from the more advanced developing countries of the world, particularly in the more labor-intensive industries such as textiles, clothing, footwear, and furniture, which threatens many of our technologically more advanced industries such as electronics; the exploitation of new mineral resources in the developing world, which in several instances has sharply reduced Canada's share of world mineral output and trade in these products; and the increased utilization of forest resources in tropical countries with implications for Canadian exports of paper and allied products.

In spite of the challenges to be faced, the recently concluded

Chart 4

Manufactured Goods: Ratio of Trade Balance to Domestic Exports 1960 to 1979

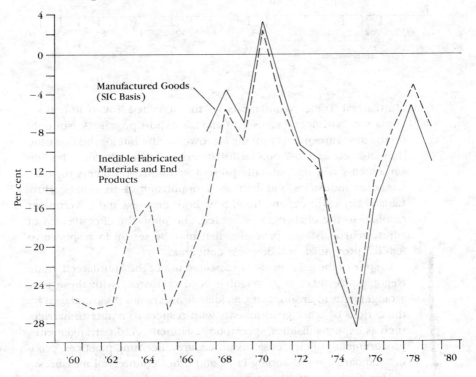

Source: Statistics Canada and the Economic Intelligence Branch, ITC.

Chart 5

Inedible End Products: Ratio of Trade Balance to Domestic Exports 1960 to 1978

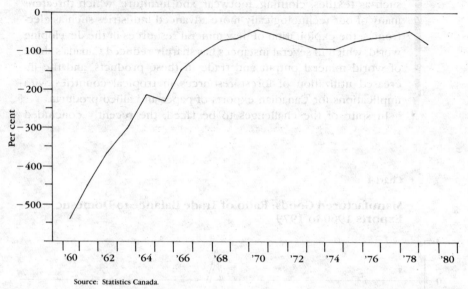

Source: Statistics Canada.

Multilateral Trade Negotiations — the so-called Tokyo Round — contain many hopeful signs for Canada's export prospects. Not only do the new agreements provide for lower tariffs, but for the first time they also cover most non-tariff barriers to trade. The new trading agreements will undoubtedly present additional problems to some Canadian industries and increased opportunities to others. How Canada fares will depend upon how both business and government respond to the challenges presented, and upon the effectiveness of adjustment assistance programs that may be set up in response to federal, provincial, and business concerns.

In spite of the gains made or expected under the Multilateral Trade Negotiations, there is an ongoing need consistent with these new arrangements to ensure that Canadian firms are not disadvantaged by the actions of other governments with respect to non-tariff barriers such as export subsidies, special tax treatment, credit arrangements, procurement policies, customs procedures, licensing practices, product standards, anti-dumping laws, and other countervail measures.

The 1960s and 1970s were not without problems, but they did not prevent Canada from having a very satisfactory trade performance.

The future too will provide its challenges, but there is no reason a determined national effort should not allow Canadians to continue to reap an appropriate share of the benefits of ever-expanding world trade.

II
Trade Theory and Canada's Comparative Advantage

B
Canadian Trade Policy

5
Economic Interdependencies in an Open Economy

Hamid Etemad

Dr. Etemad is assistant professor of international business in the Faculty of Management, McGill University. His areas of teaching and research are international marketing and international business policy.

This chapter was written expressly for this volume.

Introduction

The primary objective of this chapter is to define and examine the concept of economic interdependencies of open economies and to study their effects on the conduct of international business in those economies. To do so, the relations between external and internal balances are examined and a rather general model is presented. The implications of the model for Canada's international business managers are explored.

By definition, a closed economy (an economy with no international trade, investment and/or exchange) enjoys neither the advantages of international trade and investments, nor the problems associated with such transactions. Economic policy instruments are used to achieve internal goals or to secure a sense of internal equilibrium.

Conversely, an open economy (an economy with considerable international trade, investment and/or transactions) enjoys the fruits of international trade and investments but, in return, it must adhere to certain requirements and conventions of the system of international trade and investment. Such adherence imposes limitations on the country's policy alternatives. Sustained health of the whole system is heavily dependent upon all member countries' external balances, for the external disequilibrium of one country quickly becomes a disequilibrium in the other(s). Such interlinkages are implicit manifestations of the interdependencies of open economies.

Reorienting economic policy to correct the external balance usually affects a country's internal balance as well; and in some cases governments face a major economic dilemma: the simultaneous achievement of internal and external balance and stability seem to require contradictory use of macro-economic policy instruments.

Although Mead's classic work, followed by Levin, Mundell, Ott and Ott, and Willet provide a wealth of guidance on assigning economic policy instruments to correct economic ills and their consequent effects, the issue is still open.[1] This issue is crucial to

1. J. E. Meade, *The Balance of Payments* (London: Oxford University Press, 1951); J. H. Levin, "International Capital Mobility and the Assignment Problem", *Oxford Economic Papers*; R. A. Mundell, "The Appropriate Use of Montary and Fiscal Policy Under Fixed Exchange Rates", *IMF Staff Papers* **IX** (March 1962), pp. 70-79; T. D. Willet and F. Forte, "Interest Rate Policy and External Balance", *Quarterly Journal of Economics,* **LXXXIII** (May 1969), pp. 242-262.

international businesses, because international business is directly affected by the immediate effects of both the internal and external balances. For example, a nation's internal disequilibrium usually causes national economic difficulties and hence the national operations of multinational corporations (MNCs) (at the subsidiary level) would be affected. External disequilibrium accentuates the domestic problems even further. A national problem (or a subsidiary's problem) becomes an international problem and affects the headquarters as well. Problems at the headquarters may adversely affect future subsidiary operations.

In short, one imbalance (internal disequilibrium or external disequilibrium) is a *reasonable* cause for concern, whereas signals pointing to disequilibrium of both balances warrant serious consideration.

A simple graphical Hicksian I-S and L-M model is used to define internal equilibrium in the section 1 below. In the second section, the model is extended to cover the case of an open economy, and internal and external balances are derived. The third section examines critically the model and some of its assumptions. Its implications for Canadian business managers are explored, and conclusions are presented.

Model of a Closed Economy

In this section, a simple Keynesian model of income determination is used to show the relationship between different sectors of the economy. Hicksian IS-LM analysis characterizing equilibrium in markets for goods and services (G & S) and financial markets, respectively, is employed to define internal equilibrium. This analysis finds a pair of nominal income and interest rate for which the G & S and financial markets will be in equilibrium.

The Model
For a simple three-sector economy, the aggregate demand on the expenditure side (on goods and services) is comprised of aggregated expenditures on consumption, expenditures on investment, and expenditures by the government. Aggregate consumption is an increasing function of aggregate income (that is, consumption increases are proportional to income increases). Aggregate investment is a decreasing function of interest rates. Government expenditures are related to tax receipts or exogenously determined.

Equilibrium in the markets for goods and services, characterized by aggregate demand being equal to aggregate supply, is influenced primarily by the level of two basic economic variables, namely, the interest rate and the income level. Hence the locus of equilibrium in the G & S markets is defined in terms of those basic variables only (income and interest rate). Symbolically, this can be shown as follows:

Aggregate Demand = Aggregate Supply, or

$$\text{Agg D} = \text{Agg s}$$

Aggregate Demand = Consumption (C) + Investment (I) + Government (G), or

$$\text{Agg D} = C + I + G$$

Aggregate Supply = National Income (Y), or

$$\text{Agg s} = Y$$

Hence: $Y \equiv C + I + G$ (1)

To define Equilibrium in G & S markets:

Aggregate Consumption = An increasing function of income, or

$$C = C\,(Y) \tag{2}$$

Aggregate Investment = A decreasing function of interest rate, or

$$I = I\,(r) \tag{3}$$

Aggregate Savings = An increasing function of interest rates, or

$$S = S\,(r) \tag{4}$$

Aggregate investment = Aggregate savings, or

$$I = S$$

Government Expenditure = Tax receipts, or

$$G = T \tag{5}$$

Tax Receipts = An increasing function of income, or

$$T = T\,(Y) \tag{6}$$

Defining IS

The locus of equilibrium points for the G & S markets can be defined by a relationship between income (Y) and interest rate (r), such as:

$$f(Y, r, C_1) = 0 \tag{7}$$

Due to the fact that investments (I) are equal to savings (S) for all equilibrium points in markets for G & S, relation 7 is called the I-S curve. In $f(Y, r, C_1) = 0$, C_1 is a combination of exogenous and *fiscal policy* variables (that is, government expenditures and taxes). This relationship is depicted in Figure 1.

Figure 1

IS Curve

IS curve is a locus of equilibrium points in markets for goods and services. Government expenditures and taxes are among the parameters included in C_1. Changes in fiscal policy instruments (i.e., G & T) shift IS curve.

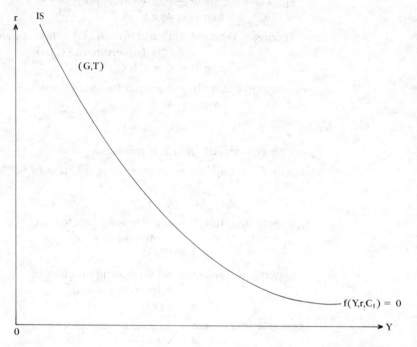

Defining LM

On the monetary side of the economy, the locus of equilibrium points in financial markets is defined by demand for money (liquid funds, L) being equal to supply of money (M) and is called the L-M curve.

It is assumed that demand for money is comprised of three parts, precautionary, transaction, and speculative. Then, demand for money, M^d, can be characterized by:

demand for money (M^d) = precautionary demand + transaction demand + speculative demand.

Precautionary demand = a constant amount (M_0).

Transaction demand = an increasing function of income (lY).

Speculative demand = a decreasing function of interest rate ($-nr$).

It will be assumed that the supply of money is controlled by monetary authorities and determined exogenously (that is, $M^s = M_0^s$). Therefore, at the equilibrium, demand (M^d) and supply (M_0^s) for money should be equal ($M_0^s = M^d$). That is:

$$M_0 + lY - nr = M_0^s \tag{8}$$

The above equation is a relationship between Y and r ($lY - nr = M_0^s = M_0$), the general form of which is:

$$g(Y, r, C_2) = 0 \tag{9}$$

C_2 represents a combination of exogenous and *monetary* policy variables (that is, money supply). This relation is shown in Figure 2.

Defining Internal Equilibrium
Simultaneous equilibrium in goods and services markets and financial markets is attainable by a combination of r and Y which satisfy both the IS and LM curves. Or, the solution to the following simultaneous equations yields the desired results — the *internal balance*

Figure 2

LM Curve

LM is a locus of equilibrium points in financial markets. Money supply (M_0^s) is among the exogenous variables included in C_2. Changes in monetary policy instruments (M_0^s) shift LM curve.

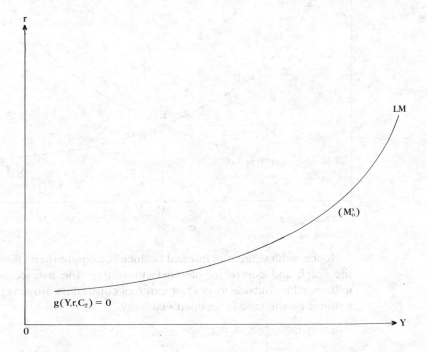

characterized by a pair of income and the interest rate (Y^*, r^*), for which G & S and money markets are in equilibrium.

$$\left.\begin{cases} \text{IS: } f(Y, r, C_1) = 0 \\ \text{LM: } g(Y, r, C_2) = 0 \end{cases}\right\} \longrightarrow \quad (Y^*, r^*) \tag{10}$$

A graphical solution to the above simultaneous set is shown in Figure 3.

Figure 3:

Equilibrium in
Financial, and Goods and Services Equilibrium
in a Closed Economy.

Financial, and goods and services markets are in equilibrium at point $E(Y^*, r^*)$.

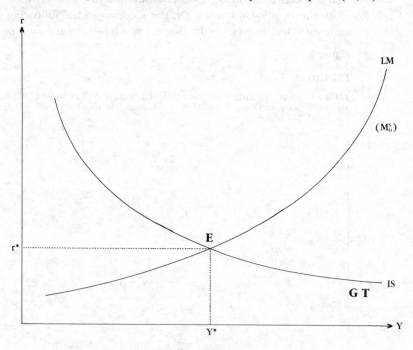

Hence, achievement of internal balance (or equilibrium) is within the reach and control of national authorities. The balance is *not* influenced by outside forces nor external constraints. However, this will not be the case in an open economy.

Model of an Open Economy

Adapting the Model

In adapting the simple model of the closed economy to an open economy, relevant effects of the economy's international transactions must be incorporated. This will be done in two parts: (1) in the goods and services markets; and (2) in the financial markets.

1. Goods And Services Markets. In a closed economy model, all entries were strictly domestic. In an open economy, however, entries have some foreign content. For example, in the level of investment, I, investment or disinvestments correspond to positive or negative addition to the stock of capital at home (in plant and equipment, buildings, consumer durables, inventories, etc.) by domestic or foreign sources. Therefore, a minimum adjustment as:

$$I = I_d + I_f \tag{11}$$

must be applied; where I_d and I_f correspond to domestic and foreign sourced investments, respectively. Hence, the level of investments is influenced by the positive or negative additions to the country's total foreign investments by changes in net debtor or creditor positions through lending, borrowing, investment, and divestment (excluding capital gains or losses). Substituting from (11) into (1) yields an equation for national income for the open economy as:

$$Y = C + I_d + I_f + G \tag{12}$$

Let the value of *all exports*, including services, be X; the value of *all* imports be M; the amount of income from foreign investments (interest and dividend payments) be D; and, the value of remittances be R. Then I_f can be defined as $(X - M + D + R)$, or:

$$I_f = (X - M) + (D + R) \tag{13}$$

Of course, I_f, I_d, I, D, and R can be either positive or negative. In equation (13), $(X - M)$ corresponds with the balance of trade and $(X - M + D + R)$ represents the major entries in the current account balance. (See Chapter 1 for definition and Canadian statistics).

Flows of imported goods and services enter into the domestic markets and are consumed similarly to domestically produced goods and services. Hence the consumption function for imports must assume a similar relation to the consumption function of domestically produced G & S, as in the case of a closed economy.

A similar argument must hold for exports. Exports produced domestically and shipped to the rest of the world (w), are consumed

similarly to other goods and services produced by the rest of the
world, and hence assumes a similar consumption function to that of
goods and services produced by the rest of the world. The above
arguments lead to:

1. Imports = An increasing function of national income, or

$$M = M(Y) \tag{14}$$

2. Exports = An increasing function of the rest of the world's
income (Y_w), or

$$X = X(Y_w) \tag{15}$$

Therefore, in a simple two-country model (the domestic economy
and the economy of the rest of the world), the locus of equilibrium
points in goods and services markets will no longer be independent
of the other countries' income level. Everything being the same,
flows of exports and imports from one country to the other establish
a certain degree of interdependence between the two economies.
Due to this interdependence, the national authorities can no longer
set their policies without attention to the behavior of the rest of the
world.

In short, increases (decreases) in the income level of the rest of
the world (Y_w) lead to increases (decreases) in their consumption of
imports. Increases (decreases) in a country's export to the rest of the
world affects primarily the aggregate supply side and in turn results
in increases (decreases) in the country's income level. Changes in
income level affect the internal equilibrium in the G & S markets. A
symbolic presentation of this dynamic process is shown below:

$$\uparrow Y_w \rightarrow \uparrow X \text{ (which is } M_w) \rightarrow \uparrow \text{ Agg Supply} \rightarrow \uparrow Y \rightarrow \uparrow M \tag{16}$$

2. The Financial Markets. On the monetary side of the economy,
international capital movements distinguish the open economy from
the closed economy. This section examines only the capital movements that are the consequences of two basic phenomena: (1)
movements due to trade account surpluses or deficits which may
result in increases or decreases in the money supply; and (2) capital
movements due to the differences between the rest of the world and
the country's interest rates.

A trade account surplus $(X > M)$ increases the money supply.
Conversely a trade account deficit $(X < M)$ drains the money supply.
Although export and import shipments affect G & S markets directly,
their associated monetary transactions influence the state of equilibrium of financial markets indirectly. As a result, two observations are
in order:

1. The distinctive dichotomy between G & S markets and financial markets, which was the case in a closed economy, will no longer exist.
2. Due to the interdependence of G & S markets with the rest of the world and the dependence of financial markets on G & S markets, all markets will be interdependent.

Capital movements in response to interest rate differentials affect the state of the financial market directly. A positive interest rate differential ($\Delta r > \Delta r_w$) attracts liquid funds and leads to an indirect increase in the money supply. However, a negative interest rate differential ($\Delta r > \Delta r_w$) may decrease the money supply. Hence, in an open economy, the interest rate differential (between the country and the rest of the world) affects the country's liquidity, money supply, and the interest rate. Therefore, the national monetary authorities can no longer set their policies independently or in isolation.

A symbolic presentation of the above process is shown below:

$$\left. \begin{array}{c} \uparrow \text{(increase)} \\ \downarrow \text{(decrease)} \end{array} \right. \text{in } Y_w \to \begin{array}{c} \uparrow \\ \downarrow \end{array} X \tag{16}$$

$$\begin{array}{c} \uparrow \\ \downarrow \end{array} \text{in } Y \qquad\qquad \to \begin{array}{c} \uparrow \\ \downarrow \end{array} M \tag{17}$$

$(X - M) \uparrow \to \uparrow$ Money supply, and also $\to \uparrow$ Agg s $>$ Agg D $\to$

$\qquad \uparrow Y \to \uparrow M \to$ LM to shift to left, and also $\qquad\qquad$ (18)
$\qquad\qquad$ IS to shift to right

$(\Delta r - \Delta r_w) \uparrow \to \uparrow$ in flow of capital, and also $\to$ $\qquad\qquad$ (19)

$\qquad \uparrow$ money supply $\to$ LM to shift right

In a closed economy, shifts in IS and LM (to the left or right) were due to changes in exogenous or policy variables (that is, changes in government expenditures, taxes, or money supply). In an open economy, however, the income and interest rate of the rest of the world (Y_w, & r_w), as explained in relation 18 and 19, may have similar effects on the country's internal equilibrium (due to shifts in IS and LM). This suggests that the effect of changes in policy variables of the rest of the world must be taken into consideration. Similar conclusions are derived from incorporating relations 16, 17, 18, and 19 into relations 13, 12, and 8. Doing so will also result in different sets of relationship for IS and LM in an open economy. They are:

$$\left. \begin{array}{l} \text{IS: } U(Y, r, Y_w, r_w, C_3) = 0 \\ \text{LM: } V(Y, r, Y_w, r_w, C_4) = 0 \end{array} \right\} \longrightarrow (Y^*, r^*) \qquad \begin{array}{l} (20a) \\ (20b) \end{array}$$

Internal equilibrium, characterized by relation 20, is shown in

Figure 4. Y_w and r_w must be viewed similarly to other exogenous or
policy variables; for their changes cause similar effects on internal
equilibrium. This similarity of effects is a central issue in economic
interdependence.

Figure 4

Equilibrium in
Financial, Goods and Services Market
in an Open Economy.

A pictorial presentation of financial and G & S market in equilibrium for an open
economy. r_w and Y_w are among the parameters that influence the equilibrium point
(E).

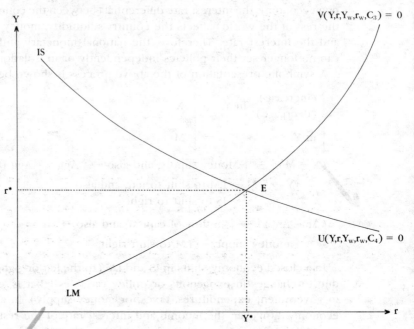

The actual amount of shifts in IS and LM due to changes in
international income (Y_w) and interest rate (r_w) depends primarily on
the degree of the economy's dependence on sensitivity to international trade and investments.

In the case of Canada, exports and imports have consistently
accounted for a large portion of the country's GNP (25.2 per cent and
24.1 per cent, respectively, in 1979). The ratio of exports and
imports to production of goods has also been traditionally high and is
rising. In 1979, the ratio of exports to production of goods increased
by 0.6 per cent to an all time high of 87 per cent. This figure is by far

the highest among all OECD countries. The ratio of imports to production of goods also increased in 1979 to an all time high of 83.3 per cent (second only to the United Kingdom).

The large size of the U.S. financial markets, traditional capital mobility between the United States and Canada, proximity of the two countries, and comparability of commercial and political risk have all contributed to a very strong interdependence between Canadian and U.S. financial markets.

International business managers, in general, must be aware of such interdependencies. Canadian managers, in particular, must consider the effects and incorporate them into their decisions.

Preliminary Discussion Of External Balance

To see the relation between the "external" and the "internal" balance as defined by the pair of Y^* and r^*, one has to re-examine the case of an open economy. Balance of payments is indeed an approximation of the external balance. Major elements of the balance of payments are:

1. The trade balance, represented by $X - M$;
2. The value of services and other unilateral transfers, represented by $D + R$ and assumed to be exogenous ($D_0 + R_0$); and,
3. Short-term capital movements represented by k ($\Delta r - \Delta r_w$).

Hence, external balance (approximated by the balance of payments) is comprised of the current account balance ($X - M + D + R$), and the capital account balance.

Symbolically, this is shown below:

BOP = current account balance + capital account balance (CAB)

$$BOP = (X - M) + (D + R) + CAB \qquad (21)$$

$$X - M = X(Y_w) - M(Y) \qquad (22)$$

$$D + R = D_0 + R_0 \text{ (exogenous)} \qquad (23)$$
$$\text{capital movements} = \text{function of interest rate}$$
$$\text{differentials } (\Delta r - \Delta r_w)$$

$$CAB = A(\Delta r - \Delta r_w) \approx A(r - r_w) \qquad (24)$$

Incorporating relations 21, 22, 23, and 24 leads to an expression for external balance (equilibrium) in which income and the interest rate of the rest of the world (Y_w, r_w) are among the explicit variables. This expression is symbolized in equation (25):

$$BOP = B(Y, r, Y_w, r_w, C_3) = 0 \qquad (25)$$

Equation (21) is a positively sloped curve and characterizes a relationship between Y and r for the economy's external balance. This curve divides the Y − r space into two regions. In the region below the curve all points represent a balance of payment deficit (BOP < O); and for the other region, all points characterize a balance of payment surplus (BOP > 0). This is shown in Figure 5.

Figure 5

Balance of Payment Curve

The balance of payments is an approximation of locus of points for which the economy is in external balance.

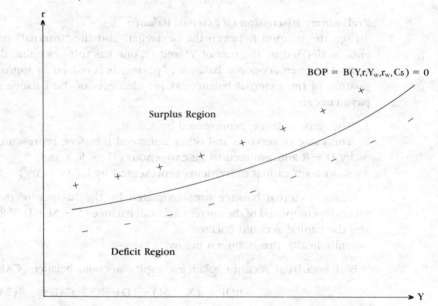

Internal Versus External Balance: A Preliminary Discussion

The overall equilibrium pair of Y* and r* is the solution of a set of simultaneous equations (that is, 20a and 20b) for which both the G & S markets and financial markets are in equilibrium. This pair may or may not guarantee equilibrium in other areas (for example, employment). Under certain conditions Y* and r* also satisfy equation (25). Under that set of special conditions, the market for goods and services, the financial market, and the balance of payments will be in equilibrium simultaneously. This is, however, a rare case. The state of equilibrium of goods and financial markets is likely to create a balance of payments deficit or surplus. A surplus case is shown in Figure 6. This surplus or deficit will force the national authorities to act to correct the situation, with the burden of adjustment traditionally falling on the deficit countries. Indeed, such countries have been forced (by the international community) to take drastic corrective actions in cases of persistent deficit. Such corrective actions (restrictions on imports, subsidies on exports, and lucrative incentives for capital investment from abroad) have broad influences on most economic sectors and this should concern everyone involved. Any major change in policy designed to correct internal and/or external disequilibrium will eventually affect the practice of international business at the subsidiary, intersubsidiary and/or subsidiary-headquarters level. For this reason, the interrelationships and their potential effects on international business must be understood.

Figure 6

Internal and External Equilibrium

Internal equilibrium ($r^* - y^*$) and the Balance of Payment (BOP) curve. The economy is in surplus position in the above case.

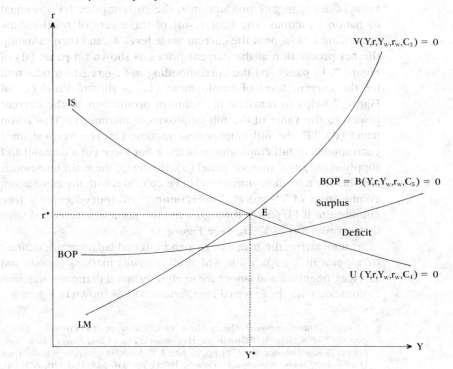

Incorporating Labor Markets Equilibrium

Introducing the concept of labor market equilibrium to the model improves the analysis considerably and adds to its complexity. Most national governments are showing much greater sensitivity to unemployment problems than to interest rate or balance of payments related aspects of their economies. Indeed, labor market equilibrium (full employment) has assumed a critical role in setting national economic objectives. Full labor employment, over-employment, and/or under-employment have been the subject of many labor economics books and articles. Any short discussion of the topic is inadequate to cover some of the complex arguments involved (consult Ackley, Branson, Elliot, and Ott, Ott and Yoo[2]). However, an attempt to derive Labor and Market Equilibrium is presented below:

The total labor input (L) is one of the major input components of the aggregate production function. That is:

$$P = P(L,K) \tag{26}$$

where the aggregate production, the total labor input, and the aggregate capital involved are represented by P, L and K, respectively. The value of net aggregate production at the current price level is equal to national income. The final result of these sets of relationships employing L of labor at the current wage level W_0 and then valuating the net production at the current prices, is shown on panel (d) of Figure 7. In panel (b) the corresponding *net* aggregate production for the current level of employment (L_e) is shown. Panel (c) of Figure 7 helps to translate the value of production, at the current prices, to the value of the full employment income, Y_0. That is, on panel (d), FE, the full employment income (FE is a vertical line) corresponds to full employment of the labor force (in a demand and supply sense) as shown on panel (a). However, the main question is whether the full employment level of FE coincides with the equilibrium combination of Y^* and r^*. The economy will indeed enjoy a true equilibrium if FE passes through a unique point characterized with the co-ordinates of Y_{te}, r_{te} (see Figure 8).

To summarize, the true external and internal balances are defined by a point in Y-r space for which all *internal* markets (goods and services, financial, and labor) are in equilibrium if that point happens to coincide with the external equilibrium. This is shown in Figure 8.

2. G. Ackley, *Macroeconomic Theory* (New York: The Macmillan Company, 1961), pp. 359-393; William H. Branson, *Macroeconomic Theory and Policy* (New York: Harper & Row Publishers, 1972), pp. 95-122; J. W. Elliot, *Macroeconomic Analysis* (Cambridge, Mass.: Wintrope Publishers, 1975), pp. 310-324; D. J. Ott, A. F. Ott, and J. H. Yoo, Macroeconomic Theory (New York: McGraw Hill, 1975).

Figure 7

Full Employment (FE) Curve.

Full employment (FE) curve in panel (d) is a reflection of labor market equilibrium. Panel (a) shows the equilibrium quantity of labor at the going wage rate for which labor market is an equilibrium in a demand and supply sense. In panel (b), through an aggregate production function this quantity is translated to aggregated production. Finally, after a transformation in panel (c), a full employment curve is derived at panel (d).

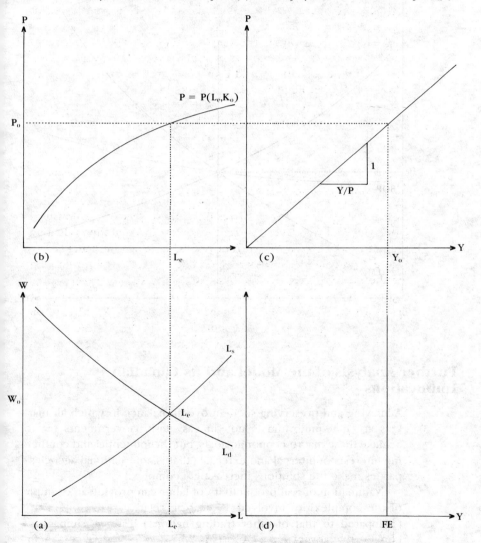

Figure 8

True Overall Equilibrium.

The equilibrium pair of r, Y, satisfy full employment (FE) in labor markets as well as balance of payments, hence all markets are in equilibrium.

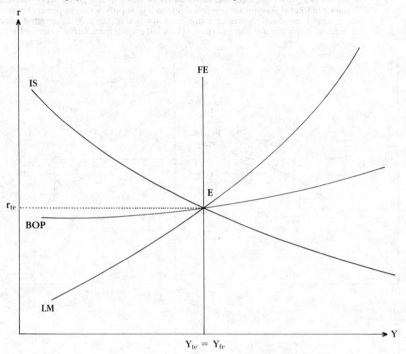

Further Analysis of the Model and Its Canadian Implications

Achieving and preserving such an overall balance in which all markets are in equilibrium is not an easy task. Governments try to achieve these macro-economic goals, but the influential and conflicting interests of internal and external (that is, international agencies) parties make the solutions increasingly complex.

Examination of real productivity of labor can provide an example of the complexities involved. Erosion in relative real productivity (compared to that of other trading nations) leads to slippage of comparative advantage in exports mainly due to relative cost inefficiency in domestic production. As a direct result, everything else being the same, exports may start decreasing. If unchecked by other policies (commercial, fiscal, and monetary) this slippage may lead to further substitution of imports for domestic production, causing a balance of payments deficit on one hand and under-employment or unemployment in the labor force on the other hand.

Comparative figures on Canada's productivity in manufacturing and unit labor costs are shown in Tables 1 and 2, respectively. Japan's economy experienced the highest productivity gains for all OECD countries between 1970-1980 (Table 1). Canada's gains were only moderate, third lowest after the United Kingdom and the United States. Real productivity in manufacturing (productivity adjusted for unit labor costs), however, provides a different picture. Canada has preserved roughly its relative position.

Table 1

Output Per Man-Hour for Major OECD Countries. Index: 1967 = 100

period	United States	France	F.R. Germany	Italy	Nether- lands	United Kingdom	Japan	Canada
1970	105.0	121.2	116.1	121.7	134.0	110.0	146.5	114.7
1975	118.8	150.7	151.3	152.9	181.1	125.3	174.6	133.7
1976	124.0	163.6	160.3	165.9	199.1	129.2	188.7	140.4
1977	127.7	171.7	169.0	167.8	206.7	128.6	197.3	148.1
1978	128.2	180.2	174.7	172.9	217.3	130.1	212.9	155.0
1979	129.2	189.9	183.8	188.0		133.0	230.5	156.3

Source: U.S. Department of Commerce, "International Economic Indicators", VI, No. 4 (Washington: December 1980). International Trade Administration.

Table 2

Unit Labor Cost in U.S. Dollars for Major OECD Countries. Index: 1967 = 100

period	United States	France	F.R. Germany	Italy	Nether- lands	United Kingdom	Japan	Canada
1970	116.5	96.7	125.7	119.2	108.7	104.8	113.2	117.7
1975	152.4	206.2	268.5	245.1	245.4	197.6	284.8	165.6
1976	158.2	195.1	265.4	212.5	238.8	182.4	285.3	185.7
1977	166.6	207.0	299.4	234.9	268.7	197.0	326.7	182.5
1978	179.4	242.6	360.5	271.7	311.8	247.5	408.7	174.3
1979	194.1	276.5	399.3	307.8		307.9	384.2	184.4

Source: U.S. Department of Commerce, "International Economic Indicators", VI, No. 4 (Washington: December 1980). International Trade Administration.

Regardless of the original cause, a balance of payments deficit may force the authorities to adopt a policy of high interest rates to attract international liquid funds, coupled with controls designed to discourage imports, to encourage exports, to stop or slow down exchange rate depreciations, and finally to minimize reserve losses. Although a monetary policy designed to raise interest rates to preserve external balance may stop the balance of payments from further erosion, it may also lead to severe unemployment of all resources, including labor in the internal market (mainly due to a drop in domestic investment, I). However, an expansive fiscal policy may succeed in correcting some of the unwanted results (for instance, high unemployment). This interrelationship of internal and external balances (and variables involved) can influence the whole system dramatically. Hence, the selection of proper macro-economic tools and policies to respond to *seemingly* unrelated and isolated problems is important.

With respect to import and export policies, Canada's high tariff barriers have traditionally discouraged imports (see Chapter 8 by Carl Beigie). Federal and provincial governments have offered and are still offering a multitude of export incentive programs to encourage exports. The absolute level of import barriers or export incentive programs, however, may not accomplish the intended results due to extreme interdependencies. Indeed, in spite of discouraging import policies of others, the most competitive and efficient set of export incentive programs will prevail. The recent aggressive approaches of the United States, Japan, France, and the Federal Republic of Germany are cases in point.

For Canadian managers, these topics assume a critical role. Given the fact that Canada's economy is a fairly open one and the United States is Canada's major trading partner, U.S. fiscal, monetary, and commercial policies affect Canadians directly. As demonstrated in this chapter, a change in one economic variable (for instance, a change in the monetary policy in Canada or the United States) will soon lead to another, and before long will affect the domestic and international operations of most firms.

In summary, a thorough knowledge of the interrelationships between the internal and external economic variables and the extent to which they can affect a firm's operations are of crucial importance to all international managers. The implication of using different policy tools, for their different effects on different markets, cannot be ignored by the businessman of fairly open market countries such as Canada. Indeed, the knowledge of these complex interrelationships and their implications, can but help managers prepare for their future unwanted consequences.

For Further Reference

Dernberg, Thomas F., "Exchange Rates and Co-ordinates Stabilization Policy". *Canadian Journal of Economics,* **III** (February 1970), pp. 1-13.

Grubel, H. G., "Internationally Diversified Portfolios: Welfare Gains and Capital Flows". *American Economic Review,* **LVIII** (December 1968), pp. 1299-1344.

Ott, D. J. and Ott, A. F., "Monetary and Fiscal Policy Goals and the Choice of Instruments". *Quarterly Journal of Economics,* **LXXXVI** (May 1968), pp. 313-325.

Tobin, James, "Adjustment Responsibilities of Surplus and Deficit Countries". *Maintaining and Restoring Balance in International Payments.* Edited by William Fellner, et al. Princeton, New Jersey: Princeton University Press, 1966.

Niehans, Jurg, "Monetary and Fiscal Policies in Open Economies Under Fixed Exchange Rates: An Optimizing Approach". *Journal of Political Economy,* **LXXXVI**, Part II (July/August 1968).

II
Trade Theory and Canada's Comparative Advantage

B
Canadian Trade Policy

6
The Legacy of Protection

Economic Council of Canada

The material in this chapter originally appeared in Economic Council of Canada, *Looking Outward: A New Trade Strategy for Canada*, 1976. Reprinted by permission of the minister of Supply and Services Canada.

Canada's economy has long been dependent on foreign trade, foreign investment, and immigration to an extent almost unequalled among nations. And, while there are differences of opinion about some aspects of this openness to the outside world, Canadians by and large recognize that they have prospered from this interchange of goods, money, population, and ideas. Given this position, the importance of global economic developments for Canada is undeniable, and recent profound changes in the international context should be examined with care. Some of these events, in the view of the Economic Council, call into question the validity of a long-standing feature of this country's economic arrangements: the use of a protective commercial policy to promote Canada's national development.

One of the most significant recent trends in world affairs is the emergence of an integrated international economic system. Whereas twenty years ago there were more than twenty economically advanced non-communist countries, each with an essentially separate economy, today there are three economic superpowers — the United States, the European Economic Community (EEC), and Japan. Other economic units appear very small in comparison with these giants. The thrust of development in these affluent economies is, on the whole, towards industrial activities that are technologically advanced or in other ways skill intensive. The key to efficiency, at least in the goods-producing sector, is a highly sophisticated organization of output, usually involving large scale and elaborate industrial plant and product specialization.

Equally significant is the emergence of a number of "new Japans" — that is, countries displaying an extensive capability for production of a range of "standard-technology" manufactured goods, such as were made in Japan in the years before the Second World War. As was the case in that country, wages paid in these industries are very low, labor is diligent, and in consequence the goods produced are extremely cheap. A large proportion of these goods is exported to the advanced countries, where they easily undersell comparable products made locally.

These developments are of particular significance to a country like Canada, which is an advanced industrial nation but a relatively small economic unit lacking the domestic scope for enhanced efficiency through large scale and specialization in the manufacturing sector. This situation limits Canada's ability to compete effectively with both the major developed countries and the newly industrializing areas of the developing world, not only in export markets but even at home. Moreover, these characteristics tend to inhibit technological and other initiatives in Canada that could offset the disadvantages of high unit costs. The competitive weakness of Canadian enterprises in turn encourages their takeover by foreign concerns more fortunately placed. Then, as subsidiaries of companies headquartered abroad, firms in Canada are operated in most cases as satellite activities outside the main areas of industrial innovation and growth. At the same time, the comparative advantage that Canada could gain through the production of those commodities that it is potentially capable of producing most efficiently is lost because of its lack of free access to larger markets.

The problems associated with this train of events can already be observed in the rather slow rate of expansion in output per person employed in Canada. Although the overall level of Canadian output has risen quite rapidly, much of this performance can be attributed to the unusually high rate of labor force growth, derived from a high birth rate in the 1950s and a large influx of immigrants. Growth in output per person employed, which is a convenient proxy for productivity or efficiency, has compared poorly with that of other countries, and the evidence is that, unless strong policy measures are taken, it may not improve very much in the future, despite the many advantages that Canada possesses.

One of the basic causes of our poor productivity performance is the type and organization of manufacturing fostered by the commercial policies adopted by Canada and other countries over the years. Such measures were aimed directly at influencing the terms under which goods and services could be imported and exported and included the use of import duties (tariffs) and non-tariff barriers to trade, such as subsidies to domestic firms, export and import licensing, and various quantitative restrictions.

Canadian governments have long employed the tariff as one of the main ways of furthering the attainment of national economic and political goals. This approach was embodied in the National Policy, which was introduced in 1879. The National Policy was a combination of protective tariffs and immigration and transportation policies that were all designed to foster the development of manufacturing, mainly in central Canada, and to stimulate the growth of population and resource-based industries in western Canada. It was a response to changing events in the external world — to the dynamic westward expansion of the United States and to Canada's failure to regain a preferential position for trade in either Britain or the highly protected U.S. market of the 1870s. Indeed, much of Canada's tariff history has been influenced by the level of tariffs in the United States (Chart 1).

Chart 1

Average Nominal Rates of Duty, Canada and United States, 1869-1973

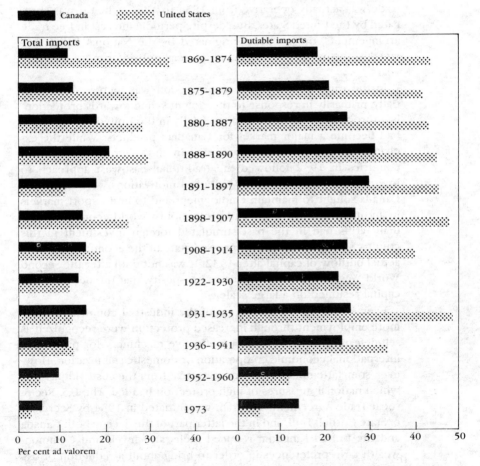

Note: The data are an average of duty collected divided by import value. The U.S. data have been adjusted to coincide with the Canadian time periods by using weighted averages. Data for 1973 were calculated by the Economic Council from official Canadian and U.S. figures.

Source: Based on H. M. Pinchin, *"The Regional Impact of the Canadian Tariff"*, a background study for the Economic Council of Canada.

The initial emphasis of the National Policy was on stimulation of east-west trade within Canada and between Canada and Europe, in order to balance the growing continental economic dominance of the United States. Around the turn of the century, for example, Canada extended unilateral tariff preferences to the United Kingdom primarily to strengthen the European orientation of Canadian trade. The east-west approach, however, did not always enjoy unequivocal support. Efforts to abandon the National Policy in favor of free trade with the United States gained a considerable following at various times, and the case for "reciprocity" was a major focus of the general elections of 1891 and 1911. These initiatives reflected the fact that, in the pre-Confederation period, a treaty for limited Canada-U.S. free trade was actually operative from 1854 to 1866, when it was abrogated by the United States. But, despite periodic interest in free trade arrangements, the concepts originated by the National Policy survived as the basis of Canadian commercial policy for more than fifty years.

In the early 1930s, Canadian protection was increased substantially, primarily in response to the violent swing towards protectionism throughout the world and especially in the United States, which had become a major market for Canadian products. While the exchange of tariff preferences with Britain and other Commonwealth countries in 1932 followed the traditional east-west approach to international trade, the major Canadian motivations were defensive. Canada sought to maintain employment and to find export markets in an otherwise depressed and protectionist world economy. Canadian tariffs had in the past stimulated foreign investment in this country's industry, but the depressed state of the economy led to an actual outflow of capital after 1932. It was not until after the Second World War, in a climate of greater prosperity, that the net inflow of capital resumed on a large scale.

Even in the 1930s, the efforts of the industrial countries to promote employment through increased protection were recognized as self-defeating, but there was no effective machinery for promoting international economic co-operation or domestic stabilization. However, some attempts were made to retreat from the costly impasse to which national measures of high protection had led. The U.S. Reciprocal Trade Agreements Program was initiated in 1934 by Secretary of State Cordell Hull, and in the latter part of the decade both Canada and the United Kingdom reduced their tariff levels and Commonwealth tariff preferences in order to bring about a reduction of U.S. tariffs.

The end of the Second World War was a turning point in Canadian international economic relations. To offset U.S. influence, strong support emerged in Canada for multilateral action to reduce world trade barriers; this was preferred over the narrower concept of a trade relationship focussing on Europe and particularly Britain. In practice, however, the United States was increasingly becoming Canada's most important trade partner and source of capital.

The multilateral approach to reduction of trade barriers came to centre around the General Agreement on Tariffs and Trade (GATT), negotiated in 1947. As one of the main initiators of GATT, Canada accepted the principle that no new preferential arrangements would be exchanged between countries, and recognized implicitly that the existing Commonwealth preferences would wither away as most-favored-nation tariff rates were reduced through GATT negotiations.[1] In common with the other members, Canada also agreed that national commercial policy measures should be used to promote the growth of world trade, international specialization, and efficiency of national production and *not* primarily to achieve high levels of employment in protected industries — the "beggar-my-neighbor" policies of the 1930s. All of the industrial countries developed increasingly comprehensive domestic instruments designed to maintain growth and employment.

Meanwhile, world economic conditions tended to increase the interdependence of the Canadian and U.S. economies. Canada provided a stable and attractive location for a growing volume of U.S. investment. The U.S. share of Canadian direct investment abroad also increased rapidly until the early 1950s and, although it has declined in relative importance since then, it still accounts for more than half of the total.

With respect to trade, both the Canadian and U.S. markets were relatively open in the 1950s when most other countries controlled imports — particularly those from the "dollar" countries — to conserve foreign exchange. And, in comparison with the war-shattered economies of the other industrial nations, both countries were in a good position to supply products that the other required. The European Economic Community and Japan grew faster than the United States in the 1960s, but their trade with Canada was modest and their investment in Canadian industry small. Moreover, Canada's competitive position in the European market deteriorated with the estab-

---

1. New preferential tariffs are prohibited by GATT, save for arrangements substantially freeing trade among countries, as in a customs union (common market) or free trade area.

lishment of the EEC and it was impaired even more by British entry into the Community in 1973.

Canada-U.S. economic integration was also reinforced through bilateral policy measures. The defence production sharing program with the United States was renewed in 1959, and the Canada-U.S. Automotive Agreement, which resulted in a major expansion of north-south trade and much closer integration of a major industry in the two countries, was signed in 1965.

More recently the interdependence of the two countries has become a matter of increasing political concern in Canada. A widely quoted statement on this issue, released in 1972 by the secretary of state for External Affairs, suggested a number of alternatives for Canadian policy with respect to the United States:

In practice, three broad options are open to us:

1. we can seek to maintain more or less our present relationship with the United States with a minimum of policy adjustments;
2. we can move deliberately toward closer integration with the United States;
3. we can pursue a comprehensive, long-term strategy to develop and strengthen the Canadian economy and other aspects of our national life and in the process to reduce the present Canadian vulnerability.[2]

The minister chose the third option as the one most likely to ensure Canadian sovereignty, independence, and distinctness. Thus, in effect, he reaffirmed his attachment to a policy of national consolidation along the east-west axis as opposed to an acceptance of the forces tending to bring Canada into a north-south "continental" economic system.

According to one interpretation of this option, Canada must, and in fact does, strongly support the multilateral approach to the reduction of trade barriers. Indeed, Canada participated in the seven GATT negotiating rounds held from 1947 to 1978. Substantial progress was made in the dismantling of Canadian import barriers in this process, so that our economy — like those of our trading partners — is much less protected now than it was in 1945. Even so, there remains a hard core of what might be described as "lingering protectionism" in this country and elswhere. There is no adequate system of regulating the widespread use of non-tariff barriers, and there is a residue of

2. Honorable Mitchell Sharp, "Canada-U.S. Relations: Options for the Future", *International Perspectives* (Fall 1972).

national tariffs that still discriminate against the import of manufactured goods.

Comprehensive and constructive negotiations on all trade barriers will be required to consolidate the gains from earlier negotiations and to prevent the world from slipping into a costly new spate of protectionism. Such backsliding would be disastrous for Canada. Without free access to foreign markets, this country cannot evolve in the direction of large-scale specialized production in the manufacturing industries and will not be able to overcome its productivity or innovation difficulties in areas of high technology and "knowledge-intensive" endeavor.

Commercial policy is thus of paramount importance if Canada is to achieve the sort of economic growth and dynamism that will provide its population with the wealth, security, and well-being that they desire for the future. This report is devoted to an analysis of Canadian commercial policy requirements on the basis of contemporary national goals. Of these goals, the most fundamental are the same basic political imperatives that were recognized a hundred years ago when the National Policy was established: national unity and independence. Today, however, they take a different form from that underlying the development strategy of the late nineteenth century. The need for unity, which then led governments to foster the construction of railways and the settlement of land, now encourages a search for greater regional representation in national decision making and for means of reducing the disparities in levels of wealth among various parts of the country. Similarly, the preoccupation with independence, which in earlier times was expressed in action to prevent physical occupation of Canada's empty spaces by Americans is today manifested in a concern to limit U.S. investment and cultural penetration.

Commercial policy must also clearly be related to a number of economic goals, the most significant of which have been subject to widespread discussion and study in recent years.[3] These include substantial increases in real living standards over time; full employment, including productive jobs for an increasingly educated labor force; reasonable stability of prices; a more equitable distribution of income among different groups and regions; and steady growth in the world economy, with accelerated progress for the developing countries.

3. Canada's economic goals have been set out in Canada, Department of External Affairs, *Foreign Policy for Canadians* (Ottawa: Information Canada, 1970); and various Annual Reviews of the Economic Council of Canada.

II
Trade Theory and Canada's Comparative Advantage

B
Canadian Trade Policy

7
Textile Import Policies: A Reappraisal

Ursula Kobel

Ms. Kobel is assistant to the manager of budgets, Canadian Pacific Enterprises Limited, and a graduate student in international business in the Faculty of Management, McGill University. She was formerly employed as economist, Textile/Apparel Department, Canadian Imperial Bank of Commerce, Montreal.

The material in this chapter originally appeared in *The Canadian Business Review*, Summer 1981. Reprinted by permission.

Canada's import restraint policies have recently been subject to much debate, especially with regard to the highly protected textile and apparel industries. This chapter discusses import policies concerning the two industries and alternative solutions to the problem.

Why Current Import Policies were Deemed Necessary

Background

The textile and apparel industries in Canada currently employ approximately 200,000 people directly, and an estimated additional 330,000 indirectly. Shipments from the two industries were expected to exceed $9 billion in 1980, with exports approaching $600 million.[1]

While there are manufacturing plants in all provinces, employment is concentrated in Quebec (60 per cent), Ontario (30 per cent), and Manitoba (4 per cent). Although these two industries account for approximately 11 per cent of all manufacturing employment in Canada as a whole, that figure approaches 22 per cent in the Province of Quebec.[2] The apparel industry is the largest employer of manufacturing manpower in Manitoba, and its importance as an employer in that province is steadily increasing.[3]

Approximately 75 per cent of textile and apparel industry employment is female. Geographic mobility is very low. A study by the Department of Manpower and Immigration (1970) indicated that employment alternatives for workers from these industries are limited for four principal reasons:

1. Average level of education is low.
2. Average age is over forty.
3. Workers are predominantly female and secondary wage earners.
4. Many workers have limited command of the English language.[4]

1. Canadian Apparel Manufacturers' Institute.
2. Government of Canada, *The Textile Industry — A Canadian Challenge*, p. 3.
3. Canadian Apparel Manufacturers' Institute, *Apparel Industry Comments on Liberal Caucus Research Bureau Paper "Special Protection for the Textile and Clothing Industries"* (November 12, 1980), p. 5.
4. Textile and Clothing Board, *Clothing Inquiry* (1977), **VI**, pp. 10-12.

In support of the argument of limited mobility, a recent government study of the 1976 closure of Associated Textiles Ltd., of Louiseville, P.Q., a town of 4,000 persons some eighteen miles from Trois Rivières, showed that of 437 people laid off as a result of the plant closure, 34 accepted early retirement. As of May 1978, 200 former employees were still unemployed, and a survey concluded that 95 per cent were not willing to move even if they were offered suitable employment.[5]

By 1960, it had already been noticed that imports of clothing and cotton textiles were cutting into the domestic market. This problem was exacerbated by the spread of man-made fibre technology to several developing countries at a time when synthetic fibres were not covered under the old GATT-sponsored long-term arrangement, and the Canadian manufacturer's share of the Canadian market began to drop.

Originally the bulk of "low-cost" imports was concentrated in the textile fabric end of the business. While there have always been problems with promotional items such as shirts and jeans, and later sweaters and outerwear, the really serious impact on clothing producers did not come until the early 1970s. By 1976, major retail stores were also firmly entrenched in direct import programs. Many manufacturers complained that department stores were ordering samples of new designs, then having them reproduced in Hong Kong, Taiwan, or other low-cost countries at a fraction of the cost for Canadian distribution. Importers of apparel and textiles were expanding their markets, and 1976 import levels exceeded the record levels of 1975 by almost 50 per cent on a unit volume basis. At the present time about 8 per cent of textile yarn and fabric imports originate in "low-cost" and state-trading countries.

Reasons for Implementation of Import Policies
The Canadian textile and apparel industries are being protected for three basic reasons:

1. *Redistribution of income and maintenance of employment.* It is feared that if the proportion of imports of apparel and textiles are permitted to increase, Canadian production will suffer, leading to plant closures and unemployment. The province hardest hit would be Quebec, where unemployment rates are already excessively high, and where additional economic problems would only add fuel to the separatist fire. The lack of geographic mobility of

5. Newall, ed. *Consultative Task Force on Textiles and Clothing* App. I, p. 19.

workers in the industry would make relocation and retraining difficult. It is, therefore, less disruptive to support the industry despite the fact that clothing costs will be forced up for Canadians as a whole, rather than support an additional 250,000-300,000 persons on unemployment.

Over the six-year period from 1970 to 1976, the number of textile and/or apparel establishments decreased by 236, despite a significant but short-lived upswing in 1974 (see Table 1). Over the same period, there was a net increase in employment of 900 persons. The statistics also show, however, a net decrease in employment of 15,200 persons from 1973, the year of peak employment, to 1976, the year of quota implementation. (1973 was a year of world shortage of textiles, and many foreign textile exporters withdrew abruptly, although temporarily, from the Canadian market.)

Table 2 indicates a rising level of imports as a percentage of apparent Canadian market (by value) from 18.2 per cent in 1970 to 25.7 per cent in 1976, while Canadian exports as a percentage of shipments decreased 0.7 per cent from 5.1 per cent to 4.4 per cent over the same period.

2. *Protection of infant industry.* Although the apparel industry in

Table 1

Textiles and Apparel Industries: Establishments, Employment, and Selling Price 1970-79

	1970	1971	1972	1973	1974	1975	1976	1977	1978	1979
No. of Establishments										
Textile	1,008	1,003	1,000	999	1,037	1,029	987	944	N/A	N/A
Apparel	2,450	2,417	2,393	2,355	2,408	2,318	2,235	1,660	N/A	N/A
Total	3,458	3,420	3,393	3,354	3,445	3,347	3,222	2,604	N/A	N/A
Employment ('000)										
Textile	76.7	77.2	83.4	86.1	85.1	79.8	76.1	63.5		
Apparel	117.8	118.5	122.1	124.7	121.4	119.6	119.5	110.5		
Total	194.5	195.7	205.5	210.8	206.5	199.4	195.6	174.0	178.0[a]	182.0[a]
Industry Selling Price (1971 = 100)										
Textile	—	100.0	98.8	108.3	129.5	132.5	142.5	150.4	159.7	180.7
Apparel	96.4	100.0	102.6	110.4	128.6	142.1	154.1	167.4	178.2	196.0
Knitting	98.0	100.0	102.1	108.6	129.9	135.7	143.0	152.0	162.6	177.9
Manufacturing						153.7	161.6	173.7	190.4	217.8

(a) Estimated

Source: Statistics Canada.

Table 2

Textile and Apparel Industries: Trade and Market Statistics 1970-79

	1970	1971	1972	1973	1974	1975	1976	1977	1978	1979
Shipments ($ million)										
Textiles	1,813	1,977	2,226	2,551	2,878	2,803	3,076			
Apparel	1,652	1,778	1,948	2,159	2,434	2,700	2,977			
Total	3,465	3,755	4,174	4,710	5,312	5,503	6,053	6,404	7,473	8,568
Exports ($ millions)										
Textiles	101	116	120	157	187	140	160			
Apparel	75	83	93	117	125	105	107			
Total	176	199	213	274	312	245	267	320	387	472
Imports ($ million) F.O.B.										
Textiles	528	613	744	862	1,057	978	1,119			
Apparel	204	238	331	406	512	617	881			
Total	732	851	1,075	1,268	1,569	1,595	2,000	1,973	2,250	2,828
Apparent Canadian Market										
Textiles	2,240	2,474	2,850	3,256	3,748	3,641	4,035			
Apparel	1,781	1,932	2,186	2,449	2,821	3,211	3,752			
Total	4,021	4,406	5,036	5,705	6,569	6,852	7,787	8,057	9,336	10,924
Imports as % of ACM										
Textiles	23.6	24.8	26.1	26.5	28.2	26.9	27.7			
Apparel	11.5	12.3	15.1	16.6	18.1	19.2	23.5			
Total	18.2	19.3	21.3	22.2	23.9	23.3	25.7	24.5	24.1	25.9
Exports as % of Shipments										
Textiles	5.6	5.9	5.4	6.2	6.5	5.0	5.0			
Apparel	4.5	4.7	4.8	5.4	5.1	3.9	3.6			
Total	5.1	5.3	5.1	5.8	5.9	4.5	4.4	5.0	5.2	5.5

Source: P. Newall, Textile Profile 8; P. Clothing Profile 12 (Statistics Canada: 1977-70).

Canada is hardly in its infancy (in the UNCTAD terminology it has moved from being "mature" to "senile"), the argument is the same — protect the industry to give it time to establish itself, to make the capital expenditures necessary to make it more productive and hence competitive with developing country imports. This argument does not apply to the textile industry, as it is more technologically advanced than the apparel industry, and far less labor intensive.

3. Political objectives. This rationale includes maintenance of essential industries in case of war, and indeed clothing may be considered essential. It is estimated that currently there is insufficient capacity in Canada to supply the necessary military clothing as well as civilian clothing.

Consumers living in our hostile climate should be more con-

cerned about Canada's long-term security of supply for clothing. Some 90 per cent of Canada's garment imports come from
developing and state trading countries. Production in a number of these countries such as Korea, Hong Kong, China, and
Taiwan could be disrupted by hostilities — yet we rely on them
for over a third of the clothing consumed in Canada. If our
apparel supply lines were disrupted, the shortfall in supply
could not readily be replaced from existing Canadian capacity
overnight — or by imports from other developed countries
because they too, rely heavily on these developing countries
for their apparel needs. . . . Sweden let itself become too heavily dependent on clothing imports and found it did not have the
ability to clothe its army. They had to invoke the GATT National
Security escape clause to rebuild their industry. . . .[6]

Canada's Import Policies on Textiles and Apparel

Canada's import policies on textiles and apparel have evolved through
three distinct phases.

Phase I — 1960-75
In the early 1960s some bilateral agreements were negotiated with
low-cost suppliers of cotton textile and apparel products, notably
Japan, Hong Kong, Taiwan, the People's Republic of China, Macao,
Singapore, and Malaysia, among others. As man-made fibres were
developed and commercially produced, these too were incorporated
into the agreements. These bilateral agreements, though, were of
little effect, and did nothing to guarantee Canadian producers a share
of their own market.

It was not until 1969-70 that the Canadian government saw fit to
introduce a textile policy "designed to bring about an orderly rationalization and strengthening of the textile and apparel industries".[7]
The policy included:

1. formation of a Textile and Clothing Board to hear industry
   problems and recommend measures of protection from injurious
   imports;
2. special adjustment assistance for workers who had to be phased
   out;
3. government assistance for productivity improvement centres.[8]

---

6. Cogit International Corporation, *The Eighties and Beyond,* p. 209.
7. *Ibid.,* p. 19.
8. *Ibid.,* p. 19-20.

This situation was temporary. When the then minister of Industry, Trade, and Commerce was not re-elected in 1972, the measures weakened; agreements were not respected, some were dropped entirely, and imports increased sharply.

Phase II — 1976-78

With the drastic increase in imports by 1976, Canadian manufacturers were failing fast, and they stepped up pressure on the government for intervention. Early in November 1976, the Textile and Clothing Board recommended the imposition of global quotas on virtually all categories of apparel products and many textile products. On November 29, 1976, the government promised five years' protection, and the quotas were introduced, limiting imports to 1975 unit volumes.

Global quotas have their advantages to the manufacturers:

• They provide an *overall* limit on imports. They are administered and allocated in Canada so there is little possibility of overshipment.

• They do not have the growth and flexibility provisions included in bilateral agreements.

• The government can set aside a reserve to take account of high fashion and special hardship cases. This comes out of the overall limit — ensuring that, at least in some of these cases, quotas are utilized to import products that cannot be or are not made in Canada, thereby reducing the imports of directly competitive products.[9]

Very soon, however, pressure was brought upon the government, principally by the United States, which was worried that the Canadian actions would eventually preclude renewal of the Arrangement Regarding International Trade in Textiles (also known as the Multi-fibre Arrangement or MFA) (see Appendix), an agreement necessary for their own textile import protection.

Phase III — 1979-81

Late in 1977, the government began negotiations aimed at reaching bilateral agreements with seven nations which together accounted for approximately 85 per cent of Canada's low-cost textile/apparel imports (Hong Kong, Korea, the People's Republic of China, Taiwan, the Philippines, Poland, and Romania). These agreements were based on 1975 levels, adjusted for the growth that was denied while global

9. *Ibid.,* p. 20-21.

quotas were in place. Agreements have been signed with all the above countries, as well as new entrants — Thailand, Macao, Bulgaria, Hungary, Sri Lanka, and Pakistan. As of the end of 1979, discussions were under way with India and Malaysia.

These agreements are administered by the exporting countries. While the Textile and Clothing Board had recommended that quotas under the bilaterals be allocated in Canada, the government found that they could not negotiate this condition. "Exporting countries took the position that it was bad enough to have to agree to limit their exports outside the usual terms of GATT without giving the import permit holder buying leverage over exporters in the restricted country."[10]

In addition to this, textiles and apparel from all sources are subject to tariffs of 22 per cent on most items.

Are Canada's Import Policies Accomplishing Their Goals?

It was suggested above that Canada implemented its import policies with respect to apparel and textiles in order to:

- maintain employment levels in the sector;
- allow Canadian manufacturers the time and support necessary to make the technological changes necessary to bring their productivity up to competitive levels;
- maintain sufficient capacity should trade be suspended.

Employment in the sector, which had been decreasing from 1973, reached a low point in 1977 and since then has been increasing at a rate of approximately 2 per cent per annum.[11] However, from the beginning of the fourth quarter of 1979 through 1980 there has been a steady reduction in activity among Canadian apparel manufacturers, reflecting the impact of the recession. Imports under quota have not declined to the same degree. Canadian manufacturers have borne the brunt of reduced economic activity.

Table 3 shows capital and repair expenditures for the textile and apparel industries. After a low point in 1977, these expenditures (in current dollars) have been increasing year after year. In constant (real) terms, while these expenditures have been increasing slowly over the past three years, they have not yet attained even the lowest levels of capital and repair expenditures evident during the three years prior to the implementation of global quotas. There are, how-

10. *Ibid.,* p. 23.
11. Textile and Clothing Board, *Textile & Clothing Inquiry* (1980), p. 18.

Table 3

Textile and Apparel Industries: Capital and Repair Expenditures 1974-1979

	Clothing			Textiles and Knitting Mills[a]			Clothing & Textiles			
	Capital	Repair	Total	Capital	Repair	Total	Capital	Repair	Total (Current $)	Total (1971 $)
	($ millions)									
1974	20.3	7.0	27.3	158.0	64.2	222.2	178.3	71.2	249.5	196.5
1975	23.1	7.7	30.8	174.2	61.6	235.8	197.3	69.3	266.6	185.1
1976	21.8	8.9	30.7	119.3	67.3	186.6	141.1	76.2	217.3	140.2
1977	21.0	8.2	29.2	87.6	68.4	156.0	108.6	76.6	185.2	110.9
1978	26.1	11.2	37.3	106.3	73.2	179.5	132.4	84.4	216.8	120.4
1979[b]	26.6	10.4	37.0	133.2	78.2	211.4	159.8	88.6	248.4	127.4

(a) Includes knitted garments.
(b) Preliminary.

Source: Statistics Canada.

ever, prospects for significantly increased capital expenditures in the apparel industry. These new technological advances offer very good prospects for increased productivity and efficiency. The pay-back periods are longer but the investments could pay off — given adequate assurances that a market will be there to serve. The Textile and Clothing Board Report, as protectionist as it might seem, will probably result in a reduction in the number of firms in the industry. There is a definite trend towards larger production units, which will be the leaders in adopting new technology. Nonetheless, one must face the fact that, no matter what technological changes are introduced in the apparel industry, it will be extremely difficult to overcome the wage advantages of developing countries. These countries are using systems which are eight to ten years behind Canada's, but the wage differentials are so great that it is economical for them to do so.

Productivity, as reflected by the Index of Real Value Added per Man-Hour Worked is shown in Table 4. We note that while productivity increased year after year, the rate of increase in all sectors except knitting and children's clothing was greater in the period 1971-76 than in the period 1976-79 during which the global quotas and bilateral agreements were in place. This also implies that productivity increases at a faster pace when capital expenditures are high.

A problem with the present import policies concerns the less affluent Canadian consumer. Low-cost imports are used to provide clothing at an affordable price to these consumers. Quotas and bilateral agreements still permit the import of low-cost clothing into Canada. However, it is only natural that the exporting company/country will maximize its receipts by exporting the top of their line, the highest margin merchandise they produce. The selling price of these products has risen not only with inflation, but also with the rapid improvements in styling and quality that come from experience.

One rebuttal quota/restraint supporters often use against consumer claims of high costs is that the selling prices of domestically produced goods has increased less quickly than that of the imports. One of the reasons is that imported items started from a lower base and quality level. The reduced value of the Canadian dollar, making imports appear more expensive, is another factor which cannot be ignored.

The industry argues that *global quotas* were beneficial to Canada's industry — they were administered in Canada, they did not provide for annual growth in imports, and they were flexible enough not to withhold imports of items not manufactured in Canada. They were, however, not in effect long enough for the results to be measurable.

On the other hand, it is argued that the bilateral agreements are administered in the exporter's country; they provide for an increase in imports annually, and, in addition, allow for entry of new exporting countries at levels of 100,000-200,000 units of each category for their initial year, subject to annual increases, thus increasing more quickly the amount of imported clothing and textiles annually. This problem is compounded during recession years. One of the inherent dangers in the quota system is that it can become a floor as well as a

Table 4

Textile and Apparel Industries: Index of Real Value Added Per Man-Hour Worked (1976-1979) (1971 = 100)

	Women's	Clothing Men's	Children's	Textile Industries	Knitting Mills	All Manufacturing
1976	130.3	119.6	114.5	127.3	110.6	118.0
1977	125.4	116.8	114.5	137.3	117.4	123.6
1978	140.0	127.6	127.9	144.0	133.8	128.6
1979	143.8	127.1	151.8	145.6	135.0	128.9

Compound Annual Growth Rate (%)

1971-79	4.7	3.0	5.4	4.8	3.8	3.2
1971-76	5.4	3.6	2.8	5.0	2.0	3.4
1976-79	3.3	2.1	9.9	4.6	6.9	3.0

Source: Statistics Canada.

ceiling. This is apparent in the manufacturing and import statistics from the fourth quarter 1979 through 1980, where the declining activity of apparel manufacturers has not been matched by a decrease in apparel imports. Another serious problem is the external administration of the agreements, especially in the case of the People's Republic of China. From the start, China did not live up to the recently signed agreement. When this was questioned, pressure from the Canada-China Trade Council and from Canadian exporters led the Canadian government to be more accommodating, permitting up to 50 per cent of the three-year-total of merchandise under the original agreement to be shipped in the first year. Imports from China during 1980 and 1981 are supposed to be reduced due to the "front end loading" in year one (1979), but Canadian manufacturers are sceptical.[12] Korea has also been accused of overshipping their quota limits.

North-South Institute Study
A recent study commissioned by the North-South Institute claims that Canadians paid $467 million more than was necessary for clothing in 1979 because of the government's import policies.

The accuracy of this study is debatable, considering many of the factors included in the study, such as:[13]

• A cost of $20.7 million attributed to the fact that consumers did not purchase as many garments as they might have at lower prices. (Ignoring the usual practice of discounting and clearance of unsold apparel.)

• A cost to the consumer of $92.8 million for tariff revenues to the Canadian government. Presumably elimination of tariff revenue would require increasing of other government sources of funds, for example, taxes.

• Assumption that other industries are capable of absorbing large numbers of displaced textile/apparel employees, given the fact that Canada has already some 800,000 unemployed persons.

• Assumption that textile/apparel workers are free to relocate. Those workers who choose to leave the industry after extended layoff (for example, women who choose to remain at home) are dismissed as voluntary withdrawals.

An interesting point concerning the costs to consumers of import protection which is seldom examined is that Canadian consumers' costs of wearing apparel are among the lowest in the world.

---

12. Canadian Apparel Manufacturers' Institute, *Apparel Industry Comments*, Annex D.
13. Cogit International, *The Eighties*, pp. 22-23.

Options

There are several options open to Canada, which cluster into two groups — those involving import restrictions over and above duties, and those that do not.

With Import Restrictions

1. *Return to global quotas.* This option would please the Canadian manufacturers and, according to the study by the North-South Institute, would reduce the costs of import restrictions for the consumer. This system has been tried in the past but was discontinued under pressure from the United States.

   The United States objected to the global quota, but for political rather than economic reasons. They did not want to risk hampering the MFA renewal and the recent round of GATT negotiations. The U.S. and Europe are looking at "globalization" as a real option. This may be one of the few ways to protect the aspirations of the poorest countries — by taking entitlements away from the more advanced developing countries such as Hong Kong, Taiwan, and Korea, in order to make room for Sri Lanka, Bangladesh and other less industrialized countries, which now are limited to very low levels due to market domination by the large exporting countries which began export programs fifteen to twenty years ago.[14]

   This type of approach, a global limit for all low-cost imports, leaving developed country exports free of restraint, could possibly work. While there is a GATT non-discrimination clause, Article II, Part IV of GATT permits discrimination in favor of developing countries; Article 6 of the MFA requires it. What would be necessary in order for this to work is a new MFA which differentiates between the powerful non-industrialized countries such as Hong Kong and Korea and the real developing countries.

2. *Continue bilateral agreements, with some amendments.* For the manufacturer, it is vital that market share not diminish. With the bilateral agreements as they now stand, new exporting countries are granted significant entry levels. These quantities are added on to levels already granted to the other exporting nations in arriving at potential import levels for Canada. This problem could be alleviated if the bilateral agreements provided for a growth in imports lower than the expected growth in Canadian demand for textiles and apparel. When new entrants are granted their quotas, they would not then cut into the Canadian manufacturers' share of the Canadian market.

14. Canadian Apparel Manufacturers' Institute, *Apparel Industry Comments.*

The problem of providing low-cost imports for low-income families is difficult to resolve. Under the provisions of GATT as they currently stand, a country cannot grant a favored status to one country over another. If this agreement did not exist, or if some conditions were changed, it would be possible to set aside larger portions of imports to new developing country entrants to the market — those which have not yet developed the technology and the expertise to produce higher quality garments, and whose costs are low enough to export low-cost, adequate quality goods. The problem with most developing countries which have been exporting apparel and textiles over a number of years is that they have achieved levels of skill and technology which approximate (indeed sometimes exceed) Canada's. They produce high-quality garments, often even "designer" models, and are interested only in exporting the top of their line.

According to some, denomination of quotas by value rather than quantity would alleviate this problem. However, the GATT Textile Surveillance Body will not approve dollar-based quotas as they do not protect the interests of the developing countries.[15]

3. *A North American Free Trade Zone.* This option would involve free trade in apparel and textiles between Canada and the United States, but would not rule out import restrictions outside of North America. Co-ordination of Canada and U.S. import policies would be a necessity and, in all likelihood, protection would be increased to U.S. levels, which far exceeded Canada's.

Free trade with the United States would greatly enlarge Canada's "domestic market", enabling certain economies of scale, especially through larger runs (primarily in the textile industry), and would reduce raw material costs where cotton yarns and certain man-made fibres not usually manufactured in Canada are concerned.

However, there are risks to consider as well as potential benefits. These would include the fact that the U.S. market is twelve times larger than Canada's. U.S. production only has to increase 10 per cent to meet Canada's needs. A 10 per cent increase in Canadian production, on the other hand, would be less than 1 per cent of U.S. production. There would have to be a transition period in which Canadian barriers would stay in place or gradually be phased out, perhaps over five years, while U.S. tariffs are reduced immediately, in order to give Canadian manufacturers time to make the adjustments necessary to service the U.S. market and to prepare for increased competition.

15. *Ibid.*

Without Import Restrictions

1. *Government subsidy of the industry.* At present, the Canadian people are subsidizing the textile and apparel industries through higher prices on wearing apparel. Certain incentive programs and development grants are currently available to the industry. Potentially, the government could subsidize the industries directly with the aim of maintaining employment and sustaining an essential industry. This approach is extremely costly and has few benefits over import restrictions other than not directly interfering with trade.

2. *Non-support of the textile/apparel industries.* This implies sink or swim for the Canadian manufacturers of textiles and apparel. Many of the existing companies would be unable to cope, leading to a drop in employment levels. This would potentially place an additional 500,000 people on the labor market. These workers would have to be retrained for other industries and, where necessary and possible, relocated (bearing in mind what has been said on this subject earlier in this chapter). If even 50 per cent of these people could be otherwise gainfully employed, there would still be another 250,000 people requiring unemployment insurance and other benefits — in effect, a subsidy of textile/apparel employees, rather than the industry.

A recent report by the National Council on Economic Opportunity asserts that:

> . . . a rise of 1 per cent in unemployment . . . is responsible for a rise of 3.4 per cent in admissions to psychiatric institutions, of about 4 per cent in suicides, of 2 per cent in deaths from cardiovascular and renal diseases and cirrhosis of the liver, of 4 per cent in state prison admissions, of 3.8 per cent in homicides, 5.7 per cent in robberies, 2.8 per cent in larcenies, and 8.7 per cent in narcotics arrests. . . .[16]

Given this scenario, tariffs on apparel and textiles could be abolished, allowing for a reduction in costs of apparel to Canadians, in part offsetting the expense of supporting the unemployed workers, if Canada is willing to incur the social costs resulting from such a move.

Should Canada's Import Policies on Textiles and Apparel Be Continued?

The existence of import controls on textiles and apparel results in

16. John Hein, "Paging Adam Smith", *Across the Board* (January 1981), p. 48.

higher prices on apparel for all Canadians. Abolition of the controls
would lead to political and social unrest. Surely it is worth something
to Canadians to promote social and political harmony. What, then, is
the solution? Will the needle trade ever be economically viable?

Import controls are meant to be a temporary measure — one
which all too often turns into a permanent situation. Permanent
import controls on textiles and apparel will not solve anything; they
just camouflage the basic problems.

Clearly though, the controls should not be terminated abruptly.
Perhaps the optimal solution is to continue import restraints in
conjunction with a North American free trade zone, for a long
enough period to give sufficient time to those sectors which have
potential for efficient, competitive operations to establish themselves, but with a definite enough withdrawal plan to avoid the influx
of new capital into a dying sector.

Appendix

International Trade Agreements Affecting Canadian Textile and Apparel Import Policy

The GATT *Arrangement Regarding International Trade in Textiles*
(MFA) came into force on January 1, 1974, providing international
sanction under the GATT for the negotiation with 'low-cost and state
trading textile exporting countries of arrangements designed to
minimize the disruptive effects of these countries' exports on the
markets of importing countries.' It is also aimed at providing a climate for the orderly expansion of international trade in textiles.[17]

This instrument permits a nation to take safeguard action of two
general types against imports:

1. It can negotiate bilateral restraint arrangements with exporting
   countries on a product-by-product basis after having established
   that the imports concerned have resulted in injury to the domestic industry.
2. It can negotiate comprehensive bilateral arrangements with exporting countries, with a wide range of products included from
   yarn to garments, without the need to prove injury.

Under (1) the restraint can be applied unilaterally if an exporter
refuses to negotiate, while under (2) restraints are permitted only if
both countries agree. Canada has followed the course of arrangements under (1). Other provisions of the MFA include such items as
the minimum annual growth rate for restrained imports at 6 per cent

17. Hein, "Adam Smith", p. 102.

or greater and rules for establishment of a base period from which restraint levels could be calculated.

Canada was not the only country signatory to the MFA to experience difficulty with it, and when the arrangement came up for renewal in 1977, major changes were proposed. At the conclusion of negotiations, however, a majority of the participants agreed to renew the MFA unchanged for a further four years (until December 31, 1981). This was accomplished by opening a protocol to the 1973 arrangement. However, accompanying the protocol were the informal notes of the negotiating group. These are considered almost as binding as the arrangement itself. In the notes, the EEC is given the right to obtain in its bilateral negotiations with exporting countries "reasonable departures" from the terms of the MFA, particularly concerning annual growth rate and base periods. The notes also underline the right of countries with small markets and high import penetrations to take import restraint action more severe than that permitted by the MFA. It is understood by many of the participants in the MFA discussions, however, that this applies to the Nordic countries alone. Many countries, including Canada, refused to sign the protocol unless the same privileges of reasonable departures were available to them.

Canada nevertheless began the negotiating of comprehensive bilateral agreements with the major low-wage countries exporting textiles to our markets on the assumption that the reasonable departures clause does apply.[18]

Article VI of the GATT provides for compensating measures to cope with material injury caused by dumping or export country subsidies. The remedy is restricted to a special duty not greater than the margin of dump for the products being dumped or the financial benefit received by the product by way of a bounty or a subsidy.[19]

Article XIX of the GATT provides for remedial action where exports are entering a country under fair competition but are causing serious injury to a Canadian producer. This article also provides that a country whose exports have been restricted may seek compensation by way of concessions in other product areas, and that any action taken under this article be non-discriminatory, that is, uniform for all countries.[20]

18. Newall, *Textiles and Clothing*, pp. 57-59.
19. *Ibid.*, p. 55.
20. *Ibid.*, p. 56.

II
Trade Theory and Canada's Comparative Advantage

B
Canadian Trade Policy

8
The Political Economy of Canada-United States Free Trade

Carl E. Beigie

Mr. Beigie is president, C. D. Howe Institute, and associate professor in the Faculty of Management, McGill University. He is an author and editor of numerous articles, monographs, and books on Canada-United States economic relations covering the auto pact, natural resources, FIRA, and future policy directions. He is a member and formerly director of research (Montreal), Canadian-American Committee.

This chapter was written expressly for this volume.

Throughout its history, Canada has contemplated and debated the most desirable state of affairs for commercial relations with the United States. No final conclusion has been possible as advocates of maximum economic efficiency through free trade have joined battle with advocates of optimum political sovereignty through restrictions on bilateral transactions.[1] Although the battle appears to have been fought to a stalemate, the reality is that the two economies have become progressively more integrated and interdependent as a result of a series of discretionary policy initiatives superimposed on a flow of activity responding to natural market forces.

Canada-United States free trade, therefore, is fundamentally an issue in political economy: it is economic in the sense that certain positive statements can be made about the costs and benefits of barriers that exist to free trade as well as about the consequences of the removal of those barriers; it is political in the sense that judgments must be made about the relative merits of economic efficiency and non-economic considerations.

This chapter is divided into four sections. The first reviews the pure economic case for free trade and assesses some of the main arguments against free trade with the United States from a strictly economic perspective. Any exercise in political economy involves the interplay of various interest groups. In the second section the conflicting motives of business as an interest group on the free trade issue are examined. The third section contains a description and analysis of the various ways that free trade might be accomplished, ranging from such sectoral agreements as the auto pact to a number of across-the-board approaches to the elimination of commercial restrictions. The final section of the essay goes beyond the pure trade dimension of the bilateral free trade issue to consider other aspects of the economic association that has evolved between Canada and the United States. Negotiations involving these other aspects will

---

1. The concept of economic efficiency lends itself to quantitative measurement; the concept of sovereignty does not. Therefore, it is appropriate to think of maximizing efficiency on some objective basis, whereas the notion of having more or less sovereignty involves inherent subjective elements.

largely determine prospects for resolving the free trade stalemate that exists in Canada.

In matters of political economy, it is very difficult to separate analysis from advocacy. While a conscious effort is made to achieve this separation in this chapter, the author has an acknowledged economic bias, which translates into a predisposition in favor of the efficiency gains that can be achieved through free trade on the broadest possible scale, not simply with the United States alone.

Free Trade: The Pure Economic Case

The essential economic argument for free trade is that barriers to the unrestricted movement of output emerging from the production process limits the real value of a nation's income and wealth. At a theoretical value, this conclusion applies to barriers among regions of a single country as well as to those among different countries.[2]

Inefficiencies arising from trade restraints occur for three basic reasons. First, these restraints prevent a country from being able to concentrate its efforts on activities for which it has a comparative advantage in relation to those in other countries. Second, they discourage firms from taking full advantage of economies of scale that would lower unit production costs. Third, they encourage firms to engage in a wasteful form of non-price competition, namely a proliferation in the range of products offered that are differentiated on the basis of superficial quality characteristics.

Taken together, the resultant inefficiencies raise prices to consumers, lower the potential value of output that can be produced from the factor inputs a country possesses, and depress the average real level of incomes. The nature and extent of these economic costs vary with the specific characteristics of a country's industrial structure; we therefore turn to a consideration of each of the three sources of inefficiencies arising from barriers to trade in the Canada-United States context.

There are certain inherent structural features of the Canadian economy that contrast sharply with those of the U.S. economy. While Canada's land mass exceeds that of the United States, it has approximately one-tenth of the total U.S. population. Moreover, even though

---

2. The free trade debate has become a major factor in the constitutional challenge facing Canada. Provincial initiatives, commonly referred to as part of an exercise in "province building" as opposed to "nation building", have had the effect of restricting the interprovincial movement of goods, capital, and labor. These restraints have income and wealth consequences within the national economy that are similar to barriers to free trade in the international system.

the Canadian population is heavily concentrated within a few urban centres, these centres are separated from each other by vast distances.[3] Again in contrast to the United States, Canada's population centres are strung out along a narrow east-west corridor that is adjacent to the U.S. border. Finally, given a larger land mass and a much smaller population base, the endowment of natural resources per capita is many times higher in Canada compared to what it is in the United States.[4]

Given these basic characteristics of the Canadian economy, natural market forces dictated that producers in Canada would seek to expand markets for their output to a relatively greater extent in a north-south than in an east-west direction. This orientation occurred both because the accessible U.S. market included a larger number of buyers and because shipments to other Canadian locations involve high transportation costs.[5] In this pursuit, resource-based production would have a natural advantage relative to general manufacturing production in competing successfully for those U.S. markets.

These basic tendencies in the Canadian economy were recognized from the very inception of Confederation in 1867. The country's first industrial strategy, embodied in Prime Minister John A. Macdonald's National Policy of 1879, sought to encourage the development of an indigenous manufacturing capacity through tariff protection and, through support of a transcontinental railway system, to foster the growth of markets for this production along an east-west axis.

The National Policy was successful in promoting a Canadian manufacturing base, although it was heavily concentrated in southeastern Ontario and, to a much lesser extent, in southwestern Quebec. It is ironic that this policy, being motivated in part by a determination that Canada must avoid being simply a resource hinterland to the United States, contributed to the rest of Canada becoming basically a resource hinterland to central Canada.

3. Victoria, British Columbia, is separated from St. John's, Newfoundland, by $5^1/_2$ time zones, whereas Montreal or Toronto is separated from London, England, by 5 time zones. In a north-south direction, Toronto finds more Americans who live within one hundred miles of its manufacturing sites than people in all of Canada.
4. There is evidence that natural resources, taken as a group, are nearly randomly distributed around the earth. Thus, while oil or tin, or zinc, for example, may occur in a few spots of heavy concentration, one square kilometre of land is just about as likely as any other to contain some form of natural resource. On this see G. J. S. Govett and M. H. Govett, "The Inequality of the Distribution of World Mineral Supplies", *Canadian Mining and Metallurgical Bulletin* (August 1977), pp. 6-12.
5. The Canadian tariff provides only limited protection to a producer operating from a single plant location. A firm in Ontario, for example, is at a disadvantage relative to a West Coast U.S. firm, despite the tariff.

Canada's general manufacturing base grew because it was protected, not because it was efficient. In part, inefficiency was the result of the Canadian market being too small and too geographically fragmented to permit scale economics to be realized in full. But size is by no means the complete picture, or even the most important part of that picture, for the domestic market is large enough to support at least one firm of minimum efficient scale in most industries, although there are a few exceptions (which include commercial and military aircraft and main frame computers). The more basic problem for most Canadian manufacturers is that the limited domestic market has been carved up among an excessive number of firms.

Canada has never had a comprehensive industrial policy. Tariffs restrained the competitive entry of imports, but throughout its history Canada has permitted, and even encouraged, an easy entry policy with respect to the establishment of new firms, both foreign and domestic owned. This is a key point regarding the structure of Canada's manufacturing industries and warrants some elaboration. Three points should be stressed.

First, Canada's approach to competition policy has been heavily influenced by developments in U.S. antitrust philosophy. In general, this philosophy is based on a structural view of the way markets should operate, with performance being anticipated to improve with a greater number of independent firms operating in any given market. This view, which is based on a theoretical model contrasting pure competition with monopoly, has contributed to a relaxed attitude toward the fragmentation of the Canadian market even though the basic philosophy originated in an economy ten times as large.

Second, Canadian policy has allowed consumer sovereignty to be given very broad expression. Canadians are constantly exposed to information regarding the range of choice available to residents of the United States. Information shapes tastes, and Canadians have come to expect that a similar range of differentiated products will be available to them. In order to supply this choice within a protected market, however, firms in Canada were forced to restrict production of any one style of product, thereby forgoing the gains in efficiency that accompany economies of specialization.[6]

Third, Canada's approach to manufacturing development encouraged U.S.-based companies to extend their oligopolistic rivalry northward. Spill over of the domestic marketing campaigns of these com-

6. A major early elaboration of this issue is D. J. Daly, B. A. Keys, and E. J. Spence, "Scale and Specialization in Canadian Manufacturing", *Economic Council of Canada Staff Study No. 21* (Ottawa: Queen's Printer, 1968).

panies into Canada helped create Canadian demand for their products. High tariffs discouraged the use of exports to meet this demand, so these companies evaluated the economics of establishing plants in Canada to serve that market. The economics were favorable, and the decision was made to set up "tariff factories".[7] Once one firm adopts this strategy in an oligopoly industry, its rivals are under pressure to follow suit to preserve their relative market shares.

The phenomenon of tariff factories and its implications are explored more fully in the next section of this chapter. The key point to note here is that the introduction of free trade to an economy with a manufacturing structure dominated by tariff factories causes far more fundamental disruptions than is commonly supposed in pure economic analyses of this option. Free trade would force greater specialization in production, and this specialization would allow scale economies to be more fully realized. As a result, Canadian manufacturing efficiency would rise and real incomes would go up in the aggregate.[8] But this outcome will require far-reaching changes in the basic structure of Canadian manufacturing. These changes will generate short-term costs, and the willingness to accept these costs will be a function of the perceived longer-term gains, once these changes have been accomplished, and the distribution of these gains among regions and sectors of the economy.

Advocates of the pure economic case for free trade advise confidence in the outcome of a pursuit of this policy strategy. To the extent they base their arguments on economic rather than non-economic grounds, critics of this case raise a number of points that are hard to respond to with full assurance in the contemporary world political economy.

The fundamental assumption of the pure economic case for free trade is that full employment can always be sustained with an appropriate set of government policies. Therefore, any unemployment resulting from unrestricted imports will be of a transitional nature, and the short-term costs of this unemployment will be greatly exceeded by the permanent gains arising from the higher efficiency

---

7. The term "tariff factory" applies to plants set up to avoid paying tariffs. These plants differ from a traditional branch plant in that the latter are closely integrated into the overall decision-making structure of the basic operation. In contrast, a tariff factory is a subsidiary established to maximize profitability within a localized planning horizon, and its activities have minimal corporate impact outside that horizon.

8. The Economic Council of Canada has estimated that the "total gains from free trade would amount to at least 5 per cent of GNP and perhaps somewhat more". Economic Council of Canada, *Looking Outward: A New Trade Strategy for Canada* (Ottawa: Information Canada, 1975), p. 81.

achieved at full employment. Even as imports cost some workers their jobs, increased export opportunities create new employment openings. At a time of high unemployment around the world, this assumption rings hollow.

In order to sustain full employment, a government must be prepared to tolerate, and if necessary to stimulate, growth in demand. With inflation a dominant preoccupation of economic officials over the past decade, however, demand restraint has become the chief strategy of most governments. A reduction of tariffs, because it lowers import prices,[9] would be a logical part of any anti-inflation program, but the accompanying pressure on jobs cannot be ignored by politically sensitive officials when unemployment is already high.

Even if unemployment were not so difficult a problem as it has been in recent years, an effective adjustment to free trade requires that the Canadian dollar be free to float, at least during a transition period, relative to the U.S. dollar. In particular, there would have to be downward flexibility to allow Canadian manufacturers to have the time to adjust the structure of their operations to meet increased foreign competition and expand into new export opportunities.

This breathing space may be difficult for Canada to obtain, given its relatively abundant resource endowment. Resource exports and foreign capital inflows motivated by the prospect of high returns in the resource sector may well keep the value of the Canadian dollar up. If so, it would force the adjustment burden onto manufacturing wages. Since these wages have proven to be fairly inflexible downward, the outcome from free trade might be a prosperous resource sector combined with a depressed manufacturing sector. Such a prospect cannot be ignored in planning a transition to free trade.

A final complication in the pure economic case for free trade to be considered here is the result of a dynamic view of the industrial process. This view is provided by an examination of the product life cycle.[10] Because of the significant role of tariff factories in Canada's

9. Tariff reductions may not be fully passed along to consumers if sales are controlled by an oligopolistic or monopolistic supplier. This is particularly the case for textile imports brought into Canada under quota by large retail chains. The gains from trade, in this case, are captured by middlemen rather than producers or consumers.

10. Raymond Vernon, "International Investment and International Trade in the Product Cycle", *Quarterly Journal of Economics* (May, 1966), pp. 190-207. In the case of a typical product, once production has reached the stage of becoming highly standardized, its production will be located in a relatively low-wage area. For situations involving tariff factories (Canada), avoidance of tariffs, not minimizing production costs, is the critical locational determinant.

industry structure, its commercial efforts have been directed more toward adoptive than toward innovative technological applications. While both domestically owned companies (for example, Northern Telecom and Mitel) and foreign-owned companies (for example, IBM and Canadian General Electric) have innovated products finding world market demand, free trade would stretch the capacity of most firms to alter quickly their entrepreneurial horizons.

These pragmatic considerations do not invalidate the case for free trade. They do indicate that the transition to a free trade environment would be a demanding process. The demands would be easier to accommodate if the transition were phased over an extended period of time, during which a broad range of assistance measures by the Canadian government would be tolerated by the free trade partner as not being inconsistent with the longer-term goals of free trade. Although the United States might not be prepared to exhibit such tolerance it is unlikely that Canada would be able to find an alternative free trade partner of even roughly similar attractiveness that would be more receptive to Canada's unique problems.

Business Perspective on Free Trade

If free trade with the United States is ever to be more than a political economy debating exercise in Canada, politically powerful constituencies must become mobilized on one side or the other of the debate. Because such constituencies have not emerged, Canada waffles. Critics of free trade seek an alternative in some vague notion of a "new industrial strategy" for the country,[11] even while the passage of time brings greater and greater Canada-United States economic integration.[12] Advocates, on the other hand, ignore the practical problems in implementing their proposals, even while indecisiveness of

---

11. Most of the basic issues in the industrial strategy debate are exposed in John H. H. Britton and James M. Gilmour, assisted by Mark G. Murphy, *The Weakest Link: A Technological Perspective on Canadian Industrial Underdevelopment* (Ottawa: Science Council of Canada, 1978); Kristian S. Palda, *The Science Council's Weakest Link* (Vancouver: The Fraser Institute, 1979); Donald J. Daly, "Weak Links in 'The Weakest Link'", *Canadian Public Policy* (Summer, 1979), pp. 307-317; A. E. Safarian, "Foreign Ownership and Industrial Behavior: A Comment on 'The Weakest Link'", *Canadian Public Policy* (Summer, 1979), pp. 318-335; and Richard D. French, *How Ottawa Decides: Planning and Industrial Policy Making 1968-1980* (Ottawa: Canadian Institute for Economic Policy, 1980).

12. See Peter Morici, assisted by Laura L. Megna, *Canada-United States Trade and Economic Interdependence,* Canada-U.S. Prospects series (Montreal and Washington, D.C.: C. D. Howe Research Institute and National Planning Association, 1980).

purpose fuels a trend toward political disintegration between the two countries.[13]

Canada may soon be unable to continue to waffle on this issue because of domestic political pressures. The West, and particularly Alberta, may be easily swayed toward active support of free trade, given that it would increase its resource export earnings and decrease the costs of most of its manufacturing purchases. The West sees tariffs as being principally a benefit to Ontario and Quebec and is growing impatient with supporting what it regards as being a form of welfare system for central Canada.

In terms of broad national interest groups, it might be anticipated that consumers would be a strong force for free trade, since restraints on commercial activities tend to raise prices and limit product choice. But most consumers are also workers, or are dependent upon the income of workers, and the perceived threat of free trade to jobs has helped to diffuse anticipated support. Agricultural interests, which have generally been in favor of free trade in the past, have also modified their position because of experience with cyclically disruptive imports and because free trade might jeopardize the income-support programs farmers have been successful in obtaining from the federal and provincial governments.

Ambivalence on the free trade issue is particularly interesting in the business sector of the Canadian economy. The only differentiation between pro- and anti-free trade camps in this sector that stands up to analysis is based on perceptions of a threat from increased competition, on the one hand, and expanded opportunities for growth, on the other. This basis for differentiation cuts across industry sectors and across ownership structures.

Tariffs have three principal effects on Canadian business. First, U.S. tariffs serve to restrict access to the large U.S. market, a situation which tends to limit the horizons of many Canadian firms to the small, protected domestic market. Second, Canadian tariffs raise the

13. Evidence of disintegration began in 1971 when the United States imposed a temporary 10 per cent surcharge on dutiable imports and refused to exempt Canada from its application. This was widely interpreted in Canada as signaling the end of a so-called special relationship between the two countries. Partly in response to the perception of a new era in the relationship, in 1972 Canada's Secretary of State for External Affairs, Mitchell Sharp, floated an article favoring a strengthening of Canada's ability to reduce its vulnerability to the United States ["Canada-U.S. Relations: Options for the Future," *International Perspectives* (Autumn, 1972), pp. 1-24]. Although nothing has occurred that could be classified as a clear break in the relationship, it has become more distant in many respects in the 1970s as both countries defined their national interests in more inward-looking terms.

cost of production in Canada to the extent that imported equipment and materials are necessary in the production process or can be obtained at lower costs (excluding the tariff) in the United States, and thus by competitors based in the United States. Third, Canadian tariffs created a margin by which Canadian prices can exceed U.S. prices for the Canadian consumer. This margin may be used in a number of ways. [14,15].

One use is simply to pad profits behind a protective wall. If profitability rises noticeably, however, new entrants will be induced to begin production in Canada. As noted earlier, entry of tariff factories into Canada has not been blocked in any systematic manner, so high profits (high in the sense of what they were in the United States) could be expected to be bid away.

Another way to use this margin is to finance inefficiency.[16] This is in fact what has happened in many of Canada's oligopolistic industries. Too many firms relative to the size of the domestic market prevent scale economies from being fully exploited. Moreover, the margin supports the use of non-price competition in the form of excessive product-line proliferation, leading to a sacrifice of the economies of specialization.

The outcome of these developments has been twofold. First, Canadian firms became hostages to tariff protection. Without it, their margin for inefficiency would disappear and they would be exceptionally vulnerable to imports, including those from the parents of U.S.-owned subsidiaries. Second, these firms were in no position to attract export markets, given the high costs their protected domestic market had encouraged.

Thus, foreign-owned tariff factories and their domestically owned counterparts were generally against free trade. In fact, heads of Canadian subsidiaries have in many cases been among the most

14. The margin for inefficiency is a function of the effective rate of protection rather than the nominal rate. Suppose Canada has a tariff on the import of a complete truck equal to 10 per cent of the cost. Suppose further that up to half the value of the truck can be imported duty-free in the form of parts. The remaining value added can then be produced 20 per cent less efficiently in Canada than in the United States without being uncompetitive with a complete truck import.

15. An extended consideration of the margin for inefficiency would include other factors that raise or lower the effective size of the margin. For example, lower fuel costs would raise the margin, as would lower wage rates. Higher interest rates would lower the margin. The margin translates into the degree to which Canada's output per unit of labor input can be less than what it is in the United States.

16. It is implicit in this discussion that the margin is fully used, which means that the price in Canada is set by the U.S. price plus the tariff, after adjustment for differences in the two currencies. If competition drives the Canadian price below this limit, the actual margin is below the potential margin.

severe critics of free trade because of a recognition that their tariff factories, with the high-prestige titles that went with their management, would become, at best, branch plants carrying less prestigious-sounding titles.

Others in the business community in Canada, in contrast, have supported free trade, at least for the sectors in which they operate. Their positions reflect one or more of the following characteristics of the environment their companies face:

- They are in the resource sector and have foreign parents that rely on Canadian exports to supply the input needs of plants located outside Canada.
- They possess resources that are in short supply worldwide, but volume and profit cannot be expanded because of import tariffs or quotas in other countries and/or export restraints in Canada.
- They have developed a unique, or highly competitive product for which foreign tariffs or non-tariff barriers restrict market expansion through exports.
- They were launched as tariff factories, or their domestically owned equivalents, but their previously protected status has been eroded *and* they want to remain in business in Canada on the basis of a new viability arising from efficiency through specialization.
- Their domestic competitiveness and market prospects are hampered by the inability to import, duty-free, key inputs to their production processes.

Given the diversity of situations in which Canadian firms find themselves, there will obviously be a state of dynamic tension in the business community over the free trade issue. This tension has been increasing and will almost certainly continue to do so as (1) tariffs fall as a result of multilateral trade negotiations; (2) newly industrialized countries (NICs) such as Taiwan, Singapore, and Brazil gain in their competitive strengths; and (3) restraints on Canadian exports proliferate in the form of non-tariff barriers. Some type of free trade relationship with the United States becomes increasingly attractive as these developments progress, but so too do appeals to shore up Canadian defences against import penetration.

Support for protectionism comes in a variety of forms, but the federal government is constrained in its response to this support by concern over retaliation, by provincial differences over the willingness to bear the costs of protection, and by the recognition that the more innovative Canadian companies have preferred to expand in the United States rather than being confined to the limited growth prospects of the Canadian market.

Therefore, free trade with the United States will continue to be an actively discussed policy option within Canada. The next section of this chapter examines the various paths that exist in moving toward free trade.

Alternative Structures for Free Trade

When free trade is discussed as an issue in political economy, it is normally in the context of an across-the-board elimination of tariffs for, say, manufactured products. Business supporters of free trade, however, generally would be satisfied with free trade for specific product sectors such as textiles, petro-chemicals, or paper products. During the recently completed Tokyo Round of multilateral trade negotiations carried on under the General Agreement on Tariffs and Trade, the Canadian government was a strong advocate of a variant of the sectoral approach to trade liberalization, but without much success.[17] The objective Canada sought to pursue was to lower the discriminatory feature of tariff escalation whereby low, or zero, tariffs are placed on imports of Canada's raw materials and progressively higher tariffs are placed on Canadian exports that involve further processing and greater labor content.[18] Also, the federal government sought, through the sectoral route, to obtain a practical approach to restricting the use of non-tariff barriers (quotas, preferential government purchasing policies, etc.) that are hindering expansion of certain of Canada's exports.

A concrete example of the advantages and disadvantages of the sectoral approach to free trade is provided by the Canada-United States Automotive Agreement of 1965, commonly referred to as the auto pact.[19] This agreement had its origins in a set of unilateral Canadian initiatives aimed at redressing the inefficiencies that were inherent in the Canadian automotive industry, a classic example of a tariff factory. Because these initiatives had their full impact, the auto pact was negotiated in an effort to head off a fullfledged bilateral trade dispute.[20]

17. For a comparison of the U.S. and Canadian approaches in the GATT negotiations, see Carolin Pestieau, *The Sector Approach to Trade Negotiations: Canadian and U.S. Interests* (Montreal: Canadian Economic Policy Committee, 1976).
18. See Louis Silver, *The Pursuit of Further Processing of Canada's Natural Resources,* HRI Observations #6 (Montreal: C. D. Howe Research Institute, January, 1975).
19. For a background of the auto pact, see Carl E. Beigie, *The Canada-U.S. Automotive Agreement: An Evaluation* (Montreal and Washington, D.C.: Canadian-American Committee, 1970), especially Part I.
20. The specific issue centred on a Canadian program whereby import duties on motor vehicles and equipment were subject to remission in return for increased automotive exports. This program was challenged by a U.S. parts producer as being in violation of U.S. law against export subsidies. Duty-remission arrangements have subsequently become fairly widespread in Canada.

While the auto pact provided for free trade between Canada and the United States, this free trade was made conditional in two important respects. First, it applied only to new vehicles and original equipment parts; used vehicles and parts for the replacement market were excluded.[21] Second, free trade was confined in Canada to vehicle manufacturers, most of whom are subsidiaries of U.S. parents, who would agree to meet certain conditions imposed to protect vehicle and parts production in Canada.[22]

The performance of the Canada-U.S. automotive industry following the auto pact has generally conformed to the expectations of free trade theorists. There has been a massive increase in the two-way flow of vehicles and parts, leading to opportunities for the Canadian sector of the industry to achieve much greater economies of scale and specialization.[23] Canadian plants now produce a greatly reduced number of models and styles, but in volumes for the entire Canada-U.S. market. As a result, Canadian output per man-hour (productivity) has improved in this industry relative to what it is in the United States, thereby providing justification for wage parity across the border.[24] Furthermore, the prices Canadians pay for a North American-type vehicle, net of federal taxes, has moved closer into line with prices Americans pay for the same vehicle.[25]

Nevertheless, the auto pact has demonstrated the kinds of problems that can be anticipated in the political economy of free trade. These problems have arisen because of both the sectoral nature of the auto pact and the inherent trade-offs that accompany a shift from an industry structure dominated by tariff factories to one dominated by branch plants.

21. Tires were included if they were mounted on new vehicles. The tire industry in Canada developed as a classic example of tariff factories with inadequate scale and specialization.
22. In brief, these safeguards required qualifying Canadian manufacturers to:
    a) maintain at least a minimum ratio between the value of vehicles produced and sold in Canada;
    b) maintain a minimum level of automotive value added;
    c) expand Canadian value added by a minimum dollar amount over a four-year period;
    d) expand Canadian value added by a fixed percentage of sales in Canada.
    For details and analysis, see Beigie, *Automotive Agreement*, pp. 45-56.
23. In just three years under the auto pact, Canada's automotive exports to the United States rose from $100 million in 1965 to $2.4 billion in 1968. *Ibid.*, p. 71.
24. This parity has been defined in terms of the two currencies. With the Canadian dollar trading at a discount relative to the U.S. dollar, there is a real wage advantage for the Canadian plants.
25. The price differential reflects the fact that individual Canadians are still not able to buy vehicles in the United States and bring them back duty-free. Extension of free trade to individuals, however, would also remove the leverage the Canadian government possesses to enforce compliance with the safeguards.

The basic difficulty with any sectoral free trade arrangement such as the auto pact is that its results are judged virtually exclusively in terms of impacts within a specific sector rather than for the national economy as a whole. What this means, in practice, is that attention focusses on the bilateral trade balance for products within the sector. A key factor motivating Canada's unilateral initiatives preceding the auto pact was an automotive trade deficit that was large and growing, with every indication pointing to the trend continuing. Canada's anticipation was that the auto pact would produce a rough balance of automotive trade with the United States, increased export competitiveness in third-country markets, and a resultant increase in job prospects in this key manufacturing sector.[26]

During the early years of the auto pact, Canada's anticipation proved justified. Largely as a result of capacity expansion from new plant construction and increased productivity, combined with a healthy rate of demand increases in the United States and Canada for North American vehicles in the second half of the 1960s and the early 1970s. Canada's automotive exports to the United States grew more rapidly than its imports from the United States. As a result, its balance on bilateral trade in automotive products moved from a deficit of $586 million in 1964 to a surplus of $197 million in 1971.[27] In the second half of the 1970s, however, Canada moved sharply back into a deficit, which reached nearly $4 billion in 1979.[28]

It is not entirely clear why Canada has fared so poorly in bilateral automotive trade. Part of the explanation is found in the weakness, to the point of a depression, in the market for North American-type cars in the late 1970s as the industry tried to adjust, after years of lack of foresight, to the end of the era of cheap energy and secure oil supplies. The industry is no longer expanding its capacity in terms of volume, but must instead expend billions of dollars to refit its plants for the production of fuel-efficient vehicles. Canada is receiving investments for this refitting exercise, the results of which will eventually show up in the production of a better match between the

26. Increased efficiency means that fewer workers are required to produce the same volume of output. Therefore, it was essential that the framers of the auto pact anticipated a fairly healthy growth in sales so that efficiency increases would not result in an absolute decline in the number of jobs in either or both countries.
27. For the 1964 calculation, see Beigie, *Automotive Agreement*, p. 87; for the 1971 data, see Canadian-American Committee, *Bilateral Relations in an Uncertain World Context: Canada-U.S. Relations in 1978* (Montreal and Washington, D.C., 1978), p. 32.
28. Canada's overall automotive trade deficit with the United States is consistently made up of a surplus on trade in completed vehicles and much larger deficit on trade in parts, many of which are imported into Canada for subsequent re-export in completed vehicles.

vehicles that are produced and the kinds of vehicles an energy-cost-conscious public wants to buy. In the meantime, the Canadian public has been greatly sheltered from the full brunt of higher fuel costs and continues to buy larger cars relative to what Americans are buying.

Canadian plants, now geared to the combined Canada-U.S. market, have continued to produce vehicles that have declined in popularity in the United States, hampering Canada's automotive exports. Canadian consumers, in turn, have continued to demand relatively more of the less-fuel-efficient cars traditional in the industry, thus helping to maintain U.S. exports. These divergent trends both contributed to a Canadian bilateral automotive trade deficit.

From an analytical standpoint, it would be premature to forecast the pattern of the bilateral automotive trade balance over many years on the basis of results during the second half of the 1970s. Rising energy prices will influence the preferences of Canadian consumers; investments for refitting plants will impact on Canadian producers' export prospects. It will take many years for these developments to work themselves out and generate some sort of long-term equilibrium. In the meantime, the auto pact will cause bilateral friction as an exercise in political economy. On the one hand, supporters of the pact will argue that the balance of trade problem is largely a transitional phenomenon; on the other hand, critics will argue that this problem is yet another example of the way Canadian interests are sacrificed to the interests of U.S.-based multinational enterprises.

There is only one way that this source of conflict can be resolved: the balance of automotive trade would have to be kept within a narrow range on either side of zero.[29] Large and growing imbalances in one direction or another would lead to challenges that the agreement was not producing "fair shares" in the distribution of output, employment, and export earnings.[30] The same kind of challenges would arise regardless of the products involved in any sectoral free trade agreement.

The key point is that while sectoral free trade might result in an improvement in the efficiency of production from a strict economic perspective, this approach to free trade would largely be evaluated on grounds other than pure economic efficiency from a political economy perspective. The auto pact applies to an industry that

29. A zero automotive trade balance would mean, essentially, that production of North American-type automotive products (measured by value added) was equal to purchases of those products in both countries.
30. Article I of the Agreement establishing the auto pact sets forth the following objective: "to [enable] the industries of both countries to participate on a fair and equitable basis in the expanding total market of the two countries".

avoided many of the problems that would normally be experienced in achieving a long-term zero-trade-balance target, because:

1. The automotive industry involves a small number of independent firms, each with operations on both sides of the border. With more firms, the task of obtaining compliance with a specific target performance either through voluntary actions or through moral suasion by government would be much harder.
2. This industry relies on inputs that are either free traded (parts) or are produced under broadly similar cost conditions (steel) in the two countries. In industries requiring inputs that are not free traded, and whose costs vary substantially between the two countries, balanced trade in output would be exceedingly unlikely.[31]
3. Workers in this industry are highly unionized in an international union. Early in the life of the auto pact the two branches of the union agreed to accept nominal (dollar-for-dollar) wage parity. If such parity had not been achieved, one side or the other of the industry would have had an advantage in a key input cost — wages.[32]

Quite apart from the inherent technical problems with sectoral free trade, the auto pact has come under considerable criticism because of the consequences of shifting from a tariff-factory to a branch-plant structure in the Canadian segment of the industry. Among the more persistent of these criticisms in Canada have been the following:

1. There is not enough research and development carried on by the industry in Canada.
2. The job mix is too heavily weighted in Canada toward lower skilled, lower paid, and unchallenging occupations.
3. Sourcing and other basic decisions have become even more concentrated in Detroit.
4. The Canadian economy has been even more closely tied to business cycles in the United States and to any managerial errors made by U.S.-based parents.

The degree of validity to these criticisms is subject to debate. It is also rather stretching a point to argue that the auto pact, per se, was

---

31. In order for free trade in output to result in maximum efficiency, there must also be free trade in inputs.
32. Given that the Canadian dollar is trading at a substantial discount relative to the U.S. dollar, that there is only nominal wage parity, and that the price and supply of energy inputs are relatively favorable in Canada, it would be reasonable to anticipate considerable strength in future for the Canadian section of the industry.

responsible for significant change in these areas. Much more to the point here, however, is that the auto pact brought about gains to efficiency in Canadian automotive production by fundamentally altering tariff factories and simultaneously increased the degree of integration of the Canada-U.S. automotive industry by converting the Canadian operations into more conventional branch plants. This trade-off of increased efficiency for decreased independence (albeit independence to product inefficiently) lies at the very foundation of the political economy issues of free trade from a Canadian perspective.[33]

One option for responding to this trade-off has been for the formation of a Canadian-owned alternative to the "Big 3" auto makers (General Motors, Ford, and Chrysler). Few observers of the industry think this option would have much feasibility, given tastes among Canadian consumers and the huge head start the Big 3 possess.[34] Nevertheless, the pressures on the long-term survivability of the gasoline engine may create new opportunities for development of alternative motive fuels by Canadian entrepreneurs.

The perceived disadvantages of traditional branch plants, on the one hand, and the constraints that would face newly established Canadian-owned companies, on the other hand, have led to attention being focussed upon a new structure for parent-subsidiary relationships — intracorporate specialization agreements (including what are referred to as "global product mandates").[35] These agreements, which have been made operational by IBM, General Electric, and Black & Decker, among others, encourage Canadian subsidiaries to develop specific product lines for sale throughout large parts of the world. The development process involves a broad range of skills and

33. It should be noted that the discussion here has focussed on static efficiency — the ability to minimize unit costs. Dynamic efficiency — the ability to extend, or at least to stay with, the technology and innovativeness of an industry — raises another set of issues. U.S.-based multinationals in some sectors have been subject to criticism for their performance in this regard and this criticism is part of the case made for greater Canadian economic independence.

34. A recent extended analysis of the Canadian automotive industry, including the prospect for a new Canadian-owned firm, is provided in the report of an inquiry headed by Simon Reisman, a retired senior federal civil servant who played a key role in the auto pact's creation. See *The Canadian Automotive Industry: Performance and Proposals for Progress* (Ottawa: Minister of Supply and Services Canada, 1978).

35. See Harold Crookell and John Caliendo, "International Competitiveness and the Structure of Secondary Industry in Canada", *Business Quarterly* (Autumn, 1980), pp. 58-64.

functions for the subsidiary, thereby responding positively to Canadian concerns about the truncation of its economic capacities.[36]

The chief purpose of intracorporate specialization agreements is to achieve the benefits of increased scale and reduced product-line proliferation within a somewhat less integrated structure than is common for traditional branch-plant operations. It is not clear, however, that such agreements will have very broad application if tariffs remain at significant levels. If a Canadian subsidiary must export its specialized product(s) over a U.S. tariff and import some of its inputs and the rest of the multinational's products over a Canadian tariff, the specialization may not be economically viable from the perspective of the multinational firms. Therefore, such agreements may be conditional upon a form of sectoral free trade, but in this case the free trade status would have to be applied on a differentiated basis between firms that do or do not formulate and implement specialization agreements meeting a basic set of criteria. It is more likely that many firms would see such agreements as being a means for adapting to eventual free trade rather than as an alternative to free trade.

Emphasis has been placed thus far on problems to be anticipated with single-sector free trade agreements such as the auto pact, and specifically the problem of achieving a mutually satisfactory bilateral trade balance within a particular sector. A possible way around this problem is to negotiate simultaneously a group of sectoral free trade arrangements, with a recognition in advance that both parties would experience trade balance strengths and weaknesses in some of those sectors.

The difficulty with such an approach would be to pick the right group of industries to generate a desired overall result. In practice, it is virtually impossible to forecast accurately the outcome of one, let alone several, sectoral free trade agreements. One way to avoid this complication would arise if one or the other party to the agreement was more concerned about a specific benefit, such as assured access to supplies of a scarce natural resource, and was prepared to risk a deterioration of its trade balance to secure that benefit. During the 1980 U.S. presidential campaign, several of the candidates, including Ronald Reagan, the eventual winner, expressed strong interest in some form, only vaguely defined, of a North American approach to

---

36. The concept of truncation, referring to gaps in Canadian economic capabilities, was elaborated in the so-called Herb Gray Report, *Foreign Direct Investment in Canada* (Ottawa: Information Canada, 1972).

energy self-sufficiency. Canada immediately expressed its lack of interest, but it may turn out that Canada will find that it is in a position to obtain an agreement beneficial in terms of many of its manufacturing goals in return for fairly modest energy export commitments. A clear formulation of Canadian priorities would, in that event, be essential.

Moving beyond sectoral approaches to free trade to across-the-board approaches introduces a host of complex strategic and tactical issues. Among the most important of these are the following:

1. To what extent should a free trade agreement with the United States be extendable to allow for inclusion of other countries?
2. Should the agreement be confined to manufacturing, or should provision be made to include natural resources and agriculture?
3. Should the agreement be for a free trade area (in which each country maintains its own trade policies with respect to other countries), or a customs union (in which the participating countries apply a common, harmonized set of trade policies with respect to other countries)?
4. To what extent should the agreement be applied to non-tariff barriers to trade?
5. What policies other than those strictly related directly to trade should be included in the agreement?

These questions relate to the substance of any trade negotiation in a political economy context. The final section of this chapter is devoted to an examination of these questions in that context.

Political Sovereignty with Economic Association[37]

This section is based on two premises. One is that the manufacturing sector of the Canadian economy, or at least that portion dominated by a tariff-factory structure is facing significant challenges. To meet these challenges one option that merits serious consideration is a carefully planned and managed move toward free trade with at least the United States. The second premise is that a move toward even more liberalized trade with the United States will meet considerable opposition within Canada, one major reason being a fear that closer economic association will jeopardize Canadian political sovereignty.

The second premise is put forward without elaboration. It could

---

37. There is a not unintended parallel to be drawn here with the issues raised by the Parti Québecois's attempt to define sovereignty association between Quebec and the rest of Canada in the late 1970s.

be subjected to strong challenge, and has been.[38] But the perception of a problem is often as important as the reality in an exercise in political economy, and this is one such instance. The first premise is not a form of advocacy for bilateral free trade; it rests on a prediction that a gradual decline in tariff protection in Canada since the Second World War, a rise in manufacturing competitiveness in certain third-world countries, and the rigidities that characterize an industry long oriented toward tariff factories will add up to a need for change. While economic logic does not suffice to predetermine the direction of that change, it will exert a major influence on the course of debate over what the change should be. Economic logic favors an attempt to negotiate a mutually acceptable free trade agreement with the United States.

There is already a strong economic association between Canada and the United States in the areas of trade, investment, technology, and so on. But this association has developed over the years within a very informal framework. In what follows, it is assumed that any negotiations aimed at bilateral free trade would have to include a much more formal framework that is responsive to Canada's desire to maintain, and strengthen, its political sovereignty.

The first issue to be considered would precede the negotiations. While efficiency gains would provide a motive for Canada to consider entering the negotiations, this is not a credible reason for expecting U.S. interest, since the United States already has the market size to attain economies of scale and specialization. Therefore, Canada would have to be prepared to offer some inducement, and the most likely canadidate would lie in the area of resource supplies. An unwillingness on Canada's part to offer such an inducement would probably prevent the negotiations from even getting started.

For most resources, the United States might be satisfied if Canada were to guarantee that it would make access to its supplies available to the United States on no less favorable terms than to any third-nation customer, without quantity expectations being specified. In the case of energy, however, the United States would probably expect to receive certain commitments regarding export volumes and might go so far as wanting limits to the difference in prices charged by Canada for its energy in the domestic and U.S. markets. Otherwise, much more favorable terms for access to supply for Canadian cus-

38. As an example, see Peyton V. Lyon, *Canada-United States Free Trade and Canadian Independence* (Ottawa: Information Canada for the Economic Council of Canada, 1975).

tomers would strongly influence location decisions of energy-intensive industries.

If the negotiations did get off the ground, the economic benefits to Canada would depend in large part on the pattern for phasing in tariff cuts. For most industries, the adjustments required in Canada would be much greater than in the United States, and Canada would seek to have this fact recognized in the negotiations of transitional arrangements.

A related issue concerns the exchange rate relationship that would be negotiated. For Canada, there would be a clear need for a highly flexible exchange rate to assist the process of industrial adjustment. While Canada has a flexible exchange rate now, in theory, its movements are managed. In a free trade agreement, especially, guidelines would have to be agreed to if charges of manipulation of the rate to gain competitive advantage are to be avoided.

During the transition, Canada would need access to U.S. investment to supplement domestic sources of finance to fund a major capital restructuring program. At the same time, Canada would want to avoid equity capital inflows, for the purpose of buying up Canadian-owned firms, which would be especially vulnerable to takeovers during the early stages of adjustment to the opportunities and challenges involved in competing within a much larger free market area. Therefore, Canada would seek agreement that it could restrict equity inflows without the U.S. restricting debt outflows. While the United States might be responsive to this Canadian concern, it would be unlikely to agree to extend such an agreement beyond a reasonable period to allow Canadian-owned firms to establish a solid base in the new environment.

Canada would be very reluctant to enter any agreement with the United States that was not open-ended, for two reasons. One is that it would be more palatable politically not to appear to be locked in with the United States; the other is that growth prospects in the United States are not as attractive as in many other countries. On this second point, the attractions for Canada of free trade with the United States lie in the process of adjusting out of an excessively inward-looking industrial structure with the help of a large trading partner that might be willing to respond to Canadian concerns with more patience and understanding than could be anticipated from other potential partners. Once the adjustment is accomplished, however, the benefits of having undertaken it would be larger the more countries that were prepared to enter into the free trade agreement.[39]

A final major issue area that would arise concerns the room for independent policies Canada would retain under a free trade agreement. While there is no inherent reason why considerable flexibility could not be accommodated, there would have to be agreement on a degree of policy harmonization in several key areas. Canada would almost certainly desire considerable flexibility regarding economic relations with third-world countries. Therefore, the agreement would more likely be for a free trade area than for a customs union. Furthermore, Canada would want to have non-tariff barriers in the agreement, but it would refuse to be overly constrained in its ability to offer such incentives as regional development grants that serve national objectives. Determining codes of conduct, in effect, to serve as guidelines in this area would be a time-consuming negotiating task.

Related to this issue area are matters such as policies regarding labor mobility across the border, policies originating in the pursuit of cultural objectives, and policies concerning the structure of taxation. Canada would wish to maximize its opportunities for independent action, but the United States would require some assurances that such independence would not produce excessive indirect effects on decisions regarding the location of production.

This listing demonstrates the complexities that would have to be addressed in a serious set of free trade negotiations. These complexities might prevent such negotiations from ever getting under way. For firms involved in Canadian-U.S. commercial affairs, and even for firms that are confined to the Canadian market, the prospect of free trade represents a major factor in the future environment they face. Although some firms might prefer that the status quo would persist, forces are at work in the world economy that are undermining the status quo: Canada must now try to determine, and implement, the new commercial framework it wants to see replace the status quo that has eroded.

39. Advanced commitment to a wider agreement would ease the "double adjustment" problem, which would arise if, after adjusting once to free trade with the United States, Canadian producers would then have to adjust again to free trade within a broader framework.

II
Trade Theory and Canada's Comparative Advantage

B
Canadian Trade Policy

9
Why a North American Common Market Won't Work—Yet

Herbert E. Meyer

Herbert Meyer joined Fortune as an associate editor in 1971. He had previously been a staff associate for the President's Advisory Council on Executive Organization and prior to that a staff reporter for the *Wall Street Journal* in New York and Washington, and a member of the staff of the *Times Herald-Record*, Middletown, New York.

Meyer is a graduate of Brooklyn College with concentration in political science and economics and attended the University of Paris where he studied diplomatic history and Soviet studies.

The material in this chapter appeared originally in *Fortune*, September 10, 1979. Reprinted by permission.

Some prominent American politicians and business executives are suddenly talking up an idea that is so arresting — and so seemingly sensible for all parties — that one wonders why nobody proposed it earlier. It is the idea of linking the U.S., Canada, and Mexico together in a North American common market. If it were to be patterned after Western Europe's Common Market, it would amount to a customs union covering the exchange of goods, the prohibition of duties on exports and imports among the three countries, and the adoption of a common external tariff in relations with third countries. It could also include the free movement of labor and capital.

Current enthusiasm for the proposal, however, has little to do with a grand design for reshaping political and economic relationships in the western hemisphere. Twenty-five years ago, Jean Monnet was thinking in those broader terms when he was calling for a European Common Market. The advocates of a North American "economic community" start from the important but narrower premise that it will somehow help the U.S. to lessen its dependence on OPEC oil. John Connally, Jerry Brown, the president of Dow Chemical Co., and others who have endorsed the common market idea seem to view it primaril᾽ ᾽s a means of increasing the flow of oil and natural gas from Canad᾽ ᾽ Mexico to the U.S.

That ᾽ᴏpe turns out to be an illusion. Formation of a common market would not automatically increase Canadian and Mexican exports of energy to the U.S. For a common market in no way gives member nations the right to help themselves to one another's natural resources. But the concept of a continental economic union deserves better than to be treated as a gimmick that will help solve our energy problems. Its champions, up to now, have done their cause a disservice by their failure to explore the grand possibilities raised by the scheme. They have also overlooked some rather formidable obstacles in the way of its being put into effect.

Imagine for a moment what a North Amrican common market would look like — in 1979 terms. Just by itself, the U.S. has a larger GNP ($2.1 trillion) than either Japan ($956 billion) or the nine-nation European Community ($1.9 trillion). Moreover, the U.S. alone produces 19 per cent of the world's grain. Join the U.S. with Canada and Mexico, and the combination creates an even more awesome colossus. With a population of 312 million, it would contain more people than the European Community (260 million). GNP would approach $2.5 trillion. Largely because of Canada's farm output, the market's share of world grain production would amount to 22 per cent. And because of their vast proven reserves of oil, gas, and coal, the three nations would have the potential of becoming self-sufficient in energy. In every way, then, a North American common market could be an alliance with plenty of economic muscle.

Since the 1980s will almost certainly be marked by ferocious competition among the industrialized countries for Third World markets and raw materials, a North American alliance would guarantee its three members at least a fair share of the pie — or at least a larger slice than each would be able to grab by itself. To be sure, free trade within the bloc would expose weak or inefficient companies to stiff new competition. That could lead to some wrenching shifts in industries and workers. But those companies that survived could compete more effectively around the world.

Within its own boundaries, a North American common market would seem to provide some rather stunning economic opportunities for its three member countries. To begin with, manufacturers in the U.S., Canada, and Mexico would gain unrestricted access to one another's markets. U.S. capital and technology would pour into Canada and Mexico and create a lot of jobs for Canadians and Mexicans. Mexico's backward agricultural sector would also benefit, and so would that country's fast-growing and underfed population. If North America actually could manage to fill all of its own energy needs, today's hemorrhage of dollars to OPEC would be permanently stopped.

Given all these advantages, one might expect that Canada and Mexico would be pro-common market. Americans who are pushing the idea seem to expect this sort of response. But along with the economic advantages come some risks that common market advocates seem not to recognize — and Canadians and Mexicans are simply not willing to take. In fact, the Canadians and Mexicans are downright scared of the prospect.

To understand that fear, just look at the continent's lopsided trade pattern, which now favors Canadian and Mexican exports to the U.S. Under the new U.S.-Canada bilateral trade agreement, negotiated this year as part of the GATT Tokyo Round, 80 per cent of all Canadian exports to the U.S. will be duty-free. Another 15 per cent will enter at tariffs of 5 per cent or less. Mexican oil and coffee beans, which represent nearly 40 per cent of that country's exports to the U.S., are duty-free. The average U.S. tariff on all other Mexican products, from machinery to cork, is 6.03 per cent.

Our own products are not nearly as welcome in our neighbors' markets. Under that new bilateral agreement, Canada will allow only 65 per cent of U.S. exports to enter duty-free. And Canada's average tariff on dutiable U.S. imports will be 8.5 per cent — down from 14.8 per cent under the old agreement but still more than double the average U.S. tariff on dutiable imports from Canada. Mexico uses a complex licensing system to bar many U.S.-manufactured products. American goods that do slip through the system are hit with tariffs ranging from 35 to 100 per cent.

What all this means, of course, is that the big winners in a common market — at least in the short run — would be U.S. manufacturers. For it is their markets to the north and south that would expand most dramatically under a duty-free customs union. For many Canadian and Mexican businesses, the removal of tariff walls would surely lead to some unpleasant consequences.

Right now, most U.S. companies that serve the small Canadian market — just 23.7 million people, or slightly more than the population of California — do so from branch plants set up in Canada in order to get over the tariff wall. This branch-plant network is far more extensive than most Americans realize. Today U.S. companies control forty-five of the one hundred largest companies in Canada. Canadian-based subsidiaries of U.S. companies account for 43 per cent of all Canadian manufacturing and 58 per cent of all oil and natural gas companies. With some justification, Canadians complain that theirs is merely a branch-plant economy, with many factories run by absentee landlords to the south. Whenever there are production cutbacks because of economic conditions, Canadians insist, American corporations invariably give priority to preserving jobs at their U.S. plants at the expense of jobholders in Canadian plants.

Removal of the tariff wall obviously would give U.S. companies the option of supplying Canada more easily from U.S.-based plants. And it's likely that some U.S. companies would abandon their branches. For one thing, plants located in the U.S. tend to be more efficient than Canadian plants because they are geared to serve a larger domestic market. Moreover, labor costs in Canada are generally higher than those in the U.S. Northern Telecom, Canada's giant communications equipment manufacturer, calculates that total labor costs at its Canadian plants range from 10 to 50 per cent higher than those at its U.S. factories.

A shift of production — and of jobs — from Canada to the U.S. would be rather like a giant version of our own Sunbelt phenomenon. This development probably would enable many Canadian workers to enjoy a higher standard of living. But to "enjoy" it, they would have to move to the U.S. — something that not many Canadians are likely to do. Nor is it a development any Canadian government would be likely to encourage. After all, any major outflow of companies and jobs would weaken the economy and contribute to a further decline in the value of the Canadian dollar.

In the long run, a southward migration might depress the Canadian dollar to such a low level that it might even become economically attractive to build plants in Canada large enough to serve the entire North American market. But quite a few Canadians — moderates, not rabid nationalists — fear that by the time that might be possible, their own country would be too far gone to save. They worry that the gravitational force of the gigantic U.S. market would be too strong ever to escape. Its pull on jobs, workers, and capital would combine to break the fragile ties among Canada's contentious provinces and, by doing so, destroy the Canadian Confederation itself.

Formation of a common market would also give U.S. manufacturers a clear shot at the expanding Mexican market. To the extent that they supplied that market from plants located in the U.S., the "victims" would include Mexican competitors that might go bankrupt and Mexican workers whose jobs would disappear. Since the unemployment rate in Mexico is currently hovering around 20 per cent — and another 20 per cent of the work force is underemployed — the social and political impact of any major job loss could be devastating.

Of course, some U.S. companies might decide to build plants in Mexico itself — perhaps even plants with export capacity. This would certainly help keep the Mexican unemployment rate from rising. But it's more likely that U.S. companies would establish themselves in Mexico by taking over their financially and technologically weaker Mexican counterparts. Mexico, like Canada, would become a branch-plant economy. And that possibility makes the Mexicans see red.

It is hardly surprising, then, that our continental neighbors are haunted by the spectre of a U.S. economic offensive. Indeed, it's fair to describe Canadian history as an unending effort to protect that country's manufacturers from U.S. competitors. The last politician bold enough to suggest publicly that Canada abandon protectionism was Prime Minister Sir Wilfrid Laurier, who campaigned for re-election in 1911 on the theme of free trade with the U.S. Laurier and his Liberals were soundly beaten by Robert Borden, whose Conservatives swept to power on a slogan of "No truck or trade with the Yankees". The rhetoric has cooled down, but even today Canada's economy remains among the most protected within the twenty-

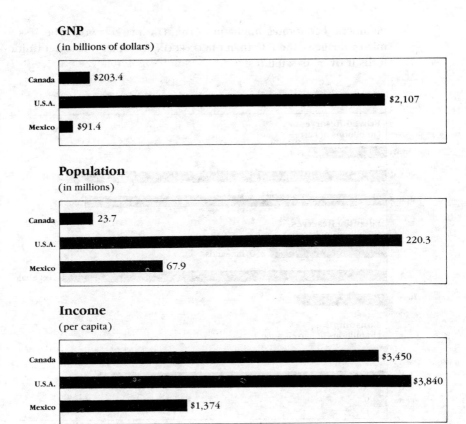

GNP
(in billions of dollars)

Canada	$203.4
U.S.A.	$2,107
Mexico	$91.4

Population
(in millions)

Canada	23.7
U.S.A.	220.3
Mexico	67.9

Income
(per capita)

Canada	$3,450
U.S.A.	$3,840
Mexico	$1,374

four-nation OECD. And Mexico makes Canada seem like a hotbed of "free-tradeism". For several decades, Mexico has been embarked on an extensive program of "Mexicanization" of its industry. So protectionist is the country that it refuses even to join the eighty-four-member GATT, although Mexico now has the world's fifteenth-largest economy.

To Canada and Mexico, the political implications of a continental union look even more hazardous than the economic ones. That's because a North American common market — unlike, say, the European Community — could never be a confederation of economic equals. After all, North America is not Western Europe, where no single country is big enough and strong enough to have its way on every decision. The U.S. would inevitably dominate a North American common market no matter how carefully its rules might be drawn, how softly its diplomats might tread, how well the other members' economies might perform. The market would be less a mirror image of the E.C. than of COMECON, in which the Soviet Union lords it over its satellites.

Oil

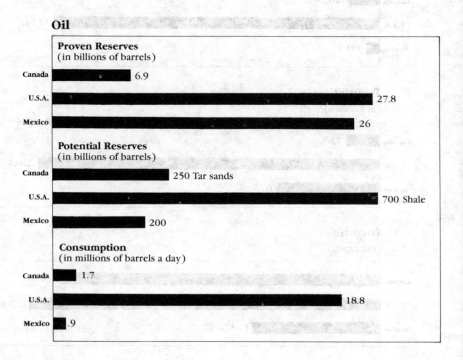

Proven Reserves
(in billions of barrels)

Canada   6.9
U.S.A.   27.8
Mexico   26

Potential Reserves
(in billions of barrels)

Canada   250 Tar sands
U.S.A.   700 Shale
Mexico   200

Consumption
(in millions of barrels a day)

Canada   1.7
U.S.A.   18.8
Mexico   .9

Gas

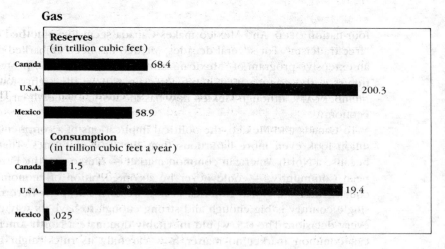

Reserves
(in trillion cubic feet)

Canada   68.4
U.S.A.   200.3
Mexico   58.9

Consumption
(in trillion cubic feet a year)

Canada   1.5
U.S.A.   19.4
Mexico   .025

All this suggests that advocates of a North American common market have missed a crucial point: Canadians and Mexicans just won't buy it. Of all the conceivable ways to secure better U.S. access to energy supplies, this is the one least likely to succeed. Considering the current political mood both north and south of our borders, it is scarcely an exaggeration to suggest that the surest way to extract more energy from our neighbors would be for us to promise that the idea of a common market will not be raised again for at least the remainder of this century.

The irony is that, whatever else it might accomplish, a common market would not guarantee the U.S. a cheaper or surer flow of energy from Canada and Mexico. If a North American common market were to follow the example of the European Community, each member country would retain sovereign control over its own resources, the rates of production, and even its choice of customers. For example, Britain limits the output of its North Sea oil, although most of its fellow E.C. members would buy as much as they could get. Moreover, Britain sells one-third of its oil to non-E.C. countries, including the U.S. So it would be quite possible to create a North American common market — every bit as formal and as comprehensive as the E.C. — in which the U.S. would receive not one more drop of oil or one more cubic metre of natural gas.

In any case, there are simpler and more direct ways in which the U.S. can enlarge its access to Canadian gas and Mexican petroleum. Several kinds of deals are possible. For instance, Canada would like its beef to be exempted from our rigid U.S. import quotas and has been trying to get the U.S. to eliminate its present 4 per cent tariff on industrial chemicals and the 10.8 per cent tariff on textiles. Why not a concession on beef, chemicals, and textiles in exchange for a specified amount of natural gas at a fixed price? Or we might persuade the Canadians to ship more natural gas by offering to establish "sectoral free trade agreements" covering chemicals and textiles, which would allow free trade within specified dollar limits. The precedent exists, since the U.S. and Canada already have two such sectoral agreements, the auto pact and the Defense Production Sharing Arrangement, which allows duty-free movement of military goods.

The U.S. also has some leverage it could apply on Mexico to increase its oil shipments. Mexico is desperate for U.S. help in solving its population problem. With the labor-force growth far outstripping the growth of jobs, millions of Mexicans are illegally flooding into the U.S. each year in search of work. It is estimated that roughly four million Mexican aliens are working illegally in this country. For Mexico, access to the U.S. job market is a vital safety valve, and the

North American Trade

(in billions)

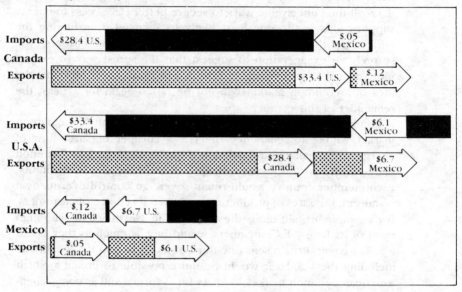

Note: Like it or not — and diehard nationalists don't — the economies of the three North American countries are already quite independent. The U.S. is the No. 1 trading partner for both Canada and Mexico. Canada is the U.S.'s No. 1 trading partner, and Mexico is No. 4. To further strengthen continental ties, Canadian groups including the Economic Council and the Senate Foreign Affairs Committee are advocating free trade between Canada and the U.S. — an arrangement far short of a common market, since it would leave each partner at liberty to set its own tariffs on third-country goods. No major Mexican groups or individuals have called for free trade, let alone a common market.

government would like us to allow millions of Mexicans to work here — legally. These are the ingredients of a deal: if the U.S. would open its borders to Mexican workers, Mexico might be willing to boost its oil production.

Mexico is also eager for the U.S. to import many more of its winter fruits and vegetables, especially tomatoes. U.S. purchases of those fruits and vegetables not only provided $300 million or so in income for Mexican farmers in 1978, but also kept thousands of Mexicans employed. Recently, however, Florida's tomato growers have been lobbying the U.S. Teasury Department to restrict Mexican tomatoes on the dubious grounds that the Mexicans are violating the 1921 Anti-Dumping Act by selling below cost. Again, some kind of agriculture-energy deal does not seem impossible.

In the interests of generally improving relations with our neighbors — and of formally ending an era in which we have often ignored them or treated them shabbily — there are several easy steps the U.S. could take unilaterally. It would help if the State Department would stop handling Canadian matters through the Bureau of European Affairs — a vestige of our dealings with the old British Commonwealth. At the same time, State could stop treating Mexico as just another desk in the Latin American bureau. Possibly the time has come to start a new North American bureau. That, at best, could encourage a more realistic approach to three-way co-operation. Perhaps, after everybody gets used to working together better, the political and other objections to an economic union may seem less formidable. But for now a North American common market is an idea whose time has not yet arrived.

III
The Challenge of Overseas Markets

Despite Canada's often protectionist import policies, public and private leaders agree on the vital role of exports in the Canadian economy. More than one-quarter of all the goods and services produced in Canada are exported to other countries, directly employing hundreds of thousands of Canadians and providing secondary or derived employment for even more, as well as the means with which Canadians can import other products produced more cheaply abroad. Yet Canadian business managers are frequently accused of being insufficiently competitive or aggressive in overseas markets.

This portion of the book contains the challenge of overseas markets and recommends means by which the export performance of Canadian firms may be improved. The views of prominent business leaders and academics are brought together to provide creative recommendations both to private firms and to government.

Crookell and Graham (Chapter 10) first provide a profile of Canadian exporters in the manufacturing and service sectors. Etemad (Chapter 11) develops a decision model which may help Canadian managers to identify and approach potential markets abroad.

Carmichael (Chapter 12) examines the competitiveness and international trade performance of individual Canadian manufacturing industries, identifying the strengths and weaknesses of each. Fodor (Chapter 13) and Nadeau (Chapter 14) offer the perspective of the chief executive officers of two small Canadian firms which have succeeded in international markets through dynamic management and innovative technology. Dagenais (Chapter 15) writes of the major international role of Canada's engineering consulting firms.

The last two chapters focus on two new marketing vehicles which hold particular promise for the international position of Canadian firms in the future. Dhawan and Kryzanowski (Chapter 16) examine the benefits and problems of the export consortium as an international marketing vehicle. McMillan (Chapter 17) discusses the pros and cons of a national export trading house.

III
The Challenge of Overseas Markets

A
Export Marketing: An Overview

10
A Profile of Canadian Exporters

Harold Crookell

Ian Graham

Dr. Crookell is director of the Centre for International Business Studies at the School of Business Administration, University of Western Ontario. He is the author of *The Role of Product Innovation in Trade Flows*, as well as numerous articles.

Mr. Graham is general manager of Graham Fiber Glass Limited, an independent manufacturer of fibre glass insulation products. His company has been in operation since December, 1979, and presently has 100 employees and $10 million in annual sales.

The material in this chapter appeared originally under the title "International Marketing and Canadian Industrial Strategy", in *The Business Quarterly*, Autumn 1979. Reprinted by permission.

It is not surprising that a country endowed as Canada is should have large and persistent trade surpluses in agricultural and raw materials-based products. Nor is it surprising that large and persistent trade deficits in secondary industry should provide the compensating balance in the trade account. This is no more than a reflection of the theory of comparative advantage. Of late, however, there has been a shift in the nation's willingness to export her raw materials — especially the non-renewable ones, but no corresponding reluctance to continue to expand finished goods imports. As a result, the trade balance has declined over $4 billion in the five-year period from 1970 to 1975. The resulting massive current account deficits and corresponding massive debt borrowings abroad have contributed to a weakening of the Canadian dollar.

There seems, at present, no prospect that the problem can be rectified by increasing exports of raw and fabricated materials. Most forecasts are for weakening metals prices and greater oil imports. Nor does there seem, at present, the will to reduce consumption of imported finished goods, and the country cannot go on for long borrowing long term to finance current consumption and retain respectability in the international economy. As a result, the focus has come down increasingly on how to get Canada's secondary and service industries to improve their international competitiveness and hence their share of foreign markets.

This chapter deals with some facets of the latter problem. Who are Canada's exporters in secondary and service industries? Where do they export or invest? What channels of distribution do they use? What is the nature of their competitive advantage? How many are foreign-owned firms? The data that follow are based on interviews with 148 firms in Canada that are active in foreign markets. The representativeness of the sample is as yet uncertain, but 119 of the firms were responsible for foreign sales of about $6.4 billion. These were not all export sales. Included were sales abroad from foreign production by subsidiaries of the responding firms. A brief statistical profile of the sample firms follows.

Table 1

Statistical Profile of the Sample Firms

Per Cent of Sales in Foreign Markets	Small Firms Sales Less than $10	Medium Firms Sales Between $10-50	Large Firms Sales Over $50	Total
Less than 25%	25	5	15	45
Between 25-50%	14	10	16	40
More than 50%	32	8	11	51
Total	71	23	42	136

Primary International Activity

	Canadian Owned	Foreign Owned
Export of Goods	71	38
Export of Services	13	2
Wholly Owned Subs.	9	1
Joint Ventures	8	—
Licensing	1	—
	102	41

Per Cent of Firms in Industry Sectors According to Their Predominant Output

		Average Foreign Sales (Millions of Dollars)
End Products	59	$ 201.1
Fabricated Material	30	149.3
Crude Materials	9	59.4
Services	21	10.0
	119	

The sample firms, on average, derived 25 per cent of their revenues from abroad in 1976. They were evenly distributed as to size. Most were Canadian-owned firms in secondary or service industries active primarily as exporters. There were however forty-two foreign subsidiaries (mostly of U.S. parents), and twenty-five subsidiaries of Canadian parents.

Aggressiveness in Seeking Foreign Markets

An overwhelming majority of respondents claimed to be actively searching for new opportunities abroad. This is a welcome and refreshing response even from a sample of firms chosen for their involvement in foreign markets. It is presumably a reflection both of the financial attractiveness of foreign markets to the firms and of the depressed state of domestic markets during 1976. As the following data show, an active search posture was claimed by both indigenous and foreign-owned firms.

Firms already heavily involved in foreign markets seemed somewhat more active in seeking new opportunities abroad than did firms not so heavily involved. The difference was not dramatic, but did seem to confirm that the experienced firms had developed better mechanisms for spotting new opportunities and were the more likely to expand international operations. In general, this finding held for foreign subsidiaries as well as indigenous firms.

Table 2

Aggressiveness of Sample Firms in Seeking New Opportunities Abroad

	Seeking Actively	Seeking Passively
Indigenous Firms	83	17
Foreign Subsidiaries	29	12

Table 3

The Effect of Experience on the Search for New Opportunities Abroad

Experience Level of Sample Firms	Seeking Actively	Seeking Passively
Foreign Revenue Less than 50% of Total	71	25
Foreign Revenue More than 50% of Total	41	4

Foreign Markets of Greatest Interest to Canadian Firms

Firms were asked to identify geographic regions where they anticipated market potential. The United States was ranked first by more than half the respondents as the market with the greatest potential for their products. Western Europe, South America, and Asia were next in preference. If one ignores the rankings and treats each response equally, the dominance of the North American market was not so evident. North America's lead fell to 21 per cent of all responses, suggesting that if it was not first choice, it was often not selected at all. Other market areas remained in the same order of preference, but the frequency of mention was impressive, reflecting broad international scope on the part of many firms.

Table 4

Market Regions of Interest to Sample Firms

Region	As Ranked First		Total Responses
	Canadian-owned Firms	Foreign-owned Firms	All Firms
North America (ex. Canada)	50	15	102
West. Europe	14	4	78
South and Central America	6	2	78
Other Asia	4	3	63
Middle East	2	2	53
Other Africa	4	—	48
East. Europe	1	1	29
Oceania	1	—	34
Total Cases	82	27	485

Table 5

High Potential Future Market Regions by Industry Sector as Ranked First

Industry Sector	Market Region					
(Per cents)	North America	West. Europe	S. & C. America	Asia	Other	Total
End Products	34	5	6	1	7	53
Fabricated Materials	24	2	0	3	1	30
Services	5	3	3	3	4	18
Food, Feed, etc.	4	4	1	2	0	11
Crude Materials	2	2	2	0	1	7
Total	69	16	12	9	13	119

Target export markets did vary according to the industry sectors in which responding firms competed. Whereas 80 per cent of firms in the fabricated materials sector said primary potential lay in the United States, the service sector was much more diverse in its interests. Only 28 per cent expressed primary interest in the U.S. Evidently consulting and other service industries find more opportunities in the developing world than in the industrialized nations.

These results do not indicate any major shifts of interest away from market regions where sample firms are currently active. The role of the U.S. as our major trading partner is clearly demonstrated in these data. Its position as a consumer of our natural resources is also markedly evident.

Personnel and Organizational Structure

The average number of employees in the sample firms was 2,200. The number engaged in international activities, however, was much smaller. About half of the firms had fewer than 6 employees spending at least a quarter of their time on international business activities.

Respondents were asked to rank the skills they felt were "most required to implement and achieve corporate objectives in foreign markets". Excluding skills specific to the technology of the firm, foreign market development and negotiation skills stood foremost. Negotiation skills were seen to be needed in a wide variety of tasks such as sales, investing, dealing with host government and foreign suppliers, licence and distribution agreements, etc. Again when total responses were examined, skill factors such as cultural adaptability, strategic planning, and international finance were frequently mentioned.

Table 6

Skill Requirements for International Personnel

Skill	First Rankings	Total Responses
Foreign Market Development	42	90
Product or Service Knowledge	26	49
Technical Knowledge	19	58
Negotiation	14	85
Strategic Planning	10	53
International Finance	5	44
Cultural Adaptability	4	53
Other	3	9
Total	123	441

When asked which skills were most urgently in need of development, executives in the responding firms referred most often to cultural adaptability and strategic planning. International finance skills were felt to be reasonably available at nominal cost through banking intermediaries.

The type of corporate organization used to cope with foreign markets varied directly with the size of the firm. The following table shows that the larger the firm the more frequently it used the more complex worldwide product division structure.

Firms tend to move to progressively more complex organization structures in response to the pressures of growth in international markets. The above results are not, therefore, surprising. What is perhaps more surprising is the number of medium and large firms with relatively simple organization structures. To some degree, these can be explained either as large firms with very little international activity or as foreign subsidiaries whose structures are determined by their relationship to their parents. For example, the foreign subsidiaries in the sample were larger firms on average than the Canadian-owned firms. However, the Canadian-owned firms were much more frequent users of the complex organization structure, as the following data show.

Undoubtedly, these results reflect a number of subsidiaries that are active in foreign markets through their parents and do not therefore require in their own organizations either the complexity of structure or the richness of skills that indigenous firms would require.

Table 7

Organization Structure by Size of Firm (Sales millions)

	Least Complex			Most Complex
Per Cent of Sales	Domestic Division	Export Department	International Division	Worldwide Basis
Small (< $10)	17	7	6	6
Medium ($10-50)	12	7	10	19
Large (> $50)	10	4	5	24

Table 8

Organization Structure by Control

Per Cent	Domestic Division	Export Department	International Division	Worldwide Basis	No. Cases
Canadian Control	26	12	12	29	89
Foreign Control	13	6	9	10	38
					127

Source of Competitive Advantage

From the view that Canada is an unlikely place from which to underprice foreign markets, one might expect that Canadian firms with a record of success abroad must have developed some distinctive competence which gave them a competitive edge in foreign markets. An attempt was made to discover how firms perceived themselves in this regard: that is, what, in their view, was their competitive edge, and how did they come to possess it? It was expected that some firms would see their competitive edge in marketing skills — as with Coca-Cola or Standard Brands, while others would see it in product innovation — such as Xerox, Polaroid, or Northern Telecom, and yet others in process engineering — such as Massey-Ferguson, Crown Cork, and Seal. Furthermore, given Canada's much publicized tradition of borrowing ideas from abroad and the tendency of foreign subsidiaries to lean on their parents for technology, it was expected that relatively few firms would have developed their key competitive edge in-house.

In this, the response of our sample firms came as a surprise. Almost 80 per cent of respondents indicated that their competitive edge was developed in-house. And product performance (innovative technology) was the most frequently mentioned competitive edge (ranked first by one-third of the sample firms.)

Table 9

Competitive Edge Most Responsible for Success in Foreign Markets

	First Ranked	Total Responses
Product Performance	45	97
Market Skills	35	97
Production Capability	30	88
Price	13	57
Parent/Affiliate Network	13	15
Total	**136**	**354**

Table 10

How Competitive Edge Obtained by Sample Firms

	First Ranked	Total Responses
Developed In-House	106	125
Acquired Through New Businesses or Personnel	4	31
Licensed from Outsiders	7	33
Licensed from Parent or Affiliate	19	30
Total	**136**	**219**

It is clear from these data that marketing skills are as important as technology for breaking into foreign markets in the view of responding firms. It also appears that in-house development of the critical "competitive edge" generates the confidence needed to enter international markets aggressively. Hence, by sampling only those firms active in foreign markets we are by selection sampling largely those whose competitive skills are developed in-house.

There also seemed to be a difference in the competitive approach to foreign markets according to the size of the firm and according to the locus of ownership. Smaller firms tended to compete more on the basis of product performance than did larger firms, which tended to emphasize production skills. There was a marked absence of price competition by smaller firms.

Table 11

Competitive Advantages Ranked First by Size of Firm ($ millions)

Per Cent of Sales	Product Perform	Marketing Skills	Price	Production
Small (< $10)	20	13	1	10
Medium ($10-50)	14	9	6	8
Large (> $50)	8	9	6	11

The foreign subsidiaries seemed to rely much more on the parent network to help them compete abroad than did the subsidiaries of

Canadian parents. It is likely that Canadian subsidiaries are more autonomous than foreign subsidiaries, but the reason, it seems, is that the foreign parent has more to offer its subsidiaries than has the Canadian parent. In cases where the Canadian parent had no international experience or presided over a loose conglomerate, there would be little it could offer its subsidiaries to help them compete in foreign markets.

Distribution Channels Used by Goods Exporters

International marketing is very different from exporting. Canada's auto producers export billions of dollars per year, but the activity leaves little residue of international marketing skill in the Canadian firms. The reason is that all are subsidiaries, and responsibility for non-Canadian sales is taken by and large by their parents. Even firms without foreign parents can export without learning a great deal about international marketing. They can export through local export agents or through import agents abroad, or they can sell to single customers abroad on a stencil brand basis. The firm that sells directly to its foreign customers through its own sales force will develop a much better knowledge of its international market and will need a broader range of in-house international marketing skills.

It was encouraging to note that the distribution channel to foreign markets used most frequently by the sample firms was, in fact, their own in-house sales organization. As the following data indicate, overseas import agents were the second most frequently mentioned channel, although in most cases they were used as a secondary rather than a primary channel — perhaps in market areas too small to support direct selling.

Table 12

Distribution Channels Used by Goods Exporters

Channel	Total Responses
In-House Sales Force	100
Import Agent	64
Parent	51
Export Agent	44
Total	**(259)**

The data also suggests that firms progress to channels closer to the market as they grow, with the exception of those foreign subsidiaries tied to parent channels. More smaller firms used export agents than did medium and large firms, while almost 80 per cent of large firms used an in-house sales force. Often there are working capital costs to in-house selling that smaller firms are hard pressed to afford.

Table 13

Sales Channel by Size of Firm—Goods Exporters

	Export Agent	Import Agent	In-House
Small	12	6	15
Medium	6	10	18
Large	5	3	16

It is interesting to note that a significant number of medium and large firms continued to use channels that tended to isolate them from their markets. This may indicate an inefficiency in their operations that could be resulting in inadequate market information and hence increased risk of being caught unawares by sudden market changes.

Summary and Conclusions

From the sample of firms studied to date, it would appear that the United States is likely to remain Canada's leading trading partner. Government moves to encourage more trade with Europe and Japan are not reflected in the strategies and forecasts of Canadian finished goods exporters.

Foreign subsidiaries in Canada are, naturally, wedded to parent channels into foreign markets and relatively few have developed international marketing skills of their own. Many indigenous firms use import or export agents to relieve them of direct international marketing responsibility. The result is a shortage in Canadian secondary industry of in-house skills in international marketing. This is not surprising. A nation with a history of exporting raw materials and primary products cannot be expected to have a rich supply of the kind of skills needed to sell differentiated finished goods abroad. Nevertheless a surprising number of the firms sampled did mention the use of an in-house sales force in at least some markets. There is clearly room here for greater management training efforts and for government policy attention.

Such policy attention as is given must discriminate between Canadian-owned and foreign-owned firms, not due to nationalistic fervor, but simply because the nature of their activities requires different stimulus to increase international sales. And the stimulus is needed whether or not Canada enters a free trade agreement with the U.S. In fact, it would make a lot of sense to provide such stimulus as a necessary prelude to a free trade agreement.

An unexpected number of firms had developed a critical competitive edge from which to sell into foreign markets despite Canada's high cost structure, and most had developed it in-house. It seems firms have trouble moving aggressively overseas on borrowed technology. Product innovation was the leading type of competitive edge, followed by marketing skills and process engineering. Perhaps the most encouraging finding of the survey was that 80 per cent of the firms sampled claimed to be seeking new opportunities in foreign markets. It would appear that constructive incentives for firms to develop in-house product development and international marketing skills would be put to use by Canada's international business community, as long as they did not consume in red tape the scarce managerial talent that needs to be out winning foreign markets.

III
The Challenge of Overseas Markets

A
Export Marketing: An Overview

11
A Decision Model for Exporting from Canada

Hamid Etemad

Dr. Etemad is assistant professor of international business in the Faculty of Management, McGill University. His areas of teaching and research are international marketing and international business policy.

This chapter was written expressly for this volume.

Introduction

The Tokyo Round of GATT negotiations, concluded in early 1979, will open the markets of many countries to Canadian firms. Tariff and non-tariff barrier walls will gradually come down.[1] While this may mean expanded opportunities for Canadian producers, it may also threaten their own previously protected domestic markets. In other words, it is a double-edged sword, which will cut both ways.

The small size of Canada's domestic market has long been blamed for lack of efficiency and economies of scale. If, indeed, that has played any role in the competitiveness of Canadian products, the results of GATT negotiations should be welcomed by Canadians. This is a real opportunity for those Canadian producers who take advantage of these expanded markets *early on* to enlarge their operations. However, for Canadians who do not, the failure to capitalize on economies of scale by producing for other markets will put them at a

1. See the following table for scheduled reduction of tariffs.

Tokyo Round's Typical Proposed Tariff Reductions for Selected Countries

	United States		Switzerland		Japan		E.E.C.	
Present Duty %	Final Duty %	% of Reduction	Final Duty %	% of Reduction	Final Duty %	% of Reduction	Final Duty %	% of Reduction
5	2.1	57.5	3.7	26.3	5.0	0	4.1	17.3
10	4.0	60.0	5.8	41.7	6.5	35.0	7.0	30.5
15	6.0	60.0	7.2	51.7	8.0	46.7	8.9	40.6
20	8.0	60.0	8.2	58.8	9.5	52.5	10.3	48.6
30	12.0	60.0	9.5	68.2	12.5	58.3	11.9	60.3
40	16.0	60.0	10.4	74.1	15.5	61.2	12.7	68.3
50	20.0	60.0	10.9	78.1	18.5	63.0	12.9	74.2

Source: Canadian Customs.

disadvantage when foreign producers try to enter the Canadian market and enhance their own competitive position.[2]

The problem is an urgent one, and time is of the essence. Those who move rather quickly, aggressively, and efficiently may have a good chance of success, and those who wait or adopt a passive stance help to ensure their own demise. Hence, at this crossroads, a prudent and expeditious strategy for Canadian firms to expand into the international market(s) is increasingly important.[3]

The primary intention of this chapter is: (1) to put forward a conceptual and comprehensive decision framework to allow Canadian producers or marketers to identify desirable international markets, and (2) to examine certain marketing principles that can help formulate a viable marketing strategy for those markets, especially for small and medium-size Canadian firms.[4]

First this chapter presents a conceptual framework which spells out broad guidelines to enable decision makers to isolate and thereby concentrate on serving particular markets or market segments. Secondly, this framework is analysed and the implications for Canadian firms, industries, and the government are discussed. Thirdly, the framework is applied to a firm in terms of a typical decision tree analysis. Finally, the framework's implications and its usefulness for application to other Canadian institutions facing the same type of decisions are presented.

A Conceptual Framework

The Model
One of the common problems of international marketers is the

2. In addition to the benefits of economies of scale, exports may stablize sales which in turn may lead to longer-run increased profits. However, the short-run experience of exporters does not support the notion of increased profits. Indeed, it is argued that export activities are indeed short-run investment for achieving longer-run objectives (profits). See, for example, Finn Wiedershein-Paul, Hans C. Olson, and Lawrence S. Welch, "Pre-Export Activity: The First Step In Internationalization", *Journal Of International Business Studies* (Spring-Summer 1978), p. 50; and W. J. Bilkey, and G. Tesar, *"The Export Behavior Of Smaller Sized Wisconsin Manufacturing Firms", JIBS* (Spring 1977), p. 93; S. Hirsch, *The Export Performance Of Six Manufacturing Industries* (New York: Praeger Publishing Company, 1971), pp. 82-95.
3. For a list of expansive international marketing strategies see Igal Ayal, and J. Ziff, "Competitive Market Choice Strategies In Multinational Marketing", *Columbia Journal Of World Business* (Fall 1978), pp. 84-94.
4. For a definition of small and medium-size companies see Chapter 13 by N. Fodor, "Canadian Small Business and International Markets" in this book.

difficulty of identifying potential international markets.[5] This difficulty becomes even more severe when domestically oriented marketers start market prospecting from a distance, applying familiar techniques used in domestic markets. The success or failure of familiar domestic techniques in other countries depends on their cultural sensitivity.[6] To identify a market, one has to examine the behavior of consumers within that market. Those techniques or measurements that have a lower cultural sensitivity stand a higher chance of success in the adversity of international markets.

It is generally held that an individual's needs, wants, and desires for a product give rise to a certain degree of preparedness or "willingness" to purchase that product.[7] When this is coupled with the "ability" to purchase the product, one can assume that the particular individual is *receptive* to stimulation.[8] Then, given proper stimulation, the individual can be included in the target market.

Hence, the necessary condition for someone to purchase a specific product may be characterized by a multiplicative relationship:[9]

$$s = g(p \cdot a) \tag{1}$$

where s represents a potential purchase or overall propensity to purchase; p is a measure of psychological propensity or preparedness based on desires, needs, and/or wants to purchase the product; and a is a measure of relative ability to purchase the specific product.[10]

5. In an exhaustive review of the literature on exporting, Warren Bilkey touches upon export "stages" which start with an unwilling firm receiving an unsolicited order, which is a passive strategy. See Warren Bilkey, "An Attempted Integration of the Literature on Export Behavior Of Firms", *Journal Of International Business Studies* (Spring-Summer 1978), p. 40. Also see William Dymza, *Multinational Business Strategy*, (New York: McGraw Hill Book Company, 1972), p. 7. However, a systematic search to identify potential international markets — an active international marketing strategy — still remains an unexplored area of international marketing.

6. For a definition of "environmentally sensitive" components of marketing strategy and, by extension, of techniques and measurements, see Robert Bartels, "Are Domestic And International Marketing Dissimilar?", *Journal Of Marketing* **32** (July 1968), pp. 56-61.

7. See J. Scott Armstrong, "An Application Of Econometric Models To International Marketing", *Journal Of Marketing Research* **VII** (May 1970), p. 191.

8. *Ibid*, p. 195.

9. A multiplicative model has several nice properties. For example, each of the elements may in turn be composed of several other elements. This allows for substantial flexibility in the analysis and use of the model. A user may choose to estimate each of the relationships individually or all at the same time. In addition, a multiplicative model can be transformed into a linear model by a logarithmic transformation.

10. In s = g (p · a), p represents a psychological propensity, whereas a represents a relative financial ability. As the result s will represent a degree of overall propensity to purchase. At best, given appropriate stimulation among other conditions, this will become a purchase; however, it will remain a potential purchase.

It is important to note that the relation (1) is not a sufficient condition for a purchase. Furthermore, it is *product* and *situation* specific. That is, given the product and the purchasing situation, 100 per cent ability along with full 100 per cent desire is a necessary condition for a purchase. But, the reverse does not hold. That is, 100 per cent ability and 100 per cent preparedness do not necessarily result in a purchase, nor do they guarantee uniformity across individuals. Some buy as soon as possible, whereas others choose to forgo the purchase, despite their ability and preparedness. This, indeed, calls for a moderating stimulus to motivate prepared and able customers.[11]

In short, then, those *properly motivated* people who enjoy a relatively *high level of preparedness and ability* can be viewed as potential customers. Required level of stimuli to motivate prepared people varies among individuals. Also, because of these variations, the general form of the relation assumes a more complex functional form as in relation (2). Its true form, however, can be estimated statistically. That is, in general:

$$f(P \cdot A) \geq T \text{ (a constant)} \tag{2}$$

where P and A represent p and a at an aggregated level, respectively.

Relation (2) belongs to the family of hyperbolas. One simple form of the family is rectangular hyperbola.[12] An isoquant of this in A − P space is shown in Figure 1. This isoquant is passing through point B with co-ordinates of P = 100 per cent = 1, A = 100 per cent = 1 and hence it is representative of A · P = T = 1. In Figure 1, A · P = 1 divides the space into two regions, namely, region 1 to the right of the A · P, and region 2 to the left of A · P = 1. Region 1 is the locus of all those points whose combined level of ability, and preparedness, is *at least* 100 per cent (or A · P ≥ 1). Stated differently, these points represent those people who are *willing* to purchase the product and enjoy sufficient economic ability to do so. Of course, higher-level isoquants represent higher values for combined level of preparedness and ability A · P = 2, 3, . . .

---

11. The moderating variables could have been incorporated into the model explicitly. For the sake of simplicity and clarity, this has not been done. However, one should easily be able to incorporate the final effects of such moderation or stimulation into the later stages of decision analysis (for instance at the decision tree stage described in this chapter).

12. With a proper scaling transformation most hyperbolas can be mapped into a rectangular hyperbola.

Figure 1

Rectangular hyperbola $A \cdot P = 1$ in $A - P$ space. $A \cdot P = 1$ divides the $A - P$ space into two regions: Region 1 and Region 2. In Region 1, $A \cdot P \geq 1$; whereas, $A \cdot P \leq 1$ for Region 2.

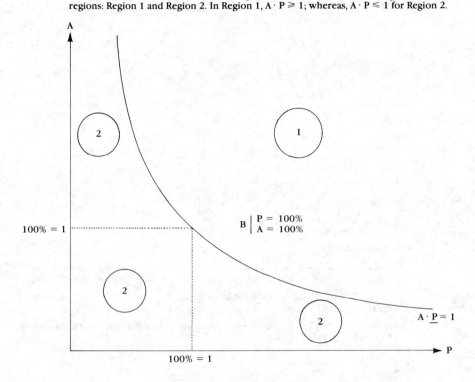

Simplifying Steps

Although the present state of numerical analysis allows for the application of highly sophisticated models, those computer-aided models are still inaccessible to the majority of small and medium-size firms. For this reason, this simplification is offered.

Simplification is based on the fact that the combination of $P = 100$ per cent and $A = 100$ per cent divides the $A - P$ space into four regions. All points in Region 1 possess a common property; namely, they all share $A \cdot P \geq 1$, since both A and P are greater than or equal to 1. This is shown in Figure 2.

Superimposition of Figures 1 and 2 on each other in Figure 3 shows that there is a substantial overlap between Region 1 of Figure

Figure 2

Combination of P = 100% and A = 100% divides the A − P space to four regions. All points in Region 1 have $A \cdot P \geqslant 1$.

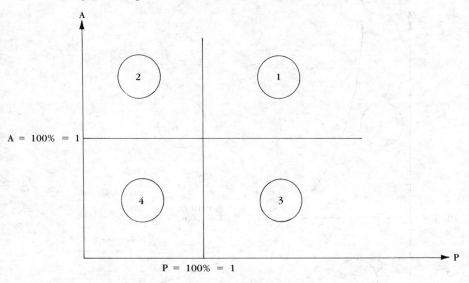

Figure 3

Region 1 of $A \cdot P = T \geqslant 1$ is the locus of points with $T \geqslant 1$ and has a substantial overlap $(A \geqslant 100\%) \; \& \; (P \geqslant 100\%)$.

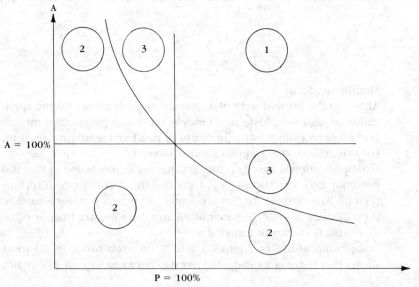

Legend: ① Overlapping area.
② Region 2 of $A \cdot P \leqslant 1$.
③ Discrepancy between $M \cdot P \geqslant 1$ and $(A \geqslant 100\%) \; \& \; (P \geqslant 100\%)$.

1 and Region 1 of Figure 2. This overlap can be taken advantage of to simplify the analysis.[13]

13. The precise amount of discrepancy (D) in the overlap areas for

$$P \cdot A = T \text{ at } P = p_0 \text{ and } A = a_0, \text{ is } \sqrt{T}(P_0 + a_0) - T\left(\ln \frac{P_0 \, a_0}{T} + 1\right)$$

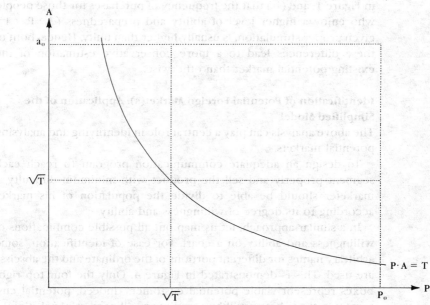

The calculations are shown below.

$$D = (a_0\sqrt{T} + P_0\sqrt{T}) - T - \int_{T/a_0}^{P_0} \frac{T}{P} \, dP$$

$$= \sqrt{T}(a_0 + P_0) - T - T \int_{T/a_0}^{P_0} \frac{dP}{P} = \sqrt{T}(a_0 + P_0) - T - T \left(\ln p\right) \Big|_{T/a_0}^{P_0}$$

$$= \sqrt{T}(P_0 + a_0) - T - T\left(\ln P_0 - \ln \frac{T}{a_0}\right) = \sqrt{T}(P_0 + a_0) - T\left(\ln \frac{P_0 a_0}{T} + 1\right)$$

for $a_0 = P_0 = 2$ and $T = 1$, $D = 3 - \ln 4$

In terms of percentage of the total area involved the discrepancy is:

$$\frac{D}{P_0 a_0} \text{ or } \frac{3 - \ln 4}{2 \cdot 2} = \% \, 15.3$$

However, the area is only a proxy and does not thoroughly reflect segment differences.

Due to substantial overlap, Region 1 of Figure 2, represented by
(A ≥ 100 per cent) and (P ≥ 100 per cent), will be substituted for
A · P ≥ 1, hereafter. However, one has to note two differences: (a)
that the area covered by (A ≥ 100 per cent) and (P ≥ 100 per cent)
— or Region 1 of Figure 2 — is smaller than the Region 1 of A · P ≥ 1
in Figure 1; and (b) that the frequency of purchases for those people
who enjoy a higher level of ability and preparedness (A · P ≥ 1),
given proper stimulation, is usually higher than unity. Hence, both of
these differences lead to a more conservative estimation of the
existing potential market than otherwise.

**Identification of Potential Foreign Market(s): Application of the
Simplified Model**
The above analysis can play a central role in identifying and analysing
potential markets.

To design an adequate communication program to reach each
segment properly and sell the product with minimum difficulty, a
marketer should be able to divide the population of his market
according to its degree of willingness and ability.

In a similar approach, let us map out all possible combinations of
willingness and ability on a chart. For ease of identification, some
arbitrary names for different portions of the ordinate and the abscissa
are used. This is demonstrated in Figure 4. Only the four top right
boxes represent viable potential customers. Indeed, potential customers in those boxes will buy readily or will need minimal stimulation to buy. For ease of reference, this market will be called an
already developed market (ADM).

People in the other segment of the market, represented in boxes 5
through 16, are not purchasing, nor are they ready to purchase
without some additional *facilitating* and *moderating* action.

Boxes 5 through 8 represent a segment of the market which
enjoys a sufficient level(s) of *psychological preparedness* or willingness but insufficient financial ability (PPS). People in boxes 9 through
12 are financially able to support their purchase(s) but are not
psychologically prepared (or willing) to do so (FPS). Finally, people
in boxes 13 through 16 are neither financially nor psychologically
prepared to justify their purchases (UPS).

Each market segment possesses different shortcomings and must
be approached differently. In formulating marketing strategy, different characteristics, including the shortcomings described above,
should be addressed accordingly. Hence, no market or market segment should be approached without a thorough cost and benefit
analysis.

Figure 4

Mapping of all possible combinations of ability and willingness.

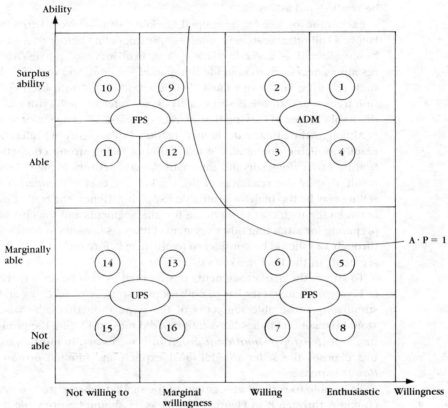

Legend: ADM = Already Developed Market.
PPS = Psychologically Prepared Segment.
FPS = Financially Prepared Segment.
UPS = Unprepared Segment.

Further Analysis of Each Market Segment

The notion of ability is a relative one. Obviously, considerably more people are able to buy a lower-priced item than a higher one. By the same token, but on a more aggregate level, more countries can afford less expensive projects than can afford more expensive projects.

Hence, identification of a market must depend not only on the nature of the product or the service, but also on the type of technological, marketing, and financial arrangements that both the buyer and the seller can provide. Among the sources of support for such arrangements are the government of the host country, banks, other international intermediaries, and members of the channels of distribution. However, such marketing and technological gaps must first be studied and assessed.

Except for the already developed markets (ADM — boxes 1 to 4 in Figure 4) all other segments require some upgrading before they can be considered as a viable market(s). A firm may not possess the resources necessary to upgrade the market segment, and the cost of such resource limitations must also be incorporated into the decision framework. In the ensuing analysis, we refer to such cost(s) as the implicit cost of serving that market or that market segment.

Although the already developed market (ADM, Figure 4) offers a readily available potential, the likelihood of facing strong competition by other domestic and international competitors is high. As a result, despite the readiness of the market, the cost of *competitive* selling may be too high for profitable exporting. Hence, the trade-offs between the high cost of servicing the ADM segments and the cost of preparing for attracting other segments (that is, segments in boxes 5 through 12) should be considered by the firm before including those segments in the final market(s).

To attract the market segments represented by FPS (boxes 9 to 12 in Figure 4), a marketer has to embark on a strategy of reaching and stimulating those able segments of the population that otherwise would remain unwilling and/or unprepared for considering the product. *An extensive promotional program* is necessary. In most cases, this exposes the seller to additional explicit and implicit *promotional* expenses.

To be able to serve that segment of the market represented by PPS (boxes 5 through 8 in Figure 4), a marketer should be prepared to provide for additional financing services. This segment is comprised of those people who are financially unable to support their purchases of the product, despite their sufficient willingness to do so. In other words, their future purchases are conditional on financial support either by the infrastructure in form of loans, credit, mortgage, outright grants, or some kind of financial provision *by the seller*. Hence, this segment will remain dormant, unless additional *financing support* is provided. This need for financing support by the PPS buyers exposes the seller to higher financing risks and/or charges. However, if extra financing arrangements are secured, the explicit and implicit costs of such arrangements must be incorporated into the decision.

Reaching the remaining totally unprepared market segment, UPS in Figure 4, requires the highest financing and the greatest promotional ingenuity of all the market segments. In most cases, this segment is not a viable market. In short, to attract people represented in the UPS segment in Figure 4 and to go beyond the first three major market segments (ADM, FPS, PPS), a marketer has to allow for additional promotional expenses *and* additional financing expenses. The development of this market should not be attempted unless a cost-benefit analysis of *all* revenues and expenses involved prove it to be a clearly viable and profitable one.

In summary, the segments have different characteristics and hence demand different approaches. A firm must consider its comparative advantage and experience and incorporate them into its market development decision. For example, firms with a clear comparative advantage in competitive selling either due to their product's superior attributes and/or highly efficient operations may find the ADM segment of the market more attractive than others. By the same token, firms with superior financing facilities and experience in providing such financing arrangements will find the PPS a more promising segment. Finally, firms with clear expertise and facility in marketing will find the FPS segment to be more advantageous.

Discussion and Analysis of the Model

Level of Analysis

On the international scale, the success of small and medium-size companies depend on the co-operative activities of several external organizations, above and beyond their own. The problem of identifying certain international markets (or market segments within those markets) on which to concentrate marketing efforts and to commit resources must be analysed on several different levels from a variety of viewpoints (objectives). A decision framework must lend itself to such varying levels of analysis.

The framework proposed earlier in this chapter is capable of satisfying the above demand. Three essential levels are discussed below.

1. *At Firm Market Segment Level.* A *firm* can consider a selected number of countries and analyse them in detail. The cost of identifying, reaching, and selling to different market segments must be balanced against the expected revenues of catering to the specific segments in each country. An overall comparison of expected net return, if returns are the primary criterion, should easily identify the best potential market(s) and market segments within it (them). Already developed segments (ADM) may offer more lucrative returns than others; but in terms of competition, quality of good, and market services, the ADM may be more de-

manding as well. The final decision on a market should not be made before a detailed study of costs and revenues is carried out. By the same token, other semi-developed segments (PPS and FPS) may not initially offer high promise, but extra effort makes them reasonably successful markets.

In considering PPS and FPS segments, *securing of additional resources (financial and/or human capital)* is the firm's first essential step; for without such resources these segments may not develop and therefore will expose the firm to unwanted consequences.

2. *At the Industry Country Level.* An *industry* can also use the analysis, but a slight modification is required. A country like Canada with many world-class industries should look at the whole world as a potential market. In the preliminary stages, ability and willingness of countries, with respect to the overall size and other specifications of the project, can be questioned. A chart similar to Figure 4 should be developed. It should not be difficult to see which countries along appropriate measure(s) of ability are capable of supporting, for example, an industrial project. After identification, the actual details of the project can be explored more explicitly with the governments of the countries being considered. At a later stage, based on those details, the members of the industry can decide which firm(s) is capable of developing the market and is willing to attack the project under the defined circumstances.

The ever-higher aspirations for growth and development in all developing areas and the desire of developing countries to attract high-technology industries can be cultivated. Countries like India, for example, do not lack industrial awareness. However, their financial inabilities are slowing down their development programs. In these cases (PPS in Figure 4), provisions for investment financing, investment guarantees, or insurance against losses may help close the deal(s) on new market development. On a global basis, these countries are analogous to those market segments which are lacking ability to finance their purchases (PPS). In short, once a financial inability of a market is identified, financing arrangements can serve as catalytic agents.

By the same token, some financially able countries (FPS in Figure 4) may still remain inactive because of present lack of need for the industry, incompatibility of the industry or the industrial project with the rest of economic infrastructure, or simply because of a country's ignorance of those industrial projects in the supplying country.

For countries for which awareness is a problem (FPS in Figure 4), a different strategy can be employed and later exploited. For example, extending an open invitation for a pre-planned tour of potentially promising Canadian industries to heads of state, leaders of the industry, industrial planners and financial elites, and financial advisors (investment and brokerage house personnel) is an elementary but essential step. This is similar to extra promotional efforts for attracting potential buyers in FPS segments (in Figure 4) in the previous case. Indeed some governmental agencies such as the Department of External Affairs (DEA) in cooperation with the Department of Industry, Trade, and Commerce (DITC) can accomplish a great deal towards developing these markets.

3. *At the Governmental Level.* Finally, on a more aggregated level of analysis, the government or governmental agencies can: (1) point out those countries which already are potential markets for certain products or industries; (2) identify the countries that can become target markets, given appropriate financial support; (3) point out the countries which have the need and financial ability but lack awareness; and (4) formulate a set of priorities as to which products, industries, and/or countries should be considered and which support services will assume higher priorities. A list of governmental priorities for supporting certain industries in certain countries, prepared by organizations like the Export Development Corporation (EDC), the Canadian International Development Agency (CIDA) and other support agencies, are extremely helpful and provide practical information for those industries concerned. The above approach is an effective way of planning (at an aggregate level) that minimizes the search time and information costs that medium and small-size companies can ill afford. It also provides a better and more competitive basis than the present system for all Canadian firms or industries that want to compete internationally. Industries and firms of other countries are enjoying similar arrangements already.

Since the support-granting agencies need some time to evaluate the request before they respond, the above suggestion will provide for a more efficient way of supporting a firm or firms in an industry. For the time being, delays are minimized and the possibility of negative response is substantially reduced.

Implication for Canadian Firms
Traditional ways of market identification can, at best, identify the market segment represented by ADM in Figure 4, because they are,

for the most part, based directly or indirectly on historical data. The market segments in ADM, as discussed earlier, are already developed and, due to relatively more intense competition, *offer lower chances of success*.

However, a program of attack on other segments, that offers higher chances of success, requires further strategic work and/or facilities. These requirements fall into two categories:

1. *For the Lower Right Section: Psychologically Prepared Segment (PPS)*. These segments, as discussed before, need additional financing due either to (relative) shortages of funds or the relatively high price tag of the product or size of the project. For those instances in which a Canadian company cannot support such heavy financing burdens, other sources of support for financing and pre-financing should be sought. Federal institutions like DITC, EDC, CIDA, and their provincial and international counterparts (for example, the World Bank) can be of considerable help. For relatively expensive items or large-size projects, a strategy of product adaptations towards less sophisticated, less encompassing, smaller portions or slightly lower quality, coupled with a lower price tag, must also be considered. Of course these can be coupled with the extra financing arrangement and carried out simultaneously, if necessary.

2. *For the Upper Left Section: Financially Prepared Segment (FPS)*. Awareness-raising promotional programs to increase the willingness of this market segment are necessary. These will require extensive information, knowledge, and expertise regarding the market (or market segments) in addition to the extra cost burden of mounting such programs. Two steps are involved: (1) proper marketing research must identify the characteristics of these segments in terms of their *life style habits, consumption behavior,* and *segment profiles*; and (2) a corresponding *communication plan* must be designed and implemented. In some cases, provisions for developing some marketing infrastructure — proper media, channels of communication, and channels of distribution — are also required. It is important to note that knowledge and human capital are the *main* ingredients here as opposed to financial capital which was the main ingredient in the previous case. For small and medium-size firms, the banding together of *complementary* companies for the pooling of their various resources or expertise is certainly recommended. However, another viable alternative on the public side is for a national trading

company(ies)[14] and/or official commercial umbrellas (for instance, Canadian Commercial Corporation)[15] to bring together all the necessary requirements or expertise. Also, export consortia[16] and similar organizations can enhance the firm's chances of final success.

Application of the Framework to a Firm — A Sample Decision Tree

In this section of the chapter, a sample application of the framework will outline the essential elements of a decision tree for carrying out the actual decision at the firm's level. It is assumed that two decisions have already been made; namely, (1) that the firm has decided to explore the international markets; and (2) that a potentially promising market has been identified. The following analysis will examine the profit potentials of different segments in that market.

Based on the conceptual model, the five broad alternatives are:

1. *Alternative 1:* Penetrating the existing and readily developed market(s). This strategy will deal with market segments 1, 2, 3, and 4 in Figure 4 (ADM).
2. *Alternative 2:* Developing the dormant section of the market in which the potential future users are capable of supporting their purchases but their level of information, awareness, and, hence, willingness is not adequate. This will cover segments 9, 10, 11, and 12 in Figure 4 (FPS).
3. *Alternative 3:* Developing that section of the market which is fully aware of the product but whose financial inability does not allow it to support its purchase. This will cover the lower right segments (PPS in Figure 4).
4. *Alternative 4:* Developing the remaining sections of Figure 4 not included in the above alternatives (UPS).
5. *Alternative 5:* Developing any combination of the above alternatives, if possible.

The decision criteria for different branches of a decision tree corresponding to the above alternatives are shown in Figure 5.

For a more detailed analysis of each alternative, see Appendix 1.

14. See the chapter by Charles McMillan, "The Pros and Cons of a National Export Trading House" in this book.
15. See the chapter, "Strengthening Canada Abroad: Summary And Recommendations" by the Export Promotion Review Committee.
16. See the chapter by K. C. Dhawan and L. Kryzanowski, "Characteristics and Experiences Of Canadian-Based Export Consortia" in this book.

Figure 5

An Application of the Framework: A Sample Decision Tree

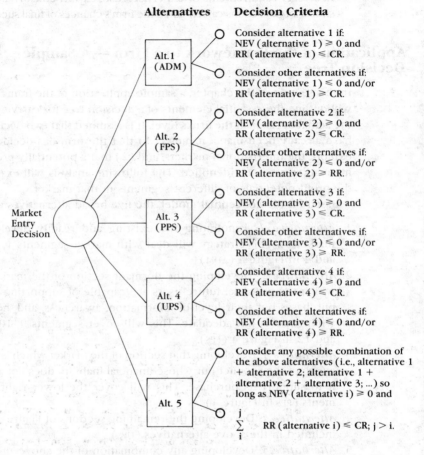

Alternatives   Decision Criteria

Alt. 1 (ADM)

Consider alternative 1 if:
NEV (alternative 1) $\geq$ 0 and
RR (alternative 1) $\leq$ CR.

Consider other alternatives if:
NEV (alternative 1) $\leq$ 0 and/or
RR (alternative 1) $\geq$ CR.

Alt. 2 (FPS)

Consider alternative 2 if:
NEV (alternative 2) $\geq$ 0 and
RR (alternative 2) $\leq$ CR.

Consider other alternatives if:
NEV (alternative 2) $\leq$ 0 and/or
RR (alternative 2) $\geq$ RR.

Alt. 3 (PPS)

Consider alternative 3 if:
NEV (alternative 3) $\geq$ 0 and
RR (alternative 3) $\leq$ CR.

Consider other alternatives if:
NEV (alternative 3) $\leq$ 0 and/or
RR (alternative 3) $\geq$ RR.

Alt. 4 (UPS)

Consider alternative 4 if:
NEV (alternative 4) $\geq$ 0 and
RR (alternative 4) $\leq$ CR.

Consider other alternatives if:
NEV (alternative 4) $\leq$ 0 and/or
RR (alternative 4) $\geq$ RR.

Alt. 5

Market Entry Decision

Consider any possible combination of the above alternatives (i.e., alternative 1 + alternative 2; alternative 1 + alternative 2 + alternative 3; ...) so long as NEV (alternative i) $\geq$ 0 and

$$\sum_{i}^{j} RR \text{ (alternative i)} \leq CR; \ j > i.$$

Notations: Alt = Alternative.
NEV = Net Expected Value = Expected Revenue − Expected Cost.
NEV (Alternative i) = Net Expected Value of Alternative i.
RR (alternative i) = Required Resource for alternative i; 1, 2, 3, 4, and 5.
CR = Company Resources.

Given limited resources and the opportunity cost of those resources, a firm must evaluate each of the above alternatives individually. Initially, any alternative with a *negative net expected value* should be rejected. However, those alternatives that meet the firm's expected rate of return and limited resources should be seriously considered. A ranking of the alternatives on the basis of their rate of return and resource requirements can help simplify the final decision.

Conclusion and Summary

Most small and medium-size companies are at a relative disadvantage when it comes to competing on a global basis and have to make prudent decisions to manage their limited resources effectively. This includes identifying markets and selecting market segments. Limited resources may force small and medium-size companies to turn to market identification from a distance. Identification of markets from a distance can be a difficult task and the results may be unreliable unless extreme care is exercised.

Identification of a market and selection of a viable market segment(s) within that market are two of the necessary steps in the process of developing international export markets. Proper identification is practically impossible without reasonable examination of the potential market segment(s); and, selection of a viable segment(s) is heavily dependent upon proper identification. In short the problem is a difficult one and the constrained resources of small and medium-size companies make it doubly difficult.

Identification and assessment of export target markets can be improved by employing a framework such as the one proposed in this chapter. However, the operational analogue of the framework — the decision tree analysis requires certain information. The decision tree analysis identifies the informational requirements and allows the firms to fully evaluate the pertinent costs and benefits of any of the strategies involved in foreign market development before they commit themselves.

In some cases, the expertise, support, and resources of several institutions external to the firm (CIDA, EDC, DITC and banks) are essential for the successful development of some of the potential markets (or market segments). A firm should not commit any resources unless such external support is already secured. Furthermore, similar analysis should be carried out by or for such external institutions. These analyses, at different levels, can reduce time delays and uncertainties that the small and medium-size Canadian firms are ill prepared to afford. As a result the export potentials of small and medium-size Canadian firms will be enhanced and hence Canadian exports will be stimulated.

Appendix I

Four decision trees, each corresponding to one of the main alternatives outlined in this chapter are shown in Figures 6, 7, 8, and 9. The results of certain elementary calculations (for instance, forecasting activities) must be known, however, before a reasonably representative and accurate decision tree can be drawn. Certain definitions are also necessary. They are:

1. *Span of Planning or Operation:* Span of planning is the length of time that a firm needs to implement its plans before the end results can be evaluated. The environmental stability of a country, the product's stage of life cycle, and the general business or marketing strategy of the firm are among the factors that can influence the length of the time span. For this example a five-year period is arbitrarily chosen.

2. *Situational Analysis:* This refers to a fair understanding of the market's *present condition* and its *future movements* over the span of planning. Forecasting of future events, especially for unfamiliar foreign markets, is not an easy task and its reliability is usually questionable. However, it is an integral part of any systematic future-oriented analysis. For ease of analysis, the five-year planning span is arbitrarily divided into two time periods — the first two years and the next three years. For each time period, an optimistic, realistic, and pessimistic forecast of total revenue with the corresponding probability of occurrence are considered. They are referred to as high, medium, and low, and denoted by H, M, and L, respectively.

3. *Feasibility Study:* This refers to the study of the standard elements of a regular pre-entry marketing feasibility study. That is, prior to entry, a firm needs to know its overall *operating, servicing,* and *production* costs for different levels of production. They are denoted by $C(O)$, $C(S,P,F)$ and $C(Q)$, respectively. Where: (1) $C(O)$, the operating cost in functional form, is generally assumed to depend on scale of operation (O); (2) $C(S,F,P)$ is the overall cost of servicing, which in turn, is comprised of the cost of selling (S), *additional* promotional expenditures (P), and *additional* financing costs (F); and (3) $C(Q)$ is the production costs which are normally a function of the production volume.

4. *Competitive Pricing:* This refers to the study of a *set* of the

Figure 6

Decision Tree for Alternative 1, Covering Market Segments 1, 2, 3, and 4 (ADM)

Values of Index i

		First Two Years		
		High	Medium	Low
Second	High	1	4	7
Three	Medium	2	5	8
Years	Low	3	6	9

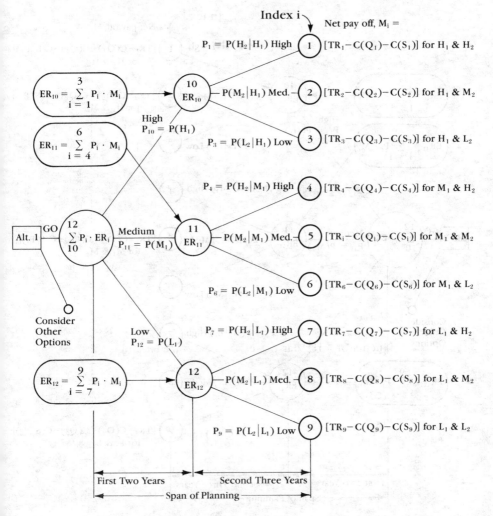

Index i

Net pay off, $M_i =$

$P_1 = P(H_2|H_1)$ High ⓵ $[TR_1 - C(Q_1) - C(S_1)]$ for H_1 & H_2

$ER_{10} = \sum_{i=1}^{3} P_i \cdot M_i$

$ER_{11} = \sum_{i=4}^{6} P_i \cdot M_i$

$\begin{array}{c} 10 \\ ER_{10} \end{array}$ — $P(M_2|H_1)$ Med. ⓶ $[TR_2 - C(Q_2) - C(S_2)]$ for H_1 & M_2

High $P_{10} = P(H_1)$

$P_3 = P(L_2|H_1)$ Low ⓷ $[TR_3 - C(Q_3) - C(S_3)]$ for H_1 & L_2

$P_4 = P(H_2|M_1)$ High ⓸ $[TR_4 - C(Q_4) - C(S_4)]$ for M_1 & H_2

Alt. 1 — GO — $\begin{array}{c} 12 \\ \sum_{10} P_i \cdot ER_i \end{array}$ Medium $P_{11} = P(M_1)$ $\begin{array}{c} 11 \\ ER_{11} \end{array}$ — $P(M_2|M_1)$ Med. ⓹ $[TR_1 - C(Q_1) - C(S_1)]$ for M_1 & M_2

$P_6 = P(L_2|M_1)$ Low ⓺ $[TR_6 - C(Q_6) - C(S_6)]$ for M_1 & L_2

Consider Other Options

Low $P_{12} = P(L_1)$

$P_7 = P(H_2|L_1)$ High ⓻ $[TR_7 - C(Q_7) - C(S_7)]$ for L_1 & H_2

$ER_{12} = \sum_{i=7}^{9} P_i \cdot M_i$

$\begin{array}{c} 12 \\ ER_{12} \end{array}$ — $P(M_2|L_1)$ Med. ⓼ $[TR_8 - C(Q_8) - C(S_8)]$ for L_1 & M_2

$P_9 = P(L_2|L_1)$ Low ⓽ $[TR_9 - C(Q_9) - C(S_9)]$ for L_1 & L_2

First Two Years   Second Three Years

Span of Planning

Note: 1 The cost of servicing, $C(S_i)$ is the normal cost of selling and does *not* include any additional charges for extra promotion or financing.

Figure 7

A Decision Tree for Alternative 2, Covering Market Segments 9, 10, 11, and 12 (FPS)

Values of Index i

First Two Years

		High	Medium	Low
Second	High	1	4	7
Three	Medium	2	5	8
Years	Low	3	6	9

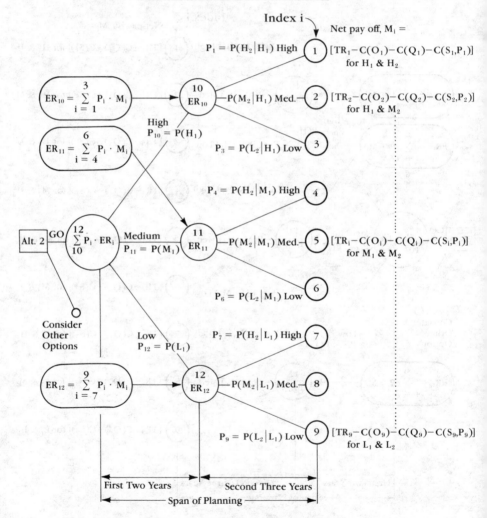

Index i

Net pay off, $M_i =$

$P_1 = P(H_2|H_1)$ High $\quad$ (1) $\quad [TR_1 - C(O_1) - C(Q_1) - C(S_1,P_1)]$ for H_1 & H_2

$ER_{10} = \sum_{i=1}^{3} P_i \cdot M_i \longrightarrow$ 10 ER_{10} $-P(M_2|H_1)$ Med.$-$ (2) $\quad [TR_2 - C(O_2) - C(Q_2) - C(S_2,P_2)]$ for H_1 & M_2

High $P_{10} = P(H_1)$

$ER_{11} = \sum_{i=4}^{6} P_i \cdot M_i$ $\qquad P_3 = P(L_2|H_1)$ Low (3)

$P_4 = P(H_2|M_1)$ High (4)

Alt. 2 | GO $\sum_{10}^{12} P_i \cdot ER_i$ $\quad$ Medium $P_{11} = P(M_1)$ $\quad$ 11 ER_{11} $-P(M_2|M_1)$ Med.$-$ (5) $\quad [TR_i - C(O_i) - C(Q_i) - C(S_i,P_i)]$ for M_1 & M_2

$P_6 = P(L_2|M_1)$ Low (6)

Consider Other Options

Low $P_{12} = P(L_1)$ $\quad P_7 = P(H_2|L_1)$ High (7)

$ER_{12} = \sum_{i=7}^{9} P_i \cdot M_i$ $\quad$ 12 ER_{12} $-P(M_2|L_1)$ Med.$-$ (8)

$P_9 = P(L_2|L_1)$ Low (9) $\quad [TR_9 - C(O_9) - C(Q_9) - C(S_9,P_9)]$ for L_1 & L_2

First Two Years $\qquad$ Second Three Years

Span of Planning

Note: 1 The cost of servicing, $C(S_i, P_i)$, allows for additional promotional costs required for attracting marget segments 9, 1
11, and 12, as well as the normal cost of selling.
2 Corresponding values of index i are given in the table above.

Figure 8

A Decision Tree for Alternative 3, Covering Market Segments 5, 6, 7, and 8 (PPS)

Values of Index i

		First Two Years		
		High	Medium	Low
Second	High	1	4	7
Three	Medium	2	5	8
Years	Low	3	6	9

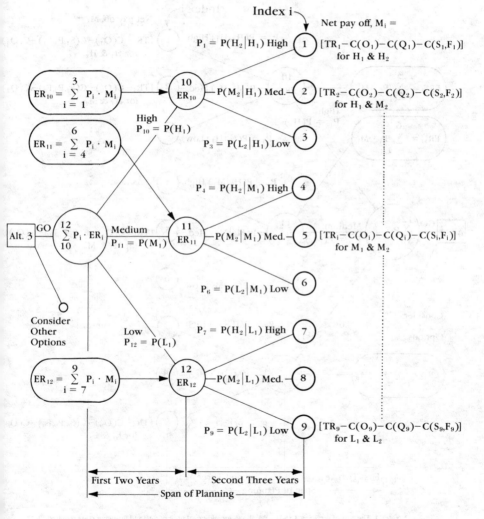

Note: 1 The cost of servicing, $C(S_i,F_i)$, allows for additional financing costs required for attracting market segments 5, 6, 7, and 8, as well as the normal cost of selling.

2 Corresponding values of index i are given in the table above.

Figure 9

A Decision Tree for Alternative 4, Covering Market Segments 13, 14, 15, and 16 (UPS)

Values of Index i

First Two Years

		High	Medium	Low
Second	High	1	4	7
Three	Medium	2	5	8
Years	Low	3	6	9

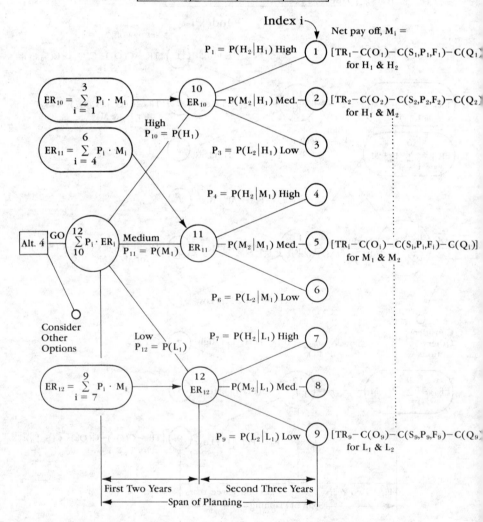

Note: 1 The cost of servicing, $C(S_i, P_i, F_i)$, allows for additional promotional and financing costs required for attracting market segments 13, 14, 15, and 16, as well as the normal cost of selling.
2 Corresponding values of index i are given in the table above.

competitive prices to clear the projected sales, given all operating and selling costs. This should result in a *set* of revenue functions. Once again, for ease of analysis, these revenue functions are simplified and denoted by TR. In reality, however, prices reflect many factors and in turn influence revenues in a very dramatic way. For the sake of clarity and ease, these complications are not introduced.

III
The Challenge of Overseas Markets

B
Marketing Strategies by Sectors

12
Can Canadian Manufacturing Compete?

Edward A. Carmichael

Mr. Carmichael is an economist with the Applied Economic Research and Information Centre at The Conference Board of Canada. His publications at the Conference Board include *The Canadian Manufacturing Sector: Performance in the 1970s*, *Reassessing Canada's Potential Economic Growth*, and *Foreign Exchange Risk Management in Canadian Companies*.

The material in this chapter appeared originally in *The Canadian Business Review*, Summer, 1978. Reprinted by permission.

Basic questions of resource allocation and efficiency — sometimes referred to as structural issues — often are most hotly debated during periods of economic recession. This is simply because the most vulnerable sectors of the economy usually are the first to be exposed by low levels of economic activity. This situation tends to complicate and confuse the debate since it is very often quite difficult to separate the impact of legitimate structural problems from the cyclical impact of weak aggregate demand. During the 1970s the discussion of structural problems has been further obscured by the persistence of rapid rates of inflation in periods of expansion and recession alike.

Much of the recent discussion of structural problems has focussed on two important related issues: the performance of the Canadian manufacturing sector and Canada's competitive position in international trade. Interest in these issues has been further stimulated by the prospect of a new round of tariff cutting as a result of the Multilateral Trade Negotiations among the members of GATT, the international body which sets and enforces the rules of world trade. Such an agreement promises to have a significant impact both on the international location of manufacturing industry and on trade flows in manufactured goods.

The purpose of this chapter is to review the international trade performance of Canadian manufacturing industries during the 1970s. The chapter provides a summary of a more detailed study undertaken at The Conference Board in Canada.[1] In the first section of the chapter some measures of international competitiveness and trade performance are reviewed for the manufacturing sector as a whole. This is followed by an examination of the trade performance of individual manufacturing industries which attempts to provide a clearer view of Canada's areas of strength and weakness within manufacturing.

Several factors influence the behavior of manufactured goods trade. These factors can be separated into influences based on demand

1. Edward A. Carmichael, *Canada's Manufacturing Sector: Performance in the 1970s*, Canadian Study No. 51 (Ottawa: The Conference Board in Canada, 1978).

conditions and influences based on supply conditions. The supply side influences are often discussed under the general heading of competitiveness. In the short run, several interdependent factors influence the competitiveness of Canadian products. These include movements in factor costs and factor productivities relative to other countries, movements in exchange rates, and the stablization policies employed by the government. In the long run, the international evolution of comparative advantage and commercial policies are important determinants of competitiveness.

Many Tests Needed

The measurement of the international competitiveness of a country's products is a complex task. While it is relatively easy to define and measure competitiveness when referring to a single internationally traded good, it is extremely difficult to measure the competitiveness of an aggregation of non-homogeneous manufactured goods. The measures which we examine include measures of price competitiveness, measures of cost competitiveness, and measures of international market shares. Each of these measures has limitations and provides only a partial picture of Canada's international competitive position. By considering all of these measures and reconciling their differences, a better understanding of the problem can be obtained.

Two measures of the evolution of Canadian relative export prices of manufactured goods are shown in the first two columns of Table 1. The relative price indices shown are based on data published by the United Nations and are the ratios of currently weighted national indices of prices of manufactured exports in U.S. dollars. Each ratio is based on a 1970 value of 100. The first column shows the price of Canadian manufactured exports relative to those of a group of fifteen major industrial countries while the second column shows the price of Canadian manufactured exports relative to those of the United States, Canada's most important trading partner.

The price competitiveness of Canadian manufactured exports appears to have improved during the 1970s relative to both the United States and the group of fifteen industrial countries. From 1970 to 1977 the relative price index of Canadian manufactured exports declined 13 per cent compared to the United States and 21 per cent compared to the group of industrial countries. It is possible that part of the decline of the relative price of Canadian exports was due to a shift in demand away from Canadian products or a shift in the composition of Canadian manufactured exports. However, the impact of the declining value of the Canadian dollar relative to the

Table 1

Indicators of Canada's Competitive Position, 1960-1977

Year or Quarter		PX^C/PX^{UN}	PX^C/PX^{US}	ULC^C/ULC^{US}
1960		1.036	1.074	NA
1965		.933	.988	NA
1970		1.000	1.000	1.00
1971		.981	1.010	1.01
1972		.947	1.029	1.05
1973		.842	.991	1.06
1974		.827	.978	1.16
1975		.780	.893	1.15
1976		.852	.918	1.26
1976	I	.865	.930	1.24
	II	.883	.940	1.27
	III	.848	.924	1.29
	IV	.801	.874	1.23
1977	I	.826	.920	1.17
	II	.807	.903	1.16
	III	.776	.862	1.16
	IV	.734	.826	1.12

Note: PXi is the currently weighted unit value index for manufactured goods of country i. ULC^1 is the currently weighted index of unit labor cost in manufacturing in country i. The superscripts denote the country or group of countries as follows: C — Canada; UN — fifteen industrialized countries including Canada, the U.S., Japan and the members of the EEC and EFTA; US — United States.

Source: United Nations; Bank of Canada; and The Conference Board in Canada.

Table 2

Market Shares of Canadian Manufactured Exports

	Canada's Share of Industrial World's Manufactured Exports	Canada's Share of Industrial World's Manufactured Exports to the United States
1960	4.5%	NA
1970	6.0	32.8%
1971	5.8	30.1
1972	5.7	30.7
1973	5.3	30.6
1974	4.7	29.2
1975	4.5	31.8
1976	4.7	32.8

Source: U.S. Department of Commerce; United Nations; and The Conference Board in Canada.

currencies of most of Canada's trading partners since late 1976 has had a visible effect in improving the price competitiveness of Canadian exports.

The evolution of the cost competitiveness of Canadian manufacturing during the 1970s has been quite different at least in terms of labor cost. As shown in the third column of Table 2, relative unit labor cost in Canadian manufacturing increased by 26 per cent compared to unit labor cost in U.S. manufacturing between 1970 and 1976. During 1977, unit labor cost rose at approximately the same rate in Canada and the United States when measured in the two domestic currencies. However, the Canadian dollar depreciated by approximately 8 per cent between 1976 and 1977, so that Canadian unit labor cost measured in U.S. dollars also dropped by approximately 8 per cent. By the end of 1977 relative Canadian unit labor cost had returned to the levels attained in 1974 and 1975 but still was 12 per cent higher than in 1970.

A comparison of the behavior of relative manufactured export prices and relative unit labor cost in manufacturing in Canada and the United States shows that — in spite of the substantial rise in unit labor cost in Canada compared to the United States between 1970 and 1976 — the relative price of Canadian manufactured exports declined substantially over the same period. A complete explanation of this experience would require an analysis of cost and price dynamics in the Canadian economy during the 1970s. However, a brief sketch of Canada's inflation experience can provide some insights.

A speech by G. E. Freeman, deputy governor of the Bank of Canada, suggests that the double-digit rates of inflation which existed in 1974 and 1975 were the result of the combined impact of the international price boom for agricultural and industrial commodities in 1972 and 1973 and the rapid expansion of the money supply which was aimed at avoiding upward pressure on nominal interest rates or on the external value of the Canadian dollar.[2] These factors combined to produce in Canada "a wage explosion of alarming proportions whereas in the United States, its major trading partner, price inflation was already abating rapidly and wage trends continued to be remarkably stable".[3]

External Pricing

The result of this wage explosion in Canada was a marked deterioration in relative unit labor cost in Canada. However, the prices of

---

2. Remarks by G. E. Freeman, deputy governor of the Bank of Canada, to the Canadian Association for Business Economics, Ottawa, May 11, 1978. Published in the *Bank of Canada Review* (May 1978).
3. *Ibid.*, p. 4.

many of Canada's exports were determined in international markets where rates of price inflation were lower than the Canadian rate of wage inflation. A deterioration of the profitability of Canadian exporting firms inevitably followed. The eventual decline in the value of the Canadian dollar in 1976 and 1977 restored much of the cost competitiveness and profitability of Canadian exporters.

Data on international market shares for manufactured exports, shown in Table 2, indicate that Canada's share in the manufactured exports of fourteen countries dropped by more than 20 per cent from 1970 to 1976. However, the Canadian share of the industrial countries' manufactured exports to the United States increased between 1971 and 1976, returning to the record level attained in 1970. Even though the U.S. market share of Canadian exports was maintained during the 1970s, the world market share declined. This occurred because U.S. demand for manufactured exports in nominal terms grew only about half as rapidly as export demand in the rest of the world. Since Canadian manufactured exports are so heavily concentrated in the United States, which exhibited slow growth of demand, a decline in the world market share of Canadian manufactured exports also occurred. The stable or improving share of Canadian manufactured exports in the United States is consistent with the earlier finding that the deterioration of the cost competitiveness of Canadian manufacturing was not reflected in a similar deterioration in the price competitiveness of Canadian manufactured exports.

The most widely used measure of trade performance of the goods-producing sector of the economy is the merchandise trade balance. Canada recorded an overall merchandise trade deficit from 1954 to 1960 and a surplus over the period 1961 to 1974. However, as shown in Chart 1, the merchandise balance began to deteriorate in 1971, and in 1975 it recorded a deficit of $1.5 billion, which represented a deterioration of $2.2 billion from 1974.[4] This deficit was short-lived as surpluses of $0.7 billion and $2.1 billion were recorded in 1976 and 1977. Although the merchandise deficit of 1975 was a concern, the continuing problem, which has given rise to the view that Canada's competitiveness in world trade has deteriorated, is the performance of the trade balance on finished manufactured goods. The trade deficit for finished goods increased from $3 billion in 1970 to $11.1 billion in 1977.

Chart 1 shows the performance of the trade balance of the four

---

4. All trade data in this study are reported on the basis of customs totals as reported by Statistics Canada. Certain adjustments must be made to meet the concepts and definitions used in the system of National Accounts.

Chart 1

Nominal Trade Surplus

(billions of current dollars)

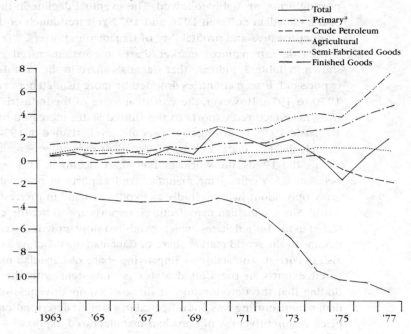

——— Total
–·–·– Primary[a]
– – – – Crude Petroleum
·········· Agricultural
–··–··– Semi-Fabricated Goods
——— Finished Goods

(a) Excluding crude petroleum.
Source: Statistics Canada: The Conference Board in Canada.

major commodity groups which make up total trade.[5] Between 1971 and 1974, there were mild improvements in the trade balances on agricultural, other primary, and semi-fabricated goods. However, these improvements were more than offset by an accelerating deterioration of the trade balance on finished goods. In 1975, the coincidence of a slight deterioration in the semi-fabricated goods trade balance, a continued deterioration on the finished goods balance and a government decision to phase out exports of oil to the United States contributed to the overall merchandise trade deficit mentioned above. During 1976 and 1977, the merchandise trade balance rebounded sharply entirely on the strength of improvements in the balances of

5. Two minor categories — live animals and special transactions — are not shown separately but are included in total trade. In addition, the crude materials group is separated into crude oil and other primary goods in Chart 1.

non-agricultural primary products and semi-fabricated goods. The trade balances on crude petroleum and finished goods continued to deteriorate over this period.

Although the current dollar merchandise trade balance is an important measure of trade performance from the point of view of balance of payments considerations, it is not well-suited to measuring trends in the international competitiveness of Canadian products. Changes in the terms of trade, the expansion of trade volume, and the influence of domestic and foreign business cycles all influence the nominal balance. In order to remove the first two influences on the trade balance, the real normalized trade balance (RNTB) for each of the major categories of traded goods has been calculated. This is done by using constant dollar import and export data to calculate the real trade balance, thereby removing the influence of changes in the terms of trade, and then normalizing the real trade balance by dividing by the total volume of trade to remove the influence of the expansion of trade volume. The results are shown in Chart 2.

Chart 2

Real Normalized Trade Balance

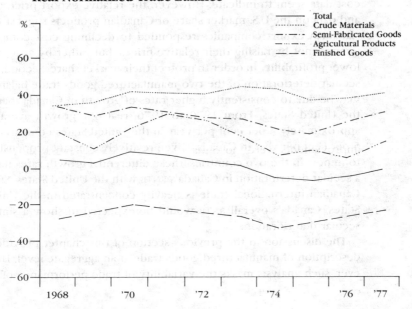

Source: The Conference Board in Canada.

Separate Causes

A comparison of Chart 2 with Chart 1 indicates that much of the deterioration in the nominal trade balance for finished manufactured goods was due to unfavorable changes in the terms of trade and expansion of total trade volume of this category. Similarly, much of the improvement in the nominal trade balance for semi-fabricated manufactured goods was due to favorable changes in the terms of trade and expansion of trade.

Much of the remaining movement of the RNTB for semi-fabricated and finished manufactured goods is explained by the influence of Canadian and U.S. business cycles. A detailed analysis of the nominal trade balances for these two categories of manufactured goods indicated that most of the change which has occurred since 1971 has been due to factors other than changes in competitiveness — namely changes in the terms of trade, trade expansion, and cyclical influences.[6] While these factors appear to explain most of the improvement in the semi-fabricated products nominal trade balance and most of the deterioration in the finished products balance, there does appear to have been some residual secular deterioration in both of these trade balances in the 1970s. Two factors could account for this deterioration. First, some Canadian manufactured products may have become less competitive during the decade as the relative unit labor cost data seem to indicate. However, the relative export price data and data on the U.S. market share of Canadian products suggest that Canadian export companies responded to declining cost competitiveness not by raising their relative prices, but rather by accepting lower profitability in order to protect their market share. Second, the secular deterioration of the two manufactured goods trade balances may be due to consistently higher rates of growth in Canada than in the United States. From 1970 to 1976, real GNP growth averaged approximately 3 per cent per year in the United States compared to 5 per cent per year in Canada. Given relatively constant propensities to import in the two countries, these differential growth rates imply a secular deterioration in Canada's RNTB with the United States. Since Canadian international trade is heavily concentrated in the United States, Canada's overall RNTB would be expected to show a similar secular deterioration.

The discussion in the previous section of this chapter provides a description of manufactured goods trade at an aggregate level. However, such analysis masks the variability of trade performance of the

---

6. Carmichael, *Canada's Manufacturing Sector.*

specific commodities (and the industries that produce them) which make up manufactured goods trade. As a measure of the trade performance of individual manufacturing industries, the change in the normalized trade balance (NTB) between 1971 and 1976 was employed. It would have been preferable to use the deflated NTB but this was not possible since import and export price deflators are not available on an industry basis. Therefore, it should be kept in mind that changes in the terms of trade may be partly responsible for changes in the NTB of a given industry.

In Table 3, Canadian manufacturing industries are divided into a group which has exhibited relatively strong trade performance in the left-hand column and a group which has recorded relatively weak trade performance in the right-hand column. To qualify as a strong performer, the industry had to exhibit a normalized trade balance which was e ,er in surplus or approximately in balance in 1971. Within this group are found Canada's traditionally export-oriented industries, such as pulp and paper, sawmills, metal mines, and the primary metals industry. Within the group of traditionally weak trade performers — that is, those which recorded a sizable normalized deficit in 1971 — are those industries which produce goods that Canada traditionally has imported. Included in this group are machinery, chemical, electrical products, and textile industries.

Within each of these two groups, industries have been further subdivided into those which showed improvement in their trade performance over the 1971-1976 period, those which suffered a deterioration in trade performance, and those which recorded no significant change. A significant improvement in trade performance was arbitrarily assumed to be represented by an increase of four percentage points or more in the industry's NTB between 1971 and 1976. Similarly, a deterioration was deemed to have occurred if the NTB declined by four percentage points or more over the period. Two categories which have not yet been mentioned are new strengths and new weaknesses. New strengths refer to industries which have moved from a trade deficit in 1971 to a surplus in 1976, and for which the improvement in the normalized trade balance was in excess of twenty percentage points. A new weakness refers to the opposite situation of an industry's trade balance moving from surplus to deficit, and a deterioration in the NTB of more than twenty percentage points.

Some Improvements

The results in Table 3 indicate that, while there are a substantial

Table 3

Trade Performance of Canadian Industries

Strong (Surplus) Industries

	Normalized Trade Balance[a] 1971	1976	Change from 1971 to 1976
Improving			
Other Transportation Equipment[b]	5.4%	10.8%	5.4%
Metal Mines	66.5	71.0	4.5
Primary Metals	44.6	49.1	4.5
Deteriorating			
Petroleum and Gas Wells	31.0	10.0	−21.0
Non-Metal Mines	− 1.6	−13.9	−12.3
Sawmills	88.8	80.4	− 8.4
Motor Vehicles and Parts	− 0.6	− 7.4	− 6.8
Leaf Tobacco	94.2	87.5	− 6.7
Agriculture	60.4	53.9	− 6.5
Pulp and Paper	91.4	86.2	− 5.2
Distilleries	56.2	51.0	− 5.2
New Strengths			
Petroleum and Coal Products	−13.2	37.9	51.1
Coal Mines	−27.0	1.3	28.3
No Change			
Slaughtering and Meat Processing	11.3	8.6	− 2.7
Asbestos Mines	98.9	98.8	− 0.1

Table 3 (continued)

Weak (Deficit) Industries

| | Normalized Trade Balance | | Change from |
	1971	1976	1971 to 1976
Improving			
Other Furniture[c]	−77.2%	−45.6%	31.6%
Rubber Products	−64.8	−34.2	30.6
Breweries and Wineries	−76.6	−53.0	23.8
Printing and Publishing	−75.9	−62.1	13.8
Selected Scientific Instruments	−46.1	−36.3	9.8
Metal Fabricating	−43.6	−38.0	5.6
Other Wood Industries[d]	−19.5	−14.4	5.1
Deteriorating			
Household Furniture	−31.0	−78.2	−47.2
Miscellaneous Manufacturing	−38.7	−61.5	−22.8
Knitting Mills	−82.0	−94.2	−12.2
Electrical Products	−41.5	−53.1	−11.6
Tobacco Products	−42.5	−54.1	−11.6
Pharmaceuticals and Medicines	−53.2	−59.7	− 6.5
Allied Paper Products	−61.1	−67.5	− 6.4
Textile Products	−69.7	−75.4	− 5.7
Leather Products	−76.9	−82.4	− 5.5
New Weaknesses			
Clothing Industry	0.0	−59.1	−59.1
Forestry	19.8	−14.6	−34.3
Veneer and Plywood Mills	21.3	− 9.9	−31.2
Other Food and Beverages[e]	11.9	−10.7	−22.6
No Change			
Other Chemical Industries[f]	−14.8	−12.8	2.0
Paint and Varnish Industry	−84.4	−84.0	0.4
Machinery Industry	−51.4	−51.1	0.3

(a) The normalized trade balance is defined as the trade balance divided by total trade and is expressed as a
       percentage.

(b) Excluding Motor Vehicles and Parts.

(c) Excluding Household Furniture.

(d) Excluding Sawmills and Veneer and Plywood Mills.

(e) Excluding Slaughtering and Meat Processing, Breweries and Wineries and Distilleries.

(f) Excluding Pharmaceuticals and Medicine and Paint and Varnish.

Source: The Conference Board in Canada.

number of industries which have shown significant deterioration in trade performance since 1971, there are also many which have shown improvement. Within the strong industry group three industries — metal mines, primary metals, and other transportation equipment (excluding motor vehicles and parts) — showed marginal improvements. Within the traditionally weak industries, seven industries showed improvement, with the rubber products industry, the other furniture industry (excluding household furniture), and breweries and wineries showing the strongest gains. In addition to these industries, the petroleum and coal products industry and coal mining showed significant improvements and are categorized as new strengths.

Many industries recorded deteriorating trade performances over the 1971 period. Within the strong industry group, the NTB of petroleum and gas wells declined by over twenty points (although this is mainly due to the phasing out of oil exports). The decline shown in the NTB for motor vehicles and parts is extremely important because of the large volume of automotive trade. The deterioration of the NTB for this industry of approximately seven points represents an increase in the nominal trade deficit of over $1 billion.

Within the weak industry group, several industries which exhibited high normalized trade deficits in 1971 experienced further deterioration by 1976. This group included such industries as the clothing industry, knitting mills, the leather products industry, the textile industry, the household furniture industry, and the electrical products industry. The combined trade balance of these six relatively labor-intensive industries deteriorated by $2.2 billion between 1971 and 1976, which accounts for approximately 62 per cent of the deterioration in the manufacturing trade balance over the period. Four industries may be categorized as new weaknesses. These include forestry products, other food and beverage industries (other than slaughtering and meat packing and alcoholic beverages), veneer and plywood mills, and the clothing industry. In the case of forestry products and veneer and plywood mills, the sharp deterioration appears to be largely a cyclical phenomenon. Rough calculations indicate that both these industries recorded trade surpluses in 1977. However, the deteriorations experienced in the clothing and other food and beverage industries do not appear to be due to cyclical conditions but rather to a secular increase in the competitiveness of imports.

In summary, the investigation of individual manufacturing industries uncovers a wide degree of variability in their trade performance. While the manufacturing sector as a whole does not appear to have suffered a serious deterioration in either its export price competitiveness or its U.S. market share, there does exist an identifiable group of industries which have serious competitive problems, often in spite of the relatively high tariff protection which they receive. These competitive problems are not a new development of the 1970s for this subset of manufacturing industries. However, some of the problems may have been masked by the favorable economic performance of the 1960s. The worldwide recession of 1974 and 1975 in combination with the general profit squeeze on Canadian exporting and import-competing industries dramatically exposed the competitive weakness of these industries.

III
The Challenge of Overseas Markets

B
Marketing Strategies by Sectors

13
Canadian Small Business and International Markets

N. J. Fodor

Mr. Fodor is president of Electrovert, Ltd., a manufacturer and exporter of electronics production equipment. His companies export 98 per cent of their production to more than seventy countries. He has served as chairman of the International Trade Committee of the Montreal Board of Trade; director of the Board of the Canadian Export Association; chairman of the Small Exporters' Committee of the Canadian Export Association; member of the Export Promotion Review Committee; chairman of the Export Council of the Electrical and Electronic Manufacturers' Association; and in many other capacities.

This chapter was written expressly for this volume.

This chapter deals with the small business aspect of exporting. This subject is usually approached from the viewpoint of the possible value of exports to Canadian small business. A less obvious approach is to explore the value which small business has for Canadian exports. This chapter is more heavily weighted in favor of the latter approach.

In this chapter, the meanings of small business and entrepreneurship are discussed. This is followed by a general discussion of small business exports and their impact on Canadian employment. Canadian innovators and export consultants are mentioned as examples of valuable contributors to Canadian exports. The chapter is concluded by highlighting the future of high-technology sectors in the world economy and the importance of small business technology companies in the export of highly sophisticated technological products.

Definition of Small Business and Entrepreneurship

Small business is not easily nor clearly defined. While number of employees may remain an important consideration, volume of sales or units of production are equally valid measures. There is no consensus on a formal definition, nor is it possible to draw a dividing line between actual firms. However, the term is used and, in general, can be understood.

Small businesses are usually thought of as enterprises with one proprietor or a small group of owners who fly by the seat of their pants most of the time. They must fight for sales and scramble for working capital in order to avoid bankruptcy. Surplus profits are seldom in evidence, especially in the early days of the small business.

The problems that befall the small business man in the day-to-day operation of his business are seldom taken as seriously by the press or by the government as are the problems of large manufacturers in areas such as the automotive industry. For example, wholesale government underwriting of small business debt is rarely available to the small business man.

Statistics show that approximately 80 per cent of small businesses fail within their first five years. Some small businesses reward their owners financially, but this is usually the result of unusual energy and innovation on the part of the owner, accompanied by high risk taking. The majority of small businesses, however, merely manage to survive until they are appropriated by a larger enterprise, merged with a healthier competitor, or fall into bankruptcy. The small business man's reward is more likely to be a gratifying sense of achievement than financial gain. Professor David McLelland of Harvard notes that the entrepreneur "has a higher-than-usual need for achievement as well as for independence". Monetary satisfactions, he claims, are quite secondary to personal fulfilment.

The strong individualistic drive of the entrepreneur is an interesting personality trait, for it is the basis of small business. In the absence of unlimited budgets for marketing, sales promotion, research and development, and equipment, small business must innovate to survive and become the birthplace of new ideas, new techniques, and new products.

The small business man generally starts out with a wish to be his own boss. In order to fulfill this aspiration, he must discover or create a product or service that other people will want to buy. In the short term, this is most easily accomplished by copying an existing product or service, but long-term success on a large scale is usually granted to those with enough innovative drive to create an original enterprise.

Although the entrepreneur wants to be his own boss, once he has begun his enterprise he soon discovers that in fact he must obey many new "bosses" — labor, government, bankers, suppliers, and, most important of all, the customer. However, the small business man tends to persist, provided he can retain a measure of independence in making day-to-day judgments and decisions. Once he has tasted success, these drawbacks become inconsequential and he is "hooked". The individual entrepreneur who treasures his own personal freedom and takes the statistically obvious risk of failure in order to keep on innovating is ultimately, if indirectly, working to benefit human progress.

The "discovery" of small business by sociologists took place in North America fifteen or twenty years ago. North America, the heartland of free enterprise, is where the small business man seems to function best. State bureaucracy does little to encourage the entrepreneur. Small business existed before it was "discovered" by the sociologists. In prehistoric times, the tribal artisan who excelled at some particular craft became the community potter or carver of implements. The other members of his community fished, or hunted, or gathered food for him in return. When the demand for his skill became so great that he could no longer fill the orders, he trained a helper and began his career as a small business man. The Industrial Revolution produced businesses which were small before they grew into the great mills and factories that kept England a world power.

What the sociologists have recently discovered is the extent to which small businesses continue to breed and grow and stimulate our economy. Small enterprises co-exist with the giants of the industrial world and make a greater contribution in terms of both jobs and the creation of economic wealth. In 1976, the top 500 American companies provided 15 million jobs. The next 500 provided 2 million more. These top 1,000 companies are here used to represent big business. Smaller businesses provided 94.7 million jobs, or nearly six times as many as the top 1,000 American companies. The Canadian situation is similar.

The discovery of the inherent economic value of small enterprise has provoked a great deal of reaction. Governments have begun to recognize the tax benefits of small, successful companies, as well as their employment and foreign exchange contributions. This enthusiastic government response is welcomed by enterprising individuals who have felt ignored for years as they struggled with the distinctive problems of small enterprises. But there is also a real danger of Big Brother smothering the little man through an excess of kindness and misdirected zeal.

Small Business Exports

Exports are generally conceived of as goods shipped out of one country to another. More specifically, exports are goods that are sent abroad for which payment is returned to the country of origin. The word "goods" is perhaps too specific in this context, as other less tangible exports do exist. For example, business consultations offered by Canadians to those in other lands and Canadian investment in overseas enterprises both earn income for Canada. Canadian exports should not only bring foreign currency into Canada, but in doing so they should also provide the maximum possible employment for Canadian citizens.

Shipments of agricultural and forest products are among Canada's most successful earners of foreign exchange, as are exports of Canada's extractive industries, especially hydrocarbons. There is a market for any oil and gas Canada cares to sell. Eager buyers in the United States guarantee Canada a market for any hydro-electric power that exceeds our own needs. Both renewable and non-renewable Canadian export products earn foreign exchange; but these exports measure poorly in terms of jobs provided in Canada.

Manufactured products provide more employment for Canadians than primary industry, though this may vary from product to product. Manufacturing, as well as primary industry, is influenced by the goals of increased productivity and reduced labor per unit of product. The Canadian economic activity which will allow us to sell our work efforts abroad in return for foreign exchange while providing jobs for Canadians at home is small business rather than primary industry or large-scale manufacturing.

In this chapter, small business is not limited to the manufacture of products, but covers all types of goods and services. Consultants export expertise. Tourism sells visitors another intangible. Some economists predict that by the year 2000 the tourist industry will be Canada's largest single source of foreign exchange funds. Measured against the vastness of our wheat, hydrocarbon, mineral, and forest product exports, this prediction is astounding. However, the world is changing and becoming increasingly affluent and mobile.

Tourism is predominantly a small business industry. Certainly it includes major airlines and giant hotel chains, but it relies upon small businesses such as shops, restaurants, motels, local air and bus services, service stations, bars, innumerable local historic sights and tourist attractions, and so on. Because the tourist market is constantly searching for "something different", this field provides a natural environment for entrepreneurs, enabling them to make significant contributions to Canadian employment and foreign exchange earnings.

Canadian Innovators and Export Consultants

Given the right economic climate, Canada can expect to continue to produce many innovators and consultants. In the past, important projects such as the Hong Kong-Kowloon tunnel were designed by Canadians, and at present Canada exports engineering, communications, and technology expertise.

Toward the end of the 1970s, a shift in Canadian exports away from agricultural and mining products towards manufactured items became evident. At that time 76 per cent of total exports was manufactured goods and nearly two-thirds of that percentage consisted of items of finished manufacture. The types of manufactured products which offer Canada the most attractive possibilities for the future are those classified as secondary manufacturing. This classification includes high-technology products (the direction of the future) and products such as arts and crafts, which are distinctive to the particular country. This latter type of manufacturing typifies the "limited market limited production" aspect of the product which is not mass-produced.

High-technology products of the future require new technology, new marketing techniques, and above all a new breed of entrepreneurs with new ideas. Some of these high-technology products are home computers,[1] electronic toys, word processors, and robot-controlled processing plants. How does a small business, particularly a Canadian small business, participate in the future-oriented segments of high-technology industries? In the next section, the author summarizes the future perspective as he sees it, based upon his personal experiences.

Future High Technology

Robert Theobald, the economist-philosopher, said nearly twenty years ago that "within the discernible future two per cent of the population will be able to produce all the goods and services needed to feed, clothe, and run our society — with the aid of machines". Where does this leave the small business man?

The push toward large-scale computerized industry has caused bankruptcy for many small businesses. Increased productivity requires larger plants, specialization, and computer-assisted technology which is usually beyond the grasp of small business. This trend can be expected to continue in the future.

In decades ahead, one may speculate that giant plants around the world will produce one product to be distributed to people all over the world. Canada, with its small population, high production costs, and vast geographical distances, is unlikely to house many of these industrial megafacilities. This vision of the future is modified by transportation costs. If energy continues to be a cause of inflation in transport cost, complete centralization of industries may be impossible. Nationalism will also have a moderating effect on centralization because people will demand a familiar product produced in their home plants.

What remains for Canadian consultants and small business men is

---

1. For a brief discussion on high-technology products, entrepreneurs, and new firms spawned by them, see an interesting article, "Small-Computer Shootout", *Time* (March 2, 1981), pp. 42-43.

the production and design of new devices to improve the productivity of the world's giant industrial plants. The technology needed to run them will not be mass-produced. An example is furnished by the present-day state of the automobile industry. Ninety per cent of the special devices and parts which make it function are produced by small and medium-size businesses.[2] In addition, services will continue to be necessary, providing entrepreneurs with another area for small business innovation.

Conclusion

This chapter has outlined a few of the benefits to Canada's economy accruing from small business. Despite these benefits, there are 5,500 Canadian business failures per year. How can government help to support small business?

Although many failures are due to inefficiency on the part of the entrepreneur, money is the key problem. Governmental tax structures that would acknowledge the service performed by the entrepreneurs for the national economy might prevent a few of these failures. More unity in presenting Canadian products as the output of a unified nation would do much to increase the success of Canadian ventures. The future survival of Canadian small business is not the responsibility of the government alone. It is the responsibility of the entrepreneur to learn new techniques and develop a world trade sense which other countries have had centuries to perfect. For individuals with innovative drive this task should not prove too difficult, as has been envisaged by Pierre E. Trudeau in a 1964 essay:

> In the world of tomorrow, the expression 'banana republic' will not refer to independent, fruit-growing nations but to countries where formal independence has been given priority over the cybernetic revolution . . . of advanced technology and scientific investigation, as applied to the fields of law, economics, social psychology, international affairs, and other areas of human relations.[3]

2. A confirmation of this scenario on the robot revolution and custom-made robots produced by brand new small companies is given in the cover story in *Time* (December 5, 1980). Also see "Japan: Fanuc edges closer to a robot-run plant", *Business Week* (November 24, 1980), p. 56.
3. Richard Gwyn, *The Northern Magus* (Toronto: McClelland and Stewart Ltd., 1980), p. 48.

III
The Challenge of Overseas Markets

B
Marketing Strategies by Sectors

14
Economic Nationalism and Canadian Exports

Bertin Nadeau

Mr. Nadeau is president and chief executive officer of La Société Nadeau Limitée, a holding company whose subsidiaries include a major Canadian furniture producer and the world's largest manufacturer of pipe organs, 90 per cent of which are exported to other countries. He was a professor of business policy at the Ecole des Hautes Etudes Commerciales in Montreal for seven years before entering the full-time business world. He is an active business and community leader, serving on a variety of governmental advisory boards and corporate directorships.

This chapter was written expressly for this volume.

The themes of economic nationalism and industrial strategies in Canada inevitably touch upon very important factors for the success of business. This is all the more true in a world where national economies are becoming more and more interdependent. The purpose of this chapter is to propose an industrial strategy for Canada, designed to give industry the incentive necessary to become competitive in world markets. The problems of the current protectionist attitudes in Canada are explored, and a framework for action is developed. What I have to say is necessarily biased by my experience as president and general manager of a medium-size company in the furniture and pipe organ sectors of industry, which employs about 500 people.

The Current Situation

Canadian industry's major problem lies with competition from the United States. By comparison, our prices are too high and our designs too imitative. This is largely explained by the size of our market, which is one-tenth the size of the American market. Because of customs protection, Canadian businesses have managed to survive for a long time, satisfied with producing for the local market products designed in the United States. On the other hand, for the past few years the efficiency of U.S. producers has been such that, in some cases, they can compete with us in our own market despite the tariff barriers. Two types of action may remedy this situation:

1. To define Canadian industry in terms of the North American market. It is only by considering the North American market as a whole that a manufacturer can hope to reach a sales figure that allows sufficient economy of scale to warrant competitive quality and prices.
2. To make our mark at the product level in both design and technology. In other words, we must make sure our products are not simply copies of U.S. products.

Up to now, Canadian economic policies have not seemed to appreciate the need for such actions. In the context of economic nationalism, which can be labelled protectionist, industrial strategy has become simply a catch phrase to justify diverse interventions.

The wealth of our society and the quality of life in Canada forbid us to overdramatize the situation. It would be ridiculous, to cry "disaster" in a society where the satisfaction of basic needs is so easily accomplished for the majority. The model of a mixed economy, established since the end of the nineteenth century, made it possible for Canadians to attain this level of prosperity. Yet one hundred years ago, none could have dreamed that such a system as ours was possible. It is only through compromise and experiment, often in opposition to prevalent theories, that the manufacturing sector has developed in partnership with governments, which were paradoxically blamed on many occasions for their interventions and reproved for their lack of action.

The Background of Economic Nationalism

Historical necessity rather than economic theories have led Canada to economic nationalism.

Before income tax was instituted, the raison d'être of customs duties was their contribution to government revenues. A series of political events caused these economic measures to evolve into protectionist policies.

Between 1854 and 1866, Canada and the United States operated under a reciprocity agreement, treating one another alike at the customs level. Canada found this arrangement so suitable that when the United States decided not to renew the agreement prime ministers Macdonald and Cartier increased their efforts in Washington to have the decision reversed. The pressure caused by U.S. protectionism and England's withdrawal of its preferential treatment forced the Canadian colonies to react. It is within this framework that we witness successive policies of growing economic nationalism.

First, in order to protect itself from the domination of U.S. business, Canada established a tariff protection policy which has since become firmly entrenched. The Liberals suffered a bitter defeat, first in 1891 and then in 1911, due to their defence of free trade with the United States. After witnessing the Liberal Party's 1911 experiences from the sidelines, Mackenzie King vowed that his party would never again challenge the necessity for tariff protection.

This type of policy provided the encouragement needed for the establishment of foreign, in particular American, manufacturing plants in Canada. As a result, Canada was forced to take a second step: the

control of foreign ownership. According to the economic nationalists of the time, not only did U.S. subsidiaries compete with our own
businesses, but their effective contribution to the welfare of Canada
was minimal. Research and development, as well as exports, were
kept within the jurisdiction of the parent companies in the United
States. Around 1960, Canada's reaction to this foreign presence was
to introduce a series of corrective measures to control foreign investments. The Foreign Investment Review Agency (FIRA) is the best
example.

When one measure is instituted to correct another, paradoxically,
new problems are often generated. The control of foreign ownership
created a problem at the balance of payments level. The government
felt the need to take further action: to work out an industrial strategy
whereby Canadian business could export to the world market. Until
this time, there had been no well-defined means of reaching this
objective. Economic planning was insufficient, and subsidies to businesses were based on criteria previously defined by the bureaucrats,
which often led to unintended results.

The Consequences of Protection

Let us take a closer look at the consequences of Canada's protectionist measures and industrial strategy. One of the results of protectionism was to limit Canadian business to an excessively restricted
market. As the Canadian market is only one-tenth the size of the U.S.
market, this has led to serious consequences in terms of size and
specialization of manufacturing plants. Moreover, protectionism has
reduced competition in the local market and led Canadian business
to survive through a "strategy of imitation". That is, manufacturers
could manage quite well by imitating products created elsewhere
and producing them for the local market. In sum, protectionism has
at least reduced the incentive for effort and innovation.

Economic development measures, that is, various government
programs of grants and subsidies, have led in some cases to beneficial
results. On the whole, however, the results have been more negative
than positive. First, they have contributed to the emergence of a
society that relies more on grants, subsidies, and other forms of
government aid to solve its problems than on its own strength.

Second, they have distorted the workings of the market, often in
favor of the weaker and the less efficient. In a democracy where one
of the government imperatives is to bring the taxpayers to accept the
way in which subsidies are granted, it is perhaps not politic to

support the strong at the expense of the weak. Yet, that is the logical path in an economic situation which requires that we compete with business the world over.

Third, by rewarding effort and action instead of results, and by distributing government aid on the basis of criteria that are arbitrary and incomplete, the programs of grants and subsidies have often had results contrary to the objectives in mind at the time the programs were conceived. The support of subsidies in certain areas has often led to aberrations on economic and social levels. The history of the trailer and the mobile home in Quebec is one example of the kind of distortion created by the system. The many government subsidies handed out for innovations or improvements in productivity without regard to the market as a whole, only managed to create an increasingly fragmented competition and led to the bankruptcy of a large proportion of the businesses in this sector.

This leads to the following observation: many government interventions, instead of being in step with the logic of the system, rather tend to throw it off balance. The effects of this lack of balance are:

1. businesses become less competitive domestically as well as outside the country;
2. the decision-making process becomes impractical;
3. initiative and productivity research are lessened among Canadians.

Plan of Action

In view of these facts, what can be done to improve the situation? It seems to me that the following premise should be the starting point of any action in this area: As Canadians, if we want to remain masters of our own house, while maintaining our standard of living, we have no choice but to take up the challenge of foreign competition and build businesses that are just as efficient, powerful, and innovative as those of the Americans, Japanese, Germans, and so on. Any other solution, however attractive it may seem, would not take the economic realities of this world into account and would lead sooner or later to bitter disappointment.

The real problem that we must try to solve, is how we can go about making our Canadian businesses more competitive in the international market place.

Corporate Strategy

There are two basic ways for Canadian companies to be competitive, depending on their field of endeavor and market sector. First, let us look at standard products which are basically undifferentiated. Competition in this area is usually based on price, implying that production costs must be as low as those of the competition. In addition to the costs of raw materials, it is obvious that the efficiency of the production system in general, and the productivity of labor in particular, are very important elements in this calculation. How can they be improved? The following factors, among others, have a predominant impact at this level:

1. The length of production runs and the specialization of the factories. (It becomes important, therefore, for our businesses to define themselves in terms of a much larger market than Canada.)
2. The existence of an industrial technology at the peak of development.
3. The presence of an attitude or a value system conducive to the emergence of a hard-working, innovative, and efficient society. (When all Canadians are convinced that the only way to increase our collective wealth is to increase our productivity, the problem will be half-solved.)

Quite clearly, it is not possible to compete with foreigners on the basis of price (production costs) in all areas, particularly with those developing countries where unskilled labor is plentiful and technology is primitive.

We are becoming increasingly aware of the fact that the gap between developed and undeveloped countries will never be reduced if we do not open our markets to those of their products which meet our standards as regards quality (for example, certain areas of the textile industry). It seems logical to help the less-developed countries in areas where they are more efficient. However, such a policy could cause a massive short-term dislocation in some of our own industrial sectors. We would have to find ways to adapt our industries and workers to the requirements arising from the eventual opening up of our borders. This leads into the discussion of the second way in which Canadian industry can be competitive.

In the case of differentiated products, it is possible to compete on a non-price basis; that is, by varying the products. If through research and development, technology and design, we succeed in creating products which offer more specific advantages to the consumer, it is possible to develop markets in areas where it would be impossible to compete on the basis of price with a "me too" product. The following examples from our own businesses illustrate this point. At the turn of the century, under the leadership of the brothers Samuel and Claver Casavant, our subsidiary, Casavant Frères Limitée, developed and refined an electro-pneumatic organ technically superior to competitive products. By taking advantage of this technological edge, the Casavant brothers climbed to the top of the world pipe organ market. This innovation gave their business the impetus that still makes it the "General Motors" of its industry. It's too bad for Canada that the Casavant brothers didn't turn to cars instead of pipe organs.

More recently, another of our subsidiaries (this one involved in the manufacturing of colonial furniture) decided to tackle the U.S. market. It had become obvious to us that if we wanted to continue to grow we had to gain some market share south of the border.

As noted earlier, the major drawback of Canadian manufacturing versus its American competition is lower productivity, which results from smaller, less specialized plants and from higher labor and material costs.

A closer analysis of the particular strengths and weaknesses of our company compared to our U.S. competitors revealed that one of our plants in New Brunswick had similar productivity and labor rates to the U.S. manufacturers making medium-high to high-priced furniture of similar style but had shorter production runs. We could compete in that price range as long as we could build up production runs enabling us to realize economies of scale. We concluded that we needed: first, a distribution channel that would enable us to have, right from the start, high volume on a small number of items; and second, a design that could differentiate our product from those already existing on the market. To be successful our sales strategy had to focus on design and quality rather than price.

We approached one of the major U.S. mass retailers, armed with an in-depth study of their needs and suppliers. They were very impressed with our quality, our design vis-à-vis their needs for the market of the 1980s, and the overall vitality of our organization as demonstrated by our professional approach. They decided to work with us to develop a small line (five items) of furniture aimed at the higher end of their product assortment. It took their marketing experts and our designers, marketing team, and production specialists months to finalize the prototypes. Prices were not discussed during that period. When the products were finalized we came up with our cost estimates, which were accepted without discussion. They decided to proceed with a market test. If successful, they estimate that their requirements will be such that our production runs will enable us to be as efficient on those products as any U.S. manufacturer could be. These examples illustrate the following points:

first, it is possible through thorough analysis to find ways to shift the focus from price competition to other factors on which we, as Canadians, do not have an a priori weakness. Quality, and product uniqueness, are two of the areas where one can find a niche in foreign markets; second, where price is a factor, a detailed analysis to discover why costs are higher can sometimes (as has been the case for us) indicate ways to minimize this disadvantage.

In the search for competitiveness in foreign markets, there are no magic formulas that will assure automatic success. What we have to develop in this country is a mentality whereby each potential exporter will dare to at least look at the foreign markets and competitors, analyse them and his own situation, and try to come up with his own formula for competition.

There are many other examples of businesses that have succeeded in making their mark on the international market due to innovation and design: Bombardier, Micom, les Meubles Rougier, Northern Telecom are a few.

Government Strategy

It is becoming imperative for Canadians to invest more seriously in research and development (including design) in order to personalize and differentiate our products. What strategy should the government adopt to give Canadian business the incentive to take up the challenge of international competition? The following five guideposts should be the basis of government action at this level.

First of all, government strategy should respect the natural workings of market and competition that control and govern economic activity. Any government participation should reinforce rather than undermine these natural interactions. This implies that government aid should be granted according to results, rather than efforts and actions. In other words, the government should let the market select the winners and the losers and then reward the winners. This approach would encourage the emergence of a value system conducive to the existence of an autonomous and efficient society that would rely on the productivity, creativity, and perseverance of its members, rather than on government action, to settle its problems.

Second, in line with the GATT principles, the government should progressively lower tariff barriers in order to subject our businesses to foreign competition and stimulate greater productivity research.

Third, our industrial strategy should progress from protectionism to expansionism. Canadian businesses should be encouraged to measure themselves internationally, by developing foreign markets for their products and by making foreign investments. In this light, research and development, design, and innovation must continue to be encouraged. Again, this must be done in terms of achievement rather than effort.

Fourth, all government aid to business should be dispensed through the taxation system. This would have a double effect. In the first place, it would help to simplify greatly aid program management, especially in the selection of those eligible for subsidies. In the second place, by rewarding results instead of effort, the workings of the market would be respected.

Finally, it is to be hoped that any government intervention policy would not be changed with every new budget or government. Obviously program continuity and the permanence of measures are vital ingredients of success.

Conclusion

Allow me to reiterate what I believe is the basic premise of any analysis aimed at outlining an industrial strategy for Canada in the 1980s: If we want to remain masters of our own house and maintain our standard of living, we have no other choice but to take up the challenge of foreign competition.

To do this, we have to measure ourselves against the international market in general, and the North American market in particular. Once and for all, we must admit that foreign business in Canada is not the problem. The problem is our own foreign development. Exports create employment. Opening up to competition would, without a doubt, help extricate our industry from its inertia. One condition for such development would be the formation of Canadian multinationals, which would extend their activities into the U.S. and other regions of the world. The government would have to intervene in a different way to develop these businesses and create propitious conditions for exports. One suggestion which, to my mind, would be very effective and would respect the five guiding principles set forth earlier is to abolish taxes on profits made by Canadian companies on foreign sales. Such a policy would undoubtedly have considerable impact on the operations of Canadian businesses. Some will certainly see difficulties in implementing such a policy. Personally, I am willing to bet on the inventiveness of the Ministry of Revenue officials and their ability to come up with the necessary procedures to put the policy into operation.

I am well aware that the fear of economic and cultural assimilation by the United States remains with us and will remain for a long time, coloring our political choices. Yet, I dare to hope that our leaders are also aware that it is not by erecting walls that we will develop. We have proved that we can be front runners on the world market in many areas. At present we can compete as equals because of our natural assets, the education level of our population, and our new spirit of entrepreneurship. Who knows? We may be the Japan of the 1980s.

III
The Challenge of Overseas Markets

B
Marketing Strategies by Sectors

15
Canada's Consulting Engineers: Prime Exporters of Technology, Goods, and Equipment

C. A. Dagenais

Mr. Dagenais is chairman and chief executive officer of The SNC Group, one of Canada's major engineering consulting firms. His company provides engineering, procurement, construction and project management services throughout the world. The SNC Group ranks among the top ten of its type in the world, with some 50 per cent of its revenues earned from operations abroad. Mr. Dagenais has served as director of the Canadian Export Association, and as a member of the Export Promotion Review Committee.

This chapter was written expressly for this volume.

Consulting engineers represent a large sector of the Canadian economy. According to a report prepared for the Department of Industry, Trade, and Commerce and the Association of Consulting Engineers of Canada published in 1978,[1] the 1,600 firms in this sector employed 40,000 people in 1977, many of them highly specialized technical staff. To cite the figures, 29 per cent were engineers, 4 per cent non-engineering specialists, 46 per cent technicians and drafting staff, and 21 per cent administrative personnel.

The sector's billings in 1977 totalled $1.2 billion. With international billings of $200 million, consulting engineers accounted for an estimated 80 per cent of Canada's exports of professional services. Their work abroad sparked the export of $350 million worth of Canadian goods and equipment. The multiplier effect of consulting engineers' international fees was estimated to have generated the sale of an additional $825 million worth of Canadian goods. Although dollar figures have undoubtedly risen over the past three years, the ratios have almost certainly remained relatively constant.

As can be seen from the breakdown of the staff of Canadian consulting engineering firms, this sector forms an important pool of technological expertise. Although consulting engineering firms seldom conduct pure research, they are experienced in the application of new technologies as their day-to-day work regularly calls for process and design improvements. They must therefore possess a comprehensive knowledge of the state of the art in their specialized fields. More perhaps than any other Canadian sector, consulting engineers are in the forefront of advanced technology. To keep them so, of course, is one of the challenges this sector has faced in the past, still faces, and will continue to face in the future. At the same time it must continue to build strength in management. Since the 1960s, Canadian consulting engineers have been developing and increasing project management capabilities. But as projects become larger and more complex, it is more essential than ever that they reinforce Canadian management ability and experience.

1. *Consulting Engineering in Canada: Overview and Prospects* (Peter Barnard Associates, 1978).

The Evolution of Canada's Consulting Engineers

It is only in the last twenty years that Canadian consulting engineers have had a substantial impact on the international market. The very fact that they were Canadian was undoubtedly a factor in their initial success. They were able to offer the developing countries North American technology without political ties and in at least two languages, French and English. They had, moreover, in some instances, developed technological expertise that was uniquely Canadian. It applied to such industries as hydro-electric power, mining and metallurgy, pulp and paper, and telecommunications. This expertise was firmly based on experience in Canada on Canadian projects.

The phrase "consulting engineers" no longer accurately describes a great many of the companies in this sector. Traditionally, consulting engineering firms were partnerships of professionals, employing other engineers, technicians, and designers, solving engineering problems for their clients, and producing engineering drawings. Their work on a project site was usually limited to supervision of quality. Today, this has changed. Though most employees in the sector are engineers, technicians, or drafting staff, it also employs economists, management specialists, urbanists, financing experts, lawyers, agronomists, linguists, and other professionals. Firms have evolved in response to clients' needs and no longer merely specialize in engineering design. They purchase materials and equipment, co-ordinate, and carry out construction. They commission and initially operate plants. Before a project starts, they conduct the technical and financial feasibility studies, establish the concept, and arrange for financing. Some companies are moving into research and process development. They do not limit themselves to exporting engineering services. They export capital goods and capital projects. Today's firms can take total responsibility for the design, supply, and execution of a project — whether it is a large dam or a huge industrial complex — and turn it over to the client as a fully operating unit. Many of these firms are no longer partnerships; they are incorporated companies and are evolving into conglomerates.

The consulting engineers' sector of the Canadian economy has enjoyed long-term growth, but it has been erratic, going from a zero rate of increase in the early 1970s to a peak of 19 per cent which has since dropped to 3 per cent. This cutback in growth reflects a decline in certain sectors of domestic industry, notably construction and municipal works, and the recent reluctance of companies to invest in Canada during a period of economic and political uncertainty. At the same time, however, the domestic energy sector has continued to grow and to provide work for consulting engineers in their home market. One positive result of the down turn in the Canadian economy has been to lead Canadian consulting engineers to explore and develop the international market. Those who were already working internationally increased their business abroad during the last decade. At present, it would probably be realistic to estimate that 30 per cent to 45 per cent of consulting engineers' billings will come from abroad in the 1980s. In Canada itself we can expect 80 per cent to 90 per cent increases in the electricity, petroleum, and natural gas sectors, and in the development of alternate sources of energy.

New Challenges to the Sector's Growth

It is most important that Canadian consulting firms participate in these large energy projects at home because it is on Canadian experience and Canadian technology that their success in the now vital international market depends. Consulting engineering firms and their associations have addressed themselves to this problem, one of our major ones, for close to two decades. It is probably not enough. For the past few years Canadian consulting engineers have been facing a new challenge, and one that, unless positive action is taken, threatens the continued growth of this sector and the very existence of a number of its firms. As the ACEC recently pointed out,[2] the industry is experiencing decreasing profitability in terms of a percentage of fee income. Expenses in terms of fee income rose from 84.8 per cent in 1974 to 92 per cent in 1978, an average increase of 1.8 per cent annually. "If this trend should continue," ACEC estimated, "the industry as a whole would be operating at a loss in 1983!" As ACEC stated, the decrease may be attributed in part to rising wage and salary costs in terms of a percentage of total expenses. Nor has the markup in professional fees charged to the client kept pace with soaring costs. However, the association tended to blame price competition in large part for the decrease. Although provincial associations of professional engineers set recommended fee schedules, the ACEC cited instances where conditions produced situations in which firms had to undercut these schedules to minimum profitability to obtain contracts. ACEC recommended rigid "selection by ability" as a remedy.

There is undoubtedly justice in ACEC's analysis, but one could cite other facts that tend to erode the profitability of consulting engineering firms. The ACEC's point about prices does, however, indicate a problem

2. "Profitability Declines in Industry", *ACEC Information* (September 1980).

of growing competition consulting engineers now face at home and abroad.

Problems of Marketing Capital Projects Abroad

For one thing, the foreign projects so important to Canada's balance of payments and its economy in general are more expensive to carry out than domestic projects, and they entail a much higher level of risk and correspondingly higher lending rates. Individual firms are now attempting to share the cost and risk of obtaining and performing such work by banding together in joint ventures and consortia. They are therefore meeting less and less Canadian competition in the international market place. Even so, international competition grows fiercer every year. On large hydro-electric projects, for example, as many as thirty international consortia may bid. Among these, European firms are highly competitive because they do not carry out the same degree of engineering or supervision as is customary in North America, and hence their initial bids are lower. Faced with competition of this nature, Canadian firms have a selling job to do that calls for more effort and more investment than it did ten or fifteen years ago, all of which is lost if they fail to win the contract.

Many countries give much more financing support to consulting engineers than does Canada, and to compete, Canadian firms must seek additional sources — from banks, private lending agencies, or international financial institutions. The large Canadian firms have been providing this service to international clients for more than a decade and have developed considerable expertise in it. Needless to say, this service calls for time, effort, and highly specialized staff.

Clients abroad are also demanding more and more turnkey packages with financing provided. The solution to part of this problem is to band together with manufacturing companies that can supply all the key equipment needed for a turnkey plant. Canadian companies have had some success in this line. Elinca Communications Limited, a consortium which groups a number of leading Canadian electronics manufacturers and the SNC Group are at present working on the PANAFTEL telecommunications link spanning five African countries. More recently, the SNC Group formed a consortium with two Canadian manufacturers of refrigeration equipment that is now beginning to obtain contracts in developing tropical countries.

Despite these moderate successes, consulting engineers have always encountered reluctance among the majority of Canadian manufacturers to participate in such consortia and to share the risks of developing a specific Canadian technology and marketing it abroad. This was brought home in the findings of the Export Promotion

Review Committee of the Hatch Commission. Many of the manufacturers represented had sold individual products abroad and had experienced success in international markets. But they were diffident about investing in research and development for the export market or in entering into consortia for the export of turnkey plants. In many instances they lacked the knowledge of how to go about putting a turnkey package together. Canada's consulting engineers, through their experience in going out and doing it, have the know-how. In a consortium, this is experience they can provide the manufacturers, if those manufacturers are interested. That so many of them are not interested can be attributed in part to the continuing high rate of foreign ownership of Canadian industry. The only really effective remedy is for more Canadians to invest in their own enterprises. It is of prime importance, too, for at the point we find ourselves today, Canadian consortia of manufacturers and engineers represent one of the most vital elements in maintaining and increasing our exports of technological goods and services. Our competitors from other countries like Japan and Germany offer such packages, and if we are to stay in the market we must do the same.

Another high risk factor consulting engineers face in overseas markets today is the growing demand for lump sum bids, often on projects that are not clearly defined at the time proposals must be submitted. This trend, if it continues, will make operations abroad increasingly precarious.

Some Possible Solutions

What can Canada's consulting engineers do to surmount these obstacles, and how can our industries and governments support our consulting engineers? You may, of course, ask why they should do so at all. The answer can be found at the beginning of this chapter, and in the fact that three years ago the 40,000 people employed in this sector brought 550 million export dollars into the Canadian economy, which in turn generated $850 million worth of additional business, most of it domestic. This adds up to a contribution of $1.4 billion to the Canadian economy in one year, or $35,000 per employee. This seems to prove that it is worth the effort of Canada's various levels of government and of all its industries to contribute, if possible, to keeping the consulting engineering sector healthy and profitable. Certainly, if this industry should become unprofitable, its owners would not go on operating.

There is, moreover, something industry and government can do to support consulting engineers that will not cost one cent. This is to employ Canadian firms on Canadian projects, and particularly on large or high-technology projects, as engineers and as project managers. As people in the industry have been saying for years, it is on demonstrable Canadian experience that they are able to market our services abroad. It is because some private and public industries at home gave Canadian engineers the opportunity to participate in large or advanced projects at home that they were able to make their first thrust into international markets in hydro-electricity, mining, metallurgy, and forest products. Recently there have been excellent signs of progress in the growing tendency of Canadian governments to insist on high Canadian content in projects here, and in the alacrity with which some Canadian companies have sensed this need and encouraged Canadian engineers and project managers. Given the vast energy developments foreseen in the 1980s, it becomes even more important that this high technology, and the expertise in the management of such large and complex projects, be Canadian. Canada is striving to become self-sufficient in energy, but it will profit the country little unless it is also self-sufficient in technology and management techniques.

Conversely, provincial or regional governments should resist the temptation to set up barriers to consulting engineers from other parts of Canada, which would brake the free flow of market exchange within our own boundaries. Unfortunately a trend toward this policy has arisen simultaneously with the encouraging increased use of Canadian talent on large Canadian projects. In the long run it can only be self-defeating, for the regions themselves as well as for the country as a whole.

The government record in supporting and co-operating with consulting engineers in their marketing effort has, in general, been good. Yet, when we compare the support other nations provide for our competitors in the international market, Canada could do more. Financial support in the cost of proposals is, generally, adequate, at least for the larger firms. But these would benefit from additional tax considerations and more all-embracing risk insurance, to cover costly marketing efforts and the risks involved, whether from penalties or from political upheavals on projects abroad. As the geopolitical scene becomes increasingly disturbed, broader and more comprehensive risk insurance becomes essential if Canadian firms are to continue to undertake large projects abroad.

On the side of financial aid, both large and small firms would benefit considerably from increased government funds being made available to finance feasibility studies and conceptual design contracts. These are not profitable contracts, particularly if conducted abroad. On the other hand, more often than not they lead to large projects.

For the larger firms, who are now in the habit of seeking and negotiating financing for their overseas clients' projects, it would be helpful to have more funds available in EDC at more competitive rates and to be able to blend these with increased CIDA funds. For smaller firms, EDC and CIDA funds are often essential if they are to venture into the international market and obtain overseas contracts.

Not Just a Sectorial Effort, but a National One

Such financial support from government is not indiscriminate largesse. It is an investment in Canada's economy. It is a short-term investment in terms of the direct benefits to the Canadian balance of payments and the stimulation of Canadian manufacturing industries that come from projects carried out abroad by Canadian consulting engineers. It is a long-term investment in terms of the experience and expertise gained by Canadians in engineering and managing large and innovative projects, and in terms of the world reputation not only Canadian engineers but Canadian manufacturers stand to gain from complex assignments well performed.

Canadian manufacturing companies can support consulting engineers, and invest in their own future at the same time, by joining with them in consortia to market and perform turnkey projects abroad. Some figures will reinforce the statement that industry stands to benefit substantially from such participation. The current average ratio of the export of Canadian goods to Canadian engineering export dollars earned varies from 1:1 to 3:1. The potential average is 8:1, and for some engineering firms it is, at present, as high as 10:1. These very high ratios, of course, are achieved where there is an equally strong commitment to the use of Canadian goods and equipment. Nowhere is this commitment stronger than where the project is carried out by a consortium of Canadian manufacturers and engineers. Indeed, it seems clear that participation in such consortia offers an unprecedented opportunity for Canadian companies to enlarge their international markets and to build future business abroad.

Through such co-operation, in which governments, manufacturers, and consulting engineers work together for the benefit of all of us, most of its practitioners feel that the consulting engineering industry will remain a healthy, aggressive, and growing sector of our economy. If they can so work together, consulting engineers will continue to be in the future, as in the past, a unique pool of high technology and creators of Canadian exports out of all proportion to their individual numbers.

III
The Challenge of Overseas Markets

C
New Marketing Vehicles

16
Characteristics and Experiences of Canadian-Based Export Consortia

K. C. Dhawan

Lawrence Kryzanowski

Dr. Dhawan is co-ordinator of the international business program in the Faculty of Commerce and Administration, Concordia University. Dr. Kryzanowski is associate professor of finance in the same faculty. The two authors have recently published the results of their work on Canadian-based export consortia in book form, *Export Consortia: A Canadian Study*. They also have been consultants to the Export Promotion Review Committee (Hatch Committee) and have written several background reports that were the basis of the Committee's publication, *Strengthening Canada Abroad*.

This chapter was written expressly for this volume.

The intensely internationally competitive export markets of the "cash rich" petroleum-exporting (OPEC) countries have continued to grow in world importance. Unfortunately for Canadian suppliers, domestic clients in these markets usually stipulate that procurement be on a fixed-price turnkey contract basis for the delivery of complete technological systems[1] (such as the multibillion dollar contract[2] for the telephone modernization program in Saudi Arabia).

While procuring contracts for, and during the delivery of, these turnkey projects[3] in the OPEC markets, Canadian and other foreign firms have encountered difficulties with: (1) unfamiliar host environments and "ways of doing business"; (2) high inflation rates; (3) manpower and shipping bottlenecks; (4) high levels of political, business, and financial risks (especially those arising from local civil work and bid and performance bonds and guarantees); (5) "scale or technology gap";[4] and (6) the highly competitive "political marketing" effort and export support programs provided by foreign governments.[5]

To overcome some of the above difficulties, Canadian firms have

1. A complete technological system is considered to be a group of technologically complex industrial, or agricultural, or infrastructural units so combined as to form a whole (or system) that operates interdependently and harmoniously.
2. For the post-award analysis of the project and some of the hypotheses offered for the loss of the project by the American firms, see "The Saudis say 'wrong numbers' to the U.S.", *Business Week* (January 9, 1978), pp. 20-21; and James Flanigan, "The Mystery of the 'Vague Specifications' or How the Americans Lost Out on a Giant Saudi Arabian Contract", *Forbes* (February 20, 1978), pp. 39-40.
3. A turnkey project involves a contractual liability incurred by a supplier to the buyer for the delivery of the pre-engineering and economic feasibility study stage to the commissioning and start-up stage of a complete technological project. Furthermore, upon start up, the operating complete technological system is transferred to the buyer (owner) and the supplier's contractual liability is discharged.
4. A scale or technology gap is defined as the difference between the scale or technology of the project to be delivered and similar domestic (or international) projects undertaken in the past by the supplier (or by any other supplier).
5. A partial listing of Middle East projects containing U.S. participants is given in an article by Searby. (See Daniel M. Searby, "Doing Business in the Mideast: The Game is Rigged", *Harvard Business Review* (January-February 1976), pp. 56-64. Furthermore, Searby argues that U.S. firms are not competing successfully for turnkey projects in the Middle East, although the firms are of substantial financial standing and financial substance.

begun to utilize innovative organizational and contractual structures, such as consortia, to obtain the necessary financial substance, risk reduction, and project delivery expertise in order to successfully obtain and discharge foreign-based project contracts.

Therefore, the purposes of this chapter are: first, to define the term "consortium" and to discuss various types of consortia classifications; second, to present some of the characteristics of Canadian-based limited liability consortia; third, to present the perceptions of consortia participants on the benefits derived by member firms from participating in a consortium; and fourth, to present the perceptions of consortia participants of the problems encountered within and by a consortium.

Definitions

A consortium has been defined as an association between selected manufacturers and a trading corporation or a number of trading corporations to co-operate on penetration, pricing, and competitive markets.[6] Unfortunately, this definition is deficient in many respects. First, it does not adequately distinguish between a cartel, a co-operative, a joint venture, and a consortium. Second, it is too restrictive in its membership criteria, for many consortia also include consulting engineers, contractors, private experts, or government agencies. Third, a consortium can be designed to pursue one or more of a large number of commercial activities such as marketing, construction, purchasing, or construction management. Fourth, a consortium can be used to conduct business in a competitive or uncompetitive market. For example, in a "mega" turnkey project, a consortium could be used, not to meet competition, but to parcel out risks and tasks in units that are palatable to individual firms.

Therefore, a more general and operational definition of a consortium is as follows: A consortium is an ad hoc or ongoing, informal or formal, sometimes "shell", association of two or more business/governmental/financial entities to profitably pursue, generally on a competitive basis, one or more common commercial activities that are either complementary to, an extension of, or in addition to the regular activities of its members.[7]

6. R. Fournier, *Market Development Group Report on Trading Houses and Export Middlemen in Canada* (Ottawa, 1972).
7. While consortia do exist in the non-profit sector of our economy (for example, in education), for our purposes these consortia are not of interest unless they become commercially export oriented.

Cartels, co-operatives, and joint ventures are therefore "special case" consortia. In particular, a cartel is a consortium designed to control the purchase or sale of a single commodity (sometimes on a worldwide basis, as in the case of OPEC). A co-operative is a consortium formed by a large number of small members operating in a similar industry to purchase or market particular goods and services on a large scale to the better advantage of its members. A joint venture is a consortium, generally of financial substance (standing), formed by two, and sometimes more, members to share in or to collectively undertake a specific, clearly identifiable project on an ongoing basis.[8]

For the purpose of this chapter, any reference to consortia is to be interpreted as any consortia that cannot be classified as one of the above "special case" consortia.

Methodology

In-depth personal interviews were utilized to collect all of the primary data used in this study. An important feature of the interviews was the fact that most were conducted by the two authors in tandem.

The interview process proceeded as follows. First, the authors conducted a number of local unstructured interviews with selected individuals from industry and government to obtain a more complete list of Canadian-based consortia. Second, one of the authors went to Iran to analyse the host environment and the nature of international competition in the Iranian market. Third, a comprehensive, personal, in-depth, structured interview guide was prepared and pre-tested.[9] Fourth, extensive interviewing was conducted across Canada with 104 senior officials of the following Canadian entities: fifteen of the twenty-four identified Canadian-based consortia, their member firms, Canadian federal and provincial governments, consulting engineering firms, trade associations, financial institutions, consulting firms, and internationally oriented potential consortia members. Fifth, concurrently with the Canadian interviews, one of the authors conducted further interviews in Iran, and both authors conducted interviews in Saudi Arabia.

8. This differs from the definition used by Daniels-Ogram-Radebaugh who view a consortium as a "special case" joint venture. More specifically, they state that "when more than two organizations participate, the resultant joint venture is sometimes referred to as a consortium". See John D. Daniels, Ernest W. Ogram, Jr., and Lee H. Radebaugh, *International Business: Environment and Operations* (Reading, Massachusetts: Addison-Wesley Publishing Co., 1976), p. 382.

9. All through the interview process, additional names of Canadian-based consortia, their member firms, and their leaders were solicited.

Classification of Possible Types of Consortia

Each of the eight classifications of possible types of consortia are discussed below.

Legal Form

A consortium can be classified by legal form as a "club" or "association", a legal partnership, or a fully incorporated limited liability company.

Expected Time Duration

Consortia can be classified by time duration as ad hoc or ongoing. An ad hoc consortium is a consortium with a limited expected life which is designed to accomplish a specific task (generally one particular transaction or project). The advantage of an ad hoc consortium is that it can be optimally designed in terms of membership, ownership, member interests, and other factors, in order to accomplish a specific task.

An ongoing consortium is a consortium designed to undertake a specific objective (such as to market prefab houses abroad or to undertake turnkey management in Iron Curtain countries). The major advantage of such a consortium is that it can develop expertise in its line of endeavor. The major disadvantage is that as it develops, the consortium is often restricted by the composition of its initial membership, its stipulated interests, and the articles of its formal agreement of establishment.

Function

Consortia can be classified by function as procurement, distribution, financial, marketing, project management, or turnkey consortia. Thus, a procurement consortium is designed to derive the benefits of economies of scale which result from large collective purchases. Generally, the benefits of such consortia are immediate, with a small initial cost outlay. Therefore, some European countries believe that firms should begin collective endeavors by forming procurement consortia.

Similarly, a distribution consortium is designed to reap the benefits of economies of scale which may result from large collective shipments of goods.

A financial consortium is designed to parcel out risk in units that are small enough to be of interest to risk averse financial firms. Financial consortia are used extensively in the banking and insurance field (for example, the Orion banking consortium).

A marketing consortium is designed to increase the marketing effectiveness of a group of firms. Marketing consortia can be further classified as single product or multiple product. Single-product consortia are popular with small firms who want to begin to export abroad, and with commodity producers during periods of oversupply. (Examples include the production of sulphur and potash.)

A project management or turnkey consortium is generally a grouping of complementary firms combined in order to supply all, or a portion, of a complete technological project (commonly referred to as a turnkey).

Absolute Size of Participants

Consortia can be classified by absolute size of participants, as small participants or large participants. A consortium of small participants generally has limited productive, financial, and marketing capability. As a result, procurement, distribution, and marketing consortia are viable operations for small participants' consortia.

A consortia of large participants is generally formed to undertake project management when the scale of the project is large (for example, construction of a metropolitan transportation system in Venezuela, construction of a paper mill complex in Iran, or a petrochemical refinery unit in Saudi Arabia).

Relative Financial Standing of Participants

Consortia can be classified by the relative financial standing of their participants, as participants of similar standing (substance) or participants of different standing (substance). Many of the operational difficulties associated with consortia occur within the latter type of consortia.

Initiator

Consortia can be classified by initiator, as manufacturer/producer initiated or packager initiated. A packager is any consulting engineer, trading house, trade association, or other entity that offers to supply a grouping or package of goods and services, which it has neither manufactured nor designed, to a client.

The distinction between manufacturer/producer-initiated and packager-initiated consortia becomes important in the area of project management. For example, the packager generally does not have the financial standing or substance to incur the liabilities necessary for the bonding or guarantee requirements of foreign turnkey projects.

Nationality of Participants

Consortia can be classified by nationality of participants as national (all members drawn from the same country) or international (members drawn from more than one country).

Operational Domain

Consortia can be classified by operational domain as pure (operating only in the export markets) and mixed (operating both in the domestic and export markets).

Classification and Characteristics of the Canadian-Based Limited Liability Consortia

Each of the twenty-four limited liability consortia identified by the authors can be classified as in Table 1.

The characteristics of the twenty-four consortia listed in Table 1 can be summarized as follows:

1. With regard to time duration, twenty consortia are ongoing, three are dormant, and one is ad hoc.
2. With regard to function, ten consortia were formed for the export of turnkey projects, two for the export of turnkey projects and multiple products, one for the export of multiple products, one for the export of project management, two for the export of project management and services, one for the export of services, and seven for the export of a single product.
3. With regard to the absolute size of participants, five consortia are comprised of small members, eight of small to medium members, one of small to large members, eight of medium to large members, and two of large members.
4. With regard to the relative standing (substance) of consortia participants, fourteen consortia have members with similar relative standing and ten have members with different relative standing.
5. With regard to initiator, thirteen consortia were initiated by a manufacturer, eight by a packager, and three by a producer.
6. With regard to the nationality of participants, all but one is national (all members drawn from Canada).
7. With regard to operational domain, all twenty-four consortia are pure.

Perceived Benefits of Marketing, Project Management, and Turnkey Consortia

A number of consortia participants were asked to rate a number

Table 1

Classification of Canadian-Based Limited Liability Consortia

Consor-tium[a]	Time Duration	Function	Absolute Size of Participants	Relative Standing of Participants	Initiator[b]
1	ongoing	turnkey projects abroad	medium to large	different	manufacturer
2	ongoing	multiple products	small to medium	different	manufacturer
3	ongoing	turnkey projects abroad	small	similar	manufacturer
4	was ongoing (now dormant)	turnkey projects abroad	small	similar	manufacturer
5	ongoing	project management abroad	large	similar	packager
6	ongoing (and ad hoc by project)	multiple products and turnkey projects abroad	small to medium	different	packager
7	ongoing	services	medium to large	similar	packager
8	ad hoc (new status now)	single turnkey project abroad	medium to large	different	packager
9	ongoing	multiple products and turnkey projects abroad	small to medium	different	manufacturer
10	ongoing	single product	medium to large	similar	producer
11	ongoing	turnkey projects abroad	small to medium	different	manufacturer
12	ongoing	single product	small to large	different	manufacturer
13	ongoing	turnkey projects abroad	medium to large	similar	manufacturer
14	ongoing	turnkey projects abroad	medium to large	similar	manufacturer
15	ongoing	single product	small	similar	manufacturer
16	ongoing	services and project management abroad	medium to large	similar	packager
17	was ongoing (now dormant)	single product	small	similar	manufacturer
18	ongoing	single product	small to medium	similar	producer
19	ongoing	single product	small to medium	different	producer
20	ongoing	turnkey project abroad	small to medium	different	packager
21	ongoing	single turnkey project abroad	medium to large	similar	manufacturer
22	ongoing	turnkey projects abroad	small to medium	different	packager
23	ongoing	services and project management abroad	large	similar	packager
24	was ongoing (now dormant)	single product	small	similar	manufacturer

(a) Identification withheld due to an expressed desire for anonymity by the leaders of most of the consortia.
(b) An "initiator" is often referred to as a "promoter".

of benefits derived by a member firm from participating in a consortium. Their responses are summarized in Table 2.

Table 2

Perceived Benefits of Marketing, Project Management, and Turnkey Consortia

(Sample Size of 15)	Rating[a]						
Benefit	Not Beneficial					Most Beneficial	
a) Rationalization of production	1	2	3	4	T	6	S
b) Strong organization for market penetration	1	2	3	4	5	S, T	7
c) Better distribution and delivery due to bulk sales	1	2	3	4	T	6	S
d) Additional revenue opportunities due to offshore sales	1	2	3	4	5	T	S
e) Elimination of intra-Canadian competition for foreign markets	1	2	3	T	S	6	7
f) Geographic diversification	1	2	3	4	T	S	7
g) Diversification through sharing of business risk	1	2	3	S	T	6	7
h) Allows entry by reducing the necessary initial investment	1	2	3	4	S, T	6	7
i) Greater ability to obtain financial backing	1	2	3	S	T	6	7
j) Improves decision making since "unanimous (or majority)" decision making protects against undesirable decisions	1	2	S	T	5	6	7

(a) S represents a consortium formed to export a single product. T represents a consortium formed to export multiple products and turnkeys.

Since "not applicable" responses are not included in the calculations, some bias is present in the ratings. However, the bias is only significant for benefits (a) and (c) for T consortia.

Other important benefits of consortium membership identified by the respondents included: (1) compensation for slack in domestic sales; (2) opportunity to participate in projects of broader scope; (3) participation in large-scale capital projects; (4) access to other skills and products; and (5) risk to be underwritten by sharing rather than by contingency markups.

The participants were also asked to rank the three most important of the ten benefits indicated in Table 2. The three most important benefits, in descending order of importance for single-product marketing consortia were: (1) better distribution and delivery due to bulk sales; (2) strong organization for market penetration; and (3) rationalization of production. For all other consortia, they were: (1) strong organization for market penetration; (2) additional revenue opportunities due to offshore sales; and (3) diversification through sharing of business risk.

Some interesting comments made by the respondents on the possible benefits from consortium participation include the following:

1. A consortium consisting of small members is not necessarily a stronger organization for market penetration if the consortium is pursuing turnkey projects. In fact, "many clients prefer to deal with a single large firm with a known record than with a patchwork (consortium) of small firms, no matter how highly competent the individual firms are".
2. Single-product (commodity) consortia obtain cost economies from better distribution and delivery due to bulk sales. For example, by pooling the product of its members, a consortium can lower freight costs by shipping via a unit train system.

Problems Encountered Within and by Marketing, Project Management, and Turnkey Consortia

The same consortia participants were asked to rate a number of problems encountered within/by a consortium. Their responses are summarized in Table 3.

Other important problems identified by the respondents included: (1) parental endorsement for participation by a subsidiary in a consortium; (2) negotiation of a project agreement; (3) funding by new participants; (4) cost escalation; (5) risk on local costs; (6) lack of delegation of management authority; and (7) "drop out" of key consortium members.

The participants were also asked to rank the three most critical of the sixteen problems shown in Table 3. The three most critical

Table 3

Perceived Problems Encountered Within and by Marketing, Project Management, and Turnkey Consortia

(Sample Size of 15)	Rating[a]						
Problem	Not Critical						Most Critical
a) Negotiation of a formal consortium agreement	1	2	3	4	T	S	7
b) Funding consortium start-up costs	1	S	3	T	5	6	7
c) Sales allocation among members	1	2	S	T	5	6	7
d) Ensuring continuous consortium participation	1	2	3	S, T	5	6	7
e) Distribution of profits	1	S	T	4	5	6	7
f) Insolvency of one or more members	1	2	S	T	5	6	7
g) Joint and several liability	1	2	3	S	T	6	7
h) Industrial espionage	S	T	3	4	5	6	7
i) Fear of government scrutiny of books	S	T	3	4	5	6	7
j) Fear of Combines Investigation Act	S	T	3	4	5	6	7
k) Characteristics of foreign markets	1	2	3	S	T	6	7
l) Possible involvement in illegal or unethical activities	1	S	T	4	5	6	7
m) Decision making	1	2	3	4	T	S	7
n) Disagreements among consortium participants	1	2	3	T	S	6	7
o) Disclosure for public participants	S	2	T	4	5	6	7
p) Performance of consortium leader	1	2	3	S	5	T	7

(a) *S* represents a consortium formed to export a single product. *T* represents a consortium formed to export multiple products and turnkeys.

Since "not applicable" responses are not included in the calculations, some bias is present in the rankings. However, the bias is only significant for problems (e), (h), (i), (l), and (o) for *T* consortia.

problems, in descending order of importance, for single-product marketing consortia were: (1) negotiation of a formal consortium agreement; (2) decision making; and (3) ensuring continuous consortium participation. For all other consortia, they were: (1) joint and several liability; (2) performance of consortium leader; and (3) negotiation of a formal consortium agreement.

Some interesting comments made by the respondents on the problems encountered within/by a Canadian-based consortium include the following:

1. If a potential member of a consortium is a subsidiary of a U.S. firm, it is unlikely to join the consortium because of the U.S. Antitrust Law. Before joining, the subsidiary usually will have to get clearance from the U.S. Department of Justice.

2. If the potential members of a consortium have had no previous experience in organizing a consortium and they do not consult an external expert, pre-incorporation is likely to be frustrating and lengthy. For example, it took one consortium under such conditions eighteen months before a consortium agreement was finalized.

3. The first pre-incorporation meeting for a consortium is used by the potential members to get familiar with each other. Then the group is addressed by a financial expert (often a banker), a representative from the Export Development Corporation (EDC), and a representative from the Department of Industry, Trade, and Commerce (IT and C).

4. The initial outlay necessary to fund a consortium's start-up costs, although small, deters many firms from joining a consortium. For example, in the initial formation of one consortium, a few firms would not participate financially. As a result, a promoter had to provide the funds for two of the consortium's members.

5. Since a particular consortium had a limited development budget of only $50,000, its manager tried to conserve funds by using one-day trips to conduct business. According to a participant from a facilitator organization, this type of consortium "can only succeed by pure luck".

6. Members of an ad hoc consortium are more likely to renege on a bid than those in an ongoing consortium.

7. Manufacturers and other members of a consortium often try to "play both ends".

8. Joint and several liability is a problem for many Canadian-based consortia because the consortia and many of their members are shell companies. On the other hand, joint and several liability is

not a problem for most foreign-based consortia since these
consortia generally contain manufacturers with substantial
financial standing.

9. Joint and several liability is a problem for most Canadian-based
consortia which have a subsidiary as a member. More specifically, the foreign parent often will not give the domestic subsidiary permission to assume liability on a joint and several basis.

10. When a member agrees to assume liability on a joint and several
basis, it is assuming its proportional share of the risk of the
weakest member(s). As a result, the consortium is not much
stronger than its weakest member.

11. Protecting against industrial espionage can be important when
the consortium consists of competing members involved in a
high-technology industry.

12. The fear of governmental scrutiny of books is important to
single-product export consortia involved in exporting natural
resources.

13. New consortia often fail because they do not understand the
characteristics of foreign markets such as the Middle East.

14. A general manager or chief officer of a consortium should be an
outsider with veto power. If this condition is not satisfied, the
general manager will not be able to resolve disagreements adequately among consortium members.

15. If the performance of the consortium leader is poor, one of the
members will become the informal leader. This informal leader
often becomes active in pursuing projects, not for the consortium, but for himself.

16. If a foreign subsidiary is a member of a consortium, it is often
difficult to ascertain whether or not it can, or wants to, bid on a
particular project.

17. With regard to turnkey projects, many clients prefer not to deal
with a consortium because this often results in "split responsibility".

18. If a consortium is involved in turnkey projects, the delineation
of responsibility among members must be clear. For example,
there must be a clearly specified agreement on who is responsible for the costs of errors.

Conclusion

In this chapter, a general and operational definition of the term
consortium, eight possible types of consortia classifications, and

some characteristics of the sample of Canadian-based limited liability consortia were first presented and discussed. Subsequently, the important benefits derived by a firm from participating in single-product, multiple-product, and turnkey consortia, and the critical problems encountered within and by these consortia were critically evaluated.

Since most of the Canadian-based limited liability consortia identified have been incorporated since 1972 and many are also unseasoned,[10] the findings of this study may be sample sensitive. A follow-up study of the consortia studied (and those more recently formed) may be required to establish whether or not the findings of this study will remain invariant over time.

10. An export consortia is unseasoned if it has never conducted business or exported abroad.

III
The Challenge of Overseas Markets

C
New Marketing Vehicles

17
The Pros and Cons of a National Export Trading House

Charles J. McMillan

Dr. McMillan is associate professor and director of the public administration program in the Faculty of Administrative Studies, York University. In addition to his teaching and research in the areas of public administration and international business, he has published several articles on the Japanese industrial system.

This chapter was written expressly for this volume.

Introduction

In recent years, Canada's chronic trade deficit in finished manufactured goods has prompted calls for various remedial policies. Not only do Canadian exports consist overwhelmingly of unprocessed raw materials and basic foodstuffs — finished end products were only 30 per cent of exports in 1978 — even for end products, 60 per cent have been in motor vehicles and 20 per cent in industrial and agricultural machinery.

In this context, there has been a major initiative to promote Canadian export trade, as announced in the Speech from the Throne on April 14, 1980. On that date, the federal government indicated its intention "to establish a national trading company . . . to improve the ability of Canadian industry to compete abroad in order to create jobs at home". Since then, the House of Commons has established a parliamentary committee to study the trading house idea, and hearings have been held in Ottawa and various cities across the country. As it happens, the U.S. Congress has also examined the desirability of the trading house approach to promote and expand U.S. exports,[1] although no legislation has been passed.

The subject of a national trading house for Canada has thus more than mere academic interest. Indeed, in some countries, most notably in Japan, trading houses are the most widely used vehicle for export trade. The subject is also timely, given the serious problems and challenges facing Canadian exporters in international markets. Foreign ownership, weak and unaggressive management, poor coordination of government export policies, problems in export finance — such are the familiar reasons often given for Canada's export plight. The trading firm concept is thus a potentially aggressive approach to promoting Canadian marketing in international trade.

This chapter examines the national trading house model as an instrument of national policy in the context of the trading house sector which already exists in Canada. Three areas are considered:

---

1. Adlai Stevenson, "Export Trading Companies and Trade Associations" (*Hearings,* Subcommittee on International Finance of the Committee on Banking, Housing, and Urban Affairs, U.S. Senate, Ninety-Sixth Congress, September 18-19, 1979).

(1) the strategy and structure of trading firms generally; (2) the model of trading houses as exemplified by their most prominent success, the Japanese *Sogo Shosha*, and their imitators elsewhere; and (3) a weighing of the pros and cons of a national trading house for Canada. Reference will be made to various initiatives taken in other countries, including new proposals for the development of export trading firms in the United States, and particular managerial issues which influence the government's role as "owner" of a trading firm.

Trading Firms: Concepts and Definitions

Historically the modern concept of the trading firm dates from the joint stock companies of the mercantile period in Britain and Europe. The main engine of growth was imperialist expansion, such that the organizational strategy of the trading concerns involved the control of end markets. In Japan, by contrast, foreign threats and geographical isolation led to the strategy of *Sogo Shosha* control of manufacturers in order to compete freely in international markets, usually with government support (*sogo* — "all around"; *shosha* — companies in foreign trade).

There is no precise definition of a trading house, since the manufacturing and marketing functions can vary tremendously, particularly when sales cross national borders, political jurisdictions, legal systems, cultural and organizational archetypes, and the like. Lancaster adopts the following definition: "A trading house is a non-manufacturing business entity conducting an international commercial activity, exporting, importing or a combination of both between two or more countries".[2] Ozawa, by contrast, defines trading firms as "industrial organizations unique to Japan, organizations whose existence is almost unparalleled elsewhere. There are literally thousands of trading companies in Japan (anywhere from 3,000 to 7,000, depending on the criteria used for classification)".[3]

In the simplest sense, a trading firm markets goods and services produced in one country to one or more other countries. Intermediary functions can be of a generalized or a specific type. For example, general functions can include the handling of paperwork for importing and exporting, obtaining foreign exchange, advising on transport

2. John Lancaster, "Sectoral Paper on Trading Houses in Canada" (Unpublished manuscript, Ottawa, ITC, 1980).
3. Terutomo, Ozawa, *Multinationalism, Japanese Style: The Political Economy of Outward Dependency* (Princeton, N.J.: Princeton University Press, 1979).

modes, arranging insurance, providing storage arrangements, and the like. Specific types of functions include obtaining and providing market research for clients, arranging financial credit, and linking clients to special agencies and new customers.

An important additional role for trading firms is to facilitate trade. Developing or actually creating trade flows can come about by identifying markets through specialized product scanning and organization unattainable by the producer at an acceptable cost. A trading firm, in short, is supply-demand-oriented rather than user- or maker-oriented.[4] In this respect, there are various possibilities. Trading houses can act for the producer as principal but on a contractual basis. For some products and markets, the trading house may itself become the principal, assuming the risks of selling to foreign markets. As will be seen below, this is the major strength of the large Japanese trading houses, although other forms exist; for example, a trading house may serve as agents for foreign buyers seeking produces in the local market.[5]

Of course, most marketing systems involve complex interactions of intermediaries, including agents, brokers, warehouses, advertising agencies, and similar bodies. The real question is to what extent does the marketing function dominate other functions in the total organization? In most North American firms, particularly those in manufacturing, the "modern" organizational design gives primacy, not equality, to marketing, as compared to production, research and development, or finance. Kotler outlines the perspective as follows:

A company can have a modern marketing department and yet not operate as a modern marketing company. Whether it is the latter depends upon how the officers of the company view the marketing function. If they view marketing as one of the several equal functions in the organization, the company is probably not a modern marketing company. If they view marketing as the hub of the enterprise, and not just one of its spokes, the company has achieved modern marketing stature.[6]

From an organizational viewpoint, there are two general perspectives of the linkage between the manufacturer and the customer. In

4. Arthur Anderson and Co., "U.S. Companies in International Markets — The Role of Trading Companies in Stimulating Exports" (*Brief* submitted to Committee on Banking, Housing, and Urban Affairs, U.S. Senate, 1979).
5. Markisa Emori, *Japanese General Trading Companies* (Tokyo, 1971) and Alexander Young, *The Sogo Shosha: Japan's Multinational Trading Companies* (Boulder, Colorado: Westview Press, 1979).
6. Phillip Kotler, *Marketing Management: Analysis, Planning and Control* (Englewood Cliffs, N.J.: Prentice-Hall Inc., 1976).

the first case, and the one prevailing in North America, the linkage should be direct with no, or at least minimal, intermediaries. Manufacturers thus desire direct access to customers and their feedback, and with it, prefer to avoid any loss of marketing control and perceived isolation. This argument for integration usually involves the range of incentives for scale economies of distribution, inventory management, and customer servicing. In short, there are high transaction costs for these functions and the typical response is to internalize them through forward integration.[7]

In the second case, the manufacturing organization specializes in the production function and "contracts" out the marketing function to an external organization, the trading firm. Conceptually, the main argument for this approach is the economies of scale in the total marketing function of many products and specialized services. For the trading firm, the major financial obstacles are high start-up costs in personnel, market research, and distribution channel information and control. Once developed, however, incremental costs of volume expansion are quite low, since the main transaction costs are informational. Properly organized for bridging information linkages between many manufacturers and many consumers, the trading firm can afford to work on high volumes and low margins, even for low value-added, standardized products. Japan historically has been the best example of this approach.

For the trading firm operating on an international basis of even minimal scale, the key operating asset is thus informational: the range and quality of trading contacts; the human capital of skills and experience in particular products, markets, functions, or services; and the hardware systems of on-line communication flows, ranging from personal meetings, telephone calls, and computer systems, to the ubiquitous Telex. In Japan, where these informational linkages easily rival most countries' diplomatic network, overseas personnel of firms like Mitsui, Mitsubishi, and Marubeni are coupled directly to their offices in Tokyo and Osaka from more than 100 countries. According to one Japanese trading firm "our company has 130 bases in the world connected by Telex. The total length of our communications network is 400,000 kilometers — equivalent to four circumnavigations of the earth. There are 20,000 messages every day. On the basis of information coming in from all over the world, many factors, such as commodities, freight charges, and foreign exchange rates, are brought together in order to conduct transactions and analyse the possibilities for long term projects".[8]

7. Oliver Williamson, *Markets and Hierarchies* (New York: The Free Press, 1975).
8. Marubeni, 1978.

This huge informational base and communication system are somewhat akin to what MacRae calls the organizational confederation of entrepreneurs,[9] since in practice, trading firms operate with a very high element of entrepreneurial decentralization. To function as such, however, trading firms need not only informational resources, but a financial asset base to provide credit, absorb foreign exchange rate risks and costs, and act as financial agent for producer firms, particularly small businesses. In some cases, the financial role may go beyond these functions to include equity investment, direct loans, or guarantee for loans, although this approach has developed only recently.[10]

The Japanese Sogo Shosha

The recurrent problems of low productivity growth in North America and the dynamism and technological sophistication of Japan have prompted the search for lessons in export trade there. Potential areas of learning from Japanese practice include methods of industrial strategy and planning[11] and the Japanese export trading houses, the *Sogo Shosha*.[12] Academic interest in the *Sogo Shosha* has been minimal, although Young's study has partly filled a void, at least from a U.S. perspective.[13] In Canada, Tsurumi provides an overview of the *Sogo Shosha* and tries to make a case for their establishment in Canada.[14] As already noted, the parliamentary hearings on the trading house idea sheds additional light on various symptoms and problems of Canadian export marketing. In all this, Japan is clearly the reference point.

In fact, Japanese trading firms trace their modern structures and policies to the early days of the Meiji Revolution in 1868. When Japan first opened the doors to international commerce, companies like Mitsui and Mitsubishi established trading houses with government support to cope with the specialized needs of both exports and imports.[15] These and other trading firms were an integral part of the

9. Norman MacRae, "The Coming Entrepreneurial Revolution", *The Economist* (December 1976).
10. Japan External Trade Organization (JETRO), *The Role of Trading Companies in International Commerce*, Marketing Series 2, Revised (Tokyo, 1980).
11. D. Horvath and Charles McMillan, "Industrial Planning in Japan", *California Management Review* (Fall 1980), pp. 1-14.
12. Yoshi Tsurumi, *Sogo Shosha: Engines of Export-Led Growth* (Montreal: IRPP, 1980).
13. Young, *The Sogo Shosha*.
14. Tsurumi, *Sogo Shosha*.
15. Hidemasa Morikawa, "The Organizational Structures of Mitsubishi and Mitsui Zaibatsu, 1868-1922: A Comparative Study", *Business History Review* 44 (Spring 1970).

pre-war industrial groups, the *Zaibatsus*,[16] although their present size, success, and prominence clearly dates from the post-war era. Actually there are three kinds of trading firms in Japan and each serves quite different needs. The first kind is the best known, namely the *Sogo Shosha*, the huge firms, nine in number, which dominate Japan's export and import trade. As shown in Table 1, the *Sogo Shosha* are not only giant firms in themselves, with total sales turn-over in excess of $220 billion, they are the central institutions in Japan's total international trade. Their activities are not just the buying and selling of goods, services, and commodities; they serve as bankers in lending credit and finance; they act as principals and co-ordinators in exporting turnkey projects and plants, establishing overseas joint ventures, and serving as a linking agency for third

Table 1

Breakdown of Top Nine General Trading Houses' Turnover in FY 1978

	Turnover	Breakdown			
		Exports	Imports	Domestic	Overseas
	(Value Y1,000 million)				
1) Mitsubishi Corp.	8,837 (100%) 19%	1,700 (19%) 18%	2,251 (26%) 26%	4,350 (49%) 19%	536 (6%) 12%
2) Mitsui & Co.	8,361 (100%) 18%	1,590 (19%) 17%	1,648 (20%) 19%	4,462 (53%) 19%	661 (8%) 15%
3) C. Itoh & Co.	6,561 (100%) 14%	1,327 (20%) 14%	994 (15%) 11%	3,456 (53%) 15%	784 (12%) 18%
4) Marubeni Corp.	6,271 (100%) 14%	1,636 (26%) 17%	962 (15%) 11%	2,837 (45%) 12%	836 (13%) 19%
5) Sumitomo Corp.	5,849 (100%) 13%	1,234 (21%) 13%	809 (14%) 9%	3,502 (60%) 15%	304 (5%) 7%
6) Nissho-Iwai	4,177 (100%) 9%	846 (20%) 9%	834 (20%) 10%	2,085 (50%) 9%	412 (10%) 10%
7) Toyo Menka	2,136 (100%) 5%	479 (22%) 5%	418 (20%) 5%	888 (42%) 4%	351 (16%) 8%
8) Kanematsu-Gosho	2,040 (100%) 4%	313 (15%) 3%	469 (23%) 5%	1,093 (54%) 5%	165 (8%) 4%
9) Nichimen Co.	1,789 (100%) 4%	479 (27%) 5%	346 (19%) 4%	694 (39%) 3%	270 (15%) 6%
Total	46,021 (100%) 100%	9,604 (21%) 100%	8,731 (19%) 100%	23,367 (51%) 100%	4,319 (9%) 100%

16. Kozo Yanamura, "General Trading Companies in Japan — Their Origins and Growth", ed. Hugh Patrick, *Japanese Industrialization and Its Social Conse- quences* (Berkeley: University of California Press, 1976).

country trade, thanks to their enormous global information systems. As such, these firms are highly diverse and operate on huge sales volumes and low profit margins. Mitsubishi, for example, had total sales in 1978 of U.S. $40 billion, but a profit margin of only .18 of 1 per cent on sales. The same small net profit also applies to the other *Sogo Shosha*, usually less than a quarter of 1 per cent, but varying by size of firm, product range, markets, and general economic conditions.

The extreme diversity of the *Sogo Shosha* contrasts with the second type of Japanese trading firm, the specialized trading house. These firms number in the thousands and limit their operations to quite specialized and focussed strategies. Some firms may handle only particular product lines in a large number of markets. Some specialize by product and market, or even a region of Japan. For example, one small trading firm concentrates only on hospital supplies manufactured goods in southern Japan for Asian markets. Another medium-size firm concentrates on motors and pumps, and focusses on the markets of the Middle East and Francophone Africa, mainly from an office in Tokyo and an agency in Paris. Almost all these specialized trading houses handle all the trading functions, from transport to freight to customs and credit.

The third type of trading firm in Japan and one of the fastest growing, are the sales arms of captive manufacturing firms, such as those in electronics, automobiles, office equipment, and precision machinery. In this category are the sales firms of the automobile firms (for example, Toyota Motor Sales) and the electronic firms (for example, Matsushita Electric). The main reason for the development of these trading firms is the need of the manufacturer to establish direct customer contact, to handle after-sales servicing, and to establish a brand name image and dealer network. As it turns out, many of these firms are branching out to other products, as well as participating in foreign ventures via direct investment.

Despite the variety of size, type, and function, the Japanese trading firms are extremely competitive, even within product groups. For example, while the *Sogo Shosha* are spread throughout Japan and around the world in a bewildering array of products, markets, services, and third nation trade flows, within specific market segments in Japan competition for trade is severe. For instance, there are one thousand small trading firms importing food products, 900 handling textiles, 500 dealing in logs and lumber, another thousand in machinery.[17] In 1980, there were more than 30,000 Japanese employed

17. JETRO, *Role of Trading Companies.*

in the overseas operations of Japan's trading houses — the nine *Sogo Shosha* alone had 908 overseas offices.

To understand the real scope and operations of the Japanese trading house sector, three points are critical. First, there must be a recognition that the entire economy runs on the basis of the trading firm model, domestic sales as well as imports and exports. This means that the corporate strategies of individual producers are predicated on the presence of the trading firms, and their provision of business credit, loans and payment guarantees, and secured market outlets. It follows, therefore, that any transfer of the trading house concept to another country, especially for a single firm, must take this cumulative impact of thousands of specialized trading firms into account.

A second fundamental consideration is the style of management and commercial expertise which is so highly developed in the trading house sector. Operating with huge volumes but very low margins, the trading firms are, in fact, collections of individual brokers and traders linked to contacts, agents, producers, and customers in international markets. Like most Japanese corporations, the trading firms recruit from the best universities, but the formal education is typically general — specialized training takes place within the firm. Canadian or even American business school education is not terribly relevant for the trading firm system of management, where the emphasis is almost exclusively on marketing, distribution, and finance. Further, the Japanese companies have centuries of traditions and practices to draw on, and these are not easily copied or transferred abroad. This organizational entrepreneurship in trading houses is not as easily exportable as management practice in manufacturing.[18]

The third basic point is that in their trading functions, the Japanese firms are not only exporters but also importers (often providing the first export sales of foreign firms). The *Sogo Shosha* account for about half of all Japanese imports (Table 2) and in some cases, 80 or 90 per cent of the imports of particular commodities. There is thus enormous concentration of economic power and potential for harmful corporate behavior from the perspective of the consumer. Obviously Japan's position as a resource-poor, "through-put" economy contributes to the concentration of the import functions of the trading firms. Such imports tend to be unprocessed, standardized commodities whose selling price is set in world markets. Dealing in high import volumes tends to cushion the financial risks of export

---

18. Charles McMillan, "Is Japanese Management Really So Different?" *The Business Quarterly* (Fall 1980).

trade, since costs of global information and distribution systems, currency fluctuations, and buffer inventories can be spread across both imports and exports. It is no accident, of course, that the *Sogo Shosha* are leading the way in Japanese direct overseas investment, often with domestic manufacturers participating in equity along with host country firms.

By the end of 1978, foreign investment by the *Sogo Shosha* amounted to U.S. $4 billion, an increase of 33 per cent since 1974. Mitsui and Co. led the way with almost 30 per cent of the *Sogo Shosha's* total investment.

Table 2

Top Nine General Trading Houses' Shares in Japan's Total Exports and Imports

	Japan's			Top 9 General Trading Houses			Ratios		
	GNP (A)	Total Exports (B)	Total Imports (C)	Turnover (D)	Exports (E)	Imports (F)	D-A	E-B	F-C
(Value Y1,000 million)									
1969	64,514	6,047	5,761	16,706	2,857	3,599	25.9%	47.2%	62.5%
1970	75,524	7,290	6,967	20,565	3,509	4,365	27.2%	48.1%	62.7%
1971	83,165	8,474	6,824	22,499	4,314	4,140	27.0%	50.9%	60.7%
1972	96,884	9,071	7,659	26,618	4,555	4,797	27.5%	50.2%	62.6%
1973	117,258	10,877	12,369	38,320	5,767	8,004	32.7%	53.0%	64.7%
1974	139,219	17,080	18,276	46,841	9,577	10,462	33.7%	56.1%	57.2%
1975	153,126	17,026	17,396	45,321	9,453	9,550	29.6%	55.5%	54.9%
1976	171,736	20,669	19,713	49,914	10,636	10,408	29.1%	51.5%	52.8%
1977	191,426	21,790	18,509	47,009	10,860	9,204	24.6%	49.8%	49.7%
1978	210,636	19,990	17,057	46,021	9,604	8,730	21.9%	48.0%	51.2%
Annual Growth (1969-1978)	14.1%	14.2%	12.8%	11.9%	14.4%	10.4%	—	—	—

Source: GNP: Economic Planning Agency; Japan's total imports and exports: Ministry of Finance.

Note: Figures of Ataka & Co., which was absorbed by C. Itoh & Co. in 1977, are included in (D), (E), and (F) for 1969-76.

The obvious scope and success of the Japanese trading firms in promoting export marketing have prompted other countries to study the Japanese model. Some countries, such as South Korea, Brazil, and Mexico have actually copied the organizational strategy and form of the Japanese trading house for domestic enterprises, and each country has had active assistance from Japanese companies. The Korean government in particular has pushed the trading house sector. Since

1975, Korea promoted the establishment of firms and adopted special policies, such as providing low-interest loans and guaranteeing quick processing of export orders through customs. Specific growth targets were set, such as the volume of total exports handled by trading firms, the numbers of items exported which exceeded U.S. $1 million, the number of overseas branches developed, and the like. By 1979, twelve major trading firms had evolved, all privately owned, and they had 302 overseas branches, of which only 25 per cent were in Asia. Nineteen per cent were in the Middle East, 18 per cent in Europe, 17 per cent in North America, 11 per cent in Africa, and 9 per cent in South America and Middle Europe. Growth rates for 1976 to 1978 were 102 per cent, 93.5 per cent, and 22.4 per cent. Of the total exports in 1978 of U.S. $3,985, not quite a third of all Korean exports that year, Dae Woo Industrial Co. was the most successful, with export sales of U.S. $705.8, a growth rate of 437 per cent in four years (Table 3).

Trading Firms in Canada

The announcement of the government's intention to establish a national trading house, and the parliamentary hearings on the subject, have served to focus attention on what hitherto has been a neglected aspect of Canada's export activities. A symptom of this problem has been the lamentable shortage of data on the size and scope of the trading sector in Canada. The Canadian Export Association publishes a directory of Canadian firms by name, product, and markets served. Lancaster carried out a survey on the sector and discovered there are about 600 trading firms operating in Canada.[19] These firms range in size from a one-man agency to a large multinational conglomerate conducting more than a billion dollars in two-way trade. Moreover, within the vast sector of Canadian wholesalers and distributors, there are about 5000-6000 firms doing an estimated $12 billion in total trade, of which about 450 do a substantial volume.

Lancaster estimates that some 10 per cent of Canada's 1978 exports were channelled through trading firms.[20] In contrast, the nine large *Sogo Shosha* handle about half of Japan's export trade. Trading firms handle about a third of exports in France and the Netherlands, about 30 per cent in West Germany, 20 per cent in Britain, and 15 per cent in Sweden. Even for the United States, where the trading house concept is not widespread, trading firms channelled between 20 and 40 per cent of all exports.

19. Lancaster, "Trading Houses".
20. *Ibid*.

By any international comparison, there is strong ground to believe that a strengthening of Canada's trading house sector is in order. Indeed several provincial governments have developed Crown corporations to improve export trade, and in recent years, many of the largest Canadian firms such as Alcan, Brascan, Inco, MacMillan Bloedel, and Noranda, have established trading arms to serve international markets. Thus there are really two questions at issue: first, how can Canada's trading sector be cultivated and improved; and second, how or why could the establishment of a national trading house improve Canada's export trade?

The only academic study to look into the second question is the recently published monograph of Tsurumi. He bases his argument for a Canadian *Sogo Shosha* primarily on the growing dependence of Canadian exporters on the U.S. market and on the implication that "Canadian manfacturing firms have not cultivated export markets other than the U.S." Tsurumi adds, "as compared with the United States, Canada does not have many medium-sized manufacturing firms that can become export-oriented very easily. Therefore in Canada much greater efforts by governments and industry should be made, not only to develop Canadian *Sogo Shosha*, but, more importantly, to link them with special policies to promote Canadian small- and medium-sized manufacturing firms."[21]

Table 3

The Twelve Largest Korean Trading Companies

Name	Capital Stock	Exports 1975	1978	Overseas Branches	Local Affiliates
	(000s of U.S. dollars)				
Korea Trading International Inc.	3,093	11.9	31.3	6	
ICC Corporation	13,773	63.7	472.3	23	17
Kumho and Co., Inc.	10,309	32.3	256.0	20	11
Dae Woo Industrial Co., Ltd.	84,124	161.0	705.8	48	24
Bondo Sangsa Co., Ltd.	8,247	31.1	329.6	23	16
Sam Sung Co., Ltd.	24,742	223.2	439.4	32	24
Samhwa Co., Ltd.	11,340	27.9	260.6	21	14
Sun Kyong Ltd.	15,464	55.8	283.4	23	8
Ssangyong Corporation	6,186	125.4	264.5	22	10
Hanil Synthetic Fiber Ind. Co. Ltd.	41,561	66.2	188.3	26	5
Hyundai Corporation	16,495	—	259.7	31	25
Hyasing Corporation	10,309	34.1	337.8	27	14

Source: Ahn, Kwon and Co., Seoul, Korea.

21. Tsurumi, *Sogo Shosha*.

Tsurumi offers three models or alternatives for Canadian *Sogo Shosha*, based on the Japanese, Korean, and Brazilian examples. The first model is to build around commodity exports, such as wheat, pulp, or raw materials. The second model is to organize a trading firm around imports, especially of standard products which do not require technical assistance or after-sale service. The third choice is to cultivate direct supply contracts with final buyers in foreign countries. Tsurumi comes to the conclusion that:

> The success of Canadian exports, independent of the American parent firms' captive purchases from their Canadian subsidiaries, depends upon independent marketing activities outside Canada by Canadian trading and manufacturing firms . . . Canada should create at least two Canadian Soga Shosha. They should be explicitly encouraged to compete with one another as well as with the Japanese Soga Shosha and foreign multinationals in Canada. Rather than colluding with Canadian Sogo Shosha, the Japanese Sogo Shosha could be counted on to provide sharp competition.

Tsurumi is not explicit on the need for a government-owned trading firm.

The main arguments in favor of a new, national *Sogo Shosha*, drawing on the foreign experience of other countries, appear to include the following:

1. It would act as a vehicle for export promotion of small and medium-size firms not now exporting.
2. It would build a high threshold level of trading expertise and market information not presently available in an institutionalized format.
3. It would overcome the problem of foreign ownership, where most foreign subsidiaries lack a mandate to export Canadian-made products abroad or to compete against the parent or other subsidiaries of the same firm.
4. It would link the financial functions of international trade with the marketing functions, and reduce perceived risks which present government export promotion policies fail to do.
5. Government backing would provide the financial muscle necessary to provide trade credits, which are the main limiting barriers to a *Sogo Shosha's* mercantile activities.

Such arguments all have the fundamental premise that the deficiency in Canada's export trade performance is primarily a marketing weakness. A rather different perspective is to consider the weaknesses in Canada's trade performance to exist in its industrial structure and system of production, particularly in the capacity to develop entrepreneurial talent, encourage new firm formation, and adopt up-to-date technology.[22] It should not go unnoticed that it is Japan where the trading firm concept is most successfully applied *and* where small business thrives in terms of employment, exports, and new company formation, despite a high bankruptcy level.

This consideration gives a different perspective to the role of the trading firm sector and Canada's trade position, but there are specific reasons for questioning the need for a national trading firm along the lines recommended by Tsurumi and political spokesmen.[23] Five major points stand out: (1) trading firms operate best with standardized, low value-added products, not high-technology products or services; (2) the financial problems of small and medium-size companies, while real, may be overcome by adding a middleman, even on subsidized terms; (3) international trade is increasingly shifting to consortia structures and turnkey "systems" projects which require novel organizational joint-venturing which even several, let alone one or two trading firms, would not be well equipped to promote; (4) trading firms develop economies on import and export trade, as well as on offshore trade, and for Canada imports are largely captive to foreign enterprises; (5) the trading corporation's incentive and motivation system are basically individual and small group oriented to particular companies, and a government corporation would be subject to extremely adverse political cross currents. Each issue will be elaborated.

Standardized vs. Value-added Products
The Japanese economy is subject to a number of shifting production trends, one of which is the emergence of high-technology manufacturing concerns which have the financial clout to develop their own international marketing expertise without their former clients, the *Sogo Shosha*. In the high-technology sector, where a product sale forms part of a package of servicing (for example, distribution) and after-sales functions (for example, repairs and provision of newer ancillary equipment), some authors see the decline of the trading firm and the pre-eminence of the manufacturer.[24]

22. Charles McMillan, "The Changing Competitive Environment of Canadian Business", *Journal of Canadian Studies* (Spring 1978) and Rein Peterson, *Small Business: Towards a Balanced Economy* (Toronto, 1977).
23. Carey French, "Trudeau Is Expected to Unveil Study on Trading Corporation", *Globe and Mail* (April 11, 1980), p. B5.
24. Kiyoshi Kojima, *Japanese Direct Foreign Investment* (Tokyo: Charles Tuttle, 1978).

For Canada, this hypothesis would argue that a public or private trading corporation would operate most efficiently in the area of standardized, low value-added products. Yet this is precisely the area where Canadian exports are concentrated. Indeed the country's export position is consistently made up of 50 per cent or more of trade in unprocessed or semi-processed products, with the primary demand influenced by economic conditions totally outside Canada's control. It remains unclear how a trading firm, even one with monopoly advantages such as those once enjoyed by Inco in nickel, would greatly increase the demand for such products.

Trading Firms and the Financial Function
There can be little question about the critical role of the Japanese *Sogo Shosha* in their financial intermediary role of providing loans and trade credits. However, to fully appreciate the financial leverage of the Japanese trading firms, one has to analyse the role of the commercial banking system and the central bank, particularly with respect to the provisions for indirect finance. Equity involvement is usually small, but possible as a last resort.[25]

In Canada, of course, the banking system operates on totally different lines and a main deficiency of export finance is in multilateral bank financing. Japan, Britain, and most European countries provide a variety of programs to assure a favorable tax and non-tax export incentive environment.[26] The evidence of such Canadian studies as that of the Export Promotion Review Committee suggest that the federal government has a way to go to fulfill this function for export promotion but there already exists a variety of institutions to cope with these problems. It remains a formidable leap in logic to argue for the need of a government-owned institution organized along the lines of the trading firm concept to compensate for the inadequacies of existing public institutions.

Consortia and Turnkey Projects
Closely related to the financial dimension in international marketing is the growing importance of "systems selling", that is the sale of complete manufacturing plants or service establishments, from telecommunication and broadcasting systems to hospitals and urban transportation networks. The sheer size of these contracts, often

---

25. Lawrence Krause and Sueo Sekiguchi, "Japan and the World Economy", ed. Hugh Patrick and Henry Rosovsky, *Asia's New Giant* (Washington: The Brookings Institution, 1976) and Yosio Suzuki, *Money and Banking in Contemporary Japan* (New Haven: Yale University Press, 1980).
26. Anderson, "U.S. Companies in International Markets".

measured in billions of dollars, usually requires consortia organizational structures, novel financial arrangements, and active involvement of domestic consulting engineering firms in the initial stages of the total project (see chapters 15, 16, 31, and 41 of this book).

In Japan, the trading firms are a natural vehicle to act as a catalyst to bring the various consulting, financial, legal, and manufacturing organizations under an umbrella framework for consortia bidding. But it remains uncertain why this would be the case in Canada, even more so in a government organization. In fact, however, the major deterrents seem to be less the presence of potential Canadian participating companies as much as the absence of competitive financial terms, insurance schemes, risk absorption measures, and willingness of major firms to act as prime contractor (see Chapter 41 of this book).

Canada's Captive Import Picture
A recurrent theme of most analyses of foreign trading firms is their key role in both imports and exports. Assuming for the moment the likelihood of one or more newly established Canadian *Sogo Shosha*, there is the question of how and where imports would enter the picture. In the case of certain strategic imports, such as oil, a basic rationale for the establishment of Petrocan was to handle government-to-government import deals. But as most Canadian imports are finished goods, controlled directly by U.S.-owned firms, there seems little room for using even government leverage to establish a dominant, let alone a secondary position, for even one Canadian trading firm.

Even for non-American trade, British, European, and Japanese firms have established very strong footholds in the Canadian market which no private or government-owned trading firm is going to supplant. In the case of the Japanese, to take one example, both Mitsui and Mitsubishi have Canadian sales in excess of $1.2 billion. Of Japan's total of 1,230 overseas projects as of September 30, 1977, there were 51 in Canada by the top ten *Sogo Shosha*, compared to only 176 in the U.S. and 112 in Europe.[27]

Incentive and Motivation Systems
Trading firms operate as a system of mini-firms specialized by function, product, or markets, blending individual incentives to market opportunities. The larger the trading firm, the more complex the range of transactions and the more specialized the trading terms of

27. Sogo Shosha Yearbook (Tokyo, Japan, 1977).

particular deals. As Tsurumi argues, it takes a particular blend of organizational talents to couple the enormous entrepreneurial initiative required of the trading firm to the special range of incentives needed to attract and keep qualified employees.[28] Nowhere is there any discussion of how this human chemistry will work within the corporate culture of a government bureaucracy, or why this form is even remotely preferable to a promotion of the existing mixture of the private trading firm sector.

The issue of incentives and rewards is most stark at the level of firm-to-firm transactions. Specialized knowledge, interpersonal trust, a long-term perspective, and a back-up of market and financial knowledge are all critical factors in any trading firm manufacturing relationship. None of these factors can be standardized or subjected to a rigid set of rules and procedures, let alone precise incentives. Yet even in only a fraction of cases, a public trading firm operating on such premises could become immediately susceptible to a bewildering array of political pressures to offer more favorable terms, alter existing terms, promote particular areas and products, package the deal in this or that format. Expecting any public corporation, subject to the slightest whiff of political input, to act other than as a political organization is probably unrealistic.

Summary and Conclusions

The dynamic influences in international trade and Canada's flexible response to them require an increasing level of sophistication and awareness, particularly when the performance of the largest trading partner, the United States, is itself facing severe productivity problems. In this regard, any proposals and policy initiatives to promote Canadian export trade should be greeted as signs of such sophistication. In the case of the *Sogo Shosha* proposal, there is almost interest by association, namely an extremely successful Japanese model in the world's most dynamic economy.

This chapter has examined the pros and cons of the national trading house model for Canada, and the trading house sector in Canada's export marketing activities. The basic argument of the chapter is that, while it is difficult to transfer the trading house model from Japan to Canada in any comprehensive fashion, there is much to be learned both about supporting and building the sector and in training managers to run it. At a general level, there are a variety of initiatives which could add to the vitality of the trading firm sector.

28. Tsurumi, *Sogo Shosha*.

There could be more innovative policies to help the financial health of trading firms, including the provisions of loans and grants hitherto limited to manufacturers. The government could act as a catalyst in promoting the formation of a sector association to provide policy input on trade policies at the federal and provincial level. There could be vastly more informational and educational resources to promote the trading company concept for small and medium-size businesses and to prepare publicity brochures, possibly along the line of Japan's External Trade Organization (JETRO). Special tax incentives might include special reserves for up front marketing costs in overseas markets, especially where, as in Japan, formidable language and distribution problems exist. Other policy considerations to develop the sector include allowing immediate tax write offs of export marketing investments, travel assistance for export promotion and industrial trade shows similar to that offered manufacturing firms, and improved information services which would bring about better linkages between potential buyers and sellers.

The training of managers could also be greatly improved on the basis of co-operation between government, universities, and business. The most acute problem is the general lack of awareness of the specialized skills of export traders. Business school courses are a good starting point for change, but trading skills need on-the-job learning as in Japan. Student apprenticeships in overseas businesses or at foreign trade desks of the Canadian government would be a good start, as would student research work on foreign trading firms, not just in Japan, but in Europe, and Third World countries.

In the final analysis, Canada's trade performance is a long-term problem which requires the treatment of real problems, not just symptoms. The trading firm sector is vital to Canada's export activities, but no single corporation, publicly or privately owned, is going to solve the basic issue of developing competitive products for the global market place. The Japanese and other models may help Canadians learn new skills, but in the long run, the only real solutions are those developed by Canadian skills and institutions.

IV
Foreign Direct Investment Theory, Impact, and Control

Foreign direct investment — in which business firms participate directly in the management and control of subsidiaries in other countries — has important consequences both for business management and for public policy. Canadian companies have direct investments in many countries abroad. Their managers are thus involved in a much wider range of complex international business management decisions than those in firms whose international activity is limited to exports. At the same time, Canada is the world's largest host or recipient of foreign direct investment by firms in other countries. Questions concerning the impact of foreign ownership, and appropriate public response, are of major concern to Canadians and the subject of current debate.

The first two chapters of this section present the theoretical foundations of foreign direct investment. Calvet (Chapter 18) summarizes the main theoretical approaches, including significant recent developments. Rugman (Chapter 19) further reviews the literature and elaborates on the theory of internalization as an explanatory model.

The following four chapters give an overview of foreign direct investment, both by Canadian firms abroad and by foreign firms in Canada. Gherson, Gratton, and McMillan (Chapter 20) profile the size and patterns of direct investments in

Canada by firms from several countries and regions. Litvak and Maule, in related chapters (21 and 22), discuss the characteristics of Canadian direct investments abroad, both by the large Canadian-based multinationals and by smaller Canadian firms. Wright (Chapter 23) focusses on the problems of managing Canadian joint-venture investments in Japan.

Three chapters discuss the impact of foreign direct investments in Canada from different perspectives. Murray (Chapter 24) describes the rise of Canadian nationalism and presents survey results which reveal Canadians' attitudes toward foreign ownership. Hurtig (Chapter 25), representing the view of many Canadian nationalists, argues that foreign domination costs Canadians jobs and undermines Canada's economic prospects. Globerman (Chapter 26) presents the contrasting results of an econometric study designed to measure the economic efficiency benefits of foreign direct investment in Canada.

The final two chapters focus on Canada's attempt to control foreign direct investment through the Foreign Investment Review Agency (FIRA). Dewhirst (Chapter 27) describes FIRA's review process and evaluation criteria. Twaalfhoven (Chapter 28) offers the critical view of a foreign business manager who has dealt with FIRA.

IV
Foreign Direct Investment Theory, Impact, and Control

A
Theory

18
Foreign Direct Investment Theories and Theories of the Multinational Firm: A Canadian Perspective

A. L. Calvet

Dr. Calvet is an assistant professor in the Faculty of Administration at the University of Ottawa. He has worked in advisory capacities to government and business in Canada and Venezuela and has published several articles in the areas of international business and finance.

This chapter was written expressly for this volume.

Introduction

The issue of multinational enterprises (MNEs) has been heartily debated over the last decade, particularly the impact of MNEs on the economies of the host countries. In addition to the research conducted on the external effects of these large firms, there have been a number of theoretical and empirical studies offering explanations for the phenomenon of international production, which have increased in frequency in recent years.[1] This chapter will classify and review these theories and identify conceptual trends likely to guide future research in this field. A secondary objective is to evaluate the relevance of these theories in a Canadian perspective.

Historically, it has been customary to distinguish between the period starting in the mid- to late 1950s during which international production, financed by foreign direct investment (FDI),[2] began to assume an impressive magnitude, and the situation prior to the Second World War, when portfolio capital flows were the dominant component of the international transfer of resources.[3] The growth of FDI brought about important changes in the composition of international resource flows and in the channels through which these flows took place.

1. See, for instance, P. J. Buckley and M. C. Casson, *The Future of the Multinational Enterprise* (London: The MacMillan Press, 1976); N. Hood and S. Young, *The Economics of Multinational Enterprise* (London: Longman, 1979); and A. M. Rugman, *International Diversification and the Multinational Enterprise* (Lexington, Mass.: Lexington Books, 1979).
2. Strictly speaking, foreign direct investment flows are capital flows involving no change in ownership, that is, foreign direct investors maintain equity-based control over foreign operations.
3. It should be emphasized that the growth of FDI after the Second World War was dominated by one home country, the U.S., and that portfolio capital flows, which are essentially financial transactions between independent lenders and borrowers, remained the main transfer vehicles for Europeans to invest in North America. See G. Ragazzi, "Theories of the Determinants of Direct Foreign Investment", *IMF Staff Papers* (July 1973), pp. 471-498. Since the late 1960s, one feature of the changing pattern of international production has been the diversification of its country of origin. For more details, see the excellent paper by J. H. Dunning, "Explaining Changing Patterns of International Production: In Defence of the Eclectic Theory", *Oxford Bulletin of Economics and Statistics* (November 1979), pp. 269-295.

Research efforts to explain the expansion of multinational production did not always meet with success. Early attempts to relate foreign direct investment to capital theory were flawed by the realization that within an MNE's network, goods, services, financial capital, information, etc., all flow between the headquarters and the subsidiaries, as well as among the subsidiaries themselves, so that the flow of capital could not be considered as being unidirectional or even of foremost importance.

Neither were references to trade theory helpful in explaining the phenomenon of international production. The reason was that international trade theory had evolved at a level of abstraction not easily compatible with the existence and role of MNEs in the world economy. The main agents in international trade are nations which engage in exchanges of goods and services, supposedly via independent domestic firms transacting at arm's length prices. In the multinational network, however, the parent firm and the subsidiaries trade between themselves mostly at prices which are internally and administratively determined. Hence, attempts to explain foreign involvement with reference to country-specific factors, that is, expressions of comparative advantage, found only limited success, for, as it has been pointed out, the real issue is not "why locate economic activity in a particular country?" but "why locate economic activity within a particular firm at a certain time?"

The previous comments suggest that rather than take a trade or capital flow approach, it is more relevant to investigate the reasons why firms expanding abroad would be more inclined to internalize their international activities than carry them out through external means — most frequently the market place, for example, by exporting or licensing to autonomous foreign partners. There is another way of phrasing this same question while making specific reference to the mode of transacting chosen: why would a firm going abroad prefer to establish a bureaucratic, hierarchical relationship based upon ownership with a foreign firm, rather than a relationship based upon arm's length contracting?

With the above question in mind, this chapter will proceed by first reviewing previous surveys of the determinants of foreign direct investment. In the second section a taxonomy based upon the market imperfections paradigm will be proposed, the existing literature will be classified, and the various theories will be evaluated as to how they can be put to use to explain FDI in Canada. The third section singles out recent contributions to the theory of MNEs and assesses their relevance for the Canadian situation. The fourth section points to areas for future study.

A Review of Recent Surveys

The purpose of reviewing previous surveys is to gain an insight into the various ways in which several authors have classified the literature on foreign direct investment and to evaluate critically which classification seems to encompass more fully the different strands of research. To do so the comprehensive surveys of Kindleberger, Dunning, Aho, and Baumann were selected.[4]

Kindleberger approached the question of direct investment from the standpoint of the perfectly competitive model of neo-classical economics, by asserting that in a world of pure competition direct investment could not exist.[5] Indeed, when all markets operate efficiently, when there are no external economies of production or marketing, when information is costless and there are no barriers to trade or competition, international trade is the only possible form of international involvement.[6] Logically, it follows that it is the departures from the model of perfect competition that must provide the rationale for foreign direct investment. The first deviation was noted by Hymer, who postulated that local firms have better information about the economic environment in their country than do foreign companies. According to him, two conditions have to be fulfilled to explain the existence of direct investment: (1) foreign firms must possess a countervailing advantage over the local firms to make such investment viable; and (2) the market for the sale of this advantage must be imperfect.[7] It was, thus, a natural step for Kindleberger to

4. See C. P. Kindleberger, *American Business Abroad: Six Lectures on Direct Investment* (New Haven: Yale University Press, 1969); J. H. Dunning, "The Determinants of International Production", *Oxford Economic Papers* (November 1973), pp. 289-336; C. M. Aho, "Foreign Direct Investment: Theories and Empirical Evidence" (Manuscript of a paper written for the Council on International Economic Policy, 1974); J. G. Bauman, "Merger Theory, Property Rights and the Pattern of U.S. Direct Investment in Canada", *Weltwirtschaftliches Archiv* 7 (1975), pp. 676-698. Other comprehensive surveys include Ragazzi, "Direct Foreign Investment"; G. C. Hufbaner, "The Multinational Corporation and Direct Investment", *International Trade and Finance*, ed. P. B. Kenen (Cambridge, Mass.: Cambridge University Press, 1975); and C. F. Bergsten, T. Horst, and T. H. Moran, *American Multinationals and American Interests* (Washington, D.C.: The Brookings Institution, 1978).

5. Kindleberger, *American Business Abroad*, p. 13.

6. J. H. Dunning, "Trade, Location of Economic Activity and the MNE: A Search for an Eclectic Approach", The International Allocation of Economic Activity, ed. B. Ohlin, P. O. Hesselborn, P. M. Wijkman (New York: Holmes and Meir Publishers Inc., 1977), p. 396. This assertion follows from the Heckscher-Ohlin theory of international trade. Trade of goods will indeed equalize factor prices in a world of factor immobility.

7. S. H. Hymer, *The International Operations of National Firms: A Study of Direct Foreign Investment* (Cambridge Mass: MIT Press, 1976). This was Hymer's MIT thesis in 1960.

suggest that market imperfections were the reason for the existence of foreign direct investment. Specifically, he came up with the following taxonomy: imperfections in goods markets, imperfections in factor markets, scale economies and government-imposed disruptions.[8] We will call this classification the "market imperfections paradigm".

Dunning's survey examined the relevance of several branches of economic analysis in identifying the factors which influence international production. His study reviewed the contributions of capital, trade, location and industrial organization theories. He distinguished between the approaches which sought to explain what causes firms to produce abroad and those approaches which tried to reason why particular foreign markets are supplied by affiliates owned and managerially controlled from a different country.[9] In drawing this distinction, Dunning anticipated most of the later research conducted on the theory of the MNE.

In an unpublished paper, Aho dealt with the theories and empirical evidence of foreign direct investment using a line of attack that was somewhat different from those of the two previous authors. He concerned himself with the foreign firms' objectives, that is, whether they wish to maximize profits or some other quantity. After discarding alternative goals such as sales or growth maximization — based upon weak empirical evidence — he chose as his unifying theme the profit maximization hypothesis. Subsequently, he distinguished among three main groups of FDI theories: (1) those where firms act as independent profit maximizers; (2) those where the essential characteristic is the interdependence involved in maximizing decisions, that is, the typical feature of oligopolistic industries; and (3) those where firms diversify abroad to minimize risk. Aho's reference to market imperfections was scant, yet he stressed that FDI theories were not in conflict with the objective of profit maximization.[10]

In a paper dealing with the pattern of FDI in Canadian industries, Baumann broached the question of direct investment in a different way. Instead of searching for the motives of the firms or for the imperfections in the market system, he noted that FDI takes place in any one (or combination) of three ways: (1) the takeover of existing domestically owned firms; (2) the establishment of *de novo* subsidiaries; and (3) the further growth of these entities relative to that of domestically owned firms (through further takeovers or investment).

8. Kindleberger, *American Business Abroad*, p. 14.
9. Dunning, *Determinants of International Production*.
10. Aho, "Foreign Direct Investment".

Based upon this taxonomy, Baumann suggested two possible theoretical avenues for researching the FDI phenomenon: the theory of mergers and the theory of investment, as they apply in an international context. He quickly discarded the latter approach as not being directly applicable to explaining the pattern of FDI, since foreign direct investment does not necessarily require real expenditures on plant and equipment.[11] Hence, he was left with the theory of mergers as a possible foundation on which to base a study of the pattern of direct investment in Canada, and to investigate what motivates foreign firms to acquire domestic companies operating in particular industrial sectors. The approach chosen by Baumann sheds further light on the FDI phenomenon by focussing on the implementation side, that is, the takeover problem, which had been very much ignored by the previous authors, and which is paramount in the Canadian case.[12]

This brief review of classification schemes for FDI theories shows that the literature has dealt mainly with: (1) the market imperfections argument; (2) the relevance of particular strands of economic analysis; (3) the practical ways in which FDI is implemented; and (4) the objectives of the firms expanding abroad. We believe it is fair to argue that the latter concern is somewhat irrelevant. Horst made this point when he stated that "differences in objectives may not lead to differences in behavior, or if they do, the differences in behavior are too subtle to be detected with existing data".[13] Therefore, the behavior of a firm may reveal little about its ultimate objective. The most one can say is that, in certain cases, foreign direct investment appears consistent with profit maximization.

The seeming preference of direct investors for acquisition of local firms offers more insight into FDI. It points to an underlying similarity between FDI and acquisition behavior that has many implications.[14] However, the takeover of a local firm is only one way of entering a foreign market, and generalizations to other means do not follow easily from the theory of mergers. As for the extent to which the

11. For a thorough criticism of the application of domestic investment modes (accelerator, neo-classical, etc.) to the question of foreign direct investment, see J. D. Richardson, "Theoretical Considerations in the Analysis of Foreign Direct Investment", *Western Economic Journal* (March 1971), pp. 87-98.
12. Bauman, "Merger Theory".
13. T. Horst, "The Theory of the Firm", *Economic Analysis & Multinational Enterprise*, ed. J. H. Dunning (New York: Praeger, 1974), p. 41.
14. There is an interesting area of inquiry about the relationship between merger waves in the U.S. and U.S. takeovers in Canada. See A. L. Calvet, "Foreign Direct Investment and Acquisition Activity in the U.S. and Canada" (Paper presented at the Eastern Economic Association Meetings, Montreal, May 1980).

various branches of economics help in understanding the phenomenon of international production, there is a broad consensus in the
literature that neither capital nor trade theory can provide a fruitful
framework for analysing multinational enterprises. And the industrial
organization approach is nothing more than the study of market
imperfections.

In all, the one perspective which seems to best stand the test of
time and repeated examination by different authors is the market
imperfections paradigm. It also seems to conform more readily to the
main theme of the inquiry about MNEs — that is, why is there internalization within a single entity instead of external, market-mediated
transactions with foreign-owned firms? For, as shall be seen shortly,
when markets are imperfect or fail to exist there are grounds for
rationalizing the existence of MNEs.

A Classification of FDI Theories Along the Market Imperfections Paradigm

To encompass new developments in the field of the determinants
of foreign direct investment, we propose a modified categorization
somewhat different from that of Kindleberger. We will distinguish
among four classes: (1) market disequilibrium hypotheses; (2)
government-imposed distortions; (3) market structure imperfections;
and (4) market failure imperfections. Some brief comments are in
order to elucidate the meaning of these four categories.

The common feature found in all the hypotheses in group (1) will
be the transitory nature of foreign direct investment. FDI is an equilibrating force among segmented markets which eventually comes to
an end when equilibrium is re-established, that is, rates of return are
equalized among countries. The unifying characteristic in group (2)
will be the role played by either host or home governments in
providing the incentive to invest abroad. Group (3) will include
theories in which the behavior of firms deviates from that assumed
under conditions of perfect competition, through their ability to
influence market prices. Finally, in group (4) we will classify theories
which depart from the technical assumptions underlying the
model of perfect markets, that is, the assumptions about production
techniques and commodity properties. This last category will deal
basically with those phenomena which lead to market failure, cases
where "the decentralizing efficiency of that regime of signals, rules,
and built-in sanctions which defines a price-market system" will
fail.[15]

15. F. M Bator, "The Anatomy of Market Failure", *Quarterly Journal of Economics*
(August 1958), p. 352.

Several factors support this classification scheme. In the first place, the order in which the categories appear corresponds roughly to the chronological order in which new explanations of the FDI phenomenon have been brought forth. They range from the old view of an integrated approach to foreign direct investment and portfolio capital flows among countries, to the more recent versions of FDI as a spinoff of welfare economics.[16] Second, most, if not all, of the literature on FDI fits into this categorization. Third, our categories are arranged roughly in the order of increasing need for control over foreign operations. The justification for controlling foreign firms becomes, as we shall see, stronger as we go from (1) to (4). Finally, note that (1), (2), and (4) are compatible with profit maximizing behavior while (3) requires a restricted version of the maximization argument, due to the typical interdependencies of oligopolistic industries. By being less restrictive, growth or sales maximization, profit satisfaction, or any other mode of behavior can be accommodated in any of the four categories.

We now turn to a detailed exposition of these categories.

Market Disequilibrium Hypotheses

The notion of a perfect economy and perfect competition requires the assumption that prices everywhere are adjusted to bring supply and demand into equilibrium. It may well be that because of segmentation in world markets, rates of return are not equalized internationally. In a disequilibrium context, flows of FDI would take place until markets returned to stability. Instances of disequilibrium conditions that provide incentives to invest abroad are numerous. They basically apply to factor markets and foreign exchange markets.

Currency overvaluation is perhaps the most salient example of these disequilibrium hypotheses. A currency may be defined as overvalued when, at the prevailing rate of exchange, production costs for tradeable goods in the country are, on the average, higher than in other countries.[17] Such an occurrence creates opportunities for profit making by holding assets in undervalued currencies with the expectation that, once the equilibrium in the foreign exchange market is re-established, capital gains will be realized. In the meantime, there is an incentive to locate production of internationally traded commodities in countries with undervalued currencies and to purchase income-producing assets with overvalued money. The important point is that, once exchange rates return to equilibrium,

16. H. G. Johnson, "The Efficiency and Welfare Implications of the International Corporation", *The International Corporation*, ed. C. P. Kindleberger (Cambridge: Mass.: MIT Press, 1970).
17. Ragazzi, "Direct Foreign Investment", p. 491.

the flow of FDI should stop. Even more, foreign investors should sell their foreign assets, pocket the capital gains, and return to domestic operations.

Foreign direct investment may be attracted towards areas where the average rates of profit are higher. This is basically the capital markets disequilibrium hypothesis. It implies that, for a given level of risk, rates of return on assets are not equalized internationally by portfolio capital flows, due to inefficiencies in securities markets (for example, thinness, lack of disclosure, etc.). Therefore, the only way that rates of return on real assets can be brought to equilibrium is by flows of direct investment. The process is, however, self-destructing since firms from low-yield countries will invest in countries with high yields until rates of return are brought to equilibrium. Then foreign direct investment will cease.[18]

The same approach has been used with respect to labor costs. Here foreign direct investment would flow from high labor cost countries to low-cost countries in the pursuit of cost minimization. This hypothesis is no exception to the transitory character of the FDI phenomenon, since the demand for labor in countries where wages are low will tend to hike up labor costs, while the lack of demand in source countries will drive wages down. The result is a finite life for direct investment.

Finally, disequilibrium situations may arise in technology markets. Rates of technical and technological innovation may vary among nations, thereby placing some countries in leadership positions with respect to new products and processes. The origins of superior knowledge can be traced back to superior R & D performance or to merely chance factors, for example, a breakthrough in scientific knowledge. In any event, firms in countries where technology is relatively advanced would find profitable opportunities abroad and would, therefore, have an incentive to invest overseas.

This review covers basically all the situations where conventional economic disequilibrium conditions can give rise to FDI flows. Regarding the relevance of these hypotheses to the Canadian situation, the following comments can be made: The currency factor can hardly be invoked since Canada has experienced flexible exchange rates for long periods of time, thus allowing its currency to reach equilibrium values. It is therefore difficult to argue that currency disequilibrium is a primary determinant of FDI into Canada. Secondly, the degree of imperfections in Canadian security markets does not

18. Hufbauer, "The Multinational Corporation". Hufbauer provides a good exposition and criticism of this hypothesis, sometimes called the differential-return hypothesis.

warrant the massive amounts of foreign direct investment reaching the Canadian economy. The argument that discrepancies between industrial risks and rates of return of enterprises and the risks and rates of return implicit in minority holdings in their securities determine FDI flows, rests on a segmentation of the Canadian capital market which has no theoretical or empirical support. With respect to lower labor costs at home, the comparison of one factor price (for example, wages) is misleading when production costs depend on a whole range of inputs, some of which are higher priced in Canada than abroad due to Canada's small scale production runs. Hence, the "cheaper labor costs in Canada" argument is untenable as a means to rationalize the inflow and subsequent growth of foreign direct investment. Finally, disequilibrium situations in technology markets, such as those existing between Canada and the United States, do not necessarily imply direct control over Canadian operations. It would seem that foreign firms would be better off selling the technology to local Canadian producers who, it may be assumed, have a better knowledge of the institutional and cultural environment in their own country. Foreign direct investment would only be justified when market imperfections impeded foreign firms from appropriating the full rent of their superior technology. However, this is no longer a disequilibrium argument applicable to a competitive environment but rather a market distortion of a different nature, as will be seen shortly. In summary, disequilibrium hypotheses share the major shortcoming of viewing foreign direct investment merely as an equilibrating capital flow, thereby ignoring the composite nature of FDI and the institution through which it takes place. Neither alone nor taken together could these hypotheses be considered the primary determinants of direct investment into Canada.

Government-Imposed Distortions

At the outset, it should be mentioned that government policies could conceivably be responsible for some of the disequilibrium hypotheses previously considered. Fixed exchange rates, wage policies, and policies regulating the migration of labor create unstable conditions apt to foster foreign investing. The main difference, however, between this category and the last is that there do not appear to be any equilibrating forces which would correct the distortions imposed by governments. That is to say, in order to nullify the incentive for direct investment, all governments would have to harmonize their policies or have no policies at all.

Tariffs, quotas, and other non-tariff trade barriers (for example, regulations on imported goods) are often regarded as a major cause of direct investment. Other things being equal, an increase in trade barriers (or the expectation of their rise) may be the necessary incentive for firms to establish a subsidiary inside the protected market, rather than export to it.

Another major government-induced distortion is the levy of taxes.[19] Not surprisingly, the incentive to invest abroad can originate in differences in the tax laws governing countries. After all, firms try to maximize rates of return after taxes. If, furthermore, the parent government tax laws encourage expatriation of capital (for example, via a deferral system), the incentive to set up foreign operations will be even stronger.

Government-related disruptions can take many other forms — from price and profit regulation to antitrust laws or any other change in the institutional setting in which business operates. All these actions can be used to rationalize the expatriation of domestic firms on the grounds that they restrict their autonomy.

The tariff argument has been extensively used to rationalize FDI into Canada. There is no doubt that tariffs are responsible in many instances for the decision to locate the production of certain goods inside the protected market. The problem with the tariff argument is that it indicates only that movements of goods via exports is denied or restricted but has little, if anything, to say about the other components of the international transfer of resources, for example, technology, managerial skills, etc. This raises questions as to why foreigners have not taken the licensing route more often to penetrate the Canadian market by selling or leasing rights to domestically owned companies — it's even more surprising when they know that Canada has no restrictions for the servicing of foreign technology. As for the tax argument, a "favorable" tax treatment in Canada would constitute an incentive for foreign producers to set up Canadian facilities only if they were able to generate profits in Canada, regardless of the fact that they must face the incremental costs of adapting to the local institutional environment.

This leads us directly into the area of industrial organization, for the foreign firm would need a countervailing advantage to compensate for these higher costs.

Market Structure Imperfections

The previous cases of disequilibrium hypotheses and government-

19. T. Horst, "The Theory of the Multinational Firm: Optimal Behavior Under Different Tariff and Tax Rates", *Journal of Political Economy* (September/October 1971), pp. 1059-1072; "American Taxation of Multinational Corporations", *American Economic Review* (June 1977), pp. 376-389; and Tax Issues, *American Multinationals and American Interests*, ed. C. F. Bergsten, T. O. Horst, and T. H. Moran (Washington, D.C.: The Brookings Institution, 1978). Horst provides the most extensive treatment of the impact of tax differentials on FDI.

induced distortions are compatible with a "relatively" competitive market structure. Market structure imperfections, on the other hand, refer to deviations from purely market-determined prices brought about by the existence of monopolistic or oligopolistic market forces. In this perspective, foreign direct investment becomes the outgrowth of industrial organization.

The recognition that foreign direct investment belongs to the realm of industrial organization goes back to the writings of Hymer.[20] Since then, it has received much attention and has become the most popular approach to date (see, for example, Bergsten, Horst, and Moran[21]). There are two essential characteristics which set oligopolistic industries apart from competitive ones. First, the former are industries where maximizing decisions — whether of profit or growth — are interdependent: each firm must speculate on the reactions of the few other firms in the industry. Second, barriers to entry are essential in order to prevent a surge of competition. As one would expect, both of these features have been extensively used to explain foreign direct investment.

Not all barriers to entry lend themselves to direct expansion abroad. Leaving aside vertical foreign investments which respond to barriers of a different kind, Caves considered product differentiation in the home market as being the critical element giving rise to foreign investment. The successful firm, producing a differentiated product, controls knowledge about servicing the domestic market that can be used at little or no cost in other national markets. This provides the motivation for investing abroad, as long as the means to protect the product exist, for example, patents, copyrights, etc.[22]

Other contributions to the oligopolistic feature of direct investment include models which explicitly take into account the interdependence of firms in the industry. The most publicized is, perhaps, the product life cycle hypothesis where firms react to the threat of losing markets as the product matures by expanding overseas and capturing the remaining rent from the product's development.[23] Variations to this approach include the "follow the leader" case, where the investment moves of one firm trigger similar moves by other leading firms in the industry,[24] and the "exchange of threats"

20. Hymer, *International Operations*.
21. Bergsten, Horst, and Moran, *American Multinationals*.
22. R. E. Caves, "International Corporations: The Industrial Economics of Foreign Investment", *Economica* (February 1971), pp. 1-27.
23. R. Vernon, "International Investment and International Trade in the Plant Cycle", *Quarterly Journal of Economics* (May 1966), pp. 192-207.
24. F. T. Knickerbocker, *Oligopolistic Reaction and Multinational Enterprise* (Cambridge, Mass.: Harvard Business School Division of Research, 1974).

hypothesis, where oligopolists imitate each other by establishing subsidiaries in each other's markets.[25]

The oligopolistic argument has been widely mentioned to rationalize the foreign domination of Canadian industries. The most famous application of this view is the concept of a "miniature replica" to depict the structure of U.S.-controlled Canadian industries based on a similar industrial pattern found in the United States, albeit on a minor scale.[26] Despite its success, there are still some unanswered questions, and recent evidence has shed some doubt on the validity of the industrial organization hypothesis. For example, this theory places too great an emphasis on sellers' concentration — a measure of oligopolistic structure — as being a main determinant of direct investment. On this point, Ragazzi reported that the degree of industrial concentration was, in general, much higher in Europe than in the U.S. in the 1950s, although the bulk of FDI was from the U.S. to Europe.[27] Kojima cast further doubts by showing that the Japanese experience points to a compatibility of international investment with a relatively competitive market structure at home.[28] As regards Canada, it is well known that foreign investors did not seek out the industries with the highest concentration.[29] These studies imply that the link between FDI and market structure, either in the home or in the host country, is not as clear as was once thought. Nor is it obvious why foreign firms would show an apparent preference for takeovers — an important facet of FDI in Canada.

Finally, and particularly in Caves's argument, the static concept of product differentiation is related to the notion of intangible capital in the form of knowledge, yet the two do not imply the same form of international involvement. Indeed, "licensing of domestically controlled firms would be a feasible alternative in industries with an unchanging product mix since quality changes, brand changes, etc. pose no difficulties for agreements."[30] However, as will be seen in the next section, the transfer of intangible capital in the form of knowledge does pose serious problems.

25. E. M. Graham, "Oligopolistic Imitation and European Direct Investment in the United States" (Ph.D. diss., Harvard Business School, 1974).

26. See H. Gray, Foreign Direct Investment in Canada ("The Gray Report") (Ottawa: Information Canada, 1972).

27. Ragazzi, "Direct Foreign Investment".

28. K. Kojima, Direct Foreign Investment: A Japanese Model of Multinational Business Operations (London: Groom Helm, 1978).

29. G. Rosenbluth, "The Relation Between Foreign Control and Concentration in Canadian Industry", Canadian Journal of Economics (February 1970), pp. 14-38.

30. Bauman, "Merger Theory", p. 683.

Market Failure Imperfections

As pointed out earlier, market failure imperfections are characteristics in production techniques and commodity properties which prevent a market mechanism from allocating resources efficiently. There are basically three types of imperfections which lead to market failures: (1) external effects; (2) public goods; and (3) economies of scale (decreasing cost industries). Under any one of these conditions, the duality between social efficiency and market performance ceases to exist.[31]

The significance of market failures as a potential explanation of FDI was not fully realized until 1970. At that time, Johnson related foreign direct investment to the welfare economics of technological and managerial knowledge as a factor of production — a typical case of market failure.[32] His ideas were based upon previous work done by Arrow on the accumulation of knowledge in society.[33] Briefly, the peculiarities of knowledge which make its markets so imperfect are:

1. the lumpiness of the inventive input necessary to produce it; and
2. the high degree of spill over or externality that accompanies the inventive process.[34]

This in turn creates problems for both the production and international transfer of knowledge. First, reasons of social efficiency would dictate that existing knowledge be made available as a free good. Hence the dilemma: how is the production of new knowledge to be motivated if no property rights are granted? Second, the natural characteristics of knowledge would favor its transfer within a single firm, hence "justifying" foreign direct investment over other alternatives of exploiting foreign markets. Indeed, if markets for knowledge are difficult to organize, internalization achieves two objectives: (1) it provides channels for the transfer of this knowledge at lower costs than via external modes;[35] and (2) it avoids or slows down the dissipation of this knowledge to competitors.

The validity of this hypothesis in a Canadian context is enhanced by the empirical findings that U.S.firms investing in Canada have high R & D intensity at home — a proxy for economically valuable

31. P. Bohm, *Social Efficiency: A Concise Introduction to Welfare Economics* (New York: John Wiley & Sons, 1973), p. 19.
32. Johnson, "Implications of the International Corporation", p. 36.
33. K. J. Arrow, "Economic Welfare and the Allocation of Resources for Invention", *The Rate and Direction of Inventive Activity* (Princeton: Princeton University Press, 1962).
34. W. D. Nordhans, *Invention, Growth, and Welfare* (Cambridge, Mass.: MIT Press, 1969), p. 36.
35. D. J. Teece, *The Multinational Corporation and the Resource Cost of International Technology Transfer* (Cambridge: Ballinger, 1976).

knowledge.[36] The emphasis that the hypothesis places on natural imperfections is also enlightening for it justifies to a certain extent the permanent nature of FDI — a facet in contradiction with earlier conceptions of FDI as an equilibrating capital flow.

We now turn to recent developments in the field of the multinational firm, of which the one common feature is "a switch in attention from the act of foreign direct investment . . . to the institution making the investment".[37]

Recent Contributions to the Theory of the MNE

Although market imperfections still underlie much of the thinking on MNEs, there has been a distinctive shift in theoretical literature towards developing a global theory of the multinational firm. It was not by chance that at approximately the same time the economic profession showed signs of a renewed interest in the economics of internal organization, a new terminology for an old area of economics evolved — the theory of the firm.[38]

In this section, we will examine three major contributions in the field: the appropriability theory, the internalization theory, and the diversification theory. The three bring new insights to our understanding of the multinational phenomenon.

The Appropriability Theory
The appropriability theory of the multinational corporation, best represented in Magee's work,[39] is a consolidation of two main streams of thought: on the one hand, the industrial organization approach to foreign direct investment; on the other hand, the neo-classical ideas on the private appropriability of the returns from investments in information. MNEs are at the crossroads of these two streams of thought for, as Magee states, the distinctive nature of these corporations resides in their being specialists in the production of "information" (technology).[40] Valuable information is generated by MNEs at

36. See, for instance, T. Horst, "Firm and Industry Determinants of the Decision to Invest Abroad: An Empirical Study", *Review of Economics and Statistics* (August 1972), pp. 258-266 and R. E. Caves, "Causes of Direct Investment: Foreign Firms' Shares in Canadian and United Kingdom Manufacturing Industries", *Review of Economics and Statistics* (August 1974), pp. 279-293.
37. Dunning, "Defence of the Eclectic Theory", p. 274.
38. The interested reader can refer to "Symposium on the Economics of Internal Organization" in the special issues of the *Bell Journal of Economics* (1974, 1975).
39. S. P. Magee, "Technology and the Appropriability Theory of the Multinational Corporation", *The New International Economic Order*, ed. Jagdish Bhagwati (Cambridge, Mass.: MIT Press, 1976); "Multinational Corporations, the Industry Technology Cycle and Development", *Journal of World Trade Law* (July/August 1977), pp. 297-321.
40. Magee, "Appropriability Theory", p. 317.

five different stages: new product discovery, product development, creation of the production function, market creation, and appropriability.

The theory then postulates that, because sophisticated technologies are less prone to imitation, MNEs are more successful in appropriating the returns from these technologies than from simple ones. Furthermore, sophisticated information is transferred more efficiently via internal channels than by market means. These two factors taken together enable Magee to assert that there is a built-in incentive in the economic system to generate sophisticated information — to the detriment in some cases of users' needs, for example, those of less developed countries. To complete the theory, Magee goes on to say that production is information saving so that, ultimately, there is a decline in the production of new information. All these considerations generate a technology cycle at the industry level; that is, young industries are those where information is being created at a fast pace, which in turn implies that the firm expands in size because of the internalization of the information produced. As the industry matures, the amount of information being created is minimal. Thus, optimum firm size diminishes accordingly. In terms of the international expansion of the firm, the assertion that optimum firm size declines after the innovation stage suggests that, at a certain point, licensing should increase relative to direct investment.

The propensity to engage in takeover activity is also an implication of the appropriability theory. On the subject of takeovers, Magee states that "takeovers of host country production facilities and mergers of multinationals with host country firms are normal consequences of the expansion in optimum size early in an industry's technology cycle". In addition, takeovers, according to Magee, "may be aimed at slowing the depreciation of the stock of information by absorbing the most likely interlopers".[41] Note that two arguments are being used: one is the higher efficiency of intrafirm transfers dictating an internal solution; the other one is the monopolistic argument of the industrial organization approach to FDI.

The Internalization Theory

The existence of imperfect markets for knowledge is the basis of Buckley and Casson's theory of the multinational enterprise. It is perhaps in their work that the notion of the multinational firm as an entity is given the most attention. The starting point of their theory is the idea that the modern business sector carries out many activities apart from the routine production of goods and services. All these activities, for example, marketing, R & D, training of labor are

41. Magee, "Appropriability Theory", p. 333.

interdependent and are related through flows of intermediate products, mostly in the form of knowledge and expertise. However, intermediate product markets are difficult to organize due to their imperfections. This provides an incentive to bypass them, and results in the creation of internal markets, that is, bringing the activities which are linked by the market under common ownership and control.[42] Finally, it is the internalization of markets across national boundaries which gives rise to the multinational enterprise. A few years earlier, McManus had already pointed out that the essence of the phenomenon of international production is not the transfer of capital but rather the international extension of managerial control over foreign subsidiaries — control which is ownership-based and through which management replaces the market as the allocator of resources.[43]

Dunning, expanding on the internalization theory, stated that the incentives to internalize activities are to avoid the disadvantages, or to capitalize on the advantages, of imperfections on external (markets and public) mechanisms of resource allocation.[44] Therefore, not only must firms possess superior resources — as in Hymer's argument — but they must have the desire and the ability to internalize the advantages which result from their possession.

Further developments on this theory are contained in the works of Rugman, whose ideas are explained in the next chapter of this book.[45]

The Diversification Theory

Up to now the concern of this chapter has been mainly the imperfections in markets for products and for knowledge. Financial market imperfections have not been generally in the forefront of the literature, "presumably because financial markets are deemed to be more efficient than markets for real goods and services".[46] However, the evidence that has accumulated recently tends to suggest that there are imperfections in financial markets, and hence advantages for the MNE in internalizing financial transactions. In his recent review of the internal financial transfers within MNEs, Lessard pointed to sources of gains stemming from exchange control arbitrage, credit market arbitrage, and equity market arbitrage. Undoubtedly the most well-

42. Buckley and Casson, *Multinational Enterprise*, p. 33.
43. J. C. McManus, "The Theory of the International Firm", *The Multinational Firm and the Nation State*, ed. C. Paquet (Toronto, 1972).
44. Dunning, "Search for an Eclectic Approach", p. 402.
45. Rugman, *International Diversification; Multinationals in Canada: Theory, Performance and Economic Impact* (Boston: Martinus Nijhoff, 1980).
46. R. D. Lessard, "Transfer Prices, Taxes, and Financial Markets: Implications of Internal Financial Transfers within the Multinational Firm", *Economic Issues of Multinational Firms*, ed. R. G. Hawkins (Jay Press, 1979).

publicized advantage accruing to MNEs is that which derives from equity market arbitrage, that is, risk reduction through diversification. Although the mechanics of diversification are well known, the application of international diversification to the MNE has not always been properly substantiated.[47] Originally the argument had been put forward by international portfolio theorists that variations in security returns across countries show less correlation than within a single country. An immediate implication is that international diversification can be used as a means of reducing the average risk faced by investors. However, there is nothing in this argument which would justify corporate international diversification, for in an integrated and perfectly competitive world capital market, individual investors can diversify their holdings at no cost. The issue which was subsequently raised in the literature concerned the existence of barriers or costs to capital transfers and the potential benefits to be derived from the indirect diversification provided by MNEs. In one of the first attempts to deal with this issue, Agmon and Lessard argued that two conditions must be satisfied before attributing the diversification motive to the MNE: (1) there must exist greater barriers or costs to portfolio capital flows than to direct investment flows; and (2) investors must recognize that MNEs provide a diversification vehicle which would otherwise not be available.[48] More recently, Errunza and Senbet, taking a more general equilibrium perspective, have been able to show, however, that the existence of barriers per se does not yield price differentials among purely domestic and multinational stocks. Consequently, the pricing effects of international involvement by the MNE become hard to verify empirically. As an alternative, these authors propose a value-based approach which allows them to isolate the benefits to be derived from financial market imperfections, over and above those to be attributed to real market imperfections.[49]

These three new approaches to the phenomenon of international production undoubtedly represent a step forward in explaining the propensity of firms to choose the foreign direct investment route

---

47. M. F. J. Prachowny, "Direct Investment and the Balance of Payments of the United States: A Portfolio Approach"; and G. Stevens, "Capital Mobility and the International Firm", *The International Mobility and Movement of Capital*, ed. F. Machlup et al. (New York: Columbia University Press, 1972); Lessard, "Implications of Internal Financial Transfers". Prachowny and Stevens concentrate on risk-reducing benefits of diversification without explaining why these are uniquely realized through the MNE. Lessard provides a good criticsm of these approaches.

48. T. B. Agmon and D. R. Lessard, "Investor Recognition of Corporate International Diversification", *Journal of Finance* (September 1977), pp. 1049-1055.

49. V. R. Errunza and L. W. Senbet, "The Effects of International Operations on the Market Value of the Firm: Theory and Evidence" (Unpublished manuscript, September 1980, forthcoming in *Journal of Finance*).

over alternative ways, such as licensing, in order to exploit foreign markets. All three theories, however, offer a double-edged view of the MNE: on the one hand, multinationals appear to take advantage of imperfections to enhance their already impressive power, on the other hand, they facilitate the transfer of factors, goods, and services, transfers which would otherwise be handled inefficiently, or not at all. Future empirical work comparable to Teece's[50] will, it is hoped, shed further light on the question of whether MNEs create, extend, and/or perpetuate market imperfections, or whether they are a vehicle for overcoming natural imperfections to the benefit of all parties.

Finally, do these theories provide us with a better understanding of the Canadian situation? The appropriability and internalization theories are particularly relevant[51] in emphasizing the very nature of MNEs, that is, large firms, the superiority of which is based on knowledge generation, be it of a technical or managerial type. These theories mitigate the usual claims about MNEs' oligopolistic behavior in goods markets, only to better illustrate their restrictive conduct in the area of knowledge. This conduct is more justifiable since it is generally recognized that incentives must be found, if new knowledge is to be generated. And these incentives, in the form of "sufficient" profits, can only be maintained if property rights and takeovers are used to prevent the dissipation of valuable knowledge. The above remarks imply that any Canadian moves in the arena of anti-combines legislation must be co-ordinated with changes in the area of patent legislation, science policy, and control of foreign direct investment. None of these aspects can be tackled independently of the others.[52]

The internalization theory also points to many aspects of the organization of productive activities where external markets are poorly suited for use as modes of transacting but where MNEs are efficient responses to market failure imperfections. Thus, there are powerful reasons for not constraining the operations of MNEs in Canada, for the alternative would not be arm's length market exchanges but rather no exchanges at all. If anything, these theories clearly indicate that one should beware of simple arguments where foreign firms are pictured as oligopolists operating in an environment that can be analysed within a narrow economic neo-classical model with no uncertainty and no transactional considerations.[53]

50. Teece, *The Multinational Corporation.*
51. The diversification theory seems less readily applicable to the case of Canada since barriers of costs to portfolio diversification are comparatively low.
52. The chapter by Alan Rugman, following in this book, addresses some of these issues.
53. These points have been developed by Calvet. See A. L. Calvet, "A Synthesis of Foreign Direct Investment Theories and Theories of the Multinational Firm", *Journal of International Business Studies* (1981).

On the other hand, more research is needed to ascertain when MNEs create market imperfections and when they respond to natural imperfections. Failure to develop this area of investigation would lead us to the equally dangerous road where all MNEs are de facto efficient responses to market failures. This need not necessarily be so.[54]

Conclusion and Areas for Further Study

We can now foresee some of the major directions for research for the 1980s. First of all, putting into perspective the three previous sections, it is clear that the trend is towards investigating the nature of MNEs, that is, the reasons for their existence. This will most likely be done by avoiding the strict neo-classical framework, which assigns an undue advantage to markets, with the idea that there are certain conditions (environmental, human, technological, etc.) which favor either the establishment of markets or of firms. We know that in situations where goods or services are well defined and the market allows for numerous producers and buyers, the price mechanism is the most efficient way to organize transactions. But we also know that when contractual obligations extend over time, refer to ambiguously defined commodities, and feature a small number of economic agents, the superiority of market-mediated transactions is not well established. Hence, an interesting area of research will be to investigate under what conditions one would expect to see the emergence of organized markets or of integrated firms.[55]

Along the same line of research, a comparative analysis of the sharing of transactions between firms and markets across industries, countries, and over time, can bring further insight to what the organization of international trade and investment will be years hence.

Undoubtedly, research into the theory of the MNE will have spill overs for our comprehension of the Canadian situation — a situation which is rapidly changing as Canadian MNEs expand in the U.S. and in other countries at a fast pace and Canada becomes a net exporter of FDI. It is hoped that this research will also be used to guide public policy decisions concerning the control of foreign business in Canada so that among the myriad of inconsequential events, the real issues concerning MNEs can be identified and tackled in the near future.

54. A sector where these theories may find difficulties in providing a defensible argument are the resource industries.
55. For an early inquiry in this direction, see McManus, "The International Firm"; also "The Costs of Alternative Economic Organizations", *Canadian Journal of Economics* (August 1975), pp. 334-350; and A. L. Calvet, "Markets and Hierarchies: Towards a Theory of International Business" (Ph.D. diss., Sloan School of Management, MIT 1980).

IV
Foreign Direct Investment Theory, Impact, and Control

A
Theory

19
Internalization as a General Theory of Foreign Direct Investment: A Reappraisal of the Literature*

Alan M. Rugman

Dr. Rugman is associate professor of business administration and director, Centre for International Business Studies, Dalhousie University. He has previously held faculty positions at Columbia University, Concordia University, and the University of Winnipeg. His publications include *International Diversification and the Multinational Enterprise*; *Multinationals in Canada: Theory, Performance, and Economic Impact*; and *Inside the Multinationals: The Economics of Internal Markets*.

This chapter is an expanded version of an article which appeared originally in *Weltwirtschaftliches Archiv.*, Vol. 116, No. 2 (1980). Reprinted by permission.

* Helpful comments on a previous version of this chapter, presented to the annual meeting of the Eastern Economic Association at Boston in April 1979 were made by Winston Brown at the conference and, on other occasions, by Mark Casson, John Dunning, Ian Giddy, Stefan Robock, and Raymond Vernon. Additional comments were made by participants at seminars at Columbia University, Concordia University (Montreal), and Dalhousie University. The author is alone responsible for the views expressed here.

Introduction

The world is characterized by imperfections in the goods and factor markets which act as barriers to the free trade of goods and services and inhibit private international financial investment. As a result neither factor price equalization nor goods price equalization has been observed. Further, there is a large volume of foreign direct investment and international production by the multinational enterprise (MNE), an activity which cannot be explained readily by conventional trade theory alone.

A large literature has developed in order to offer explanations of the phenomenon of foreign direct investment (FDI) and the reasons for international production by the MNE. It is argued in this chapter that the existing theories are basically subsets of the general theory of internalization. This theory was first advanced by Coase in a domestic context[1] and by Hymer in an international dimension.[2] It is synthesized by Buckley and Casson and by Dunning.[3] Internalization serves to determine the reasons for the foreign production and sales of the MNE, namely that these activities take place in response to imperfections in the goods and factor markets.[4]

1. Ronald H. Coase, "The Nature of the Firm", *Economia*, N.S. 4 (London, 1937), pp. 386-405. Repr. in: *Readings in Price Theory*, ed. George J. Stigler and Kenneth E. Boulding (Homewood, 1953), pp. 331-351.
2. Stephen H. Hymer, *The International Operations of National Firms: A Study of Direct Foreign Investment* (Cambridge, Mass: MIT Press, 1976).
3. Peter J. Buckley and Mark Casson, *The Future of Multinational Enterprise* (London 1976); John H. Dunning, "The Determinants of International Production", *Oxford Economic Papers*, N.S. 25 (Oxford, 1953), pp. 289-336.
4. The concept of internalization has been developed by economists associated with the University of Reading in England. A clear statement of the benefits and costs of internalization appears in Buckley and Casson, *Future of the Multinational Enterprise*, see esp. ch. 2. A more extensive and rigorous treatment is in Mark Casson, *Alternatives to the Multinational Enterprise* (London, 1979), chs. 2-3. The work of John Dunning has always sought to integrate the theories of FDI, and it is instructive to contrast his comprehensive survey of the field in "The Determinants of International Production", in which internalization is not mentioned, with his major unifying synthesis in "Trade Location of Economic Activity and the MNE: A Search for an Eclectic Approach", in *The International Allocation of Economic Activity*, ed. Bertil Ohlin et al. (London, 1977), pp. 395-418, where it is the central concept. Many of the ideas expressed in this chapter originate from either the written work of Casson and Dunning, or from conversations that I have enjoyed with them.

The main point of this chapter is its argument that most of the existing literature on the theory of the MNE consists of specific explanations and models developed by individual writers who have spotted one or another of these many imperfections which exist in world markets. For example, several writers have discovered imperfections in the markets for knowledge and information, while others have focussed upon imperfections in the capital markets, or upon indivisibilities, scale economies, and other firm specific externalities. Here these imperfections are identified by author and are then shown to be different examples of the general theory of internalization.

In this chapter the theory of internalization is explained and then it is applied in a new manner to suggest a possible integration of the theories of FDI advanced by writers such as Vernon, Kindleberger, Caves, Aliber, Johnson, Magee, Kojima, and others in recent years.[5] In a related work, Dunning refers to the need for an eclectic approach to the theory of FDI.[6] His approach can be reconciled with the proposition advanced here, namely that internalization provides an integrated theory of FDI by the MNE. For additional surveys of the recent literature on FDI see Dunning, Hufbauer, Rugman, Vernon, Giddy, Hood and Young, and Casson.[7]

5. Raymond Vernon, "International Investment and International Trade in the Product Cycle", *The Quarterly Journal of Economics,* **80** (Cambridge, Mass., 1966), pp. 190-207; Charles P. Kindleberger, *American Business Abroad: Six Lectures on Direct Investment* (New Haven, Conn., 1969); Richard E. Caves, "International Corporations: The Industrial Economics of Foreign Investment", *Economica*, N.S. **38** (London, 1971), pp. 1-27; Robert Z. Aliber, "A Theory of Direct Foreign Investment", *The International Corporation: A Symposium*, ed. Charles P. Kindleberger (Cambridge, Mass., 1970), pp. 17-34; Harry G. Johnson, "The Efficiency and Welfare Implications of the International Corporation", *The International Corporation*, ed. Kindleberger, pp. 35-56; Stephan P. Magee, "Information and the Multinational Corporation: An Approbability Theory of Direct Foreign Investment", *The New International Economic Order: The North-South Debate,* ed. Jagdish N. Bhagwati, pp. 317-340; Stephan P. Magee, "Multinational Corporations, The Industry Technology Cycle and Development", *Journal of World Trade Law*, **II** (Twickenham, 1977), pp. 297-321; Kiyoshi Kojima, *Dirct Foreign Investment: A Japanese Model of Multinational Business Operations* (London, 1978).
6. Dunning, "Trade, Location of Economic Activity and The MNE".
7. Dunning, "The Determinants of International Production"; Gary C. Hufbauer, "The Multinational Corporation and Direct Investment", *International Trade and Finance: Frontiers for Research*, ed. Peter B. Kenen (Cambridge, 1975), pp. 253-319; Alan M. Rugman, "Motives for Foreign Investment: The Market Imperfections and Risk Diversification Hypotheses", *Journal of World Trade Law*, **9** (Twickenham, 1975), pp. 567-573; Raymond Vernon, *Storm over the Multinationals: The Real Issues* (London, 1977); Ian H. Giddy, "The Demise of the Product Cycle in International Business Theory", *The Columbia Journal of World Business*, **13** (New York, 1978), pp. 90-97; Neil Hood and Stephen Young, *The Economics of Multinational Enterprise* (London, 1979); Casson, *Alternatives to the Multinational Enterprise*. Two recent textbooks in economics also contain good surveys of the pre-internalization literature on FDI: Herbert G.

Free Trade or the Multinational Enterprise

The first premise of this chapter is that the theory of FDI is the converse of the pure theory of international trade. If the world were characterized by a model of free trade, there would be no need for the MNE. In a traditional Heckscher-Ohlin model of free trade, perfect goods and factor markets are assumed, as are zero transport costs, identical tastes, constant returns to scale, and so on. In such a first best Paretian situation global welfare is maximized by nations producing according to their relative comparative advantage, where this is determined by a difference in factor endowments or some other reason which sets the international price ratio at variance with the domestic price ratio.[8]

It can be shown, within the same theoretical framework, that relaxation of some of the assumptions of the trade model, for example, to allow for scale economies or transport costs, still generates gains from trade. Such assumptions must be relaxed sequentially, and for each case the rest of the system must be in perfect competition. Then any one of these potential situations is a reason for trade due to a difference between the domestic and foreign price ratios. Yet when the underlying basic conditions of perfect goods and factor markets do not hold, free trade is destroyed and is replaced by second best solutions such as the MNE.

The modern theory of FDI suggests that the MNE develops in response to imperfections in the goods or factor markets. Then the country specific advantage of a nation — which leads to trade — is replaced by a firm specific advantage internal to an MNE — which leads to FDI. When there is an advantage specific to a firm, such as knowledge or other special information, it can be transported between the home and host nation within the internal market of the MNE. The MNE is a substitute for free trade, in the rigorous terms of economic theory.

If there is an imperfection in the goods market, such as a tariff, then free trade is replaced by the MNE. A tariff imposed by a nation to

Grubel, *International Economics* (Homewood, 1977); and H. Peter Gray, *International Trade, Investment, and Payments* (Boston, 1979). Unfortunately most writers in international economics and international business have either neglected the theory of the MNE as a separate topic, despite the great importance of MNEs in trade and exchange, or (at best) have incorporated it as a section in long-term capital flows, whereas it belongs on its own with its distinctive theoretical rationale, namely internalization.

8. For evidence of a similar approach see Jurg Niehans, "Benefits of Multinational Firms for a Small Parent Economy: The Case of Switzerland", and Michael Adler, "Comment", *Multinationals from Small Countries*, ed. Tamir Agmon and Charles P. Kindleberger (Cambridge, Mass., 1977).

support its domestic industry will attract the subsidiaries of MNEs, since they can avoid the customs duty by replacing exports with host nation production. Canada is a prime example of a nation in which protection has led to foreign ownership of most of its manufacturing industry and nearly all of its resources. Presumably the MNEs would not have been attracted into Canada if it had not been for the barriers to trade erected by the federal government. In a continental economy, domestic corporations of either Canada or the United States could sell to an integrated market and such free trade would be efficient.[9]

Imperfections in the factor markets, especially in the market for intermediate goods, always lead to the development of MNEs. The major point of Hymer's seminal thesis of 1960 is that the MNE has a firm specific advantage, developed in reponse to one or another market imperfection.[10] Hymer demonstrates that market advantages are achieved if the MNE can acquire factor inputs at a lower cost than its rivals; if it has better distribution and marketing facilities; if it has a monopoly advantage in information, research, knowledge or some other aspect of the production process; or if it makes a differentiated product. Hymer recognized that in these situations the firm can create an internal market to substitute for, or supersede, the regular external market. The MNE is a response to some sort of externality. It overcomes the externality by internalization. If there were perfect goods or factor markets in the first place then there would be no reason for an MNE to develop and free trade would exist. In this theoretical situation, we have free trade being determined by country specific factors or a world of market imperfections in which the MNE operates due to firm specific factors. In practice, there are elements of both country specific and firm specific factors in existence, so the MNE is more important when there are relatively greater restrictions on free trade than when such barriers are assumed away, as in the Heckscher-Ohlin world.

The Theory of Internalization

Internalization can occur in response to any type of externality in the goods or factor markets. As discussed above, a tariff, or other type of distortion in the goods market, will induce FDI and multinational activity. The essence of internalization theory is the explicit recog-

9. For an extension of this point see Alan M. Rugman, *Multinationals in Canada: Theory, Performance and Economic Impact* (Boston, 1980).
10. Hymer, *International Operations*.

nition of these worldwide market imperfections which in practice prevent the efficient operation of international trade and investment. Following this line of thinking it can be argued that the MNE has developed in response to both exogenous government-induced regulations and controls as well as other types of market failure which have destroyed the theoretical reasons for free trade and private foreign investment. The process of internalization permits the management of the MNE to overcome such externalities and governmental regulations in the product market.

In addition, the MNE has been an efficient response to nongovernment market failure in areas of the factor market such as information and knowledge. Imperfections in this factor market, at an international level, tend to generate the MNE. Of particular interest is the lack of regular markets for intermediate products such as research, information, and knowledge. These markets cannot be found in international trade because of the risk of loss of the knowledge advantage if direct sales were made in another nation.

Information is an intermediate product par excellence. It is the oil which lubricates the engine of the MNE. There is no proper market for the sale of information created by the MNE, and therefore, no price for it. There are surrogate prices; for example, those found by evaluating the opportunity cost of factor inputs expended in the production and processing of a new research discovery or by an ex post evaluation of the extra profits generated by that discovery, assuming all other costs to remain the same. Yet there is no simple interaction of supply and demand to set a market price. Instead the MNE is driven to create an internal market of its own in order to overcome the failure of an external market to emerge for the sale of information. This internal market of the MNE is an efficient response to the given exogenous market imperfection in the determination of the price of information. Internalization allows the MNE to solve the appropriability problem by assigning property rights in knowledge to the MNE organization.

The MNE will organize and administer its internal market for information in the best manner it can, subject to the traditional accounting practices and other conventions, which have to be followed. Once an internal market is in place, it becomes an integral part of the firm. Then it becomes difficult to distinguish aspects of the firm's organizational structure from its internal pricing. They are now interdependent. The possession of an internal market gives the MNE the ability to produce and distribute goods and services which are intensive in the use of information. It is this ability to effectively utilize information (an intermediate product) on an international level which distinguishes the MNE from other domestic corporations. It explains why the MNE has an advantage in foreign operations, since it can use overseas subsidiaries to produce goods similar to those developed in the home market, where these products all make use of the information monopoly of the MNE.

The creation of an internal market by the MNE permits it to transform an intangible piece of research into a valuable property specific to the firm. The MNE will exploit its advantage in all available markets and will keep the use of information internal to the firm in order to recoup its initial expenditures on research and knowledge generation. Production by subsidiaries is preferable to licensing or joint ventures since the latter two arrangements cannot benefit from the internal market of an MNE. They would therefore dissipate the information monopoly of the MNE, unless foreign markets were segmented by effective international patent laws or other protective devices.

Coase was the first to recognize "that the operation of a market costs something" and that the internal organization of a firm can be an efficient method of production.[11] There are transaction, contracting, and co-ordinating costs in using the price mechanism which lead frequently to vertical integration within the firm. The four types of costs are: the brokerage cost of finding a correct price; the cost of defining the obligations of parties in a contract; the risk of scheduling and related input costs; and the taxes paid on exchange transactions in a market. To avoid these costs the management team of the firm (or entrepreneur in the original Coasian conception) can use administrative fiat to set internal (transfer) prices. The firm can then control the production and marketing of an intermediate product through its vertically integrated structure. It is more efficient for the firm to set prices internally only when there are high transactions costs in using a regular market or when such a market cannot exist. Since the creation of a market by the MNE is not costless it is entitled to a fair return for doing internalization.

These fundamental insights of Coase are readily applicable to the MNE. There are presumably more imperfections and greater transactions costs in international than in domestic markets. These give rise to the MNE. It can enjoy worldwide economies of internal organization. These internal advantages must be sufficient to offset the additional costs of operating abroad in unfamiliar political and economic environments in order to have FDI replace potential indigenous production. Once established abroad the MNE will then use its inter-

---

11. Coase, "The Nature of the Firm", *Readings* (1953), p. 338.

nal organization to defend its market advantage. This advantage may have been generated, for example, in the firm specific use of knowledge, information, management, or marketing skills. Furthermore, the process of internalization by the MNE is a dynamic one. The MNE attempts to prevent dissipation of its knowledge (or other type of) advantage by maintaining control over the production and sales of final products which incorporate this firm specific advantage. Frequently, FDI is preferable to licensing since the latter process involves the risk of dissipation of the knowledge advantage.[12]

The genesis of the concept of internalization can be traced back to Hymer. His theoretical conception was used by Kindleberger to build up a modern theory of FDI based on product and factor market imperfections, scale economies, and government regulations, taxes, and tariffs.[13] These all serve to induce FDI by the MNE rather than portfolio investment or exporting. While these authors make market imperfections the centre of their theory, neither specifically identifies internalization as a paradigm for the theory of FDI.

The first explicit treatment of the relationship between knowledge market imperfections and internalization of markets for intermediate goods is in Buckley and Casson.[14] There is also an excellent synthesis of the modern literature of FDI, built around the concept of internalization, in Dunning.[15] The most rigorous treatment of internalization yet has appeared in Casson.[16]

Others to recognize the applicability of the Coasian model of the firm to the MNE are McManus, and Brown.[17] Unfortunately their contributions have been largely ignored by other economists and they had no impact on the separate development of internalization as a paradigm for FDI by economists associated with the University of Reading, such as Dunning and Casson. With the benefit of hindsight we can now see that it is a short step to move from analysis of one particular imperfection towards the development of a general theory

12. These points are explored in greater detail in Ian H. Giddy and Alan M. Rugman, *A Model of Trade, Foreign Direct Investment and Licensing* (Mimeo., Graduate School of Business, Columbia University, New York, 1979).
13. Kindleberger, *American Business Abroad*.
14. Buckley and Casson, *Future of the Multinational Enterprise*; reviewed in Giddy, "Demise of the Product Cycle", and ably summarized in Hood and Young, *Economics of Multinational Enterprise*.
15. Dunning, "Trade, Location of Economic Activity and the MNE".
16. Casson, *Alternatives*.
17. John McManus, "The Theory of the International Firm," *The Multinational Firm and the Nation State*, ed. Gilles Paquet (Toronto, 1972); Wilson B. Brown, "Islands of Conscious Power: MNCs in the Theory of the Firm", *MSU Business Topics*, 24 (East Lansing, 1976), pp. 37-54.

of FDI, in which all of the reasons for market failures are related to the internal organization of the MNE.

Internalization as a General Theory

It has now been shown that internalization is a refinement of the market imperfections approach, and that it explains why the MNE has a firm specific rather than a country specific advantage. Internalization is a synthesizing explanation of the motives for FDI. To demonstrate that the existing theories of FDI are really sub-cases of the theory of internalization it is now necessary to examine the more important versions of some of the important but apparently different models of FDI.

One of the most influential treatments of externalities and market imperfections is that of Caves.[18] He is able to link the imperfect market for knowledge with arguments which suggest that the MNE will respond to such an imperfection by engaging in product differentiation and horizontal integration, the latter to extend its monopoly advantage into world markets. The MNE tends to operate in oligopolistic markets and these encourage it to differentiate its product, or to utilize scale economies or some other firm specific advantage. The "Caves economies" of product differentiation advantages and horizontal integration can be contrasted with the "Coase economies" of information and knowledge advantages which occur under vertical integration. Both types are stressed here since they are the essence of internalization. The MNE is usually both vertically and horizontally integrated, so it is able to maintain its firm specific advantage quite readily.

Other writers have focussed upon the imperfect nature of the knowledge advantage of the MNE, without relating this explicitly to internalization. Johnson has shown that knowledge is a public good with a zero social price but a non-zero private cost which is borne by corporations as they engage in research and development.[19] To substitute for the missing regular market for knowledge production the MNE can create an internal market of its own in which the use of information by foreign subsidiaries can be monitored and repaid by fees payable to the parent firm (or other knowledge generator). Magee extends Johnson's analysis to deal with the appropriability problem of new information and technology for which there is no regular market.[20] These ideas are synthesized by Casson who demon-

18. Caves, "International Corporations".
19. Johnson, "Efficiency & Welfare Implications".
20. Magee, "Information and the Multinational Corporation"; "Multinational Corporations".

strates, in perhaps the most rigorous explanation of internalization to date, that the use of an internal market permits the MNE to retain control over its advantage in proprietary information.[21] Production by subsidiaries is preferable to licensing since the latter method involves a probable loss of control of the information monopoly obtained only at considerable expense by the MNE. Internalization allows the MNE to appropriate a fair return for its costly knowledge expenditures.

In an interesting paper, Hirsch has developed a model of international trade and production.[22] In it he explores the conditions required for exporting or FDI by a firm endowed with a firm specific knowledge advantage, K. Although not stated explicitly, his model treats K as an intermediate product which is internalized in the structure of the MNE. Hirsch unfortunately does not consider explicitly the conditions for licensing, the third possible method of serving a foreign market, along with exporting or FDI. This third option, of licensing, is viable at the end of the firm's technology cycle rather than at an early stage of foreign activity as is sometimes argued in the literature on international business. Hirsch also largely ignores the dynamic nature of technology; that is, the changing conditions under which the MNE can appropriate its firm specific advantage in K.

In this classic statement of the product cycle model, Vernon offers a powerful generalization of the process of FDI.[23] As is well known, he identifies three stages of product development and uses these to explain the crossover of exports and imports for three types of nations, over time. Initially the new product is produced by the home nation (often the United States) and exported to other nations. Next, as the product matures it starts to be produced by other (advanced) nations, often by subsidiaries of the home nation's MNEs. Finally the good becomes a standardized product, that is, one where no monopoly in information or other firm specific advantage is retained. In this third stage, production can start up in less-developed nations, continue in other advanced nations, but will decline in the home nation so that it now imports a product which was once exported.

The relevance of the internalization theory to Vernon's product cycle model lies in the basic motivation of research and knowledge generation which promotes a new product. The appropriate questions to ask are: what generates the initial research discovery in the home nation, and how can there be successive waves of product

21. Casson, *Alternatives*.
22. See Hirsch, "An International Trade and Investment Theory of the Firm", *Oxford Economic Papers*, N.S. **28** (Oxford, 1976), pp. 258-270.
23. Vernon, "International Investment".

cycles once such research discoveries continue on a dynamic basis? Clearly the dynamic nature of research generation lies at the heart of the theory of internalization, so the product cycle model is a subcase of it. Once the motivation of research is explained by internalization then everything else in the product cycle model follows.

Similarly in his latest work, Vernon is concerned about the spectre of entropy facing MNEs.[24] The MNE is in one of several categories; that is, in an innovation-based oligopolistic framework, or in a mature oligopoly or a senescent oligopoly. Vernon argues that the firm specific advantage of an MNE is in constant danger of being eroded and that the firm needs to overcome entropy to generate new advantages. Again the basic motivating factor for FDI can be seen to be the need for an MNE to generate firm specific advantages in a dynamic manner — the essence of internalization. Giddy has recognized this in a paper which relates the product cycle model to the theory of internalization.[25]

Defensive FDI is often undertaken by MNEs in an oligopolistic industry. They are concerned with protecting their market shares on a worldwide basis as well as on a domestic one. The concept of defensive investment was first postulated by Lamfalussy for domestic investment and has been applied in an international context, where it has received its most detailed treatment, by Knickerbocker.[26] The latter author found that foreign subsidiaries of firms in an oligopolistic industry tended to be established in clusters; that is, once one MNE set up a subsidiary in a nation then its rivals responded by opening their own affiliates in that market. Using an entry concentration index for each industry, Knickerbocker found that half of the two thousand U.S. foreign subsidiaries established between 1948 and 1967 were formed in three-year industry clusters and that three-quarters of the total were formed in at least seven-year clusters. He used data from the Harvard multinational data bank for the 187 U.S. multinationals identified by the project to confirm the oligopolistic reaction hypothesis.

The theory of defensive FDI and oligopolistic reaction by the MNEs is explained by the general theory of internalization. In the first place, there must exist an initial imperfect market, such as an oligopoly with price leadership or some collusion, in order to generate the concern with market shares on a world basis. If this oligopoly struc-

24. Vernon, *Storm over the Multinationals*.
25. Giddy, "Demise of the Product Cycle Model".
26. A. Lamfalussy, *Investment and Growth in Mature Economies: The Case of Belgium* (Oxford 1961); T. Frederick Knickerbocker, *Oligopolistic Reaction and Multinational Enterprise* (Boston, 1973).

ture exists in a domestic industry and a firm engages in FDI to secure its share of a foreign market then it is clearly attempting to retain its firm specific advantage, as will any MNE. Therefore, the theory of oligopolistic reaction is yet another example of firm specific advantages being exploited through FDI. Second, what the theory fails to explain is the reason for an initial foreign investment decision by one of the members of the oligopoly, to which the other members react. This initial FDI is explained by some other theory such as the product cycle model in which one firm generates a technological advantage, or by an attempt of the firm to differentiate its product and segment markets. In short, many of the reasons for the motivation of FDI can be applied here as explanations of the initial foreign investment. Since these reasons for FDI have already been shown to be part of internalization theory then the oligopolistic reaction hypothesis is another sub-case of internalization.

Kojima has proposed a "Japanese model" of FDI which is trade biased, that is, one in which FDI in resources, or other sectors where Japan has a comparative disadvantage, acts as a complement to trade.[27] He used a modified Heckscher-Ohlin model in which management skills and knowledge appear as a factor input — a specific factor model. Kojima argues that American FDI is trade destroying since it typically occurs in sectors where the United States has a large comparative advantage. Here FDI substitutes for trade, serves to export employment abroad and results in balance of payments problems. Kojima is extremely critical of the product cycle model and its variants which he terms the "American model" of FDI, since this model acts as an apologia for the transfer abroad of those industries in which the United States has a comparative advantage — due to its technological superiority.

The main problem with Kojima's analysis is that it is set in the static framework of trade theory. His model needs perfect markets and the assumptions of a Heckscher-Ohlin world. Clearly it is a mistake to regard technology as a homogeneous product over time and to ignore the dynamic nature of the technology cycle. It is probable that the United States has a comparative advantage, not in technology itself but in the generation of new knowledge. Therefore it is feasible for U.S. FDI in technology to take place to secure new markets on a continuous basis, as successive stages of the technology cycle are exploited, first in domestic markets and then in foreign ones.

Contrary to Kojima's allegations, most American FDI is not trade

27. Kojima, *Direct Foreign Investment.*

destroying but, in general, is undertaken to replace free trade. There are major barriers to trade in technologically advanced goods, due both to exogenous government imposed controls and also to endogenous restrictions imposed by the MNE. The latter restrictions are necessary since knowledge is a public good and only through the process of internalization is it feasible for a firm to organize a market for new technology. The MNE will seek out foreign markets in which price discrimination can be practiced in order to maximize its return on the information monopoly internal to the firm. Control over the use of information is necessary for the MNE to appropriate a private return for its investment in knowledge creation. FDI is a superior device to licensing since production and marketing by subsidiaries allow the MNE more successfully to avoid the risk of dissemination of its technological knowledge. FDI also replaces exporting once the latter is denied by tariffs, controls and other government imposed barriers to free trade. This FDI is trade replacing rather than trade destroying.

The location economics approach to FDI can also be regarded as an aspect of internalization, this time in a spatial context. The MNE can save transport costs by setting up an overseas subsidiary rather than relying on exports from the home nation. This spatial cost saving is another example of a firm specific advantage internalized by the MNE. As Robock demonstrates the location economies are more important for market-oriented MNEs than for ones in the aircraft or heavy engineering industries, since the latter types of product can achieve only a limited saving in transport costs.[28]

The location economics approach fails to recognize that international production is done by the MNE, so a firm specific explanation of the reasons for international activity is required. This explanation is that most MNEs are attempting to produce, and market, differentiated products; or they are creating an internal market for an intermediate good. In these cases the spatial dimension of MNE activity complements the other firm specific advantages characteristic of multinationals. Location theory is not an independent explanation of FDI but one which serves to reinforce the powerful predictive nature of internalization theory. Within the MNE knowledge is internationally mobile, transported by its internal market. While the sourcing of production by the MNE to service its foreign markets is often determined by location economies, the overall structure and operations of the MNE are determined by firm specific advantages. Ultimately, the MNE is always a creature of internalization.

28. Robock, *International Business*, ch. 3.

In a slightly different context, Leff has hypothesized that the imperfect goods and factor markets of poorer nations can be somewhat overcome by the "group" form of industrial organization.[29] The group is a multicompany firm run by owners and/or managers from a common cultural background and is frequently an association of individuals or families who are wealthy, relative to their neighbors. The group performs as an intermediary in pooling risks and in reducing information costs. It appears, therefore, to be a primitive type of Coasian firm searching for the benefit of an internal market. It is not clear if Leff firms are purely domestic ones, or if they have international activities. If they are not MNEs then the potential benefits of internalization are limited to the gains from avoiding market imperfections within the domestic economy. Clearly there are greater gains to be made on an international scale, given the lack of perfect integration of the economic and financial markets of poorer and richer nations.

Aliber makes an interesting attempt to introduce foreign exchange risk into the theory of FDI.[30] He assumes a world with different currency areas in which an MNE is able to borrow funds more cheaply than potential competitors in host nations since there is a premium on the currency of the home nation. This enhances the income stream of the MNE and permits it to engage in risky investments in the host nations. In effect, the MNE has a lower cost of capital due to its lower perceived foreign exchange rate risk. This model was postulated at a time when there was a premium on the U.S. dollar, and it appeared to explain the relatively large FDI by U.S.-based MNEs fairly well. Further, the model helps to explain recent developments such as the rapid growth of European- and Japanese-based MNEs, given the change-over to a premium on their currencies compared to the U.S. dollar. However, the model does not explain the continued net outflow of FDI from America in recent years, albeit at a reduced rate compared to the 1960s.

In any event, Aliber's model can be interpreted as another example of a firm specific advantage being internalized by the MNE. Here the advantage is in borrowing local funds in the host nation, given a strong home nation currency. The MNE enjoys this advantage in raising capital due to its internal structure which transcends national capital markets and permits it to calculate the risk and return of

29. Nathaniel H. Leff, "Industrial Organization and Entrepreneurship in the Developing Countries: The Economic Groups", *Economic Development and Cultural Change*, **26** (Chicago, 1978), pp. 661-675.
30. Aliber, "Theory of Direct Foreign Investment".

alternative investment in a broader manner than is possible for a uninational firm.

The theory of internalization can also be applied to the area of international diversification. The recent literature on international diversification has demonstrated a superior stock market performance for MNEs compared to uninational firms, after allowing for size and industry differences.[31] This superior performance is due to the advantage of the MNE in its exploitation of information through an internal market. The role of the MNE as a surrogate vehicle for individual international diversification in a world of capital market imperfections is intimately related to its ability to create an internal market which bypasses such imperfections. Here, as in the areas of imperfect markets discussed before, the MNE is responding in an efficient manner to an exogenous market imperfection.

International diversification has been a very useful addition to the literature on the MNE, since it directs attention toward the risk (variability) of earnings as well as their level (and most other theories ultimately show how the profit rate of the MNE is affected by the relevant market imperfection). Clearly the MNE only needs to be regarded as an indirect vehicle for international diversification when individual investors are confronted with financial market imperfections which make it impossible for them to build up efficient world portfolios themselves. Therefore the imperfections in the world's capital markets (or, at least, their lack of perfect integration) are another example of market failure leading to internalization (this time financial, rather than real) by the MNE.[32]

If a more interdisciplinary view is taken, the relevance of internalization as a central theory is retained. For example, much of the work by behavioral scientists focusses upon the strategy and structure of management decision making within the MNE — a clear emphasis upon the internal market activity of the MNE. Similarly research by those in marketing and management science frequently seeks to evaluate the success of the global planning of the MNE or examines various other aspects of the organization and operation of the MNE's internal market.[33] It will probably be some time before a truly

31. Alan M. Rugman, "Risk Reduction by International Diversification", *Journal of International Business Studies*, 7, No. 2 (Newark, 1976), pp. 75-80; "Risk, Direct Investment and International Diversification", *Weltwirtschaftliches Archiv* 113 (1977), pp. 487-500.
32. These points are discussed in more detail in Alan Rugman, *International Diversification and the Multinational Enterprise* (Lexington, 1979).
33. Some of these issues are examined by behavioral scientists and economists in *Functioning of the Multinational Corporation: A Global Comparative Study*, ed. Anant R. Negandhi (New York, 1980).

interdisciplinary approach to the MNE can be worked out but at least internalization is a promising route to follow.

Conclusion and Implications

The theory of internalization explains that the MNE develops an internal market in response to an externality. In the case of a classic externality — the failure of the market mechanism to set a price for the private production and dissemination of knowledge — the internal market of the MNE allows proprietary information to be used efficiently. The MNE can overcome an exogenous market imperfection governing the production of knowledge or another intermediate good by internalizing this externality. In a similar vein the concept of internalization can be applied to other areas of market imperfection, including those in international goods, labor, and capital markets. The same implication is reached, namely that the MNE is a device for the formation and exploitation of internal markets.

One of the problems in modelling the MNE is that it has the power, on occasions, to endogenize an imperfection and perpetuate a firm specific advantage. This is inefficient. Yet most market imperfections that exist in the real world are truly exogenous or are erected by governments. It is the latter imperfections, such as tariffs, taxes, and controls on international capital, that are of particular relevance in explaining the rise of the MNE. While the formation of the internal market is usually in response to a market imperfection, the continued exploitation of the firm specific advantage by the MNE often serves to maintain the advantage in an endogenous manner. Thus the MNE is both a victim of external market imperfections and a villain in seeking to retain them.

The process of internalization explains most (and probably all) of the reasons for FDI. Previous writers in the literature on the motives for FDI have tended to identify one or more of the imperfections in factor or product markets, or have noticed a response by the MNE to government-induced market imperfections such as tariffs, taxes, and capital controls. All of these types of market imperfection serve to stimulate one sort of MNE or another. The MNE is in the business of internalizing externalities. It is now time to recognize that internalization is a general theory of FDI and a unifying paradigm for the theory of the MNE.

A Note on the Theory of Internalization in a Canadian Context[34]

How does the new theory of the multinational enterprise developed by Buckley and Casson, Dunning, Casson, and Rugman apply to the Canadian situation? Canada is one of the primary examples of a host country rather than a home country from which the MNE originates. This dependence on net foreign direct investment is, in fact, being reduced and Canada today engages in substantial international production and sales through its own MNEs. As the Canadian economy increases in wealth, such multinational activity by its firms, and especially by its banks, is also likely to increase, perhaps even at a faster rate. However, for the purpose of this analysis it is useful to picture Canada in its traditional guise as a large net importer of foreign capital and as a repository for the branch plants of MNEs, over 80 per cent of which have historically been of American origin. In the sense of Agmon and Kindleberger,[35] Canada is a "small" nation. It is open to trade, MNEs, and foreign influence. Other examples are Australia and Switzerland.

The basic fact of Canada's being a host nation to the MNE demonstrates the relevance of the theory of internalization, a point anticipated by McManus in a neglected paper which extended the Coase theorem internationally.[36] For example, it reveals that the original research and development, and indeed the ongoing knowledge generation, it most likely centred upon the parent firm of the MNE, based in the United States. The MNE sets up and maintains subsidiaries in Canada in order to service the local market. The Canadian tariff has for a hundred years been an effective additional cost of export marketing facing the U.S. firm. The tariff has consequently not protected indigenous Canadian industry but instead has attracted American FDI.

Potential rival Canadian firms are only likely to license technology and knowledge advantages from U.S. firms at a stage in the technology cycle when there is little risk of the MNE losing these advantages through dissipation. Johnson and Magee have recognized this knowledge externality and the associated problem of appropriability.[37] Due to the difficulty of setting the correct price for a licence, the MNE may well prefer FDI to licensing. FDI avoids the risk of undercharging

---

34. This section is a revised version of Rugman, *Multinationals in Canada*, pp. 59-62. Reprinted with permission.
35. *Multinationals from Small Countries*, ed. Agmon and Kindleberger.
36. McManus, "Theory of the International Firm".
37. Johnson, "Efficiency and Welfare Implications"; Magee, "Information and the Multinational Corporation".

for the licence as well as the probability of dissipation of knowledge. These are some of the implications to be drawn from the Giddy-Rugman model.[38]

Other factors can possibly be identified as important causal events attracting FDI: horizontal and vertical integration, for example,[39] or market imperfections.[40] Yet, apart from the location variable, that is, the obvious geographical proximity of Canada to the U.S. (which is as much an advantage for potential Canadian exporters as it is for American ones) most of these can usually be identified as subordinate explanations to the generalized theory of internalization. For example, international tax rate differentials, or an occasional period of effective currency exchange controls, may have induced the MNE to use transfer prices in order to maximize its earnings. Such internal prices are an efficient response by the MNE to exogenous market imperfections imposed by government regulation. Canada is unlikely to be used for offshore assembly of goods by U.S. MNEs (as its labor costs now exceed those of the U.S.A.), but the assembly argument is another example of the use of internal administrative fiat by the MNE.

The nature of the Canadian federation is also partly responsible for the large amount of American foreign ownership of its industry and resources. The federal government is not as powerful as the national governments of Britain or the United States. Many economic powers, especially the control of land, minerals, and other resources, reside with governments of the provinces. They give incentives to FDI and encourage foreign firms to enter their particular province to bring rates of output and opportunities for more regional employment. Unfortunately, there is insufficient harmonization of tax policy (and other regulations affecting corporations) between federal and provincial governments. This leads inevitably to a morass of market imperfections and the now classic response of internalization by the MNEs.

The non-uniform nature of the Canadian economy and federal-provincial efforts to reduce regional income disparities have led to industry location incentives and other policies for regional economic development. These, and other, subsidies to industries have encouraged MNEs to open branch plants that they probably would have been happy to establish anyway. Provincial governments have tried to outbid each other in fighting for the establishment of a subsidiary in their own territory. Their political leaders are aware of the benefits in terms of employment creation, tax revenue, and output genera-

38. Giddy and Rugman, *A Model of Trade*.
39. Caves, "International Corporations".
40. Hymer, "International Operations".

tion provided by the MNE subsidiary. These provincial leaders have many economic levers to pull in order to attract the MNE — possibly too many for the good of the country as a whole.

In the area of research and science policy there are similar lessons to be drawn by application of the theory of internalization. The majority of Canadian industry is foreign owned. If the theory of internalization tells us anything it is that the initial and ongoing knowledge generation takes place in the U.S. parent firm and not in the Canadian subsidiaries. Yet Canadian science policy attempts to encourage research and development by Canadian industry at large. It is, therefore, doomed to failure, since the majority of firms receiving funding are the subsidiaries of the U.S. MNEs. These subsidiaries, by definition of their role, are not geared for original or even innovative research. Neither are they likely to have a comparative advantage in knowledge generation, although Canada itself may have some such (unrealized) potential.

The failure of Canadian science policy to generate any substantive indigenous technology advantage has been documented by Safarian and McFetridge,[41] and is related to tariff policy in an imaginative study by Daly and Globerman.[42] An implication of the theory of internalization is that Canadian funding for research should be directed toward independent local firms only, or to universities and specialized research centres. Basic research can be stimulated in the latter, and product innovation conceivably can be generated in truly indigenous firms. In turn, the latter will become prototypes for the Canadian MNEs of the future.

The forgoing is a type of infant technology argument for a subsidy. It is related to the infant industry argument for a tariff, but it actually has a better economic rationale. The infant technology argument is in the form of a subsidy rather than a tariff, so it avoids the secondary distortions that arise once a tariff alters the relative prices of traded to non-traded goods. Johnson and Corden have shown that the unforeseen secondary distortions of the tariff in a general equilibrium system are to be avoided whenever possible.[43]

If the objective of Canadian public policy is to promote technological advantages in domestic industry, then the correct economic

41. D. G. McFetridge, *Government Support of Scientific Research and Development: An Economic Analysis* (Toronto: University of Toronto Press, 1977); A. E. Safarian, *Foreign Ownership of Canadian Industry* (Toronto: McGraw-Hill, 1966).

42. D. J. Daly, and S. Globerman, *Tariff and Science Policies: Applications of a Model of Nationalism* (Toronto: University of Toronto Press, 1976).

43. Max Corden, *Trade Policy and Economic Welfare* (Oxford: Oxford University Press, 1974); Johnson, "Efficiency & Welfare Implications".

way to proceed is by a direct subsidy to indigenous industry rather than by the tariff or the regulation of FDI. In the case of transfer of technology it is possible to apply the theory of internalization in a Canadian context to demonstrate that a public subsidy may conceivably generate a firm specific knowledge advantage. In time, the incipient Canadian-based MNEs may rival the more established U.S.-based MNEs, which continue to dominate the Canadian economy at the present time.

Future empirical work using internalization as a seminal base is required before the implications drawn here can be accepted with greater certainty. Such empirical work should consider the firm's choice between the modes of exporting, FDI, or licensing. It can do this in a logical fashion by a comparison of relative net profits of each mode. Additional information can come from data on relative R & D expenditures at firm level and from analysis of royalties and licence fees, or an evaluation of transfer pricing.

Public policy in Canada would do well to recognize the special role of the MNE in Canadian industry. It is an organization with a knowledge advantage and Canada is just one market to be serviced in an efficient manner. The Canadian tariff has denied exporting to the U.S. firms, and licensing is perhaps a risky option, so the firm is left with FDI. Over the years, Canada has maintained market imperfections such as tariffs and non-tariff barriers to trade which have, if anything, encouraged the MNE to internalize markets. The more recent introduction of FIRA acts on another market imperfection which attempts to regulate the effect (multinational firms) rather than the cause (tariffs). Unless there is a dramatic change in the direction of Canadian public policy, it would appear that FDI will continue to respond to such government-induced externalities, as well as such natural externalities as knowledge and technology. All our theory indicates that the MNE will continue to use the process of internalization to service the Canadian market in the future.

IV
Foreign Direct Investment Theory, Impact, and Control

B
Patterns

20
Foreign Investment in Canada: An Overview by Source

Joan Gherson

Gilles Gratton

Carl H. McMillan

The Japanese and U.S. sections of this chapter were written by Joan Gherson, an economist with the Research and Analysis Branch of the Foreign Investment Review Agency. The East European section was written by Carl McMillan, director of the Institute of Soviet and East European Studies of Carleton University. The West European section was written by Gilles Gratton, editor of *L'investisseur étranger*, which is the French counterpart of *Foreign Investment Review*.

The sections of this chapter appeared originally as separate articles in *Foreign Investment Review* in Spring 1979, Autumn 1979, and Spring 1980. Reprinted by permission of the minister of Supply and Services Canada.

Japanese Investment in Canada*

A significant development in recent years has been the growing importance of Japanese overseas investment. Although Japanese capital represents only a small fraction of all foreign investment in Canada, several features have made it unique and interesting, including a tendency toward loans rather than equity, a high incidence of minority holdings and joint ventures, and a marked orientation toward western rather than central Canada, which has been the usual target for foreign investment in this country.

From 1970 to 1978 nearly $27 billion was authorized for overseas investment by Japanese companies. This represents an average annual investment exceeding the cumulative total of the previous two decades. Even though actual investment falls short of the licensed amount because some approved projects fail to materialize, the rate of growth has still been remarkable, raising Japan from a negligible foreign investor to one of the foremost in the course of a decade. If the current annual level of investment is maintained at over $4 billion, Japan could become the world's second largest investor in the 1980s.

Japanese licensed investment in Canada also increased substantially and at a faster pace overall than that of most other investing countries. From a total of only $113 million in 1969, accumulated investment grew to $715 million by 1978-79.

Despite its considerable growth record, Japanese investment in this country has not kept pace with total Japanese investment overseas. From 1951 to 1970 the Canadian share of the total was nearly 6 per cent of all licensed Japanese foreign investment. For 1970 alone, when investment for that year nearly equalled the total of the previous two decades, it accounted for a remarkable 10.8 per cent of Japanese overseas investment. Since then, however, Canada has had a substantially smaller share. This country now accounts for only 3 per cent of all outstanding Japanese foreign investment, ranking eighth in the scale of recipients. Changing Japanese priorities account for that

* "Japanese Investment in Canada", by Joan Gherson.

decrease. During the 1970s worldwide Japanese investment in mining and forest products, the two most important targets for investment in Canada, grew more slowly than total Japanese investment. The manufacturing sector, on the other hand, increased its share of the total, but that investment was largely directed towards the developing countries.

Besides being a small proportion of total Japanese investment, the Canadian share represents a small proportion of total foreign investment in Canada. Though Japan ranked seventh among investing countries in 1975, it accounted for less than 1 per cent of all foreign direct investment (based on actual, rather than authorized, investment and excluding portfolio investment). Later figures are not available, but applications under the Foreign Investment Review Act indicate a continuing low level of Japanese-controlled investment. From 1976 to 1978 only 2 per cent of the applications were from Japan and allowed Japanese investments accounted for a mere 0.3 per cent of the total value of investments allowed.

Characteristics of Japanese Investment
Japanese investment is unlike traditional foreign investment in Canada. A high proportion of it is in the form of loans rather than equity, and the Japanese often take minority holdings or enter joint ventures. Another unique characteristic is the extensive participation of the large Japanese trading houses. In addition, while most foreign investment is destined for central Canada, Japanese investment is earmarked mainly for western Canada, particularly British Columbia and Alberta.

Just over half of Japanese investment in Canada is in equity. The rest is mainly in the form of loans, including corporate bonds and debentures, with a very small amount in real estate and branches. This distribution almost exactly parallels that of Japan's worldwide investment but differs markedly from its pattern in the United States where 70 per cent is in equity. In forest products and metal fabricating, the chief focus of Japan's manufacturing investment in Canada, the ratio of loans to equity is higher than the average, whereas in the principal non-manufacturing sectors, mining and trade, it is lower. In the trade sector, equity accounts for over 90 per cent of the investment.

As mentioned above, the high incidence of joint ventures is a distinctive feature of Japanese investment. On a worldwide basis, only about 10 per cent of subsidiaries are wholly Japanese owned and less than one-third are majority owned. Canadian experience confirms this general pattern, and it is one of the reasons why

Figure 1

Cumulative Japanese Investment in Canada by Industry Sector December 1978

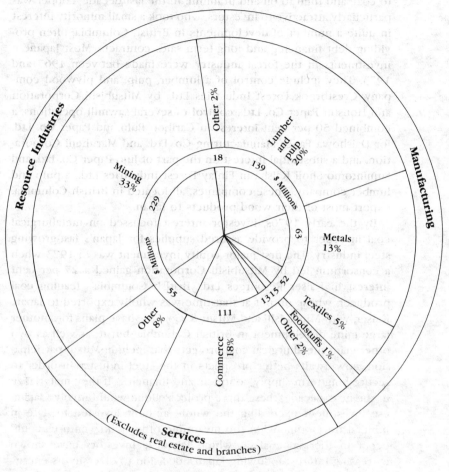

Canadian data on foreign direct investment, which does not include portfolio investment, show Japanese investment to be less than half the licensed investment.

Investment by Sector
Resource development and resource-related industries account for more than half of Japan's accumulated investment in Canada. Of these, mining is the most important (33 per cent), followed by forest

industries (20 per cent). Since Japan's investment in resources is mainly motivated by its industry's need for raw materials, its targets have changed over time from non-ferrous metals and forest products to coal, and then to oil and uranium. In the last decade, copper was particuarly attractive to investors, who took a small minority interest in quite a number of developments in British Columbia, often providing debt financing and long-term sales contracts. Most Japanese investments in the forest industry were made between 1967 and 1973. They include control of a lumber, pulp, and plywood company, Crestbrook Forest Industries Ltd., by Mitsubishi Corporation and Honshu Paper Co. Ltd., control of several sawmill operations, a combined 50 per cent interest in Cariboo Pulp and Paper Co. Ltd. for Daishowa Paper Manufacturing Co. Ltd. and Marubeni Corporation, and a substantial interest on the part of Jujo Paper Co. Ltd. and Sumintomo Shoji Kaisha in Finlay Forest Industries Ltd., a pulp and lumber company. These companies, all located in British Columbia, export most of their wood products to Japan.

By the early 1970s, investor interest focussed on metallurgical coal in order to provide assured supplies for Japan's fast-growing steel industry. The first major equity investment was in 1973 when a consortium led by Mitsubishi Corporation gained a 27 per cent interest in Kaiser Resources Ltd., British Columbia's leading coal producer, whose output at that time was wholly exported to Japan. Kaiser, with Mitsubishi and Mitsui & Co. Ltd., have plans for another large mine development in British Columbia, but it, as well as two other giant metallurgical coal projects that include Mitsui participation, now awaits better prospects in the steel industry in order to secure long-term supply contracts and financing. If they materialize in the next decade, these three projects alone would involve Japanese investment exceeding the whole amount invested to date in mineral development. In the meantime other joint ventures could occur in thermal coal, in which Japanese investors have shown increasing interest following Japan's decision to diversify its energy sources.

High-priced oil and diminishing reserves of conventional oil have sparked great Canadian and foreign interest in non-conventional oil resources in Alberta. Two Japanese companies, both controlled by the Japan National Oil Company, are now involved in important projects for developing in situ technology for oil recovery from these resources. One, a joint venture between Japan Oil Sands Co. Ltd. and Norcen Energy Resources of Canada, is concluding a pilot program using steam injection for heavy oil recovery; a decision about commercial production has not yet been made. In another joint venture with Petro Canada and other partners, Japan Oil Sands Alberta Ltd. will invest at least $75 million over the next fifteen years to develop new technology for recovering oil from oil sands by electrical induction.

Reflecting their substantial commitment to nuclear energy for generating electricity, the Japanese are also engaging in exploration for uranium. PNC Explorations (Canada) Co., a newly formed subsidiary of the Japanese government agency, Power Reactor and Nuclear Fuel Development Corp., has several projects in Canada, including a partnership with Eldorado Nuclear Ltd. and Saskatchewan Mineral Development Co. (SMDC) at Beaverlodge, Saskatchewan and a 45 per cent interest, also in partnership with SMDC, at Wollaston Lake. With an annual budget of only $2.5 million, however, PNC's expenditure is but a very small part of the nearly $70 million spent last year on uranium exploration in Canada.

Except in pulp and paper, Canada has not been as successful as Europe or the United States in attracting Japanese capital in manufacturing. The few Japanese companies that are in Canada, however, produce a wide range of products, from Japanese milk products to plastic products and color televisions. Many of them are joint ventures, combining Japanese technology and financing with Canadian market access. Titan Steel and Wire Co. Ltd., a large cable manufacturing company, is one such Japanese-Canadian venture, in which Kobe Steel Ltd. and Mitsui Corporation are the Japanese partners. Another is Sekine Canada Ltd., which makes bicycles for the Canadian market using Japanese Sekine Industries Ltd. technology. There are also a number of joint ventures in textiles, mainly in Quebec, the largest being Fuji Dyeing and Printing Limited, engaged in dyeing, printing, and finishing textiles. The Japanese partners in this venture are C. Itoh & Co. Ltd., Seiren Co. Ltd., and Teijin Ltd. An important manufacturer of ball and roller bearings with substantial world exports is NTN Bearing Mfg. Canada Ltd. Beginning as a joint venture with Canadian-owned CAE Industries Ltd., the firm is now Japanese controlled.

There are also substantial Japanese investments in some food processing activities, mainly oil seeds and fish products. The several minority interests and joint ventures in western Canada oil seed processing plants all date from 1973-76. Interest in fisheries began much earlier. Marubeni Corp.'s 50 per cent holding in Cassiar Packing Company Ltd. dates from 1962, while Taiyo Fishery Co. Ltd. has been established on the east coast since 1966. Recently, Japanese investors have shown renewed interest in this resource.

One investment intention which could dwarf all previous invest-

Table 1

Japanese Applications to the Foreign Investment Review Agency*

	Acquisitions	New Businesses
Number of Applications		
Allowed	13	15
Disallowed	2	1
Withdrawn	3	5
Allowed Applications by Sector		
Resources	2	1
Manufacturing	2	4
Services	9	10
Allowed Applications by Region		
British Columbia	5	7
Prairie Provinces	1	—
Ontario	5	6
Quebec	2	1
Atlantic Provinces	—	1

*To March 31, 1979

Chart 1

Japanese Licensed Investment in Canada (million dollars)

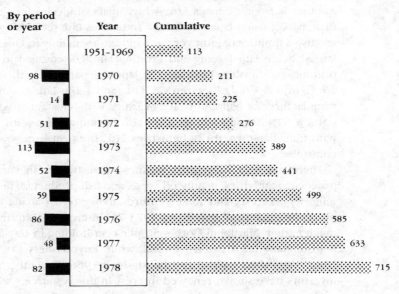

By period or year	Year	Cumulative
	1951–1969	113
98	1970	211
14	1971	225
51	1972	276
113	1973	389
52	1974	441
59	1975	499
86	1976	585
48	1977	633
82	1978	715

Source: Japanese Ministry of Finance.

ment in manufacturing is the $225 million Petrochemicals Alberta Project (Petalta), a world-scale benzene plant, in which Mitsubishi Corp. is a partner.

In terms of the number of investments, the service sector, which covers trade, warehousing, banking, and other activities, is by far the largest. Nearly 40 per cent of licensed investments have been in this sector. Moreover, since they more often involve Japanese control, these investments represent an even higher proportion of cases reviewed under the Foreign Investment Review Act. Of the twenty-three Japanese investment proposals allowed under the Act between 1974 and 1978, nineteen were attributed to service industries. Their average value, however, is small and consequently services account for only about a quarter of the value of licensed investment. This sector includes the captive distributors of Japanese manufacturers and the Canadian subsidiaries of major Japanese trading companies who play a major part in servicing the $1.7 billion import and $2.5 billion export trade with Japan. Annual revenues of the three largest of these companies, Mitsubishi Canada, Mitsui & Co. (Canada), and Marubeni Canada, place them in the top 100 firms in Canada, according to the Canadian Business Magazine listing. Nissan Automobile Co. Canada, which imports Datsun cars and trucks, Canadian Honda Motors Limited, and Canadian Motor Holdings Ltd. (Toyota), are in the top 200 companies. Most of the other well-known Japanese manufacturers such as Sony, Panasonic, Hitachi, Yashica, Noritake, as well as some lesser known firms, also have substantial distributing companies in Canada. This trading group includes most of the wholly owned Japanese companies in Canada, although some have Canadian partners. It also represents the oldest Japanese investments in Canada, many dating from the early 1950s when Japanese trading companies began to establish themselves around the world.

Increasing travel between Canada and Japan has encouraged investment in tourism. C. Itoh & Co., for example, has a minority interest in a company selling package tours between the two countries and Prince Hotels Inc. owns a hotel in Toronto. In the financial sector, several Japanese banks have established representative offices in Canada.

Outlook for Japanese Investment
The slower growth rate of the past several years and the decreases in 1974 and 1977 have deflated previous Japanese investment forecasts which were based on annual increases of 20 per cent or more. Nevertheless, many factors point to continued high levels of Japanese foreign investment over the next several years. Foreign invest-

ment by Japanese companies is being encouraged by the Japanese government to help reduce the large accumulation of foreign exchange reserves and to offset protectionist measures against Japanese exports. At the same time, the relatively high exchange value of the yen makes foreign investments increasingly attractive to Japanese firms. In addition, rising Japanese labor and electricity costs have made manufacturing more competitive in some foreign locations and growing environmental concern in Japan may limit further industrialization at home. Finally, Japanese fiscal policy and the establishment of the EXIM bank favor new investment in resource projects. The increase in overseas investment in 1978 has also encouraged expectations for a period of renewed growth.

The outlook for Japanese investment in Canada is also quite favorable. One hopeful sign was the slight rise in Canada's share of total Japanese foreign investment in 1978 after several years of steady decline. That decline was largely attributed to the slower growth of Japanese investment in the resource sector. Worldwide Japanese investment in resources is not expected to accelerate, but there are a number of reasons why a larger proportion could be directed to Canada. First, Japanese investments in this country's resources have been increasingly directed to energy resources. The outlook for this sector, and for fisheries, in which there is increasing Japanese interest, is more favorable than for other raw materials, though much will depend on Canadian investment and export policies in these sensitive areas. Another factor that favors Canada for resource investment is its reputation as a stable and reliable source of supply. In a recent survey, Japanese investors ranked Canada higher than any other resource area in terms of investment climate.

While investment in Canadian resources should grow despite a general slowing of Japanese resource investment growth, the manufacturing sector could benefit from the trend towards establishing new plants, particularly for consumer durables, in developed countries. Thus far, the United States and Europe have been the chief beneficiaries of that investment, but the recent improvement in Canada's competitive position, a result of the lower exchange level of the dollar and increased industrial productivity, could spark new interest. Specific measures, such as the remission of duty on certain imported manufactures in return for purchases of Canadian components, could also encourage the production in Canada of parts for export. For manufacturing generally, Canada's resource base and its relative advantages in energy will be important factors in future development. Greatly increased contact between Japan and Canada, not only of officials, both federal and provincial, but also of busi-

Figure 2

Some Japanese Trading Companies[a] and Their Canadian Investments

Mitsui & Co. Ltd. — trading, minerals, warehousing, wire manufacturing, venture capital.	**Nissho-Iwai Co., Ltd.** — trading, oil seed processing.
	Sumintomo Shoji Kaisha Ltd. — trading, lumber, minerals
Marubeni Corporation — trading, fish processing, construction, wire products, minerals, oil, and gas	**Kunematsu-Gosho Ltd.** — trading
Mitsubishi Corp. — trading, oil seed processing, minerals, pulp, lumber, beef processing, venture capital	**Toyo Menka Kaisha Ltd.** — trading
	Itoman & Co. Ltd. — trading
C. Itoh & Co., Ltd. — trading, oil seed processing.	

(a) Includes subsidiaries

nessmen, through trade and investment missions and the Canada-Japan Business Co-operation Committee, are fostering a greater awareness of the mutual benefits of investment.

Soviet and East European Direct Investment in Canada*

In March 1978, the Economic and Social Council of the United Nations published the conclusions of its first major re-examination since 1973 of the role of the transnational corporation in world development. The report revealed that from 1967 to 1976 the relative importance of foreign direct investment from both developing and socialist countries had increased. Canada has been one of the countries affected by increased socialist foreign investment.

The socialist countries of Eastern Europe (USSR, Bulgaria, Czechoslovakia, German Democratic Republic, Hungary, Poland, and Romania) have been following over the past decade a strategy of re-entry into the world economy. An important facet of this strategy has been the establishment of companies in the West, either wholly owned or owned jointly with local or other foreign partners. Most of these companies have been formed in industrialized Western countries, but an increasing number of direct investments have been made in developing countries. The East-West Project in the Institute of Soviet and East European Studies at Carleton University in Ottawa has

* "Soviet and East European Direct Investment in Canada", by Carl H. McMillan.

identified 356 companies in the OECD countries in which equity was held at the end of 1978 by state enterprises of the USSR and its six East European partners in the Council for Mutual Economic Assistance (COMECON). In addition it has found 179 Soviet and East European direct investments in developing countries. Of the 356 OECD companies 23 per cent are wholly owned by socialist parent enterprises. The socialist share amounts to 50 per cent or more in all but 15 per cent of the remaining mixed equity companies.

The major socialist investors in the industrialized West are the USSR (91 companies), Poland (87), and Hungary (57). They have invested mainly in Germany, France, the United Kingdom, Austria, Italy, the Benelux countries, and Sweden. By end-1978, 39 Soviet and East European companies had been established in North America, 15 in Canada and 24 in the United States. Ten of the U.S. companies were founded after 1975 (2 in 1978), whereas only 1 new company was established in Canada during that period.

Information on the book value of socialist direct investment in the West is fragmentary. Carleton's East-West Project estimates the assets of companies in the industrialized West, in which there is socialist equity, at more than $750 million. Much of this is concentrated in the 23 banks and insurance and leasing companies owned by the socialist countries. The average assets of the remaining companies barely exceed $1 million.

The reason for the small average value of the assets of most socialist companies abroad is that they are concentrated in the service sector, especially in marketing and transportation. Socialist investments in the West, however, are becoming more diversified with a growing number of banks and more investments in the extractive and manufacturing industries.

Soviet and East European Investments in Canada
The 15 Soviet and East European companies in Canada are relatively new, the exceptions being Omnitrade Ltd. and Pekao Trading Company which were founded in the early post-war period. Most of the companies, representing investments by the Soviet Union, Hungary, Czechoslovakia, Romania, and Bulgaria, were founded between 1971 and 1976.

In 12 of the companies, socialist equity represents a majority share and, in eleven, 95 per cent or more. The capital invested in these companies is not great, however, with individual investments ranging from $25,000 to $1 million. While balance-of-payments data specifically on direct Soviet and East European investment in Canada are not available, Statistics Canada estimated the book value of direct investment by the "centrally planned economies" from 1971 to the end of 1975 at $20 million, including long-term loans from parent to subsidiary as well as equity capital invested by the controlling country. Most of this investment was from the USSR (which accounted for more than half), Czechoslovakia, and Poland with most of it occurring in 1974 and 1975. Since 1975, the socialist countries have apparently not found that the state of the Canadian market justified significant new investments. Furthermore, socialist practice is to support the development of existing companies, wherever possible, through the reinvestment of profits or through local borrowings.

Fourteen of the companies were established to market products exported to Canada by the socialist parent or by other enterprises in the home country. The other, also in the service sector, is an agent for Soviet shipping on the Pacific coast.

In contrast to the trading firms established earlier, all of the companies founded in the 1970s are specialized by product. The majority, moreover, specialize in the marketing of machinery and equipment such as agricultural implements, machine tools, electric turbines, and aircraft. The higher capitalization of some of these companies shows that product modification and servicing are an important adjunct to their sales. For example, the Soviet machine-tool firm, Stan-Canada Machinery Ltd., has an impressive headquarters in Toronto with large showrooms and built-in warehouse and staging areas. It also has similar though smaller facilities in Montreal.

Soviet and East European investments in Canada could gradually extend to other sectors, the most probable being fisheries, mining, manufacturing (assembly of imported machinery and equipment components), and even banking, if the relevant amendments to the Bank Act are adopted. Several cases suggest such an extension. Polish-Canadian fishing ventures have been discussed. The Czechoslovak company Omnitrade Ltd. in Montreal has extended its activities to production (mining machinery) through the acquisition of a local manufacturing firm. The Soviet-owned Moscow Narodny Bank Ltd. of London has long considered establishing a North American branch. Finally, the Romanians are reported to be interested in gaining access to supplies of Canadian metallurgical coal. They might take an equity interest in a Canadian operation, as they sought to do in the United States in the development of the Island Creek Coal Co. in Virginia, a subsidiary of Occidental Petroleum. U.S. tax regulations discouraged the Romanians from investing directly in the Island Creek operation, and they settled for a $53 million advance payment in return for guaranteed annual shipments of metallurgical coal at agreed terms over a period of thirty-five years.

In the case of mixed equity companies, the Canadian partners are frequently individuals (company lawyers or former agents) who are senior executives or directors. In other cases, the partners are usually small Canadian companies with prior association as representatives in Canada of the socialist parent enterprise. Allarco Developments Ltd. is the only well-known Canadian joint investor, its subsidiary, International Jet Air, owning one-third of Socan Aircraft Ltd. of Calgary, which was established to market a small Soviet passenger jet aircraft called the Yak-40.

The staff of a socialist company in Canada is a mixture of Canadians and nationals from the home country. The nationals usually occupy some of the principal management and most technical positions, while Canadians are usually in sales, public relations, and clerical positions.

Investor Motives

The principal motive for Soviet and East European investments in Canada has been to facilitate the sale of socialist products or, as in the case of Morflot Freightliners Ltd., services in the North American market. The new socialist external strategy in the 1970s has involved a major drive to expand manufactured exports. While traditional socialist exports to the West have been primary products that can be marketed through trade missions or local agents, more effective marketing techniques are needed to expand exports of diversified and sophisticated manufactured products and related services.

New objectives require new instruments. Development of a permanent market in the West for industrial machinery and equipment or consumer goods requires not only detailed knowledge of customer needs and preferences, but rapid and flexible servicing of their demands. Trade mission officials do not have either the specialized knowledge or the time required by such markets. Local agents have also been increasingly regarded as unsatisfactory, their interests frequently conflicting with those of their socialist employers. By pursuing their own profits, local agents frequently overlook socialist manufactured goods in favor of the more marketable goods of other clients, sometimes the direct competitors of the socialist enterprises. Furthermore, direct investment is necessary to establish an effective infrastructure, including the marketing and servicing of machinery and equipment, warehousing and support facilities, dealer networks, and technical service centres.

The decision to take on a local partner is basically the same for socialist and capitalist investors, both having to weigh the advantages of association with a materially interested partner who has local contacts and expertise, against those of full control. In the case of East-West partnerships, however, investors must consider additional factors. Socialist products, developed in a very different economic environment, can confront special problems on Western markets which a partnership, with its greater local identity and know-how, may help to overcome. On the other hand, the bureaucratic nature of the socialist parent and the centralized system of state planning and control under which it operates can make joint equity ventures particularly difficult.

Policy Issues for Host Countries
The growth of direct investment by Soviet and East European state enterprises raises certain policy issues for Canada and other Western host countries. While Soviet and East European direct investment in Canada is presently insignificant relative to other international investment flows, it seems likely to continue to grow rapidly and diversify as the socialist countries pursue new markets and sources of supply in the West. Trends in the internalization of production suggest that Soviet and East European investment will increasingly extend to the extractive, processing, and manufacturing industries as the socialist countries become increasingly involved in the world economy. Though ownership and management of productive assets in a capitalist economy create serious ideological problems for socialist countries and persistent hard-currency deficits constrain their ability to undertake major capital investments in the West, they will have to expand and diversify their foreign investment in order to meet the requirements of international sourcing and more effective servicing of foreign markets.

A second cause for concern is the potential political influence that could be exercised by the socialist countries through direct ownership and control of companies abroad. This could lead to actions contrary to the interests of host countries. Direct foreign investment by state-owned corporations, however, is not limited to East-West relations, but is also common to relations among Western countries. Moreover, there have been well-publicized instances of private Western multinationals being used by governments for covert political activities in host countries. Nevertheless, Soviet and East European investors cause special concern because they are subject to a more centralized governmental control and their national objectives are more likely to conflict with those of host countries in the West.

In these circumstances, the operational record of the companies in question is crucial. Evidence indicates that Soviet and East European companies in Canada follow familiar commercial norms and that

Table 2

Soviet and East European Companies in Canada

Company	Head Office	Year Established	Socialist Partner	Socialist Equity	Issued Share Capital	Principal Activity
Omnitrade Ltd.	Montreal	1947	Transakta (Czechoslovakia)	100%	$1,000,000	Sells and services wide range of industrial products.
Pekao Trading Company Canada Ltd.	Toronto	1956	Bank Polska Kasa Opieki (Poland)	99%	$ 25,000	Sells consumer and manufactured products.
Dalimpex Ltd.	Montreal	1965	DAL (Poland)	95%	$ 150,000	Sells and services wide range of consumer and industrial products.
Cebecom Ltd.	Toronto	1965	Bulgarkonserv (Bulgaria)	50%	$ 47,600	Sells fruits, conserves, and other food products.
Motokov Canada Inc.	Montreal	1966	Motokov (Czechoslovakia)	100%	$ 725,000	Sells and services Czech motorcycles, bicycles, and mopeds.
Superlux Canada Ltd.	Montreal	1967	Glassexport (Czechoslovakia)	100%	$ 100,000	Sells products of Czech glass industry.
Morflot Freightliners Ltd.	Vancouver	1971	Sovinflot (USSR)	95%	$ 100,000	Agent for Soviet shipping to Canadian west coast.

Company	City	Year	Exporter (country)	%	Value	Description
Belarus Equipment Ltd.	Toronto	1972	Traktoroexport; Zapchastexport (USSR)	100%	$ 500,000	Sells and services Soviet agricultural equipment in Canada.
Stan-Canada Machinery Ltd.	Toronto	1972	Stankoimport (USSR)	100%	$ 900,000	Sells and services Soviet machine tools in Canada and the United States.
EMEC Trading Ltd.	Vancouver	1973	Energomachexport (USSR)	95%	$ 414,000	Sells and installs electrical generators and turbines.
Omnitrade Industrial Co. Ltd.	Montreal	1973	Transakta (Czechoslovakia)	100%	$ 50,000	Sells and services textile machinery and other products in the United States through operating divisions in New York and North Carolina.
Hungarotex-Canada Ltd.	Montreal	1974	Hungarotex (Hungary)	50%	$ 50,000	Sells Hungarian textiles in Canada and abroad.
Terra Power Tractor Company Ltd.	Saskatoon	1974	Universal Tractor (Romania)	100%	$ 100,000	Sells and services Romanian agricultural equipment in western Canada.
Socan Aircraft Ltd.	Calgary	1975	Aviaexport (USSR)	67%	$ 50,000	Sells and services Soviet aircraft.
Ascott Equipment Ltd.	Sherbrooke	1976	Universal Tractor (Romania)	49%	$ 150,000	Sells and services agricultural equipment in eastern Canada.

Source: Information on file in the East-West Project, Institute of Soviet and East European Studies, Carleton University.

their operations do not differ markedly from those of other foreign-owned firms. Furthermore, there have been no publicized cases of subversive behavior.

The commercial objectives of the socialist companies are compatible with Canadian interests, their primary purpose being to adapt their products and services to Canadian needs. The benefits of Canadian imports from the socialist countries should therefore increase. In the case of countries such as the USSR, who have persistently had large trade deficits with Canada, their expanded exports are a means of creating a better balance of trade and a more stable base for the further expansion and normalization of trade relations.[1]

West European Investments in Canada*

In recent years, European multinational corporations have been gaining significant ground on their U.S. counterparts. European firms have taken the lead in some sectors and have significantly improved their rank in many others. For example, Hoechst and BASF have become world leaders in the chemical industry; Philips (Netherlands) and Siemens (West Germany) now rank third and fourth as producers of household appliances and electronic equipment; Gutehoffnung-shutte and Brown Boveri are second and third in general engineering; Flick and Reed have joined Bowater in the top ten of world paper production; and Hoechst, Bayer, and Ciba-Geigy are the leading pharmaceutical producers, ahead of Johnson & Johnson. Recent trends of European investments in Canada must be viewed in light of this international background.

West European investments in Canada have increased significantly since the Second World War. Their rate of increase has actually surpassed that of U.S. investments. This comparison, however, can be misleading because the European base in Canada is very much smaller than that of the United States. Nevertheless, the European presence is growing as a result of the increasing international strength of

---

1. For further information see, A. V. Engibarov, Smeshannye obshchestva na mirovom rynke, Moscow, 1976; Carl H. McMillan, "Direct Soviet and East European Investment in the Industrialized Western Economies" (Working paper No. 7, East-West Commercial Relations Series, Institute of Soviet and East European Studies, Carleton University, Ottawa, 1978); Bruce Morgan, ed., Directory of Soviet and East European Companies in the West, Institute of Soviet and East European Studies (Ottawa: Carleton University, 1978); United Nations Economic and Social Council, Transnational Corporations in World Development: A Re-examination (New York: United Nations publication No. E/C 10/38, 1978); and Jozef Wilczinski, The Multinationals in East-West Relations (London: Macmillan, 1976).
   * "West European Investments in Canada", by Gilles Gratton.

European multinationals, their search for secure supplies of primary resources and the view of some of them that Canada is a good place to enter the North American market.

The Early Role of British Investment
In any survey of European investment in Canada, the role of British capital deserves special mention because of its importance in the early commercial development of the country. Two corporate giants, the Hudson's Bay Company and Canadian Pacific, both formerly predominantly British owned, serve as reminders of the early pre-eminence of British investment in Canada. But it is not as well-known that the London bond market was the principal source of foreign capital for the development of Canada until well into the current century. Indeed Britain remained the largest single foreign investor in Canada until about 1920.

The book value of British capital invested in Canada in 1930 amounted to $2.8 billion. Thereafter, through the 1930s and 1940s little new investment flowed from Britain to Canada, and as much of the earlier financing had been through bonds, repayments, and some defaults in the depression years greatly reduced the stock of British-owned capital in Canada. By 1950 the book value of British investment in this country had declined to $1.8 billion of which under $500 million represented direct investment (that is, investment in British-controlled companies) and $1.3 billion represented portfolio investments.

This investment pattern changed dramatically in the 1950s. From 1950 to 1960, the value of Britain's direct investments increased from under $500 million to $1.5 billion, while its portfolio investments rose from $1.3 billion to $1.8 billion. In 1960, British interests controlled almost 1,400 firms in Canada, including 400 manufacturing firms, 430 commercial businesses and about 250 financial institutions. Most of the investments were made in the oil, forest products, textile, chemical, and transportation equipment industries. The 12 largest accounted for over $1 billion of the total. The latter included British Petroleum, Shell, Bowater, Reed, C.I.L., Imperial Tobacco, Tate and Lyle, Cadbury, Rowntree, A. V. Roe Canada, Vickers, and Rio Tinto. During the 1960s and 1970s many of the British firms in Canada strengthened their position in the North American market through expansion and diversification.

Investment from Continental Europe
European (other than British) investment in Canada only began to be significant in the early 1960s. Before then, most European capital

came to Canada in the form of portfolio investments, but even these were very small. By 1946, for example, the value of European direct investments had reached only $63 million, with only $11 million going to manufacturing and over $40 million, to financial institutions. In all, there were approximately 80 European firms, most of them financial institutions. The 1950s, however, saw the value of European direct investments rise sharply from $80 million in 1950 to $800 million in 1960 while the number of continental European firms rose to 300 in 1955, and to over 500 in 1960. In this period, Belgians were the leading European investors, with investments totalling about $225 million. They were followed by the French ($180 million), the Swiss ($150 million), the Germans ($110 million), the Dutch and the Swedish ($35 million). Though a large proportion of the investments were still destined for financial institutions, other trends were already becoming apparent. Half the manufacturing investments were earmarked for the development of the non-metallic mineral industry, mainly cement, and oil refining. Furthermore, direct investments in primary metals manufacturing were increasing.

In addition to being highly concentrated in a limited number of industrial sectors, the bulk of European investments were confined to a very limited number of large corporations. Most Belgian investments, for example, were being made by Petrofina, the Société générale de Belgique, the Cimenteries CBR, and the Empain Group who together accounted for $175 million of the $225 million invested by 1960. This concentration was also true of French investments which were mostly accounted for by Air Liquide, Lafarge, and a few financial institutions. Dutch investments were largely concentrated in four companies: Shell (a Dutch-British firm), Philips, Nationale Nederlanden N.V., and the Patino Group.

Like the British, continental European investors considerably expanded their Canadian activities in the 1960s and 1970s. The two most significant developments of the 1970s were: (1) the establishment of an increasing number of small- and medium-size European firms in Canada, active mainly in the manufacture of machinery, electrical products, and chemicals; and (2) the considerable increase of European investment in energy exploration, principally uranium and petroleum. Equally of note, the rising number of acquisitions of U.S. firms by European companies had repercussions in Canada, where European firms indirectly acquired Canadian subsidiaries of American firms, For example, when Thyssen, a company which already had significant interests in Canada, acquired control of the Budd Company of the United States, it also acquired an interest in the

Canadian subsidiary, Budd Automotive of Canada, which produces automobile chassis for General Motors.

A measure of the importance to Canada of European investment can be gained from the fact that European investors, or companies controlled in Europe, have accounted for just under 30 per cent of the takeover proposals and over 35 per cent of the proposals to establish new businesses submitted to date for review under the Foreign Investment Review Act.

Though European investments in Canada, including those by British investors, have been expanding rapidly, they have attracted considerably less attention than U.S. investments. This can be attributed to the relatively smaller volume of European investments compared to those of the United States, their concentration in industrial sectors and, with few exceptions, their very limited participation in the production of consumer products in Canada. The consumer products they are associated with, such as Lipton soups, Philips home appliances, Nestlé foods, and Unilever's Lux soap, have been in Canada for so long that most Canadians are no longer aware of their foreign roots. By far the greatest part of European manufacturing investment is still in the production of industrial products such as cement, machinery, chemicals, and electrical equipment. The leading European investors in these areas are the Germans (Kugelfischer, Siemens, Klockner-Moeller, Demag, Klockner-Humboldt-Deutz and O & K Orenstein and Koppel), and the French (Leroy-Somer, Linier, HES Machine Tools, Levage Sepa, and Moteurs Drouard). Other Europeans in this sector are the Italians, Danish, and Dutch (Dikkers, Hughes-Owens, and others).

Europeans have become important in the construction and construction products sectors as well as in the manufacturing of industrial products. Many European firms were active in Canada's industrialization, especially in the development of an infrastructure and extensive power network. The construction firms of Camus, Dumez, Grands Travaux de Marseilles, Franki, and Impreglio-Spino all participated in the development of highways, roads, bridges, and hydroelectric dams. Impreglio-Spino, an Italian-Canadian firm in which three big construction firms from Milan (Impresit, Girola, and Lodigiani) have interests, holds the largest contract in the multi-billion dollar James Bay hydro-electric project.

Europeans also have an important stake in the building materials sector. For example, the Canadian cement industry is almost entirely controlled by European firms: Lafarge, which controls about 40 per cent of the market and has successfully penetrated the U.S. market, Genstar (Société générale de Belgique and Associated Portland

Cement Manufacturers of Great Britain) and Ciments Saint-Laurent (Holderbank of Switzerland). In the construction products manufacturing sector, one finds German (Danzer, Manessmann, August Thyssen-Hutte, and a few others) and Dutch firms, including Hunter-Douglas. Didier recently established a $25 million plant for producing firebricks near the SKW works in Bécancour. The Canadian cement, steel, non-ferrous metal, and chemical industries will now be able to obtain supplies in Canada which they previously had to import. Furthermore, 80 per cent of Didier's products will be exported.

In the past few years, European manufacturers have set up firms to produce equipment for the mining, oil, and chemical industries. Examples are Fried Krupp of Germany and Nuova Raccordi Forgiati of Italy. This Italian firm is associated with a new $30 million joint venture (Uniracor Ltd.) to produce steel pipe fittings. These products, which have been mostly imported at a cost of about $45 to $60 million, are used in the chemical and petro-chemical industries, and in nuclear facilities.

Prominent European chemical firms are also well established in Canada. They include Imperial Chemical Industries of England, Ciba-Geigy, Pechiney Ugine Kuhlmann, BASF and Hoechst. More recently KemaNord AB of Sweden has announced that it will build a sodium chlorate plant, making possible a reduction in imports of that product, which is used in paper production.

European Investment in Resource Development
European investment in the exploration and development of Canada's mineral and oil resources has also grown, mainly since the 1950s. It is interesting to note that a number of the European firms in this investment field are either state controlled or have some state participation. A 1977 Canadian government survey showed that no less than forty-five European-controlled firms in Canada in resource development had some form of foreign government participation.

BP, Shell, and Petrofina are the largest European companies involved in Canadian oil and gas exploration and development. Total Petroleum, a subsidiary of the Compagnie Française des Pétroles, also has an important stake in numerous oil and gas fields. Elf and Aquitaine, whose Canadian assets are valued at almost $500 million, are each carrying out aggressive exploration programs. Aquitaine, moreover, holds a 75 per cent interest in a major gas processing plant. The Italian group ENI has exploration rights off the Atlantic coast, while a consortium of German firms, Deminex, is exploring frontier zones.

European firms have been particularly visible in uranium explora-

Table 3

Foreign Direct Investment in Canada

	Book Value in Millions of Dollars				Per Cent Increase		
	1930	1945	1955	1965	1975	1945 -55	1955 -65	1965 -75
U.K.	392	348	890	2,033	3,717	156	128	83
Other Europe	42[a]	61[a]	325[a]	1,131	3,207	432	248	184
U.S.A.	1,993	2,304	6,513	14,059	32,194	183	116	129

(a) Includes a small amount of non-European investment

Source: Statistics Canada.

Table 4

Distribution of Foreign Direct Investment in Canada by Industry, 1975

	United States Per cent	United Kingdom Per cent	Other Countries Per cent
Manufacturing	42.9	32.6	32.3
Petroleum and Natural Gas	24.2	20.0	25.5
Mining and Smelting	11.4	7.6	9.9
Utilities	1.7	0.1	0.9
Merchandising	6.5	8.6	6.3
Financial	9.4	27.2	21.6
Other	3.7	4.0	3.5
	100. 0	100.0	100.0

Source: Statistics Canada.

tion. Amok, a French company, has initiated a large-scale production program in Saskatchewan involving the investment of about $130 million over the next two years. Seru Nucléaire (Canada), a subsidiary of the Société d'Études et de Recherches d'Uranium de France, is co-operating with Canadian interests in the exploration of the James Bay area. Uranerzbergbau and the government of Saskatchewan are jointly involved in the $100 million development of a new mine. BP is carrying out extensive uranium exploration and subsidiaries of the Italian Ente Nazionale Indrocarburi have concluded joint venture agreements with Canadian firms to explore for uranium. Indeed as interest in uranium exploration has quickened in recent years, a sizable number of consortia involving Canadian and European investors have been formed to search for this valuable resource.

European firms are also active in other mining sectors. They include Patino N.V. with copper-gold mines in Quebec and Elco Mining Ltd., a consortium of six European firms involved in the development of coal properties in British Columbia, as well as firms active in mineral exploration, such as Metallgesellschaft and Pechiney Ugine Kuhlmann.

European Investment in Finance
The financial sector has traditionally been one of the most active destinations for European capital in Canada. In fact, well over 20 per cent of European direct investment is in this sector. One has only to think of the British insurance companies, Norwich Union Life, Commercial Union Assurances, Royal and Standard, and Prudential. In addition, the Crédit Foncier Franco-Canadien, was established at the end of the nineteenth century, with the participation of European investors. Others who have established themselves in this country are l'Abeille and La Paix which are known in Canada as the Victoire Group. The Nationale-Nederlanden, N.V. also has considerable holdings, as do Holland Life Insurance and Ennis N.V. of The Hague.

The European industrial presence in Canada and the internationalization of financial transactions have drawn a significant number of financial institutions, affiliated with European banks, to Canada. At present Canadian legislation places restrictions on foreign ownership of Canadian chartered banks. No shareholder or his associates (whether Canadian or non-resident) may hold over 10 per cent of the voting stock of a bank and the collective holdings of non-residents are limited to 25 per cent. Foreign banks, however, did contribute to the formation of the two newest Canadian banks. The British bank S. G. Warburg and the Paribas International Group each acquired an interest in the share capital of the Commercial and Industrial Bank, and the Deutsche Genossenschaftsbank is also a shareholder in the Northland Bank. As well, a considerable number of affiliates of European banks are providing, either alone or in partnership with others, a variety of financial services in Canada — the making of loans, leasing, factoring, and venture capital activities. In addition many prominent European banks have established representative offices in Canada. Proposed changes in Canadian banking legislation will permit the establishment of wholly foreign-owned banks in Canada. It is expected that a number of European banks will seize this opportunity to gain a stronger foothold in the Canadian financial sector.

Joint Ventures
One interesting feature of recent European investment in Canada has been the growing frequency of joint ventures with Canadian firms. A survey of the main European investment projects (from $5 million up) underway in Canada in 1978 shows that many are being carried on in conjunction with Canadian entrepreneurs. Some of these projects and the European investors involved are: a new plant to manufacture automobile engine components (CAE — Montupet Diecast) in which the Société Industrielle et Financière Montupet has a 20 per cent interest; a new sawmill (Houston Forest Products) joint venture with Eurocan Pulp and Paper Co., owned by two Finnish companies; and a project to manufacture speciality steel (Les Forges HPC Ltée) in which the Société de Forgeage de Rive de Gier has a 60 per cent interest.

An earlier joint venture that has proved particularly successful is that formed in 1965 between the Compagnie Générale d'Électricité and the General Investment Corporation of Quebec, a Quebec government agency, to manufacture electrical insulators and switch components. These products are found today on 80 per cent of all electrical energy transmission networks in Canada and the technology developed is now exported to South Africa and Brazil. In partnership with other subsidiaires of the Compagnie Générale d'Électricité, the joint venture is developing new technologies in manufacturing low- and medium-voltage cells.

Other European companies have concluded licensing agreements with Canadian entrepreneurs. For example, Bombardier is making generators designed by the Italian firm Grandi Motori, while Marine Industries is producing electric turbines from French technology. In 1977, the Ontario Ministry of Industry and Commerce recorded about a dozen major manufacturing agreements between industrial firms in that province and European firms.

Over the years Canada has derived considerable benefit from European investment. Besides providing an alternative source of funds for the development of Canadian industry and resources, Europeans have often brought new technology and management skills. Canada still seeks investments that can contribute to the achievement of its economic objectives. That goal and the increasing strength and investment vigor of European multinationals suggest that the European presence here will continue to grow.

U.S. Investment in Canada*

To many Canadians, foreign investment is synonymous with American investment, and indeed, there is good reason for that impression. U.S.-controlled firms are the major foreign presence in Canada, controlling nearly half of all capital employed in the manufacturing and natural resource sectors. Although the American presence has been paramount for only the latter half of this country's 114-year history and in recent years has shown some slight sign of diminution, its importance and influence have made it the subject of intense study both in Canada and in the United States. This section of the chapter outlines the history, size, and concentration of that investment.

Though the United States has always had a profound influence on cultural and commercial life in Canada, it has not always played a major role as a source of investment funds in this country. In fact, up to the middle of the nineteenth century the role of foreign creditor was almost entirely borne by Great Britain in Canada just as in the United States itself. It has been estimated that at least 90 per cent of the $200 million of total foreign investment in Canada in 1867 originated in Britain. Most of that investment was portfolio investment, largely government and railway bonds. Direct investment amounted only to about 20 per cent of the total, Britain being also the foremost direct investor.

Britain's dominant position changed only slightly during the period leading up to the First World War in spite of the substantial increase in foreign borrowing, particularly between 1900 and 1913 when approximately $2.5 billion worth of foreign capital entered Canada. While securities, chiefly of government origin, continued to be the major financial vehicle, with Britain still the leading source of funds, U.S. investment stock was growing twice as fast as British investment. By 1914 the British share of total foreign capital in Canada had declined to about 72 per cent, whereas the U.S. share had increased to about 23 per cent. It was during this period that the United States supplanted Britain as the leading source of direct investment, most of the U.S. capital going into forestry and mining, and some into manufacturing.

While the more rapid growth of American investment was already evident before 1914, it was overshadowed by the dominant size of British investment. This situation changed, however, during and after the war. The British began to liquidate outstanding government and

* "U.S. Investment in Canada", by Joan Gherson.

railway debt and Canadian governments and corporations began to turn to New York instead of London for funds. From 1914 to 1926 U.S. portfolio investment in Canada increased from approximately $250 million to $1.8 billion; it was the major factor in the rapid increase of total U.S. investment during that period. This, coupled with the more than doubling of U.S. direct investment, made the United States Canada's principal creditor by 1926, the first year for which official Canadian data on foreign investment are available. The United States maintained this position in spite of a slight increase in British investment in the late 1920s and a modest decline in U.S. investment in the 1930s. With the further erosion of British investment during the Second World War, much of it replaced by U.S. sources, the positions of the United States and Britain as Canada's creditors were, by 1946, exactly the reverse of what they had been in 1914; that is, some 72 per cent of the $7 billion of foreign capital was owned in the United States and about 23 per cent in Britain.

The 1950s and 1960s were decades of massive influxes of foreign investment in Canada, foreign long-term investment increasing by over $30 billion. In 1967, Canada's centenary, the U.S. share of foreign capital in this country peaked at 80 per cent. The 1970s, however, were an even more dramatic period of increasing foreign investment, averaging $6 billion per year between 1970 and 1976. So great was the increase that, although the U.S. decreased to below 75 per cent by 1976, its value had more than doubled since 1966.

Characteristics of U.S. Investment
The principal characteristic of U.S. investment is its sheer size. With a book value in 1977 of over $65 billion, it represents nearly 75 per cent of all foreign investment in this country. Moreover, Canada is also the chief locus of U.S. external investment, accounting for 25 per cent. In fact, Canada's share of U.S. external funds during this century has stayed consistently in the 25 per cent range, even in the early years when Britain was the major source of funds. The present size of U.S. investment in Canada is due, therefore, not to any increase in concentration in Canada, though that was a factor in the 1950s and 1960s, but to the remarkable growth of U.S. investment worldwide and Canada's consistent share of that investment.

A second and long-standing characteristic of U.S. investment is the high proportion represented by direct investment involving ownership or control of Canadian industry. Between 1900 and 1913, for example, about 55 per cent of U.S. investment was direct investment, compared with only 11 per cent of British investment. After 1914 the proportion fell below 50 per cent but resumed its predominance after 1945. Between 1946 and 1974 the book value of U.S. investment increased by nearly $44 billion of which nearly $27 billion or 62 per cent was due to increased direct investment. Although portfolio investment was again relatively stronger in 1975 and 1976, the proportion of direct investment in the total stock was still 58 per cent at the end of 1976. By comparison, only 40 per cent of other foreign investment was direct investment. One consequence of the size and age of U.S. direct investment is its ability to grow from earnings generated in Canada. In recent years retained earnings of subsidiaries have been the principal source of additions to foreign direct investment in this country. Thus, the early establishment of American companies enabled them to consolidate their position and in some cases to inhibit the entry of others because the size of the market would not support new producers.

Historically, the two principal motives for U.S. direct investment have been to secure supplies of raw materials for its industries and their subsidiaries, and to extend the market for U.S. products. The first can be attributed to the close proximity and the complementarity of Canadian resources. It has led to large-scale investment in Canada's natural resources and, consequently, to an orientation of Canada's exports towards raw materials and towards the United States. Canada's forest industries were the first to attract large investments. Beginning with purchases of large timber tracts in the last century, that investment moved into sawmills, pulp mills, and newsprint as export restrictions, tariffs, or relative costs of production made these desirable or imperative. Securing a captive source of raw materials has increasingly been an important element in mineral developments such as iron ore, asbestos, and petroleum. In other cases, however, where the gain to be had from the development of rich deposits was the only force motivating Americans to become principal investors, the existence of a large market to the south has always been an important underlying factor.

The second motive for direct investment, to extend the market for the products of American industry, is responsible for the vast number of American branch plants in Canada. Strong evidence suggests that the Canadian tariff, and later the Commonwealth Preferential Tariff, stimulated that development. But as the relative importance of the tariff declined, other factors, such as the considerable growth of the Canadian market, special market characteristics requiring modification of the American product and service needs, contributed to the continued growth and expansion of the American branch-plant presence.

Figure 4

Percentage Distribution of U.S. Investment in Canada — 1976

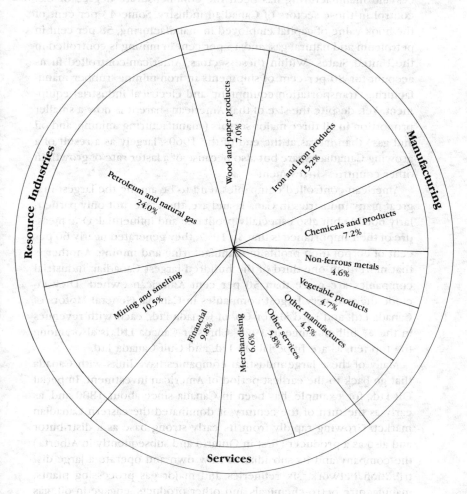

The predominance of the two motives identified above has been so strong that, by 1975, resource development and secondary manufacturing together accounted for 78.5 per cent of the book value of all U.S. direct investment in Canada. As much as 43 per cent of that investment was in the manufacturing industries, 24 per cent in petroleum and natural gas, and 11 per cent in mining.

U.S. Control in Canadian Industry

One of the results of the high concentration of investment in resources and manufacturing has been the commensurate degree of U.S. control in those sectors of Canadian industry. Some 43 per cent of the book value of capital employed in manufacturing, 58 per cent in petroleum and natural gas, and 45 per cent in mining is controlled in the United States. Within these sectors, American-controlled firms account for 80 per cent of shipments in iron-mining, rubber manufacturing, transportation equipment, and electrical industrial equipment. Yet, despite the size of that American share it is now a smaller proportion in all three major sectors (manufacturing, mining, and oil and gas) than it was at the end of the 1960s, largely as a result of a growing Canadian share but also because of a faster rate of growth in other countries' investment.

American-controlled companies tend to be among the largest in a great many industries in Canada and are, therefore, not only particularly notable but also especially profitable and influential. One measure of their importance is that, in 1977, they generated nearly 60 per cent of corporation profits in manufacturing and mining. Another is that more than one-third of the hundred largest Canadian industrial companies are more than 50 per cent American owned. They include the two very largest companies in Canada, General Motors of Canada Ltd. and Ford Motor Co. of Canada Ltd., each with revenues in the $7 billion range in 1978. Chrysler Canada Ltd. is also among the top ten, as are Imperial Oil Ltd. and Gulf Canada Ltd.

Many of these large industrial companies have links with Canada that go back to the earliest period of American investment. Imperial Oil Ltd., for example, has been in Canada since about 1880 and, as early as the turn of the century, it dominated the eastern Canadian market. Growing rapidly from its early strong base as a distributor and also as a producer (first in Ontario and subsequently in Alberta) the company and its subsidiaries now own and operate a large distribution network, six refineries and major gas processing plants, manufacture petro-chemicals and other products, engage in oil, gas and other mineral exploration and development, and have major interests in pipelines.

Among the hundred or so other companies that were here before 1900 are the two leaders in the electrical apparatus industry, Canadian General Electric Co. Ltd and Canadian Westinghouse Co. Ltd., as well as the Canadian branches of Sherwin-Williams Company, for long the largest American-owned paint company, The Singer Sewing Machine Company, Ingersoll Rand, and the International Paper Com-

Chart 2

Book Value of U.S. Investment in Canada

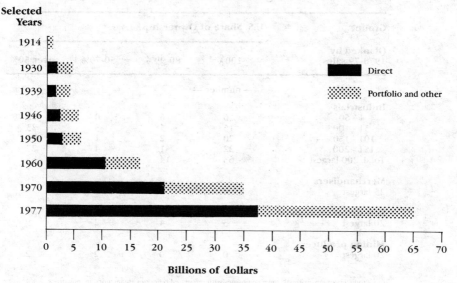

Selected Years

Billions of dollars

pany. Only slightly later, in the early years of this century, came the two largest automotive companies, Ford and General Motors, though neither were in the first instance organized by the parent company. Ford, the earliest, was started by a Canadian, with 51 per cent of the initial capitalization given to the American company in return for rights and processes. The predecessor of General Motors was also started by a Canadian, who maintained control until the First World War. Also established before 1914 were the Ontario Paper Company, owned by the Chicago Tribune, the first explosives plants of the DuPont Company, the Otis Elevator Company, the Goodyear Tire and Rubber Company, and the two large agricultural implement manufacturers, International Harvester and John Deere. Indeed, the early decades of this century were years of prolific branch-plant development. By the mid-1930s, the list of American companies had grown to well over a thousand. Only slightly set back by the depression, the growth has continued until over 4,000 corporations are now classified as being American controlled. Still more spectacular than the increase in numbers has been the growth in assets through expansion and acquisition.

Table 5

U.S. Control of Largest Canadian Companies

Group	U.S. Share of Ownership			
(Ranked by 1978-79 sales)	100%	80-99%	50-79%	over 50%
	— number —			
Industrials				
1 - 50	6	6	0	12
51 - 100	15	5	3	23
101 - 150	20	2	1	23
151 - 200	22	1	4	27
Total, 200 largest	63	14	8	85
Merchandisers				
25 largest	8	0	1	9
Petroleum producers[a]				
20 largest	3	4	2	9
Mining producers[a]				
20 largest	0	0	2	2

(a) Producers of raw materials only; companies with integrated refineries are included in industrials.

Source: The Financial Post.

Regional Distribution

Although there are American companies in all regions, the investment is concentrated in Ontario, Quebec, and Alberta where 81 per cent of the taxable income of U.S.-controlled non-financial corporations was generated in 1976. A breakdown by source of income shows that U.S.-controlled mineral (including oil and gas) investment is mainly in Alberta, while manufacturing investment is predominantly in Ontario and, to a considerably lesser extent, in Quebec.

That this regional concentration of investment is vitally significant for provincial economies is evident from the fact that U.S.-controlled companies earned 58.5 per cent of all corporate taxable income in Alberta and 45 per cent of the total in Ontario. This is also true for other provinces, where American investment is considerably smaller, because its concentration in either mining or manufacturing can make it particularly important to the economy.

Outlook

The magnitude and evident profitability of U.S. investment in Canada shows that this country has been a good place for American capital.

Table 6

U.S. Applications to the Foreign Investment Review Agency

Since the inception of the Foreign Investment Review Act Americans have been responsible for 61 per cent of all reviewable applications. In terms of the value of assets acquired or new investment proposed, the U.S. share is smaller, though the difference is slight. This U.S. share, whether in terms of number of applications or the value of investment involved, is substantially less than the U.S. share of the value of all foreign direct investment in Canada, which exceeds 80 per cent. That difference undoubtedly reflects the fact that a large part of the increase in the book value of U.S. investment is due to the growth and expansion of existing U.S.-owned businesses.

	Acquisitions[a]	New Businesses[b]
	— number —	
Reviewable Applications	950	675
Allowed	732	548
Disallowed	78	42
Withdrawn	64	53
	874	643
Reviewable Applications by Sector	— per cent —	
Primary	7.8	5.5
Manufacturing	49.0	25.9
Services	43.2	68.6
	100.0	100.0
Reviewable Applications by Region		
Atlantic provinces	2.5	1.9
Quebec	15.7	10.1
Ontario	57.0	64.3
Western provinces & Territories	24.8	23.7
	100.0	100.0

(a) April 1, 1974 to December 31, 1979.
(b) October 15, 1975 to December 31, 1979.

But the very size of that investment and changes in the world investment picture such as tariff reductions, which diminish the advantage of branch plants, put the future rate of growth in question. The huge post-war influx of American capital has subsided in recent years and a plateau may have been reached in the establishment of new American manufacturing plants. Though the U.S. presence continues to grow in Canada, that growth is increasingly financed from Canadian sources, principally the retained earnings of subsidiaries, and its rate has declined. The U.S.-controlled share of the total capital employed in manufacturing, mining, and oil and gas has also been declining. This is partly due to repatriation of a number of American-controlled investments, notably in resource industries, but also in manufacturing. Another factor is the more rapid growth in investment from other countries, including the acquisition of American parent companies by non-Americans and the resulting change in ownership of Canadian subsidiaries. Yet, it would be unwise to conclude that present trends will continue. More than forty years ago an important study of Canadian-American industry concluded, in similar circumstances, that because American industry had nearly reached "saturation", its rate of increase must in future be much slower. Instead, in the ensuing years, a new surge of development brought new investment to unprecedented levels.

IV
Foreign Direct Investment Theory, Impact, and Control

B
Patterns

21
The Emerging Challenge of Canadian Direct Investment Abroad

Isaiah A. Litvak

Christopher J. Maule

Dr. Litvak is a professor in the Faculty of Administrative Studies, York University. He has authored and edited numerous books and articles with Dr. Maule. His recent research has focussed on international business and government-business relations.

Dr. Maule is professor of economics and international affairs at Carleton University. In addition to his research and publications with Dr. Litvak, he has published in the area of industrial organization. He has lectured extensively in North America and Europe, and has acted as a consultant to both government and business.

This chapter is a revised version of an article which appeared originally in *The Business Quarterly*, Spring 1978. Reprinted by permission.

Introduction

Direct investment abroad by Canadian companies is fast emerging as a major topic for debate in Canada. The concern expressed is two-fold: first, such investment by Canadian businessmen is viewed as a vote of non-confidence in the state and future of Canada's economy. Press announcements of Canadian firms acquiring, or establishing new, commercial operations abroad, particularly in the United States, have become a common feature in the daily newspaper. The firms identified include both giant corporations such as Inco, acquiring ESB a major battery manufacturer in the United States, as well as small firms like Hobarth and Association Studio in Montreal, which intends to open a $300,000 photo products plant in the State of New York.

Secondly, attention is drawn to the potential negative impact of such investment on Canada's economy. For example, expanding abroad can be an alternative to expanding at home. By producing abroad to service local markets, unions and politicians have argued that domestic employment is being exported. Moreover, it is contended, that such investment will result in a significant drop in Canada exports and thereby result in further deterioration of Canada's balance of payments. Both consequences are being highlighted in the context of Inco's recent announcement to cut back nickel production and employment in Canada, while bringing on stream its new nickel deposits in Indonesia and Guatemala.

The negative view of the impact of such investment on the capital exporting country is not unique to Canada. A similar debate occurred in the United States with much greater intensity in the early 1970s. In response to such charges, especially those triggered off by unions, the U.S. government launched a major study to examine the impact and effects of direct investment abroad. The findings refuted most of the charges, claiming that such investment was indeed beneficial to the U.S. economy.[1]

---

1. United States Tariff Commission, *Implications of Multinational Firms for World Trade and Investment and for U.S. Trade and Labor* (Washington: U.S. Government Printing Office, 1973).

The purpose of this chapter is to present some important data on Canadian direct investment abroad, to highlight the key characteristics of Canada's major corporations with investments abroad, and to draw some observations and generalizations concerning the overseas operations of these companies.

Nature and Extent of Canadian Direct Investment Abroad

Canadian direct investment abroad (CDIA) increased more than five times from $2.5 billion in 1960 to $13.4 billion in 1977.[2] By the end of 1977, the United States accounted for 52.3 per cent of total CDIA, United Kingdom 10.5 per cent, the European Economic Community (excluding the U.K.) 6.2 per cent, Australasia 3.6 per cent, and Japan 0.5 per cent (see Table 1). As a group, developed countries accounted for 76.2 per cent of CDIA. Thus, most of CDIA is in developed economies. The industrial distribution of CDIA in 1977 was 48.2 per cent in manufacturing, with more than half of it centred in the United States; 22.0 per cent in mining and petroleum; 13.2 per cent in utilities; 3.3 per cent in merchandising; and the remainder in other industrial categories.

Four key observations can be made with respect to CDIA: first, most of it is located in the developed world; second, the United States, with more than one-half of the total, is the major geographical area of concentration; third, the manufacturing sector is the prime area for such investment, much of it centred in the United States; and fourth, most of the investment is held in subsidiaries which are 100 per cent owned by the Canadian parent company.

Two further observations should be noted. In 1969, approximately 40 per cent of CDIA was made by enterprises in Canada which were controlled abroad, for example, Ford Motor Company of Canada.[3] In the intervening years, this figure has declined for two reasons: investment abroad is being undertaken by more Canadian-based and controlled firms, both large and small; and, some of the previously non-Canadian-controlled firms have acquired the status of "Canadian"-controlled firms because of a change in their ownership composition and/or by virtue of a reclassification of their status by Canada's Foreign Investment Review Agency. The implications for Canada of the foreign-controlled component of CDIA may differ from that of CDIA which is Canadian controlled and which is the subject of this chapter.

2. *Statistics Canada Daily*, Cat. 11-001E (August 18, 1980), p. 3.
3. I. A. Litvak and C. J. Maule, "Canadian Investment Abroad: In Search of a Policy", *International Journal*, **XXXI**, No. 1 (Winter 1975-76), p. 161.

Table 1

Canadian Direct Investment Abroad by Location of Investment in 1977

Location	Year Ended 1977	% of Total
North America and Caribbean:		
United States	7,027	52.3
Mexico	65	
Bahamas	148	
Bermuda	408	
Jamaica	112	
Trinidad and Tobago	29	
Other	154	
Sub-Total	7,943	59.1
South and Central America:		
Venezuela	22	
Argentina	57	
Brazil	1,403	
Other	121	
Sub-Total	1,603	11.9
Europe:		
United Kingdom	1,410	10.5
European Economic Community:		
(excluding the U.K.)		
Belgium and Luxembourg	48	
France	187	
Italy	74	
Netherlands	176	
West Germany	190	
Denmark	70	
Ireland	84	
Sub-Total	829	6.2
Switzerland	184	
Norway	69	
Spain	84	
Other	84	

Finally, CDIA is highly concentrated in a few large enterprises. Statistics Canada revealed in 1968 that twelve large Canadian enterprises accounted for about 69 per cent of total CDIA.[4] Based on data collected by the authors, this figure may in fact understate the current high level of concentration of CDIA in a handful of "Canadian"-based and controlled enterprises.

The data obtained by the authors differ significantly from the

4. Litvak and Maule, "Canadian Investment", p. 16.

totals compiled by *Statistics Canada*. For 1974, $9.3 billion of CDIA has been reported. This figure is compiled on the basis of flows and claims between all Canadian parent companies and their foreign subsidiaries. The data surveyed and compiled by the authors include all corporate assets located abroad, including those foreign-held assets acquired through local (foreign) financing. The difference between the balance of payments calculation of direct investment and that of the overseas corporate assets is best demonstrated in a benchmark study of foreign direct investment in the United States.[5] At year-end 1973, the U.S. government estimated that Canada's direct investment position in the United States was $5.2 billion compared to $3.9 billion estimated by *Statistics Canada*, while the balance sheet assets of Canada's U.S. affiliates according to the U.S. study totalled in the neighborhood of $24 billion. These are the data which must be collected in order to examine the full public policy implications of CDIA. For example, related to the U.S. "assets" figure for Canada, 175,973 people were employed by the U.S. affiliates of Canadian-based companies.

The Corporate Landscape

Canada is atypical because so much of its industry is owned and controlled by foreign investors. This phenomenon can be quickly gleaned by examining *The Financial Post Top 200* industrial Canadian companies ranked by sales for 1976/77: Of the 200 companies, "68 are wholly owned by foreign parent companies, 47 are 50 per cent or more owned, and there are another 20 where there is substantial, sometimes controlling, foreign interests".[6] About 75 per cent of these 135 foreign-owned/controlled firms have their headquarters in the United States.

A commonly accepted definition of a multinational enterprise is one that has "controlled manufacturing subsidiaries in six or more countries".[7] The parent companies of most of these large foreign-

5. The difference between the Canadian and U.S. calculations re: Canadian direct investment in the United States is due to the difference in the definition of what constitutes direct investment; a lower percentage of foreign equity ownership is employed in the case of U.S. data to indicate direct investment. The Canadian figure is taken from *Statistics Canada Daily*, Cat. 11-001E (September 14, 1976) p. 4. For the U.S. data, see Report to the Congress, *Foreign Direct Investment in the United States* 2 (Washington: U.S. Department of Commerce, April 1976).

6. *The Financial Post 30C* (Summer 1977), p. 19.

7. Raymond Vernon, *Sovereignty at Bay* (New York: Basic Books, 1971), p. 11.

   (a) All companies on the list must have derived more than 50 per cent of their sales from manufacturing and/or mining. Figures exclude intracompany transactions and include subsidiaries more than 50 per cent owned, either on a fully consolidated or prorata basis.

   (b) As shown at the company's year-end.

controlled Canadian firms meet this condition, and the majority of them are either listed on the *Fortune 500* Largest U.S. or non-U.S. Industrial Corporations.

Canada placed 39 firms on the *Fortune 1976* list of the "500 Largest Non-U.S. Industrial Corporations"; however, only 22 of these firms are Canadian controlled, and they form the basis of our study of CDIA. Table 2 identifies the "Canadian contingent" by sales, assets, and

Table 2

Canadian-Controlled Firms on the Fortune List of Largest Non-U.S. Industrial Corporations

Company	Sales[a]	Assets[b]	Employees
	(- - - $000 - - -)		
Massey-Ferguson	2,771,696	2,305,145	68,200
Alcan Aluminum	2,656,072	3,090,239	60,000
Canada Pacific Investments	2,152,259	4,046,339	36,948
Seagram	2,048,910	2,161,193	17,000
Inco	2,040,282	3,628,311	55,767
Canada Packers	1,609,089	314,975	15,000
MacMillan Bloedel	1,542,022	1,268,155	23,601
Steel Co. of Canada	1,379,267	1,823,723	22,691
Noranda Mines	1,250,079	2,073,207	32,649
Northern Telecom	1,127,966	698,482	25,277
Moore	1,053,241	764,262	25,964
Dominion Foundries and Steel	916,845	1,023,543	11,500
Genstar	901,097	1,221,378	10,695
Domtar	899,494	760,763	17,520
Abitibi Paper	892,984	891,000	22,000
Cosolidated Bathurst	755,887	735,760	17,557
Burns Foods	732,178	162,425	6,971
John Labatt	683,336	446,626	12,150
Molson	663,015	428,063	10,695
Dominion Bridge	543,994	357,270	10,313
Hiram Walker-Gooderham and Worts	543,955	912,388	7,500
Dominion Textile	472,915	360,702	13,130

Source: *Fortune* (August 1977), pp. 226-235.

employees. The leading "Canadian-owned" firm is Massey-Ferguson which ranked 80th on this *Fortune* list, and was a distant fifth to General Motors of Canada which ranked 32nd. General Motors of Canada had sales of approximately $5.3 billion in 1976 almost twice the total of Massey-Ferguson, and it is the first company in Canada to exceed the $5 billion sales figure. The other non-Canadian-controlled companies whose sales exceed Massey-Ferguson were as follows (in rank order): Ford Motor of Canada, Imperial Oil, and Chrysler Canada.

To what extent are Canadian-controlled firms multinational? Based on the Harvard criteria of "manufacturing subsidiaries in six or more countries", many of the "Group of 22" could not be considered "Harvard Multinational". On the other hand, if the criteria were altered to include firms which operate subsidiaries in at least two foreign countries, then most of these firms could be viewed as multinational.

Rather than formulate a convenient criterion to fit the "Group of 22", the authors conducted a short survey in 1977 to ascertain the companies' geographic breakdown of sales, assets, and employees for 1975/76 (see Table 3). In the case of Canadian Pacific Enterprises, a holding company, data was obtained for two of its more important subsidiaries — Cominco and Algoma. A number of interesting observations can be made concerning the overseas operations of these firms.

Sales — In the case of nine companies, non-Canadian sales exceeded sales in Canada as a percentage of total corporate sales. Some of the comparisons are quite extreme, viz., Massey-Ferguson 92 per cent vs. 8 percent; Alcan 83 per cent vs. 17 per cent; Seagram 94 per cent vs. 6 per cent; Inco 89 per cent vs. 11 per cent; Moore 90 per cent vs. 10 per cent; and Hiram Walker 88 per cent vs. 12 per cent. In every case, U.S. corporate sales equalled or exceeded company sales in Canada. Five of the nine companies had non-Canadian sales in excess of $1 billion: Massey-Ferguson, Alcan, Seagram, Inco, and MacMillan Bloedel.

Assets — Unlike the sales situation, fewer companies hold more of their assets outside of Canada: Massey-Ferguson, Alcan, Seagram, Moore, and Hiram-Walker. Other companies with significant assets abroad are Inco (47 per cent), MacMillan Bloedel (39 per cent), Noranda (25 per cent), Northern Telecom (20 per cent), Abitibi (22 per cent), Dominion Bridge (40 per cent), and Dominion Textile (31 per cent). Cominco, a subsidiary of Canadian Pacific Enterprises, has 37 per cent of its corporate assets abroad. In the case of Massey-Ferguson, Seagram, and Moore, U.S. corporate assets exceed the Canadian totals.

The corporate process of internationalization has moved more rapidly in the functional area of marketing (sales) than in (assets). This may be attributed to a combination of the following reasons: first, extended and extensive exporting of goods from Canada is often a precursor to undertaking substantial investments abroad; second, Canadian-controlled firms in manufacturing are relatively

Table 3

Canadian-Controlled Companies on the Fortune List of Largest Non-U.S. Industrial Corporations 1976
Geographic Distribution of Sales, Assets, and Employees

Company	Sales Total ($000)	Can. %	U.S. %	U.K. %	Other %	Assets Total ($000)	Can. %	U.S. %	U.K. %	Other %	Employees Total ($000)	Can. %	U.S. %	U.K. %	Other %
Massey-Ferguson	2,771,696	8	23	8	61	2,305,145	11	26	15	48	68,200	12	9	17	62
Alcan Aluminum	2,656,072	17	21	15	47	3,090,239	48	9	16	27	60,000	31	6	14	49
Canada Pacific Investments (a)	2,152,259	--	N.A.	--26--	--	4,046,339	--	N.A.	90[b]	--	36,948	--	N.A.	90[b]	--
Seagram	2,048,970	6	68	12	27	2,161,193	10	23	9	15	17,000	10	27	15	12
Inco	2,040,282	11	50	4	7	3,628,311	53	23	5	10	55,767	46	1	6	14
Canada Packers	1,609,089	85	4	9	22	314,975	82	3	13	3	15,000	79	1	7	1
MacMillan Bloedel	1,542,022	24	45	--4--	--	1,268,155	61	23	--	--	23,601	77	15	7	1
Steel Co. of Canada	1,379,267	88	8	--	--	1,823,723	96	4	--	--	22,691	99	1	--	--
Noranda Mines	1,250,079	25	25	7.5	42.5	2,073,207	75	12.5	--	12.5	32,649	85	7.5	--	7.5
Northern Telecom	1,127,966	86	9	--5--	--	698,482	80	15	--5--	--	25,277	80	12	--8--	--
Moore	1,053,241	10	63	7	20	764,262	9	61	11	19	25,964	9	51	15	25
Dominion Foundries	916,845	90	5	1	4	1,023,543	98	2	--	--	11,500	100	--	--	--
Genstar	901,097	80	18	--	2	1,221,378	85	12	--	3	10,695	89	10	--	1
Domtar	899,494	78	15	7	--	760,763	94	3	3	--	17,520	93	2	5	--
Abitibi	892,984	40	48	--12--	--	891,000	78	22	--	--	22,000	91	9	--	--
Consolidated Bathurst	755,887	55	20	5	20	735,760	90	--	--	10	17,557	85	--	--	15
Burns Foods	732,178	95	2	--	3	162,425	100	--	--	--	6,971	100	--	--	--
John Labatt	683,336	93	6	--1--	--	446,626	90	5	--	--5--	12,150	95	5	--	--
Molson	663,015	96	3	1	--	428,063	95	4	1	--	10,695	97	2	1	--
Dominion Bridge	543,994	67	33	--	--	357,270	60	40	--	--	10,313	55	45	--	--
Hiram-Walker	543,955	12	58	3	27	912,388	16	33	25	26	7,500	25	23	24	28
Dominion Textile	472,915	60	25	3	12	360,702	69	21	1	9	13,130	79	18	--	3
Cominco (a)	725,005	25	39	16	20	973,205	63	18	1.5	17.5	10,696	80	9	.5	10.5
Algoma Steel (a)	584,835	78	21	--1--	--	928,248	89	11	--	--	12,200	91	9	--	--

(a) Cominco and Algoma Steel are controlled by Canadian Pacific Investments Limited (CPI) which in turn is a subsidiary of Canadian Pacific Limited.

(b) Largely in the U.S.

Source: *Fortune* (August 1977), and Company Survey.

late entrants as multinationals, compared to their European and U.S. counterparts; and, third, many of these firms are in resource-based industries, they are highly capital intensive in Canada, and until recently were largely export oriented.

This scenario is changing as more Canadian companies are vertically integrating forwards and diversifying their operations through foreign acquisitions and the formation of new establishments abroad. At present, four Canadian companies have corporate assets in excess of one billion dollars located outside of Canada: specifically, Massey-Ferguson, Alcan, Seagram, and Inco. Moreover, they are among the more aggressive Canadian companies currently expanding abroad.

Employees — As one might expect, the distribution of employees parallels the geographic breakdown of corporate assets. In addition to Massey-Ferguson, Alcan, Seagram, Moore and Hiram-Walker, Inco had more employees working for the corporation abroad than in Canada (54 per cent vs. 46 per cent). Generally speaking, these six companies are the most internationally diverse of the "Group of 22". A key characteristic of Canadian multinationals is that the domestic market declines rapidly in importance as they internationalize their operations, and the contribution of Canadian sales to total corporate (global) sales drops significantly behind the U.S. figures.

As previously noted, four Canadian companies have overseas assets valued in excess of $1 billion each. These may be viewed as members of the Canadian billion dollar club when dealing with CDIA. Before proceeding to highlight the historical evolution of these companies, it should be noted that Brascan, a Toronto-based firm, could also satisfy the billion dollar criterion. Since it is primarily a regulated utility distributing company, it was excluded from the *Fortune* list. At this time, Brascan could be described as a binational firm, Canada and Brazil — with most of its operations based in Brazil, e.g. 90 per cent+ of sales and employees, and 80 per cent+ of assets. Another potential club member is Bata Shoes, a privately held corporation, with headquarters in Toronto. Most of this company's activities and investments are also based abroad, but unlike Brascan they are geographically diverse.

The Billion Dollar Club

Alcan and Aluminum
In the Western world, six large multinational companies with vertically integrated operations control approximately 80 per cent

of the aluminum smelting capacity. These six producers are Alcan
(Canada), Alcoa, Reynolds and Kaiser (U.S.), Pechiney (France), and
Alusuisse (Switzerland).

Two of the characteristics of the North American industry are its
dependence on imported sources of bauxite and/or alumina, which
the major firms have traditionally owned or controlled, and the large
number of independent fabricators that manufacture aluminum
products often in competition with the major producers. In Canada,
these characteristics are accentuated even further. The Canadian
aluminum industry is entirely dependent on imported bauxite; smelting capacity is owned 85 per cent by Alcan and 15 per cent by
Canadian Reynolds; Canadian consumption of aluminum products
is supplied about 68 per cent by Alcan, 20 per cent by Canadian
Reynolds and 12 per cent by imports and secondary aluminum. A
very high proportion of aluminum produced is exported from Canada. Consequently, the Canadian aluminum industry can be closely
identified with Alcan, and the livelihood of this industry can be seen
to be very dependent on external factors.

Measured in terms of capital employed and sales of aluminum, 42
per cent of Alcan's fixed capital was outside of Canada, and 83 per
cent of sales were realized in foreign markets. In addition, 69 per
cent of the approximately 60,000 Alcan employees work outside of
Canada.

Alcan's subsidiary and related companies have bauxite holdings in
seven countries, produce alumina in six, smelt primary aluminum
in ten, fabricate aluminum in thirty-four, have sales outlets in over
one hundred, and maintain warehouse inventories in the larger
markets.[8]

Is Alcan a Canadian company? Many Canadians and foreigners
alike perceive Alcan to be an American firm, not a Canadian company.
However, judging by the criteria of registered ownership, location of
headquarters organization, and nationality of senior management and
the board of directors, Alcan is a Canadian multinational corporation.
In mid-1976, the registered ownership of the more than 40 million

8. The following books provide an historical overview of the four Canadian multinational corporations: I. A. Litvak and C. J. Maule, *Alcan Aluminum Limited: A
Corporate History* (prepared for the Royal Commission on Corporate Concentration, Government of Canada, 1977); Samuel Bronfman, *Little Acorns* (Personal
history of Seagram Co., included in the company's Annual Report of 1970); E. P.,
Neufeld, *A Global Corporation* (Toronto: University of Toronto Press, 1969);
O. W. Main, *The Canadian Nickel Industry* (Toronto: University of Toronto Press,
1955).

shares of Alcan Aluminum Limited (the parent holding company) then outstanding was 49.0 per cent in Canada, 37.3 per cent in the United States and 13.7 per cent in other countries. Moreover, the majority of the directors and officers of Alcan are citizens of Canada. In 1976, the Canadian government, through the Foreign Investment Review Agency, classified Alcan as a "Canadian" company, not bound by its regulations governing acquisitions and new investments into related and unrelated areas of Canadian business activity by "foreign-owned" firms.

The perception of Alcan as an American company has risen from the knowledge that its corporate roots were in the United States, and that there was majority U.S. ownership in the company until the late 1960s. At the turn of the century (July 3, 1902), the Aluminum Company of America (Alcoa) established a Canadian affiliate under the name of the Northern Aluminum Company, Limited. Some twenty-three years later on July 8, 1925, the corporate name was altered to the Aluminum Company of Canada, Limited, hereafter referred to as Alcan Canada, which on May 31, 1928 became the principal operating subsidiary of Aluminium Limited, the holding company known as Alcan. This Canadian incorporated company was assigned all of Alcoa's foreign holdings except for its bauxite operations in Surinam.

The first "corporate separation" between Alcoa and Alcan appears to have been prompted more by managerial ambition, rather than possible U.S. antitrust action. Arthur Vining Davis was Chairman of the Board of Alcoa in 1928, when two of his subordinates were competing for the presidency of the firm: Roy A. Hunt, son of Captain Alfred Hunt, a founding member of Alcoa, and E. K. Davis, Arthur's younger brother. The split between Alcoa and Alcan allowed A. V. Davis to appoint his brother, E. K. Davis, to the presidency of Alcan, while Alfred E. Hunt was named president of Alcoa.

On assuming the presidency of Alcan, E. K. Davis brought with him to Canada a small group of Alcoa-trained personnel who collectively were responsible for the emergence of this company as a giant industrial enterprise in Canada. Some of the Alcoa-Alcan pioneers were visible and dominant in a number of the key managerial positions and board rooms of Alcan and its key operating subsidiary Alcan Canada up until the late 1960s.

Running parallel with the managerial changes, significant antitrust developments dramatically altered the U.S. ownership composition of Alcan, and its links to Alcoa. In April of 1937, the U.S. Department of Justice filed a complaint under the U.S. antitrust laws naming as defendants Aluminium Company of America (Alcoa), twenty-three of its subsidiaries and affiliated companies including Alcan and thirty-seven of its directors, officers, and shareholders. The complaint alleged that Alcoa monopolized the manufacture of virgin aluminum ingot, and the sale of aluminum sheets, alloys, bars, etc. in the United States. The case was formally ended twenty years later in 1957.

Although no wrongdoing was proven by the antitrust authorities, the Court ordered in June of 1950 that "the shareholders of Alcoa be required to dispose of their stock interests either in Limited (Alcan) or Alcoa", to ensure the future competitiveness of the U.S. aluminum industry. All the principal shareholders, except E. K. Davis, elected to sell their Alcan shares, and by December 1957 the disposition order, with a small balance of shares outstanding, was completed.

Alcan has grown rapidly from a relatively small firm to one of giant proportion, even in global terms — second only to Alcoa. The company's corporate thrust has changed from being chiefly a producer and exporter of primary aluminum to a large vertically integrated producer which increasingly consumes its own primary aluminum output in its worldwide fabricating plants, producing a myriad of industrial and consumer goods manufactured out of aluminum. A major ingredient for the success of this strategy rested on Alcan's investment and penetration of the U.S. market.

Alcan's U.S. subsidiary, Alcan Aluminum Corporation (Alcancorp), which was nothing more than a sales subsidiary in 1944, emerged as the fourth largest aluminum fabricator in the United States, and its sales in 1976 would have easily placed it on the *Fortune* list of the 500 largest industrial corporations in the United States.

The importance of Alcan's U.S. subsidiary cannot be underestimated: in 1976, sales to third parties in the United States accounted for about 21 per cent of Alcan's total worldwide sales, and for approximately 9 per cent of Alcan's total capital employed. Similarly, the importance of Alcancorp's contribution to Alcan Canada, and hence its impact on Canada cannot be overemphasized: "approximately 75 per cent of U.S. ingot imports comes from Alcan and 80 per cent from Canada as a whole". As a result of Alcan's investment into fabrication in the United States, there is a very high degree of corporate interdependence and integration between Alcan Canada and Alcancorp. This explains why Alcan actively encourages the creation of a North American free trade arrangement, at least in primary aluminum.

In recent years, the shape of a new corporate strategy appears to be emerging; a strategy that will not necessarily be linked to the requirements of Alcan Canada, that is, consumption of largely Canadian produced primary aluminum. In 1971, David M. Culver, currently chief executive officer of Alcan Canada, projected a scenario in which Canadian smelter production would be geared essentially to North American requirements, especially those of the United States, and would play a marginal role as a supplier to other foreign markets.

Traditionally, competitive pressures have led Alcan to erect abroad local smelting operations in order to protect its dominant local position. Currently, in order to enter certain new markets or retain its position in existing markets, Alcan is being pressured into establishing fully integrated aluminum industries (self-contained ingot and fabricating systems) even in those countries where the importation of Canadian primary aluminum might make the venture more efficient. These investments are being made because of their strategic and economic importance to the general competitiveness of Alcan as a multinational enterprise, of which Alcan Canada is a part, albeit a critical one.

Inco and Nickel

Inco is the world's largest producer of nickel, a substantial producer of copper, which is associated with nickel in the nickel-bearing sulphide ore mines in Canada, and a major producer (from its Canadian ores) of six platinum group metals — platinum, paladium, rhodium, ruthenium, iridium, and osmium. The company also produces iron ore pellets and limited quantities of gold, silver, sulphur, selenium, and tellurium. In addition, through its rolling mills division with plants in the United States and Great Britain, it produces wrought nickel, high nickel alloys, and welding products; and since 1974, Inco has become a major producer of automotive battery products.

In 1975, Inco supplied 38.5 per cent of the "Free World's" nickel consumption. Its major customer is the United States which accounted for 41 per cent of the company's metal sales in dollars, followed by Europe with 39 per cent, and Canada with 11 per cent. Inco supplies approximately two-thirds of U.S. nickel requirements. Although Inco has operating facilities in more than twenty countries, the bulk of its nickel is mined in Canada, and it appears that Canadian nickel deposits will continue to be an important element of the company's operations. The company is making substantial investments in developing nickel deposits in Indonesia and Guatemala and is engaged in seabed exploration for nickel.

There appears to be an historical parallel between the emergence of Inco and Alcan as major Canadian-based multinational companies. Both are of U.S. origin, the year 1902 is a critical one in their respective development, and the U.S. steel industry played a significant role in their establishment. The International Nickel Company was formed in 1902 through the merger of a number of firms in Canada and the United States, under the sponsorship of J. P. Morgan and Co. and the U.S. Steel Corporation. The head office was centred in New York, and seven of the ten members of the first corporate board of directors came from major U.S. steel firms, as did the first president of the company.

In 1916, the International Nickel Company incorporated its Canadian subsidiary, the International Nickel Company of Canada, Ltd., and partly in response to Canadian government and public pressures to refine mine output locally, it built a refinery at Port Colborne, Ontario which came on stream in 1918.

The year 1928 is a major landmark in the emergence of Inco as a Canadian-based company. Through an exchange of shares, Inco (Canada) became the parent company, and Inco (U.S.) the subsidiary. It is interesting to note that on May 31, 1928, Aluminum Limited (Alcan) was incorporated in Canada to engage in the international aluminum business. In both instances, however, while Inco and Alcan were legally incorporated in Canada, Inco's head office was based in New York, and Alcan's most senior personnel were resident in the United States as well in 1928.

Through a combination of acquisition, expansion, and modernization, Inco, at the time of the Second World War, was the Western world's largest wholly integrated nickel producing complex, from mining to refining and primary fabrication, with subsidiary operations located on two continents, and company personnel scattered in twelve countries. An interesting similarity between Alcan and Inco arises from the fact that these two companies looked to Canada for their raw material source — in the case of Alcan, it is cheap hydroelectric power, and for Inco it is the nickel ore body. To this day, approximately one-half of the corporate assets for both firms are located in Canada, and the bulk of their Canadian output is exported to sister subsidiaries and affiliated companies, largely in the United States and Europe.

Inco, unlike Alcan, however, has been more active in diversifying its activities away from the company's traditional metal base of operation. The first major step in Inco's diversification program was the acquisition in mid-1974 of ESB Incorporated, one of the world's leading battery companies. This U.S. company is a subsidiary of Inco-Canada's U.S. subsidiary, International Nickel Company, Inc. Sales of ESB Incorporated were $598 million in 1976, accounting for about 30 per cent of worldwide corporate sales in 1976. ESB, in its own right, is a major U.S-based multinational firm with ninety-eight plants in seventeen countries.

As a result of the ESB acquisition, the strategic importance of the

U.S. market in terms of sales, assets, and employees is now greater for Inco than Alcan: sales — 50 per cent vs. 21 per cent; assets — 23 per cent vs. 9 per cent; and employees — 27 percent vs. 6 per cent. In terms of ownership, the two companies exhibit similar characteristics; at year-end (1976), "Canadian residents of record held 49 per cent of the shares outstanding, United States residents of record 36 per cent, and residents of record in other countries 15 per cent".

Unlike Alcan, however, Inco only recently (1972) moved its head office organization from the United States (New York) to Canada (Toronto). It was in the late 1950s that the most senior executives of Alcan moved from the United States to their head office in Canada (Montreal). Inco, like Alcan, was recently judged by FIRA to be a "Canadian-controlled firm"; but in the case of both firms, the chief executive officers have been and are to this day citizens of the United States, although the boards of the two companies continue to be "Canadianized".

Massey-Ferguson and Farm Machinery
Massey-Ferguson Limited (M-F), headquartered in Toronto, is one of Canada's oldest and largest multinational operations. As an international organization, it can trace its corporate thrust into international business as far back as the 1880s. The predecessor of M-F was the Massey Harris Co. Limited which merged with Harry Ferguson Limited in 1953 to form Massey-Harris-Ferguson whose name was changed to Massey-Ferguson Ltd. in 1958. M-F is a holding company with over one hundred subsidiaries incorporated in different national jurisdictions. The company operates worldwide through subsidiaries and through associates in which it holds minority interests; it manufactures in 18 countries and sells farm machinery, industrial and construction machinery, and diesel engines through subsidiaries, associated and franchised distributors and dealers in more than 130 countries.

With a sales volume of $2.8 billion in 1976, corporate management contends that it is the largest manufacturer, in the Western world, of agricultural tractors and sugar cane harvesters; that its aggregate sales in agricultural equipment is exceeded only by the sales of two U.S multinational competitors; and that it manufactures more high-speed diesel engine units, worldwide, than any other competing producer. M-F is not only one of the biggest firms in Canada, it also ranks as one of the world's largest manufacturers of agricultural equipment. This distinction is an important one to bear in mind when one compares the size of Canadian MNCs with those of the United States. The largest manufacturers in the United States tend to rank high among the largest worldwide, but the largest in Canada only rank high in the context of industry/product specific categories.

The growth of M-F since the mid-1960s has been triggered off by an active program of acquisition, expansion, and integration. Most of the acquisitions took place in the industrialized West, for example, United States, U.K., Italy, and Germany. In 1976 M-F had a manufacturing base of some fifty plants containing 25 million sq. ft., situated in twelve countries. This is the core of the company's manufacturing system; in addition, through corporate arrangements with associate companies or licensees, M-F manufactures in eighteen other countries.

M-F has pursued a program of corporate integration in all key areas of commercial activity; however, it is in production and sourcing that the company has gained considerable success and business acclaim. The corporate policy is designed to promote maximum interchangeability of component parts, especially for tractors and combines, in order to increase production efficiencies on a worldwide basis. In the company's 1975 Annual Report, management stated:

> Highly productive results have been secured from each major capital investment through the use of our worldwide production scheduling system and our logistics network of multinational sources. In addition, product costs continue to be kept under control by product integration — switching from buy to make . . . through product design and manufacturing planning, emphasis continues to be placed upon interchangeability and commonality to obtain cost benefits and sourcing flexibility.

M-F's strategy aims at sourcing complete machines for specific markets from those M-F plants which can supply them at the lowest cost. Flexibility, via interchangeability of component parts of the machine, is not simply realized by plant location, but also by phase of manufacturing which takes place in the individual plant. Corporate integration is especially evident in the North American operations of M-F, because there are no tariffs on shipments of agricultural equipment between Canada and the United States. For this reason, a group of M-F operating subsidiaries conduct the company's business in this combined market with some products manufactured in the United States and others in Canada.

In 1976, the relative corporate importance of Canada and the United States, measured in terms of sales, assets, and employees, was as follows: 8 per cent vs. 23 per cent (sales); 11 per cent vs. 26 per cent (assets); and 12 per cent vs. 9 per cent (employees). Employing the same metre stick for the two country comparison (Canada vs. United States), the 1966 figures were as follows: 10 per cent vs. 31

per cent (sales); 18 per cent vs. 16 per cent (assets); and 17 per cent vs. 11 per cent (employees). In that ten-year interval, North America's share of the company's total sales dropped from 41 per cent to 31 per cent while Latin America, Asia, Africa, and Australia increased their relative sales importance. But in terms of assets, both globally and in the context of the company's North American operations, the picture is different: the United States now accounts for slightly more than one-quarter. The sales to assets ratio is approximately 1:1 and it appears that even though free trade exists between the United States and Canada, the company has opted to service the U.S. market largely from U.S. plants. While transportation costs may be a ready made explanation for establishing and acquiring U.S. plants, rising Canadian labor costs and the lower productivity of its Canadian plants led M-F's Canadian management to invest more heavily in recent years in the United States.

M-F's entry into the U.S. market parallels the approach favored by many of today's companies which invest in the United States; namely, the acquisition route. In 1910, M-F acquired an implement manufacturer located in Batavia, New York. On the other hand, M-F's rationale for first investing in the United States is somewhat atypical. E. P. Neufeld in his study of M-F notes:

> When it did obtain its first manufacturing facilities in the United States it was, paradoxically, because of the fear of free trade and not because of any attempt to circumvent the tariff. This is how it happened. Potential competition from the United States threatened to change with the 1910 campaign for reciprocity, that is, for free trade between Canada and the United States. Massey-Harris (M-F) seemed to fear that if the campaign were successful, its Canadian market would be threatened by a flood of imports from the United States. Such fears were not entirely ill-founded. To protect itself from such competition, Massey-Harris hurriedly established itself in the United States by buying into the Johnston Harvester Company. . . .

> Among North American multinationals, M-F is a pioneer; by 1908, it realized approximately one-half of its corporate sales outside Canada. This achievement took place without the benefit of significant sales to the U.S. market. This is no longer the case; sales in the United States are significant, accounting for about one-quarter of total corporate sales; and M-F's U.S. subsidiary, Massey-Ferguson Inc., placed eighteenth in sales on the list of the hundred largest foreign-owned companies in the United States.

Seagram and Liquor

The Seagram Company Ltd., like M-F, is a holding company. It is headquartered in Montreal, and multinational in scope, with operating subsidiaries and affiliates in 23 countries. The company produces a complete line of whiskies, gins, rums, brandies, vodkas, other spirits and wines, and markets its brands in over 130 countries. In addition, through its subsidiaries, the company is engaged in the exploration for and development, production, and sale of crude oil, natural gas, and related products. A further similarity between Seagram and M-F is that in addition to being one of Canada's largest firms with a 1976 sales volume of approximately $2 billion, Seagram is also the world's largest producer and marketer of distilled spirits and wines.

The history of the present day company dates back to 1928 when Samuel Bronfman and his brothers acquired the shares of Joseph E. Seagram and Sons Ltd. of Waterloo, Ontario. This Waterloo-based firm began its operation in 1857 and by 1928 was a highly respected firm. The 1928 purchase was combined with the Bronfman's owned and managed company, Distillers Corporation Ltd., to establish a new public company, Distillers Corporation Seagrams Ltd.

Bronfman's entry in the U.S. market took place some five years later (November 1933) when a distilling plant in Lawrenceburg, Indiana was purchased. Thus, the acquisition route was again employed by yet another Canadian multinational. Joseph E. Seagram and Sons Inc. was formed to operate the distillery and has since become the parent company in the United States. Expansion in the U.S. market has continued rapidly ever since. In 1976, the U.S. market accounted for 68 per cent of total company sales and Joseph E. Seagram and Sons Inc., incorporated in Indiana in 1933 and head-quartered in New York, is now an operating and holding company in its own right. It controls through stock ownership all of the affiliated distillery operations and sales companies in the United States.

In 1975, the U.S. subsidiary of Seagram Company Ltd. of Canada had a sales volume of approximately $1.6 billion, ranking third on the list of the one hundred largest foreign-owned companies in the United States. The relative commercial importance between the head office in Canada and its U.S. subsidiary head office can be whimsically contrasted from the following quote excerpted from the company's 1975 Form 10-K report, under Item 3, entitled:

Properties:
The company's executive offices are located in a four-storey office building which the company owns at 1430 Peel Street, Montreal,

Quebec, and Joseph E. Seagram's executive offices are located in a thirty-eight-storey office building which it owns at 375 Park Avenue, New York, New York.

That this is the case is not surprising since 68 per cent of Seagram's sales are realized in the United States while only 6 per cent are earned in Canada. Nonetheless, Seagram's market share in each country is comparable — 20 per cent in Canada and over 19 per cent in the United States.

Since the Second World War, Seagram's has been actively expanding its overseas operations (non-North America), while in more recent years it has been engaged in a significant diversification program away from its traditional business of distilled spirits and wines. With reference to its policy of growth through internationalization, the M-F strategy of interchangeability and flexibility appears to characterize the Seagram corporate strategy. Sam Bronfman, who until his death was synonymous with "Seagram", offered the following explanation for the emergence of his company as one of the world's leading multinationals:

> I have always considered it most important that our business between the countries in which we have interests should be on the basis of a "two-way street". Let me explain. We ship our Canadian, American, and Scotch whiskies to France and Italy, for example, and we ship our French and Italian products to Canada, the United States, and Great Britain. This "two-way street" premise extends to all the countries where we have facilities. It is this policy which is the spine of our business. It brings and holds together our worldwide operations.

Inasmuch as 94 per cent of company sales are realized outside of Canada, and only 10 per cent of the company's assets are located in Canada, with the United States accounting for well over one-half of total corporate sales and assets, it is not surprising that a U.S. subsidiary of Joseph E. Seagram & Sons, Inc. handles international sales. Seagram Export Sales Co. Inc., established in New York, was formed and given responsibility for sales in over one hundred countries.

In 1953, a major change in the company's activities was initiated. In that year the Frankfort Oil Co. of Oklahoma was purchased. In the words of Sam Bronfman:

> Foreseeing the requirements for energy in the 1950s and 1960s, and the almost unbelievable demand of the 1970s, I was motivated in 1953 to cause Joseph E. Seagram & Sons, Inc. to begin investing in the petroleum industry — the energy business.

Growth through diversification received its biggest boost in 1963 when Seagram acquired Texas Pacific Coal and Oil Co., now known as Texas Pacific Oil Company, Inc. (incorporated in Delaware). This company generated total revenues of $140 million in fiscal 1975, ranking it among the top five independent producers in the United States. This Dallas-headquartered firm does no refining or consumer marketing itself; instead, it concentrates exclusively on finding, developing, and producing hydrocarbons. Its major preoccupation today is with expansion.

In 1975, exploration and development property was held in twenty states of the United States and in Alberta (by Seafort Petroleum). North American holdings, largely U.S., totalled 2.5 million net underdeveloped acres, while overseas acreage amounts to 8.1 million net acres. Spain, Dubai, the North Sea, Kenya, and the Philippines are some of the areas in which the Seagram's subsidiary, alone or in partnership, is pursuing its exploration activities.

The management of Seagrams is committed to developing the company's oil and gas business. Business and political events since 1953 strengthened management's conviction that the need for and value of new reserves would continue to grow. This conviction involves further exploration in the United States, but Seagram also accepts the larger risks, both political and economic, that are involved in international exploration. Management believes that it is overseas where the discoveries of world-ranking new reserves will probably be made, and that this will influence Seagram's investment in the future. Current investment and Seagram's corporate strategy for the future appears to be U.S. and non-Canadian oriented, albeit, multinational in scope.

Summary Observations

CDIA is occurring with increasing frequency through the establishment of new facilities, takeover of foreign firms, and involvement in joint ventures. Much of this investment is financed through borrowings in foreign financial markets, and by investing the retained earnings of existing foreign affiliates abroad. Domestic market saturation, drive for growth, relative scarcity of production factors (labor, capital, land, and intermediate products), access to foreign markets, need for certain raw materials, and tax and other financial advantages are some of the reasons offered by Canadian businessmen for investing abroad.[9]

9. See I. A. Litvak and C. J. Maule, "Canadian Multinationals in the Western Hemisphere", *The Business Quarterly* 40, No. 3 (Autumn 1975), pp. 30-42.

In the 1960s, corporate motivation for investing abroad was largely viewed in positive terms, that is, to grow big enough to compete successfully internationally meant the firm had to break through the small Canadian market syndrome. The bulk of this investment was undertaken by resource-based firms in Canada as a means of diversifying their operations both in geographic and product terms. Motivation for investing abroad in the late 1970s has been greatly accelerated by negative considerations as well, such as Canada's high inflation rates; government controls on prices, profits, and executive salaries, strikes, union militancy, and poor labor-management relations; federal-provincial jurisdictional disputes in mining and expropriation; and the general political and economic uncertainties surrounding Quebec.

The corporate vignettes of Canada's four major multinationals indicate that regardless of their historical roots, Canadian or U.S., their investment and involvement in the United States is substantial, increasing and critical to the success of their corporate strategies. Moreover, the performance of the Canadian part of the operation is affected by what happens in the United States. While the corporate relationship between the Canadian and U.S. entities within the Canadian multinational corporation are to varying degrees interdependent, they are also asymmetrical; as is the case between Canada and the United States in terms of trade and capital. Thus, although the headquarters of each of the four corporations is based in Canada, the sensitivity of the corporate executive in Canada to what happens in the United States is very great.

In the context of the present politico-economic environment in Canada, including poor government-business relations, it is worth noting that Alcan and Inco were originally of U.S. origin. For this reason, it is not difficult to imagine that these two firms might wish to transfer their headquarters again; this time back to the United States. The move would not be a difficult one to make. Similarly, Seagram and Massey-Ferguson might see the merit of moving their headquarters. Some would argue that such a move would be more "de jure" than "de facto"; and the most likely site would also be the United States.

The probability of the forgoing scenario materializing at this time is not great, but it cannot be ruled out. If the present poor investment climate in Canada continues to deteriorate because of political as well as economic circumstances, the current transfer of headquarters' organizations between provinces, for example, Quebec and Ontario, may in due time be overshadowed by moves involving some of Canada's largest industrial enterprises with substantial operations in the United States, to the United States.

The authors are currently examining the policy implications of Canadian direct investment abroad for corporations and governments in Canada.

IV
Foreign Direct Investment Theory, Impact, and Control

B
Patterns

22
Canadian Small Business Investment in the U.S. — Corporate Forms and Characteristics

Isaiah A. Litvak

Christopher J. Maule

Dr. Litvak is a professor in the Faculty of Administrative Studies, York University. He has lectured extensively in North America, Europe, and Africa. In addition to being an executive member of various learned societies and serving on the editorial boards of several journals, he is an active consultant to government and business.

Dr. Maule is professor of economics and international affairs at Carleton University. He is co-author with Dr. Litvak of *Alcan Aluminium Limited: A Corporate History*; *Corporate Dualism and the Canadian Steel Industry*; *Foreign Investment: The Experience of Host Countries*; *Dual Loyalty: Canada-U.S. Business Relations*; and other publications.

This chapter is a revised version of an article which appeared originally in *The Business Quarterly*, Winter 1978. Reprinted by permission.

Introduction

Domestic economic and political circumstances are largely responsible for the public concern expressed regarding the motivation for Canadian direct investment abroad (CDIA) and its probable impact on Canada. Expanding abroad is seen by many as an alternative to expanding in Canada. Consequently, such corporate investment is perceived to be bad because of the probable loss of Canadian jobs, exports, and the exportation of technology and capital. Canadian direct investment abroad quadrupled from $2.5 billion in 1960 to $10.7 billion in 1975 and to $13.4 billion in 1977.[1] The United States accounted for approximately one-half of total CDIA, and since Canada's export trade is heavily dependent on the U.S. market, this type of corporate investment is viewed with alarm in some Canadian quarters, specifically among unions and governments (federal and provincial).

There appears to be particular cause for concern when CDIA involves small and medium-size Canadian-owned firms in the secondary manufacturing sector, which is the focus of this study. The reasons for this concern are many; however, the following two are generally considered to be among the more important:

1. The secondary manufacturing sector is currently experiencing problems so that any corporate expansion outside of Canada by firms based in this sector is viewed as a loss to the Canadian economy.

2. The high level of U.S. investment in the Canadian manufacturing sector has prompted Canadian governments in recent years to develop policies and programs aimed at encouraging the "start up" of new Canadian entrepreneurial ventures, as well as to "dissuade" foreign investors from acquiring such enterprises. The latter policy may be partially blunted by horizontal investments undertaken by small and medium-size Canadian firms in the U.S.; for if they are successful, the end result will be an "Americanization" of their corporate strategy and structure. The consequences of

1. *Statistics Canada Daily* (Dec. 12, 1977), p. 3.

such actions may limit the immediate economic contribution to
Canada by the companies in question.

The Study

During the summer of 1978, the authors conducted a survey designed to provide empirical data about the reasons small and medium-
size Canadian firms invest in the establishment of affiliate operations
in the United States, about the corporate form of their investment,
the impact of such investment on their corporate operations, and the
implications for Canada.

The group of firms examined consists of twenty-five Canadian-
owned firms with one or more affiliate operations in the United
States. Each of these firms exhibit three key characteristics: (1) they
are located in the secondary manufac ring sector; (2) they are small
or medium-size operations; and (3) they are all deemed to be
technologically based firms: that is, companies which emphasize
research and development or which place major emphasis on exploiting new technical knowledge.

Information about these firms and their U.S. affiliates was obtained
primarily through personal interviews conducted in the field, supported with material obtained from Canadian and U.S. government
agencies, associations, and chambers of commerce. A questionnaire
guide was used to direct the company interview. The companies
requested that their names not be identified in the study for fear of
being unfairly criticized for investing in the U.S. at a time of high
unemployment in Canada.

The Companies

The geographic distribution of the head offices of the twenty-five
secondary manufacturers is as follows: Ontario — fifteen; Quebec —
six; and the West — four. Table 1 gives a breakdown of their sales,
assets, and employees.

In 1977, five of the twenty-five firms had sales volume of less than
$5 million; eighteen firms had an annual sales volume between $5
million and $49.9 million; and two firms had sales in excess of $100
million a year, and at first glance might be termed large. Upon further
examination, these two firms were viewed as borderline cases, ex-
hibiting more of the characteristics of a medium-size firm, than a
large mature corporation. For example, the two firms are owner-
managed, recent corporate entrants, and not ranked among the
hundred largest Canadian firms. In fact, one of the two firms is a steel

Table 1

Corporate Sales, Assets, and Employees for the Year Ending, 1977

Sales (in million $)		Assets (in million $)		Employees (in hundreds)	
Less than 1	(2)	Less than 1	(4)	Less than 100	(4)
1 - 2.9	(2)	1 - 2.9	(3)	101 - 199	(3)
3 - 4.9	(1)	3 - 4.9	(2)	200 - 499	(9)
5 - 9.9	(3)	5 - 9.9	(5)	500 - 999	(4)
10 - 24.9	(7)	10 - 24.9	(8)	1000 - 1999	(3)
25 - 49.9	(8)	25 - 49.9	(1)	2000 - 4999	(2)
50 - 99.9	(0)	50 - 99.9	(0)	5000 - 9999	(0)
100 +	(2)	100 +	(2)	10,000 +	(0)

producer and is one of the smallest enterprises in its industry. Firms that appear large by Canadian standards are often small by international standards.

Reasons for Investing in the United States

All twenty-five companies have affiliate operations in the United States. What is particularly significant is that the opening date of their operations took place during the past decade, none before 1967; for example, two between 1967-1970, nine during 1971-1974, two in 1975, three in 1976, two in 1977, six in 1978, and one slated to be opened in 1979. Thus, the executives were in a relatively good position to explain their reasons for investing in the United States. Table 2 provides a frequency distribution of the reasons, and their relative importance at the time the decision was taken.

Market Considerations

Home markets are rarely saturated, except in a relative sense. In this context, it is argued that when the cost of developing new business is greater in Canada than, say, in the United States, the Canadian company may contemplate investing in the U.S. Such a "situation develops most commonly in a mature domestic corporation which has surplus funds and management capability for which it foresees only marginal opportunities"[2] in Canada. The literature on foreign direct

2. United States Tariff Commission, *Implications of Multinational Firms for World Trade and Investment and for U.S. Trade and Labor* (Washington: U.S. Government Printing Office, 1973), p. 119.

investment suggests that the benefits from investing abroad include the following: promote new growth from a low market share position, which can be quickly achieved through the acquisition route; management and technical know-how from the parent company can be readily transferred via a few parent company employees who may form the nucleus of the new subsidiary management team; foreign markets can be better serviced by a local subsidiary which provides a complete line of services in support of the company's marketing program; profitability is often higher in the foreign market; and by expanding the domestic company's operations beyond its national boundaries, management can take greater advantage of product and marketing innovations.[3]

While these observations help to explain the foreign investment motivation and strategies of large mature Canadian corporations with affiliates in the U.S.,[4] they do not characterize the operations of our sample of companies, nor do they explain their reasons for investing in the United States. In the first place, none are large and mature; second, only a few had surplus cash at their disposal; and, third, all were involved in the manufacture of very narrow product lines. The last feature distinguishes the operations of small and medium-size firms in Canada and is critical to understanding their marketing motivation for investing in the United States.

The data in Table 2, under the market classification, show that the first five (a, b, c, d, and e) considerations were judged to be among the most important reasons for establishing a U.S. affiliate. This is not surprising since similar findings would apply to large mature Canadian companies. In the case of the latter type of firms, however, their product range tends to be much broader and more diversified.

The majority of the companies interviewed realized for themselves a particular niche in the Canadian market, through the design and development of a limited product line as "measurement sensors and computer control systems for the paper industry". In this product category, as is the case with many of the other corporate interviewees, the company occupies a dominant market position, and is not in competition with large firms. The drive for growth led this company to invest in replicating its strategy and operations in the U.S., although it readily acknowledged the existence of opportunities to diversify its product line in Canada, for example, in terms of other industry applications.

3. See *Implications of Multinational Firms* **II**, ch. 1.
4. See I. A. Litvak and C. J. Maule, "Canadian Multinationals in the Western Hemisphere", *The Business Quarterly* **40**, No. 3 (Autumn 1975) pp. 30-42 and "The Emerging Challenge of Canadian Direct Investment Abroad", *The Business Quarterly* **43**, No. 1 (Spring 1978), pp. 24-37.

Table 2

Reasons for Investing in the U.S. (Ranked in order of importance)[a]

	1	2	3	4
Market Considerations				
a. Maintain or increase market share in the U.S.	22	—	—	3
b. Faster sales growth in U.S. than in Canada	21	2	1	1
c. Difficult to reach U.S. market from Canada because of tariffs, transportation costs, or nationalistic purchasing policies	16	4	3	2
d. Diversify product line/geographic market	18	2	1	4
e. Increase responsiveness to U.S. customer demands and improve servicing capability	12	10	2	1
f. Integrate forward/backward	1	1	0	23
g. Promote exports from parent Canadian firm through U.S. subsidiary	2	2	0	21
h. Secure U.S. sources of materials supply	2	2	3	18
i. To export from U.S. to third countries	4	1	2	18
U.S. Production/Cost Factors				
a. Availability of advanced technology	3	1	1	20
b. Availability of natural resources	1	0	2	22
c. Availability of fuel	1	0	1	23
d. Availability of stable labor force	9	6	2	8
e. Availability of managerial talent	4	4	5	12
U.S. Politico-Economic Environment				
a. General political stability	3	5	5	12
b. Trade unions' attitudes	5	3	4	13
c. More favorable taxation policies	5	3	5	12
d. Relative freedom from regulatory constraints	5	3	2	15
e. Easier access to financing	5	2	5	13
f. Wage/Price policies	7	2	5	11
g. Federal government economic incentives	0	2	1	22
h. State government economic incentives	2	1	1	21
i. Buy American policies	7	3	1	14
Firm's Canadian Corporate Resources and Capabilities				
a. Possession of superior technology	21	4	0	0
b. Growth in experience in international business	17	6	2	0
c. Growth in corporate capacity to finance investment via retained earnings/borrowing/issue of new equity	4	9	9	3
Canadian Politico-Economic Environment				
a. General political climate	3	6	4	12
b. Quebec-Canada constitutional debate	3	4	3	15
c. Trade unions' attitudes	4	3	5	13
d. Taxation policies	4	3	7	11
e. Regulatory constraints	4	2	4	15
f. Access to financing	5	3	5	12
g. AIB controls	3	2	5	15
h. Federal government policies	5	3	3	14
i. Provincial government policies	3	2	1	19

(a) Rating Scale: 1 — very important; 2 — important; 3 — of minor importance; 4 — unimportant.

The unwillingness to diversify in Canada was attributed to a number of factors such as reticence to enter a new product market, especially if there is probable competition from large firms, many of which are U.S. owned; the cost of building up a new product line in the area of manufacturing, sales, and distribution; as well as general hesitation to engage in new business fields, especially if the corporate waters are uncharted. For these and other reasons, many of the companies elected to probe the U.S. export market as a means of increasing company sales.

The third (c) market consideration is often pivotal because it pushed a number of Canadian companies into setting up U.S. subsidiaries. For example, a Canadian manufacturer of automotive parts explained,

> The American people are very proud, and there is a great tendency on their part to identify an American factory as being inherently or automatically better than a foreign factory as a source of goods they are going to buy. I think that is a very big factor. People in the United States, if they know you are going to supply them with goods from a Canadian factory, seem to feel that in some way these goods will be inferior.

Most interviewees stressed that a major objective for their U.S. subsidiary is to project to their American customers the image of a U.S.-oriented company. For example, companies which have U.S. sales offices and warehouse facilities, but no U.S. plant, often maintain a direct tie line between their U.S. office and their main plant in Canada. Thus, U.S. customers calling the "U.S. sales office" can be linked into the main Canadian plant and frequently are not aware of the fact that they are talking to someone outside the U.S. All catalogues, literature, and direct mail pieces sent to U.S. customers make no mention of the fact that the company is Canadian.

A key finding under the "market" heading is that few firms with U.S. subsidiary manufacturing operations saw the establishment of such facilities as a means of promoting Canadian exports to the U.S.

U.S. Production Cost Factors and Politico-Economic Environment

The relative size and growth potential of the U.S. market is the major reason for investing in the United States — a view shared by most Canadian firms, regardless of size.[5] Our study does not contradict

---

5. See Report to the Congress, *Foreign Direct Investment in the United States.* **5**, Appendix G, ch. 7: Canada (Washington, D.C.: U.S. Department of Commerce, April 1976), pp. G-210 to G-256.

this contention; however, our findings suggest that the difference between the Canadian and U.S. politico-economic environments was also a critical consideration in many of the investment decisions. The environmental factors included the following: higher profit expectations in the U.S. because of lower relative political and economic risks; lower cost and greater availability of financing; lower relative production costs attributed to less labor unrest and increasingly more favorable labor costs; superior productivity growth related to lower labor costs and more aggressive management arising from a stronger commitment to the free enterprise system; and less governmental intervention which promotes greater investment security for business.

The costs of production including land, labor, material, capital, and management seldom constituted the major rationale for the U.S. investment decision. For example, all interviewees claimed that labor costs were lower in the U.S. — from 15 per cent to 40 per cent; however, only a few were involved in labor-intensive manufacturing activities, that is, where labor costs represent a high proportion of the value of output.

The production cost comparisons were rarely judged to be the predominant reason for investing in the U.S. as opposed to investing in Canada. Certain executives remarked that the impact of inflationary forces, price stabilization activities of governments, wage agreements, or changes in taxation, tariff, and foreign exchange rates can quickly nullify or aggravate differences in the relative costs of production.

If, however, the production costs included the cost of doing business in the U.S. (for example, exporting to versus manufacturing in the U.S.) then tariff and non-tariff barriers, ease of financing and related considerations would have to be included in the total cost calculation. In this instance, the combination of the two groupings — U.S. production cost factors and U.S. politico-economic environment — was considered to be of comparable importance to the "market factors" by a number of interviewees, the majority of whom are based in Quebec and the West.

Canadian Corporate Capabilities and Politico-Economic Environment

Superior technology and international business experience, but not financial resources, were among the important corporate capabilities which led many of the interviewees to establish U.S. subsidiaries (see Table 2). This finding should not be surprising since a major weakness of most small and medium-size firms in Canada is a lack of capital.[6] Obviously, this limitation is not a sufficient condition to dissuade the companies from investing in the U.S.

The key point made was that their competitiveness in Canada, possibly their survival, hinged on achieving market success in the U.S. In brief, geographical diversification was regarded as the route to getting bigger in the confines of the small Canadian market; however, only a handful of firms exhibited financial strength, and viewed this corporate feature as one of the "very important" pre-conditions to going abroad.

Not one interviewee singled out the present Canadian politico-economic difficulties as the sole reason for investing in the United States. Nonetheless, all six Quebec-based companies admitted that the domestic political climate played a key role in their U.S. investment decision, but only after due consideration was given to the probable marketing and manufacturing implications for their Canadian operations.

As for the other interviewees, the majority of whom are based in Ontario, the environmental considerations were examined in relative terms, vis-à-vis the United States. On the whole, the United States was regarded as the more attractive site for corporate investment.

One symptom of the current economic and political difficulties experienced in Canada is the decline in value of the Canadian dollar. The actual extent to which capital flows may or may not be influenced by the undervaluation or the overvaluation of the Canadian dollar is virtually unquantifiable. Opinion is divided on the extent to which the 1978 exchange rate realignments may reduce the size of corporate capital outflows in the form of direct investment. While there may be some reduction, our findings indicate that corporate capital migrates for a host of other reasons, and that the current exchange rate fluctuations have a limited impact on the U.S. investment decisions of small and medium-size Canadian firms.

The U.S. Subsidiary

Canadian companies which establish subsidiaries normally do so after having exported to the U.S. for a few years. The typical sequence is one of exporting first, usually through distributors in the United States; followed by setting up a sales subsidiary with or without

---

6. See I. A. Litvak and C. J. Maule, "Government-Business Interface: the case of the small technology-based firm", *Canadian Public Administration* **16**, No. 1 (Spring 1973), pp. 97-109.

warehouse facilities; which may lead to the establishment of a plant for local assembly and/or full production. At the outset, the U.S. plants may engage in the partial manufacture of the Canadian parent company's product line, the items produced are often few in number and not always the most profitable. U.S. tariff and non-tariff barriers, transportation costs and U.S. customer service requirements are among the key factors which dictate the product mix to be manufactured.

All twenty-five companies had sales in the United States: in ten cases, 50 per cent or more of total corporate sales were realized in the U.S. and only five companies had U.S. sales which accounted for less than 10 per cent of total sales (see Table 3). Nineteen of the twenty-five companies were also marketing their product line outside of North America, and for six of these firms more than one-quarter of their total sales were generated offshore. Geographical diversification is obviously the road to corporate growth, and the U.S. market appears to be the major target for this drive.

All twenty-five companies invested in some physical operating presence in the United States. Fifteen of the twenty-five companies had U.S. manufacturing plants, but only three of them had more than one plant. Of the remaining ten companies, four were essentially sales subsidiaries which owned, leased, or rented warehouse facilities. The geographical breakdown of the assets and employees of the "Group of 25" bears witness to the foregoing finding. Eighteen of the companies had declared assets in the United States, but only in thirteen cases could it be considered significant, that is, in excess of 10 per cent of total corporate assets. As for employees, fourteen of the companies employed 10 per cent or more of total corporate personnel in the United States (see Table 3).

The geographic location of the Canadian-owned operations in the U.S. was widespread: six in New York State, three in the Carolinas; three in California; two each in Colorado, New Hampshire, and Texas, and one each in Florida, Georgia, New Jersey, Ohio, Pennsylvania, Tennessee, Utah, Vermont, Washington, and Puerto Rico.

Management Control and Finance

Twenty-four of the twenty-five companies have wholly owned subsidiaries, and one of them also has a partially, but majority-owned subsidiary. The one remaining company has a majority-owned subsidiary in which key U.S. personnel have some equity participation. This finding should not be surprising, since the companies are in the small-medium-size category and tend to be owner-managed. Man-

Table 3

Geographic Distribution of Corporate Sales, Assets, and Employees for the Year Ending 1977 (in percentages)

a) Sales

Canada		United States		Other Countries	
90 +	(2)	90 +	(1)	90 +	(-)
75-89	(4)	75-89	(3)	75-89	(-)
50-74	(6)	50-74	(6)	50-74	(4)
25-49	(6)	25-49	(2)	25-49	(2)
10-24	(6)	10-24	(8)	10-24	(4)
1-9	(0)	1-9	(5)	1-9	(9)
0	(1)	0	(0)	0	(6)

b) Assets

Canada		United States		Other Countries	
90 +	(15)	90 +	(1)	90 +	(-)
75-89	(4)	75-89	(0)	75-89	(-)
50-74	(2)	50-74	(2)	50-74	(-)
25-49	(2)	25-49	(3)	25-49	(1)
10-24	(1)	10-24	(7)	10-24	(3)
1-9	(1)	1-9	(5)	1-9	(1)

c) Employees

Canada		United States		Other Countries	
90 +	(10)	90 +	(1)	90 +	(0)
75-89	(8)	75-89	(0)	75-89	(0)
50-74	(4)	50-74	(0)	50-74	(0)
25-49	(2)	25-49	(6)	25-49	(3)
10-24	(-)	10-24	(7)	10-24	(2)
1-9	(1)	1-9	(4)	1-9	(1)
0	(-)	0	(7)	0	(19)

agement of such firms like to maintain personal control over their operations,[7] and since their U.S. subsidiaries are relatively young, it was charged that it would not be smart business to go public in the U.S. with an untested and unknown company operation.

The concern with control is not only reflected in the ownership of the subsidiary, but also in its reporting relationship to the Canadian parent. Seventeen of the twenty-five Canadian companies designated a "president" for their U.S. subsidiaries, and of the remaining eight, there were four vice-presidents and four general managers. Thirteen of the twenty-five chief executive officers were American nationals, ten were Canadians and two were British. With one exception, the

7. See I. A. Litvak and C. J. Maule, "Profiles of Technical Entrepreneurs", *The Business Quarterly* (Summer 1974), pp. 40-49.

U.S. chief executive officers reported directly to senior executives of the Canadian parent company on all important matters — strategic and tactical. Much of the reporting was done along functional lines, for example, manufacturing, marketing, and finance.

The U.S. subsidiaries enjoyed little autonomy, and only four of the twenty-five Canadian companies maintained a formal management contract with their U.S. operations covering such areas as research and development, and exporting. The formal approach was considered unnecessary since all key management decisions were taken in the Canadian parent company. Furthermore, for reasons of taxation and finance, it was felt that the informal approach is more practical since it allows for maximum flexibility to decide when, how much and for what activities the U.S. subsidiary should be charged.

The financial structure of the U.S. affiliates varied substantially from company to company. In terms of the mix of debt and equity, the ratios ranged largely from 2:1 to 10:1. There were also significant differences in the extent to which debt was local or imported. A key finding is that most companies prefer high-debt ratios and a minimum of equity capital for their U.S. subsidiaries, with much of the debt capital raised in the U.S.

The preference for this type of financing is not surprising since many of the firms are privately held, and those that are public are closely held by a few individuals. The preoccupation with control is a key reason why the U.S. subsidiaries are thinly capitalized and thus highly leveraged. The relative ease of financing in the U.S. is the major reason for borrowing locally. The experience of all interviewees is that the U.S. unit banking system is more responsive to the financial needs of small and medium-size firms, the collateral requirements are less exacting and the interest rates are generally lower in the U.S. than in Canada.

Fourteen of the twenty-five companies raised most of their capital requirements in the U.S., and of the remaining eleven, six of the companies financed their U.S. operations wholly in Canada through the use of corporate funds and debt capital obtained from Canadian financial institutions. The cost of establishing the U.S. subsidiary ranged anywhere from $50,000 to $15,000,000, but most of the operations fell significantly below the $1 million level.

Acquisition of an existing U.S. operation and the establishment of a new facility are generally the two ways of physically expanding into the U.S. Only three of the twenty-five companies studied employed the acquisition strategy, while many of the other companies set up their U.S. operations through a combination of lease/rental arrangements. This approach was the dominant one because it was the least costly and risky. Moreover, it was also one of the few ways in which a Canadian company, financially strapped, could expand its operations into the U.S.

Manufacturing

Fifteen of the twenty-five companies had manufacturing plants in the U.S., and three had multiplant operations. The three included a steel producer, a mobile home manufacturer, and a telecommunications equipment manufacturer. The square footage of these plants ranged from a low of 4,000 to a high in excess of 200,000 with most concentrated around the 100,000 mark. The staff employed at these plants were as few as 10 in one instance, and as many as 800 in another. In only three cases were the U.S. subsidiary operations, in size and output, larger than their Canadian parent.

These three companies included an Ontario-based steel producer, a Quebec hardware manufacturer, and a British Columbia aircraft designer. The steel producer has one mini-steel mill in Canada but two in the U.S. While the combined output of tonnage of the U.S. mills exceeds the Canadian total, the plant staff employed in both countries are comparable in size. In the case of the hardware manufacturer, U.S. acquisitions and the concentration of their manufacturing activities in one new large plant has made the American operation larger than the Canadian. However, as in the case of the steel producer, the size of the Canadian labor force exceeds that of the U.S. The differences may be explained in terms of the relatively more modern U.S. plants, and the greater degree of specialization, because fewer products are manufactured, and their production runs are significantly longer than in the Canadian parent operations.

The aircraft example is a special case. The company was incorporated in 1970 to build a prototype STOL aircraft. In 1971, management decided to produce the prototype in the State of Washington to qualify for FAA certification and because aircraft expertise was readily available from Boeing in Seattle. Thus, the Seattle operations became significantly larger than the total equivalent Canadian base. The original idea was to do the manufacturing in Canada, once the prototype flew. In 1974, however, management decided that manufacturing should also take place in the U.S. because of a lack of Canadian government financing and the higher costs of manufacturing in Canada.

Impacts

The probable impact of the Canadian-U.S. business arrangements on the Canadian economy can be highlighted in the context of the employment and balance of payments effects.

Employment Effects

Three employment effects can be readily identified. First, there is the production displacement impact on employment in Canada. The assumption here is that employment would have occurred in Canada had the production of the U.S. subsidiaries been carried out in Canada. The assumption underlying the production displacement effect was questioned in fifteen of the twenty-five companies interviewed, namely, those that engage in some manufacturing activity in the U.S. This was done by ascertaining the corporate motives which prompted these firms to establish U.S. manufacturing affiliates. As previously noted, the key reasons were largely market considerations and the choice was rarely between expanding production in Canada and producing in the United States, but between supplying the U.S. market or dropping out.

The second major employment effect has to do with export stimulation. The literature on direct foreign investment indicates that a significant amount of domestic employment is generated through the production of goods which result from the establishment of overseas affiliate operations. The U.S. Department of Commerce notes three reasons why foreign investments stimulate U.S. export trade.[8] First, if a significant part of overseas investment is made through an export of U.S. capital equipment, this will usually require some continuous supply of replacement equipment. This generalization does not apply to our group of Canadian companies. The equipment and machinery employed in the Canadian parent company plants were largely sourced in the United States, Europe, and Japan. Thus, it is not surprising that most of the equipment and machinery installed in the U.S. subsidiaries were leased or purchased from manufacturers based in the United States.

Second, U.S. studies show that many U.S. parent companies export parts and components for further assembly. This situation is apparent in our sample of companies because most are engaged in partial

8. See U.S. Department of Commerce, *Studies on U.S. Foreign Investment Re: The Multinational Corporation*, 1972 **1** and **2**.

manufacturing activities in the U.S. Third, an important volume of U.S. exports to foreign affiliates is resold with minimal assembly activity. This finding applies to our sample of companies as well. Sales organizations of U.S. subsidiaries are more effective than non-affiliated U.S. distributors in merchandising Canadian-made products in the U.S. The existence of U.S. sales facilities, warehouses, and trained personnel help to facilitate not only the affiliates assembled and/or manufactured goods, but those of Canadian parents as well.

The third major employment effect has to do with whether the establishment of U.S. subsidiaries provides job opportunities for Canadians in the U.S. The major difference between the "home-office" employment effect and the "displacement" and "export stimuli" effects is that in the case of the latter two, the occupational coverage largely consists of semi-skilled and skilled occupational classes. In the case of the former, the jobs are primarily managerial, clerical, and professional.

Most U.S. subsidiary personnel were recruited in the United States. With few notable exceptions, minimal employment in Canada was created for companies which service the operations of Canadian parent firms with U.S. subsidiaries. These firms engage in such activities as engineering, public relations, law, management consulting, finance, and banking. U.S. provincialism and nationalism, superior expertise, lower rates, and Canadian ignorance of U.S. laws were among the reasons cited for employing U.S. firms in support of Canadian activities in the United States.

Balance-of-Payments Effects

The corporate reasons for establishing U.S. manufacturing facilities have been examined. By highlighting the impact of such investment on the Canadian company's manufacturing and exporting activities, one can gain some appreciation of the differing effects this type of investment may have on Canada. For a start, one key benefit generally associated with U.S. outward investment is only minimally realized; specifically, an increase in the export of Canadian-made machinery and equipment, and related support services. The explanation offered is that Canada lacks a sophisticated secondary manufacturing capability, a fact which is readily evident in the foreign-made equipment and machinery installed in Canadian plants.

Companies with manufacturing affiliates tend to reproduce their operations in the United States. During the initial phase of setting up the U.S. subsidiary, parent company exports may increase significantly because of the expanded and more aggressive activities of the company's U.S. sales organization. Canadian exports will include both finished products as well as components to be assembled in the U.S. plant. However, as the U.S. subsidiary strengthens and expands its manufacturing capability, increasing reduction in exports from the Canadian parent is likely to take place.

This seems to be a common event for a number of corporate interviewees, whose U.S. manufacturing operations have been in place for some years, that is, in excess of five. The cause is explained in terms of the tendency for Canadian companies to replicate their operations in the U.S.; specifically around product lines previously exported to the United States. At first glance, this appears to be a "miniature replica" scenario in reverse involving Canadian parent companies. There is one major difference: if the subsidiaries in the U.S. are successful, they are anything but "miniature" compared to the scale of their parent company operations in Canada because of the size of the U.S. market.

The interviewees' U.S. experiences were not universally profitable. Some encountered serious difficulties such as a Quebec manufacturer of radio telephone systems who closed his plant in New York and had the following observations to offer:

Quite a few small Canadian firms which recently opened assembly-manufacturing subsidiaries in the U.S. closed them down because of high and unforeseen costs which arise from running a plant in another country, even if it is next-door to you. These costs are seldom realistically computed and often exceed the benefits gained from the lower wages paid to U.S. workers. But the most important lesson learned is that if you phase out your U.S. production from your Canadian plant to the new U.S. operation, unless the gap in production is filled with new domestic or export business, parent plant costs will increase and the subsequent result will be an increase in overall manufacturing and sales costs, and a deterioration in the financial capability of the company.

In the case of an Ontario-based firm, management felt it had to manufacture in the U.S. or face the prospect of losing its U.S. market to its competitors. The company recognized that the loss of production to the Canadian plant would have to be made up by increasing its offshore sales. This option was not so apparent to some of the other interviewees who elected to limit their U.S. operations to warehousing and assembly, even under the threat of losing their sales to U.S.-based manufacturers.

A differential impact on Canada's balance of payments will also

occur with the type of financing undertaken. Where the U.S. investment is financed largely from sources in the U.S., there will be little
initial outflow affecting Canada's balance of payments. At the same
time, there will be little inflow of earnings on the equity invested by
the Canadian firm. Both the debt/equity ratio in the capitalization of
the U.S. subsidiary and the source of debt and equity will affect the
flow of capital between Canada and the U.S.

In our group of companies, there is a high proportion of debt to
equity, with much of the debt raised in the U.S. This means that
Canada will not receive much in the way of earnings on the investment for some time. In fact, there appears to be a net outflow
because most of the affiliates were recently established, so it is too
soon to tell whether they will be profitable, and some are already
experiencing serious difficulties requiring further financial assistance.

Summary

International business expertise was common to all companies. The
executives generally believed that in order to sustain their competitiveness in Canada they had to achieve sales success in the United
States. Partly in response to this concern and challenge, our group of
small and medium-size companies established U.S. subsidiary operations. While the motivation for such investment may be viewed as
being part of a defensive marketing strategy, it is equally important to
recognize that the formulation of this strategy was accelerated by
deteriorating economic and political circumstances in Canada.

The establishment of the U.S. subsidiary normally took place after
exporting for a few years to the U.S. market. Initially, most of the
subsidiaries were sales and warehousing operations, leading to assembly, partial or full manufacturing organizations. Since the firms in
question were generally small and recent U.S. corporate entrants,
only a few had U.S. plants which manufactured in full their Canadian
developed and designed products. Most, however, hoped that success in the U.S. would lead them in this direction, that is, the opening
up of a "manufacturing" plant.

The U.S. subsidiaries were tightly controlled by their Canadian
parents, and all key decisions were made by executives in Canada,
particularly those involving financial outlays. While the amount of
capital invested outside of Canada by our group of companies was
not significant, two important observations can be made about such
investment in terms of its impact on small business in Canada.

First, the financial resources of small and medium-size firms are
generally limited. Thus, if a company expands into the U.S., its

financial ability to pursue similar investment opportunities in Canada will be constrained, because it will have had to mortgage most of its assets in support of its U.S. project. Raising the capital in the U.S. may reduce the impact of such investment on capital outflows, but it will hardly improve the financial capability of the Canadian firm to raise capital in Canada or elsewhere for other investment undertakings.

Second, the limited size of the Canadian market and the general reservation about growing through product diversification prompts small and medium-size firms to consider investing in the United States. If such a decision leads to the establishment of a manufacturing plant in the U.S., the former Canadian-U.S. export business is normally transferred slowly to the U.S. operation. The new "gap" in Canadian production can be either filled through an increase of Canadian or offshore sales. If this result is not forthcoming, the competitiveness of the Canadian firm can be jeopardized, particularly at a time when its resources are strained because of the competing demands emanating from its newly established U.S. subsidiary.

IV
Foreign Direct Investment Theory, Impact, and Control

B
Patterns

23
Canadian Joint Ventures in Japan

Richard W. Wright

Dr. Wright is associate professor in the Faculty of Management, McGill University. He is actively involved in research, training, and consulting activities throughout the world, including Japan. He has published widely on Japanese finance and management practices and has recently spent a year as advisor and visiting professor at the Institute for International Studies and Training, Fujinomiya, Japan. His newest book, *The Economic Impact of Japanese Business in Canada*, will be published by the Institute for Research on Public Policy in 1982.

This chapter is a revised version of an article which appeared originally in *The Business Quarterly*, Autumn 1977. Reprinted by permission.

Business activity between Canada and Japan has grown enormously in recent years. In 1973, Japan became Canada's second most important trading partner, and in 1980 consumed $4.37 billion worth of Canadian exports.[1] With easing of foreign investment controls in Japan, businessmen in Canada and elsewhere increasingly are eying the massive Japanese economy as a target for direct investment, particularly through joint ventures.

This article reports on the most comprehensive study to date of the Canadian joint venture experience in Japan. The author conducted in-depth interviews with executives of the Canadian investor companies, the Japanese partners, and the local subsidiary managers of fifteen Canadian joint venture operations in Japan. The sample includes all significant Canadian joint ventures existing in Japan at the end of 1976.[2] Additional interviews were conducted in a variety of other organizations to gain a broader understanding of the economic, political, and cultural conditions affecting joint ventures in Japan.

General Patterns

The total value of Canadian equity investment in joint ventures in Japan as of 1978 was approximately $83 million. Six of the joint venture companies are in the primary metals or metal products sectors; five in manufacturing; and four in services. The recent pattern of Canadian investment activity in Japan reveals several significant general trends:

- *Dominance of the joint venture form.* Except for two Canadian firms (Bata Shoe Co., and Emco-Wheaton, Ltd.) with small manufacturing operations in wholly owned subsidiaries, nearly all of Canada's direct investment in Japan is in the form of joint ventures with Japanese companies.

1. Department of Industry, Trade, and Commerce, 1981.
2. Excluded from the study were branch offices of Canadian firms; subsidiaries serving only a distribution function; and investments made by Canadian subsidiaries of non-Canadian companies.

- *Increasing rate of joint venture formation.* Of the fifteen Canadian joint ventures in Japan identified in the present study, ten had been in existence for less than four years.
- *Sectoral changes.* With a single exception, the Canadian joint ventures formed in Japan prior to 1970 were in the areas of metal refining or processing of metal products. Since 1970, most new Canadian investments in Japanese joint ventures have been in the manufacturing and service areas.
- *Participation of smaller firms.* All of the Canadian firms which formed joint ventures in Japan prior to 1970 were among the large Canadian multinational companies. Since 1970, most of the new joint ventures have been formed by smaller Canadian companies, some privately held.

Reasons for Investing in Japan

Canadian firms seeking involvement in Japan generally have a choice of at least three major strategic routes for entering the Japanese market: (1) to service the Japanese market through export or licensing arrangements; (2) to create a wholly owned processing or manufacturing subsidiary in Japan; or (3) to invest in a joint venture operation in partnership with a Japanese firm. The reasons which lead Canadian companies to seek direct investment in Japan fall into two main groups, according to whether the investing companies are primary metal companies, or whether they are manufacturing or service companies.

The raw materials and metal producing companies invest in Japan mainly to increase their sale of raw materials. Japan is viewed as a large and rapidly growing potential market. But the Canadian raw material producers find it difficult to service the Japanese market via the export of raw materials because of cultural and economic barriers. The most important of these is the need for identification with the Japanese market. These companies feel that potential customers in Japan, as well as the Japanese government, favor Japanese companies. By investing in Japan, the Canadian raw material supplier becomes identified more closely with the Japanese economy. High shipping costs and high tariffs are other incentives to invest in smelting or refining operations in Japan. Shipping costs for ore are often less than those for metal. Similarly, Japanese tariffs are lower on the import of concentrate than on the import of metal or manufactured metal products. For these reasons, it may be more economic to ship the ore to Japan for processing, rather than to process in Canada and ship the finished goods to Japan.

For Canadian manufacturing and service companies, the dominant objective of investing in Japan is to increase the return on scarce knowledge or skills by generating a flow of dividends back to the parent company in Canada. Seeing enormous potential in the Japanese market, these companies wish to participate more fully in the long-run growth via direct investment, rather than by contractual licensing and sales arrangements.

While dividend income is the major objective of Canadian manufacturing and service firms investing in Japan, other factors cited, in approximate order of importance, are as follows:

- *Protection of know-how.* Several firms with scarce technology or skills have general policies of exploiting their advantages abroad only through investment positions rather than contractual arrangements, in order to ensure control and security.
- *Economic and political stability.* Several Canadian executives report that whereas they might generally favor arm's length relations in foreign markets, their perception of economic and political stability in Japan influenced their decision to invest directly there.
- *Sale of machinery or equipment.* In the case of several Canadian investor firms, the opportunity to sell their machinery or other equipment to the Japanese affiliate was an important, but not decisive, influence on their investment decision. (In a couple of cases, the Canadian firms' ability to supply essential physical components enabled them to acquire equity with a very low cash input.)
- *Tariffs and shipping costs.* Two manufacturing firms cited the combination of high tariffs and shipping costs as an important influence on their decision to invest in Japan.

Reasons for Choosing Joint Venture Form

Given that many Canadian firms prefer some form of investment rather than export or licensing arrangements, their reasons for choosing joint ventures rather than wholly owned subsidiaries vary, depending mainly on the time when the joint venture arrangements were first formed.

In the case of all Canadian joint ventures formed in Japan prior to the early 1970s, government restrictions precluded the use of wholly owned subsidiaries or majority controlled joint ventures in Japan by foreign firms. Most of the Canadian firms which invested in Japan in joint ventures during that period report that they would have preferred a wholly controlled subsidiary. It is significant, however, that in two of those cases, the management of the Canadian partner companies now report that they are pleased with the joint venture form and, in retrospect, prefer the joint venture to a wholly owned subsidiary.

The choice of a majority controlled subsidiary or a wholly owned subsidiary has existed for most Canadian companies investing in Japan since 1972. Despite the liberalization of investment restrictions, however, there are only two significant manufacturing companies in Japan which are wholly owned by a Canadian parent company. This research reveals a wide variety of reasons for choosing the joint venture form.

In the case of raw materials companies, the most important motive for joint venturing was the earlier government restriction on foreign-controlled subsidiaries. Another major incentive for joint ventures was the perceived need of raw materials companies to be identified with Japan. The joint venture provides a more intimate and secure long-term relationship for the sale of material than does an arm's length contractual arrangement, while at the same time retaining the "Japanese identity" more than would be possible in a wholly owned subsidiary.

The incentives for joint ventures are more diverse in the manufacturing and service sectors. Major reasons cited by these Canadian firms for joint venturing in Japan are as follows:

- *Complexity of the Japanese business system.* The cultural and behavioral aspects of manufacturing and marketing in Japan are seen as much too complex for the foreigner to try to handle himself through a wholly owned subsidiary. Canadian firms wishing to invest in Japan often choose the joint venture form as the only perceived means of operating effectively in the Japanese business environment and with the Japanese government.
- *Synergistic advantages.* Several Canadian executives stressed their belief that the joint venture form, in general, combines the expertise and skill of two different organizations while helping to ensure that both parties work toward the same objectives. This cannot be achieved in a wholly owned subsidiary; nor could it be easily achieved in a contractual arrangement under which a Canadian company would license a Japanese company to manufacture its products.
- *Availability of competent and reliable partners.* Several Canadian executives who would normally insist on wholly owned or controlled subsidiaries abroad feel comfortable entering into joint ventures in Japan because they consider Japanese businessmen to be sophisticated managers who can effectively implement policy.

- *Diversification of risk and return.* For some Canadian manufacturing firms, the joint venture form appears to be the most
profitable opportunity in proportion to the amount invested. By
becoming a partner in a Japanese joint venture, the Canadian firm
can take a risk position in a share of the long-run profits, as well as
realize immediate income through licensing and royalty payments
from the joint venture company.
- *Sequential involvement.* Some Canadian manufacturing firms prefer to enter the Japanese market in stages, and the joint venture
provides a feasible means of doing this. In several of the joint
ventures, the plan was that the Japanese partner would first import
finished manufactured goods from the Canadian parent company
and distribute them in Japan. Then as the market became established, the joint venture company would assemble products in
Japan. Finally, the joint venture company would manufacture the
whole product in Japan.

The author also questioned the Japanese partners in the joint
ventures to determine their objectives in participating in the Canadian investments. In almost all cases, the principal objective of the
Japanese participation was to gain access to technology or know-how
which the Japanese companies themselves did not possess. In some
cases, particularly where a Japanese trading company participated as
a minority partner, a secondary objective was to gain commissions
from handling the subsidiary's supply and sales functions. In a couple
of cases, the Japanese partners mentioned the possibility of additional benefits accruing to them because the joint venture operations
would lead to increased volume and/or profit in other units of
their Japanese industrial group. Finally, some Japanese companies
saw the joint venture as a means of obtaining a secure source of raw
material.

Choice of Partner

Because of the enormous cultural barriers to doing business effectively in Japan, most foreign companies with joint ventures there
find it necessary to surrender much more operating authority to their
local partners than they would in other countries. Thus, the choice
of a reliable and compatible joint venture partner is probably of even
greater importance in Japan than elsewhere. While the procedure
and the criteria for partner selection vary with each Canadian joint
venture, three main groups can be identified.

First are the large, internationally known Canadian manufacturing firms. For these companies, partner selection in Japan is less of a

problem than for other companies. In the case of most of the big-name firms, the potential Japanese partners approached the Canadian firms first, because the Canadian firms were so well-known. The Japanese firms also were reasonably large, well-known companies. The choice among the various potential partners generally was made on the basis of the size and the financial soundness of the potential Japanese partner. Managers of these firms indicate that they consider it much easier to find sophisticated and reliable partners in Japan than in many other countries.

A second major type of partner selection process occurs generally with the raw materials companies. In most cases, the Canadian company had a prior relationship as a materials supplier to the Japanese company which eventually became the joint venture partner. The existence of an earlier supplier or licensor relationship appears to be an important influence on joint venture success, providing a "courtship" period in which the potential partners can work together and develop mutual trust before entering into a long-term joint venture "marriage".

For the smaller Canadian manufacturing and service companies forming joint ventures in Japan, the partner selection process is more difficult and less sophisticated. In two cases, the Canadian company was introduced to the Japanese company which ultimately became its joint venture partner through the Canadian embassy in Japan. In another case, the Canadian and Japanese partners-to-be met at a technical conference in Ottawa sponsored by the Canadian government. In the remaining cases, the parties were brought together through other intermediaries. In several cases, these intermediaries were Japanese trading companies, which subsequently took minority positions in the joint ventures that were formed.[3] In two cases, the Canadian and Japanese partners-to-be were brought together by individuals who had formerly been associated with one of the companies. It is significant that in the case of most smaller Canadian firms that have formed joint ventures in Japan, the parties were *not* well-known to each other prior to beginning the joint venture negotiations, nor had any prior supplier or licensor relationship existed. In general, smaller Canadian firms appear to have bypassed opportunities to form working acquaintances through contractual arrangements prior to entering into long-term joint venture commitments.

3. The most prominent trading company for Canadian joint ventures in Japan is Mitsui and Co., Ltd. Mitsubishi, Marubeni, and C. Itoh have also been major participants, as have smaller trading companies such as ABC Trading Co., and Tokyo Maruichi Shoji Co.

Negotiating Process

For the larger Canadian firms with international experience, negotiating a joint venture in Japan was no more difficult than similar negotiations elsewhere would be. Many of the firms report initial disagreements over specific features such as the rate of royalty fees charged by the Canadian company, the value of capital equipment supplied from Canada, etc. Perhaps the most striking common feature of these negotiations was the gradual acceptance by the Canadian companies that effective operational control of the joint venture company would have to be left in the hands of the Japanese because of the complexity of the Japanese business system.

For smaller Canadian firms, cultural differences fundamental to the negotiating process itself have become major problems. A particular problem is in the speed of negotiation. Several times, Canadian executives expecting to conclude joint venture agreements swiftly have perceived the Japanese as unwilling or unable to make firm decisions. Thus, joint venture negotiations have dragged on much longer than anticipated, causing anger and frustration. According to the Japanese partners who were involved in the negotiations, the Japanese were not trying intentionally to delay. They emphasize that in Japan, it is much more essential that a close personal relationship be established before the business negotiations can be concluded, and this necessarily takes time. Also, the consensus decision-making process in Japan requires much more discussion and study than in the West (but once the decisions are made, Japanese companies are usually able to implement them more quickly than Western firms). Similarly, Canadians negotiating with high-level Japanese executives have been frustrated to learn that even the most senior officials in Japan often lack authority to make commitments binding upon their companies.

Another fundamental negotiating difference between the Japanese and the Canadians, particularly in smaller companies, is in the role of written contracts. Several negotiations have been frustrated by what the Canadians see as an unwillingness of the Japanese to enter into precise contractual agreements. Japanese negotiators often prefer to keep joint venture agreements very brief and general and "vague". This appears to reflect a fundamental cultural difference.[4] Compared to North Americans, Japanese place relatively little emphasis on written contracts. Rather, mutual understanding and personal

4. For an excellent discussion of the Japanese view of contracts, see Jiro Tokuyama, "The Japanese Notion of Law: An Introduction to Flexibility and Indefinitude", *Nomura Investment Report* (December 13, 1973).

agreement play a much more important role. (This further under-
scores the importance in Japan of selecting a partner with whom one
can work and trust in the long run). As one negotiating intermediary
said to a Canadian negotiator who was particularly frustrated by the
inability to come quickly to precise written agreements: "As long as
the music plays and the heart is in the right place, you will make a
deal. Just listen to the music, not the words."

Joint Venture Arrangements

The actual agreements arrived at have various forms. In all cases,
there is a basic joint venture agreement that provides for the formation and structure of the joint venture company. The basic agreements tend to be very brief (as short as six typewritten pages) and
general, reflecting the tendency in Japan for business relationships to
be formed and conducted by general agreement and understanding,
rather than by detailed contract. Typically, operational authority is
left in the hands of the local joint venture management. Certain key
decisions on technical matters, dividends, major capital expenditures, and changes in financial structure, may be reserved for prior
approval of the joint venture board of directors or the parent companies.

The basic joint venture agreements are usually supplemented by
some combination of the following:

- *Technical agreements.* These provide for the transfer of technical
  knowledge to the joint venture company, and for the payment of
  royalties for the patents and services provided. Several of the
  technical agreements, which originally provided only for the flow
  of information from Canada to Japan, are presently being revised
  to accommodate two-way flows.
- *Supply and sales contracts.* Supply contracts are particularly important for Canadian raw materials companies. Joint venture companies smelting or processing in Japan may be obligated under the
  contracts to purchase all or most of their inputs from the Canadian
  partners, usually according to a formula based on prevailing world
  prices. The sales contracts typically state that the joint venture
  company will service the domestic Japanese market and will consult with the Canadian parent about export marketing. Perhaps
  unique to Japan is the role of trading companies in the joint
  ventures. Where a Japanese trading company holds a minority
  partnership position, the contracts may grant it exclusive rights
  as the supply and sales agent of the joint venture company. Thus,

benefits may accrue to a Japanese partner from the trading activities of the joint venture, which are quite separate from the profit position of the joint venture company.

* *Management contracts.* Several of the joint ventures have management agreements under which the Japanese partner provides management to the joint venture company, usually priced at cost.

In practice, Canadian firms joint-venturing in Japan rarely exercise the degree of managerial control and participation to which their proportion of equity ownership or the contractual arrangements entitle them. This is due mainly to the complexity of the Japanese business system and to the enormous difficulty of effective cross-cultural communication. Even where the joint venture agreements specifically provide for prior consultation or approval, these rights are often waived in practice because of the feeling by both sides that excessive delay and complication in the decision-making process would result. The prevailing attitude among most Canadian firms with experience in Japan was summed up by one executive: "The only way to run a joint venture in Japan is to leave it up to the Japanese. We give them advice, but we let them run the show."

Political and Economic Constraints

The influence of constraints from Japanese government controls and regulations is mainly a function of when the joint venture was formed. Measures to liberalize inward investment have been introduced progressively over the past several years. In the final phase of liberalization, now in effect, foreign investment is prohibited in nuclear energy, power and light, gas supply, and the manufacture of aircrafts, armaments, and explosives. Foreign investment is subject to case-by-case approval in four other cases: mining, petroleum, agriculture, and leather products.[5] Except for these sectors, a foreign company may receive "automatic approval" to acquire up to 100 per cent of the equity stock in a Japanese company, through application to the Bank of Japan.[6] It cannot be assumed that approval will always be granted even in those sectors which are 100 per cent liberalized. The relevant industrial association in Japan may lobby against a proposed foreign investment, and if the ministry responsible for that industry determines that the investment would be "disruptive", ap-

5. Business International, *Investing, Licensing, and Trading Conditions Abroad —
   Japan*, Business International Corp. (July 1, 1975), 6-7.
6. Ministry of Finance (International Finance Bureau) and Bank of Japan (Foreign
   Department), *Manual of Foreign Investment in Japan* (March 1976).

proval may still be denied.[7] However, the recent experience of Canadian investors suggests that as the formal restrictions have been relaxed, approvals are forthcoming accordingly. None of the Canadian investors experienced any additional constraints or delays in government approval beyond those formally stated in the foreign investment laws.

Although the most important governmental constraint has been in limiting the degree of foreign ownership, there are isolated reports of other governmental actions adversely affecting the management of the joint ventures. No significant import restrictions are reported, but several managers feel that unreasonably high tariffs are imposed. One Canadian partner company reports that they wish to introduce more stock to the joint venture on consignment, but the Japanese government discourages that through permit requirements. Several Canadian firms experience constraints imposed by the Japanese government on the licensing arrangements that accompany the joint ventures, specifically in refusing approval for high royalty payments and in using "administrative guidance" to pressure the joint venture companies to lower existing royalty payments to the Canadian partners. In two of the joint ventures, the Canadian parent companies report being legally precluded from restricting the market areas of their Japanese joint venture companies.

Both Canadian and Japanese participants in the joint ventures expressed some reservations about the future political climate for Japanese business, particularly in light of the reversals suffered by the pro-business Liberal Democratic Party in the 1976 elections. But the possibility of a coalition government in Japan, while disturbing, is not of major concern, and appears unlikely to affect the long-run investment plans of any of the joint ventures studied.

Overwhelmingly, the main economic constraint for recent Canadian joint ventures in Japan has been the recent Japanese business recession. Nearly all of the joint venture companies with Canadian participation have shown lower profits, or losses, in the last two or three years. The effect of the Japanese business recession has been particularly severe for the newer joint ventures, formed within the past three or four years. In nearly all of these cases, realized cash flows are at least a year behind projected cash flows, causing a continuing lack of profit and increasing indebtedness. While this situation has seriously affected the profitability of the joint venture

---

7. A recent case example is that of Dow Chemical Company. See "Japan's Liberalization: MITI Can Slam the Door and Sometimes Still Does", *Business International* (November 28, 1975) 377-8.

operations in Japan, it is emphasized that these are not problems internal to or unique to the joint ventures, but rather to all business operations in Japan. Both the Canadian and the Japanese participants in most of the joint ventures which remain unprofitable feel that the current unfavorable situation is merely temporary; that their joint venture operations are essentially healthy; and that performance will improve once the economy picks up again.

Cultural Constraints

The most critical constraints and problems for Canadian joint ventures in Japan are caused by differences between the Japanese and the Western character, which in turn are reflected in differences in the business systems and in approaches to specific management practices. These types of environmental constraints appear far more significant to Canadian investments in Japan than do constraints from the political or economic environments. The most common areas of conflict or problems resulting from such cultural and business differences are the following:

- *Difference of objectives.* The most fundamental problems of Canadian joint ventures in Japan appear to arise from differing objectives between the Canadian and Japanese partners. Where the main objective of both parties is to participate in a flow of dividends, the problem is minimal. But in many of the joint ventures, either the Canadian partner or the Japanese partner may view other benefits as equally important or more important than the stream of dividends, thus creating a conflict of objectives. This is particularly true in the case of Canadian raw materials suppliers, whose main objective in a joint venture may be to earn profit from the sale of raw material. In such cases, a Japanese partner whose sole benefit is the dividend resulting from the profitability of the joint venture company, has objectives which are different from and likely antagonistic to those of the Canadian partner. Similarly, in several of the joint ventures the Japanese partners view their investment as a means of generating more activity and profit somewhere else within the related cluster of companies that form industrial groups in Japan. While such fundamental differences are discussed openly in only one or two of the joint ventures, it appears that many of the disagreements and difficulties experienced in the joint ventures result from the fact that the objectives of the partners were at least partially incompatible from the start.

- *Growth versus profit orientation.* Even where the objectives of both partners focus on the performance of the joint venture company, there is often a fundamental cultural difference between the Canadian orientation toward profit maximization and the Japanese orientation toward growth of sales volume and market share. This difference appears to stem from several conditions unique to the Japanese business system. Because of the lifetime employment tradition in most large Japanese companies, continued growth in the size of the company is important to maintain morale among managers and employees. Continued growth is sustained by the extremely high financial leverage of Japanese companies. In some cases this difference in orientation is evident at the outset as a conflict in target growth objectives; in others it emerges only later, when profit retention decisions must be made.

- *Communication barriers.* Most of the Canadian firms in Japan experience major communication problems because of the language barrier and the great distances involved. Even beyond these obvious difficulties, however, is a much more fundamental problem rooted in cultural differences. A basic characteristic of Japanese life is an emphasis on harmony. In Western cultures, it is common to identify a problem or conflict area and bring it into the open for resolution. In Japan, conflicts and problems tend to be kept beneath the surface; confrontation is avoided. This difference is seen in the reluctance of Japanese managers to admit that problems exist. Canadian executives express frustration at their belief that problems must exist in their Japanese operations, which should be dealt with, but which are not identified by the joint venture managers or the Japanese partners. The only effective way to bridge this information gap appears to be for the foreign firm to have its own representative permanently at the scene of operations in Japan. However, this costs well over $200,000 per year, clearly more than the smaller Canadian ventures can support.

- *Flexibility of contracts.* Problems arise in a number of the joint ventures because of differences between Japanese and Western emphasis on written agreements. Whereas Western companies are accustomed to operating with detailed and enforceable written contracts, the Japanese place relatively less emphasis on written agreements. This appears to be due in part to the Japanese desire for harmony, discussed previously. Detailed written contracts are too precise to be used comfortably in the Japanese system. In the event that conditions of a legal contract are violated, responsibility must fall on one party or the other, violating the important Japanese principle of "saving face". This difference causes misunderstanding and problems both in the negotiating process and during the subsequent operation of the joint ventures. In the view of several experienced Canadian managers, the Japanese are much too willing to let conditions drift away from those specified in the joint ventures contracts. There is very little that the Canadian firms can do in such a situation, other than to take legal action against the Japanese partner, an extremely difficult process. Instead, several Canadian companies report that once the initial contractual arrangements of the joint venture are finalized, they are put away and virtually ignored during the subsequent operation of the joint venture. From the viewpoint of the Japanese partners, this is quite satisfactory. They stress that contracts in Japan must be regarded as very flexible documents, and that any foreign company insisting on following a contract to the letter in Japan will encounter problems. Rather, the foreign firm involved in the joint venture in Japan should recognize that the contract represents only the conditions of understanding at the time the joint venture was formed, and these terms and conditions will evolve over time.

- *Selling methods.* One of the most common sources of conflict is in selling methods. These conflicts appear to result from basic cultural differences in the business systems. Whereas many Western firms are accustomed to high-pressure selling methods and quick sales, in Japan it is customary to build a more intimate long-term relationship with a customer. This may require more contact with the customer before the sale is made, less pressure to sell, and more follow-up activities to cultivate the long-term relationship. Several Canadian managers report that they consider their Japanese partners too humble and timid in selling. On the other hand, several Japanese managers consider Canadian selling methods too aggressive for Japan, and they are upset by what they see as attempts by the Canadian partners to shove their marketing techniques onto the Japanese. Japanese managers emphasize that the Canadian partners should recognize that selling methods appropriate to the Japanese culture are very different from those of the West, and they should not try to export their sales methods to Japan.

- *Cost control.* In most of the larger Canadian joint ventures in Japan, the joint venture operation was created as a distinct entity, separated completely from the Japanese parent company in terms of physical facilities and personnel. With smaller Canadian joint ventures, however, the high cost of space and manpower in Japan often requires operating the joint venture under the wing of the Japanese parent company, and in many cases, the Japanese parent supplies managerial and technical personnel to the joint venture company. In these situations, the problem of cost control becomes very important for the Canadian partner. Managers of several smaller Canadian companies acknowledged that they have little basis on which to judge whether the costs being charged to the joint venture company by the Japanese parent are realistic or not. In most cases, the Canadian partners must simply rely on the good faith of their Japanese partners in regard to cost control. One or two Canadian joint venture partners report having difficulty in getting effective and meaningful audits accomplished in Japan.

* *Materials pricing.* Particularly in those joint ventures in the raw materials and metal industries, contractual arrangements may obligate the joint venture companies to secure raw materials from the Canadian partners. While the price charged by the Canadian parent company to the Japanese joint venture company is usually a function of the world price, there is considerable room for negotiation. In several cases, significant disagreements have occurred between the Japanese partner and the Canadian partner regarding the pricing of raw materials supplied to the joint venture company. The Japanese partner, relying on the profit of the joint venture company as its primary source of return, may want the joint venture company to pay the lowest feasible price for materials purchases. The interests of the Canadian partner, on the other hand, may be furthered by charging the highest possible price. While disputes over materials pricing do not appear to have been critical to any of the Canadian joint ventures in Japan, it is a fundamental and ongoing problem in several of them.

* *Personnel policies.* Some difference of opinion between Canadian and Japanese partners is reported in the Japanese personnel practices of lifetime employment and high employee benefit. Representatives of two of the Canadian partner companies report that they would prefer to see employees of the joint venture company laid off, particularly during the recent and current recession. Because of the tradition of lifetime employment in most Japanese companies, the Japanese partners have been reluctant to accomplish this. In most cases where there was difference of opinion in this respect, the Canadians have ultimately accepted the prevailing Japanese practices. Several Canadian firms also feel uncomfortable at the Japanese partners' insistence on very high employee benefits and amenities, which tend to be much more important in Japan than in North America. Again, these differences of opinion are generally resolved by Canadian acceptance of the prevailing Japanese practices.

Recommendations

Attractive opportunities remain for further Canadian participation in Japan. But serious potential problems exist. The recent experience of Canadian companies has important lessons for other firms — particularly smaller manufacturing and service companies — considering entering Japan in the future.

- *Be sure you really want a direct investment position.* The large size and rapid growth of Japan's economy instinctively appeal to foreign companies wishing to participate fully via direct investment. But if the Japanese market is one of the world's most attractive, it is also one of the most complex and difficult to operate in. Where direct investment is not really necessary to serve the Japanese market, Canadian firms may be better off staying with contractual licensing arrangements.
- *If possible, enter gradually.* The most successful joint ventures are those in which the partners moved together in progressive stages over time — first with an arm's length licence or supply agreement, then with a joint venture to assemble or distribute, then with a full joint venture manufacturing or processing company. This provides opportunity for the partners to move together gradually, as mutual trust and confidence develop.
- *Avoid wholly owned subsidiaries.* Trying to "do it yourself" is exceedingly difficult and risky in Japan. The foreign firm operating alone lacks access to marketing channels, financial institutions, industrial associations, and government agencies. For all but the very largest firms with highly needed technology, the skills and contacts of a Japanese partner are essential.
- *Get acquainted with the culture.* This seems an obvious lesson, but probably is the least appreciated. The culture of Japan is profoundly different from that of the West, and the effects of those differences permeate every management decision and every business relationship. The study of Japanese history and customs is not only interesting. It is also good business.
- *Ensure that objectives are compatible.* Problems frequently occur in Japanese joint ventures because the partners had divergent objectives from the outset, which were either not recognized or ignored. If either partner is to receive benefits other than dividends from the joint venture company (for example royalties, supply or sales commissions, sale of raw materials), this should be recognized at the outset and arrangements made to avoid future conflict. Even where the joint venture performance is central to

both partners, very careful attention must be given to the potential conflict of growth versus profit maximization.

- *Allow much more time than usual for preliminary meetings and negotiations.* Joint venture negotiations in Japan are likely to require more trips abroad, for longer periods of time, than in most other countries. By anticipating this, the Canadian manager can budget for the additional time and expense that will likely be required, as well as minimize discouragement and frustration. Extra patience may have other long-run benefits by providing more opportunity to develop personal relations and clarify objectives.

- *Consider contracts to be general and flexible.* In Japan, the written contract is more a symbol of a desire to work together than a real working document. The handshake is more important than the written agreement. Canadian companies negotiating in Japan should be willing to accept contracts that are more general and fluid than what they may be accustomed to. They should also be prepared for frequent changes in the contract terms.

- *Separate personnel and facilities from those of the local partner.* The high cost of space and manpower in Japan provide a strong incentive to economize by operating the joint venture under the wing of the Japanese parent. But sharing people and facilities leads often to severe cost allocation problems, which are particularly difficult to handle effectively in Japan because of the dearth of information available to the Canadian partner. Where possible, the Canadian partner should seek clear separation of the joint venture, even at a higher cost.

- *Have a full-time representative in Japan, if possible.* The barriers to effective communication and information flow between a Japanese joint venture and a Canadian parent are enormous. Canadian managers who try to keep abreast of joint venture developments through reports and/or visits to Japan — however frequent — are nearly always frustrated. A permanent representative in Japan can significantly enhance the flow of information. The catch: a cost of at least $200,000 per year.

- *Let the Japanese run the show.* The Japanese business system is so unique and so complex that only the Japanese can understand how to operate effectively in it. Even a Canadian firm owning 50 per cent or more of the joint venture equity should realize that exercising effective control is difficult if not impossible, and should leave operational authority to the Japanese.

Table 1

Principal Canadian Joint Ventures in Japan (As of 1977)

Joint Venture Company	Year of Formation	Activity	Canadian Partner	% Canadian Ownership	Japanese Partner(s)
Asia Gestalt Co., Ltd.	1975	Aerial Photo Maps	Gestalt International Ltd.	50%	Asia Air Survey Co. Ltd./Mitsui & Co. Ltd.
Canada Foods Ltd.	1974	Meat Products	Burns Food Co., Ltd.	49%	Tokyo Maruichi Shoji Co., Ltd.
Daido Special Alloys, Ltd.	1974	Nickel Alloys	International Nickel Company of Canada Ltd.	50%	Daido Steel Co. Ltd.
Gifu-Husky Co., Ltd.	1973	Injection Molding Machines	Husky Injection Molding Systems Ltd.	25%	Gifu Die and Mold Co./Mitsui Mining Co., Ltd.
Intalite Co., Ltd.	1972	Luminous Ceiling Systems	Integrated Lighting Canada Ltd.	50%	ABC Trading Co., Ltd.
Kirin-Seagram Ltd.	1973	Distilled Spirits	Joseph E. Seagram & Sons Inc.	50%	Kirin Brewery Co., Ltd.
Mitsubishi Cominco Smelting Co. Ltd.	1965	Lead Smelting	Cominco Ltd.	45%	Mitsubishi Metal Corporation Ltd.
Nippon Fibracan Co., Ltd.	1975	Plastic Containers	Fibracan Inc.	50%	Fujimori Co., Ltd./Marubeni Co. Inc.
Nippon Light Metal Co., Ltd.	1952	Aluminum Smelting	Aluminum Company of Canada Ltd.	50%	Nippon Light Metal Co., Ltd.
Pacific Creative Tours, Ltd.	1974	Travel Services	C.P. Air	60% [a]	C. Itoh & Co. Ltd.
Pizza Patio Japan Inc.	1974	Food Services	Pizza Patio Management Ltd.	50%	Individuals
Shimura Kako Co., Ltd.	1972	Nickle Refining	International Nickel Company of Canada Ltd.	30%	Mitsui & Co., Ltd./Others
Tokyo Nickel Co., Ltd.	1967	Stainless Steel	International Nickel Company of Canada Ltd.	45%	Shimura Kako Co., Ltd./Mitsui & Co. Ltd.
Toppan-Moore Business Forms Co., Ltd.	1965	Business Forms	Moore Corporation	45%	Toppan Printing Co., Ltd.
Toyo Aluminum Co., Ltd.	1931	Aluminum Foil	Aluminum Company of Canada Ltd.	50%	Light Metal Educational Foundation/Sumitomo Light Metal Co., Ltd./Others

(a) Pacific Creative Tours, Ltd. is a 100 per cent-owned subsidiary of Transpacific Tours Ltd. which is owned 60 per cent by C.P. Air and 40 per cent by C. Itoh & Co.

For Further Reference

Abegglen, James C. *Business Strategies for Japan*. Tokyo: Sophia University, 1970.

Baker, James C., and Takao Kondo. "Joint Ventures in Japan and How to Obtain Managerial Control". *MSU Business Topics*, XIX, No. 1 (Winter 1975), pp. 47-54.

Ballon, Robert J. ed. *Joint Ventures and Japan*. Tokyo: Sophia University, 1967.

——, "Understanding the Japanese: Preparation for International Business". *Business Horizons*, XII, No. 1 (June 1970), pp. 21-30.

Ballon, Robert J., and Eugene H. Lee, eds. *Foreign Investment and Japan*. Tokyo: Sophia University, 1972.

Bank of Tokyo, *Setting Up Enterprises in Japan*. Tokyo: The Bank of Tokyo, Ltd., 1977.

Drucker, Peter F. "What We Can Learn From Japanese Management". *Harvard Business Review* 49, No. 2, (March-April, 1971), pp. 110-122.

Government of Japan. *Manual of Foreign Investment in Japan*. Tokyo: Ministry of Finance (International Finance Bureau), and Bank of Japan (Foreign Department), 1976.

"How Companies Resolve Common Problems in Japanese Joint Ventures". *Business Asia* (September 10, 1976), pp. 289-291.

Japan External Trade Organization, *A Case Study of Foreign Investment In Japan*. Tokyo: JETRO Business Information Series, No. 5

"Joint Venture Problems in Japan". *Economist* (May 14, 1977), pp. 100-1.

Kraar, Louis. "Japan is Opening Up for *Gaijin* Who Know How". *Fortune* LXXXIX, No. 3 (March, 1974), p. 146 ff.

"A Study of Failures of Foreign Companies in Japan". *Nikkei Business* (August 30, 1976). (Translated by Boston Consulting Group, Tokyo).

Tharp, Mike, "Uneasy Partners: More U.S. Firms Drop Joint Ventures with Japanese". *Wall Street Journal* (November 8, 1976), p. 1.

Tokuyama, Jiro. "The Japanese Notion of Law: An introduction to Flexibility and Indefinitude". *Normura Investment Report* (December 13, 1973).

Van Zandt, Howard A. "How to Negotiate in Japan". *Harvard Busines Review* 48, No. 6 (November-December 1970), pp. 45-56.

——, "Learning to Do Business with Japan Inc.". *Harvard Business Review*. 58, No. 4 (July-August 1972), pp. 83-92.

IV
Foreign Direct Investment Theory, Impact, and Control

C
Impact

24
Canadian Attitudes Toward Foreign Ownership

J. Alex Murray

Dr. Murray is professor of international business operations in the Faculty of Business Administration, University of Windsor. He is also director of the Institute for Canadian-American Studies, a policy-oriented institute focussing on North American topics for business and government audiences. He has published a number of books and academic papers in the area of multinational business. His particular interest has been U.S./Canadian business problems, in addition to attitudinal studies of Canadians on economic, social, and international issues.

This chapter was written expressly for this volume.

Introduction

Much of the ongoing debate over the multinational enterprise is due to the large amount of foreign investment in Canada. Currently, over 75 per cent of Canadian rubber, automobile, chemical, and electrical apparatus manufacturing industries are owned by foreigners. These types of statistics have provided fuel for nationalists who favor tighter regulation of multinational corporations headquartered outside of Canada.

At the same time, the high degree of interdependence between Canada and the United States is jointly responsible for the popular feeling that offshore companies were headquartered in a friendly domain. Given the small size of the Canadian population and the geographical spread of her markets, Canadians usually felt that national control over her economy was something to be dealt with at the federal level, with only passing attention being given to it by provincial or local governments. It was not until the strong national-ist sentiment was raised by Walter Gordon and a number of his followers that Canadians began to formulate opinions toward spe-cific public policies dealing with the regulation of incoming foreign investment. In this vein, the contribution of public opinion to the formation or maintenance of specific foreign investment policies, was very problematic. In the area of foreign policy, for instance, it is generally conceded that the contribution of public opinion is mar-ginal, and shifts in public opinion are often seen to follow rather than precede changes in government policy on such issues.[1] In addition, affairs are seen as preoccupations of an elite. Nevertheless, in certain areas where foreign policy touches directly on the domestic affairs of the country, and/or when international issues assume greater salience for the general public, the impact of public attitudes in the policy

1. For a general discussion of the linkages between public opinion and foreign policy, see James N. Rosenau, *Public Opinion and Foreign Policy* (New York, 1961). See also Barry Farrell, *The Making of Canadian Foreign Policy* (Toronto, 1969), Bruce Thorardson, *Trudeau and Foreign Policy: A Study in Decision Making* (Toronto, 1972), and John Holmes, "The Impact of Domestic Political Factors on Canadian-American Relations", *International Organization* **38**, (1974), pp. 611-636.

process may be greater. This is not to suggest that under such circumstances public opinion will of itself determine the direction of policies, but rather that democratic governments must of necessity be responsive over time to changes in "public moods". It is most interesting to note that public opinion in Canada has shifted, and the changes in these shifts are being noted by foreign policy decision makers and observers alike. As a result, a close linkage can be seen between the recent government policies affecting multinational corporations and foreign investment generally, and changing public attitudes over the past decade. Most recently, the question of Quebec separatism and Confederation has introduced new dimensions to internal Canadian politics and nationalism for the multinational corporation. How critically current issues will affect previous investment decisions is yet to be seen. In this chapter, however, we will, with the aid of national opinion survey data, explore the shifting patterns of public attitudes toward foreign investment in Canada, and the relationship between changing climates of opinion and shifts of government policy in the area of foreign investment.[2]

A Conceptual Examination

In order to argue that there has been a measurable change in Canadian nationalism, we must examine the inputs which have prompted this change and influenced the determination of the government's posture on certain policy matters. In particular, political support for trade and investment decisions provides a mini-lesson in the dynamics that give government the (political) support needed to develop strong nationalistic policies.

The specification of the inputs have been diagrammed in Figure 1, which describes the major flows that influence a government's pol-

2. The data reported here have been obtained from surveys conducted annually by Elliott Research Corporation (Toronto, Ontario), and the International Business Studies Research Unit at the University of Windsor (Windsor, Ontario). The surveys are based on national quota samples of approximately 3,000 respondents, controlled for province, rural-urban location, age, and sex. Some reports which have utilized data from past surveys in this series are J. Alex Murray and Mary C. Gerace, "Canadian Attitudes Toward the U.S. Presence". *Public Opinion Quarterly* 36 (1972), pp. 388-397; J. Alex Murray and Lawrence LeDuc, *Canadian Public Attitudes Toward U.S. Equity Investment in Canada*, Ontario Economic Council Working Papers Series, 1975; Lawrence LeDuc and J. Alex Murray, "Public Attitudes Toward Foreign Policy Issues", *International Perspectives* (May-June 1976), pp. 38-40; Terence A. Keenleyside, Lawrence LeDuc, and J. Alex Murray, "Public Opinion and Canada-United States Economic Relations", *Behind the Headlines* 35 (1976), No. 4; J. Alex Murray and Lawrence LeDuc, "Public Opinion and Foreign Policy Options in Canada", *Public Opinion Quarterly* 40 (1976), pp. 488-496.

Figure 1

Dynamics of Trade and Investment Policy Decision

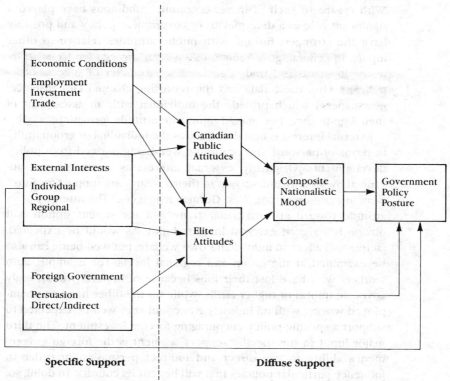

icy posture. Easton has argued that in order to examine the political support system in which popular policies have their underlying foundation within the nation state, one must distinguish support at two major levels: specific and diffuse.[3] The uniqueness of each of these two levels can be viewed from perspective of their inputs and time horizon. Specific support assumes that certain members of state have sufficient political awareness to be able to associate satisfaction with a particular action, and they make certain rational calculations in order to test the results of government efforts. While diffuse support is much more lasting, it is not as particularized, as it deals with a general attachment or powerful feelings towards individuals and issues that have been nurtured over a longer period.

3. David Easton, "A Re-Assessment of the Concept of Political Support", *British Journal of Political Science* 5 (October 1975), pp. 435-457.

The interrelated inputs of trade and investment policy suggest that specific support is generated from three major inputs: economic conditions, external interests, and foreign government persuasion. With regard to each of these, economic conditions have played a significant role as a determinant of government policy and possibly have the strongest linkage with public attitudes relative to other inputs. In general, government policy is most receptive to inflation, unemployment, and trade figures as a barometer of success of its policies. Also, these data and the reporting channel (for instance, newspapers) which provide the individual with an assessment of their significance, become an input into attitude formation.

External interest is best described as the individual or group utility in terms of personal and economic well-being derived from policy developments. Originally, external interest as a variable was advanced by Mennis and Sauvant in their research on support for European integration among West German managers.[4] The intensity of an attitude toward any particular trade and investment option will obviously have an external interest input. As would be expected, factors will affect an individual's own welfare, but well-being can also be examined at the group and regional levels. For example, auto workers who have lost their jobs because of imports will strongly advocate quotas or higher tariffs, while on the other hand an unemployed worker with no industry ties could very well be expected to support a specific policy encouraging foreign investment. The third major input in the specific support segment is the foreign government's ability to use direct and indirect persuasion in order to influence particular policies that will benefit its country. In doing so, the government sometimes uses intermediaries (that is, bureaucratic or business elites) to legitimize their case. Litvak and Maule have shown this in relations between the United States and Canada, where subsidiary operations of multinational corporations were used as vehicles to implement U.S. foreign trade policy toward enemies. This has sometimes been referred to as extra-territoriality, or offshore policy implementation.[5]

Although we have diagrammed these as mainly specific support variables they are also influencers of the major diffuse support components — attitudes. For example, external interests can be located on two fronts: influencing elites to support a certain policy, and

4. Bernard Mennis and Karl P. Sauvant, "Multinational Corporations, Managers, and the Development of Regional Identification in Western Europe", *The Annals* **403** (September 1972), pp. 114.
5. I. A. Litvak and Christopher Maule, "Conflict Resolution and Extra-territoriality", *The Journal of Conflict Resolution* **XIII**, (September 1969), pp. 305-319.

making a direct contact with government decision makers. In a broader context, diffuse support is far from being a short-term phenomenon. It is built from childhood and continues to be shaped through adult socialization of new experiences. Support of this type is of a durable quality, and these powerful feelings can reinforce or repudiate a particular government posture on trade and investment. At the same time, significant swings in attitudes have preceded the formation of policy. The components of diffuse support are generally identified as public and elite attitudes. Public attitudes can be defined as the formation of a number of opinions on questions dealing with situations that have either a direct or indirect effect on the welfare of the public being surveyed. Because these attitudes have been partially established over a longer period of time, their direction and intensity are paramount for political support. At the same time, public attitudes are influenced in the immediate period by economic events, and the personal well-being of the respondent toward any particular issue or object. It is often argued that public attitudes tend to follow the lead of government, rather than to precede the formation of policy. This can easily be documented. However, on those occasions when foreign policy touches directly on the domestic affairs of the country, then the impact of public opinion tends to be greater. Governments, of necessity, tend to be responsive over time to significant changes in the public "mood" or what are sometimes called by opinion analysts "climates of opinion".[6] In Canada, one area in which the public has seen foreign policy directly relevant to the domestic situation has been that of Canadian-American relations.

Elite attitudes are usually considered to be the informed opinions of those individuals whose influence is much broader than their immediate circle of acquaintants. These elite attitudes are derived from images that the individual has developed over a long period of time. These images may or may not reflect the real situation, but they do suggest preferences for the formation and implementation of certain types of policies.[7] Together with public opinion, elite attitudes help to form a composite mood. A measure of this mood toward broad foreign trade and investment policy decisions can provide a barometer of the strength of nationalistic feelings on economic matters. Government policy on any particular issue will be influ-

6. Terence A. Keenleyside, Laurence LeDuc, and J. Alex Murray, *Public Opinion and Canada-United States Economic Relations*, in the series *Behind the Headlines* **XXXV**, 1976, p. 3.
7. R. B. Byers, David Leyton-Brown, and Peyton V. Lyon, "The Canadian International Image Study", *International Journal* **XXXII** (Summer 1977), pp. 605-671.

enced by this composite nationalistic mood. In addition, other inputs have been incorporated into the composite mood, such as interest groups which may have broad public support.

This framework is presented to indicate the importance of public attitudes as political support mechanisms with respect to government policy on trade and investment matters. There are a number of instances that demonstrate that public attitudes do influence particular policies, especially when there are strong domestic repercussions attached to the policy. Recent reports have suggested that both federal and provincial governments are conducting regular opinion polls to measure the pulse of the public on selected subjects. This being the case, it would appear that, at least on the Canadian scene, more attention must be given to public attitudes as a major component of the composite mood index and as an indicator of what policy postures the country can expect from the government.

The Rise of Canadian Nationalism

In the decade of the 1950s and during the early 1960s, government policies generally tended to reflect the public's favorable view of close relations with the United States (or vice versa), particularly in the economic sphere. There was, in this period, little evidence of public concern with the extent of American economic influence in Canada. From 1948 until the mid-1960s, for example, public opinion polls generally indicated that at least half of those surveyed did not think that the "Canadian way of life" was being unduly influenced by the United States.[8] In 1956, 63 per cent of those surveyed by the Canadian Institute of Public Opinion felt that there was not too much American influence, while only 27 per cent expressed concern (Figure 2). This concern rose through most of the 1970s and took a dip in 1976. Sixty-six per cent of a national sample in 1976 felt that Canada's relationship with the United States was basically a healthy one.[9] With respect to trade relations, a 1956 government report cited a poll showing that 68 per cent of those surveyed supported the idea of free trade with the United States.[10]

8. John H. Sigler and Dennis Goresky, "Public Opinion and the United States/ Canadian Relations", *International Organization* **28**, (1974), pp. 656-659. Also see, Terence A. Keenleyside, Lawrence LeDuc, and J. Alex Murray, "Public Opinion and Canada-United States Economic Relations", *Behind the Headlines* **35** (1976), No. 4, pp. 8-10.

9. USIA Study, "Canadian Attitudes Toward the U.S. Economic and Cultural Presence in Canada", (Research report, R-35-78, 1978), p. 53.

10. As quoted in Mitchell Sharp, "Canada-U.S. Relations: Options for the Future", *International Perspectives* (Autumn, 1972, special issue), p. 11. See also Sigler and Goresky, "Public Opinion", pp. 652-655.

Figure 2

Per Cent Indicating That There Is "Too Much U.S. Influence in the Canadian Way of Life", 1956-76

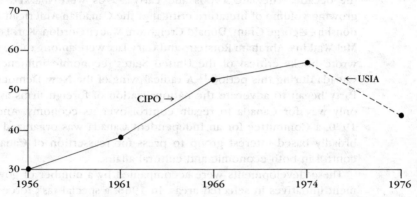

Sources: CIPO, *The Gallup Report* (May 25, 1974); and John H. Sigler and Dennis Goresky, "Public Opinion on United States-Canadian Relations", *International Organization XXVIII* (1974), p. 658, USIA Study, "Canadian Attitudes Toward the U.S. Economic and Cultural Presence in Canada", (Research report, R-35-78, 1978), p. 35.

It was not until the publication in 1958 of the report of the Royal Commission on Canada's Economic Prospect (The Gordon Commission) that signs of government concern with the then-existing state of Canadian-American relations began to arise. Although the Diefenbaker government talked of transferring some 15 per cent of Canadian trade with the U.S. to Britain, little came of such proposals. Most government efforts in the area of Canadian-American relations in that period were intended to emphasize Canada's *political* independence from the United States, and the Canadian posture during the Cuban missile crisis and at the United Nations began to reflect this attitude. There were, however, limited moves toward restricting foreign ownership in television broadcasting (1958), and restrictions were placed on the granting of oil and gas leases in territories under federal jurisdiction (1960) during this period.

With the return of the Liberal party to power in 1963, the first major initiative directed at the problem of foreign ownership of Canadian business was undertaken. Walter Gordon, then finance minister, introduced a 30 per cent "takeover tax" to be levied on the value of shares of Canadian firms acquired by non-resident corporations, but the tax was withdrawn under strong pressure from the financial community and the suggestion of an absence of widespread public support.

Public attitudes toward the United States' economic influence in Canada were, however, gradually changing during the late 1950s and early 1960s, and these changes began to accelerate by the middle of the decade. The late 1960s and early 1970s were marked by a growing volume of literature critical of the Canadian-American relationship. George Grant, Donald Creighton, Walter Gordon, Kari Levitt, Mel Watkins, Abraham Rotstein, and Gary Lax were among those who wrote books critical of the United States' economic influence in Canada during this period.[11] A radical wing of the New Democratic Party began to advocate the nationalization of foreign firms as the only way for Canada to regain control over its economy. And, in 1970, a Committee for an Independent Canada was organized as a broadly based interest group to press for reassertion of Canadian control in both economic and cultural affairs.

These developments were accompanied by a number of government initiatives in selected areas. In 1968, a special task force created by the federal government issued a report (the Watkins Report) which put forward several policy proposals intended to enhance Canadian economic independence. In 1972, the Trudeau government tabled a long-awaited report on foreign direct investment (the Gray Report) which recommended a plan for dealing with foreign investment by means of a government screening agency. A new quarterly journal entitled *Foreign Investment Review* is now being used as a vehicle for communicating recent government initiatives in controlling and directing foreign-controlled investments.

All of these events led to increased media attention throughout the late 1960s and early 1970s on the state of Canadian-American relations particularly in the economic sphere. The cumulative effect of the growing awareness of this area of Canadian public policy was a body of public opinion increasingly critical of the Canada–U.S. relationship. Thus, while in 1956 only 27 per cent of the respondents in the CIPO poll cited earlier felt that there was "too much American influence", the figure climbed steadily to 57 per cent by 1974 (see Figure 2). The 48 per cent who in 1963 felt that Canadian dependence on the United States was basically a good thing was down by 34 per cent by 1972.[12] The 46 per cent who felt that there was enough U.S. capital in Canada in 1964, climbed to 67 per cent in 1972.[13]

11. George Grant, *Lament for a Nation* (Toronto, 1965); Donald Creighton, *Canada's First Century* (Toronto, 1970); Walter Gordon, *A Choice for Canada* (Toronto, 1966); Kari Levitt, *Silent Surrender* (Toronto, 1970); D. Godfrey and M. Watkins, ed., *Gordon to Watkins to You;* and Abraham Rotstein and Gary Lax, ed., *Independence the Canadian Challenge* (Toronto, 1972).

12. CIPO, *The Gallup Report* (August 26, 1972).

13. CIPO, *The Gallup Report* (February 12, 1972).

In that same year, while the discussion of an agency to screen foreign investment was under way, in a CIPO poll 69 per cent were found to favor the creation of such an agency.[14]

With respect to Canada-U.S. trade relations, there was not the same shift of opinion over this period that is discernible in the other data. For example, the 54 per cent of a CIPO sample who had been found in 1953 to favor a free trade agreement with the United States had remained virtually constant at 56 per cent when CIPO last asked this question in 1968.[15] A 1965 CIPO survey found Canadians equally divided between favoring more and less trade with the United States, as did our own 1975 survey of 5,000 Canadians which examined attitudes toward the Canada-U.S. auto agreement.[16] We found 27 per cent pro and 28 per cent against additional trade agreements, with 30 per cent indicating that it depended on the industry.

Parallel to shifting public attitudes toward the U.S. economic influence in Canada were a modest flow of new policies growing out of the various government studies and reports mentioned earlier. Until 1972 the approach was highly selective, designed primarily to protect specific sectors of the Canadian economy from undue foreign influence. Amendments to the Insurance and Loan and Trust Companies Act, restrictions on the tax deductibility of advertising in newspapers and magazines, and the blocking of the sale of a large uranium mine (Dennison) to a U.S. corporation are examples of specific initiatives taken during this period. Perhaps because of the unhappy experience with the proposed takeover tax in 1963, more comprehensive measures to deal with U.S. economic influence were not considered. Then, in 1972, the government introduced legislation to create a Foreign Investment Review Agency (FIRA), which was to make all new foreign direct investment in Canadian companies subject to government review. This legislation was passed in 1973, and was hailed as a significant initiative in attempting to confront the problem of foreign investment in the Canadian economy (see the other chapters in this book by Dewhirst and Twaalfhoven on FIRA).

At about the same time, significant initiatives were also being taken in the foreign policy sphere. Mitchell Sharp, then secretary of state for External Affairs, released a paper entitled "Canada-U.S. Relations: Options for the Future", which sought to identify three options that the country might pursue vis-à-vis the United States These were identified as (1) maintenance of the existing relationship

---

14. CIPO, *The Gallup Report* (February 12, 1972).
15. CIPO, *The Gallup Report* (May 18, 1968).
16. CIPO, *The Gallup Report* (January 29, 1969). See also, Keenleyside, LeDuc, and Murray, *Public Opinion*, pp. 20-22.

with the United States with a minimum of policy adjustments; (2)
movement toward closer economic integration with the United States;
and (3) the reduction of Canada's dependence on the United States
through the cultivation of closer ties with other countries, and the
development of a comprehensive strategy to develop and strengthen
the Canadian economy. The paper, together with the discussion that
followed, left little doubt that the last of these, or the "third option"
as it came to be identified, was the one favored by the government.[17]
Slowly, the third option attained the status of official government
policy, a position finally made explicit by Sharp's successor, Allan
MacEachen, in 1975. Over the past two years, however, the level of
commitment of the government to a third-option policy appears to
have waned somewhat.

It is impossible to discern exactly the role of public opinion either
in the development of a comprehensive foreign investment policy or
in the evolution of the "third option". That both of these developments were accompanied by an escalating public concern for Canadian economic independence, however, is evident from the survey
data. It also seems reasonable to argue that the government was slow
in adopting a comprehensive policy until it was convinced that
public opinion was supportive, perhaps because of the negative
experience with the 1963 takeover tax. There is, in addition, some
specific evidence of government awareness of the climate of public
opinion with respect to the proposed third option. In his initial
paper, Sharp cited the "growing public awareness of concern" about
the trend of Canadian-American relations, and stated that the public
was prepared to "contemplate and support reasonable measures".
In announcing the third option as official government policy, Mac-
Eachen referred specifically to trends in public opinion (diffuse
support), even citing the polls.

This new feeling of being Canadian is reflected very sharply in the
economic field. The issue is our economic independence. I have
already cited figures showing the degree to which we are dependent on the United States in trade and investment. A cross section of
various polls taken in Canada in 1972 indicated that 88.5 per cent
of Canadians thought it important to have more control over our
economy, and that two out of every three Canadians considered
the level of American investment in Canada too high.[18]

17. Sharp, "Options for the Future", p. 17. See also Denis Smith, "Nationalism and the
    Third Option" (Paper presented to the Conference on Canada-U.S. Relations,
    Dept. of External Affairs, February, 1975).
18. Department of External Affairs, Ottawa, *Statements and Speeches,* No. 75-1.

Foreign Investment: Some Recent Trends

It is impossible to ascertain the extent to which public opinion influenced the various initiatives in the area of Canadian-American relations outlined above. That the measures taken were accompanied by a gradually escalating public concern with respect to Canadian economic independence is, however, clear from our survey data collected over this period.[19] The percentage of successive national samples willing to categorize U.S. investment as basically a "good thing" for the Canadian economy declined steadily throughout this period, reaching its lowest point of 45 per cent in the 1974 survey, one year after the passage of the Foreign Investment Review Act (Figure 3). This proved however to be the end of the period that might loosely be categorized as one of rising Canadian nationalism and decreasing support for closer trade and investment relations with the United States. Slowly, throughout the middle and late 1970s, public opinion began to reverse, and the percent of the population who felt that U.S. investment was good for the Canadian economy

Figure 3

Per Cent of National Sample Who Believe that U.S. Investment, in Canada Is a "Good Thing" 1970-1980

(Excludes "No Opinion" and "Qualified" Answers)

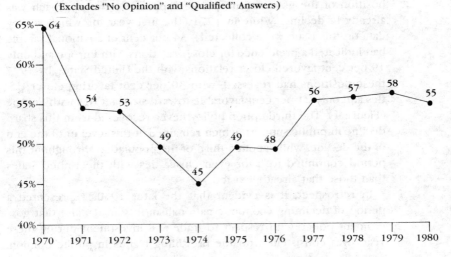

19. Lawrence LeDuc and J. Alex Murray, "Public Attitudes Toward Foreign Policy Issues", *International Perspectives* (May-June, 1976), pp. 38-40.

returned to majority status and remained at this level until the end of the decade. At the same time, the new policies which had been aggressively pursued by the federal government under the Foreign Investment Review Act were quietly set aside, and critics charged that FIRA was "falling apart in the face of corporate obstinacy and government indifference".[20] Herb Gray, the author of the Gray Report and father of FIRA, was dropped from the cabinet and ministers less sympathetic to the goals of the Foreign Investment Review Act, such as Jean Chrétien, first as trade minister and later as finance minister, became responsible for its implementation and enforcement.

Similarly, the "third option" fell into decline as a goal of Canadian foreign policy almost as soon as it was given official sanction in 1975. A much heralded "contractual link" between Canada and the European Common Market, one of the few tangible elements of the third-option policy, failed to have any real impact on Canada's trade relationships or on other areas of government policy.[21] It became increasingly evident that the government did not intend a major re-orientation of Canadian foreign or trade policy, in spite of statements made in support of the various government reports on this subject.

The survey data for this period suggest the reasons behind this cautious approach to the issue of Canada's foreign policy orientation. At the time that the third-option policy was announced as the official position of the government, public support for this approach was already in decline. While in 1974 (the first year for which survey data on this issue were collected), 34 per cent of a national sample had indicated a preference for closer relations with Europe and only 19 per cent favored closer relations with the United States, by 1977 these positions had reversed, with 30 per cent favoring closer U.S. ties and only 21 per cent favorable toward stronger ties with Europe (Figure 4). The third-option policy never recovered from this sharp decline in public support, which remained at this level until the end of the decade, while about a third of the population throughout this period continued to favor even closer ties with the United States than those that already existed.

In retrospect, it is evident that the later 1970s represented a period of declining economic nationalism in Canada, and that government policy with respect to trade and investment during these years was consistent with the prevailing trends in public opinion.

20. Ian Urquhart, "FIRA: Watchdog or Lapdog?" MacLeans (July 11, 1977), pp. 18-20.
21. "Canada's Link with Europe Still Not Widely Understood", International Perspectives (March-April, 1976), p. 33.

Figure 4

Per Cent of National Sample Favoring a Change in Canadian Foreign Policy: 1974-1980

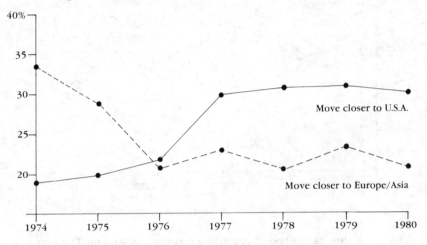

Government policies intended to increase Canada's control over its own domestic economy and to lessen its trade dependence on the United States were initiated at a time when public acceptance of Canada-U.S. economic interdependence was declining, and these same policies were later curtailed as public attitudes toward the Canadian-American relationship grew more favorable.

Now, as we enter the 1980s, there are signs that a revival of the nationalism of the early 1970s may be beginning. The evidence to this effect in the survey data reported thus far is slight but nevertheless unmistakable. Following five consecutive years of increasingly favorable public attitudes toward the role of American investment in the Canadian economy, there has now been a small but statistically significant decline in the proportion of Canadians who regard U.S. investment as a "good thing" for the Canadian economy (Figure 3). At the same time, the proportion of Canadians who regard foreign investment as a "serious problem" has risen to a level only slightly below that recorded in 1976 (Figure 5). In short, there is evidence that the level of foreign investment in Canada may once again become a viable political issue, inviting new government initiatives of the type begun in the early 1970s.

With regard to the overall orientation of Canadian foreign policy, the survey evidence is less clear but similar in direction to the

Figure 5

Per Cent of National Sample Who See Foreign Investment as a Serious Problem at the Present Time, 1980

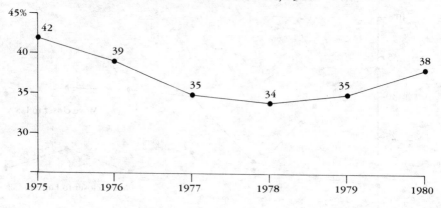

attitudes expressed regarding foreign investment. The proportion of Canadians who favor closer relations with the United States (what might now be called a "continentalist" approach, although this term was not used in any of the surveys) has failed to rise further following its sharp increase in 1977, and has declined slightly since the 1979 survey (Figure 4). Although support for a third-option-type policy of trade diversification has also not increased in the last several years, the percentage of Canadians favoring the status quo in trade policy has risen slightly from the   vel of one year ago.

Recent trends in the posture of the federal government toward trade and investment issues have been cautiously more nationalistic, perhaps reflecting this shift in public opinion. Following the Liberal defeat in the 1979 federal election, pressures developed within the party for policies which more clearly reflected a concern for the level of foreign investment in the Canadian economy and the degree of Canadian trade dependence on the United States. Following the Liberal return to power in 1980, these policies gained wider accept-ance within the cabinet. The return to prominence of ministers such as Herb Gray and Allan MacEachen may also be considered as indica-tive of a "tilt" in the direction of more nationalistic trade and invest-ment policies, in line with the new trends in public opinion noted earlier.

It should, of course, be noted that the modest resurgence of nationalism evident in the most recent survey data is not completely uniform throughout the country, although there is surprisingly little variation in the overall pattern. The largest year-to-year decline in the proportion of respondents who see U.S. investment as good for the Canadian economy has taken place in Ontario and in the Atlantic provinces, but the actual percentage varies only from a low of 45 per cent in British Columbia to a high of 51 per cent in the prairie provinces (Table 1). Nevertheless, these two regions both display statistically significant changes from the pattern of one year ago.

As in previous surveys, young people are among those more likely to express negative attitudes toward foreign investment. Forty-one per cent of those respondents under thirty years of age in the most recent survey rated U.S. investment in Canada a "bad thing" as compared with 24 per cent of those over fifty years of age expressing a similar opinion. Women (38 per cent) are slightly more likely than men (36 per cent) to feel that U.S. investment is bad for Canada, and there are modest relationships between the socio-economic status of respondents and attitudes expressed toward this issue, with the lowest income groups expressing the most strongly positive attitudes toward American investment in Canada.[22] There are also, as

Table 1

Per Cent of National Sample Who Believe That U.S. Investment in Canada Is a Good or Bad Thing for the Country, by Region, 1980

	Atlantic	Quebec	Ontario	Prairies	British Columbia	Total Canada
(1979 shown in parentheses)						
Good thing	46 (53)	50 (49)	49 (53)	51 (50)	45 (44)	49 (50)
Bad thing	42 (33)	32 (35)	37 (33)	37 (40)	44 (46)	37 (36)
Qualified	5 (4)	8 (6)	9 (6)	8 (5)	7 (8)	8 (6)
No opinion	8 (9)	9 (12)	5 (7)	4 (5)	4 (3)	6 (8)
N (1980)[a]	199	854	1,136	505	344	3038

(a) Weighted.

22. These socio-economic findings coincide with the "eldorado" theory tested by Carl J. Cuneo, "The Social Basis of Political Continentalism in Canada", *Canadian Review of Sociology and Anthropology* 13, 1976, pp. 55-70. The eldorado proposition suggests that underprivileged groups in Canada will support political union because of their relative isolation from dominant Canadian institutions and their resultant discontent.

might be expected, relationships between attitudes toward foreign investment and more fundamental political attitudes, with supporters of the New Democratic Party expressing the highest proportion of negative attitudes toward American investment (48 per cent). Both Liberals and Conservatives are more positive (56 per cent and 52 per cent respectively). The overall pattern of these relationships has persisted over a number of surveys, suggesting that, although these attitudes may change over time, they are not subject to wide and frequent fluctuations.

The distribution of reasons given by respondents to support their position on the foreign investment issue has likewise not changed appreciably over the period during which this question has been included in our annual surveys. Respondents who feel that U.S. investment in the Canadian economy is basically a bad thing tend to give general nationalistic responses ("Canada should control its own affairs", "should be more independent", etc.) or to cite the pervasiveness of U.S. influence in Canada. Those, on the other hand, who feel that foreign investment is basically a good thing for the country tend to cite economic growth and development reasons (Table 2). Nearly half of the respondents in this group gives answers specifically relating to employment or unemployment, and many more mention reasons such as resource development or the improvement of living standards.

Similar patterns may be observed in the responses to the question measuring the extent to which foreign investment in Canada is seen as a "problem" for the country (Table 3). The increase in the proportion of respondents who see foreign investment as a serious problem may be observed in each region of the country except Quebec, and in virtually every socio-demographic group.[23] Although there are variations between the regions, the largest year-to-year increases in the percentage of respondents defining foreign investment as a serious problem may be found in Ontario and the Atlantic provinces, a pattern similar to that observed for the foreign investment issues more generally. British Columbia, however, continues, as it has in previous surveys, to contain the largest absolute proportion of respondents who see foreign investment as a problem which must be dealt with in Canada.

The recognition of foreign investment as either a present or future problem by many Canadians has not generally been accompanied by widespread public support for direct government action to control

---

23. This should be qualified for business executives, who have in the past generally supported foreign investment. In 1980, 63 per cent had a positive attitude.

Table 2

Reasons for Believing That U.S. Ownership of Canadian Companies Is a Good or Bad Thing for the Canadian Economy, 1980

Reasons for a Good Thing	Total Canada	Reasons for a Bad Thing	Total Canada
Creates more employment 49%		U.S. taking over Canadian economy; Canada/Canadians should control their own business/economy 37%	
Need outside investment for expansion/development of industry/resources 18		Profits/money leave the country; does not benefit Canada; U.S. profits from Canada's resources 35	
Brings more into Canada; more money is circulated 16			
Raises/expands the economy (better standard of living; helps Canada/Canadians) 15		Canadians can do it themselves; should be more independent (not depend on United States) 12	
Canadians are not willing to invest too cautious — need a push), if United States did not do it, some other country would 12		Take jobs/business away from Canadians 9	
Creates a friendly relation-ship/co-operation; stabilizes; keeps Canada par with United States; help each other 6		Canadians take risk/initiative/invest in their own country; keep Canadian investment in Canada 9	
Most of what we have now is because of U.S. investing; Canadian economy is based on U.S., could not operate without United States 5		No employment security; they can move out any time it suits them especially when going gets rough 4	
Better/more products; world market, more to export/trade 3		Tend to "Americanize"/change Canada/Canadian methods; will lose Canadian identity 3	
Miscellaneous reasons 4		Discrimination; unequal trade; do not get a square deal; Canadians pay more; manpower drain, etc................. 2	
N = 1,145		Miscellaneous reasons 5	
		N = 886	

Percentages total more than 100 because multiple responses to the survey question were permitted.

Table 3

Per Cent of National Sample Who See Foreign Investment as a Serious Problem by Region, 1980

	Atlantic	Quebec	Ontario	Prairies	British Columbia	Canada
(1979 shown in parentheses)						
Yes, a serious problem	40%	37%	36%	38%	46%	38%
	(34)	(39)	(30)	(33)	(43)	(35)
Might be in future	20	26	24	24	22	24
	(22)	(25)	(25)	(27)	(25)	(25)
No, not a problem	30	27	33	32	26	30
	(31)	(25)	(38)	(32)	(26)	(32)
No opinion	10	10	8	6	7	8
	(13)	(11)	(8)	(9)	(7)	(9)
N (1980)[a]	199	854	1,136	505	344	3,038

(a) Weighted.

foreign investment. In previous surveys, only a minority of those identifying foreign investment as a problem were found to favor direct government regulation through agencies such as FIRA, although some favored selective controls in certain industries. More have supported incentives for Canadian business or alternate investment schemes such as the Canadian Development Corporation. In the most recent survey, the proportion of respondents favoring government regulation has increased slightly from its low point of 1980 (Table 4), but is still favored by no more than 26 per cent of those who see foreign investment as a problem. However, this increase followed several years of successive declines in the percentage of the population favoring government controls, and is indicative of the modest resurgence of nationalism found generally in the 1980 survey data. As noted earlier, this slight shift in opinion has been accompanied by policy and personnel changes which may suggest a strengthening of FIRA and a new resolve on the part of the federal government to limit the extent of new U.S. investment in Canada.

The same general observations may be made regarding the orientation of Canadian foreign policy as for the foreign investment issue. The proportion of Canadians who favor closer ties with the United States

Table 4

Proposed Solutions to the Foreign Investment Problem Responses for Selected Years

	1980	1979	1976
(Only respondents who viewed foreign investment as a problem)			
More support for Canadian business	32%	35%	34%
Government regulation	26	24	31
Canada Development Corporation	20	18	17
Selected industry controls	13	13	14
Investment from many countries	7	9	7
All other	1	2	2
No opinion	4	2	2
	N = 1,874	N = 2,354	N = 2,300

Percentages total more than 100 because multiple responses to the survey question were permitted.

Table 5

Preference of National Sample for Three Foreign Policy Options, By Region, 1980

	Atlantic	Quebec	Ontario	Prairies	British Columbia	Total Canada
(1979 shown in parentheses)						
Stay as we	40%	38%	42%	34%	35%	38%
are	(38)	(40)	(35)	(36)	(29)	(36)
Move closer	31	29	29	32	33	30
to U.S.	(38)	(31)	(29)	(34)	(31)	(31)
Move closer to						
Europe/Asia	22	20	20	25	26	21
	(13)	(18)	(26)	(21)	(32)	(23)
No opinion	7	12	8	8	6	9
	(11)	(11)	(10)	(10)	(7)	(10)
N (1980)[a]	199	854	1,136	505	344	3,038

(a) Weighted.

has levelled off in recent surveys, following a sharp rise in 1977. Although it too has declined slightly in the most recent survey, this decline from one year ago is statistically insignificant on a national basis (Figure 4). There are, however, modest variations in this pattern by region (Table 5). The percentage of respondents favoring closer relations with the United States has declined more sharply in the Atlantic provinces but has shifted only slightly in the rest of the country. In all parts of the country except Quebec and the Prairies, the percentage of the sample favoring maintenance of the status quo in foreign policy has risen significantly. The levelling off of the proportion favoring closer ties with the U.S. has thus not been accompanied by a resurgence of pro-European sentiment and does not therefore in itself suggest a revival of the third-option policy. Rather it suggests increasing caution in Canadian foreign policy and a scepticism regarding the desirability of closer economic ties with either the United States or other countries. Support for the status quo in current foreign policy may therefore reflect not satisfaction with existing policy but dissatisfaction with the two major alternatives which have been propounded in recent years.

The socio-demographic correlates of attitudes toward foreign policy have generally been similar to those for the foreign investment issue. Younger people have been somewhat more favorable toward the third option, with 23 per cent of those under twenty-one years of age in the most recent survey favoring this approach while only 21 per cent of this group favor closer ties with the United States. Thirty-five per cent of the respondents over fifty years of age, however, favor closer U.S. ties, while only 16 per cent prefer the third option. Men (34 per cent) are slightly more favorable toward closer relations with the United States than are women (27 per cent), a pattern also observed in previous surveys. There are no significant relationships, however, between socio-economic status variables such as income or occupation and attitudes toward foreign or trade policy.

Conclusions

The pattern of attitudes on these several issues suggests that for many Canadians attitudes toward issues such as foreign investment in the economy or the orientation of the nation's foreign relations are based not on emotions but on more practical considerations. Often, issues involving elements of nationalism might be expected to be highly emotional and related to more deeply held feelings.

Undoubtedly, there are many Canadians who are "nationalists" in this sense. But there appear to be more who are characterized by a highly pragmatic attitude toward these types of issues. Just as there are substantial numbers of people who recognize foreign investment as a "problem" but nevertheless consider it a "good thing", there are significant numbers who favor closer ties with the United States in general terms in spite of a negative attitude toward American investment specifically. The fact that a number of combinations exist in itself suggests that such attitudes are not uni-dimensional in character, and the fact that opinion has been shifting in both areas in recent years suggests that much of the public may be more heavily influenced by short-term policy considerations than by deeply held beliefs or emotions which are, by definition, more resistant to change.

Earlier, we speculated that the apparent decline in public support for government regulation of foreign investment and of public support for a "third option" in foreign policy might be related to the slackening of the Canadian economy and more specifically to growing unemployment. Certainly, the same surveys which have documented the trends in opinion on these two policy issues have also disclosed that economic considerations occupy a much higher priority for most Canadians than do issues such as foreign investment or the contractual link with the EEC (Table 6). In particular, the last three surveys have detected a reawakening concern of the Canadian public with respect to high unemployment, even as unemployment rates have steadily risen. It is understandable then, that much of the public may see these issues in economic terms, and that a more favorable attitude toward foreign investment and/or toward closer ties with the U.S. may be seen by some as "necessary" in a period of economic slow down. Mr. Chrétien, the minister previously responsible for the enforcement of FIRA, was recently quoted putting these tradeoffs succinctly, in stating that "a continuing inflow of direct investment from abroad is an essential condition of continuing economic progress in Canada". On the other hand, Mr. Trudeau is activating a new campaign to raise Canadian control of the oil and gas industries from 36 per cent at present, as measured by assets of Canadian-held companies, to at least 50 per cent by 1990.[24] Canadian public support for this initiative will be measured in the coming months.

The broader question of the relationship between policy making

24. "Trudeau's Drive to Canadianize Industry", *Business Week* (October 6, 1980), pp. 126-131.

Table 6

Most Important Issues Facing the Country, 1978-80

	Most Important			Total Mentions		
	1980	1979	1978	1980	1979	1978
Inflation	50%	43%	36%	83%	83%	79%
Unemployment	18	30	38	65	78	81
Environment and Pollution	11	8	7	33	29	26
Energy	8	2	3	42	19	25
Provincial-Federal Relations	4	4	4	19	22	18
National Unity	3	6	8	19	25	32
Taxation	3	3	3	23	28	25
U.S. Investment	3	3	3	14	15	13

N (1980)[a] = 3030

Totals to more than 100 per cent because multiple mentions were permitted in the survey.

(a) Weighted.

and public opinion in this area is somewhat more problematic. These are issues which are not by themselves highly salient to much of the public, although they are bound up with larger, more conspicuous economic policy questions. Thus, on the one hand a government may have considerable freedom of action in an area such as foreign policy at one particular point in time, but may on the other hand have to subordinate its initiatives in this area to other shorter-term considerations. It would be going beyond the limitations of the data reported here, however, to infer that on issues such as FIRA or the third option, the Canadian government has taken a new offensive in the face of changing public opinion; or alternatively that changes in government policy themselves have had an effect on public opinion. Rather, it seems more likely that at least part of the change in public opinion is accounted for by an overriding concern for the health of the economy and that the government, like the public, has simply had its attentions focussed elsewhere, at least temporarily. As Mr. Humphreys has noted, the government has made no real attempt to "sell" the contractual link with the EEC to the Canadian public as yet, and its pursuit of the third option has been extraordinarily low key of late. But an attempt to enlist public support behind such a policy, or to strengthen FIRA as Mr. Gray is now suggesting, could well be decisive, particularly if such action were initiated in an improved economic climate.

IV
Foreign Direct Investment Theory, Impact, and Control

C
Impact

25
Canada on a Platter

Mel Hurtig

Mr. Hurtig is president of Hurtig Publishers Ltd., an Edmonton publishing house. He is a founding member and past national chairman of the Committee for an Independent Canada and a leading spokesman for the cause of economic nationalism.

The material in this chapter appeared originally in *Canadian Business*, July 1979. Reprinted by permission.

By 1971, the level of foreign ownership in Canada had surpassed that of all of Western Europe combined, including Scandinavia, with Japan thrown in for good measure. It has reached a level that no other government, or citizens of any other country would even dream of allowing.

In every single year since 1971, the annual growth of foreign ownership in Canada has set new records — as it will again this year. Ten years ago, I said we would soon find that imported foreign direct investment would be replaced by the expansion of foreign ownership, not through money coming into Canada, but through retained earnings and through funds foreign corporations raise here from Canadian savings — mostly from our ever-so-friendly and obliging five big and remarkably profitable Canadian banks. Today, we know that well over 80 per cent of the expansion of foreign ownership in this country during the 1970s has been financed with funds obtained here in Canada.

I also said then that our huge annual outflow of interest payments would soon be exceeded by the pay out of even larger dividends — profits made in Canada flowing out of the country — and that both interest payments and dividends would soon be less than the ballooning multinational service charge manipulation, which even then had begun to show up in ominous multibillion-dollar figures in Statistics Canada's annual reports.

In 1978, every hour of every day, an average of $845,000 flowed out of Canada, mostly to the United States, in payment for our total services deficit. In 1979 the net outflow exceeded $1 million an hour, or almost $9 billion for the year. By 1981, it will be at least $13 billion.

For most of three decades now, the Bank of Canada, the Department of Finance, our federal and provincial leaders, our top businessmen, and senior financial executives, have followed or advocated policies based on our supposed heavy dependence on imported foreign capital. Last winter former finance minister Jean Chrétien said in New York: "Canada has continued to benefit substantially from the inflow of long-term capital. . . . I can state categorically that the government of Canada welcomes foreign investment . . . Some years ago our government rejected the demands of some Canadians for drastic curbs on foreign investment. . . . The record clearly shows that the Foreign Investment Review Act is not being used to block foreign investment."

Let's look at the result.

For the past thirty years, Canada has had a net capital inflow of some $34 billion. We took in that money primarily through extremely high interest rates. Those interest rates slowed the Canadian economy and substantially increased our rate of inflation. At the same time, federal and provincial governments either actively encouraged, via direct solicitation, or did nothing to inhibit the growth of foreign ownership.

Today, non-Canadians control more than $110 billion in Canadian assets at book value. The real market value is of course considerably higher. They control 65 per cent of all of our combined manufacturing, mining, petroleum and natural gas; 98 per cent of our rubber industry; 82 per cent of chemicals; 46 per cent of pulp and paper; 61 per cent of agricultural machinery; 74 per cent of the electrical apparatus industry; 59 per cent of transportation equipment; 96 per cent of the automobile and parts industry; and annually increasing percentages of wholesale and retail business, food processing and agricultural distribution, grain handling, forest products, and fishing.

Grim as they are, these figures are actually underestimated. The Corporations and Labor Unions Returns Act annual reports, and other Statistics Canada figures, are most often based on 50 per cent-or-over ownership. In reality, hundreds of important so-called Canadian corporations are effectively foreign controlled through minority ownership in widely held companies.

Let's have a look at what that ownership is really costing us.

In the same thirty-year period, the outflow of interest payments and dividends, mostly dividends, was more than $40 billion. And the outflow of those easy-to-fiddle service payments from subsidiaries to foreign parent companies was a colossal $44 billion.

In other words, the cost of the $34 billion in inflow was a gigantic $84 billion in outflow, plus foreign control of Canadian assets with a market value of at least $145 billion.

When huge foreign economic control occurs, the costs always escalate like an historical graph of the world's population — relatively flat at first, then upwards, climbing at a steeply accelerating angle. Let's look only at the most recent five years for which complete, reliable numbers are available, 1973 to 1977. The total of imported, new, foreign direct investment was a very modest $1.4 billion for the five years. The net import total of all long- and short-term capital flows was $12.8 billion.

Figure 1

The Foreign Piece of the Economic Pie

Who makes the money:
Foreign-owned companies account for more than half the sales and profits reported by
Canada's Top 500 non-financial corporations.[a]

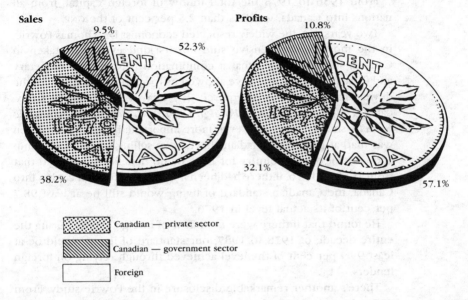

Sales

9.5%   52.3%   38.2%

Profits

10.8%   32.1%   57.1%

▓▓▓ Canadian — private sector

▧▧▧ Canadian — government sector

☐ Foreign

(a) All data are for 1976.

Source: Statistics Canada.

For the same five years, the assets of foreign-controlled corporations in Canada grew by some $42 billion. The outflow of interest
payments and dividends was more than $15 billion, and the outflow
of other foreign ownership and foreign investment-related service
payments was a staggering $20 billion. Last year, the outflow of
interest payments and dividends jumped 88 per cent over the average of the previous five years. Figures released in March 1978 show
that foreign-controlled corporations in this country receive half of
the total taxable income in Canada. They paid 86 per cent of their
dividends and 78 per cent of their business service payments to
non-residents!

For as long as I can remember, our chambers of commerce and
boards of trade, the Canadian Petroleum Association presidents, the
Conference Board in Canada, and almost all our daily newspapers
have been telling us how much we depend on the U.S. After all, they
supply us with the capital we need. They're our major trading

partner. They account for about 70 per cent of our exports and more than 70 per cent of our imports. Whatever we do, *we must be careful*. We're vitally dependent on that two-way relationship, and we mustn't rock the boat.

But again, let's have a closer look.

From 1950 to 1978 the total inflow of foreign capital, from all nations into Canada, was less than 2.5 per cent of the GNP.

Two years ago, the widely respected economist Dr. Thomas Powrie, in the most comprehensive study of its kind ever undertaken in Canada, showed clearly that a combination of Canadian monetary and fiscal policies would have allowed us to supply virtually all of the development capital we required. His heavily documented study, called *The Contribution of Foreign Capital to Canadian Economic Growth*, showed something even more important. Its major conclusion was that, at best, we Canadians have been selling off the ownership and control of our country for little or no benefit. He showed that from 1950 to 1976, if there had been *no* inflow of foreign capital into Canada, the Canadian standard of living would still be at least 98.7 per cent of its actual level in 1976.

He found that if there were no inflow of foreign capital during the entire decade of 1978 to 1987, our standard of living would be at least 99.9 per cent of the level achieved through relying on foreign lenders.

There's another remarkable disclosure in the Powrie study. From 1973 through 1976, the growth of foreign ownership in Canada through retained earnings — that is, only the growth financed by profits made here in Canada — was greater than the entire growth of foreign ownership for the period of 1950-70.

The Powrie study, combined with the first-class work of the Science Council of Canada, together present a crystal-clear picture:

* Foreign ownership in Canada is *causing* unemployment.
* It is *increasing* inflation.
* It is *decreasing* the money supply for Canadians.
* It is *reducing* skilled job opportunities.
* It is badly *damaging* the nation's economy.
* It is *lowering* our standard of living.

Not only have we sold off our country, but we've sold it off for nothing.

Canada is caught in a huge whirlpool, trapped into quickening, deepening current account deficits caused primarily by the massive outflow of interest payments, dividends and service charges, and by an unnatural and unnecessary excessive inflow of imported goods

Figure 2

Where the Pay Outs Go

Canada's Top 500 companies make the vast bulk of their dividend and business service payments to non-residents.

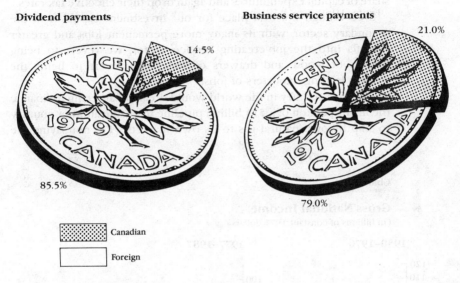

Dividend payments

Business service payments

14.5%

85.5%

21.0%

79.0%

▨ Canadian

☐ Foreign

and services. Current account is the national profit and loss. And our growing deficit produces the worst kind of multiple reactions, produces policies that would seem inconceivable if viewed objectively from outside this country.

To try to balance our ballooning deficits, we've made certain that future deficits will be even worse by raising interest rates to attract even more foreign capital. With massive unemployment, we raised interest rates six times in one year to all-time record heights, guaranteeing a multiplier inflationary effect throughout the economy. In an economy working well below capacity already, we've severely curtailed demand through expensive money and inhibited our ability to compete with the rest of the world.

As our own interest rates go up, federal, provincial and municipal governments, corporations, and individuals borrow more money abroad, and more foreign capital comes in. It comes in not mainly to bolster productivity, but mostly to service our huge past debts.

Our perpetual deficits have an even worse result. We know we're in trouble, so we look around desperately for solutions. And the quickest, most expedient solution is to dig up more of Canada. We rush into huge capital-intensive — not labor-intensive — projects so that we can export even more of our non-renewable natural resources. We amend and weaken our natural gas protection formula so that we can ship out more gas. We increase the resource sector share of capital expenditures and again drop their effective tax rates.

Even though the best place for our investment capital is in the secondary sector, with its many more permanent jobs and greater spinoffs into the job-creating service sector, we revert to being hewers of wood, and drawers of water. We revert to being the world's leading exporters of jobs!

No other country in the world would dream of agreeing to finance the major portion of a $14 billion pipeline to enable another country to ship its own natural gas to its own markets. (I'm not saying the

Chart 1

Gross National Income
(in billions of constant 1971 dollars)

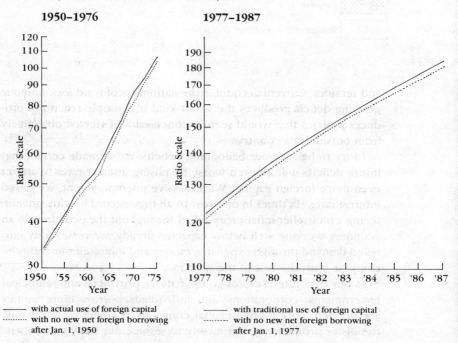

1950–1976	1977–1987

——— with actual use of foreign capital
·········· with no new net foreign borrowing
        after Jan. 1, 1950

——— with traditional use of foreign capital
·········· with no new net foreign borrowing
        after Jan. 1, 1977

Source: T. L. Powrie, The Contribution of Foreign Capital to Canadian Economic Growth.

According to the Powrie report, our vast borrowings of foreign capital have had — and will continue to have — a negligible effect on our standard of living.

pipeline shouldn't be built, but we could have done it on terms far more advantageous to Canada.) And no other country with the natural gas surpluses claimed by the petroleum industry, and with our unemployment, would seriously entertain the idea of an expensive Arctic LNG development or an Arctic Islands-Hudson Bay pipeline. Such a proposal would be laughed out of the local equivalent of NEB hearings.

Instead we continue to overdevelop our dependency on natural resource exports and then complain that we've vulnerable to the export of many of the same resources from low-wage countries.

We're already among the world's greatest exporters. Last year we had a surplus of $15 billion in agricultural products, metals, minerals, and semi-fabricated goods. We've already exported too much oil. We've already driven Canadian domestic prices far too high for several commodities by exporting too much. We already export more per capita than the U.S., West Germany, Japan, France, the U.K., and Italy.

And while last year we recorded an all-time merchandise trade surplus, we also had an all-time record *deficit* in finished products. The difficulty is, with 60 per cent of our manufacturing foreign controlled, there's little chance that we can increase the export of labor-intensive finished products. Branch plants were never intended to compete for exports. Branch plants are meant to consume: to consume parts, components, and services from their parents at high transfer prices. They provide a guaranteed market for home factories, and they rarely innovate distinctive products. Hardly ever do they have the capability or even the desire to be externally competitive, no matter what R & D incentives you try to package. It's simply not their job. And branch plants producing the same products are springing up all over the world in countries with lower wages than ours.

Since Richard Nixon's 1971 restrictive trade policies, since the establishment of the Domestic International Sales Corp. (DISC) and other U.S. incentives for domestic production, the multinationals have steadily transferred their manufacturing away from Canada and back to the U.S.

In 1953, manufacturing provided 26 per cent of all jobs in Canada; today it's down to 19 per cent. In 1955, we were second only to the U.S. in our per-capita manufacturing. Today we're down to ninth in the world. In 1970 our manufactured goods accounted for 21 per cent of our exports. Today it's 10 per cent. In 1973 we made 600,000 television sets. Today we make only about 130,000. Once, we made a lot of tractors. Now Massey-Ferguson Ltd. imports its finished product from Detroit.

In the fall of 1974, there were 115,000 job vacancies in Canada. In February of 1979 there were only 41,000.

In 1970, we had a huge and worrying $3 billion deficit in fully manufactured goods. Last year it was $11.5 billion. Foreign imports account for almost one-third of our domestic market.

Economists have calculated that the $8 billion increase in our finished product trade deficit corresponds to the loss of 400,000 jobs for Canadians. Not only, then, are we among the world's greatest exporters of jobs for other people, we are the world's leading *importer* of jobs for other people!

With 60 per cent of our manufacturing foreign controlled, there's no possible way our export ambitions can, in themselves, be a long-term solution to our huge international deficits.

So what do we do? Our myopic strategy is to raise interest rates to attract more foreign capital, to allow more massive foreign ownership, to accelerate more exports of our depleting non-renewable resources via new capital-intensive projects. And that means borrowing much more foreign money — at extremely high interest rates. It means selling off more of Canada, and it means a scarcity of development capital (or, when it is available, more expensive capital) for the job-creating sectors of the economy.

A nation careening madly downhill (perhaps in one of Mr. Horner's famous three-million-ton trucks) has decided to throw the brakes and steering wheel out the window over the edge of the cliff. Current account deficits that increase the way ours have ($4.5 billion in 1977, $5.3 billion in 1978) mean certain downward pressure on currency. The greater the deficits, the greater the pressure.

No matter how carefully I've searched the explanations, no matter how many economists, government officials and businessmen I've talked to, the only conclusion I can reach is that we have been ridiculously foolish in our reaction to the downward pressure on the Canadian dollar.

The overwhelming reason for the drop in the dollar has been our growing current account deficits, deficits caused mainly by the enormous foreign control of our economy, the resulting services outflows and our excessive merchandise imports.

The reason the Canadian dollar was up at $1.03 — and so unrealistically high to begin with — was simply our decades-long policy of encouraging the inflow of foreign capital through high interest rates. The greater the inflow, the more the demand for the Canadian dollar. The greater the demand, the higher the value of the dollar. The higher the value of the dollar, the greater the detriment to all of our labor-intensive industry, to manufacturing, to mining, to forestry, to agriculture, to all of our export-oriented industries. The Canadian dollar never had any business being up there in the first place. Good management, sound economic policy, would never have permitted it.

And in response, the Finance Department and the Bank of Canada use up $5 billion in our foreign exchange reserves, then arrange to borrow $5 billion more (at a cost of $575 million a year), and legislate so that we can borrow another $10 billion to artificially sustain the dollar's value, at the cost of another billion and a half in our current account deficit. Yet still we have a dollar down 7 per cent in a year against the U.S. dollar, and down 9.5 per cent against ten major currencies.

But, again, here is Mr. Chrétien: "The depreciation of the Canadian dollar has contributed to a much-improved competitive position for Canada in international markets . . . . Over the last year I have emphasized the advantages of the lower Canadian dollar. There is no doubt in my mind that the depreciation of the dollar has been extremely beneficial to Canada in terms of increased jobs, increased investment, increased trade."

Why would the Bank of Canada and the Department of Finance want to keep the level of the dollar artificially higher than they fear market forces might otherwise dictate, especially since the lower value means increased exports? The reason, of course, is those expensive imports — mostly from the U.S., mostly sold by parent companies to their subsidiaries, mostly labor-intensive products. Head office tells branch office where to buy and what to buy and at what prices.

This year we will import more than $50 billion worth of goods. So we borrow more money and deplete our foreign currency reserves, trying to keep the dollar's value high so the huge imports won't add too much to inflation. Or so Mr. Bouey and Mr. Chrétien have told us. Joining the chorus is the Conservatives' Sinclair Stevens, who says the dollar should be higher because "its reduced purchasing power is driving up the costs of imports and contributing to inflation".

Never mind that most of the imports are already purchased at non-arm's length inflationary pricing to begin with. Never mind the further downward pressure on the dollar that will surely result from our new extra borrowing costs. Never mind the fact that the government's own analysis shows that even an 80¢ Canadian dollar would add only 1-2 per cent to inflation, while high domestic interest rates are at least as inflationary, severely hinder domestic production, and encourage even more imports.

Speculation and downward pressure on the dollar would probably disappear if the bank and government announced a hands-off policy. Ironically, by all international GNP and productivity comparisons, right now the Canadian dollar is about where it really belongs.

How do we get the Canadian economy rolling again? How do we create more jobs, and better jobs? How do we become less dependent, less vulnerable to the decisions, to the mistakes, to the naturally self-concerned policies of others? How can we restore our own confidence in our own future, the confidence that's essential in any attempt to rekindle the nation's spirit?

First, jobs now will mainly be found in the secondary and tertiary sectors. Manufacturing will have the greatest spin off into services. Change tax policies. Identify the major unnecessary sources of our end products deficits. Use incentives, low-interest loans, deferred taxation, and other incentives, particularly in product development. Use them selectively, only for Canadian-owned and -controlled companies. Concentrate on the production of finished goods that can be produced competitively on economies of scale for our own domestic market first and foremost.

We need a strategy of substituting for imports instead of escalating resource exports. At the very worst, we could cut our imports of finished products by one-quarter and create 300,000 new jobs, less unemployment, higher productivity, less unemployment insurance and greatly reduced current account deficits.

Second, leave the dollar alone. Let it find its own true value, which is somewhere between U.S. 80¢ and 85¢. Reduce interest rates accordingly.

Third, our banks. Canadians are among the highest per-capita savers in the world. Our 1978 personal savings accounts held more than $47 billion. The big five Canadian banks administer assets of more than $171 billion. And these banks have been using that money and their own huge annual profits to finance the sell-out of our own country. Bring in legislation to gradually increase loans to Canadians, gradually decrease loans to foreigners. Even a 5 per cent per year shift would make a vital difference. We could require banks and other financial institutions to report annually their total loans to Canadians, and to non-Canadians inside and outside of Canada. One hundred per cent penalties would apply to all loans exceeding the annual quota for loans to foreign corporations or individuals.

Fourth, announce a long-term policy package of gradual decreases in tax rates for Canadian-controlled firms, and gradual increases for foreign-controlled companies. This in itself would likely ensure an end to the growth of foreign ownership in Canada. The emphasis is on the words "gradual" and "long-term". Massive overnight changes are impossible. But a dedicated government with a policy for tax rates truly beneficial to Canadian-owned companies would bring about a smooth transfer of the assets of foreign-controlled corporations to Canadians capable of and prepared to do the job, and to do the job with a far greater net benefit to Canada.

And change tax policies so that far more middle-income Canadians could become shareholders and investors through employee profit-sharing schemes and other investment incentives. Election campaign promises by both the Liberals and Conservatives in this area would produce only a further accumulation of wealth for the top 5 per cent of Canadian taxpayers, and further concentration of ownership. What is needed instead are tax investment incentives for middle-income Canadians, the majority, so that as foreign ownership is reduced, millions of Canadians will benefit, and have the pride and incentive of ownership of Canadian industry — capitalism for the masses, instead of a small handful of families.

Fifth, establish policies of federal, provincial, and municipal government purchasing of Canadian goods and services wherever possible and wherever logical. Even if at first it will mean paying somewhat higher prices in some areas, certainly in the long run, and quite likely very soon, all Canadians will benefit. In the long run lower prices will often be the result. The Science Council has estimated that Canadian products up to even 76 per cent more expensive than a foreign product can still provide significant net public benefits which outweigh the additional short-term costs to the taxpayer.

Sixth, stop the stupid policy of giving Ford Motor Co. $68 million and General Motors Corp. $86 million, making huge multimillion-dollar public handouts, and giving tax concessions to the subsidiaries of multinationals such as Exxon Corp. (1978 sales $65 billion), Crown Zellerbach International Ltd., Shell Petroleum, NV or IBM Corp. Federal and provincial government grants, when they are necessary, should be made exclusively to Canadian-controlled companies.

Seventh, save Canadian taxpayers millions of dollars and simply abolish the Foreign Investment Review Act. Since FIRA was established we have succeeded in breaking new foreign-ownership growth records every year. In the last fiscal year this Mickey Mouse agency approved a record number of takeovers. This year, the number is one-third higher. Last year it approved 96 per cent of all new U.S. takeovers and investment applications. Get rid of the absurd, useless bureaucracy and replace it with legislation that simply says: I'm sorry, we already have far too much foreign ownership, and we don't want any more.

Eighth, GATT, reciprocity, tariffs. Canada already has the lowest effective tariff rates on manufactured products of any of its major trading partners. For example, in 1976, of some $14 billion worth of manufactured goods entering Canada, more than 63 per cent entered completely duty-free. Certainly we believe a time will come when we will wish to reduce our trade barriers, along with all of our trading partners. But not now — not when our country has, as the Science Council puts it so well, a "technologically backward branch-plant economy" in a "de-industrializing" nation. Tariff reductions now, as Science Council Vice-Chairman John Shepherd has so aptly put it, "would be like opening the window on a pneumonia patient. Sure it's fresh air, but it's going to kill him." We should consider tariff reductions and other trade moves only when our own secondary sector is more competitive, and only then when our major trading partner allows reciprocal access to its markets for our finished products. The GATT negotiations prove how ill prepared Canada is in its role as one of the world's trading nations.

In the vital field of technology, we could develop more of our own specialized technology, and import the foreign technology we do need on much more advantageous terms.

There are many other things Canada could do. We could much better use our *genuinely* surplus natural resources as trading tools. We could continue to keep foreign banks out of regular banking in Canada. (But instead we're about to do exactly the opposite). We could engage in reciprocally advantageous energy swaps. (But instead we're foolishly about to export low-priced, accessible, high-quality natural gas without a swap agreement.) We could concentrate on the development of distinctive Canadian products for mining, transportation, communications, the North, instead of producing carbon copies of U.S. designs in our branch-plant component-assembling factories.

We could carefully examine the remarkable success of the 98 per cent Canadian-controlled steel industry, now operating at 100 per cent capacity — an industry more competitive, more profitable, more productive (with higher wages and job increases) than any of its major international competitors. Listen to the president of the Steel Co. of Canada: "The Canadian steel industry is almost alone in the world operating at capacity and operating at a profit. . . . We have avoided slumps encountered by other steel producers because our production is geared primarily to Canadian requirements."

What we desperately need is a new national strategy in the interests of the nation — not isolated, modest changes, but a package of important new policy initiatives. The package I've sketched out here might not be perfect, but this I know for sure: there are a hell of a lot better ways of doing things than the way we've been managing.

And I know for certain that if we don't make the necessary changes soon, we can say goodbye forever to the dreams and aspirations of so many who have worked long and hard for Canada. If we continue giving away the shop and giving away the country, we can say good-bye to the whole idea of Canada.

IV
Foreign Direct Investment Theory, Impact, and Control

C
Impact

26
Foreign Direct Investment and "Spill Over" Efficiency Benefits in Canadian Manufacturing Industries*

Steven Globerman

Dr. Globerman is professor of economics at York University. He is the author of several monographs and articles on foreign direct investment, including *U.S. Ownership of Firms in Canada: Issues and Policy Approaches*, published by the C. D. Howe Institute.

The material in this chapter appeared originally in *The Canadian Journal of Economics*, Februrary 1979. Reprinted by permission.

* This chapter is part of a larger study sponsored by the Canadian American Committee. The committee is in no way responsible for the analysis or conclusions contained herein. The author thanks two unidentified references for important criticism of an earlier chapter. Helpful comments were also received from Bernard Wolf.

Introduction

The issue of foreign ownership in Canada has spawned an extensive literature on the effects of foreign direct investment. However, existing research has concentrated, by and large, on identifying the conceptually relevant costs and benefits.[1] A few studies have empirically evaluated the performances of foreign-owned and domestically owned firms, paying particular attention to specific performance measures such as R & D expenditures,[2] adoption of new technology,[3] specialization and efficiency,[4] profitability,[5] and exporting and importing intensities among others.[6]

It is recognized that from the perspective of the host country external benefits of foreign direct investment are relevant in evaluating the net benefits of foreign investment. More specifically, it is the present value of returns not directly captured by the foreign investor that comprises the relevant benefits package for the host economy. Analogously, it is the present value of costs not directly borne by the foreign investor that constitutes the relevant comparison to the benefits' package for the host government.

1. Foreign Direct Investment in Canada (Ottawa: Information Canada, 1972); H. G. Johnson, "Economic Benefits", Nationalism and the Multinational Enterprise, ed. Hahlo, Smith, and Wright (Dobbs Ferry: Ocean Publications, 1973); J. Fayerweather, Foreign Investment in Canada (New York: International Arts and Science Press, 1973); H. F. English, "Canada-United States Relations", Proc. of the Academy of Political Science 2 (1976), pp. 68-79.
2. A. E. Safarian, The Performance of Foreign-Owned Firms in Canada (Montreal: Private Planning Association of Canada, 1969); J. D. Howe and D. G. McFetridge, "The Determinants of R & D Expenditures", Canadian Journal of Economics 9 (1976), pp. 57-72.
3. S. Globerman, "Technological Diffusion in the Canadian Tool and Die Industry", Review of Economics and Statistics 4 (1975), pp. 428-434; "New Technology Adoption in the Canadian Paper Industry", Industrial Organization Review 4 (1976), pp. 5-12.
4. Safarian, Performance; R. E. Caves, Diversification, Foreign Involvement and Scale in North American Manufacturing Industries (Ottawa: Information Canada, 1975).
5. Safarian, Performance; A. Raynauld, "The Ownership and Performance of Firms", The Multinational Firm and the Nation State, ed. Gilles Pagnet (Don Mills: Collier-Macmillan, 1972).
6. Safarian, Performance.

A number of potential indirect (or "spill over") economic benefits of foreign direct investment have been identified in the literature. It has been suggested, for example, that foreign direct investment promotes greater efficiency throughout the economy by increasing competition levels in domestic industries.[7] Indirect benefits may also be realized from non-specific human capital investments made by foreigners that, as a result of labor migration, are ultimately utilized within domestically owned firms. Other hypothesized indirect economic benefits of foreign ownership include faster adoption of new technology by domestically owned firms, improved management practices throughout the domestic economy, and increased mobility of domestic resources, particularly financial capital.

On the other hand it is also argued that foreign direct investment contributes to a "truncated" managerial structure in Canada, whereby important administrative and technological functions are centralized in the home country. The centralization of substantive managerial decision making in the parent firm is alleged to encourage a net migration of talented managers and technicians out of Canada, thereby reducing productivity throughout the economy. It is further argued, particularly by the Science Council of Canada (1977), that foreign direct investment contributes to the fragmented structure of Canadian manufacturing industries.[8] Fragmentation can be viewed as a condition of too many firms below optimal size producing too diverse an array of output which contributes to lower productivity in both foreign- and domestically owned firms.[9]

Considering that the components of foreign direct investment spill overs are both diverse and difficult to measure, it is not surprising that empirical estimates of them are lacking in the literature. For Canada, one available set of estimates is provided by Caves.[10] The premise underlying Caves's estimates of the indirect economic benefits of foreign direct investment in Canada is that if foreign invest-

---

7. This consideration is particularly relevant if entry into concentrated industries is easier for foreign-owned firms than for domestically owned firms. For affirmative evidence on this point see P. Gorecki, "The Determinants of Entry by Domestic and Foreign Enterprises in Canadian Manufacturing Industries: Some Comments and Empirical Results", *Review of Economics and Statistics* 4 (1976), pp. 485-488.
8. This claim continues to be made notwithstanding the evidence cited in D. J. Daly and S. Globerman, *Tariff and Science Policies: Application of a Model of Nationalism* (Toronto: University of Toronto Press, 1976) and elsewhere most fragmentation is largely attributable to Canada's tariffs and competition policy.
9. A comprehensive catalogue of the indirect effects of foreign direct investment would also include any external social and political works and benefits associated with such investment.
10. R. E. Caves, "Multinational Firms, Competition and Productivity in Host-Country Markets", *Economics* 41 (1974), pp. 176-193.

ment contributes to increased allocative efficiency, the profit rates of domestically owned firms should be inversely related (ceteris paribus) to the competitive pressure supplied by foreign firms. For a sample of forty-nine manufacturing industries, Caves's dependent variable was defined as the average profit before taxes on equity over the period 1965-67 for corporations with less than 50 per cent foreign ownership. The competitive pressure supplied by foreign firms was measured by the subsidiary share of sales as well as by the subsidiary share of assets in an industry. Caves concludes that both share variables have negative signs and, in simple specifications, are statistically significant; however, when the relative size of domestically owned firms to foreign-owned firms in an industry is included in the regression, the significance of the share variables is destroyed.[11] Alternative specifications which embody the notion of a threshold level of foreign competitive pressure provide no significant improvement to the specification. Thus, Caves's results provide, at best, very weak support for the presence of external benefits to foreign direct investment in Canada.

The somewhat inconclusive results cited above may reflect the use of a profit rate variable as an indirect measure of productivity. Accounting profit rates are a notoriously unstable measure of industry performance, and interindustry differences in profit rates may vary substantially over the business cycle. Furthermore, one can imagine the existence of productivity spill overs which both reduce costs in domestically owned firms and increase industry competition. In such cases the external economic benefits of foreign direct investment might escape measurement by Caves's dependent variable. Indeed, Caves acknowledges the limitations imposed by his measure of external benefits and, in the same study, estimates comparable indirect benefits for Australia by focussing on labor productivity differentials in domestically owned firms.[12]

Employing recently reported data from Statistics Canada (1977a), this chapter attempts to provide estimates of spill over benefits to Canadian manufacturing industries employing a specification similar to that found in Caves's (1974) analysis of Australian industries.

The Sample and Research Approach

Recent reports prepared by Statistics Canada provide data about the

11. Caves, "Multinational Firms", p. 182.
12. More affirmative evidence on the presence of external benefits to direct investment is provided in the case of Australia. Differences in specification prevent direct comparison of the results for the two countries.

foreign control of manufacturing plants in Canada,[13] as well as manufacturing activity data comparable to those published in the annual *Census of Manufactures*. The data indicate that output per employee is higher for plants controlled in the United States than for those controlled in Canada, both on an aggregate basis and on an industry group basis, except for the petroleum and coal products industries. Other foreign-controlled plants have in total about the same ratios as U.S.-controlled activity, but the industry group breakdown differs considerably.

United States-controlled plants are, on average, larger and more capital intensive than domestically controlled plants, a fact that contributes to an explanation of observed labor productivity differentials between the two sets of plants. Analysis of the precise determinants of productivity differentials between ownership groups could provide some insight into whether external economic benefits are associated with foreign ownership. For example, evidence that labor productivity differentials between foreign- and domestically owned plants are largely explained by differences in relative factor intensities and output scale would minimize the a priori significance of productivity spill overs. More specifically, the empirical relevance of the spill overs argument is conceptually related to transfers of nonconventional factors of production, including technology, management skills, and motivation between foreign- and domestically owned firms.[14]

Unfortunately, potentially significant differences in valuation methods used by foreign- and domestically controlled firms militate against direct comparisons of labor productivity differentials across industries. In particular, census value added for both Canadian-controlled and foreign-controlled plants includes the value of purchased services, including any services obtained by subsidiaries from foreign parents. In the case of Canadian-controlled plants, the employment involved in creating these services may well be included in the data of a Canadian head office, laboratory, or other reporting unit included in the industry's totals. However, the employment involved in creating a comparable amount of value added for the foreign-controlled plant may be located at a foreign head office or auxiliary unit outside the scope of census data.[15] Furthermore, the existence

---

13. *Domestic and Foreign Control of Manufacturing Establishments in Canada* (Ottawa: Information Canada, 1976-77).
14. Such factors comprise the determinants of the residual in total factor productivity estimates.
15. Another potential source of reporting difference is associated with the greater use of short-form data reporting by Canadian companies, which excludes purchased services from value added. A discussion of more points is in *Domestic and Foreign Control* (1976), pp. 13-15.

of productivity spill overs would reduce the observed productivity differentials between foreign- and domestically owned firms, thereby contributing to a downward bias in any estimates of productivity differences related to foreign ownership.

A direct approach to evaluating the significance of economic externalities might involve specifying and estimating a labor productivity equation for domestically owned manufacturing plants including some measure of potential spill over benefits as a variable. Such an approach was chosen for this study. The sample of four-digit Canadian manufacturing industries was chosen to satisfy the following constraints: requisite data were available for all relevant variables and a percentage of industry output greater than zero was produced in foreign-owned plants, with the percentage separately identified from output produced in domestically owned plants.

The Model

While we would ideally construct our productivity measure as the ratio of net output to an index of total factor inputs, available data permit only the construction of a partial (for instance, labor) productivity index. Our dependent variable is therefore defined as the ratio of total value added (in thousands of dollars) in domestically owned manufacturing plants to the total number of employees in domestically owned manufacturing plants for the year 1972.[16] This specification is identical to Caves's dependent variable in the model dealing with Australian industries.[17]

Our partial productivity measure will be a function of a number of factors including differences in factor proportions, quality of inputs, scale economies, and technological efficiency. More specifically, since capital and labor are complementary inputs, value added per unit of labor will be positively related to the ratio of capital services to labor services.[18] Data on gross (or net) capital stock are not available for disaggregated Canadian industries. One possibility is to employ a measure of "capital rentals" (that is, value added minus payroll) divided by wage payments as a direct measure of the capital to labor input ratio in an industry. This specification would raise potential problems of simultaneity, however, since value added, the dependent

16. Precise data sources for all variables employed are provided in the Appendix.
17. Caves, "Multinational Firms".
18. Our use of a value added specification of output obviously ignores considerations of separability in aggregate production relationships: that is, does a value added function exist in Canadian manufacturing industries? For recent evidence on this point see M. Denny and D. May, "The existence of a Real Value-Added Function in the Canadian Manufacturing Sector", *Journal of Econometrics* 1, pp. 55-69.

variable, includes both wage and non-wage payments. An alternative approach is to use the capital/labor ratio in the comparable United States industry as a proxy for the ratio in Canadian-owned plants in Canada. The variable K_i was defined specifically as the ratio of the gross book value of depreciable assets at the end of 1971 (in millions of U.S. dollars) to the total number of employees (in thousands) in 1972 for the comparably defined U.S. industry. The use of this measure involves two important assumptions. One is that differences in capital/labor ratios between Canadian and comparable U.S. industries are randomly distributed across our sample of Canadian industries. While evidence suggests that the levels of capital stock per person employed are higher in Canada than in the United States, especially for structures,[19] there is no reason to believe that these differences vary systematically across manufacturing industries. Another assumption is that capital service flows are roughly proportional to capital stocks. While this condition is likely violated for individual industries, there is, again, no reason to suspect that a systematic bias obtains across our sample.

Differences in measured labor productivity in domestically owned plants will be influenced by differences in labor quality. A standard measure of labor quality used in productivity studies is average wages. However, regressing a value-added-based measure of productivity on average wages raises potential simultaneity problems, since value added includes wages as a component. Furthermore, it might be argued that higher average wages are both a result and a cause of higher productivity in production plants. As a result of the potential least squares bias associated with using measured average wages as a proxy for labor quality, a number of alternative instrumental variables were employed. In one case, the ratio of total salaries and wages ($000) to total number of employees in foreign-owned plants in 1972 (L_{1i}) in the ith Canadian industry was used as a measure of average labor quality in domestically owned plants in the same industry. More specifically, differences in the L_{1i} variable across industries were taken to reflect corresponding differences in the (unobserved) quality of labor in domestically owned plants. Since differences in L_{1i} across industries may reflect the systematic influence of factors unrelated to labor quality, the choice of this instrument might prove to be less than satisfactory. Thus, an alternative exogenous instrument employed was the percentage of total male employees who had some university education or a university degree in the ith Canadian industry in 1971, L_{2i}. This instrument was employed as a proxy for the stock of human capital in an industry,

19. Daly and Globerman, *Tariff and Science Policies.*

which should, in turn, be related to labor quality. A third approach involved the use of two-stage least squares estimation, where the instrument L_{3i} was obtained as the forecast value of the average wage variable from the first-stage regression.

Measured labor productivity differences across domestically owned plants could conceivably be affected by differences across industries in average hours worked. Our dependent variable standardizes value added by total employees, thereby raising the possibility that systematic differences in overtime work, vacation periods, etc. contribute to interindustry differences in value added per employee. Unfortunately, data on total paid man-hours are available only for production and related workers. The ratio of total man-hours paid for production and related workers (thousands) divided by the total number of production and related workers in 1972 for domestically owned plants M_i was assumed to reflect the average hours worked by nonproduction workers and therefore by all employees in an industry.

Differences in labor productivity across manufacturing plants can be related conceptually to differences in scale economies. Economies of scale may in turn be plant and (or) product specific. Plant-scale economies include those deriving from indivisibilities, increased specialization, and the like. Product specific economies relate to production lengths of run, total planned output, and the rate of output per unit of time. In practice, the nature of available scale economies will depend in part upon the production method used, although a number of observers have argued that product specific economies of scale are generally more significant than plant specific ones in the Canadian context.[20] Gorecki's recent evidence suggests that the importance of plant and product specific economies of scale varies considerably between industries.[21] Thus, there is some question whether an average scale coefficient estimated across a sample of industries has meaning. In this regard, Gorecki's finding[22] that minimum efficient plant size is positively related to total industry employment for fifty-six Canadian manufacturing industries suggests that systematic differences in plant-scale economies may be related to differences in plant size. Furthermore, a number of case studies indicate that product diversification is a source of higher production costs in many secondary manufacturing industries. In short, it does not seem inappropriate to ascribe differences in plant-level produc-

20. D. J. Daly, B. A. Keys, and E. J. Spence, *Scale and Specialization in Canadian Manufacturing* (Ottawa: Information Canada, 1968); Economic Council of Canada, *Interim Report on Competition Policy* (Ottawa: Queen's Printer, 1969).
21. P. Gorecki, *Economies of Scale and Efficient Firm Size in Canadian Manufacturing Industries* (Ottawa: Research Branch, Bureau of Competition Policy, 1976).
22. Gorecki, *Economies of Scale*, 43.

tivity ratios to estimates of plant- and product-scale economies for a sample largely composed of secondary manufacturing industries.

In the absence of engineering cost estimates for our sample industries, an imputed measure of plant-scale economies must satisfy. Caves, Khalilzadeh-Shirazi, and Porter note that most statistical studies share a common approach to measuring minimum efficient scale (MES) in assuming that the larger plants in an industry exhaust available plant-scale economies.[23] Clearly this assumption is reasonable when considering large industrial countries. For countries with small domestic markets, such as Canada, the use of MES estimates derived from U.S. results is suggested. Scherer provides reassuring evidence that differences in transport costs and factor prices impart only minor differences in MES plants for a sample of industries in a number of developed countries, including the United States and Canada.[24] Estimates of MES plants for our sample of Canadian industries were obtained by calculating the average size of the largest plants accounting for 50 per cent of value added in comparably defined U.S. industries for 1972. This measure is quite close to that employed by Comanor and Wilson and others.[25]

In many cases, the average size of the plants accounting for 50 per cent of net output had to be estimated from discrete data providing the cumulative value added accounted for by specific percentages of total industry plants. Thus, we frequently possessed direct estimates of the number of plants accounting for percentages of industry value added above and below 50 per cent. In those cases we estimated the number of plants accounting for 50 per cent of value added by linear interpolation over the two value added percentages. In a small number of cases, the only estimate directly available was for a percentage of value added in excess of 50 per cent. For those cases estimates of the number of plants accounting for 50 per cent of value added were also obtained by linear interpolation. In most cases the range over which we interpolated was relatively small. Furthermore, differences across industries in estimated MES plants are quite substantial. Thus, the somewhat arbitrary procedure employed to estimate MES plants should not impart serious measurement errors to that variable. The extent to which the "typical" domestically owned Canadian plant captured available plant-scale economies E_i was, in turn, measured as the ratio ($U.S. 000) of the average value added in

23. R. E. Caves, J. Khalilzadeh-Shitazi and M. Porter, "Scale Economies in Statistical Analyses of Market Power", *Review of Economics and Statistics* 2 (1975), pp. 133-140.

24. F. Scherer et al., *The Economics of Multi-Plant Operation* (Cambridge, Mass.: Harvard University Press, 1975).

25. W. S. Comanor and T. A. Wilson, "Advertising, Market Structure and Performance", *Review of Economics and Statistics* 49 (1967), pp. 423-440.

domestically owned plants in 1972 to our MES plant estimate for the comparable U.S. industry.[26]

The absence of direct measures of product-scale economies imposes the need to construct an acceptable statistical proxy. Unfortunately, available data do not permit the utilization of U.S.-based measures, as was the case in estimating MES plants.[27] The model of the protected oligopoly, developed by Eastman and Stykolt and supported by Bloch's empirical results,[28] posits that excessive product diversification is characteristic of concentrated industries that enjoy significant levels of import protection. Thus, it might be argued that the extent to which firms exploit available product-scale economies is inversely related (ceteris paribus) to the joint levels of concentration and tariff protection in an industry. If potential product-scale economies were identical for all industries, an interaction variable between industry concentration and the domestic tariff level might adequately proxy the desired variable. While it is unlikely that potential product-scale economies are indeed identical across industries, no clearly preferable and easily specified alternative hypothesis is readily apparent. Rather than experiment with alternative statistical proxies for a variable of secondary interest, we specified product-scale economies attained by domestically owned plants as an interaction variable I_i between the estimated nominal tariff rate for the industry in 1963 and a Herfindahl concentration measure based upon value of shipments for the industry in 1965.[29] More specifically, the Herfindahl measure was multiplied by one if the industry's nominal tariff rate was above the median rate for all sample industries, and zero otherwise. Clearly, estimates of the I_i parameter must be evaluated with caution.

To the extent that foreign direct investment provides spill over benefits to domestically owned factors of production, one would anticipate a positive relationship between labor productivity in domestically owned plants and some measure of foreign ownership in an industry. The precise form of the relationship is not obvious, however, on an a priori basis. Caves suggests that the competitive spur

26. Canadian dollar values are converted to U.S. dollar values using the average exchange rate for 1972.
27. To some extent product-scale economies will be related to plant-scale economies since larger output volumes (holding product mix constant) imply longer output runs.
28. H. C. Eastman and S. Stykolt, *The Tariff and Competition in Canada* (Toronto: Macmillan, 1967); M. Bloch, "Prices, Costs, and Profits in Canadian Manufacturing: The Influence of Tariffs and Concentration", *Canadian Journal of Economics* 4 (1974), pp. 594-610.
29. The statistical results to be discussed indicated no difference in results depending upon whether estimates of nominal or effective tariff rates were employed. Hence, we restrict our consideration to nominal tariff rates.

to greater efficiency supplied by foreign firms is proportional to the
share of an industry's sales controlled by subsidiaries.[30] Furthermore,
a larger population of subsidiaries in an industry will foster transfer
of technology to competing domestically owned firms. This view of
the spill over mechanism argues for using some measure of foreign
share as the appropriate foreign ownership variable. Thus, one proxy
for the spill over benefits provided by foreign direct investment was
the ratio of value added produced in foreign-owned plants to total
industry value added in 1972 F_{1i}. One could plausibly argue, however,
that the influence of foreign subsidiaries does not vary continuously
with the market share they command, but rather that any influence
becomes visible only as the foreign share gets relatively large. A
version of this hypothesis was tested by measuring the external
benefits of foreign direct investment as a binary variable F_{2i}, taking a
value of one if the share of industry value added produced in foreign-
owned plants exceeded 50 per cent in 1972 and zero otherwise.

Still a third specification of the productivity foreign investment
relationship can be justified which relates external benefits to the
absolute amount of foreign-controlled activity in an industry. Specifically, the value added in a domestically owned plant DV_j might be
assumed to be related to spill over benefits B_j by some simple and
direct transformation, e.g. $DV_j = \alpha B_j$, where α is constant for all
plants. The spill over benefits captured by a plant in industry i are in
turn assumed to be directly proportional to the amount of economic
activity accounted for by foreign-owned plants FV_i in the ith indus-
try.[31] Thus, $DV_{ji} = \alpha \cdot \delta(FV_i)$, where δ is the transformation relating
spill over benefits to subsidiary production, and

$$\sum_{j=1}^{N} DV_{ji} = N\alpha\delta(FV_i),$$

where N is the total number of domestically owned plants in the ith
industry. Dividing both terms by the number of employees in domestically owned plants implies the following relationship: labor productivity in domestically owned plants in the ith industry (the dependent variable) is a positive function of value added by foreign-owned
plants ($000) divided by total employees in domestically owned
plants F_{3i} in the ith industry for 1972.

30. Caves, "Multinational Firms", p. 178.
31. The assumption that spill overs captured by each domestically owned plant in an
   industry are directly proportional to the amount of subsidiary production in the
   industry embodies the notion that such spill overs have a public goods nature:
   that is, consumption by one domestically owned firm does not reduce the amount
   available for other firms.

Estimation and Statistical Results

We summarize the preceding discussion in the following functional form:

$$V_i = f(K_i, (L_{1i}, L_{2i}, L_{3i}), M_i, E_i, I_i, (F_{1i}, F_{2i}, F_{3i})),$$

where V_i is value added ($\$000$) in domestically owned plants in 1972 divided by total employees in domestically owned plants in 1972, and the independent variables are as previously defined. Table 1 reports results obtained from estimating alternative linear specifications of the basic productivity equation. The number of sample industries associated with the various estimations reflects the greater availability of data for certain variables than for others. In each equation the maximum number of industries was fixed by the constraint that data were available for all variables.

Equations (1) through (3) report results associated with different specifications of the foreign ownership variable and the L_{1i} specification of "labor quality". It can be seen that estimates obtained from the various equations are quite comparable. In all cases, the signs of the estimated coefficients are as expected; the K_i and E_i parameters are statistically significant at the 0.01 level. All other estimated parameters in all three equations are statistically insignificant at anything higher than the 0.10 level. The adjusted coefficients of determination are similar across the equations. On the basis of the overall and individual goodness-of-fit statistics there is somewhat greater support offered for the binomial specification of the foreign ownership variable. However, the efficiency of the F_{1i} and F_{3i} coefficients may suffer from mild collinearity between the two foreign ownership variables and the I_i variable.[32] Collinearity between the L_{1i} and the K_i variables may also be contributing to the inefficient estimates obtained for the L_{1i} variable.[33]

The results provided in equations (1) through (3) are essentially unaffected when the L_{2i} variable is substituted for the L_{1i} variable in the basic estimating equation.[34] Specifically, the parameters for the K_i and E_i variables are positive in sign and statistically significant at the 0.01 level in equations (4) through (6). The M_i and F_{2i} variables are

32. The zero-order partial correlation coefficient between F_{1i} and I_i equals 0.360, while the coefficient between F_{3i} and I_i equals 0.406.
33. The zero-order correlation coefficient between L_{1i} and K_i in equations (1) through (3) equals approximately 0.5.
34. In equation (4) through (10), the statistically insignificant interaction variable was dropped from the basic estimating equation to facilitate an increase in sample points and degrees of freedom. Nevertheless, restricted availability of data for the L_{2i} variable limited the number of sample industries to forty-two in equations (4) through (6).

Table 1

Regression Results for Sample Year 1972

Equation [industries]	Constant	K_i	L_{1i}	L_{2i}	L_{3i}	M_i	E_i	I_i	F_{1i}	F_{2i}	F_{3i}	$\bar{R}^2$
1 [49]	−12.3464	0.1331 (3.899)	0.4777 (1.332)			8.0749 (1.510)	7.1042 (2.964)	−0.0013 (0.362)	0.0269 (1.456)			0.650
2 [49]	−13.8229	0.1303 (3.818)	0.5924 (1.653)			8.6958 (1.624)	6.9726 (3.004)	−0.0014 (0.384)		1.4664 (1.635)		0.654
3 [49]	−8.7827	0.1357 (4.015)	0.4692 (1.303)			6.9087 (1.292)	6.4869 (2.849)	−0.0011 (0.300)			0.0123 (1.402)	0.648
4 [42]	−9.2293	0.1755 (5.689)		1.6352 (0.229)		8.6202 (1.735)	5.6316 (2.482)			1.7286 (1.710)		0.703
5 [42]	−7.4469	0.1699 (5.293)		1.1236 (0.146)		7.3711 (1.424)	6.1524 (2.511)		0.0324 (1.465)			0.697
6 [42]	−6.4943	0.1737 (5.376)		3.4451 (0.468)		7.3992 (1.382)	5.4335 (2.469)				0.0112 (1.113)	0.689
7 [61]	−8.7826	0.1393 (4.727)			0.8119 (1.905)	6.0798 (1.378)	4.5610 (2.125)			1.1688 (1.745)		0.654
8 [61]	−6.6259	0.1387 (4.744)			0.6551 (1.721)	5.6215 (1.190)	4.7984 (2.228)				0.0131 (1.946)	0.658
9 [61]	−8.9469	0.1384 (4.706)			0.6332 (1.654)	6.3479 (1.336)	5.3388 (2.331)		0.0259 (1.849)			0.656
10 [61]	−8.2599	0.1371 (4.623)	0.4125 (1.703)			7.0007 (1.579)	6.1864 (3.002)				0.0124 (1.840)	0.659

Note: t — statistics in parentheses; $\bar{R}^2$ is the adjusted coefficient of determination.

statistically significant at the 0.05 level in equation (4) but are insignificant in equations (5) and (6). The L_{2i} variable is statistically insignificant in all three equations. The insignificance of the L_{2i} variable might be taken as evidence that formal eduction measures, by ignoring on-the-job training and experiential learning, are bound to be poor proxies for embodied human capital in manufacturing establishments. Once again, the binomial foreign ownership variable outperforms the continuous specifications, although all three specifications are consistent in direction with the notion that foreign ownership provides spill over productivity benefits.

In equations (7) through (9), the labor quality parameters were estimated by using two-stage least squares.[35] The performances of both the labor quality and foreign ownership variables represent a substantial improvement over earlier equations. More specifically, coefficients for both variables are statistically significant at the 0.05 level, with the exception of the L_{3i} variable in equation (9). The K_i and E_i variables remain strong, although the efficiency of the E_i coefficient diminishes somewhat from earlier equations. The improved performances of the L_{3i} and F_i variables presumably reflect the salutary influence of added degrees of freedom in the presence of modest intercorrelation among various independent variables. This presumption is reinforced by equation (10), which indicates that the L_{1i} parameter is statistically significant at the 0.05 level for the full potential sample of industries.[36]

In reviewing the statistical results, we are led to conclude that the evidence for the existence of spill over efficiency benefits is ambivalent. However, the preponderance of evidence, particularly for the larger samples of industries, suggests that such benefits do indeed exist. Our results offer stronger support for the spill over benefits hypothesis than Caves was able to provide previously.[37]

Summary and Concluding Comments

Cross-section analysis of differences in labor productivity among Canadian-owned plants supports the notion that such differences derive in part from spill over efficiency benefits associated with foreign direct investment. Labor productivity differences are also

35. The instrumental variable for the second stage was obtained from the first-stage estimation in which total salaries and wages in domestically owned plants ($000) divided by total number of employees in domestically owned plants in 1972 was regressed against the L_{1i}, F_{3i}, E_i, and K_i variables.
36. The F_{3i} parameter remains statistically significant at the 0.05 level in equation (10).
37. Caves, "Multinational Firms".

related to an industry's capital intensity, plant-level economies of scale, and (less important) to average work hours per employee and proxy measures of labor quality. While the precise nature of such external benefits is not revealed by our statistical analysis, the large sample results suggest that foreign direct investment spill overs are related in a continuous fashion to foreign ownership in an industry.[38]

Some notion of the relative importance of intra-industry external benefits of foreign direct investment can be gathered by calculating mean elasticity coefficients for the foreign ownership variables and comparing them to similar coefficients calculated for the K_i and E_i variables. Estimation results for equations (8) and (9) establish representative values for the F_{1i} and F_{3i} specifications. The results (summarized in Table 2) indicate that the productivity effects of foreign investment spill overs are modest in comparison to the productivity effects of capital deepening. They are somewhat smaller

Table 2

Estimated Elasticity Coefficients

Equation	$\dfrac{dV_i}{dK_i}\dfrac{\overline{K_i}}{\overline{V_i}}$	$\dfrac{dV_i}{dE_i}\dfrac{\overline{E_i}}{\overline{V_i}}$	$\dfrac{dV_i}{dF_{1i}}\dfrac{\overline{F_{1i}}}{\overline{V_i}}$	$\dfrac{dV_i}{dF_{3i}}\dfrac{\overline{F_{3i}}}{\overline{V_i}}$
8	0.1631	0.0489		0.0335
9	0.1627	0.0546	0.0506	

than the productivity effects of increasing average plant size. However, there are reasons to believe that the spill over benefits estimated in this study understate the true magnitude of such benefits. For one thing, indirect benefits contributing to improving output quality or higher wages (and other payments to domestic factors) will not be directly captured by the productivity measure employed. For another, the estimation procedure captures intra-industry but not interindustry productivity spill overs.[39]

Quite clearly we need to know more about the precise nature and

38. It is not possible on the basis of our estimation results to determine unambiguously whether spill overs are more appropriately specified as a function of the absolute or relative amount of foreign ownership in an industry. In any case the two measures are highly correlated over our sample of Canadian manufacturing industries.

39. Conceptually one might attempt to estimate interindustry spill over benefits by utilizing intput-output flows among industries to estimate indirect foreign-owned production. Requisite data, however, are not to my knowledge available at the detailed industry level employed in this study.

magnitude of the indirect benefits of foreign ownership. Results in this chapter provide a firmer basis (than heretofore provided) for arguing that such benefits do indeed exist in Canadian manufacturing industries.

Appendix: Sources of Data

Variables
1. Total value added ($000) in domestically owned plants divided by total employees in domestically owned plants, 1972: Statistics Canada, *Domestic and Foreign Control of Manufacturing Establishments in Canada* (Ottawa: Information Canada, 1977), table 3.
2. Gross book value of depreciable assets at the end of 1971 ($ millions) divided by total employees 1972 (000s) in a comparably defined U.S. industry: Bureau of the Census (U.S.), *Annual Survey of Manufacturers 1970-71* (Washington: U.S. Government Printing Office, 1973), ch. 7, table 1.
3. Total salaries and wages ($000) in foreign-owned plants divided by total number of employees in foreign-owned plants, 1972: Statistics Canada, *Domestic and Foreign Control* (1977), table 3.
4. Total number of male employees with some university or with a university degree divided by total number of male employees, 15 years and older, 1971: Statistics Canada, *1971 Census of Canada*, (Ottawa: Information Canada, 1977), Vol. 3, pt. 5, table 1.
5. Total paid man-hours for production and related workers (000s) divided by the total number of production and related workers: Statistics Canada, *Domestic and Foreign Control* (1977), table 3.
6. Value added in U.S. plants for different percentages of total industry plants ($ millions), 1972: Bureau of the Census (U.S.), *Census of Manufacturers 1972*, Vol. 6 (Washington: U.S. Government Printing Office, 1975), table 8.
7. Nominal tariff rate, 1963: J. R. Melvin and B. W. Wilkinson, *Effective Protection in the Canadian Economy* (Ottawa: Queen's Printer, 1968), table 1.
8. Herfindhal concentration index based upon value of shipments, 1965: *Concentration in the Manufacturing Industries of Canada* (Ottawa: Minister of Consumer and Corporate Affairs, 1971), table A-1.
9. Total value added in foreign-owned plants (000s) in 1972: Statistics Canada, *Domestic and Foreign Control* (1977), table 3.

IV
Foreign Direct Investment Theory, Impact, and Control

D
Controls

27
The Foreign Investment Review Act

G. H. Dewhirst

Mr. Dewhirst is director general of the Policy Research and Communications Branch, Foreign Investment Review Agency. He was employed for a number of years as an economist with the Bank of Montreal. He joined the federal public service in 1967 and held a number of positions before moving to the Foreign Investment Review Agency in 1974.

This chapter was written expressly for this volume.

The Foreign Investment Review Act, while the subject of much debate since its inception in 1974, still generally remains a misunderstood piece of legislation. Contrary reports as to its purpose, its procedures, and the role of its major participants has led to a great deal of confusion among the public, the press, and the business community.

This chapter attempts to remove some of the misunderstandings by presenting a brief historical background to the act, the major provisions embodied in the act, and a description of the administrative processes involved.

An Historical Background

Throughout most of Canada's history, there were no restrictions on the flow of capital into Canada. In fact, most of Canada's earlier policies, including Sir John A. Macdonald's National Policy, were directed to encouraging capital inflows as a means of developing the Canadian economy. The first major investors were the British, whose funds were largely in the form of portfolio investments. But shortly after the First World War, the United States became the largest investor, for the most part establishing wholly owned or majority-owned Canadian subsidiaries.

This heavy influx of American foreign direct investment accelerated after the Second World War and was joined in the mid-1950s by similar types of investments from Europe. By 1970, 36 per cent of all assets in Canadian non-financial corporations were controlled by foreigners, including 69 per cent in the mining sector and 58 per cent in the manufacturing sector.[1] The United States controlled over 75 per cent of all foreign investments in the country.

The increased levels of foreign direct investment led to concern by many Canadians as to the possible harmful effects which such investments may cause for the Canadian economy. In response to this concern, the federal government commissioned four successive

1. Corporation and Labour Union Returns Act, *Annual Report, 1970*, Statistics Canada, Cat. #61-210 (March 1973), p. 12.

studies which, at least in part, discussed the effects of foreign investment — the Gordon Report (1958), the Watkins Report (1968), the Wahn Report (1970), and the Gray Report (1972).[2]

It is the last study, the Gray Report, which is the most significant in terms of current Canadian public policy. The report concluded that foreign direct investment has played, and will continue to play, an important role in Canada's economic development. However, accompanying foreign direct investment are often negative side effects which can be harmful to the long-term growth and development of the Canadian economy. The Gray Report therefore favored an administrative procedure which would allow for a case-by-case review of the benefits and costs of each individual investment. Those which were determined to be of overall benefit to Canada would be allowed to proceed while those which were not would be refused.

The Canadian government accepted this recommendation and introduced the Foreign Takeovers Review Bill in 1972. The bill only provided for the review of the acquisitions of companies in Canada by foreign interests. The bill died on the order paper, before it could obtain third reading. However, in the following year, another bill was introduced which provided not only for the review of acquisitions but also for the review of the establishment of new businesses by foreign-controlled interests. This bill was enacted by Parliament in 1973 and was entitled the Foreign Investment Review Act.

The Key Elements of the Act

The Foreign Investment Review Act applies to two forms of foreign investment:[3]

1. the acquisition of control of a Canadian business enterprise by foreign individuals, corporations, governments, or groups containing foreign members, through the acquisition of shares or of the property used in carrying on the business; and
2. the establishment of a new business in Canada either by foreign persons who do not already have an existing business in Canada, or by foreign persons who have an existing business in Canada,

---

2. *Royal Commission on Canada's Economic Prospects* (Ottawa: The Queen's Printer, 1958) (Commonly referred to as the Gordon Report); M. Watkins et al., *Foreign Ownership and the Structure of Canadian Industry, Report of the Task Force on the Structure of Canadian Industry* (Ottawa: The Queen's Printer, 1968); *Wahn Report, Eleventh Report of the Standing Committee on Defence and External Affairs Respecting Canada-U.S. Relations* (Ottawa: The Queen's Printer, 1970); Government of Canada, *Foreign Direct Investment in Canada* (Ottawa: Information Canada, 1972) (Commonly referred to as the Gray Report).
3. *Foreign Investment Review Act* (December 1973), Sections 3 and 4.

if the new business or expansion is unrelated to the existing business.

The act is not concerned with the acquisition of shares where the acquisition does not constitute control, as is the case with most portfolio investments. Nor is it concerned with the expansion of foreign-controlled businesses already in Canada into the same or related activities as their existing Canadian operations.

All foreign investments subject to the act must be reviewed by the government. If the government determines that an investment is of "significant benefit to Canada", then it is allowed to proceed. The act specifies five factors to be taken into account in assessing "significant benefit". These factors or criteria are:

1. the effect of the investment on the level and nature of economic activity in Canada, including the effect on employment, on resource processing, on the utilization of parts, components, and services produced in Canada, and on exports from Canada;
2. the degree and significance of participation by Canadians in the business enterprise and in the industry sector to which the enterprise belongs;
3. the effect on productivity, industrial efficiency, technological development, innovation, and product variety in Canada;
4. the effect on competition within any industry or industries in Canada; and
5. the compatibility of the investment with national industrial and economic policies, taking into consideration industrial and economic policy objectives enunciated by a province likely to be significantly affected by the proposed investment.[4]

The factors are, of course, given different weights according to the circumstances of individual cases. The types of industry in which the investment falls, the region in which the investment is being made, and the solvency of the company being acquired in acquisition cases will all affect the relative weights placed on the factors. It is not necessary that an investor demonstrate benefits with respect to each factor. Indeed, in the case of many investments, some of the factors may not even be relevant.

The act provides for the establishment of the Foreign Investment Review Agency to advise and assist the minister responsible for the administration of the act.[5] The responsible minister has always been the minister of Industry, Trade, and Commerce.

4. *Foreign Investment Review Act* (December 1973), Section 2(2).
5. *Foreign Investment Review Act* (December 1973), Section 7.

The minister is given a significant role in the administration of the act. Among other tasks, he is required to give individual opinions as to whether the investor is or is not a "non-eligible person" (that is, non-Canadian) and as to whether a proposed new business is or is not "related" to the investor's existing business in Canada.[6] He can issue a demand that a notice be filed when he has reasonable grounds to believe that a reviewable transaction is contemplated or has taken place.[7] It is also the minister who has the legal responsibility to review and assess each application and to make a recommendation to the governor-in-council (the cabinet) on whether to allow or disallow the transaction.

Finally, the minister is also empowered under the act to issue guidelines to clarify the intended interpretation of the various provisions of the act.[8] Guidelines have been issued concerning the application of the act to real estate transactions, certain transactions in the oil and gas industry, corporate reorganizations, and certain venture capital investments. The minister has also issued guidelines indicating how he intends to interpret the terms "new business" and "related business" for purposes of the act.

The final decision as to whether to allow or disallow a transaction lies solely with the governor-in-council. In fact, if one were to put in simple terms the process, one would note that *the agency advises*, *the minister recommends*, and *the governor-in-council decides* all cases subject to review. (For cumulative data on reviewable cases for acquisitions and new business, see Tables 1 and 2 at the end of this chapter.)

The Review Process

In the fiscal year 1979-80, 745 cases went through the review process including the governor-in-council's decisions to allow or disallow. Another 52 cases were withdrawn before a decision was made. In order to handle the substantial case load, the agency and the government have developed procedures which allow for as swift as possible processing of cases, given the need for consultation with provincial governments and other federal government departments. The procedures can be grouped into four categories: (1) the rulings process, in which it is determined whether a transaction is reviewable; (2) the assessment process, in which an application is assessed

6. *Foreign Investment Review Act* (December 1973), Section 4(1).
7. *Foreign Investment Review Act* (December 1973), Section 8(3).
8. *Foreign Investment Review Act* (December 1973), Section 4(2).

for significant benefit; (3) the decision-making process, in which the minister recommends and the governor-in-council makes the decision to allow or disallow the investment; and (4) the enforcement process, in which allowed investments are monitored to ensure that the investor's plans and undertakings are followed and in which disallowed investment proposals are watched to make certain that the investment does not take place. These processes are described briefly below.

The Rulings Process

Many companies or individuals approach the agency each year to find out whether their planned investment would be subject to review under the Foreign Investment Review Act. Their inquiries take one of three forms — an informal discussion on the intended meaning of the act or its guidelines, a request for an agency opinion, or a request for a ministerial opinion.

Generally, informal discussions take place over the telephone between the company or its legal counsel and one of the agency staff. Often company names are not mentioned. After the informal discussion, the company or its legal counsel would in most cases feel confident in determining whether or not the planned investment is reviewable. If not, then either an agency or ministerial opinion would be the next step.

There is no statutory authority for the offering of agency opinions. They are offered solely as a guide to the legal and business community and they are in no way binding on the minister. In other words, even after the agency has expressed an opinion that a transaction is not reviewable, the minister still has the option to require the investor to file an application if he concludes that the proposed investment is reviewable. However, in practical terms this is unlikely to occur as the minister has traditionally depended on agency personnel to offer expertise in the area of reviewability. On average, over 400 agency opinions regarding reviewability are given each year.

The issuing of ministerial opinions, on the other hand, is provided for in the act. Under Section 4(1), such opinions are binding on the minister for a period of two years provided that all material facts have been disclosed and the facts remain substantially unchanged for that period of time.

On the average, there have been about thirty applications for ministerial opinions per year. The vast majority of these have been for a ruling on whether an investor is a "non-eligible person". Many of these requests for eligibility rulings stem from a desire by a company to know its status vis-à-vis the act, but where no immediate investment is intended.

In fact, one of the side effects of the act has been that several firms have taken steps to "Canadianize" themselves so as to be free to invest without FIRA review. Slater, Walker of Canada Ltd., Bramalea Consolidated Developments Ltd., Dome Petroleum Ltd., and Dome Mines Ltd. are companies which have all stated so publicly. It is likely that others have done so but have not made their reasons public. In addition, firms newly established in Canada may have altered their original investment plans in order to become exempt from the act. Frequently, the agency is consulted by these firms to find out what is required to sufficiently "Canadianize" themselves.

On occasion, foreign investors planning to make a reviewable investment fail to file notice of their intention with the agency as required by law, usually because they are not aware of the existence or requirements of the act. For this reason, the agency has a surveillance division which keeps informed of new investments through the newspapers and other public sources. This task is aided by members of other government departments or by competitors of the investor who may inform the agency of the investment.

The Assessment Process

When it is clear that an investment is reviewable, it is then referred to the assessment branch of the agency. The functions of the assessment branch are to assist the investor (now called the applicant) in presenting the maximum significant benefit possible, to consult with provincial and federal government departments concerning the compatibility of the application with the government's economic and industrial policies for which they are responsible, to assess the degree of significant benefit which the application offers as defined in the act, and to express an opinion to the minister as to whether the significant benefit test has been met. Two established procedures have evolved, based on the size of the investment, which permit the expedient review of applications. These procedures are outlined below.

The Small Business Procedure. For those investments involving less than $2 million in assets and less than one hundred employees, since March 1977 the applicant only needs to fill out a shortened form requiring substantially less information than the standard long form. Over three-quarters of all investment proposals are under these threshold levels.

After formal receipt of the completed application, the minister has only ten days to decide whether the information provided in the abbreviated form will be sufficient to enable him to recommend that the investment be allowed. If such a recommendation is not forthcoming, the applicant is required to submit the standard form and go through the longer review. Generally, the small business procedure does not result in a veto, rather the applicant is referred to the standard procedure.

When an application is reviewed under the small business procedure, the agency notifies by Telex the governments of any province that may be significantly affected by the investment and any federal government department which may have a policy interest. Through prior arrangements with the federal and provincial departments, the agency has one contact within a federal department or provincial government to whom all required information will be sent. Within forty-eight hours, these departments must inform the agency if they have cause for concern about the investment or if they feel that they require more information.

Meanwhile the agency carries out its own evaluation. An assessment officer may contact the applicant for further information or may ask for certain commitments if the investment is allowed. Because of the shortness of time, there is rarely a chance for a meeting to be held, so contact with the applicant is normally over the telephone. After the responses from the provinces and federal government departments have been received, a decision is made whether to recommend to the minister that the case be allowed or that the applicant be required to submit the longer standard form (under Section 6(4) of the Foreign Investment Review Regulations). If the latter, the minister is sent a summary description of the case stating the reasons for recommending that more information be required. Normally no more than a week will have passed from the time that the application is received until a recommendation is made to the minister.

The Standard Procedure. For those applications involving investments which involve either more than $2 million in assets or more than one hundred employees, or for those applications referred from the small business procedure, the standard procedure is employed.

In this procedure, the entire application is sent out to the provincial governments where the investment is taking place. Provincial contacts are usually in the Department of Industry or its equivalent. It is the responsibility of these contacts to inform any departments within their provincial government who may have some interest in the decision. Provincial views, if any, are an important consideration in the decision of the governor-in-council to allow or not to allow a particular investment proposal.

Agency statistics show the percentage of disagreement between the provinces and the federal government to be extremely low. A recent internal survey showed that in over 97 per cent of the resolved cases the final decision to allow or disallow a particular transaction has been in agreement with the opinion expressed by the province or provinces consulted. Even then, in almost one-third of the cases where disagreement occurred, more than one province was consulted and the opinions offered were not in agreement with each other. Therefore, no matter what the final decision was, a federal/ provincial disagreement would have arisen.

The internal survey noted several reasons for the high degree of consensus. Among the reasons suggested were the tendency of both the federal and provincial governments to support investment in general; the fact that many of the provincial responses are neutral in tone, being couched in such terms as "not incompatible with" or "not opposed to"; and the attempts by the agency to reconcile differences, possibly through the obtaining of certain undertakings.

Other federal government departments are also consulted. For instance, all standard procedure cases are sent to the Department of Consumer and Corporate Affairs for comment on the effect the investment will have on competition. The Department of Industry, Trade, and Commerce, as the department most responsible for industrial policy, receives the majority of cases. Other departments often consulted, but much less frequently, are the Department of Energy, Mines, and Resources, the Department of Regional Economic Expansion (which is consulted on all cases in which there is also an application before it), the Department of Communications, and the Secretary of State.

Meanwhile the agency works closely with the applicant, or its legal representative. The way negotiations are carried out will vary with individual circumstances. However, in the majority of standard procedure cases, the following pattern occurs. When the application has been certified as complete, the agency invites the applicant to Ottawa for a meeting. The applicant is normally represented by someone knowledgeable about the parent company operations, by someone knowledgeable about the new business or the business being acquired, and by legal counsel. The agency is usually represented by two assessment officers.

The meeting normally commences with a brief description of the parent operations and of the planned investment. The applicant's representatives state why they believe the investment could benefit

Canada. The agency personnel may suggest ways in which the proposal could be improved to show significant benefit to Canada. Every effort is made to assist applicants to make investment proposals as complete and precise as possible. While commitments or undertakings by the applicant are not mandatory, it is obvious that this can often help the applicant to make his proposal complete and precise, and thus allow the government to assess with greater certainty the effects of the investment. Undertakings are, of course, binding on the applicant if the investment is allowed, and there are provisions in the act whereby, in case of non-compliance, the minister *may* apply to the courts for remedial orders. But it has been made clear that the government recognizes that plans and undertakings are inevitably based, to some extent, on conjecture as to future conditions. Accordingly there is an obligation on the government to take reasonable account of unforeseen changes in conditions or prospects in considering cases of non-compliance. So far all instances of non-compliance with undertakings have been dealt with (sometimes through the re-negotiation of undertakings to reflect changed conditions) without recourse to the courts.

Undertakings are only one of the elements which must be assessed. Certain features of an investment may be found to be of significant benefit to Canada without being specifically covered by undertakings. For example, a proposal to establish a new business which uses important new technology might be seen as intrinsically beneficial through its contribution to technology development. Similarly, a proposal by one small business to merge with another in an industry dominated by a few large firms might well be seen as likely to increase effective competition in that industry. Again there would hardly be any need for an undertaking to that effect.

The assessment officer, in some ways, wears two hats. While he is there to assist the applicant in making the best investment proposal possible, he is also the first step in the evaluation of the proposal for determining significant benefit. This has some practical advantages in that the assessment officer has a good understanding of what kinds of undertakings would be required in a particular case to tip the scales in favor of allowance.

Usually after the initial meeting, the applicant and his lawyer will draw up a list of undertakings for submission to the agency. Another meeting may be required, although more often further negotiations are handled over the telephone and confirmed by letter or Telex.

If, within sixty days from the date of certification, the minister is unable to complete an assessment or make any recommendation to the governor-in-council or he is unable to recommend allowance, a notice is sent out informing the applicant and advising him of his right to submit representations. This notice is required under Section 11(1) of the act.

The type of Section 11(1) notice sent out is dictated by how the application is faring. Most Section 11(1) notices state that the minister "is unable to complete the assessment with regard to the investment" which generally means that the applicant has not yet completed his undertakings or that the application has been delayed for some other reason. But if the Section 11(1) notice states that the minister "is unable to make any recommendation to governor-in-council regarding the investment . . ." then it suggests to the applicant that he should strengthen his undertakings. In the case of very weak undertakings, the Section 11(1) notice will state that the minister is "unable to recommend to the governor-in-council that the investment . . . be allowed". Generally, all cases which are heading towards a disallowance are sent a Section 11(1) notice with the invitation to the company to make further representations.

When the agency has completed its analysis, agency officials draft a memorandum for the minister's signature. The degree of detail of the memorandum depends on the size and importance of the case (as will be discussed in the next section). Within the memorandum is the agency opinion on whether or not the proposal meets the test of "significant benefit to Canada". With the assessment procedure completed, the application moves to the political forum, where the ultimate decision to allow or disallow rests.

The Decision-Making Process

As noted above, in order to meet the statutory requirements as specified in the Foreign Investment Review Act, the minister must, for each case, review the information gathered by the agency, assess the level of significant benefit in light of the five factors stated in Section 2(2), and make a recommendation to the governor-in-council as to whether the application should be allowed or disallowed.

Of course, the minister has the choice of accepting or rejecting the advice of the agency. However, addressing the House of Commons Standing Committee on Finance, Trade, and Economic Affairs, Mr. Gorse Howarth, the commissioner of the agency, said, "Without attempting any precision I would give as an indication that probably in 96 or 97 per cent of cases the advice given by the agency is compatible with the minister's recommendation to his colleagues."[9]

9. The House of Commons Standing Committee on Finance, Trade, and Economic Affairs (April 11, 1978).

The high degree of consensus should not be surprising. The agency does not work in a vacuum. It is aware of the minister's concerns about certain criteria (such as research and development or exports), about certain industries, and about certain sensitive cases. In addition, the minister is kept aware of sensitive cases on a continual basis and may offer comments as the case is proceeding through the assessment process.

Once the minister has decided upon his recommendation, the application proceeds to cabinet. The procedure used by the cabinet depends basically on the size of the case. For most cases involving under $2 million in assets and under one hundred employees, a summary sheet with the minister's recommendation and all the salient details is prepared and sent to the Special Committee of Council for governor-in-council approval. While there may be some brief discussion, most of the minister's recommendations are approved without comment. Approximately three of every four cases are handled through this summary procedure.

For the larger cases, for cases where there is provincial disagreement, or for cases where the minister wishes to consult with his colleagues, a detailed memorandum to cabinet is prepared. The memorandum is sent to the Cabinet Committee on Economic Development, where a serious evaluation takes place. After the committee makes a decision, the application is passed on to cabinet for ratification.[10]

When a governor-in-council decision is taken, the agency telephones or sends a Telex to the applicant informing him of the decision. About a week later, a certified copy of the order in council is sent out to the company. A copy is also sent out to the provinces. The press and the public are informed the day after the decision by means of a press release issued by the minister.

The case then becomes the responsibility of the enforcement division of the agency, the fourth and final procedure relating to the administration of the Foreign Investment Review Act.

The Enforcement Process
The enforcement process embodies two major monitoring responsibilities. For those cases which are disallowed, the agency must make certain that the investment does not take place, or if it already

10. For a more detailed discussion of the decision-making process, see R. Schultz, F. Swedlove, and K. Swinton, "The Cabinet as a Regulatory Body: The Case of the Foreign Investment Review Act", (Working Paper #6, Economic Council of Canada, Regulation Reference, August, 1980).

has, that there be compliance with the disallowance order. For those which are allowed, it must ensure that plans and undertakings offered by the applicant are put into force. With about 2,500 decisions made under the act by the end of March 1980, the enforcement process is arduous, yet significant.

The most difficult enforcement procedure probably involves divestiture of investments in certain disallowed cases. A letter is sent from the agency four to six weeks after the disallowance asking the applicant to state his plan for compliance. The applicant has three choices. He may attempt to sell the target company or new business to a third party. He may consider submitting a second application to the government with improved undertakings. Or, he may wish to wind down the investment — an alternative which the government finds least desirable.

A survey of sixty-four disallowed acquisition cases was carried out by the agency and reported in its 1977/78 Annual Report.[11] In seventeen of the cases (or about one in four), the original applicant subsequently made another application. Fifteen of these were allowed and two were disallowed. In sixteen other disallowed cases, the acquiree businesses were subsequently purchased by other investors, fourteen of whom were Canadian-controlled companies. In only four of the cases did the target business cease operations. The survey notes that "each of the four was a small business, averaging $0.5 million in assets, and each had been unprofitable for some time".[12]

Obviously, a company faced with divestiture requires time to find a buyer and to sever past ties. The agency has shown a willingness to meet with the companies involved and to work out a timetable with which the company can live. Divestiture may take anywhere from a month to a few years. For example, a case which attracted a great deal of publicity was the N.V. Indivers attempted acquisition of Canadian Vac-Hyd Processing Limited. Indivers acquired a 52 per cent interest in Canadian Vac-Hyd in 1975, when it acquired control of Vac-Hyd Processing Corporation of the United States. However, the case was disallowed by the federal government in May of 1976. It was not until March of 1978 that Indivers was able to come to an agreement with a Canadian buyer. In the press release issued by Canadian Vac-Hyd of the announced Canadian purchase, the assistance of the Foreign Investment Review Agency was recognized.

11. Foreign Investment Review Agency, 1977/78 Annual Report (Ottawa, October, 1978), pp. 21-23.
12. 1977/78 Annual Report, p. 23.

The monitoring of plans and undertakings offered by applicants is the most time-consuming task in the enforcement procedure. One year after the date of allowance, the agency sends the investor a form setting out his plans and undertakings and requesting a performance report on compliance to date. This procedure is followed until all the plans and undertakings have been met.

While in most of the cases written statements from the company are accepted without further verification, random on-site spot checks are conducted by enforcement personnel to confirm that the responses are accurate. Enforcement officers also conduct investigations of "problem" cases and have on a number of occasions used the statutory investigation provisions (Section 15 of the act) to conduct formal inquiries.

In some cases, non-compliance will occur because of an unexpected downturn in the investor's market, a factor which is beyond the investor's control. In situations such as this, the agency has followed the statement of Mr. Gillespie, then minister of Industry, Trade and Commerce, to the Standing Committee on Finance, Trade, and Economic Affairs. He stated, "If, however, the failure to comply with an undertaking is clearly the result of changed market conditions — for example, the undertaking to export frisbees is followed by the collapse of the frisbee market — the person would not be held accountable."[13]

If full compliance of the undertakings is not waived, the agency may attempt to renegotiate the undertakings package. The key to the renegotiations, as far as the agency is concerned, is that the new undertakings package would be equal, if not superior, to the original undertakings in terms of benefit to Canada. Failure to meet one type of undertaking can be compensated for by improving on another type.

13. House of Commons, Standing Committee on Finance, Trade, and Economic Affairs Proceedings No. 26 (June 5, 1973), p. 6.

Table 1

Acquisitions — Reviewable Cases

Status of Cases by Applicant's (Apparent) Country of Control from April 9, 1974 to June 30, 1980

	Total Number of Cases	Allowed	Disallowed	Withdrawn	Total	Unresolved
United States	1049	817	92	70	979	70
United Kingdom	228	178	17	15	210	18
Other Europe						
Austria	1	1	—	—	1	—
Belgium	9	7	—	2	9	—
Denmark	5	4	—	1	5	—
Finland	3	2	—	1	3	—
France	39	28	5	4	37	2
Germany, W.	80	68	3	5	76	4
Greece	1	1	—	—	1	—
Italy	11	9	—	1	10	1
Liechtenstein	7	4	—	3	7	—
Luxembourg	4	4	—	—	4	—
Netherlands	28	20	4	3	27	1
Norway	2	1	—	1	2	—
Spain	1	—	—	1	1	—
Sweden	37	32	—	—	32	5
Switzerland	43	29	4	4	37	6
Sub-Total	271	210	16	26	252	19
All Other						
Non-Resident Cdn	8	7	—	—	7	1
Argentina	1	1	—	—	1	—
Australia	10	7	2	—	9	1
Bahamas	1	1	—	—	1	—
Bermuda	5	4	—	1	6	—
Brazil	1	—	—	1	1	—
Czechoslovakia	1	1	—	—	1	—
Hong Kong	2	—	1	1	2	—
India	1	—	—	1	1	—
Iran	2	2	—	—	2	—
Japan	21	15	2	3	20	1
Jordan	1	1	—	—	1	—
Kuwait	2	1	—	1	2	—
Lebanon	1	1	—	—	1	—
Malaysia	1	1	—	—	1	—
Mexico	1	—	—	1	1	—
Panama	3	2	1	—	3	—
Saudi Arabia	3	3	—	—	3	—
South Africa	4	4	—	—	4	—
Tanzania	1	1	—	—	1	—
United Arab Emirates	1	—	—	—	—	1
Sub-Total	71	52	6	9	67	4
Total	**1,619**	**1,257**	**131**	**120**	**1,508**	**111**

Resolved Cases Only

	U.S.A.	United Kingdom	Other Europe	All Other
Allowed	83.4%	84.8%	83.3%	77.6%
Disallowed	9.4%	8.1%	6.4%	9.0%
Withdrawn	7.2%	7.1%	10.3%	13.4%
Total	100.0%	100.0%	100.0%	100.0%

Table 2

New Business — Reviewable Cases

Status of New Business Cases by Applicant's (Apparent) Country of Control from
October 15, 1975 to June 30, 1980

	Total Number of Cases	Resolved Cases				Unresolved
		Allowed	Disallowed	Withdrawn	Total	
United States	789	639	46	57	742	47
United Kingdom	138	112	7	9	128	10
Other Europe						
Austria	4	4	—	—	4	—
Belgium	7	7	—	—	7	—
Denmark	21	18	1	1	20	1
Finland	11	8	—	1	9	2
France	63	56	4	1	61	2
Germany, West	97	83	4	6	93	4
Gibraltar	1	—	—	—	—	1
Greece	3	1	—	1	2	1
Ireland	2	2	—	—	2	—
Italy	46	36	1	6	43	3
Liechtenstein	3	3	—	—	3	—
Luxembourg	1	1	—	—	1	—
Monaco	1	1	—	—	1	—
Netherlands	16	12	—	—	12	4
Norway	9	6	—	1	7	2
Portugal	1	1	—	—	1	—
Spain	6	6	—	—	6	—
Sweden	30	22	2	3	27	3
Switzerland	47	40	1	5	46	1
Sub-Total	369	307	13	25	345	24
All Other						
Non-Resident Cdn	6	6	—	—	6	—
Argentina	1	—	—	1	1	—
Australia	12	10	1	—	11	1
Bahamas	1	1	—	—	1	—
Bermuda	2	2	—	—	2	—
Brazil	2	2	—	—	2	—
Cuba	1	1	—	—	1	—
Ecuador	1	1	—	—	1	—
El Salvador	1	1	—	—	1	—
Guadalope	1	1	—	—	1	—
Guyana	3	3	—	—	3	—
Haiti	1	—	1	—	1	—
Hong Kong	16	12	1	1	14	2
India	6	5	—	1	6	—
Indonesia	1	1	—	—	1	—
Iran	3	3	—	—	3	—
Israel	3	3	—	—	3	—
Japan	38	25	6	6	37	1
Jordan	2	2	—	—	2	—
Korea	4	3	—	1	4	—
Kuwait	2	1	—	1	2	—
Lebanon	2	2	—	—	2	—
Mexico	4	3	—	1	4	—
Netherlands Antilles	3	3	—	—	3	—
New Zealand	1	1	—	—	1	—
Pakistan	1	1	—	—	1	—
Philippines	3	2	1	—	2	1
Singapore	3	2	—	—	2	1
South Africa	10	8	2	—	10	—
Taiwan	4	3	—	1	4	—
Trinidad	1	—	—	1	1	—
Turkey	1	1	—	—	1	—
USSR	1	—	—	1	1	—
Yugoslavia	2	1	—	—	1	1
Sub-Total	143	110	12	15	137	6
Total	1,439	1,168	78	106	1,352	87

Resolved Cases Only

	U.S.A.	United Kingdom	Other Europe	All Other
Allowed	86.1%	87.5%	89.0%	80.3%
Disallowed	6.2%	5.5%	3.8%	8.8%
Withdrawn	7.7%	7.0%	7.2%	10.9%
Total	100.0%	100.0%	100.0%	100.0%

IV
Foreign Direct Investment Theory, Impact, and Control

D
Controls

28
Foreign Investment Review Act: Comments by a Concerned Dutch Party

Bert Twaalfhoven

Mr. Twaalfhoven is president and founder of N. V. Indivers, Amsterdam, a company with eighteen plants in seven countries specialized in servicing the engine market and the aluminum and plastic industries through its tooling companies. A graduate of Harvard Business School, he worked for Alcan in Montreal for three years before founding an aluminum extrusion company in 1959, the first Canadian-Netherlands joint venture in the Netherlands since the war. His present company, N. V. Indivers, was founded in 1963 and has grown rapidly through acquisitions and new activities.

The material in this chapter appeared originally in *The Business Quarterly*, Spring 1978. Reprinted by permission.

Introduction

Foreign investors, who want to establish a new business in Canada or acquire an existing Canadian business, need the approval of the Canadian Federal Cabinet according to the Foreign Investment Review Act.

We, Indivers, a Dutch firm, purchased in 1975 a U.S. corporation Vac-Hyd Processing Corporation. With this purchase we acquired indirect control of Vac-Hyd's successful subsidiaries in Canada and Germany, which are involved in the business of treating metal for aerospace and industrial purposes. As our case has dragged on in FIRA for more than a year, we have had the opportunity to closely watch the workings of the law and the agency and can now present our views.

The Growing Dilemma

Since Canada — as well as the Netherlands — is greatly dependent on import and export, it cannot live without free trade. Foreign investment in Canada is essential if Canada is to:

—develop its manufacturing industries;
—reduce regional disparities;
—achieve its energy and production goals;
—attract sufficient financial resources
  • for maintaining growth
  • for providing employment opportunities;
—secure international exchange of entrepreneurship and technology;
—provide for continuation of the increase of the per capita income
  (400 per cent over the last ten years, against 250 per cent in the
  U.S.A., not adjusted for inflation).[1]

	Canada	U.S.A.
1967	$2,095	$3,279
1977	$8,406	$8,697 (preliminary estimate)

1. U.S. National Bureau of Statistics.

Furthermore, the semi-annual survey of capital investment intentions of major businesses in Canada, carried out by the Department of Industry, Trade, and Commerce, indicates that foreign-controlled firms included in the survey are planning to increase their capital expenditures at a much faster rate than are Canadian-controlled firms (manufacturing sector 1976 + 33 per cent/ + 20 per cent, non-manufacturing sector 1976 + 41 per cent/17 per cent).[2] Generally speaking, it appears to have always been federal government policy to recognize the necessity of foreign investment and the investment climate has always been attractive for foreign — mostly U.S. — investors due to:

—Canada's wealth in minerals, energy, food products, and timber;
—Canada's population density and location[3]
  • with only 0.06 per cent of the world's population, Canada has 6.8 per cent of the world's land,
  • the population is concentrated in certain areas: 50 per cent of Canada's people live within 125 miles of the U.S. Border, 90 per cent within 225 miles, so the market is not as costly to reach as the population density would suggest. This market is a fast growing, relatively high-income market as appears from the GNP per capita figures;
—Canada's tariffs: a foreign producer might find it advantageous to move behind this barrier and take advantage of it rather than try to export from plants in the home country.

Canada's need for foreign investment and the attractive investment climate — as described — have resulted in a precarious relationship for the autonomy of Canada's economy between local and foreign control of Canada's entire manufacturing industry.

Almost 60 per cent of Canada's entire manufacturing industry is controlled by non-Canadians. About three-quarters of the permanent capital employed in Canada's petroleum and natural gas industry and more than half of the permanent capital employed in mining and smelting is controlled by residents of other countries. The figure of 60 per cent in manufacturing is, of course, an average which conceals some even more startling characteristics. Ninety-nine per cent of the permanent capital employed in Canada's rubber industry, for example, is controlled by non-residents. For automobiles and parts the percentage is 96, for chemicals and pharmaceuticals it is 86 per cent,

2. Notes dictated for an address delivered to a Harvard Business School Seminar on Canadian-U.S. relations, Nov. 3, 1976.
3. Harvard Business School, "The Canadian Development Corporation", 1-375-133/ REV 9/75, p. 2.

and for electrical apparatus it is 73 per cent.[4] Roughly 80 per cent of the non-resident controlled capital invested in Canada represents U.S. investment. One recognizes that foreign control can impose serious limitations on the ability of Canadians to pursue economic policies geared to their own needs and objectives, a reason the Canadian federal government — understandably — interfered especially with respect to "direct" or equity investment, which involves ownership and control and consequently foreign domination.

Why FIRA?

A number of reasons can be listed why Canada wants to slow down foreign investment:

— The high and growing degree of foreign control of Canadians' business activity can affect the balance between the manufacturing and resource sectors of the Canadian economy, and between the various sectors of manufacturing.
— The investment decisions of foreign-controlled corporations tend to reflect the laws and industrial priorities of foreign governments and economics which, in turn, influence Canadian industrial priorities.
— The anticipated high level of demand for resources by foreign economies could lead to undue emphasis on resource development in the coming decades; this, in turn, could impose major limitations on the ability of Canadians in the future to formulate an industrial development policy geared to Canada's own particular growth and employment objectives.
— Since the balance of interest and dividend is larger than the balance of trade (export suplus) foreign-controlled manufacturing industry results in fund outflow.

Export 1976: C. $37,976 billion, Import C. $36,886 billion, so while the Canadian balance of trade is about in balance, Canada sells 2½ times as much to Holland as it buys from Holland. The trade position of Canada with Holland is relatively more favorable to Canada than with almost any other country.

The transfer of interest and dividends is highly negative. In 1976 Canada:

	Received	**Paid**
Interest and Dividends	C.$853 million	C.$3.344 million[5]

4. An address delivered to a Harvard Business School Seminar, 1976.
5. *London Economist Weekly*.

—However, it is dangerous to generalize about the behavior of foreign-controlled companies. Many Canadian subsidiaries of foreign corporations enjoy a considerable degree of autonomy, are managed by Canadians, include Canadians among their shareholders, and in general have the freedom to operate and develop in response to market forces in much the same way as domestically controlled corporations. But there are also some subsidiaries of foreign companies in Canada which have no Canadian shareholders, which do not disclose any financial information on their Canadian operations, which import most, if not all, of their parts and services from their parents, which rely entirely on their parents for research and development and which are restricted from doing business except in certain designated marketing areas. The managers of the parent company could in such cases be concerned primarily with increasing profits of the enterprise as a whole, and with its long-term growth.

This shows the dilemma with which Canada is currently faced. The main question "does Canada wish to sacrifice the high standard of living for an economy more controlled by itself?" is a question that needs to be answered selectively. As appears from the following points, Canada's investment climate continues to slump seriously, although investment is currently picking up all over the world.

—Direct foreign investment in Canada dropped from $925 million in 1971 to $670 million in 1975. The federal control program began in 1975; the inflow in Canada since then has dropped to $245 million[6] in 1977.

—Canadian investors are joining the trend, sending their money out of the country; direct investments by Canadians abroad has been increasing steadily from $230 million[7] in 1971 and $795 million[8] in 1975 to $565 million[9] in 1977. This increase in capital outflow for direct investment might also lead to the conclusion that the business community including Canadians themselves, has felt that the investment climate is more promising in other countries.

—Furthermore, the "high" rate of inflation, escalating wages and costs of production, lagging productivity, an artificially high interest rate structure, the government freeze on corporate profits and the restriction on dividend payments, increasing government intervention and the even louder growl of Canadian nationalism, accompanying actions against foreign interests in Canada, do not

6. *Ibid.*
7. *Ibid.*
8. *Ibid.*
9. *Bank of Canada Review* (December 1977).

contribute currently to the attractiveness of the Canadian investment climate.

—Finally, transfer of ownership of the foreign parent and with the
parent the Canadian subsidiary, involves reviewing by the FIRA as
well. In principle, the transfer of ownership can be blocked:
instead of approving the transfer, the review agency can seek out
an alternative Canadian purchaser (see the case of the blocking of
the transfer of ownership in Canada, when White Industries U.S.A.
acquired control of the appliance division of Westinghouse worldwide).

Under the recent development of trade restrictions and nationalistic
development is there not a risk that *countermeasures* will be taken?
To illustrate: Suppose Holland has the same legislation as Canada, and
suppose Alcan Montreal buys Reynolds Virginia, the Dutch government
would have jurisdiction over the subsidiary in Holland (Reynolds
Harderwijk) and could say that since the takeover does not contribute
to the benefit of Holland, we restrict the sale to Dutch nationals. This
kind of protectionist measure prevents companies that will invest in
Canada with probably vast benefits for the country from action that
internationally oriented countries like Canada and the Netherlands
need. Export/import is 60 per cent of GNP in the Netherlands, 25
per cent in Canada. Both are dependent on free world trade, Canada
being too large for the Canadians, the Netherlands being too small
for the Dutch. Since the number of Canadian candidates is limited,
the value of the investment decreases in case of a possible takeover of
the parent.

Questions Raised by the Dutch Case: Indivers Vac-Hyd

In the case of Indivers, we purchased a U.S. company that founded
and owned the Canadian enterprise. Legally there is no change in
ownership. Canada claims jurisdiction. Does this mean that the transfer of one U.S. enterprise to another with Canadian subsidiaries can
be challenged by FIRA, Ottawa, even though the transaction has taken
place outside of Canada? Does the business community in the U.S.
and Europe realize that in the future any such transaction could affect
the value of their Canadian subsidiaries to a serious extent? How can
any foreign enterprise invest substantially in Canada even with approval of FIRA, if there is no guarantee that several years later they can
sell their company or transfer their company to another outsider?
Particularly in the area of specialized multinational industries the
price of such investment in Canada would decline substantially if the
company can only be sold to local interested parties.

It must be made clear that I certainly do agree that some government control of foreign investment in Canada is necessary, however, one should not kill the goose that lays the golden eggs. The one solution I see to effectively control foreign investments is openly clarifying all the aspects leading to the decision. The current secrecy and confusion about takeover rules do not give companies an opportunity to adapt to the requirements for foreign investment. At this moment:

—the reasons for principle approval or disapproval are too general;
—the reasons underlying the cabinet's decision are secret. Therefore it becomes impossible to adapt the undertaking for the benefit of Canada.

Reasons Underlying the Decision Are Too General

Lawrence A. Wright already pointed out in his articles on FIRA in *The Business Quarterly* of Autumn 1976 and Autumn 1977 that the foreign investor should prepare for the review process of his application not by developing plans which may legally fit within the statutory factors, but by preparing a proposal:

—which stresses that the company's goals are not to control the Canadian market;
—which demonstrates significant benefits for Canada in general and for the provinces affected by the proposed investment in particular.

As a result of Wright's experiences and dealings with the agency, and his study of the review process, he made some ten observations concerning "significant benefits".[10] According to our opinion, our undertakings answered most of the requirements, for example:

—Indivers limits dividends to 20 per cent of net earnings; the remainder of cash flow — net earnings and depreciation — will be re-invested in the company. Beyond this the controlling company undertakes to invest substantial funds in the Canadian subsidiary for expansion and updating equipment and techniques.

   Indivers' track record can be witnessed from the following: it started its activities in 1963 with 5 employees, provides employment today for 610 persons and exports to thirty-two countries. Investments of U.S. $3 million were made in 1977, some of it diverted from original plans destined for Canadian Vac-Hyd.

10. *The Business Quarterly* (Autumn 1977), pp. 17 and 91.

—Indivers included in the proposal the establishment in Canada of some research and development facilities: it proposed to spend 1 per cent of net sales on research and development to be conducted in Canada.

—Indivers also answered the requirements of Canadian management creating employment and relying on Canadian materials. The two factories concerned are managed by Canadian citizens; on the board of directors of Canadian Vac-Hyd, the majority are Canadian citizens. The above-mentioned investment programs will increase employment 100 per cent in the following two years. As for the "snowball effect": it is the company's policy to continue to rely on Canadian materials to the fullest extent.

—Also the development of export markets mentioned by Wright was included in the proposal: As Canadian Vac-Hyd has not exported significantly in the past — while the controlling company is strongly export-oriented (70-75 percent of total sales volume), the concept and approach of export marketing will be stressed; a new function — export sales manager — will be introduced in the Canadian subsidiary.

Although the benefits for Canadian Vac-Hyd and the Canadian economy from a continuous link with the U.S.-based parent company of Canadian Vac-Hyd and the internationally active Indivers Group were extensively highlighted, the proposal has been disapproved. Furthermore, Vac-Hyd is not a dominant force in the market place in terms of Canada's competition legislation and is not an industry which should be the preserve of Canadian-controlled firms. On the contrary, the industry needs to be international to be viable. From our point of view, the general principles underlying the government's decision on Vac-Hyd seem to have been met and in spite of this the proposal has been refused.

Missed Opportunities in the Indivers Vac-Hyd Case

Being the FIRA guinea pig had — and still increasingly has — a very unsettling and adverse impact on our Canadian business. During this period the development of a five-year plan and strategy to the benefit of the company could not be made; the Department of Trade of Ontario withdrew a major subsidy for new investment; results declined drastically and opportunities were missed. While the other Indivers and Vac-Hyd activities have expanded sustantially, the sales of Vac-Hyd Canada dropped 14 per cent in 1977 while profits have declined by 87 per cent.

Since the Indivers takeover, sales of the Vac-Hyd operations in Germany have increased by 51 per cent and employment by 84 per cent; sales of the Indivers Turbine Division have increased by 250 per cent and employment has increased by 40 per cent. We know that Canadian Vac-Hyd would have experienced similar increases if we had been permitted to carry out our undertakings to FIRA. Furthermore, with the opening of the Vac-Hyd plant in Singapore in January 1978 a further export market would have opened up to Canadian Vac-Hyd.

The Reasons Underlying the Cabinet's Decision Are Secret

It is difficult to predict whether the Canadian federal cabinet will approve a foreign investment as being of signficant benefit to Canada within the meaning of the Foreign Investment Review Act because:

—Cabinet deliberations are secret;
—Anticipation of the decision is not possible;
  —reasons for disapproval can even be political, regardless of the merits of the application on an economic basis;
  —reasons for disapproval are not given, not even to the parties directly involved in the review process;
  —reasons for approval, if published, are of no assistance in terms of establishing guidelines as to the federal cabinet thinking.
—Applicants have no opportunity to counter representations from outsiders, who may be opposed to the investment (if they are aware that such representations are made!); experience has indicated that opposition from a province or local Canadian management will very likely be fatal to the success of an application.
  The provincial governments where the factories are to be established or operate, are all-powerful in the decision whether to admit or reject foreign companies. While Indivers at no time had an opportunity to discuss in detail its contribution to Canada with the province, the province did decide on the basis of *local* representations that the entry of Indivers is not beneficial. While the province is understandably subjective, in our opinion a chance should be given for comparing benefits contributed to Canada by Canadians vis-à-vis benefits contributed by an outsider.

The above mentioned secrecy about takeover rules, the absence of clear guidelines, the inaccessibility of criteria on how and why the agency and the cabinet arrive at decisions, the so-called confidentiality of the process of screening foreign takeovers of existing Canadian companies and the involved red tape and discouraging delays make the foreign investors hesitant, including those that could contribute significant benefits to the Canadian economy.

Until the air can be cleared with respect to the practical implications of the FIRA, the outlook facing new foreign investment — still most desirable for further economic development in Canada — will remain clouded. Canada's nationalistic policy to help slow foreign economic control is necessary, but needs to move out of the cocoon of secrecy if "significant benefit" investors will be helped to direct their commitments in the direction that is favorable to Canada. The agency staff, supported by the province, should make an effort to tell the foreign investor what would be acceptable, or when the proposal will be approved, provided the foreign investor does this or that. Only then can the agency play an active role in the controlling and redirecting of foreign investments, thus ensuring that such investments benefit Canada; selected and controlled foreign investment enhances Canadian entrepreneurship and encourages Canadian investment.

A Foreign Investor Cannot Determine How to Adapt

Since the FIRA is not a tribunal that has decision-making powers and since the minister of Industry, Trade, and Commerce does not always make recommendations to the cabinet according to the advice of the FIRA, the FIRA cannot be considered as being of much assistance to the foreign investor. Furthermore the FIRA plays the role of negotiating party, trying to maximize the benefits and minimize the costs from the point of view of Canada. So the foreign investor has to determine himself:

—how to maximize the benefits and minimize the threats of the investment for Canada;
—how to prevent opposition from a province or local Canadian management;
—the reasonableness and profitability of the return on his investment in the light of the restrictions with respect to a possible sale or merger of the (foreign parent) company in the future.

As appears from the Indivers case, this determination process is quite an impossible activity, since the results of this process did not seem to help the re-application. If an open dialogue could have taken place between Indivers and all interested parties, especially the province, a more objective review of the case could have been established.

If we had been given an opportunity by both federal and provincial governments to respond to statements made by outsiders about Indivers and its capabilities, mistaken facts and impressions could have been corrected and a different result from FIRA might have been received.

If these opportunities were offered, the Canadian government could get a real grip on the activities of foreign-controlled companies without scaring beneficial foreign prospects out of the country.

It is better for Canada to adapt the working out of FIRA halfway than to persevere in an error. The present functioning of FIRA leads to a reduction of beneficial investments in Canada, the same investments which in the past have contributed so much to the rising standard of living. If countries like Canada and the Netherlands do not defend an open economy, what will be the consequences in the long term for the world's economy in terms of retaliatory practices?

V
International
Operations
Management

Part III of this book dealt with effective marketing strategies for the export of Canadian goods and services abroad. But many Canadian firms are involved in international business activities other than arm's length exports; Part IV, for example, discussed the nature and patterns of international direct investments. In addition, Canadian firms are increasingly involved in other, newer types of international business activity such as turnkey projects and technology licensing agreements. This section of the book looks at strategies for overseas expansion by Canadian firms, and at key decision areas in the management of international business operations. Emphasis is on the current concepts and developments that will shape Canadian international management policies and practices in the years ahead.

The first four chapters consider international expansion strategies for Canadian firms. Bata (Chapter 29) discusses the relationship between nationalism and international strategies from the perspective of the management of a major Canadian multinational. Wright (Chapter 30) develops various types of international business arrangements which appear to be emerging in importance for the future. Detailed attention is then focussed on a new vehicle of particular importance to Canadian firms: the capital-equipment of turnkey project. Wright (Chapter 31) discusses the concept and nature of such projects; Dhawan and Kryzanowski (Chapter 32) offer practical suggestions for turnkey project contract procurement.

Three chapters focus on technology and research-and-development management in Canadian firms. Bones (Chapter

33) examines the impact of foreign control on the domestic innovative capacity of Canadian firms. Killing (Chapter 34) discusses the variables which Canadian managers should consider in choosing between joint ventures and licensing agreements for acquiring technology from abroad. Kirpalani and Macintosh (Chapter 35) present the results of their study of the international marketing effectiveness of small- and medium-size technology-oriented firms in Canada.

Three subsequent chapters develop an important new management concept linking foreign ownership in Canada with Canadian competitiveness abroad: the world product mandate (WPM). The Science Council of Canada (Chapter 36) presents an overview of the potential role of the WPM in Canada. Rutenberg (Chapter 37) considers the implication of WPMs for Canadian managers. Witten (Chapter 38) relates four specific examples of Canadian firms which have successfully adopted the WPM model.

The international financial environment — especially exchange rate behavior and sources of financing — is of major concern in managing international business operations of whatever sort. Abdel-Malek (Chapter 39) relates the Canadian experience with floating exchange rates to the financial management of Canada's international business operations. Bishop and Prefontaine (Chapter 40) trace the development of the international monetary and exchange rate systems, with particular attention to their relevance for Canadian international managers. Dhawan (Chapter 41) discusses sources of financing for Canadian exports. Tang (Chapter 42) surveys international transfer pricing practices, comparing the policies of Canadian managers with those of other countries.

The three concluding chapters look to the future, offering suggestions both to business managers and to public officials. Daly (Chapter 43) draws on his analysis of Canada's comparative advantage to form recommendations for Canadian industrial strategy. Ross and Banting (Chapter 44) structure priorities for policy development, and future research, based on the results of a Delphi survey of business, government, and academic leaders. The last Chapter (45) presents the summary and recommendations of a major report completed recently by the Export Promotion Review Committee.

V
International Operations Management

A
International Expansion Strategies

29
Economic Nationalism and International Strategies

Sonja A. Bata

Mrs. Bata is a director of Bata Limited, the international footwear manufacturing organization. She is also a member of several other business boards, including Alcan Aluminium Limited, Canadian Commercial Corporation, and Urban Transportation Development Corporation. She was chairman of the National Design Council of Canada and is active in cultural organizations nationally as well as internationally.

This chapter was written expressly for this volume.

This chapter deals with some aspects of foreign investment and economic nationalism that have affected the Bata organization. Some examples of the ways that government policies in various countries have encouraged or discouraged business enterprise over the last thirty years will be presented. These will range from policies favoring a totally free market system to those favoring protectionism, economic nationalism, and state socialism. This chapter takes issue with those policies that result in the long-term protection of inefficient industries in the name of economic nationalism and encourage narrow provincialism at the expense of the contributions that must be made in this decade to world trade and worldwide economic progress.

We live today in an interdependent world where more and more decisions are taken which transcend national interests. The great number of international organizations dedicated to building bridges of understanding between countries and economic regions and keeping barriers of all types to a minimum, attests to the general awareness in world forums that we are entering a new era in which affairs will be decided by consensus and governed by contract. This will involve fundamentally new economic arrangements and relationships.

Certainly, all the great economic thinkers of the recent past — Keynes, Freidman, even Marx — have made reference to the need for a shared and more rational management of the world's economy. While there may be set backs, the world of the 1980s and beyond will have to recognize and respond to these global influences.

The loudest voices on the global scene calling for change are going to be those of the Third World, where development at all levels will be significant. Bata operates in many developing countries and we spend a great deal of time in close proximity to the problems of these nations. In many instances, we talk directly with the leadership and participate actively in various commissions which contribute to the ongoing dialogue between the developed and the developing nations. We call this the North-South dialogue, though that name is no longer accurate since there is a whole new class of nations such as Mexico and Brazil, which do not qualify for inclusion in either group.

It is difficult for people living in the north to fully comprehend the extent of the poverty in some of the Third World countries. Although they have been assisted by aid programs, especially those which help to build infrastructure, improve agriculture, and provide technical education, this has barely scratched the surface of the problem. Real progress for these nations will only be achieved when they are able to build their own industrial base and trade among themselves and with the rest of the world. Industrialization, not only on a large-scale level, but also at the cottage and small-scale level, and improvement in the agricultural sector are key elements. Development is needed not only to create economic improvement but to restore human dignity, security, justice, and equity to people — and to create a class of entrepreneurs.

Today the Third World still produces less than 10 per cent of the world's industrial output. If we really want to create a more equitable and balanced world, then we must be willing to encourage the rapid growth of industries in the south, mainly to satisfy their own increasing consumption. As their standards of living rise, the developing countries will need more and more sophisticated goods and services. The developed world will profit from this evolution because of increased export opportunities.

Trade must be a two-way process. The developing nations cannot buy unless they export at least part of their output. If protectionism and narrow economic nationalism in the north prevent the Third World from selling in our market, they will also prevent it from buying, and that will put a great many northern jobs in peril.

Today, industrialized nations export nearly 100 billion dollars more in manufactured goods to the south than they import. In 1977, developing countries took as much as one-third of the total export of the United States, EEC countries, and Japan. Official estimates have shown that between 1973 and 1977 one million more jobs were created per year in industrialized nations to take care of this expanding trade. There are various economic studies which prove that trade between the north and the south, far from hurting northern labor, is creating more jobs than are lost.

While the competition from low-cost countries makes the headlines, and therefore forces politicians to act, many more jobs are lost because of advances in technology. A German study shows that between 1962 and 1975, forty-eight jobs were lost through new technology for every one lost as the result of imports from developing countries.

Many believe that the future of our industrialized society depends increasingly on acceptable levels of co-operation and involvement with the poorer nations. The 1980s will be a decade of negotiation and compromise between the north and south. It will be a difficult, often intensely painful, exercise with charged emotions on both sides. I hope that what will emerge will be a greater appreciation of our mutual dependency and, I hope, an enormous improvement in the standards of living in Third World countries.

Yet today, strong forces against the evolution of the world system are building up in the current atmosphere of uncertainty and instability which began with the quadrupling of oil prices in 1973, and which is continuously being aggravated by further increases in OPEC prices. Following the conclusion of the latest round of GATT negotiations, known as the Tokyo Round, Olivier Long, GATT's director general, said, "Despite the success of the talks that will result in reducing trade barriers and regularizing world trade, there is strong evidence the ground swell of protectionism is growing."

Discussions are going on between the heads of the three major American automobile companies, the representatives of the major automotive union, and the U.S. government about the difficult situation in their industry. Protection of some sort for the U.S. industry will be the likely result.

While the desire for protection can be understood (after all, unemployment figures in the industrial world climbed to 17 million in the early 1970s, roughly double the level of the early 1960s) nevertheless in these difficult economic times the temptation to isolate ourselves and our industries over the long term must be resisted. Although we in the footwear business have suffered more than any other industry from cheap imports, this is still my opinion.

When we talk about protection or economic nationalism we are talking about official policies. Before discussing how government policies have affected the economies in some of the countries in which we operate, let me present some background on the Bata organization. Bata employs 85,000 people who manufacture footwear in ninety-two countries and sell close to 300 million pairs a year around the world. The business was started in Czechoslovakia by my father-in-law. In the 1930s, the Czechoslovak factory was by far the largest in the world, employing some 28,000 people. It was a highly centralized organization. All decisions about research, personnel training, finance, production, and so on were made centrally. Foreign sales offices were staffed mainly by Czechoslovaks and shoes were exported from Czechoslovakia to many countries.

The depression of the 1930s caused increased duties and quotas to an extent that our exports were affected, and we had to start local production in other European countries to serve their markets.

These units were what would be called today typical branch operations. The war took a very heavy toll. The Czechoslovak factory was confiscated by the Communists and the branch system was, in effect, left headless. My husband, who had come to Canada in 1939, decided that he would not rebuild the organization based on the old system. Instead, he developed the new philosophy that each Bata Company should be independent to the largest possible extent. That is why today our headquarters in Toronto is more a training and service operation than a conventional head office.

Another important decision made at that time was to participate in the economic development of the new countries, which were gradually gaining independence. While most people were sceptical about their viability, we concluded that the emancipation of the people in these new countries was reaching a stage where they would take more pride in their personal appearance and well-being. We also realized that their income levels would not allow them to pay prices which reflected high European wages, transportation costs, and often high, fiscally inspired, customs duties. We, therefore, decided to manufacture locally, mostly from inexpensive, indigenous materials which would make our shoes affordable.

A favorable impact on the balance of payments, the generation of employment, the training of technicians, the development of local management skills, the stimulation of local suppliers and service operations were just some of the ripple effects from the establishment of a Bata factory. If our enterprise was successful, others would be encouraged to come. At an early stage, we appointed local directors to our Bata Boards.

It is interesting to note that we have never built factories purely for export purposes, for the simple reason that they are too vulnerable to changes of official policy which can eliminate them — and the jobs they create — with the stroke of a pen. Our expansion has always been based on growth in local markets and trade primarily between the companies in Third World countries. The stimulation that results from trade between Third World countries is extremely important as they slowly evolve to full partner trading status, and our policy is to do everything we can to make a contribution to this evolution.

While there have been many problems to overcome, our experience in developing countries continues to be a rewarding one. We have at the moment four factories under construction, three at the planning stage, and expansion of existing factories in twelve countries. Some of this expansion Bata is doing alone, others with local shareholders and an affiliate of the World Bank — and some even with government or "parastatal" organizations.

As far as government policies are concerned, our experience has varied a great deal. On the whole, we have found that where there was political stability and clear corporate rules we have been able to adapt and grow with the country. Some of these countries, especially the smaller ones, used protectionism to help their new, struggling industries gain a secure footing. In my opinion, that is a perfectly reasonable policy provided it is in force only for a limited time.

In other countries, well-intentioned economic nationalism started them on a slippery slope towards excessive government interference and loss of freedom through state control. In recent times, the belief that government should own all industry and trade has given way to more balanced views in many instances, even in cases where the ruling authority espouses Marxist-type philosophies.

During the last few years, our companies in Indonesia, Zaire, Uganda, and Sudan have been denationalized. There is an increasing interest and desire to work with responsible international companies. Unfortunately, high petroleum prices are playing havoc with the development aspirations of most of the Third World countries. The shortage of foreign exchange for materials, machines, and spare parts which must be imported is desperate, and in many countries the infrastructure, built up over the years at great costs, is beginning to deteriorate.

In preparing this chapter, I searched for an example of two countries which started in the 1950s from the same base and which, because of different government policies developed in different ways. My choice fell on Malaysia and Sri Lanka. Both are roughly the same size and both went through periods of turmoil; Malaysia with its Communist guerrilla uprisings, and Ceylon with the fierce hatred between the Sinhalese and Tamils which led to bloodshed.

Malaya, and afterwards Malaysia under Tunku Abul Rahman and later Tunku Razak, welcomed foreign investment with open arms. Thousands of industries were established and the standard of living rose sharply across the whole country. The local business community developed, and the public service became one of the best in the Far East. Today, Malaysia is a booming nation, and although it is now more particular about its foreign investment and more insistent about having Bumiputras (Malaysian Malays in contrast to Chinese Malays) in decision-making positions, it remains open to world trade and eager to participate in it.

Ceylon in the 1950s had a similar history to Malaya under Senanayake and Kothalawela but gradually adopted a policy of economic nationalism under the Bandaranaikes, and finally converted to state socialism. Government controls increased resulting in nationalization. Penal taxation on business and individuals was introduced, along with almost total import restriction, and restrictions on development and proliferation of state enterprises. The whole economy slowly wound down. The resulting hardships have brought change. Since 1978, when Jayewardene came to power, official policy has changed, but recovery is slow because many stagnating government enterprises continue to make embarrassing losses. Politically, handing over control to the private sector presents enormous obstacles because renewed foreign investment flow is difficult to generate.

The difference between these two countries can be illustrated by an example from the footwear industry. Sri Lankans bought an average of 0.87 pairs of shoes in 1979 while Malaysians bought an average of 3.1 pairs. The difference between Sri Lankan and Thai statistics is even more illustrative. Thais bought twice as many pairs of shoes as did Sri Lankans. In other words, in 1979 a Thai bought 1.8 pairs a year as compared to the above mentioned 0.8 for Sri Lanka. Thailand, like Malaysia, followed an open investment path. In other words, the standard of living had gone up in Thailand to a point where a person could afford to buy almost two pairs every year compared with less than one pair for Sri Lanka. Other industries have had similar experiences.

A typical example of economic nationalism as we in the footwear industry experienced it occurred in Nigeria, a country with enormous potential. Several years ago the Nigerian government asked us to give up partial ownership to local shareholders. We had hardly complied with that request when the government decided that the majority of shareholders should be Nigerians. Then we were told that the distribution system was to be reserved exclusively for Nigerians. That was followed by a rule that the majority of board members must be Nigerian. Most recently a new rule decreed that at least two Nigerian executives should be on the board of directors. We would probably have done most of these things as we went along, but this constant government intervention makes us wonder where it will all end. Nigeria is keen to get more foreign technology, but our own enthusiam has been dampened. I suspect that other investors share our concern because, although Nigeria is an oil exporter, its balance of payments is not healthy and foreign investment in manufacturing has diminished. Protectionism is, of course, not the sole prerogative of developing nations. There are plenty of examples to be found in the developed world too. New Zealand and Australia are good examples. New Zealand is a small country with a good standard of living. Salaries are high, and labor unions are strong. The market is too small and insular for industry to be internationally competitive, and without protection it would not have been able to survive. Of course, a price has had to be paid. In our business, duties on shoes amount to 49 per cent, and quotas are small. The result of this long-term history of protection is that the industry has stagnated and fallen far behind world fashion. The best-selling lines in New Zealand include black lace-up shoes for girls and felt slippers. During a visit in April, we had the opportunity of speaking with Mr. Muldoon, the prime minister. He told us that he is considering liberalizing the import quotas to some extent to try and shake New Zealand out of its insularity. He is motivated by the fact that New Zealand is developing its hydro-electric power and wants to attract substantial foreign investments.

Australia is a large country with small markets — very similar, in fact, to Canada. Like New Zealand, it followed restrictive policies for many years although recently attitudes have been changing. I had an opportunity to attend a luncheon in Canberra in April at which Prime Minister Fraser made a speech stressing the vital importance of foreign investment because of the country's need for new technology and managerial skills. He made a particular point of how important it would be for the foreign investor to make a profit in Australia. In his words: "If foreign investment does not make a profit, it will not attract further foreign investments."

Looking more closely at the Australian foreign investment laws one finds that Australia has its own FIRA for businesses of over 5 million Australian dollars. They also indicate that they do like Australian participation, although their investment policy will be administered in a flexible manner.

To give you a feeling of the present atmosphere in Australia, I would like to quote the minister of Industry:

> We cannot hope to insulate ourselves from change by the creation of artificial barriers; indeed we must strive to maximize the benefits from participation in the growth of expanding markets in our region. This will require our industries to adopt new attitudes towards change and competition, to look increasingly beyond the limit of the Australian market and gradually come to rely less on government support.

An even stronger statement was made by secretary of the Treasury, J. O. Stone, at the Australian Institute of Management in Sydney recently.

> Economic growth is not to be seen as something which can be obtained by some process of manipulation by an all-wise or all-powerful government. The more a government sets itself on that road, whether in response to please inefficient industries or spend-

thrift bureaucracies, the more it builds a ball and chain around the leg of the more productive sectors. It does so not merely through the multiplication of bureaucracy which that spawns, but also because every decision to award a licence to print money in one direction denies the opportunity to make an honest profit in another. Every inefficient firm propped up is a debit in the profit and loss accounts of all the efficient firms which, directly or indirectly have to pay for that.

Later in his speech, he urged a lowering of import protective barriers to compensate for expected large increases in exports during this decade:

Far from destroying the Australian industry, the lowering of import barriers would serve in the short and longer runs to make Australian industry more productive and thereby improve our future capacity to increase the real incomes of Australians as a whole, and thereby to provide these jobs, the provision of which is interminably put forward by those who argue for protection.

Let me sum up some of the points from our past experience which we feel are important considerations for the future:

1. The 1980s and beyond will be an era of negotiation between the north and south. There will be strong global trends influencing our national economies that will be beyond the powers of the nation state.
2. A bitter struggle is shaping up for world markets. Canada, which is one of the few industrialized nations without access to a market of 100 million people or more, will be disadvantaged if it cannot find solutions. It is in the interest of Canada to develop multilateral trade.
3. Foreign investment is necessary to stimulate economic progress. It not only supplies capital but, in most cases, also supplies technological know-how and managerial skills. In today's world we cannot afford to be insular; we must keep up with the continuous flow of ever changing technologies and skills.
4. Economic growth is best achieved through private initiative. The less government interferes, the more dynamic business becomes.
5. There is a general trend that sees governments trying to gain greater direct control over their national economies. While this is an understandable tendency, past history has shown that countries that put up too many restrictions were left behind and the standard of living of their people did not rise. The forces of

economic nationalism can dissuade investors from pursuing opportunities.

6. Protectionism has a role to play for limited periods, so that local industry either can develop to a certain internationally competitive strength or, if that is not possible, reorganize itself. Extended protectionism leads to stagnation.

7. The development of R & D programs either from scratch or based on known imported technology, is of great importance to a country with high labor costs. There are R & D areas where government stimulation and help is necessary because of the high-risk factors. But in most other areas if the general environment is such that people can make a solid profit, many more firms would be able to afford their own R & D programs.

8. To be competitive on the world market, an international outlook is basic. Protectionism and economic nationalism have a tendency to make people inward looking and to sap their international competitiveness. If in Canada we are made to read only Canadian magazines and see only Canadian television, it will not help our general awareness of international matters.

In a speech recently, Dr. Keng Swee, the deputy prime minister of Singapore, said:

Those who have been ill advised enough to believe that the government is the source of all wisdom in economic growth and should, therefore, be allowed to control the economy in detail, have shown the least progress. Governments of the ASEAN states have understood that economic growth is best achieved through private initiative and that the government's role should be largely confined to the encouragement of private enterprise and the provision of infrastructure — communications, transport, power, public utilities, and such like.

This statement accurately reflects my own feelings, and echoes the conclusion to which I have come.

V
International Operations Management

A
International Expansion Strategies

30
Evolving International Business Arrangements

Richard W. Wright

Dr. Wright is associate professor in the Faculty of Management, McGill University where he has served for several years as co-ordinator of international business studies. He has conducted extensive research on international joint ventures and contractual international business arrangements. His publications include four books and numerous articles in academic and professional journals. He is also a consultant to governments and business firms, both in Canada and abroad.

This chapter was written expressly for this volume.

Sweeping changes are taking place in the world business environment. Nationalistic forces are on a collision course with international business firms. This may spell not only a slowdown of traditional foreign trade and direct investment, but their replacement by entirely new forms and relationships of international business activity.

Nature of the Conflict

Traditionally, the main thrusts of private international corporate activity have been toward *pure trade* and/or *full direct investment*. Each of these forms has brought benefits and costs to the host or recipient countries.

Pure trade activity brings the benefit of increased product consumption, by making available to the importing country a wider variety of goods at lower costs than could be produced domestically; or, in the case of a country exporting raw materials through international corporations, by providing foreign exchange with which to purchase goods and services from abroad. Indirectly, trade activity also increases the level of skills consumption in the importing country, through the consumption of goods which have incorporated skills in their production elsewhere. But pure trade has one dominant disadvantage: while it may permit greater consumption of skills by a host country, it involves no transfer of skills for long-term purposes. The stock of skills available and employed locally does not increase when a final product is imported or when a raw material is exported. Mainly for this reason, national governments are acting to modify traditional trade activity by creating new barriers to the import of finished goods and the export of raw materials, and by offering powerful inducements for local processing, with the object of increasing value added locally.

Full direct investment, likewise, brings benefits to host countries: capital, technology, management skills, access to global marketing systems, etc. But the costs to a host country of direct investment from abroad are increasingly recognized: a foreign corporation gains a high degree of control over an economic entity in the host country, often indefinitely, with a resulting loss of ability by the host government to control its domestic economic destiny and to influence business activity toward the achievement of national goals. Recognition of the costs of yielding effective and permanent control of economic activity to outsiders is leading host governments throughout the world to adopt a variety of new measures to modify full direct investment activity: screening mechanisms, local ownership requirements, divestment programs, "creeping" expropriation, and outright seizure. While the more extreme moves occur mainly in the less developed countries (LDCs), steps to modify direct investment activity of international companies are by no means confined to developing areas. Measures to control foreign investment have, for example, been introduced recently in Australia, France, and Canada.

Thus, the main thrusts of international business activity are increasingly seen as unsatisfactory and unacceptable to the host or recipient countries. The traditional forms of international corporate activity are on a collision course with national objectives. Governments are intervening more effectively than ever before to force international corporations away from their "all-or-nothing" alternatives of overseas involvement through pure trade or through full direct investment.

If the objectives of host nations and international corporations are to be mutually satisfied, new forms of relationships will have to evolve. Their directions will be determined by the changing views and objectives of the host nations and the companies.

Objectives of the Host Nations
Host nations have a variety of objectives in their relations with international corporations: the supply of lower-cost goods, the creation of local employment, foreign exchange earnings, access to overseas markets, etc. Recently, however, two new considerations increasingly dominate the traditional concerns:

- The determination of host countries to retain or regain control of economic decisions in order to ensure that these decisions are compatible with national objectives.
- The realization that a sufficient quantity and quality of high-level technical and managerial skills must be acquired to make effective control possible.

The host country viewing relations with a foreign firm seeks to minimize the surrender of *control* to foreigners, while maximizing the extent of *skills* acquisition and employment.

Perceptions of the International Firms

Basic factors such as return on investment, commercial risk, market share, and secure sources of supply continue to be of fundamental concern to any firm. However, two further considerations are becoming even more volatile and command particular attention in the present international environmental circumstances:

- The maintenance by the firm of effective control over operations in the host countries.
- The risk of impairment of earning power or outright seizure of assets through unilateral host nation action.

The international firm could at one time achieve and maintain control of its overseas operations with relative ease. Today, these control objectives are often in direct conflict with those of host nations, and the accustomed degree of control is increasingly difficult to achieve. The risk element, also, has been a fundamental consideration of the international firm. But in the past, risk was viewed primarily in terms of normal commercial risk. The newer, more volatile risk element is that of seizure of assets or impairment of earning power as a result of actions by the host governments. Such risk is particularly real in light of the developing nations' new-found sense of national sovereignty, and their determination that the fruits of enterprise should be directed purposefully toward the host country needs. The international firm approaching operations abroad, particularly in developing nations, is increasingly concerned with maintaining its *control* of foreign operations, while minimizing the *risk* of impairment or seizure.

The Critical Variables

Three key variables in the relationship between international firms and host nations are probably crucial to the future of international business: corporate control, equity risk, and skills transfer.

These variables are by no means independent. They are highly interactive, particularly when coupled through some form of firm/host nation collaboration. For instance:

- Skills transfer to the host nation is a prerequisite to the ability of many countries to achieve and maintain effective control of their economies.
- Some degree of host nation control is increasingly required by host countries before they will allow the corporate involvement which would lead to skills transfer.
- The desire of host countries for control often leads to sanctions

against the foreign firm which drastically alter the risk complexion of the firm's operations.
- Increased risk for the firm intensifies the firm's desire to maintain or strengthen control over its operation.
- Control by the foreign firm is in direct conflict with the desire of the host nations to achieve control.

Whose ends is the operation to serve? The host nation controls the environment in which the foreign firm seeks to operate. The firm must thus recognize and respond to the host country's demands for increased skills transfer and decreased foreign control. Conversely, the international firm controls the skills and market resources needed by many host countries, and national governments must recognize and respond to legitimate demands of the firm for some measure of control and for low risk of impairment.

Basis for Collaboration

Based on divergent objectives but continued interdependence, new forms of sharing arrangements are gaining importance in international business. Collaborative efforts aim mainly at limiting the degree and duration of foreign corporate involvement. While the gamut of business relationships is infinite between the extremes of pure export and full direct investment, several main trends are emerging.

Franchising

In a franchise agreement, the international company grants the use of some asset to a franchisee abroad, and agrees to supply on a continuing basis some important ingredient — either a component or a service — for the end product. The franchisee is a person or legal entity abroad that is granted the right (franchise) in a specified territory to conduct business under the trade name, trademarks, and other property for which franchise fees or royalties are paid to the franchisor. In a sense, the franchisor and franchisee act almost like a vertically integrated firm: both are interdependent, and each party produces part of the good or service that ultimately reaches the customer. A franchisor may or may not own an interest in the franchisee.

The myriad problems and risks of international expansion into a variety of business climates, legal systems, and economic and social environments have led many U.S. companies to establish international franchising networks in recent years, particularly in food services and business services. Examples:

- Holiday Inn grants franchisees the good will of its reputation, plus the support service to get started, such as appraisal of a proposed hotel site. As part of the continuing relationship, Holiday Inn offers reservations service and training programs to help assure the venture's success.
- Muzak gives franchisees permission to use its name when selling taped musical programs to business and industry, in addition to supplying the scientifically programmed tapes.

For host countries, particularly LDCs, franchising is an effective means of developing new management techniques and distribution systems to help the small local businessman operate more efficiently. The local franchisee is generally provided with management and technical training; given assistance in locating, equipping, and decorating business premises; and sometimes given financial asistance. The independent businessman, as franchisee, can overcome some of the difficulties created for him by the growth of huge corporations, by gaining access to economies of volume purchasing, standardized operating procedures, co-ordinated advertising and sales promotion, etc. At the same time, he retains the psychological incentive of owning and controlling his own small business. For the host government, the franchise system avoids the politically undesirable features of direct investment because equity remains in local hands.

The international company with management know-how and a proven way of marketing can use franchising to expand its business and derive profits with a minimum of investment through sharing with a local independent businessman the entrepreneurial risk involved in marketing a product or service. Manufacturers can assure the creation of new business and the protection of future markets, diversify their methods of creating business, sell surplus production, hedge against seasonal fluctuations, and minimize capital investment. This is particularly true in countries with stringent exchange, repatriation, and profit restrictions. Through profit-sharing arrangements with franchisees, a franchisor can avoid national restrictions on alien ownership, as well as the political and labor problems provoked by the establishment of subsidiaries. Fears of expropriation are greatly reduced.

Although franchising may be an effective method for rapid international growth, it also tends to limit the franchisor's profit. The franchisor could retain a larger percentage of after-tax profits if international growth were achieved through owned outlets. In addition, franchising may create new competitors. In the absence of legal constraints, a disenchanted franchisee could terminate an agreement and begin a similar business entirely on his own, carrying with him the managerial know-how imparted by the franchisor, as well as any trade secrets that may have been revealed during their relationship.

Turnkey Projects
Turnkey projects involve the construction of operating facilities that are transferred to the owner when the facilities are ready to begin operations. The turnkey project is typically a medium-term arrangement under which a foreign firm or consortium contracts to develop or construct a specific facility such as a harbor, bridge, railway system, factory, or steel mill. The company involved may be an equipment manufacturer, a construction firm, a consulting firm, or another manufacturer who does not find an investment of its own to be feasible. The customers for turnkey projects are often governments which have decreed that a given product must be produced locally and under public auspices. Unlike the licensing arrangement or the management contract, where an existing company or governmental agency abroad needs additional technology or management services, the turnkey project generally involves the creation of an entirely new entity. The project is often coupled with a management contract or a licensing arrangement where training or technology inflows may continue after the project has been installed and commissioned. Where the venture is of major financial dimensions it may be supported by public credit financing, often by the government of the company installing the system.

Recent examples of turnkey projects include the construction of a railway system in Indonesia by Canadian Pacific Railway, steel mills in India by the USSR and by Anglo-German consortia, and an automobile manufacturing plant in the Soviet Union by Fiat Motor Company.

The turnkey project is attractive to host countries for both economic and political reasons. In a turnkey project, the host country receives an operational plant or system without having to develop the indigenous skills needed for its construction or installation. Skills necessary for the operation and maintenance of the facility are transferred to local personnel during the construction period. The cost is known in advance, in contrast to the open-ended dividend pay out commitment which would exist had the international firm retained ownership. Perhaps most important, ownership and control of the facility are entirely in local hands once the installation is completed.

Firms performing turnkey operations are frequently industrial equipment manufacturers who supply some of their own equipment for the project. For example, Northern Telecom of Canada supplied most of the equipment for the telecommunications system it installed in Liberia. The potential returns to the international company may take several forms:

- Direct payment under the terms of the contract for the construction and installation services provided.
- The sale of equipment and replacement parts in a market from which it might otherwise be excluded.
- The good will of the host government, which could open future trade, contractual, or investment possibilities in the host country.

A problem for the international firm is that by building a turnkey facility, it may be developing a future competitor. Because of unusually long lags between conception and completion, the company performing the turnkey operation is exposed to the risks of default or currency rate fluctuations for an extended period. Since the final payment is made only if the facility is operating satisfactorily, it is essential to delineate what is satisfactory. A particular problem in turnkey projects is the "commissioning gap" — a divergence between the international firm and the host country as to the nature and extent of skills transfer needed for a complex system to be operated indigenously. The international firm, often viewing the turnkey project as a prerequisite for the sale of its equipment overseas, may find that in spite of its training of local nationals, local skills are insufficient to operate the facility independently once it has been constructed or installed. While the international firm may feel that it has fulfilled the conditions of the contract, the host government may feel that the firm has failed to train sufficiently. Bitterness and recrimination may result.

Licensing Agreements
In a licensing agreement, the international firm separates technical knowledge as a distinct commodity from its total package of corporate resources. The licensor grants rights to patents, trademarks, and know-how to a company or goverment abroad. Such rights may be exclusive or non-exclusive. The licensor generally receives payment in the form of a royalty based on an agreed percentage of the licensee's sales resulting from the transferred technology. There is usually little risk concerning the nature of the benefits, their magnitude, or their timing. Hence, the most critical issues usually centre on the direct cost of the licences and the degree of restrictions that the licensee must agree to.

- The outstanding example of a country which has grown through the acquisition of foreign technology is Japan. The use of licensing has enabled Japan to catch up quickly with the world leaders in the industries involved; to concentrate their scientific and engineering talent on devising commercially valuable incremental improvements on the basic innovations licensed from abroad ("beginning by standing on the foreigners' shoulders", as one Japanese put it); and to assess the best developments in all countries before choosing whichever seem most attractive and appropriate for Japan.

• Communist bloc countries are entering increasingly into arrangements by which they license Western technology for a fee, in order to gain Western products and services with high technology inputs while minimizing the outflow of hard currencies.

• Many less developed countries import technology through international licensing for the development of indigenous firms, rather than relying on the import of technologically based finished goods or on technology transfer via foreign-owned subsidiaries.

The greatest potential problem for countries receiving technology via licence is the restrictive convenants which often accompany licence agreements, particularly as to whether local production may be exported. There may also be less commitment by the international firm to transfer new technology and provide broader assistance to a licensee than to an owned subsidiary. Finally, a licensee risks having a licensor as a competitor upon a licence's expiry, for if a brand name or trademark is involved the licensee who has developed consumer loyalty has to see the fruit of his labor turned over to the licensor.

Licensing offers many attractions for the international company:

• For small firms especially, it can establish a foothold in foreign markets without large capital outlays.

• Returns are apt to come more quickly than with manufacturing ventures.

• Income from foreign licensing helps to underwrite costly research programs.

• A firm may be able to retain markets otherwise lost by import restrictions or because it is being underpriced.

• A foreign market can be tested and then serviced without costly additions to production or detracting from the supply available for local customers.

• Good will is built for other company products.

• In hazardous situations, a local base is provided without expropriation risk.

• The licensing relationship may lead eventually to joint business ventures and the possibility of fuller involvement and higher profits.

International licensing also poses concerns for the licensor. Foremost is the risk of developing a future competitor after a licence agreement expires, since the licensee may be able to exploit the technology long after the agreement's termination. In markets where patent laws are weak or unenforceable, the licensor risks the leaking of its technology. Weak licensor control over the licensee's manufacturing and marketing operations could result in damage to the international company's trademarks and reputation.

Management Contracts

In a management contract, as in a licensing agreement, the firm separates from the bundle of corporate resources a particular resource — in this case, management skills — to sell to a company or government overseas. The international company's return is not an entrepreneurial one for risks taken, but a contractual one for services rendered. Under the terms of the contract, the international company may undertake to manage anything from an entire company or project to a specified, limited management function. The contract covers a specific period of time, typically three to five years, and provision is usually made for renegotiation of terms at specified intervals. In addition to the actual management services provided, an important dimension of almost all management contracts is the training of local personnel to eventually be self-sufficient. Thus a successful management contract should eliminate the need for its own existence.

- A typical example is the arrangement under which the government of Ethiopia hired Trans World Airlines to help establish and manage the government-owned Ethiopian Airlines. The contract was signed at a time when TWA had abundant management capacity that could not be employed by domestic expansion due to U.S. government regulations. Since the Ethiopian government would not allow foreign ownership in its national airline, TWA obtained earnings from the operation in the only way possible.
- Socialist bloc countries such as Yugoslavia and Hungary have relied on management contracts with a number of Western firms to build industrial capacity, utilize under-employed resources, and create import substitutes.

The management contract appeals particularly to nationalistic or socialistic governments because the involvement of the foreign firm is explicitly constrained to accomplishing a particular task and then leaving. Many government enterprises in LDCs are faced with a dearth of adequately trained management, often in spite of the possession of capital and technology. Management contracts are a vehicle for importing management skills unavailable locally and for building up the supply of indigenous skills without having to surrender ownership or control to the foreign company.

International companies seldom prefer management contracts to owned subsidiaries. Where full ownership is precluded, however, the management contract may provide an attractive alternative:

- The company gets a direct return for the management and training services it provides under the contract.
- By keeping a contractual relationship with a local company or government, the company may help to secure raw materials or market outlets for itself.
- The company may be able to utilize excess managerial resources from its domestic operations.

A disadvantage of the management contract for many firms is that it draws most heavily upon management skills, which may be a scarce company resource. Another possible disadvantage is the creation of future competitors. An example is that Ethiopian Airlines now flies across the North Atlantic in competition with TWA. However, if TWA had not entered into the agreement, another established airline probably would have with the same competitive result. The crucial problem of training is that the host governments often differ with the incoming firm on how quickly training and the transfer of responsibility can occur.

Contractual Joint Ventures

The contractual joint venture is a risk-sharing venture in which no joint enterprise with separate personality is formed. It is a partnership in which two or more companies (or a company and a government agency) share the cost of an investment, the risks, and the long-term profits. The contractual joint venture may be formed for a particular project of limited duration, or for a longer-term cooperative effort, and the contractual relationship may terminate once the project is completed. Contractual joint ventures are recognized as a means of sharing resources and spreading risk even among firms in industrialized countries.

- In publishing, for example, an American publisher and a European publisher may jointly publish a book, sharing the risks and profits.

As no new legal entity is created, the partnership may terminate on completion of the venture.

- Similarly, banks in different countries may pool revenues and risk in contractual consortium ventures to finance large loans.

Even stronger inducements for contractual joint ventures exist in developing countries, particularly in the resource sectors. In their determination to maintain sovereignty over natural resources and to resist foreign domination in general, LDC governments increasingly view contractual joint ventures as a desirable substitute for ownership relations. This is well illustrated in the petroleum industry, where contractual joint ventures between the international petroleum companies and oil producing countries are replacing earlier joint equity relationships, as in the recent agreements between Saudi Arabia and the Arabian American Oil Company (Aramco).

From the LDC viewpoint, the contractual joint venture serves four essential purposes:

- It engages the use of local capital in productive enterprises which will likely be profitable.
- It helps to develop a nucleus of experienced management personnel, while advancing the training of the local population.
- The contractual nature of the agreement means that the accord can be broken with a minimum of bad feeling.
- There is no foreign ownership.

The contractual joint venture offers major advantages for the international company:

- It is a more flexible form than the equity joint venture, with few corporation formalities.
- If the wrong partner is chosen, the agreement precludes long-term losses.
- Particularly where the partner is a government agency, the host country's fear of foreign economic domination is minimal and therefore the probability of expropriation is low.

The main problems of contractual joint ventures lie in the looseness of the partners' relationship. Particularly for multinational corporations that need to maintain trade names and quality standards on a global basis, the necessary degree of operational control may be difficult to obtain. Because the contract can be relatively easily terminated, the international company's planning horizon is necessarily truncated. The resulting challenge is to find ways to effectively integrate loosely associated affiliate enterprises with tightly controlled subsidiaries.

Equity Joint Ventures

The equity joint venture is a company owned by more than one organization. It is generally a separate company formed as a subsidiary by two or more corporations, or by a corporation and a governmental agency. Each partner holds stock in the subsidiary, and each gains ownership rights over natural resources, plant and equipment, goods produced, marketing territories, and profits.

For host countries, equity joint ventures provide access to the resources of international companies on a long-term basis, while preserving greater local control and sharing more fully in the benefits than is usually the case with wholly owned subsidiaries. The equity joint venture is particularly attractive when the total "corporate skills package" is needed rather than particular skills or components, as in many developing countries. Because the international firm is sharing in the risk and profit of the joint venture subsidiary on a long-term basis, it is more likely to devote serious attention to the long-run success of the local venture than it might in a contractual relationship. The existence of local partners, particularly in majority positions, helps to ensure that the actions of the subsidiary are consonant with the national objectives of the host country.

An international company may choose the equity joint venture form for a number of reasons:

- It may wish to enter or remain in an overseas market where full ownership of subsidiaries is prohibited, as in Mexico.
- It may lack capital or personnel for overseas expansion or be unwilling to bear the entire risk alone.
- It may need the services (particularly local market expertise) of a local partner.

The equity joint venture offers the international company an opportunity short of full direct investment for major overseas involvement of unlimited duration. The role of the international company can range from that of a relatively inactive minority position to that of the controlling senior partner, and the relative positions of the partners can change over time. Where full direct investment is prohibited, the equity joint venture may be the fullest form of overseas participation available to the firm. Even where full ownership is permitted, the joint venture may be the most sensible form of involvement, particularly for smaller international companies. The equity joint venture permits equity participation with a minimal outflow of scarce capital, particularly where the company can capitalize non-capital inputs such as technology or skills. Where expansion overseas is limited by the scarcity of management skills, the equity joint venture commits the skills of the local partner on a long-term basis. The risk of nationalization may be reduced by the presence of local partners; and the size of the firm's exposure to equity risk is in any case less than in a full direct investment.

The problems of equity joint ventures stem mainly from the difficulty of reconciling the divergent objectives of the partners. For example, a frequent problem area is dividend policy, where one partner favors a quick pay out while the other may wish to re-invest profits for long-term growth. The principal concern for the international company is that it is making a long-term commitment of resources without retaining full control. This is particularly relevant in larger multinational companies seeking to rationalize operations on a global basis, where the desire of the firm to shift sourcing, transfer pricing, or allocation of markets from one subsidiary to another may conflict directly with the interests of the local partner.

Corporate Strategic Paths

The strength of economic nationalism and the determination of host countries to reshape international business to suit their own needs will put growing pressure on international companies to move away from pure trade and full direct investment into collaborative business relationships. Companies which resist these pressures and continue to rely on traditional international business arrangements are likely to encounter increasing impairment of their activities and diminished profit. A more fruitful response is for management to recognize the priorities of host countries and to plan now for the eventual transition to collaborative arrangements that will serve the interests of both sides. This evolutionary process may occur along a number of possible strategic paths.

As host governments strengthen their restrictions on the export of raw materials and on the import of finished goods, pure trade will become increasingly costly and difficult for many international companies. Faced with impediments and incremental costs, companies which traditionally import raw materials for manufacture at home may consider entering into turnkey projects and other contractual arrangements to create or develop refining and processing operations in the host countries. In so doing the company will earn revenue for the services it provides. Furthermore, the contractual links with the local processors may actually give the company a more secure source of supply than it would have in a pure trade relationship. Similarly, companies which traditionally export finished goods will encounter increasingly restrictive barriers. The firm which helps to create local manufacturing capacity abroad through licensing arrangements, management contracts, and other intermediate forms will receive income for its services, and may also help to ensure a long-run position for its products in the host country market.

Initial involvement abroad through limited, arm's length contractual arrangements may subsequently evolve into fuller and more durable relationships. For example, the company building a manufacturing facility abroad in a turnkey project may sign a licensing agreement or management contract with the newly created entity which provides for its continued involvement over an extended period. Alternatively, the international company in a turnkey project may receive part of its compensation in the form of equity shares in the new operation, leading to an equity joint venture. Similarly, initial involvement with a local firm via franchise or licence may lead to some form of joint venture arrangement as the partners gain mutual trust.

From the other extreme, international companies which traditionally go abroad with full direct investments in manufacturing or extractive subsidiaries will find both pressures and inducements to move toward collaborative relationships. More and more markets will be closed altogether to the establishment of wholly owned affiliates, as in Mexico and India. In some areas, governments are even moving to force divestment of already existing subsidiaries, as in the Andean Common Market. Rather than waiting for increasingly constrictive controls, forced divestment under unfavorable conditions, or even outright seizure, the international company may protect its long-run position by planning for orderly divestiture which will gradually transform wholly owned subsidiaries into equity joint ventures. As the equity control of the international company diminishes, it may be replaced by contractual arrangements such as licence agreements or management contracts. The total profit earned by the company from its overseas activity will probably diminish as it moves away from wholly owned operations. But in so doing the company can gain the major new advantages of lower equity exposure, reduced likelihood of impairment, and fewer operational problems.

Many companies are reluctant to move from the familiar mechanisms of pure trade and full direct investment into relationships which may appear less certain. But considering the balance of earnings and risk, the long-run well-being of the international company may best be served by charting a strategy of evolution toward the collaborative arrangements.

Summary

Key variables in the international environment appear crucial in influencing the future directions of international business activity: corporate control, equity risk, and skills transfer.

The traditional alternatives of pure trade and full direct investment are unsatisfactory to host countries. National governments increasingly are acting to force their modification. A variety of forms of international corporate involvement are emerging in the middle ground between the two traditional extremes, among which franchising, turnkey projects, licensing agreements, management contracts, contractual joint ventures, and equity joint ventures are prominent. Although different in substance and situation, these intermediate forms share certain important characteristics:

- They may exist individually or in a variety of combinations.
- They emphasize the transfer abroad of particular skills or services, which can be separated from the total package of corporate resources.
- They tend toward arm's length relationships of limited time duration.
- They are better suited than traditional forms to fulfil simultaneously the needs of both the international corporations and the host nations.

International business in the 1980s and 1990s is likely to be very different from what we have known. Effective corporate managers seeking profit in foreign markets will require sensitivity to the demands of nationalism, and flexibility to respond with collaborative relationships better suited to fulfilling concurrent needs for material well-being and national dignity.

V
International Operations Management

A
International Expansion Strategies

31
Turnkey Projects: Canada's Route to Third World Markets

Richard W. Wright

Dr. Wright is associate professor of international business and finance in the Faculty of Management, McGill University. His publications in the international business area include *International Business Research: Past, Present, and Future; Nationalism and the Multinational Enterprise: Legal, Economic, and Managerial Aspects; The Economic Impact of Japanese Business Activity in Canada*; and numerous articles in academic and professional journals. He also has broad experience as a consultant to governments and industries.

The material in this chapter appeared originally in *The Business Quarterly*, Spring 1981. Reprinted by permission.

Foreign markets play a prominent role in Canada's economy, with nearly 30 per cent of Canadian GNP derived from exports (compared to 11 per cent in the U.S. and 18 per cent in Japan).[1] But these exports have been predominantly raw materials and agricultural goods. In 1978, for example, only 30 per cent of Canada's exports were fully manufactured.[2] This is felt to be undesirable for at least two important reasons: many raw materials exist in finite quantities and face eventual depletion; and the extraction and export of primary goods generates relatively little employment in Canada.

This chapter explores the prospects for expanding the export of Canadian capital goods to Third World countries[3] via turnkey projects. Areas of potential Canadian competitiveness are identified; characteristics and requirements of Third World markets are discussed; problems experienced in Canadian turnkey project participation are explored; and recommendations are made to both the private and public sectors.

Untapped Potential

Wide attention is currently focussed on the pressing need for a national industrial strategy which will identify Canada's main strengths and promote innovative development of competitive sectors. A recent study by the Export Promotion Review Committee (Hatch Report) observed:

> The lack of innovation in Canadian secondary industry reflects not only a lack of research and development in Canada but, more significantly, a lack of in-house product design and engineering

---

1. Data Resources of Canada, *Canadian Review* (June/July 1980), p. 321; Data Resources, *Review of the US Economy* (May 1980), p. 171, DRI/NIKKEI, *Japanese Economic Review* (April 1980), p. 33.
2. Bank of Canada, *Bank of Canada Review* (October 1980), pp. 72-74; and Export Promotion Review Committee, *Strengthening Canada Abroad* (November 30, 1979), p. 16.
3. Third World refers, generally, to regions other than North America, Europe, Japan, Australia, and the Socialist bloc. As used here, the term refers in general to the developing nations and the OPEC countries.

capability in Canadian firms. The Committee recommends that greater incentive be provided . . . for firms manufacturing in Canada to design, develop and market their own unique products. The intent in so recommending is to promote the development of more exportable products.[4]

One impediment to economic success in Canadian manufacturing is the tendency of many Canadian firms to rely on the relatively small, highly protected domestic market rather than to pursue potential markets overseas. In seeking to explain the low proportion of manufactured goods in exports by Canadian firms, the Lamontagne Commission observed:

Many secondary manufacturing firms feel limited by the size of the domestic market and the declining share of the market that is available to them. They assert that if the Canadian market were larger and better protected against foreign competition, the flow of technological innovations and R & D activities they could afford to fund would increase substantially. This may well be true. But if these two conditions were the only possible solutions to the improvement of their innovative capacity, there would be grounds for pessimism, because our domestic market is not going to grow rapidly in the short term, and it is not realistic to expect higher protection in Canada.[5]

Underscoring the need for a new international marketing outlook in Canadian firms, Mr. V.O. Marquez of Northern Telecom has stated that "the problem in Canada is at least partly a matter of national attitude". Canadian industry has developed "the kind of mythology . . . which says that industry can only be developed if it can be supported on a domestic base". He illustrates his point:

One of our greatest competitors in our field, the L.M. Ericsson Company in Sweden, gets 20 per cent of their business in Sweden. This is their point of view, this is the base from which they start. This never has been the base from which Canadian industry has started.[6]

Canada will never be able to compete successfully on the international scene in all industrial sectors. But there are certain industries in which Canada, because of its unique geographic situation and its

4. Export Promotion Review, *Strengthening Canada Abroad*, p. 10.
5. Senate Special Committee on Science Policy, *A Science Policy for Canada: Targets and Strategies for the Seventies* 2, p. 501.
6. *Ibid*, p. 501.

resource orientation, appears to possess special expertise which can stand up to the challenge of global competition. Among such industries frequently identified are:

- electric power generation and transmission
- telecommunications system
- transportation systems
- pulp and paper manufacture
- airport construction
- nuclear power generation
- offshore mining and drilling equipment
- navigational instruments

While the list is far from definitive, there are industrial sectors of particular Canadian expertise. Moreover, these sectors tend to share certain important characteristics:

- They are oriented toward natural resources, energy, transportation, and communication — areas that have been developed in response to the demands of Canada's unique geographic setting and resource endowment.
- They involve highly sophisticated capital equipment.
- They emphasize process as well as product; that is, the equipment involved in such industries generally functions in complex systems rather than as isolated pieces of equipment.
- They are related to activities which, in many economies, fall within the public or quasi-governmental sector.

Unquestionably, it is in the interest of Canadians that these and related industries based on unique Canadian experience and using Canadian skills and technology, be developed. Given Canada's small domestic market, one important means of accomplishing this is through active development of overseas marketing opportunities. Expansion of Canada's capital equipment exports would stimulate employment, particularly employment of sophisticated skills. Moreover, export expansion in these areas would broaden the sales base for the research and development which Canadian industry requires to remain innovative and competitive.

The Third World Market

For the Canadian capital equipment exporter (the manufacturer of power-generating equipment, telecommunications equipment, transportation facilities, or basic industrial machinery) the Third World represents a vast and tantalizing potential market. Growth rates in many of the developing countries far outstrip those of the industrial states. Brazil's GDP, for example, is expanding at a real rate of 9.8 per cent per annum; Saudi Arabia's, at 12.3 per cent.[7] Moreover, this growth is based largely on the development of infrastructure or the exploitation of natural resources, and on the building of related primary industry. These nations are in the process of pushing back their frontiers — a process that Canada has pursued since Confederation, and is still pursuing actively today in the Canadian North.

Third World demand is thus intense for capital equipment in areas where many Canadian firms are in a position to supply a combination of product, expertise, and relevant experience. It is estimated that over the next five years Saudi Arabia alone will spend $113.9 billion on capital expenditures for development, most of which will be spent in foreign markets.[8]

What makes this Third World market even more significant is the fact that markets for capital equipment in industrialized countries are increasingly closed to Canadian manufacturers. The U.S., Europe, and Japan have local industrial capabilities which prosper in their domestic markets on the bases of transportation economies, servicing capabilities, established and highly developed systems of standards, and buy-local incentives from home governments. In the Third World, local capital equipment industries do not generally exist. Shipping costs and servicing capability from Canada are comparable to those from other industrialized nations and, as a rule, developing countries are not as firmly locked into rigid specifications and standards which would preclude Canadian products without significant redesign.

While much attention has been focussed on the nature and extent of international corporate activity in the Third World, this enormous potential market has been largely neglected by Canadian manufacturing firms. In 1977, Third World markets accounted for only 10.9 per cent of Canada's fully manufactured exports.[9] Except for a small number of firms, direct investment by Canadian manufacturers in the Third World is neglible.

Environmental Changes
Over the last decade, awareness of the potential of the Third World market has coincided with the corporate finding — often through painful experience — that direct foreign investment involving full

7. United Nations, *Statistical Yearbook* (1978), p. 738.
8. *The Europa Yearbook 1980 — A World Survey* 2 (London: Europa Publications Limited, 1980), p. 1286.
9. United Nations, *1978 Yearbook of International Trade Statistics* 2, p. 54-60.

ownership (and in many cases even simple export) is increasingly unacceptable to the host nation. Traditional ideas regarding corporate involvement in developing nations are being forced to change. No longer can a corporation arrive in a developing nation with a predetermined package of resources, expecting concession and franchise in perpetuity. No longer can a capital equipment manufacturer assume that it can ship its product to the Third World as a simple export. Rather, corporations are finding that successful involvement in the Third World market must be based on the existence of mutual interests. In addition, corporation-host nation relationships can no longer be static but must be adjusted as local conditions, capabilities, and requirements develop.

Three factors have been particularly significant in modifying the environment of the Third World market to preclude the corporation's continuing reliance on simple export or on direct investment involving full ownership. The first has been the rising tide of nationalism, which since the Second World War has brought independence to scores of former colonies in the developing world. There has followed a sustained increase in the degree to which these nations have been motivated to achieve rapid and sustained economic growth aimed at true economic independence. The corporation with its direct investments is increasingly perceived as an inefficient contributor to this goal.

A second factor has been the recognition that ambitious economic development goals, particularly those of OPEC countries, imply the need for a massive inflow of technical and managerial skills. While such skills are to a large extent inseparable from the corporations processing them, it is increasingly recognized that, with ingenuity, the corporate skills package can be imported independently of the corporation's products, its capital, and its control.

A third factor affecting the emergence of new forms of corporate involvement has been the increasing technical complexity of much of the equipment exported to the Third World. This factor is particularly significant in areas such as power generation, telecommunications, transportation, and the basic production facilities required by those nations as a development base. Such equipment cannot simply be shipped to the Third World in "brown paper parcels", f.o.b. the home port. With the shortage of local skills in the developing nations, it must be installed on site and made to work as a system. Local technicians and managers must be trained and an organization must be created — often from scratch — to maintain and operate the system once it has been put into service. As one seasoned executive has warned:

If an exporter merely pops into a (Third World) country, puts some of his hardware down in its midst, and pops out again, . . . he will have inscribed himself and his country in the unlamented ranks of others who have hit and run before him.[10]

The response of the developing nations to these three factors has been a drive toward modifying the foreign corporation's involvement according to the following criteria:

1. Minimize the amount of foreign control in order to:
   (a) allow integration of economic activity under national development plans;
   (b) ensure investment in areas of greatest social rather than commercial productivity;
   (c) maintain full sovereignty;
   (d) satisfy nationalistic sentiments.
2. Increase the efficiency of transfer of resources specifically required for development.
3. Increase the efficiency of corporate skills transfer to minimize the time over which:
   (a) foreign exchange will have to be spent on importing such skills;
   (b) control of operations will lie in expatriate hands.

Independence, national sovereignty, and a more representative and sophisticated national leadership have made feasible the aggressive pursuit of such criteria. The developing nations are increasingly in control of the natural resources and the markets sought by foreign corporations. While they are still dependent on such corporations for many of the factor inputs to development, the balance of power has swung inexorably in favor of the host nation. Increasingly, corporations are forced to meet the market through forms of involvement which explicitly consider the developing nations' concern for retaining local control of economic activity.

The Turnkey Project

The impact of these tendencies on the capital equipment exporters of the industrialized world has been significant. No longer is the market demanding the corporation's equipment. Rather, it is de-

10. Joseph W. Halina, "Canada in the World of Export" (Luncheon address delivered at the Canadian Manufacturers' Association Conference on International Marketing, Toronto, February 10, 1970).

manding *fully integrated systems and the skills to operate and maintain them*. A drastic product redefinition is implied.

In the case of large and complex capital projects and high technology systems, the turnkey contract has been used extensively as the corporate answer to the Third World market demand for product redefinition. A turnkey operation involves the construction under contract of a project up to the point of operation, at which time it is turned over to the customer. The contractor (usually the manufacturer of some segment of the project equipment) undertakes full responsibility not only for providing equipment, but also for engineering the system, financing the project, arranging the supply of complementary equipment, implementing the project, and ensuring successful operation as a whole upon completion. It also undertakes to provide the corporate skills required by the customer to operate and maintain the system following its completion.

From the developing nation's point of view, large capital projects in such areas as power generation, telecommunications, and basic industry are crucial to the development effort. Yet local skills resources are generally insufficient to support the implementation of such projects, and much valuable time would be lost in attempting the massive investment required to establish skills self-sufficiency. Nor is it generally possible to engage large numbers of expatriates individually or to generate among such individuals the capabilities required to execute a large and complex project. Even a management contract may be inappropriate, for while it is possible to separate the supply of money capital from the supply of skills, it is often difficult to separate the supply of tangible capital from the corporate skills required for its incorporation into a system.

From the corporate point of view, a turnkey contract ensures that equipment can be installed, tested, and adjusted to operate in the total system in accordance with performance specifications. It also allows the firm to establish a medium-term presence in what is generally a growing market for its equipment. Finally, the turnkey operation permits the corporation to trade directly in the resource in which it has its greatest comparative advantage — its own unique package of corporate skills.

Turnkey Project Problems
Offsetting the many advantages of turnkey projects in the Canadian business context are the various problems encountered frequently by Canadian firms looking to this method of foreign involvement.

1. *Market Knowledge.* Although many Canadian firms are actively

seeking foreign projects, they are hindered by Canada's generally poor representation in the financial institutions through which many foreign capital projects emerge. The result, in many cases, is that negotiations with other countries are already in progress before the Canadian firm becomes aware of the opportunity.

Greater co-ordination between Canada's aid activities and its trade strategy could assist domestic enterprises in their foreign endeavors by guaranteeing greater Canadian content in projects to which the aid agencies contribute. Although Canada is one of the largest supporters of multinational agencies,[11] it also has one of the poorest records in procuring contracts through them.[12]

2. *Political Marketing.* Many of Canada's competitors are adept at using high-level government support to substantiate their efforts. This technique is not widely supported by Canadian politicians who tend to remain on the sidelines until a contract is awarded. The Hatch Report observes:

Other countries frequently provide high-level political support to their firms when major projects are at stake. Prime ministers, presidents, and monarchs all have been used for this purpose. Major turnkey projects, because of their sheer size and their impact on technology and employment in the country of the successful bidder, have become politicized. It is time that Canadian political leaders added their weight to the efforts of Canadian firms. Historically, they have tended to accompany Canadian bidders on a ceremonial basis only when the contract was won. There is need in Canada to recognize that firms pursuing major contracts abroad deserve to be treated as "national champions" carrying the Canadian flag as it were. They should receive consistent, high-level ministerial support in the selling process as well as the contract signing ceremonies.[13]

3. *Negotiations.* Lack of experience in negotiating often works to Canada's detriment, especially when competing against other nations which, through colonial links, have acquired a better feel for foreign markets and for cultural differences in the negotiating process. Furthermore, Canadian executives are not accustomed to the very sub-

---

11. Multilateral assistance accounted for 40 per cent of CIDA's disbursements in 1976, compared to 14 per cent for France, 25 per cent for Germany, 30 per cent for the U.K., 32 per cent for Japan, and 34 per cent for the U.S. (*Strengthening Canada Abroad*, p. 38.)
12. "Opportunities seen for investors in Asia", *Financial Post* (July 23, 1977), p. 9.
13. Export Promotion Review, *Strengthening Canada Abroad*, p. 39.

stantial effort and on-the-spot presence required during long negotiations to compete with aggressive project development teams from
Japan and Europe who "camp" on projects until they are won. This
requires sustained top executive involvement through the entire
period from feasibility study to final turnkey contract.

4. *Anti-boycott legislation.* Canadian companies are winning more
contracts in Saudi Arabia and other Arab countries, but moves to
introduce anti-boycott legislation in Canada could prejudice their
chances.[14] Canada currently enjoys an advantage over U.S. companies
in the Middle East due to the U.S. anti-boycott legislation. However,
rumblings by the federal government of proposed legislation and of
withdrawal of government services for those not complying with
boycott clauses could adversely affect Canadian negotiating teams'
efforts.

5. *Risk Exposure.* One financial executive has identified four principal obstacles to participation in Middle Eastern projects:

> (1) the unusually large size of the projects; (2) the long time
> required to complete them; (3) the unusually expensive and risky
> bank guarantees required by the governments of Middle Eastern
> countries; and (4) the financial support that the foreign competi-
> tors . . . are receiving from their governments.[15]

The large size and long time frame of most turnkey projects results
in great risk of a magnitude that dwarfs the asset base of most
Canadian firms.[16] In the first place, bid preparation costs may total
hundreds of thousands of dollars, all spent against an uncertain
outcome. Half of these expenses are eligible for reimbursement
through the Program for Export Market Development (PEMD), although the actual reimbursement is generally limited by regulatory
procedures to approximately 40 to 45 per cent of costs *directly
related to a specific project.* General overseas marketing and market
monitoring expenses, despite their importance in pinpointing potential contracts and despite their magnitude, are not covered by the
PEMD.

The risks of winning the contract may far exceed the risk of
bidding. At present, no insurance exists against cost escalation due to

---

14. "Anti-boycott moves by Canada awaited", *Middle East Economic Digest* (April 5,
    1979), p. 13.
15. Daniel M. Searby, "Doing Business in the Middle East: the Game is Rigged",
    Harvard Business Review (January-February 1976), p. 58.
16. Export Promotion Review, *Strengthening Canada Abroad*, p. 38.

inflation or currency fluctuations (not only during the term of the contract, but also during the often lengthy period between the tendering of the bid and awarding of the contract), and unforeseen occurrences such as delays due to equipment lost in transit.

The Canadian Commercial Corporation (CCC), which has operated traditionally as a procurement agency for foreign governments seeking Canadian suppliers of goods, was given an expanded mandate in 1978. Its extended responsibilities are:

1. to continue as a procurement agency through the Export Supply Centre;
2. to serve as prime contractor for capital project exporters who need a government-to-government arrangement; and
3. to share the unusual risks that are inherent in large overseas projects.[17]

Once operational, this should provide some much needed support in the area of risk sharing.

The Export Development Corporation (EDC) has in its mandate to "facilitate and develop export trade by the provision of insurance, guarantees, loans, and other financial facilities". While the EDC covers certain types of commercial and political risks, it does not include insurance coverage against cost escalation due to extreme inflation, nor against foreign exchange fluctuation.

One of the major repercussions of lack of proper insurance agencies is the uncompetitiveness of many bids tendered by Canadians who are forced to include larger contingencies to cover risk.

6. *Financing.* In addition to the risk aspect of the project, the firm must arrange financing. The EDC also supplies long-term financing for export projects. However, a study by the U.S. Export-Import Bank shows that of seven countries studied (U.S., Canada, Germany, France, Italy, Japan, and the United Kingdom), effective "interest" rates (including all fees and premiums) in July 1977 were up to 1 per cent higher for Canadian companies. Even this is an improvement over 1976, when a similar study showed that the cost of borrowing for the Canadian exporter ran 0.7 per cent higher than the *next highest* interest cost country, and 2.7 per cent higher than the lowest interest cost country. Additionally, only 85 per cent of the contract price will be financed by the EDC (compared to 100 per cent in France and Japan, the most competitive countries). No short- and medium-term financing is available through the EDC.[18]

17. *Ibid*, p. 38.
18. *Ibid*, p. 24.

The problem of expensive and risky bank guarantees required by many Middle Eastern governments applies to all countries involved in extensive capital projects in the region. It is not uncommon for a Middle Eastern country to require confirmation by a local bank of a loan guarantee coming from a Western bank — at a cost of approximately 12 per cent per annum over and above the standard Western bank charges of approximately $3/4$ of 1 per cent for the same guarantee. In addition, performance bonds demanded are often open-ended, putting the foreign firm in an uncomfortably risky position.[19]

7. *Skills Transfer.* There is a widespread corporate tendency, when selling a turnkey project, to deliver an equipment-oriented package which fails to leave the customer with the skills required for independent system operation and maintenance at the time of project completion. Patch-up and stopgap programs follow, in which various combinations of operating contracts, management contracts, and/or technical assistance programs are invoked in an attempt to effect the corporate skills transfer originally envisioned under the turnkey operation itself. Bitterness and recriminations often result. Apart from the direct financial losses involved, there is considerable risk that the marred corporation-host-nation relationship will weaken the company's future market in the area.

This "commissioning gap" is largely a function of a number of conditions prevalent in the Third World market. The first and most general is the existence of a multitude of individual, organizational, and/or environmental barriers to skills transfer.[20] They are generally complex and interrelated, and may render inoperative a corporate training program which in the domestic market would be fully successful. In addition, there is a tendency for the corporation to assume that what is required in the way of skills transfer is technical knowledge relating to the system. In fact, the crucial requirement is often for the transfer of organizational attitudes — in some cases, for the building of the customer's organizations from scratch. This is consistently overlooked by Canadian corporations contemplating turnkey contracts in the Third World.

Matching the unrealistic assumptions of the corporation, the host nation often exhibits its own distorted views of reality. The first is a tendency to be overconfident in the capabilities of its personnel, their capacity for learning, and the stock of skills available in the local

19. Searby, *"Doing Business"*, p. 59.
20. See particularly Colin S. Russel, *Turnkey Operations and the Transfer of Corporate Skills to the Developing Nations* (MBA thesis, McGill University, 1971), pp. 78-85.

society. While pride in local abilities is understandable, it can lead to unrealistic assessment of skills transfer requirements.

Too often, systems sold are copies of those in the industrialized world, designed to meet performance standards which are unnecessary in the Third World setting. For the corporation, this involves minimum equipment redesign and maximum equipment sale. For the host nation, it often satisfies a strong desire for a system which avoids any connotation of being backward but rather stands as a monument to the progress of the nation. However, excessive sophistication also multiplies the problems associated with a commissioning gap and can delay effective takeover of system operating responsibilities for many years.

A related problem involves turnkey contract negotiations which focus invariably on performance, delivery schedule, and price — not on skills transfer. The former factors are significant, quantifiable, and relatively easily expressed and understood. But skills transfer is difficult to describe in operational terms. A tendency toward lack of concern is encouraged by the corporation's feeling that if the training envisioned proves inadequate, it can always sell further training programs at a later stage to bail the customer out. Similarly, the customer feels that extra expatriate technical assistance can always be arranged if absolutely necessary.

The abdication of both partners from the skills transfer problem must be emphasized. Skills transfer objectives too often are ill-defined and non-operational.

Adapting Products to the Changing Market

There are already signs that corporations and host nations alike are modifying their approaches to capital investment projects. With increasing experience in project planning and project management, and with a growing stock of local technical and managerial skills, the more advanced of the developing nations are in a position to purchase segments of their large capital projects and technical systems as equipment packages (as opposed to complete turnkey projects), carrying out much of the project management themselves with the judicious use of consultants. Such a tendency coincides with the feeling in some corporations that if, in accepting their equipment, the Third World market demands their wider involvement, then they are not interested in the Third World market.

The tendency away from full turnkey projects toward equipment packages is particularly significant to Canadian corporations, which often lack the vast resources and the product breadth on which to base full turnkey operations. For Canadian subsidiaries of multinational corporations, in particular, the recent trend towards global rationalization through the granting of "product franchises" and world product mandates[21] is significant in this respect. Westinghouse, for example, has given its Canadian subsidiary a global franchise for certain classes of steam and gas turbine equipment. Similarly, Philips in Canada is developing a range of instrument landing systems for the world market. These examples are representative of a broad range of Canadian firms that will be increasingly capable and willing to supply highly competitive equipment packages, as opposed to full systems. In the airport equipment field, for example, a Canadian firm might be eager to supply runway lighting equipment or a baggage handling facility, but would be unlikely to want to undertake responsibility for an entire airport development project. It is important for such firms to realize, however, that the product demanded is a package, including installation and training, rather than simply a piece of equipment delivered to the purchasing nation.

For independent Canadian manufacturers, consortia have been proposed as a logical approach to large projects in the Third World — a vehicle for smaller, specialized Canadian firms to participate in the capital projects so often the preserve of the multinational giants.[22] In practice, however, the problems of co-ordinating effort and of defining responsibility and accountability for the various project segments have often proven too great for this approach to be viable. Individual firms tend to perceive such arrangements as unduly complex and exceptionally risky.

In the future, government mechanisms for facilitating the formation of consortia may develop in Canada as they have so successfully in Europe. In the near future, it is more likely that engineering and management consulting firms will provide a growing proportion of the project management and assistance with organizational development required by the Third World market. Canadian consulting firms are becoming increasingly aware of this market.

Supplementing Corporate Capabilities

The trend toward equipment packages and the use of consultants in

21. Science Council of Canada, *Multinationals and Industrial Strategy: The Role of World Product Mandates* (Ottawa: Science Council of Canada, 1980).
22. See K.C. Dhawan and L. Kryzanowski, *Export Consortia: A Canadian Study* (Montreal: Dekemco Ltd., 1978).

assisting nations towards self-sufficiency should continue over the long term as levels of development increase. There still remain, however, many countries in which inadequate skills resources and poorly developed organizational structures require more fundamental attention than can be reasonably supplied by equipment manufacturers or project consultants, and where the risks of bidding and/or currency fluctuation are too great to be borne by one firm alone.

In order for Canada to increase its exports of manufactures to these rapidly expanding markets, Canadian firms will need the support of their government, both through the physical presence of members of the Canadian government (political marketing) and through the forms of direct and indirect support.

Direct Government Support

There is no doubt that Canadian development assistance agencies could play a larger role in assisting Canadian firms in their attempts to obtain contracts for projects abroad. The area most in need of public sector support is that of risk — not only commercial risk, but also the risk of high inflation and currency devaluation. In its report to the minister of Industry, Trade, and Commerce, The Export Promotion Review Committee proposed a new public-private facility for evaluating and assuming major risks on large capital projects undertaken in foreign markets.[23] The proposed characteristics of the joint facility include:

• Majority ownership to be initially held by the federal government which would set up a $100 million risk fund for contingent liability.
• Profit sharing in direct proportion to risks underwritten on a project-by-project basis.
• Assistance for private consortia or individual Canadian firms requiring support in capital projects abroad valued at more than $50 million.

The role of the EDC would be far more valuable if it were amended to include short- to medium-term (one-to-five year) fixed rate export financing, directly or through guarantees to Canadian chartered banks, and earlier entry of the EDC into the negotiating process with foreign customers. Additionally, cheaper sources of capital should be sought in order to provide exporters with financing at rates comparable to those provided by competing countries. Failing this, some form of government subsidy should be considered.

23. Export Promotion Review, *Strengthening Canada Abroad*, p. 39.

The role of the Canadian International Development Agency could also be more related to the private sector by giving greater priority to the funding of projects in which Canadian firms would participate.

Indirect Government Assistance

At least three areas can be identified in which the resources of Canadian development assistance agencies can affect the ability of Canada's capital equipment manufacturers to meet the demand of Third World markets, particularly with regard to skills transfer. The first such area is the definition of "true" host nation needs. While pre-investment studies of development assistance agencies traditionally stress a requirement for skills transfer, recommendations tend to be vague and non-operational, focussing on activity rather than on results. There is a need for development assistance agencies to expand their pre-investment studies of skills-resource development requirements in areas related directly to proposed capital projects and to express the results of such studies in a form that is actionable by corporations subsequently undertaking the project.

A second area which would benefit greatly from co-operation between corporations and development assistance agencies is that of planning, funding, and implementing relevant background education and training programs supportive of the project training effort. Corporate resources are inefficiently used when directed at basic education and the transfer of technical background, areas which often represent the most serious barriers to the transfer of higher-level corporate skills.

A final area where increased support is urgently required relates to the more general problem of organization building. The commissioning gap is often characterized by a persistent lack of productive attitudes, which prevents newly acquired skills from being applied on the job and developed into a solid capability on the part of an organization. In such cases, import of foreign skills is required over an extended period to bridge the gap. During the planning stages of a turnkey operation, serious consideration should be given to the need for a period of foreign involvement beyond the turnkey project in a technical, assistance-oriented management contract, involving an entity having solid experience in operating, maintaining, and managing comparable systems. Ontario Hydro in the field of power generation, Canadian National in transport, and Bell Canada in telecommunications, for example, have ventured into activity of this sort. Public financing should be made far more readily available to cover such additional contracts. Where a substantial commissioning gap is anticipated, refusal by development agencies of such support is entirely inconsistent with the support given to the purchase of equipment and its installation.

What is suggested here is integration through the greatly increased involvement of development assistance agencies in skills transfer prior to, during, and following capital projects. Canadian development agencies should join the corporations in recognizing that what is being supplied to the developing nations in a capital project is not just equipment but a system — and those vital skills necessary to maintain and operate it following its completion. The Canadian capital equipment manufacturers, too, must reassess the challenge of the Third World market and adapt their product — their equipment and their skills — to meet the challenge.

V
International Operations Management

A
International Expansion Strategies

32
Turnkey Project Contract Procurement: A Canadian Perspective

K. C. Dhawan

Lawrence Kryzanowski

Dr. Dhawan is associate professor of international business and marketing at Concordia University. His research, publications, and consulting work have dealt with international business acquisitions and divestments, individual investors' attitudes towards small business investment, enterpreneurship, and business ethics. He has co-authored *Export Consortia: A Canadian Study* with Dr. Kryzanowski.

Dr. Kryzanowski is associate professor of finance at Concordia University. His publications include: *Export Consortia: A Canadian Study*, *Principles of Managerial Finance*, and a number of journal articles on regulation, capital investments and capital markets. He has consulted for organizational entities and individuals, primarily in the area of financial economics.

This chapter was written expressly for this volume.

In the intensely competitive export markets of the "cash-rich" petroleum-exporting countries, North American-based suppliers have encountered numerous difficulties in procuring and satisfactorily discharging contracts for the delivery of complete technological components, packages, and projects (henceforth, referred to as CPPs).[1]

The following two cases illustrate these difficulties:

— In Saudi Arabia, after several years of intense competition with a number of British, German, Japanese, Dutch, French, Swedish, and Canadian multinational firms, the American multinational firms were not awarded the multi-billion dollar contract for the Saudi Arabian telephone modernization program.[2]

A brief historical account of the project award is as follows. The thirteen components of the project were packaged into two fixed-price project contracts in order to minimize "split responsibility" during project delivery. The first contract, with an estimated value of 300 million dollars, was for the delivery of a microwave telecommunications network; the second contract, with an estimated value of three billion dollars, was for the delivery of an automated telephone network. International consultants from the U.S. and Norway were retained by the Saudi government to assist in the development of technical specifications and to advise on contract award. In mid-1977, the Saudi government rejected all of the preliminary bids since they were deemed to be unreasonably overpriced, and there had been a "successful" U.S. lobby for a rebid for all, or a portion, of the contract. In June 1977, the specifications for the entire project were reissued. Subsequently, many of the world's largest equipment suppliers formed consortia in order to procure the contract. Despite continued and intense lobbying, and the use of political marketing by the U.S. firms, the project was awarded in January 1978 to an ad hoc consortium of three multinational firms from Sweden, Holland, and Canada.

1. The definitions of these (and other) terms used in this chapter are given in the next section of this chapter.
2. For the post-award analysis of the project and some of the hypotheses offered for the loss of the project by the American firms, see "The Saudis Say 'Wrong Numbers' to U.S.", *Business Week* (January 9, 1978), pp. 20 and 21; and James Flanigan, "The Mystery of the 'Vague Specifications' or How the Americans Lost Out on a Giant Saudi Arabian Contract", *Forbes* (February 20, 1978), pp. 39-40.

— In the Middle East, Japanese-based firms have utilized two innovative marketing techniques to procure CPP contracts. The first is to conduct feasibility studies and to develop the technical specification for high-technology projects at no cost to their clients. Generally, this has given these firms the following competitive advantages: (1) the buyer becomes favorably biased towards the procurement of goods and services from these firms (the "good will" value of the study); (2) since the recommendations of these feasibility studies have an "author bias", the project design and specifications in the tender document are generally biased towards the goods and services that can be sourced from these firms; and (3) the bids submitted by these firms are generally superior to those submitted by the competitors, since the preparation of the study/specifications generally provides these firms with access to non-public information and valuable contacts.

The second technique is an informal co-ordination of all the bids submitted by Japanese firms, so that no more than three official bids are submitted for each CPP contract. More specifically, one low-, one medium-, and one high-priced bid, with a corresponding range of technical capabilities, is often submitted in order to increase the probability that the successful bidder will be a Japanese firm. If the successful bidder is a Japanese firm, then the project delivery is subdivided and subcontracted to all of the interested Japanese firms.

Based on the above illustrations, it is apparent that suppliers have experienced difficulties in both of the two steps in CPP delivery: the procurement of the contract, and the fulfilment of the terms of the contract. Although both steps are important, the first, as a necessary prerequisite for the second, is the topic of this chapter.[3] More specifically, the major purposes of this chapter are: (1) to discuss the six phases involved in the procurement of a contract by a company, or a group of companies; (2) to critically analyse the difficulties encountered by companies during each of these phases; and (3) to propose alternate strategies for overcoming some of these difficulties. Before proceeding to the definition of a number of terms used in this chapter, it should be emphasized that this study is based on 104 personal in-depth interviews conducted by the authors in Canada, Saudi Arabia, and Iran.

---

3. The second step is dealt with in K.C. Dhawan and Lawrence Kryzanowski, *Export Consortia: A Canadian Study* (Montreal, Quebec: Dekemco Ltd., 1978).

Some Definitions

Complete Technological Project
A "complete technological project" involves a contractual liability incurred by each "prime" supplier to the buyer (client) for the planned undertaking ("carry out") of the stages necessary to deliver an economically viable complete technological system (such as a pulp and paper complex). A complete technological project also generally involves a contractual liability incurred by each "sub" supplier to its corresponding prime supplier and a contractual liability incurred by the members of each prime supplier to each other. (The latter only applies to those situations where the prime supplier is a grouping of firms such as a consortium.)

Project Component
A "project component" involves a contractual liability incurred by a supplier to the buyer for the delivery of no more than one stage of a complete technological project. Some examples of a project component include the provision of capital equipment and the provision of a feasibility study.

Project Package
A "project package" involves a contractual liability incurred by a supplier to the buyer for the delivery of two or more stages of a complete technological project. For example, the sale and installation of a power generator would be considered to be a project package.

Turnkey Project
A "turnkey project" involves a contractual liability incurred by a supplier to the buyer for the delivery of the pre-engineering and economic feasibility study stage to the commissioning and start-up stage of a complete technological project. Furthermore, upon start up, the operating complete technological system is transferred to the buyer (owner) and the supplier's contractual liability is discharged.

Process Followed in the Procurement of a Foreign-Based Complete Technological Project Contract

Suppliers generally follow six often overlapping phases in the competitive procurement of contracts for foreign-based CPPs (components/packages/projects). These phases are as follows:

1. Project identification;
2. Packaging of potential participants into an organizational and contractual structure based on the use of "one firm as prime and other firms as subcontractors" or "consortium as prime and individual firms as subcontractors" structures;
3. Pre-qualification (the process and criteria used by the buyer during this phase often affect the previous phase);
4. Bidding, which includes such considerations as bid specifications, cost bases, nature of competition, type of technology, product and service offered, "scale or technology gap", arrangement of financing, determination of the bid price, importance of minimizing bid-price errors, identification of risks, determination of the cost of goods and services supplied, cost of agent fees, availability and cost of bid and performance bonds and guarantees, risk contingency reduction through risk transfer, risk contingency reduction through risk sharing, determination of a premium for all remaining risk contingencies, co-insurance of residual risks, determination of the profit markup, and cost of bid preparation;
5. Short listing[4] (sometimes short listing is a prerequisite for bidding); and
6. Project award or non-award (includes such considerations as contract negotiations and the contract).

Each of these phases, together with the associated problems for the foreign supplier, is discussed below. (However, due to space limitations, only phases (2) and (4) are treated extensively in this chapter.)

Project Identification
Many Canadian suppliers identify projects that are worth pursuing as follows: First, a company employee (or consultant), using secondary sources, identifies and evaluates potential growth areas and projects. Factors considered, among others, include the nature of competition, the proximity of the project, the size of the project, the availability of financing, the requirements of the project, the viability of the customer (determined through the trade service and commercial sources), the priorities of the supplier, the risk exposure to the supplier, and the supplier-sourced content of the project. Second, if the project meets this initial screening, it is submitted for consideration at a meeting of the board of directors. Third, if the board similarly agrees that the project is worth pursuing, the board decides

4. Short listing is a screening mechanism used to restrict the number of potential bidders.

not only who will take charge of the initial pursuit of the project, but also which firms are potential participants in the project if the effort is interfirm. Fourth, the individual responsible for the project travels to the foreign country to obtain further information on the project. Fifth, if the project is of interest, it is resubmitted to the board for consideration for a pre-qualification bid. Sixth, if the board similarly agrees and the effort is interfirm, then the packaging of potential participants begins. Since this packaging process is affected by the pre-qualification process and criteria to be used by the buyer, such information should be obtained and evaluated before proceeding to the next phase.

Packaging of Potential Participants

Since a small number of Canadian firms are individually able or willing to undertake large foreign-based projects, an interfirm (package) approach is generally necessary.[5]

The first step in such an approach is to determine the required mix of participants. Firms with large-project experience suggest that the required mix of participants is a number of large equipment manufacturers, a contractor, and possibly a consulting engineer. (There appears to be little agreement on whether or not a financial institution or a governmental agency should be included.)

The second step in a packaging approach is to determine the type of organizational and contractual structure that should be used. For illustrative purposes, two organizational and contractual structures are presented and evaluated below.

One firm as prime and other firms as subcontractors. Under this organizational and contractual structure, one firm acts as the prime contractor for the entire project and other firms are hired as subcontractors for various project components (see Figure 1).

Since the prime contractor incurs liability for all of the risks inherent in the entire project (such as business risk, other commercial risks, cost escalation risk on site, political risk, and exchange rate risk), the prime contractor is responsible for obtaining all of the required bonds and guarantees. However, by accepting this contractual liability towards the client, the prime contractor gains the right to choose its own project manager and subcontractors.

Each subcontractor incurs liability to the prime contractor on the basis of project participation. As a result, each subcontractor must furnish bonds or guarantees equivalent to the required contingency

---

5. This was confirmed by the in-depth personal interviews.

Figure 1

"One Firm as Prime and Other Firms as Subcontractors" Organizational and Contractual Structure for Foreign-Based Projects

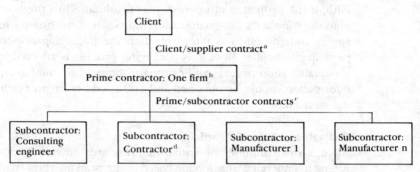

(a) In the client/supplier contract, the firm acting as prime contractor assumes 100 per cent of the bonding/guarantee requirements of the client. The firm's liability is incurred to the client.

(b) The prime contractor, in increasing order of capacity (standing), can be: a consulting engineer, a contractor, an equipment manufacturer, or a governmental agency such as the Atomic Energy of Canada Ltd. (AECI), Canadian National (CN), or Canadian Commercial Corporation (CCC).

(c) In the prime/subcontractor contracts, each subcontractor assumes x per cent of the bonding/guarantee requirements, where x is equivalent to the required contingency for the business risk inherent in the subcontractor's portion of the project. Each subcontractor's liability is incurred to the prime contractor. Typical values for x are 10 per cent for consulting engineers, 50 per cent for contractors, and 10 to 50 per cent for a manufacturer.

(d) The subcontracting contractor can be home country sourced, foreign sourced, or host country sourced. Difficulties associated with each of these sources are discussed in the chapter.

for the business risk inherent in its portion of the project (that is, its project component).

The major strengths of this organizational and contractual structure are: (1) from the client's perspective, the structure does not result in "split (divided) responsibility" for the project; and (2) project participants are not required to incur liability on a joint and several basis.

The major weakness of this structure is that only a small number of Canadian-based firms have the required financial standing to act as the prime contractor for large foreign-based projects.

Consortium as prime and individual firms as subcontractors. Under this organizational and contractual structure, a consortium acts as the prime contractor for the entire project, and individual firms (members or non-members of the consortium) are hired as subcontractors for various project components (see Figure 2).

The major strength of this organizational and contractual structure is the major weakness of the previous structure. More specifically,

Figure 2

"Consortium as Prime and Individual Firms as Subcontractors" Organizational and Contractual Structure for Foreign-Based Projects

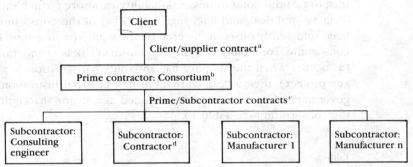

(a) In the client/supplier contract, the consortium acting as prime contractor assumes 100 per cent of the bonding/guarantee requirements of the client. The consortium's liability is incurred to the client.

(b) The effectiveness of the prime contractor, which is a consortium depends upon the prime contractors capacity (standing). For further details on the standing of individual members, see note (b) in Figure 1.

(c) In the prime/subcontractor contracts, each subcontractor assumes x per cent of the bonding/guarantee requirements, where x is equivalent to the required contingency for the business risk inherent in the subcontractor's portion of the project. Each subcontractor's liability is incurred to the consortium (of which the subcontractor may be a member). Typical values for x are 10 per cent for consulting engineers, 50 per cent for contractors, and 10 to 50 per cent for a manufacturer.

(d) The subcontracting contractor can be home-country-sourced, foreign-sourced, or host-country-sourced. Difficulties associated with each of these sources are discussed in the chapter.

the major strength of this structure is that the entity acting as prime contractor (the consortium) can be packaged so that it has the financial standing necessary to obtain foreign-based project contracts.

The major weaknesses of this organizational and contractual structure are the major strengths of the previous structure. These weaknesses are as follows: (1) from the client's perspective, the structure may result in "split responsibility" for the project; and (2) members of the consortium will have to incur additional project liability, either on a joint but not several basis where the maximum incremental liability exposure of a member is its pro rata share of the project, or on a joint and several basis where the maximum incremental liability exposure of a member is the total project liability incurred by the consortium.[6]

6. Incremental liability incurred by a member (shareholder) of a consortium is any liability that a member would not generally incur by being a member (or equity shareholder) of a limited liability company.

Incurring additional firm liability is not a problem for a firm if: (1)
the majority of the total liability exposure of the consortium consists
of business risk and this business risk has been sufficiently offset or
covered by the bonds and guarantees provided by the subcontractors; or (2) the non-business risk liability exposure (which includes
financial, political, and exchange rate risks) of the consortium has
been sufficiently offset or covered by the equity participation in the
consortium. For example, if the non-business risk is mainly financial
(as occurs when the supplier has an equity participation in a turnkey project), then a "capital-rich" firm, a financial institution, or a
governmental agency could be included as a major shareholder in
the consortium (see Table 1).

Table 1

**Possible Equity Participation in a Turnkey Consortium
Where All Risks Other Than Financial Risk Have Been Offset
or Covered**

Member	Equity Participation (Percentage)
Contractor	25
Equipment supplier 1	10
Equipment supplier 2	10
Consultant	5
"Capital-rich" firm[a]; financial institution[b]; or governmental agency, department, crown corporation, or regulated firm[c]	50[d]

(a) The firm could be "capital-rich" either because it has an excess of liquid assets or it has unused debt capacity.
(b) Many foreign-based consortia include one or more financial institutions as members. More specifically, this includes the heavy involvement of Japanese banks in Japanese-based consortia, and the equity participation of some U.S. financial institutions in a number of Iranian agro-business consortia.
(c) This refers to such Canadian entities as CN, AECL, CCC, and Bell Canada. By their nature, these firms are either directly or indirectly backed by the financial standing of the Canadian government and public.
(d) The loss of control by the other members to this large shareholder (because of the unequal equity participation in the consortium) could be offset by an agreement that each member has an equal vote. This would ensure that the appointed project manager is accountable to all members of the consortium.

The final step in a packaging approach is the internal pre-qualification of members, the procurement of commitments from the members
that pre-qualify, and the appointment of a project leader or director.
Specific problems encountered by firms in packaging participants
include: (1) manufacturers are generally unwilling to assume any

engineering or specification risk; (2) if a foreign subsidiary is a participant, it is difficult to ascertain whether or not the subsidiary really wants to bid;[7] (3) since the few qualified contractors in the home country with sufficient financial standing are often asked to bid on projects with conditions under which they would not bid domestically, they are reluctant to participate; and (4) if a foreign-based contractor is a participant in the package, then an additional political or business risk must be assumed by the home-country-based participants.

Pre-Qualification

After the potential project participants have been packaged, the grouping often must file pre-qualification documents with the buyer before it can bid on a CPP. This generally involves a detailed descriptive summary of each participant firm (including such aspects as the qualifications of personnel assigned to the project, past work undertaken by each firm, and financial and operational information on the relative standing of each firm). Furthermore, for the Middle East markets, a firm or grouping generally needs a letter from the home country government attesting to: (1) the nationality of the firm or grouping; and (2) the fact that the firm or grouping has the required capacity to undertake the project successfully.

Pre-qualification is costly and extremely competitive internationally. For example, a Canadian-based firm was one of ninety international firms that recently filed pre-qualification documents on a large turnkey project.

Bidding

If the firm or grouping pre-qualifies (and in some cases is short listed), then it can submit a bid for the CPP.

Bid specification. The bid specifications for a CPP are given in the tender document. Generally, the tender document has clauses dealing with such items as the cost basis, financing, and the detailed specification of the CPP to be delivered. Furthermore, in Iran and Saudi Arabia, there are also clauses in the tender document dealing with bid and performance bonds or guarantees.

Cost bases. There are four major cost bases for a bid. The first cost basis is the fixed-price, fixed-charge, or lump-sum basis, which re-

---

7. In Canada, the experience has been that a subsidiary will generally only pursue a project if it is in the corporate (parent's) interest; for example, when the project is part of Canadian "tied aid".

quires the supplier to deliver a specific CPP at a specified fixed price.

The second cost basis is the guaranteed maximum basis, which requires the supplier to deliver a specific CPP for no more than a specified maximum (that is, upper) price.

The third cost basis is the target-price, charge, or lump-sum basis, which requires the supplier to deliver a specific CPP at a specified fixed target price and actual costs under or over the target price result in higher or lower fees (that is, returns) for the supplier. Stated differently, the fees earned by the supplier are graduated to the losses or savings on the project, when measured using the targeted cost as the reference point.

The fourth cost basis is the cost-plus basis, which requires the supplier to deliver a specific CPP at cost plus reimbursables plus either a fixed or percentage fee.

Nature of competition. A determination of the nature of competition for a CPP sale is important because it affects the following considerations in a bid preparation: the type of technology, product, and service offered; the bid price; costing; the techniques utilized for risk contingency reduction; the size of the premium for uncovered risk contingencies; the size of the profit markup; the nature and terms of financing offered; the nature and cost of bid bonds and guarantees; the utilization of agents; and the time and effort expended in bid preparation.

Type of technology, product, and service offered. The type of technology, product, and service offered in a bid must first satisfy the bid specifications in the tender document. In addition, they should reflect the local environment, because to disregard environmental factors, especially in a competitive environment, will result in either non-award of contract, or in major problems during the delivery and operation of the CPP supplied.

Before proceeding to a determination of a bid price, the supplier should determine: (1) whether or not an unacceptable "scale or technology gap" exists; (2) whether or not the supplier will be required to participate financially or arrange financing; and (3) whether or not any required financing is both available and competitive.

Scale or technology gap. A "scale or technology gap" is defined as the difference between the scale or technology of the CPP to be delivered and similar domestic (or international) CPPs undertaken in the past by the supplier (or by any other supplier). Although no specific measurement criteria or cutoff rules have been developed either in theory or in practice, it is generally believed that the larger the scale or technology gap the higher the probability of a non-award of contract and/or major problems during the delivery and operation of the CPP supplied.

Arrangement of financing. In addition to price, quality, technical adequacy, and delivery time, the availability of internationally competitive export credit insurance and export financing are often factors that determine whether or not a supplier will be awarded a CPP contract. The availability of internationally competitive export financing is especially important because the supplying firm or consortium often has to arrange financing for the buyer and/or itself (for funding equity in a non-pure undertaking, or for funding working capital in all undertakings).

The major Canadian source for export credit insurance is the EDC (Export Development Corporation). The major Canadian sources of export credit/finance are the EDC and the chartered banks.[8]

Determination of the bid price. Since the bid price is often crucial in contract award, the determination of the bid price is an important decision in procuring a contract. In general, the bid price is calculated as the estimated cost of all goods and services to be supplied, plus the estimated cost of all agent fees to be paid, plus the estimated cost of all required interim financing,[9] plus a contingency premium for all identified risks which have not been externally shared, transferred or covered, plus a profit markup.

Identification of risks. The risks associated with the delivery of a foreign-based CPP can be classified by nature (as political or commercial), by time duration (as short term, medium term, or long term), by user (as private buyer, public buyer, or seller), by location (as pre-delivery or post-delivery), or by source (as domestic-sourced or foreign-sourced). The most common of these is the identification of risk by nature.

The cost consequences of each of the risks under different economic scenarios must first be determined. Then, based on a cost-benefit analysis of each alternative, each risk must be (1) covered or offset externally (for example, through EDC insurance); and/or (2) costed into the bid price (via a risk contingency loading); and/or (3) borne by the supplier (referred to as co-insurance in the case of a group effort).

8. An extensive comparative analysis of the export credit insurance programs and of the export finance/credit programs of a number of major industrial countries is given in Dhawan and Kryzanowski, *Export Consortia,* pp. 100-115.
9. This can be caused, for example, by a "hold back".

Cost of agent fees. Agent fees are costed into the bid price as follows: (1) any fees that are tax deductible are costed at cost; and (2) any fees that are not tax deductible (no proof of payment) are costed at cost multiplied by one plus the firm's marginal tax rate.[10] For the latter, the required disbursement by the firm includes the actual fees paid and the taxes paid on the taxable revenue that was overstated by the amount of the non-deductible agent fees paid.

Availability and cost of bid and performance bonds and guarantees. A bid bond or guarantee is a bond or guarantee issued by an issuer (generally a third party) to the buyer for the following purposes: (1) to assure the buyer that the successful bidder will make a bona fide effort to fulfill satisfactorily the terms of the contract for the delivery of the particular CPP; (2) to commit the supplier financially to the satisfactory delivery of the particular CPP; and (3) to indemnify the buyer for any losses caused by any unsatisfactory performance by the supplier in fulfilling the contract to deliver the particular CPP.[11]

Specific problems that may be encountered by a firm with bid or performance bonds or guarantees include the following:

1. *Counter-indemnification:* "Counter-indemnification" is an agreement indemnifying the bidder or supplier against loss, damage, penalty, or default caused by the client. If possible, the bidder or supplier should obtain counter-indemnification from the client for the wrongful call of all bonds or guarantees provided. Unfortunately, many buyers will not agree to a counter-indemnification agreement.

2. *Cross-indemnification:* "Cross-indemnification" is an agreement among bidders or suppliers, indemnifying the members against loss, damage, penalty, or default caused by one or more of their members (for example, by a member going bankrupt).

   For firms of similar relative financial standing, cross-indemnification causes no unique problems since any problems that may arise can be resolved legally.

   For firms of different (or limited) relative financial standing, cross-indemnification causes no unique problems if cross-bonding is both available and reasonably priced. However, bonding companies are generally reluctant to cross-bond any members of

---

10. In the Netherlands, for example, both a ship handler and an interior decorator won court judgments that allowed deductions without proof for domestic bribes.
11. For an extensive discussion of the characteristics of bid and performance bonds and guarantees, the interested reader should refer to Dhawan and Kryzanowski, *Export Consortia.*

limited financial standing, since the probability of successful recourse for the bonding firm decreases as the probability of a member firm's bankruptcy increases. Since a bond is generally secured by a general subordinated lien on a member's assets, the bonding company does not have any priority as a creditor upon member bankruptcy.

3. *Limited domestic bonding capacity:* If a bidder or supplier has "heavy" bonding requirements, it will generally have to go to a syndicate based in London, Zurich, or New York. For internationally sourced bonds, the domestic bidder or supplier is generally at a competitive disadvantage for the following reasons: (a) since foreign issuers of bonds are more familiar with their domestic firms, they can provide cheaper bonding to these firms; and (b) foreign issuers of bonds are more likely to give their domestic firms both preferential access to bonds and bond rates.

4. *Impairment of working capital:* Since a guarantee reduces or impairs the bidder's or supplier's working capital, the bidder or supplier may become working-capital-poor or deficient. A potential solution to this problem is to recruit a governmental agency, department, or crown corporation (or even a regulated firm) to be the prime contractor for the delivery of the CPP. Thus, the governmental agency, department, or crown corporation would provide the guarantees required by the client and each subcontractor would cross-indemnify the prime contractor through bonding (see Figure 2 and 3 for greater detail). Therefore, this solution would eliminate the working capital impairment to the non-governmental bidders or suppliers.

One of the major factors considered by an issuer before issuing a bond or guarantee is the future cash flow of the firm (or firms) to be bonded or guaranteed. In particular, many issuers use a "spread-sheet approach" to evaluate the cash flow coverage over time, for both the domestic (production or pre-delivery) and foreign (implementation or delivery) aspects of the CPP delivery.

Risk contingency reduction through risk transfer. The supplier can reduce the risk contingency to be costed into the bid and/or borne by the supplier by transferring some of the risks to a third party. Three methods for such a transfer of risks are:

1. The supplier can attempt to obtain fixed forward price contracts for needed goods and services from a third party (or non-member if the supplier is a consortium). Unfortunately, most potential suppliers will not provide fixed forward prices for periods beyond six months.

2. The supplier can attempt to subcontract all high risk components or packages (especially local civil work) at a fixed price to a third party. However, this method has the following potential deficiencies: (a) either no third party may be willing to become a subcontractor for a risky component or package at a fixed price, or any third parties that are willing may not be able to procure the cross-indemnification necessary to protect the prime supplier; and (b) if the subcontractor is foreign, he may renege "when the going gets tough".

3. For short- and medium-term contracts, the supplier can eliminate all of the foreign exchange risk by using the forward market. For long-term contracts, the supplier can reduce, but generally not eliminate, his foreign exchange risk by using the forward market, since it is difficult to obtain U.S. forwards of five years or more.

Risk contingency reduction through risk sharing (insurance). The supplier can reduce the risk contingency to be costed into the bid and/or borne by the supplier by sharing (insuring) one or more risks with third parties. More specifically, conventional and "custom" export insurance packages are available from insurance brokers and consultants such as Marsh and McLennan Ltd. and Reed Shaw Stenhouse Ltd.

Whether or not a supplier should insure depends upon whether or not the insurance premium is less than the contingency loading which would be included in the bid or tender price. It should be noted that many of the businessmen interviewed considered the costs of such insurance to be high.

Determination of a premium for all remaining risk contingencies. The remaining risk contingency composite and its cost consequences must be estimated. This can generally be determined most effectively by a risk analysis simulation (as proposed by Hertz[12] and applied and evaluated by Kryzanowski-Lusztig-Schwab[13]) in which one of the outputs is a distribution of possible gains and losses (that is, the difference between the possible future costs and the bid price).

Subsequent to the estimation of the distribution of losses and gains, the supplier must add a risk premium to the bid price. The size of the risk premium is generally dependent upon four factors: (1) the

12. David B. Hertz, "Risk Analysis in Capital Investment", *Harvard Business Review* 42 (January/February 1964), pp. 95-106; and "Investment Policies That Pay Off", *Harvard Business Review* 46 (January/February 1968), pp. 96-108.

13. Lawrence Kryzanowski, Peter Lusztig, and Bernhard Schwab, "Monte Carlo Simulation and Capital Expenditure Decisions — A Case Study", *The Engineering Economist* 18 (Fall 1972), pp. 31-48.

probability of incurring losses; (2) the magnitude of such losses; (3) the risk-taking characteristics of the bidder or supplier; and (4) competitive considerations.

Three common problems encountered in determining the risk premium include:

1. Suppliers may add in a risk contingency premium at each stage of the bid preparation. As a result, contingencies at later stages may be costed against contingencies added at earlier stages.
2. Suppliers may use "ignorance" costing of risk contingencies. For example, some suppliers arbitrarily add a 100 per cent contingency to the price of a bid.
3. Many suppliers cannot comprehend that some residual risk will always remain uncovered. If a bid is to be competitive, it cannot have a risk contingency premium which covers the entire risk of the CPP delivery.

Co-insurance of residual risk. Any risks that remain after a risk contingency premium has been costed into the bid price must be borne by the bidder or supplier. For an interfirm (group) approach, this residual risk must be borne by the members and is referred to here as "co-insurance". The organizational and contractual structures that can be used to deal with the co-insurance of residual risk, along with their major strengths and weaknesses, have been discussed earlier in this chapter.

Determination of the profit markup. The profit markup should be a reasonable and competitive rate of return on the CPP supplied. A major problem to be avoided in determining the profit markup is to ensure that the profit markup of the individual suppliers is profit, and not profit plus contingency.

Short Listing

If the bid of the firm or grouping passes the buyer's pre-screen, it is put on what is referred to as a "short list". (It should be noted that sometimes being put on the short list is a prerequisite to being able to submit a formal bid for a project. That is, the buyer may sometimes use a short list to solicit a limited number of bids from well-qualified bidders.)

Often, at this stage, the client will notify the bidders on the short list that the client cannot proceed with contract award for one or more of the following reasons: (1) all bids were too expensive; (2) all bids failed to meet one or more of the conditions of the tender document; and (3) firms were not packaged in such a way as to

ensure satisfactory delivery of the CPP. However, it should be remembered that often the true rationale for such a non-award of
contract is an attempt by the buyer to obtain contract concessions.

Project Award/Non-award

If the buyer is not satisfied with any of the bids and cannot obtain
sufficient concessions, then the buyer has the right to refuse all bids.
Subsequently, the buyer can reopen the tender process.

   If the buyer is satisfied with at least one of the bids, then the buyer
"awards" the contract and the difficult negotiation procedure begins.

Contract negotiations. Contract negotiations invariably concentrate
on performance, delivery schedules, price, type of goods and services supplied, and buyer audit and control. Furthermore, contract
negotiations are generally protracted and frustrating.

The contract. The contract is generally very specific and exhaustive.
Some topics included in most contracts are: (1) amount and timing
of payments; (2) nature of "holdbacks" (for example to ensure
"satisfactory" delivery of the CPP); (3) performance bonds and
guarantees; (4) specification of "satisfactory" performance; (5)
procedures for the resolution of contract disputes; and (6) cultural,
political, and religious restrictions such as the conditions under
which the supplier's personnel stationed in the buyer's country can
take vacations.

Summary and Implications

Canadian companies have encountered serious impediments and
intense international competition in their attempts to procure contracts for components, packages, and projects in foreign countries.
Some of the impediments that have been identified and assessed in
the chapter include: the packaging (grouping) of participants, the
organizational and contractual structures associated with such groupings, the fixed-price nature of some foreign contracts, scale and
technology gaps, costing of agent fees, the availability and cost of bid
and performance bonds and guarantees, and the reduction and co-
insurance of the risk contingency associated with project delivery.
   Two important implications of this study are as follows. First,
Canadian business executives must become familiar with and use
their competitor's strategies and innovative techniques for negotiations, for bidding, for packaging of participants and for the procurement of insurance, bonds and guarantees, and financing. Second,
Canadian business executives must become more aggressive towards

the procurement of foreign-based contracts and they must exhibit greater "staying power" during the lengthy and difficult negotiation process that leads to such contracts.

V
International Operations Management

B
R & D Management

33
Are Foreign Subsidiaries More Innovative?

Herman P. Bones

Mr. Bones is a senior economist with the policy research group, Industry Branch, Ministry of State for Science and Technology.

The material in this chapter appeared originally in the *Foreign Investment Review*, Spring 1980. Reprinted by permission of the minister of Supply and Services Canada.

Past investigations have generally concluded "that subsidiaries per-form either as well as or better than Canadian-owned firms in terms of R & D".[1] Such findings, however, have been based either on highly aggregate statistics, which do not distinguish Canadian from foreign-controlled firms, or on sample surveys and case studies, the validity and representativeness of which it has been difficult to determine. Data allowing direct comparisons of the R & D activities of Canadian- and foreign-controlled firms have only recently become available.[2]

Analysis of the new data shows that more than 80 per cent of industrial R & D is performed by manufacturing and is concentrated in seven key industries — aircraft and parts, electrical products, petroleum, machinery, chemicals, primary metals, and pulp and paper. These industries, although accounting for just 40 per cent of manu-facturing value added, make up 85 per cent of manufacturing R & D. In addition, when their R & D expenditures are related to overall measures of industry size (sales, value added), they are the most research intensive (see Table 1).

Manufacturing also accounts for 60 per cent of all foreign control in the economy, and it is the only sector, other than mining, in which foreign-controlled firms are predominant, with the level of control reaching 57.7 per cent in 1975. Foreign control is highest in the most research-intensive industries, with foreign-controlled firms account-ing for over 80 per cent of sales in 1975.

The predominance of foreign-controlled firms in the research-intensive industries does not mean that they are necessarily more research intensive than their Canadian-controlled counterparts but only that they tend to be concentrated in those industries where most R & D is performed. For example, Table 2 relates the R & D ex-penditures of Canadian- and foreign-controlled firms in the research-intensive industries to their respective level of sales in 1975. Where possible, industries have been further disaggregated to produce more

1. M.H. Watkins, *Report of the Task Force on Foreign Ownership and the Structure of Canadian Industry* (Ottawa: Privy Council Office, 1968), p. 211.
2. Statistics Canada, *Annual Review of Science Statistics,* cat. no. 13-212, 1977, Annual.

Table 1

Foreign Control and Research Intensity by Research-Intensive Industry, 1975

	Foreign Control of Industry Sales %		R & D/Value Added (total industry) %
High Research Intensity		**82.0**	**4.2**
Aircraft and Parts	82.7		11.0
Electrical Products	65.6		5.1
Petroleum	96.0		4.6
Machinery	67.5		3.2
Chemical Products	82.9		2.5
Medium Research Intensity		**32.4**	**1.2**
Primary Metals	17.1		1.8
Paper and Allied	43.6		0.7
Other Manufacturing		**51.6**	**0.3**
Total Manufacturing		**57.7**	**1.3**

Source: Statistics Canada.

Table 2

Relative Sales and R & D by Research-Intensive Industry, 1975

	Canadian-Controlled			Foreign-Controlled		
	% Sales		% R & D	% Sales		% R & D
Pulp and Paper		**56.4**	**67.2**	**43.6**		**32.8**
Primary Metals		**82.9**	**86.0**	**17.1**		**14.0**
Ferrous	87.0		88.8	13.0	11.2	
Non-Ferrous	78.6		85.2	21.4	14.8	
Electrical Products		**34.4**	**59.2**	**65.6**		**40.8**
Machinery		**32.5**	**31.4**	**67.5**		**68.6**
Business Machines	14.8		11.3	85.2	88.7	
Other Machinery	35.0		43.8	65.0	56.2	
Chemicals		**17.1**	**31.7**	**82.9**		**68.3**
Pharmaceuticals	13.2		29.3	86.8	70.7	
Other Chemicals	18.3		33.2	81.7	66.8	
Aircraft and Parts		**17.3**	**41.9**	**82.7**		**58.1**

Note: The petroleum industry is excluded since the data on R & D by firm group is confidential.

Source: Statistics Canada.

precise results. With one minor exception, these data show that even in the most research-intensive industries, the R & D expenditures of Canadian-controlled firms are higher relative to sales than their foreign-controlled counterparts.

Despite their lower R & D-to-sales ratio, it would be premature to conclude that foreign-controlled firms are less technology intensive than their Canadian-controlled counterparts. R & D expenditures do not account for a foreign-controlled company's access to imported technology. The importance to subsidiaries of parent technology is reflected in their payments to non-residents for technology-related services. While the notion of "technology-related payments" is imprecise and while there often is no explicit charge associated with transfers of technology with multinational corporations, the figures that are available seem quite striking. Even when the analysis is limited to visible payments for patents, industrial designs, royalties and scientific and research services (which excludes the more general categories of engineering services, and professional and management services), and when these are added to firms' R & D expenditures, the divergence between Canadian and foreign-controlled firms disappears in a most systematic manner (see Table 3). Because of the statistical and definitional problems mentioned above, probably not too much significance should be attached to the precise figures in Table 3. However, they do tend to confirm that foreign subsidiaries are no less and, in fact, probably more technology intensive than their Canadian-controlled counterparts, and that their access to foreign technology is the principal reason for their lower research intensity.

The stronger economic performance of Canada's technology-intensive industries is now well documented. They have been shown to have higher aggregate rates of growth in output, employment, and productivity, and lower rates of price increases.[3] In a similar fashion, it seems that foreign-controlled firms' access to imported technology gives them a competitive edge over their Canadian-controlled counterparts. They are much larger in size and "labor productivity in foreign-owned firms is higher (and) . . . foreign-owned corporations tend to earn higher profits".[4]

At the same time, foreign-controlled firms would appear to export less than Canadian-controlled ones. Table 4 compares U.S.-controlled firms' share of sales and exports in the most research-intensive

3. U.K. Ranga Chand, "Does R & D Boost Industrial Growth?" *The Canadian Business Review,* **5**, No. 3 (Summer 1978), pp. 27-31.
4. Economic Council of Canada, *Fifteenth Annual Review* (Ottawa 1978), p. 29.

Table 3

Relative R & D (including R & D and technology-related payments to non-residents) by Research-Intensive Industry, 1975

	Canadian-Controlled Firms		Foreign-Controlled Firms	
	Sales	R & D	Sales	R & D
Pulp and Paper	56.4	52.7	43.6	47.3
Primary Metals	82.9	78.9	17.1	21.1
Electrical Products	34.4	53.2	65.6	46.8
Machinery	32.5	25.0	67.5	75.0
Chemicals	17.1	19.7	82.9	80.3

Note: If Northern Telecom were excluded, Canadian-controlled firms' share of sales and R & D in Electrical products would be roughly equivalent, about 20 per cent in each case.

Source: Statistics Canada.

Table 4

Relative Export Performance in the High Research-Intensive Industries, 1970

	U.S. — Controlled Firms		Other Foreign-Controlled Firms		All Foreign-Controlled Firms	
	% Sales	% Exports	% Sales	% Exports (est.)	% Sales	% Exports
Electrical Products	55.0	25.9	8.0	3.8	63.0	29.7
Machinery	70.6	33.6	6.4	3.0	77.0	36.6
Chemicals	59.2	29.3	23.3	11.5	82.5	40.8
Total	61.3	30.8	12.7	5.0	74.0	35.8

Note: Total exports from these industries accounted for 15 per cent of all Canadian exports and 40 per cent of end product exports in 1970.

Source: U.S. Tariff Commission and Statistics Canada.

industries and, although data are unavailable, it seems reasonable to assume that a similar pattern would exist for other foreign-controlled firms as well. On this basis, it is seen that foreign-controlled firms, although accounting for almost 75 per cent of sales in 1970, were responsible for only 35 per cent of exports.

The poorer export performance of foreign-controlled firms may seem paradoxical in light of their better profit and productivity record. To a large extent, this reflects the impact on their more diversified production activities of the historically high levels of tariffs imposed on manufactured goods both in Canada and abroad. In fact, it has recently been shown that Canadian-controlled firms, because of their more limited product range, are generally more specialized than their foreign-controlled counterparts.[5] The findings in this paper indicate that they are also concentrated in relatively less technology-intensive areas. Accordingly, in their own product fields Canadian-controlled firms are probably competitive both domestically and abroad but, because of their greater specialization, the Canadian market accounts for a relatively smaller proportion of their overall sales.

There has been a tendency on the part of some observers to attribute the more fragmented production structure of foreign-controlled firms, and their subsequent lack of exports and R & D, to foreign ownership per se instead of more fundamental causal factors. It is important to note in this context that similar variations in product diversification occur among firms even in countries where foreign investment is insignificant. Thus it is unlikely, given the small domestic market and significant domestic and foreign trade barriers, that the behavior of these more diversified firms would be very different, even if they were Canadian-controlled and the necessary technology had been acquired through other channels such as licensing agreements and joint ventures.

Japan is often cited as a case where an indigenous innovative capacity has been developed by retaining domestic control of industry while relying on licensing arrangements with foreign firms for technology. However, this overlooks the fact that the national market in Japan is sufficiently large to allow domestic producers to achieve the minimum critical size required for meaningful R & D programs, despite the existence of trade barriers. A strong case can be made that the licensing option would have left Canada relatively worse off, given its small internal market. Licensing agreements generally preclude exports to a much greater degree than parent/subsidiary relationships, and provide no access to other types of foreign expertise in areas such as marketing, administration, production control, and personnel training.

It has been argued in the past, given the higher profits and productivity and the greater technological intensity of foreign-controlled firms, that the substitution of more domestic R & D for

5. Richard E. Caves, *Diversification, Foreign Investment and Scale in North American Manufacturing Industries,* (Ottawa: Economic Council of Canada, 1975), p. 4.

imported technology would be inefficient, since Canada would only be duplicating at much greater cost and risk that which is already available from foreign sources. This fails to recognize, however, that the divergence in the research activities of Canadian- and foreign-controlled firms is more than just a quantitative one.

R & D covers a wide range of activities, and firms with comparable expenditures may be involved in fundamentally different types of work. For example, considerable emphasis has been placed in previous studies on the tendency of foreign subsidiaries to use the basic designs and processes of their parents, while concentrating their own R & D efforts on adapting this technology to the special requirements of the small Canadian market. In fact, the relationship between subsidiaries and their parent corporations can vary widely, from one of relatively complete autonomy to that of largely dependent branch plants with limited decision-making and policy-making authority. Similarly, in the conduct of R & D, examples can be found of firms doing relatively independent research projects. Despite extensive work, therefore, no clear impression has emerged of the degree to which R & D expenditures of foreign subsidiaries reflect adaptation functions, as opposed to truly innovative activities, and there is even less agreement on what would constitute the optimal mix.

The data now available confirm that subsidiaries draw heavily on the technology of their parents. Of course, access to imported technology does not necessarily mean that foreign-controlled firms' R & D expenditures are qualitatively different from those of Canadian-controlled firms. However, the small size of most Canadian markets, relative to the number of products and production runs, has generally been viewed as insufficient to support extensive R & D programs.[6] This has led to the observation that firms with large R & D expenditures, although servicing the domestic market, must also strongly orient themselves toward export markets. On the basis of their export performance, therefore, there is little doubt that R & D in most subsidiaries is not only quantitatively less, but also qualitatively different.

Overall, the lack of specialization by foreign subsidiaries has tended to reduce their level of R & D expenditures because domestic sales have generally been insufficient to support the R & D required to develop new products and production techniques. More funda-

6. H.E. English, "Industrial Organization and Technical Progress", ed. T. N. Brewis, *Growth and the Canadian Economy* (Toronto 1968), pp. 131-2.

mentally, however, it also affected the qualitative make-up of the remaining R & D effort, directing it toward adaptive functions for the domestic market, as opposed to more innovative work aimed at exports.

No country is technologically independent and, because of Canada's small size, imported technology will continue to account for a significant part of its technological base. However, it seems clear from the preceding analysis that the net gains from both imported technology and domestic R & D performed by foreign-controlled firms, have not been maximized due to insufficient opportunities for greater specialization.

The need for greater rationalization in Canadian manufacturing has long been recognized. The evaluation of this question, however, has been discussed almost exclusively in terms of the free trade issue. The proponents of free trade, although clearly showing the efficiency losses inherent in limited scale and specialization, have tended to focus on the overall gains in the long run of economy-wide tariff cuts. The problem with this approach is that it tends to ignore the path of adjustment to this better position, specifically in terms of the impact on those individuals and industries who would lose at least in the short run as a result of these measures.

The somewhat narrow perspective of the free trade literature is unfortunate since the most significant gains from increased specialization would occur within industries, especially on the part of foreign-controlled firms in the technology-intensive sector. Of course, because the decision by foreign firms to locate in Canada has commonly been attributed to the influence of tariffs, it has often been asserted that trade liberalization would result in their departure, with Canadian operations reverting to a simple distribution function for imports.

This view fails to account for the significant changes which have occurred in the Canadian economy over the last twenty-five years. A well-educated and highly trained labor force, a sophisticated service economy, especially in financial and capital markets and in the supporting infrastructure of transportation and communications, and a relative abundance of increasingly scarce energy sources, especially in hydro-electricity and natural gas, combine to give Canada a comparative advantage which did not exist many years ago. Indeed, many foreign-controlled firms, as a result of tariff reductions in the 1960s, have already started to rationalize at least parts of their operations, and they are becoming more research intensive and export oriented.

The further reduction of both domestic and foreign tariffs, as a result of the most recent GATT negotiations, should provide additional incentive and opportunities for greater rationalization in the technology-intensive sector. This is the area where tariffs have had their most detrimental effect and where the potential for export growth is greatest, given current trends in international trade. The achievement of greater specialization in the technology-intensive industries would require some restructuring in the current pattern of production but, fortunately, these adjustments could be handled largely within existing firms. More importantly, however, the benefits of increased specialization would be clearly visible in the form of overall increases in employment and production.

More efficient use would be made of highly qualified manpower, as resources now engaged in adapting imported technology would be released for more innovative work in those fields where firms chose to specialize. In this manner, access to foreign technology could be maintained, but it would act to complement and not distort or substitute for domestic R & D. In addition, the growth in new exports of technology-intensive commodities would reduce the current account deficit in end products, and the overall increase in national productivity would act to strengthen even further Canada's international competitive position.

In brief, it is time to recognize that Canada, although benefiting enormously as a consumer of technology-intensive products, has hardly started to exploit the pay-off from their production to its full potential.

V
International Operations Management

B
R & D Management

34
Technology Acquisition by Canadian Firms

J. Peter Killing

Dr. Killing is associate professor of business policy in the School of Business Administration, University of Western Ontario. Since producing his thesis, *Manufacturing Under License in Canada*, in 1975, his research has focussed on the management of joint ventures. He is also an active consultant to business and government.

This chapter is a revised version of an article which appeared originally under the title, "How to Buy Technology", in the *Columbia Journal of World Business*. Reprinted by permission.

Canadian businessmen have been chastised by academics and government officials for some years for not carrying out "enough" in-house research and development. The chorus became particularly loud following a 1969 OECD publication[1] which noted that Canada was at or near the bottom of each of five measures of technological innovation. The Science Council of Canada added fuel to the fire in the 1970s with publications such as *Innovation in a Cold Climate,*[2] *Innovation and the Structure of Canadian Industry,*[3] and more recently, *The Weakest Link.*[4] Businessmen have been remarkedly unimpressed by this flow of words and only a little more moved by the Canadian government's research and development support programs. They have continued to survive by copying others'[5] products after they are on the market, using licence agreements, and in general, avoiding the high risks and inevitable mistakes of trying to be first with a new product.

This chapter offers Canadian businessmen help with something they do seem interested in, the purchase of technology. Canadian managers who buy technology feel that it is often an underpriced commodity, especially considering that market assistance as well as product and process specifications may be included in the package. They argue that buying technology is much cheaper than learning from one's own mistakes. However, absorbing knowledge from a firm technologically superior to one's own requires some specialized attention and skills; hence, this chapter. Working with data collected from seventy-four Canadian and British licensees and thirty managers of joint ventures formed between North American and Western European firms, this chapter considers the conditions under which a firm seeking technology should try to acquire it using each of two

---

1. OECD. *Gaps in Technology Between Member Countries: Analytical Report* (Paris: OECD, 1969).
2. Science Council of Canada, *Innovation in a Cold Climate: The Dilemma of Canadian Manufacturing* (Ottawa: Science Council of Canada, 1971).
3. Pierre L. Bourgeault, *Innovation and the Structure of Canadian Industry*, Special Study No. 23 (Ottawa: Science Council of Canada, 1972).
4. J.N.H. Britton and J.M. Gilmour, *The Weakest Link*, Background Study No. 43 (Ottawa: Science Council of Canada, 1978).
5. OECD, *Gaps in Technology*.

types of licence agreement and two types of joint venture. These are described below.

Mechanisms for Acquiring Technology

The Current Technology Licence Agreement
This type of licence agreement gives the licensee access only to technology which is in existence at the time the agreement is signed. If the licensee wishes to remain abreast of technological changes it will need to do its own development work, or negotiate further licence agreements with the licensor as new developments are made.

The Current and Future Technology Licence Agreement
In such an agreement, new development work done by the licensor in a specialized product area during the life of the agreement, as well as the existing current technology, will be transferred to the licensee. The current and future technology agreement offers a much greater opportunity for contact between licensor and licensee personnel than does the current technology agreement, as meetings may take place for a number of years. A 1975 study of current and future technology agreements revealed an average yearly contact time between licensor and licensee, of 45 man-days, with a range from 0 to 275.[6] In a current technology licence agreement, whatever contact there is between firms — the exact amount will depend upon the complexity of the technology — will take place in the first year of the agreement. In such an agreement, the licensor will not assign personnel to the licensee to assist with information transfer. This seldom happens, even in current and future technology agreements. Licensees have been known, however, to assist the information flow in current and future technology agreements by permanently assigning a man to the licensor's plant.

A second difference between these two kinds of licence agreements lies in the incidence of export restrictions, which are much higher on current and future technology agreements and in the age of products licensed. Current and future technology agreements do not tend to be available for newer products. Data are shown in Table 1.

The Locally Controlled Joint Venture
In this type of joint venture, the local firm (the technology-dependent firm) owns 70 per cent or more of the voting shares of the venture. It

6. Peter Killing, "Manufacturing Under Licence", *Business Quarterly* (Winter 1977).

Table 1

Export Restrictions and Product Age

	Allowed to Export[a]		Product Age[b] (years)		
	Yes	No	0-3	4-10	10+
Current Technology	18	6	20	4	3
Current and Future Technology	6	26	5	14	20
	24	32	25	18	23

(a) The export statistics relate only to products manufactured by Canadian licensees. It is illegal for a licensor to restrict a British licensee from exporting within the EEC.
(b) Product age is the time in years between a product's first world introduction and its introduction by the licensee.

Source: P. Killing, "Manufacturing Under Licence", *Business Quarterly* (Winter 1977).

runs the venture just as it would a wholly owned subsidiary, using the foreign firm supplying the technology as it would a licensor. One difference is that the foreign parent is much more likely to lend or permanently assign technical employees to the venture than it would to the licensee. The figures below show, however, that a permanent assignment of technical personnel is much more likely in a shared joint venture. In comparison with these data, it should be noted that in only one of the seventy-four licence agreements examined was an employee permanently assigned to the licensee by the licensor.

The Shared Joint Venture

The shared joint venture is more truly "joint" than the locally con-trolled venture, with the local parent controlling 50-55 per cent of the voting shares. Such a venture is typically managed with input from each parent and, as shown in Table 2, the foreign parent usually assigns functional executives to the venture. In fact, it was surprising that as many as four shared ventures (16 per cent in the category) did not have lent or assigned personnel from the technology supplier. However, two of these ventures were so small that they had no permanent employees, and were using part-time help from the local parent. A third was performing extremely poorly, and the Canadian manager attributed this poor performance directly to the fact that the foreign parent had not lent his company a technical man for the first few years.

A third type of joint venture, in which the Canadian technology-dependent firm is the passive minority partner, will not be discussed

Table 2

Personnel Transfers

	Employees from Technology Parent			
	Visits Only	On Loan	Permanently Assigned	Total
Locally Controlled Joint Venture	1	2	2	5
Shared Joint Venture	4	4	17	25
Total	5	6	19	30

here, because, in such a situation, the firm would not be acquiring technology as much as making a portfolio investment.

A Prescriptive Model

The following normative model suggests the conditions under which technology-deficient firms should and should not make use of current technology licence agreements, current and future technology licence agreements, joint ventures in which they own a strong controlling interest, and joint ventures in which they share control with the technology supplier. This model is based on an underlying proposition:

> The more a firm needs to learn about the business to which the acquired technology relates, the stronger the relationship it needs to form between its personnel and those of the technology supplier.

The first part of this proposition deals with the need for learning on the part of the technology-dependent firm. The degree of learning required will depend on the extent to which the firm is moving away from its established base of knowledge and skills. The further it moves away, the more learning is required. Figure 1 has been created with the idea that the major areas of learning in relation to a new product are technology and marketing, and in each of these, the skill needed for the new product can be identical to a firm's existing skills, related to existing skills, or unrelated to existing skills. Four strategies of diversification have been identified.[7]

Unrelated diversification means that neither the technology nor

----

7. The skills concept of diversification is an outgrowth of the thesis of Leonard Wrigley, *Divisional Autonomy and Diversification*, Business School, Harvard (Ph.D. diss., 1970). For further elaboration, see Peter Killing, "Diversification Through Licencing", *R & D Management* (June, 1978).

Figure 1

Relationship Between Existing Skills and Those Required for the New Product

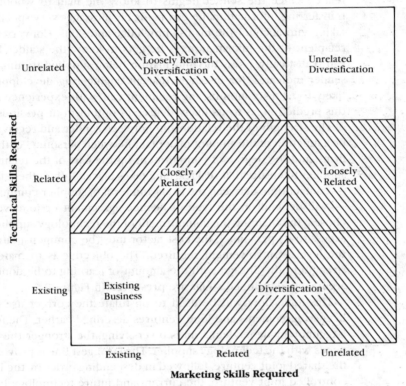

Marketing Skills Required

the marketing skill needed for the new product is related to skills existing in the firm. *Loosely related* diversification indicates the situation in which either the marketing or the technical skills needed are unrelated to those existing in the firm, but not both. When either or both needed skills are related to those in the firm (and neither is unrelated) the strategy will be one of *closely related* diversification. The final category, *existing business*, is used to denote the situation in which both the needed technical and marketing skills already exist in the firm.

The second part of the proposition deals with the relationship between the personnel of the firm using technology and those of the technology supplier. It is easy enough to transfer hardware — blueprints, specifications, price lists, and product samples — but much harder to ensure the transmission of the intangible "know-how" which is in the minds of the men who use the hardware. Effective transfer of know-how requires a strong personal relationship between sender and receiver, and it is to this fact that the proposition relates. Once the sender begins to know the man to whom he is transferring information, he can tailor his messages very specifically, taking into account the man's knowledge and skills. Conversely, the recipient of the information, as he gets to know the sender better, can realistically assess the information being supplied to him. If the sender indicates, for instance, that an engineering development is likely to take six months, the recipient can, with experience, assess this prediction, as to its likely degree of optimism or pessimism.

The strength of the relationship between sender and receiver will be a function of the amount of contact between personnel of the two firms, and the degree of commitment on the part of the technology supplier to ensure that real learning takes place. Both of these factors — contact time between the firms and level of supplier commitment — will depend on the type of licence agreement or joint venture chosen. In obtaining the commitment of the technology supplier and access to its personnel, the cost factor must be commensurate with the level of involvement required. The objective is to match the strength of the linkage with the amount of learning to be done. The arguments developed so far are presented in Figure 2.

This logic flow will be used to postulate the correct use of the licence agreements and joint ventures described earlier. The further a technology-dependent firm is diversifying, the stronger the link it needs with the technology supplier. The strongest link is provided by the shared joint venture, followed in descending order by the locally controlled joint venture, the current and future technology licence agreement, and the current technology licence agreement. The model presented in Figure 3 reflects this hierarchy, and also the belief that firms should be more conservative as the financial investment which they are making in their diversification rises. That is, if the diversification involves a small capital outlay, the firm might risk a less strong link with its technology supplier. Thus, using Figure 3, one would recommend that a firm planning a small-scale, closely related diversification choose a current or current and future technology agreement, whereas a large-scale, closely related diversification should be implemented via a current and future technology licence or a majority joint venture.

The boundaries shown in Figure 3 between the four types of agreements are not intended to be exact. They have been constructed on the principle that as a project increases in scale and degree of diversification, the necessary strength of relationship between the

Figure 2

Logic Flow

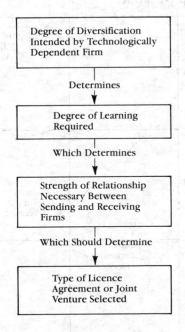

```
┌─────────────────────────────┐
│ Degree of Diversification   │
│ Intended by Technologically │
│ Dependent Firm              │
└─────────────────────────────┘
            │
        Determines
            ↓
┌─────────────────────────────┐
│ Degree of Learning          │
│ Required                    │
└─────────────────────────────┘
            │
      Which Determines
            ↓
┌─────────────────────────────┐
│ Strength of Relationship    │
│ Necessary Between           │
│ Sending and Receiving       │
│ Firms                       │
└─────────────────────────────┘
            │
    Which Should Determine
            ↓
┌─────────────────────────────┐
│ Type of Licence             │
│ Agreement or Joint          │
│ Venture Selected            │
└─────────────────────────────┘
```

parties increases, and the type of agreement specified reflects this. The following sections explore whether or not firms actually behave as this model states that they should.

Licensing Practice

With the exception of some firms which are using licence agreements to pursue unrelated diversification, a phenomenon discussed subsequently, the data presented in Table 3 suggest that firms using licence agreements do behave much as the model predicts they ought to. As the degree of diversification increases, so does the proportion of current and future technology agreements. In the simplest situations, small and moderate expansions using existing skills, no current and future technology agreements are being used at all. To implement loosely related diversification, many more firms are using current and future agreements rather than current agreements, and few licence agreements are used at all in projects of any magnitude. The only surprise is that firms are using current technology agreements to effect closely related diversification.

Figure 3

Prescriptive Model

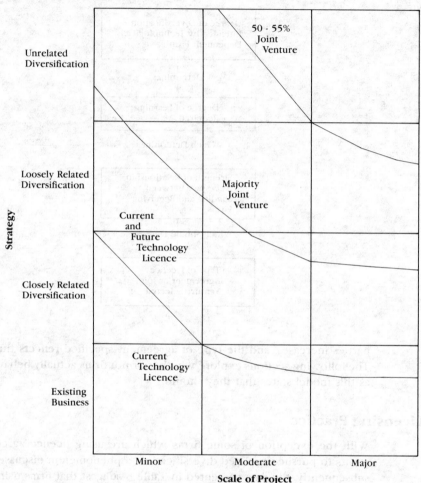

Scale of Project

A close examination was made of the licence agreements used in unrelated diversification situations. It was found that in the largest of these projects, the licensees had taken unusual steps to increase the strength of the bond with the licensor. In one case, the licensee stipulated that a senior executive of the licensor must come to work for the Canadian firm for a period of two years, to be replaced by one of his fellow workers when his term expired. This agreement was the only one of the seventy-four in which such a loan took place. In the other large, unrelated project, the two companies were situated in immediately adjacent cities on either side of the Canada–United States border. Telephone communication between the firms took place, right down to the level of draftsman. Many problems were solved over a downtown lunch. These examples reinforce the underlying principle on which Table 3 was constructed.

Table 3

Licensing Data

	Investment ($000)			
	<50	50-499	500 +	Totals
Unrelated	c = 0	c = 2	c = 0	c = 2
	c + f = 0	c + f = 0	c + f = 2	c + f = 2
Loosely Related	c = 1	c = 1	c = 0	c = 2
	c + f = 28	c + f = 2	c + f = 2	c + f = 32
Closely Related	c = 1	c = 4	c = 7	c = 12
	c + f = 3	c + f = 5	c + f = 2	c + f = 10
Existing Product	c = 5	c = 6	c = 1	c = 12
	c + f = 0	c + f = 0	c + f = 2	c + f = 2
Totals	c = 7	c = 13	c = 8	c = 28
	c + f = 31	c + f = 7	c + f = 8	c + f = 46

Note: c = current technology agreement;
      c + f = current and future technology agreement.

Use of Joint Ventures

The sample of twenty-eight joint ventures shown in Table 4 which was available for examination is significantly smaller than that used to examine licensing practices but is large enough to demonstrate conclusively that the model of Figure 3 does not accurately predict the situations in which firms will use the two types of joint ventures in question.[8] Shared joint ventures were commonly used in situations in which it was predicted that only current and future technology agreements or locally controlled joint ventures would be used. On the other hand, only one firm attempted a large-scale, unrelated diversification using a shared joint venture, the application for which it was expected most shared ventures would be used. Another striking observation was that only five of the twenty-eight were locally controlled joint ventures.

8. For similar observations, see Piero Telesio, "Licensing Policy in Multinational Enterprises" (Ph.D. diss., Harvard University, 1978).

It was discovered through further questioning that the underlying cause of both the relatively low use of majority joint ventures and the seemingly inappropriate use of shared joint ventures was the same. *Many firms with valuable technology will not supply it to a joint venture in which they own less than 50 per cent.* Thus, the market contains a significant discontinuity. Many technology-seeking firms try to set up joint ventures in which they will be the majority owner, but are offered only fifty-fifty joint ventures. Faced with no other choice, or perhaps only an opportunity to enter an equally inappropriate licence agreement, firms opt for the fifty-fifty joint venture. Thus, the frequent use of shared ventures in situations in which less strong linkages seem to be called for is explained.

The Market for Technology

In the process of talking with managers of both technology-dependent firms and technology suppliers in an effort to understand the results in Table 4, a number of factors must be considered concerning the market for technology. The overwhelming impression is of a small, fragmented, inconsistent market in which both buyers and sellers operate with little information. Several characteristics of the market

Table 4

Joint Venture Data

	Investment ($000)			
	<50	50-499	500 +	Totals
Unrelated	0	0	shared = 1 L.C. = 0	shared = 1 L.C. = 0
Loosely Related	shared = 1 L.C. = 0	shared = 1 L.C. = 0	shared = 1 L.C. = 2	shared = 1 L.C. = 2
Closely Related	shared = 2 L.C. = 0	shared = 4 L.C. = 0	shared = 5 L.C. = 2	shared = 11 L.C. = 2
Existing Product	0	0	shared = 1 L.C. = 1	shared = 1 L.C. = 1
Totals	**shared = 3 L.C. = 0**	**shared = 10 L.C. = 0**	**shared = 10 L.C. = 5**	**shared = 23 L.C. = 5**

Notes: (i) "Shared" denotes a joint venture in which the technology-dependent firm owns between 50 per cent and 55 per cent.

(ii) "L.C." (Locally Controlled) denotes a joint venture in which the technology-dependent firm owns 70 per cent or more. In each of these ventures, technology was supplied by the foreign parent.

which seem particularly relevant to managers of firms wishing to buy technology are discussed below.

The High Cost of Search
The major companies in an industry do not, as a general rule, want to sell their technology. They might sell technology in a fringe area into which they ventured by chance, but they would usually rather capture for themselves the return on technology relating to their major business. Thus, their preference is to serve a foreign market through exports or direct foreign investment, to the extent that it is feasible to do so, considering the economics of the situation and the attitude of the foreign government involved. The implication for a potential technology purchaser is that it will have to look among the smaller firms in the industry and at firms in different industries to find willing technology suppliers.[9] This search process is not easy. It is made even more difficult by the fact that many firms with good technology, which they would be willing to sell, do not consider the sale of information to be a particularly lucrative activity and, thus, do not advertise their position, or even make it easy for a buyer to negotiate a sale. They have more important things to worry about. Thus, the size and nature of the market is determined by the thoroughness and aggressiveness of the potential purchaser. The difficult decision which technology buyers often face is whether to accept the deal they are currently being offered (which does not quite fit their needs) or to keep on with the search.

Disparate Choices
If a firm is persistent in its search for a supplier of technology, it may well end up with several very dissimilar offers for obtaining the same technology. In 1977, a Canadian firm was attempting a loosely related diversification of moderate scale; a situation which, according to Figure 3, would call for a majority joint venture, or possibly a current and future technology agreement. However, one European firm offered the Canadians a current technology agreement with a royalty rate of 2-3 per cent of sales, while a second suggested a fifty-fifty joint venture in which the partner would supply machinery (rather than cash) as equity, and would provide two executives for the joint venture. Neither choice was ideal, in the Canadians' view: one offered too much liaison with the technology supplier, and the other not enough. However, because the firm felt it needed more help than was available with the current-technology licence agree-

9. Telesio, "Licensing Policy".

ment, it chose the joint venture. A Canadian competitor subsequently picked up the licence agreement. Two years later, the joint venture was liquidated, a victim in part of the lack of flexibility caused by having a partner thousands of miles away who needed to be consulted on decisions which the market demanded be made quickly. The competitor with the licence agreement has flourished.

The most difficult choice of supplier appears to arise in situations in which the quality of the technology varies between suppliers, as well as the price and administrative mechanism (licence agreement or joint venture) demanded. A typical example would be one in which the firm with what appears to be the better technology will supply it only to a fifty-fifty joint venture and demands a higher price for it. The firm with the weaker technology is more flexible and offers a lower price. The buyer's indecision is often compounded by the fact that it is not completely confident of its assessment of the relative merits of the two technologies.

Price is Negotiable
Neither buyers nor sellers of technology seem to have a clear idea of the value of the commodity in which they are trading. A European firm recently asked to be given 40 per cent of the equity of a new North American joint venture to which it was supplying technology. The North American manager was not at all certain what the European technology was worth, but decided to make a counter offer of 15 per cent. The negotiation ended when both sides agreed on a final figure of 20 per cent. This reduction from 40 per cent to 20 per cent on the part of the technology supplier was very significant, as this was not a small joint venture. Another example of the uncertainty surrounding the price of technology was provided in the mid-1970s when a major U.S. company was trying to attract partners into a joint venture in which it would supply the technology. The approach of this billion-dollar company was to say, "Here is the work we have done over the past ten years; what do you think it is worth?" At least one new entrant was astounded by this procedure, observing that if the creator of the technology could not put a value on it, how did it expect outsiders to do so?

Another sign of the confusion in the market is that current and future technology licence agreements, which appear to offer more to the licensee, do not carry higher royalty rates. The following data were collected from British licensees by the author in 1976:

Table 5

Royalty Rate and Licence Agreement Type

Royalty Rate	Current Technology	Current and Future Technology	Total
Less Than 2%	2	2	4
2-4.9%	6	9	15
5-10%	7	18	25
More Than 10%	1	1	2
Total	16	30	46

A second test was carried out to see if royalty rates were a function of product age or the uniqueness of the technology. They were a function of neither, leading one to speculate that royalty rates may be simply a function of the negotiating skills of the parties involved.

Implications for Technology Buyers

Develop a Minimum Level of Technical Competence
To venture unprotected into an unstructured market like that described above is foolhardy. To function effectively as a technology buyer, a firm needs a certain technical competence. Otherwise, it cannot begin to evaluate what it is being offered. Once a deal is signed, technical competence will again be useful in sorting out information coming from the technology supplier. One cannot simply accept uncritically all suggestions and technical specifications coming from a firm which may be a significantly different size than one's own and located in a different country. Many technology purchasers also find that transfer of technical ideas is much more effective if they have someone on staff who is trained in the relevant discipline, and thus "speaks the same language" as the engineer who is sending information from the supplying firm.

One particularly successful Swedish joint venture included in this study had by 1980 built up a staff of eighty technicians and engineers. Their job was to scrutinize the information coming from the American parent and to adapt it to best serve the needs of their particular operation. They were so successful at this that in some years their operating performance was superior to that of the U.S. divisions which were supplying the technology. American visitors became a common sight in the Swedish plant, not only to teach, but also to learn the differences in operating procedure which had increased the Swedes' efficiency.

Know Your Needs

When shopping in a market as diverse and unpredictable as that for technology, a firm should have a very good idea of just what it needs in the way of help. Is marketing assistance needed, or just production process specifications? What about product design changes in coming years? Can the firm keep up to date on its own or will it need continuing help from the technology supplier? As stated above, the firm looking for technology is likely to be offered alternatives with radically different costs and implications. Unless one is very well aware of his firm's strengths and weaknesses, and in particular its ability to learn with and without help, these choices will be very difficult.

In addition to being able to size up his own firm, a manager should also be capable of assessing the character of a potential technology supplier. Is the firm used to transmitting its knowledge to others? Is it jealous of its technology or open with it? Will it be easy or difficult for the firm to gain the attention of employees of the technology supplier once a deal is made? Some managers explain that a joint venture, with senior members of the technology supplier on its board, can readily get the attention of division managers and engineers; whereas the same may not be true if the only link between buyer and seller is a licence agreement.

Consider the Fifty-Fifty Joint Venture

In the course of identifying the thirty joint ventures referred to in this study, the researcher interviewed more than one hundred managers in North America and Western Europe to discuss their joint venture experiences.[10] One clear conclusion is that many managers, particularly in North America, will not enter fifty-fifty joint ventures. They view such ventures as too ambiguous, too inflexible, and all too likely to end in stalemated confusion and disaster. As the data in this paper suggest, however, any firm which wishes to buy technology but arbitrarily decides that it will not enter fifty-fifty joint ventures is severely restricting its options. Fifty-fifty is as far as many firms with technology will go in terms of allowing their local partners an equity holding.

One reason for the aversion to fifty-fifty ventures is that their potential difficulties are well-known, and the tales of a few spectacular disasters are widespread. Less well-known are the successes and

---

10. The joint venture data were collected as part of an ongoing study on the management of joint ventures. The intended result is a book, *The Design and Management of Joint Ventures*, for which 1981 publication is planned.

the incredible benefits which can accrue to a firm which is in an equal partnership with a world leader in the technology in question. The effort made by the technology supplier in such a situation to ensure that information is properly and completely transferred to the joint venture is equivalent to that which it would make for a wholly owned subsidiary. One leading German company spends $250,000 annually developing technology for, and supplying it to, a fifty-fifty joint venture in the United States. In addition, it has supplied two full-time managers to the venture, carries out training programs for American personnel both in Germany and the U.S., and, on a monthly basis, sends news of competitors, new product applications, and tests of new products to the joint venture. In four years, the venture's sales have doubled to $80 million. The problems of managing a fifty-fifty joint venture can be significant but so can the rewards. Firms seriously interested in buying technology cannot afford a "hands-off" attitude to these ventures.

Summary

Buying technology can be a viable corporate strategy and may be one of particular relevance to Canadian firms. To use it effectively, however, a firm must have some minimum level of technical competence. The market is small and fragmented, and the deals which a technology-seeking firm uncovers will be largely the result of its own hard work. Firms with technology that they would be willing to sell seldom advertise the fact. When deciding whether or not to enter a particular deal, a manager should have closely estimated the amount of help he is going to need in the new product area, and also should know the different degrees of access to the supplier's personnel his employees will get under various types of licence agreements and joint ventures. To be successful, a manager needs to know his firm's requirements and have the perseverance to locate a supplier who can meet them.

Many firms with technology will not enter joint ventures in which they own less than 50 per cent of the equity. Thus, technology buyers may be faced with situations in which their only options are either a closer relationship with the technology supplier than they would prefer or no deal at all. Firms that seriously wish to pursue a strategy of technology acquisition need to develop the management skills necessary to handle fifty-fifty joint ventures.

V
International Operations Management

B
R & D Management

35
International Marketing Effectiveness of Technology-Oriented Small Firms

V. H. Kirpalani

N. B. Macintosh

Dr. Kirpalani is professor of marketing in the Faculty of Commerce and
Administration, Concordia University, and a Fellow of the Oxford Centre for
Management Studies. He is the author of a large number of publications.
Before becoming an academic, he had wide business experience with the
Swedish Match Company, A. B. Electrolux, and Du Pont of Canada Ltd.

Dr. Macintosh is associate professor in the School of Business, Queen's
University. He has also been director of the MBA program. He is the author
of a large number of publications and has worked extensively with the
accounting profession.

This chapter is based on an article which appeared originally in *Journal of
International Business Studies*, Winter 1980. Reprinted by permission.

Introduction

The factors that make for successful international marketing for large organizations have been the subject of considerable research. A great deal of knowledge in this area has emerged through a cycle of attempts at theory development, empirical findings, testing, refining, and retesting. The conventional wisdom that seems to have developed from these efforts is that high technology, substantial research and development (R & D) expenses, sophisticated marketing, and advanced forms of organizational design are key contributors to international marketing success for large firms.[1,2] The consequence of this conventional wisdom has been that governments have been prone to provide incentives for R & D efforts particularly for sophisticated technological developments.

The small manufacturer who exports has not been the subject of much research. These firms, limited by size, are usually not multinationals but mainly exporters who market to third parties. What determines the international marketing effectiveness of technology-oriented small and medium-size firms in regard to exporting from the home base? This chapter is the outcome of a study which attempted to answer that basic question. The findings should be of use to small and medium-size firms and to governments which provide assistance for improving international marketing effectiveness. This chapter has three further sections. The first describes the methodology; the second states the findings and interpretations; and the third contains the conclusions.

Methodology

The research design, data collection, and data analysis were devised to enable an exploratory test to be made of the relationship of

1. John D. Daniels, Ernest W. Ogram, Jr., and Lee H. Radebaugh, *International Business: Environments and Operations,* 2nd ed. (Reading, Mass: Addison-Wesley Publishing Company 1979), p. 564.
2. Raymond Vernon, "Future of the Multinational Corporation", *The International Corporation,* ed. Charles Kindleberger (Cambridge, Mass: M.I.T. Press, 1970), p. 389.

effective international marketing (the dependent variable) with several descriptive and policy variables (the independent variables). Because the study was exploratory, no specific hypotheses guided the research design. Rather, a research methodology was selected so a wide range of independent variables could be tested for their relationship with the dependent variable. In order to prevent researcher bias from entering into the consideration, a heavy reliance was placed on statistical analysis to uncover the fundamental underlying relationships in the survey data. In sum, a research design was attempted which would let the data speak for themselves.

Sample

The firms included in the sample were small to medium size. Various parameters can be used to prescribe size. The simple parameter used was a firm with less than $30 million annual sales. Most of the sample firms had less than $10 million. Nine of the firms were parts of larger corporations but claimed to operate as profit centres and distinct parts differentiated from other parts of the body corporate. The other basis of selection was a non-random difference in characteristics between the firms, which better enabled investigators to test whether independent variables were having an impact on the dependent variable.[3] Consequently, the sample had a wide variety of manufactured products and services ranging from simple technology products (such as windshield wipers, hose clamps, key blanks, display shelves, and frozen potatoes), through medium-technology products (such as capacitators, voltage transformers, seismic service supply products, electro-chemical plant equipment), to higher-technology products (such as, acoustic-optics, avionics, numerical control equipment, and sonic products). The firms in this sample also varied considerably in terms of manufacturing technology. Twenty-four of the firms were Canadian and ten were American.

Measurement

The unit of analysis for this study was the firm. The interview guide contained seven questions which included factual data (such as, sales volume and number of plants in the world) and perceptual data (such as, credit policy relative to competition and satisfaction with government programs). The interview guide was administered, in all but three cases, to the president of the firm. In the other cases, senior administrators were interviewed.

---

3. H. M. Blalock, *Social Statistics* (New York: McGraw-Hill, Inc., 1974), and R. H. Hall, "Intraorganizational Structure Variation", *Administrative Science Quarterly* (September 1969), pp. 366-376.

The information gathered during the interviews was then transposed into ratio or interval scale data so that appropriate statistical tests could be conducted. This was accomplished in two ways. First, the actual numbers were used for the factual data. Second, the perceptual data (such as, use of government information and degree of sophistication of production machinery) were converted into discrete measures on five point Likert scales. As a general protection against interviewer bias, all interviews had been conducted by two interviewers, each of whom took separate notes for completion of the interview guide. Later, after becoming familiar with all the firms in the sample, each interviewer, working independently, transposed the interview guide information into the appropriate interval scale data. A third researcher read both interview guides and also transposed the information into interval scale data. Then the average score of the three researchers was used as the final measure of each item. Third, some information was of the yes-no type and was measured as binary variables.

Fifteen items were dropped because they dealt with general opinions such as protectionism and domestic image due to foreign operations. The remaining fifty-nine items were factor analysed in six groupings — outcome, situational, marketing, product, manufacturing, and general organizational. The factor analysis was conducted by groups to overcome the statistical degrees of freedom problem occasioned by the sample size being smaller than the number of variables. The principal components with varimax orthogonal rotation method of factor analysis was employed.[4] Factors in each group with eigen values of less than 1.0 were dropped from the data base. As can be seen in Table 1, the factor analysis reduced the data to twenty-one composite factors. Only those original items with substantial loadings on a given factor were retained. The original items retained were converted into statistically standardized form to remove the effect of size and different quantities and to provide the means of combining continuous and discrete items into composite variables.

Finally, the retained items for each factor were combined into a composite variable. This was accomplished by pooling these retained items for each factor into a composite score; this method had the advantage of "cleaning up" the factor and made it possible to understand the composite variable more clearly. The pooling was done by arithmetically averaging the standardized form of the retained original items.

4. N.W. Nie, et al, *Statistical Package for the Social Sciences* (New York: McGraw-Hill Inc., 1975).

Table 1

Results of Factor Analysis of Original Items

Composite Factor Variables		Eigen Value	Factor Loading	Original Items	
Name				Description	Measure
Success		2.2	.69	**Rate of sales growth in recent past**	**percentage**
			.79	**Export activity relative to domestic competition**	**1-5 scale**
Situational					
a) Size		3.9	.81	Number of countries for products	actual
			.83	Number of plants in world	actual
b) Government Assistance		2.6	.75	Use of government information	1-5 scale
			.65	Use of government finance and insurance	1-5 scale
			.60	Use of government for foreign contacts	1-5 scale
			.63	Satisfaction with government progress	1-5 scale
			.62	Quality of government information	1-5 scale
c) Age		1.2	.50	Age of firm	log of age
Marketing					
a) Customer Service		2.8	.40	Adequacy of dealers, inventory, and parts	1-5 scale
			.57	Quality of customer service	1-5 scale
			.79	Pricing of customer service	1-5 scale
b) Promotion		2.7	.54	Industrial promotional effort	1-5 scale
c) Mass Media		2.1	.66	Use of mass media relative to foreign competitors	1-5 scale
d) Pricing		1.8	.62	Prices relative to competition	1-5 scale
			.48	Discounts relative to competition	1-5 scale
			.74	Credit policy relative to competition	1-5 scale
e) Advantage		1.4	.76	Export price relative to domestic price	1-5 scale
			.81	Export profitability relative to domestic profitability	1-5 scale
f) Distribution		1.3	.48	Quality of distributors and dealers	1-5 scale

		Description	Scale
	.85	Compensation of dealers, relative to competition	1-5 scale
	.49	Adequacy of dealers, inventory, and parts	1-5 scale
Products			
a) Sophistication	2.3		
	.92	Extent product is a part versus a system	1-5 scale
	.72	Extent product is standard or tailor-made	1-5 scale
	−.51	Capital intensity of value added	1-5 scale
b) Line	1.8		
	.81	Width of product line	1-5 scale
	−.68	Complementariness of products	1-5 scale
c) Type	1.4		
	.47	Position on product line cycle	1-5 scale
	.50	Product modification for export	1-5 scale
	.56	Market share of most significant foreign market	1-5 scale
Manufacturing			
a) Manufacturing	1.6		
	−.43	Direct labor intensity	1-5 scale
	.76	Per cent of material imported	percentage
	.69	Per cent of foreign sales from domestic manufacture	percentage
b) Production Sophistication	1.4		
	.74	Value added as a per cent of final cost	percentage
	.47	Sophistication of manufacturing equipment	1-5 scale
General Organizational			
a) Information for Control	2.0		
	−.97	Frequency of control reporting for international division	weeks
	.50	Quality of control reports	1-5 scale
	.87	Closeness of monitoring of international organization	1-5 scale
b) Export Organization	1.9		
	.98	Maturity of international organization structure	1-5 scale
	.49	Professionals in international organization	number
c) R & D Effort	1.5		
	.70	R & D as a per cent of sales	percentage
	.49	Professionals in R & D efforts	number
d) Export	1.3		
	.64	Successful new product development	1-5 scale
	.65	Use of government for foreign contacts	1-5 scale
e) Top Management Effort	1.1		
	.52	Experience in international markets	1-5 scale
	.72	Per cent of president's time spent on international business	percentage
f) Forecasting	1.0		
	.81	Quality of forecasting international markets	1-5 scale

Success Variable

The success variable, for example, was created by pooling the original items: the rate of growth in sales over the past five years, an objective measure, and the firm's level of export activity, ratio of export sales to total sales relative to the average among its domestic competitors, a subjective rating made initially by the interviewee.

How should the success variable be correctly defined? If export sales growth in only the past five years were taken, one would have to ignore recent exporters. Because this was an exploratory study of variables associated with export success, it was decided to include recent exporters and to use the proxy of growth in total sales, domestic plus exports, over the past five years. The data showed that the rates of export sales growth in large part parallelled the rate of total sales growth for most of the sample. Further, the researchers decided, on the basis of logic and factor analysis, that a success variable incorporating both sales growth and level of export activity relative to competition was a more appropriate measure than using either one above. Sales growth by itself would mask the proportionate split between export and domestic sales; moreover, the level of export activity alone may not have been a sufficient indicator of effective international marketing.

Data Analysis

Correlation and multiple regression analysis were employed. The correlation coefficient gives an indication of the simple association between the variables. Multiple regression has the additional advantage of enabling the researcher to develop a theoretical model to explain the behavior of the dependent variable. The sample size virtually prohibited doing a simultaneous multiple regression of all twenty independent variables. To overcome this problem, each of the five general clusters of independent variables was analysed separately.

Findings and Interpretations

An interesting general finding is that although some individual companies may have suffered, the average for the total sample showed that profits on exports were above those on domestic sales. This was the result of the averages of export prices and export costs being wider apart than in the domestic market. The actual responses indicated that export prices were, in the majority of cases, equal to domestic prices or higher, while costs tended to be equal or not to rise very much. The response to cost was requested after considering that the export product would not have to bear domestic promotion, transport, and distribution costs but would replace these with costs necessary to service export markets.

Situational Variables

The statistical analysis of the relationship of age, size of firm, and government assistance with SUCCESS shows that age emerges as the only one which is significantly associated with SUCCESS, but the association is negative. This result suggests that the older the firm, the less successful it fares in international marketing. Newer firms, it seems, do better than older ones. This may mean that newer firms are more anxious to expand and thus seek growth through international markets.

Size is not significantly associated with SUCCESS — an important finding because the firms in our sample ranged from seventeen to over one thousand employees. This means that, regardless of size, any given firm has a chance to compete successfully for international markets.

Government assistance also had no significant association with SUCCESS. This may mean that government assistance is a sort of hygiene factor in the sense that it is a necessary condition for small firms to compete in international markets, but not a sufficient condition for success. This finding, however, might also mean that government assistance, as currently carried out, is not an important factor. As will be discussed later, when the final model is reviewed, this may not be surprising. The key success factors that emerge in the model are elements of international marketing which the government does little, if anything, to aid directly.

Marketing Variables

Pricing and promotion were associated significantly with SUCCESS. The pricing variable is a composite of policies regarding prices, discounts, and credits relative to competition. Evidently price shaving is an important factor. Apparently firms can arrange a price "package" which is attractive to customers in the export market. The firm, it seems, can develop alternative mixes of price, discount, and credit so that the final effect gives the foreign customer an attractive total deal. The effect of this price factor is consistent with price theory and many examples of business practice.

Promotional effort, as distinct from advertising, showed a strong positive association with SUCCESS (B = .49, p < .05). The executives interviewed also stressed that promotional efforts were critical to successful international marketing efforts. Interestingly, distribution (quality and compensation of dealers, and adequacy of stocks and parts) did not have a significant relationship with the dependent variable.

Product Variables

Three product variables were tested for their association with SUCCESS. Product sophistication (the extent to which the product is a relatively simple part, such as a lock blank, versus a complex system, such as a flight simulator; the extent to which the product is standard versus tailor-made; and the capital intensity of the value added which is an indication of the sophistication of the product) had a very modest negative association with SUCCESS. This suggests that simple products which likely are well established in broad-based mature markets succeed better than do products of a higher-technological type.

Product line (width and complementariness of product line) was negatively associated with SUCCESS ($B = -.29$, $p < .10$). This means that firms with one or a few products are more successful than those with a broad line of complementary products. Product type (position on the product life cycle, extent of product modification for export, and market share of most significant foreign market) also was associated with SUCCESS ($B = .42$, $p. < .05$). It seems mature products, modified for export, can compete very successfully in international trade. These results suggest that firms with a few, simple products which are well established in broad-based mature markets fare well in foreign markets.

It is not necessarily a comfort to know that simpler products do better on average than sophisticated ones but it may be at least an agreeable surprise. It means that competently managed firms with standard traditional products of acceptable quality can compete successfully for a place in world markets. In fact, our data indicate that more sophisticated products may be even a handicap in this direction.

Manufacturing Variables

Neither of the two manufacturing variables, manufacturing (unit labor costs relative to competition, per cent of material imported, and percentage of foreign sales from direct manufacture) and production sophistication, which emerged from the factor analysis, were associated significantly with SUCCESS, although production sophistication (value added as a percentage of cost and the degree of sophistication of manufacturing equipment) has a weak negative association with SUCCESS. Both of these variables, especially production sophistication, appear to be indirect measures of the degree of sophistication of the production process of the firms. It would appear, then, that the sophistication of a firm's manufacturing process is not an element in international marketing success. This in itself, however, is an interesting finding. It means that, at least for smaller-size firms, products may be successfully marketed internationally regardless of the capital intensity or sophistication of the firm's manufacturing process.

Organizational and R & D Variables
The general organizational group of variables was the only group from which a significant multiple regression equation emerged ($R^2 = .67$, $F = 6.5$, $p < .01$). The results of this analysis are shown in Table 2, where the obvious implication is that management and organizational practices are critical for successful international marketing — more so than situational, marketing, product, and manufacturing policies.

Information for control reporting (quality of information, frequency reporting, and closeness of monitoring of foreign operations) emerged as the independent variable with the strongest relationship to SUCCESS ($r = .64$, $B = .44$, $p < .001$). This evidence indicates that an effective control system is a key factor for competing in international markets. Good quality information and control seem essential.

Top management effort also had a significant relationship with SUCCESS ($r = .44$, $B = .25$, $p < .10$). It would seem that commitment and effort by top management, which for most of the firms in the sample means the president himself, is a crucial factor. This is not unexpected because top management support seems almost mandatory for the success of any venture. Nevertheless, it is worthwhile to state that it is unlikely that firms will have success in international markets without top management effort and backing. Export experience (use of government for contracts and experience in international markets) also showed a significant relationship with SUCCESS. This indicates that government contacts and experience in exporting are helpful. It appears that these two variables — top management effort and export experience — were connected closely ($r = .25$, $p < .08$) because in many firms it was the president who had the experience and worked with the government. Thus, it seems that top management support and backing of export experience hold potential for high pay-offs in international marketing.

Export organization (the degree of structuring and maturity of the international division or unit and the quality of staff in the export unit) is also associated with SUCCESS ($r = .32$, $p < .05$). The strength

Table 2

Multiple Regression Analysis of General Organizational Variables with SUCCESS

Independent Variables	All Variables Analysis						Best-Fit Analysis			
	r	b	β	e	F	ΔR²	ΔR²	β	e	F
1. Information for Control Reporting	.64[c]	.44	.36	.22	3.9[c]	.41	.41	.44	.19	8.3[c]
2. Export Organizations	.32[b]	.10	.10	.16	.3	.01	Dropped			
3. R & D Effort	-.21	-.25	-.24	.18	2.0	.05	.05	-.23	.15	2.5[a]
4. Export Experience	.46[c]	.14	.15	.16	.18	.02	Dropped			
5. Top Management Effort	.45[c]	.30	.38	.13	5.7[c]	.10	.10	.42	.12	8.1[c]
6. Forecasting	.26[a]	.20	.25	.12	2.6[a]	.03	.03	.24	.12	2.6[a]
R^2			.62				.59			
F			5.2				7.8[c]			
d/f			6120				4129			

r = product moment correlation coefficient
b = partial multiple regression coefficient
β = standardized b
e = standard error
F = F-ratio
R² = explained variation
d/f = degrees of freedom
ΔR² = additional explained variation as independent variables are added in the stepwise regression process
[a] p < .10
[b] p < .05
[c] p < .01

of this association, however, lessens when the other variables in the group are controlled for. This may be due to the association of export organization with top management effort ($r = .32$, $p < .03$) and R & D ($r = .38$, $p < .02$). Consequently, interpretation of the importance of the export organization must be treated as tenuous. The data, however, indicate that a well-developed, separate international marketing organization, staffed with well-trained personnel is a valuable aspect of successful international marketing. Ability to forecast international markets has a positive, but weak association with SUCCESS.

The other variable in this group was R & D (R & D expenditures as a percentage of sales, the number of professional people involved in R & D efforts, and a scale of new product development success). Surprisingly, R & D is negatively related to SUCCESS but not significantly. Interpretation of this result will be controversial because of a widely held belief that R & D is an important factor for successful exporting.

A recent study by Hanel concluded, for example, that exports of Canadian manufacturing industries are associated positively with R & D effort.[5] This study, however, used industries, not firms, as the unit of analysis. Curiously, closer examination of the results reveals that for several dependent variables (including: exports per employee, exports as a percentage of sales, and exports as a percentage of total exports of the country) statistically significant results did not emerge for Canadian industry. In any event, the data in the Hanel study were dominated by large firms aggregated to the industry level whereas this study focusses on smaller firms with the firm itself as the unit of analysis. Our data indicate that for smaller firms, R & D is not an important factor.

Discussion and Conclusions

A definite conclusion emerging from the findings is that the inputs which determine international marketing effectiveness for the small firm could be different from those that apply to the large MNC. The success of large MNCs is said to depend on high technology, substantial R & D, sophisticated marketing, and advanced forms of organizational design. In contrast, the propositions that technological leadership and substantial R & D are important for international success

5. P. Hanel, *The Relationship Existing Between the R & D Activity of Canadian Manufacturing Industries and Their Performance in the International Markets* (Ottawa: Department of Industry, Trade, and Commerce, August 1976).

seems to have limited relevance for internationally successful small manufacturing firms which market simple- or medium-technology products.

The concept of the international product cycle,[6] whereby the technological level reflected in new products generated by a firm gives it an edge in exports, is often not applicable to a small firm with small R & D capacity and budgets. Obviously, a country which invests heavily in technology through large R & D expenditures is bound to develop a host of new products and of skilled people. This technological innovation thrust will presumably carry over into international success; thus, the finding that small firms with simple- and medium-technology products can also be very successful internationally should be seen as placing technological innovation in perspective on two dimensions. One is that technological innovation leadership may be a vital input only for firms in high-technology sectors. Two, that heavy national R & D expenditures can lead, after a substantial time lag, to international marketing success through products that have by this time become standardized to the point of being classified as simple- and medium-technology.

The question remains: how can simple- and medium-technology product manufacturers be successful in international marketing? The conclusion from the findings of the present study is that a competitive price "package" and promotional effort are important. Further, what seems critical for success is a well-designed information and control system and a sound organizational structure for the international side of the business, as well as a great deal of top management effort and commitment to international marketing. Interestingly enough, these are the very same components that have contributed to the success of the Japanese Sogo Shoshas, the large trading companies. These Sogo Shoshas are known for excellence in their information and control reporting system, sound organizational structure, top management effort, and commitment to international marketing. The Sogo Shosha's strength does not lie in R & D or manufacture but in specializing in export and import business, which is trading. The Sogo Shosha finds diverse products from numerous suppliers scattered all over Japan and identifies wants in all the countries of the world; it then fits the numerous products to the numerous wants. The Sogo Shosha, in effect, trades in goods, serv-

6. Raymond Vernon, "International Investment and International Trade in the Product Cycle", Quarterly Journal of Economics (May 1966), and Louis Wells, Jr., The Product Life Cycle and International Trade (Cambridge: Division of Research, Harvard Business School and Harvard University Press, 1972).

ices, and information.[7] The *Sogo Shosha*'s distinct advantage is its territorial knowledge of international markets, which enables it to benefit small- and medium-size manufacturing suppliers for whom a real barrier to entry into international markets is ignorance of existing market opportunities, distribution contacts, trading procedures, and financial requirements.

Last, two points are worth emphasizing. One, this was an exploratory study on a limited sample; the findings now provide useful hypotheses for further research. Two, the sample demonstrates that small and medium North American firms can penetrate world markets successfully with products as commonplace as frozen vegetables and fruit, hub caps, windshield wipers, display shelves and kiosks, key blanks, and lock components and sets, to name a few. This is interesting in itself although in no way does it down play the success of firms in products such as avionics, flight simulators, and petroleum exploration supplies.

Relevance to the Canadian Scene

The emergence of managerial technology and marketing skills as the most important factors has important policy implications for Canadians. Small and medium-size Canadian firms are likely to have more opportunity to acquire these characteristics, rather than large funds of capital and scale operations typically associated with large multinational firms. Further, it suggests that Canadian government efforts should be directed towards helping small firms acquire the necessary managerial and marketing skills and attitudes for international competition. One initiative would be to establish Canadian trading companies to perform international marketing functions for small firms until their products become accepted in international markets. Another is the establishment of a small firm international management training centre. A third recommendation is to support a research study focussing on the international managerial and marketing technology employed by successful small firms in other comparable countries. A final recommendation is to begin development of a real time, data base, information system on major world markets for selected products which are presently being produced by small Canadian firms. Such a data base would include information on factors such as prices, distribution channels, and market size.

---

7. Yoshi Tsurumi, "Sogo Shosha: Institutional Engines of Industrial Growth" (Unpublished manuscript, Pacific Basin Economic Study Center, U.C.L.A., Los Angeles, 1979).

V
International Operations Management

C
Global Product Mandating

36
Multinationals and Industrial Strategy: The Role of World Product Mandates

Science Council of Canada

The material in this chapter appeared originally as a portion of Science Council of Canada, *Multinationals and Industrial Strategy: The Role of World Product Mandates*, 1980. Reprinted by permission of the minister of Supply and Services Canada.

For more than a decade, the Science Council of Canada has been concerned with issues relating to the formulation and implementation of an industrial strategy for Canada. Given the high levels of foreign ownership present in the Canadian economy, much of the analysis of Canada's industrial problems has stressed the effects of foreign ownership on our international competitive capacity. Primary attention has been given to the structural consequences of foreign investment, notably the failure, under prevailing conditions, of subsidiaries to innovate and develop distinctive products geared to export markets. This failure has been a major contributor to Canada's serious and deteriorating balance of trade in end products (manufactured goods), a deficit that amounted to $17 billion in 1979.

The dismal trend in this trade is of profound concern. Primarily it reflects the low level of competitiveness of much of our manufacturing sector as compared with those industrially developed countries, such as the United States, Japan, and West Germany that supply most of our manufactured imports. Equally pertinent, the progressive reduction of tariff barriers during the next few years, combined with recent significant changes in foreign industrial policies and the structure of the international economy, suggest this trade balance will deteriorate further unless a substantial effort is made to correct the imbalance by increasing the international competitive capacity of our manufacturing sector.

Major changes are taking place in the international trading system.[1] First, over the past two decades, the number of second-rank industrialized countries and newly industrialized countries (NICs) has increased greatly. (The first category includes countries such as Spain, Greece, and several East European nations. Among the NICs are countries such as Hong Kong, Taiwan, South Korea, and Brazil.) Over the longer term, industrial production from these rising industrial countries threatens to overwhelm that of our manufacturing industries that produce conventional mature products using standardized

1. Science Council of Canada, *Forging the Links: A Technology Policy for Canada*, Science Council Report No. 29 (Ottawa: Supply and Services Canada, 1979), pp. 30-34.

production technologies. Products from these countries have already had a significant impact on several Canadian industries. The fear of a greater impact has led more recently, in cases such as footwear, textiles, and clothing, to the use of quotas and the negotiation of voluntary export restraints. But today's events are merely precursors of problems to come. The developing industrial countries are moving up the "technological" ladder and widening their product range. Some of the NICs are producing quite sophisticated machine tools and are moving into products such as consumer electronics and automotive parts. Great difficulty lies ahead for many industries of central importance to our economy.

Second, to overcome difficulties arising from market saturation in many conventional goods, from excess production capacity in many industries, and from the challenge of low-cost imports from the NICs and second-rank industrial nations, the advanced industrial countries are moving increasingly into the knowledge- and technology-intensive phases of industrial production. Dynamic firms are concentrating production in areas dominated by product and systems innovations growing out of their highly organized research, development, and design activities. They are moving to take advantage of changing world markets through rapid product differentiation. They are also giving emphasis to quality, reliability, and automated assembly in the manufacture of consumer durables, high value added in chemicals and other intermediate products, and the incorporation of electronic technology into capital goods.

Finally, it is becoming clear that our traditional reliance on resource exports to counterbalance deficits in manufactured imports is not likely to succeed. As our traditional advantage in several resource sectors diminishes, our growth in goods production seems to be unable to keep pace with growing imports of manufactured goods and services. Further, our mineral and raw material resources are facing increasingly tougher international competition. Fortunately, we have major strengths in oil and gas.

It is evident that our high-wage economy cannot readily compete with the low-cost industrial countries on most mass-produced, conventional-technology products. At the same time, a very large number of the foreign subsidiaries in Canada are technologically dependent upon their parent firm and confine their sales to the Canadian domestic market. In addition, Canadian-owned firms are often small and heavily reliant upon purchased or licensed technology. Thus, while currently classed in the "second division" with the United Kingdom and Italy among others, we appear to be in a situation that significantly limits our prospects of entering the "first division" of industrial countries. Very few firms in Canada have the "in-house" technology base necessary to produce goods competitive with those now imported. Neither do they have the capabilities essential for an effective response to the problems facing advanced country manufacturing. As international competition sharpens and advanced industrial countries rest their future on technology-intensive products and services, these weaknesses become even more critical.

Foreign-owned subsidiaries comprise a major and key proportion of the Canadian manufacturing sector. Therefore, attention must be devoted to finding mechanisms to increase the net benefits that these subsidiaries contribute to the Canadian economy. Surprisingly, policy makers have only recently attempted to use some of the attributes of multinational corporations to promote a more favorable industrial structure and performance in Canada.

The traditional reason for the dominance of multinationals in Canada has been their ability to use the resources gained from their world-scale operations to establish a domestic production facility, usually with the support of high tariff barriers. Their financial power is then used to capture a significant share of a particular domestic market, with the assistance of parent-developed products or technology. The result is truncated subsidiaries, with little export potential. Such subsidiaries manufacture internationally standard products for our domestic market and operate with a management team that is largely under the direct administrative control of the parent firm and has little autonomy.

Changing circumstances raise the prospect, however, that the presence of branch plants in the Canadian economy can be turned to greater mutual advantage by using the multinational's strength in creating world markets for certain goods as a device to increase productivity, to improve performance, and to expand the industrial capabilities of the subsidiaries. In effect, such a strategy would use the international market power of a multinational to sell a specific product, or product line, manufactured by a single subsidiary on a worldwide basis. It is, in fact, a strategy that some multinationals have recently followed with respect to their Canadian subsidiaries; a strategy that has come to be known as "world product mandating". So far, however, very few subsidiaries have world mandates in products accounting for more than a minor proportion of the subsidiary's total output.

In its full form, a product mandate is obtained by a subsidiary from its parent firm to manufacture a product for world markets, thus increasing the scale of the subsidiary's production operations and lowering its unit costs. Significant benefits may be gained in terms of increased output, profitability, and employment. Furthermore, when other product lines within the subsidiary share components or assembly techniques with the world product mandate, the costs of products aimed solely at the domestic market may be significantly reduced. Just as important as the cost reduction implications are the attitudinal and role changes that world product mandates may generate in branch plants. The focus of management is shifted from day-to-day operational problems and domestic market needs alone to the exploitation of longer-term and export opportunities.

A world product mandate may also allow a subsidiary to source a greater quantity of its components from local suppliers. The anticipated scale of orders is sufficient to allow local firms to bid successfully for contracts with long production runs, and hence become cost competitive with potential foreign-based component suppliers who traditionally work on high production volumes. Such a process increases the positive employment impact on the subsidiary's operations and reduces the balance of payments implications of significant component imports. In addition, the expanded operations usually require the establishment of specific R & D facilities for further product development and the establishment of engineering, design, and marketing capabilities.

In this sense, the world product mandate differs significantly from a simple "rationalization" of a subsidiary's operations to serve a North American market, as in the case of the Canadian subsidiaries of the American "Big Three" car makers in the context of the auto pact. In that continental rationalization scheme, the primary emphasis has been to narrow the product mix and expand the scale of production runs in automotive assembly operations for efficiency reasons. No unique product mandates have been assigned to the Canadian subsidiaries. Instead, truncated manufacturing operations have developed, which perform no R & D and export in large part to one country on an administered market basis. Furthermore, the products manufactured require components to be imported on such a scale that automotive trade is now a significant drain on Canada's current account balance of payments.

Finally, world product mandates offer the prospect of a much more secure and stable economic future for branch plants in Canada than either continuance of the status quo or rationalization on a continental basis. By emphasizing the development of specific corporate capabilities to market a category or range of manufactured goods, world product mandates can provide local managers with the opportunity to develop their own skills, to adapt to changing international competitive conditions, and to find international market niches for their products. Therefore, unlike the traditional branch plant or the rationalized subsidiary, such firms may prove less subject to retrenchment strategies of the parent firm in times of economic recession.

The concept is hardly new to Canada. A type of world product mandate was advocated by the minister of Industry, Trade, and Commerce in 1975 when he published a statement entitled *New Principles of International Business Conduct*. More recently, the Science Council endorsed the concept in its 1979 report, *Forging the Links: A Technology Policy for Canada*.[2] Since then, the concept has been increasingly mentioned by policy makers as an interesting and useful instrument for dealing with the problems posed by a branch-plant manufacturing sector. Recently, a task force was established by the government of Ontario to investigate world product mandates. Despite the concept's widespread endorsement, however, little has been published on the subject, and no level of government has provided a clear set of policies for the promotion of world product mandating among multinational firms with subsidiaries in Canada.

2. *Ibid.*, p. 55.

V
International Operations Management

C
Global Product Mandating

37
Global Product Mandating

David Rutenberg

Dr. Rutenberg is professor of international business and operations research in the School of Business, Queen's University. He has worked for and consulted with several large international companies, and he taught for ten years at Carnegie-Mellon University. He is the author of many articles and a forthcoming book, *Multinational Management*.

This chapter was written expressly for this volume.

paradigm

The stages of corporate organization constitute a familiar paradigm of business policy. The proprietor's casual organization gives way to a functional structure with vice-presidents of marketing, production, development, and finance. This structure is efficient so long as the corporation maintains a narrow product line (though it is not a structure that nurtures general managers). To cope with the variety of many product lines, most corporations have found it necessary to reorganize into product divisions. Each product division manages its own marketing, production, and product development. However, instead of having a treasurer, banker, and board of directors, the product division faces a corporate financial staff (who, ideally, bring more analytical skill to bear, are willing to fund sensible new ventures, and have fewer compunctions about closing down divisions whose prospects are unprofitable). In a multinational corporation, each product division takes global responsibility for its product. This means that in any nation, several product divisions operate rather independently. Operationally, the subsidiary product managers report to their product division; legally the product lines in the nation, usually constitute one legal subsidiary with its subsidiary president who handles government relations and treasurer who handles banks. There is usually some friction between the operational structure (by product) and the legal structure (by nation), which is resolved by means of co-ordinators, dotted line relationships, or a formal matrix organization.

A global product mandate (sometimes called a "world charter" or "an assigned product family") reiterates the need for a product division with global responsibility. However, the realization that the management of the product division need not reside in the headquarter's nation is a new one. Among U.S. corporations, it has long been corporate practice to spread product divisional managements around the country, rather than insisting that they be adjacent to the company headquarters. Thus, the headquarters of General Electric is in Connecticut, while GE's Medical Systems Division is in Wisconsin. The headquarters of Westinghouse is in Pittsburgh, and its Steam Turbine Division, which controls plants in South Carolina, California, and Virginia, is centred in Philadelphia. Given this precedent of operating autonomy, it is a small step to move the management of a product division from the United States to another safe and comfortable nation.

Global product mandating is a new term for an old practice. European multinationals such as N.V. Philips of Holland or Hoffman La Roche of Switzerland have not hesitated to locate product divisions where it makes most sense. For example, N.V. Philips tape cassettes are manufactured in Austria, where the management team improves manufacturing processes and controls product specifications in every nation. Hoffman La Roche's U.S. subsidiary has had its own research laboratories and product development programs for many decades as have a few U.S. companies. Since the beginning, the affiliated petroleum companies of Exxon have each had a research department to perform technical service and tailor product specifications. Fundamental research was performed by Esso Research and Engineering in New Jersey. But the affiliated companies had hired bright and energetic scientists for their laboratories, who refused to be restricted to technical service. After painful attempts at solution had failed in the 1930s and 1940s, it was agreed that each affiliate would assume worldwide responsibility for a particular technical problem in addition to routine technical service and product tailoring, as an outlet for its scientific creativity. Thus, Esso France became the centre for process-control electronics and Imperial Oil in Canada the centre for mercaptan chemistry.

Control Through a Product Life Cycle

The executives of multinational corporations are sometimes wary of control. They lost their flexibility long ago and now are concerned that they are losing influence over their corporations. Not only is the corporation's internal bureaucracy complicated, but contracts, agreements, and understandings have been reached with thousands of national, regional, and local governments, as well as with intergovernmental agencies and advisory bodies. The exercise of control by top corporate executives is to a great extent, it appears, a political process.

Headquarters has less control over those products which are managed abroad (as global product mandates). But a multidivisional multinational produces hundreds of product lines, only a few of which need be managed abroad. The familiar concept of a product life cycle provides a simple means to categorize products.

Early in the life of a new product family, there is a dearth of information on which to base business decisions. Essentially, product development means finding ideas and continuing the negative cash flow until the project has yielded just enough information to justify cancelling it. This need to have the power to cut off funding requires a closeness that seems incompatible with global product mandating.

The second phase of a product life cycle is, however, quite compatible with global product mandating. The rate of product design improvements has slowed sufficiently to allow the corporation to research manufacturing processes, and even to redesign parts of the product to accord with manufacturing processes. Cash flow required still exceeds profitability, but in amounts that can be forecasted. Usually at this stage less established competitors with higher cost are dropping out (or deciding not to enter the competition).

The corporate advantage of globally mandating a product line at this stage of its development is that by being abroad it is removed from the organizational politics that can bedevil any large organization. So long as the mandate is clear enough so that boundary poaching by adjacent divisions of the corporation is not a persistent problem, then being abroad can allow management to get on with the job of improving the manufacturing process, the product design, and the marketing needed to secure world markets.

Later in the product life cycle, the product design stabilizes, as does the manufacturing process. Once the manufacturing process has sufficiently stabilized, it becomes possible for the corporation to move manufacturing to low-cost sites around the world. The notion of the global product mandate then becomes the headquarters for a miniature multinational, with satellite plants around the world. As the product evolves to become a commodity, there is less to gain from expensive central direction.

Relevance to Canada

Since the days of the Bennett tariff, foreign corporations have built manufacturing plants in Canada. Tariffs were only part of the reason. Canadian raw material costs were low and availability high. Canadian cities and manufacturing plants were intact at the end of the Second World War. Years of high growth in Canada nourished the expectation that high growth would continue. Thus, market share in Canada was a valuable asset, to be protected by a Canadian plant even if that plant had to be built prematurely. Rivalry between oligopolists thus led to miniature replica plants producing the same variety of items, each having a very short production run.

Austere growth prospects for the decades to come have reduced the value of market share in Canada. Multilateral tariff negotiations will reduce the tariff component of logistics costs, which have already (though less visibly) been reduced by improved inventory control. The rising cost of energy is resulting in an increased emphasis on manufacturing productivity, crudely defined as "working both smarter and harder". Multinational corporations are now starting to rationalize their global production and are becoming less inhibited about closing uneconomical facilities.

Plant location decisions centre on the balance between economies of scale and logistics costs. During the last thirty years, logistics costs have decreased, and the ability to design and control large manufacturing facilities has greatly increased. Thus the term "world-scale plant" has come to mean an ever larger facility. So while the Canadian market has grown in the last thirty years, the size of a world-scale plant has grown faster. In many industries, the total Canadian market is smaller than one world-scale plant.

U.S.- and European-based multinationals used to compete on the basis of marketing insight and flair. They are increasingly being challenged by Japanese multinationals with plants in Malaysia, Korea, and so on, which are competing on the basis of product quality and cost. Therefore, it seems reasonable to predict that headquarters management will scrutinize the existence of uneconomical plants anywhere in the world. Miniature replica plants in Canada may be transformed:

1. Some will be closed. As plants are closed and put up for sale, the market price of plants will drop. Those corporations that delay closing may as well use their plants as warehouses.
2. Some will become focussed factories. After being gutted of general purpose machinery and executive offices, the shell of the factory will receive special purpose machinery for a select few products or sub-assemblies.
3. Some will receive a global mandate for a product. Corporate headquarters always control key personnel and capital appropriation decisions. However, headquarters is usually willing to allow product divisions to make marketing, manufacturing, and product development decisions. Global product mandating means moving the product divisional management to Canada.

Focussed factories should become appreciably more productive than miniature replica plants. Nevertheless, Canada must restrict itself to industries in which it has comparative advantages. If a multinational, designing a factory in which semi-skilled labor assembles a component for the world, were to design the factory identically whether it is to be built in Singapore or Canada, then it would likely have similar productivity and hence be able to afford similar wages. If a wage differential is to be maintained between Singapore and Canada, the factory will have to do one or more of the following:

1. It can use inputs other than labor which are cheaper in Canada than in the rest of the world.
2. It can take advantage of the lower logistics cost of delivering to the U.S. market, so long as the U.S. remains the world's focal market.
3. It can have its design tailored to the peculiarities of Canadian workers so as to achieve a higher productivity for the same investment.

Except for products near the beginning of their life cycle, where the product design is still evolving and substantial improvements in manufacturing processes remain to be discovered these are quite stringent conditions. Global product mandating of such products from Canada makes sense.

Where learning by doing and economies of scale are significant, a business will not be viable unless its product can capture a significant share of the world market. To this end, the established sales subsidiaries of a multinational corporation are a vital outlet. They complement the marketing analysis, engineering design, production process development, and entrepreneurial management of a Canadian team which has a global product mandate. The multinational corporation's established sales force and trusted brand names constitute a significant real asset, an asset that has proven particularly expensive to build on a global basis. For such products it seems to make sense to strive for global product mandating from Canada.

Even though a subsidiary in Canada gets a global mandate, the subsidiary managers nevertheless have to work in conjunction with national executives in each market. A multinational corporation functions as a matrix organization whether that structure is a formal one or whether it is an informal amalgam of dotted line and solid line relationships. Therefore, underlying the business work has to be the political activity of keeping in touch with a worldwide constituency for this product.

The first business function is market research, leading to redesigned products and fitting the right product to each niche in each market. There is a power balance within each national market, and the Canadian product specialist has to understand each local market.

The second business function is to redesign the product and manufacturing processes to increase productivity worldwide. This calls for the best in engineering design and cost accounting disciplines.

In addition to technical service on the existing worldwide facilities, the group has to experiment imaginatively to meet tough targets. Part of the group's work involves reverse engineering on competing products from each nation.

The third business function is to manufacture the product. The possessor of the global product mandate must be a productive producer (necessary if it is to be accepted as the role model), and simultaneously it must be the flexible pilot plant in which to develop and debug yet more productive processes. It appears as though many Canadian miniature replica plants have flexible union arrangements and general purpose machinery that is quite compatible with the pilot plant role.

The fourth business function is the political task of maintaining support in headquarters. In concrete terms, this fourth task is manifested in capital appropriation requests to headquarters, detailed business plans, and usable explanations of deviations from plan. The fact that Canada is so close to U.S. corporate headquarters means that this fourth function can be carried out with ease.

Examples of global product mandating occur in many industries. A 1978 report by the Canadian Ministry of Industry, Trade, and Commerce gave both examples and recommendations.

There has already been a significant amount of consolidation and rationalization in the Canadian electrical industry. Furthermore, a number of free-standing product lines have been developed through Canadian R & D or by assignment from parent company of world charter. Examples are water-wheel generators; bulk oil and air blast power circuit breakers; drive systems for mine, mill, and transportation systems; industrial gas turbines and small steam turbines; hydraulic turbines; HVDC, EHV, and UHV power transformers; solid-state excitation systems for hydraulic generators; and a variety of utility control and instrumentation systems.... An improved investment climate achieved through government action on R & D incentives and internationally competitive taxation and trade policies will greatly assist Canadian subsidiaries in their efforts to earn additional world charters for selected product lines from within their multinational structure. Such action could also attract new R & D centres or manufacturing facilities to locate in Canada.[1]

Dozens of Canadian subsidiaries have global product mandates. Pratt & Whitney Canada develops and produces small gas turbine

1. Sector Task Force Report, *Canadian Electrical Industry* (Ottawa: Ministry of Industry, Trade, and Commerce, 1978).

engines for all of United Technologies. Garrett Manufacturing has the Signal Corporation mandate for aircraft temperature control systems, micro-electronics, and emergency beacons. Raybestos Manhattan has a mandate in large brake shoes. The Canadian General Electric mandate in water-wheel generators and other products was described in the Ministry of Industry, Trade, and Commerce report.[2] Honeywell Canada specializes in electric thermostats, as does Johnson Controls. Canadian Westinghouse has the Westinghouse mandate in gas turbines and other products.

The Science Council of Canada's 1980 statement on global product mandating consists of corporate descriptive case studies of Black & Decker Canada Inc., Westinghouse Canada Inc., Garrett Manufacturing Ltd., and Litton Systems Canada Ltd. A clearly delineated mandate is that of Westinghouse Canada:

The third step in the evolution of the gas turbine world product mandate for the Canadian subsidiary resulted from a further initiative on the part of Westinghouse Canada. The Canadian firm anticipated a substantial market for a range of high efficiency industrial turbines (up to 40,000 HP) for mechanical drive applications. This conviction, coupled with the parent firm's decision to concentrate on the large models used by hydro utilities, resulted in an opportunity for the Canadian firm to capture a further world charter assignment in 1973. A proposal was made to the parent that Westinghouse Canada take on charter responsibility for the design, development, and manufacture of a new family of two-shaft turbines. This proposal included a substantial investment in the R & D phase by the Canadian government. Because of the parent's decision to invest heavily in a new line of larger single-shaft turbines and the availability of a Canadian government grant, the proposal was accepted and the world product mandate assigned.[3]

Role of Governments

As the Canadian government is encouraging global product mandating it is competing with other governments. Fortunately for corporations, governments are different, so they include different elements in their cost-benefit analyses and plan to different time horizons. The most rudimentary "mandates" achieve a better balance of

2. Ibid.
3. Science Council of Canada, *Multinationals and Industrial Strategy: Role of World Product Mandates* (Ottawa: Science Council of Canada, 1980), p. 34.

trade. A 1971 case study, "Two-Ply Manufactures, Inc.", chronicled the Mexican joint venture which Two-Ply, a Toledo, Ohio tire company, had been induced to establish with an industrial banker, Sr. Mendoza:

> Hardly a year after the doors of the plant were opened in 1965, Wilson received word that the Mexican subsidiary, Llantas Superiores, was being faced with some new restrictions at the border. The tire fabric, it appeared, could no longer be imported from Toledo but would have to be manufactured in Mexico. What is more, synthetic tire cord would be available only in limited quantities; to the greatest extent possible, Llantas Superiores would be expected to use Mexican cotton for the manufacture of the fabric. Sr. Casas proved to be no help in the crisis. Pressure from the Agriculture Ministry and the Ministry of Industry simply had been too strong. Nor could Sr. Casas provide any part of the added capital that would be needed to expand the Mexican enterprise. Since no profits had as yet been generated, Two-Ply simply would have to enlarge its loan to Sr. Casas in order to have him retain the needed 51 per cent ownership. . . . (Shortly thereafter price controls were imposed.) This time, when Wilson arrived on the plane from Chicago, Sr. Casas proved to be an immediate help. Appointments were promptly arranged with key officials in the Ministry of Industry, who proved not unsympathetic to Wilson's plight.
>
> On the other hand, the officials also proved fairly knowledgeable about the tire business. What would prevent Two-Ply, they inquired, from placing a full production line in Mexico, capable of operating at a technically satisfactory level of output? Could not Two-Ply take some specialty tire, with a good deal of hand labor and relatively short runs, and have the Mexican plant specialize in that line for North America? If the production required some imports of specialized cord, synthetic rubber, or special chemicals, these could certainly be arranged on a duty-free basis — provided, of course, that the exports of finished tires from Mexico more than compensated for the added imports. True, the U.S. duty and extra transport costs might present a small problem for such exports. But on the other hand, the lower labor cost in Mexico might well turn out to more than offset those added costs. In short, both Mexico and Two-Ply could benefit.[4]

This Mexican example is a typical incident, familiar to every

---

4. Raymond Vernon, "Two-Ply Manufacturers, Inc." (Boston: Intercollegiate Case Clearing House 9-371-349, 1971).

multinational executive, of government intervention for the purposes of increasing employment and exports. Doz and Prahalad quoted a top manager of a multinational confronted with a lot of government carrots and sticks:

In the long run, we risk becoming a collection of inefficient government-subsidized national companies unable to compete on the world market. Yet, if we rationalize our operations, we lose our preferential access to government contracts and our R & D subsidies.

So we try to develop an overall strategic plan that makes some competitive sense, and then we bargain for each part of it with individual governments, trying to sell them on the particular programs that contribute to the plan as a whole. Often, we have to revise, or abandon, parts of our plan for lack of government support.[5]

Although it seems that all governments are alike in wanting to expand employment, they differ in the weights they apply to unskilled labor, white collar jobs, and research positions (the "shadow prices" in the benefit-cost analysis language).[6] Even within one government, different agencies perceive different weights as a comparison of the emphases of the Canadian Department of Regional Economic Expansion with those of the Science Council or even the Foreign Investment Review Agency.

The relationship between the corporation (with many product lines) and the many governments can be perceived in game theory terms. The corporation can see the profit consequences of transferring each product line to every nation. Each government has its preferences over product lines and can express these preferences in cost-benefit terms. If the data existed, the problem could be solved quite easily as a weighted distribution problem (sometimes called a machine loading problem). Each nation product assignment gives a profit to the corporation and a utility to that government. If we set the thresholds to the utility that each government requires, then the problem can be not only solved, but also explored by parametric analysis on the governments' utility thresholds.

The actual dynamics are appreciably less mechanical. The Canadian government has no formal policy of encouraging global product mandates but does so in the process of encouraging the Canadianiza-

5. Yves Doz and R. Prahalad, "How MNCs Cope with Host Government Intervention", *Harvard Business Review* (March/April) 1980.
6. John Hansen, *Guide to Practical Project Appraisal: Social Benefit - Cost Analysis in Developing Countries* (Vienna: United Nations, 1978).

tion of decision making. Government officials have this opportunity when companies apply for such government grants as those from the Enterprise Development Program or the Defence Industries Productivity Program. In essence, the head of the Canadian subsidiary is caught between his corporate headquarters and the industry sector branch officer of the Department of Industry, Trade, and Commerce. As a go-between he has to maintain the trust of both parties, rather like a labor mediator. His behavioral problems are difficult and awkward. Time is an important dimension of negotiations. Corporate executives appear to feel that they are under tighter time constraints than government officials.

Conclusions for Corporations

Because a government official is forced to be fair to all corporations in his purview, he has to view them as interchangeable, alternate means to a social end. Cost-benefit analyses can be applied.

Unfortunately corporate managers tend to view their divisions as unique and unmeasurable for cost-benefit analysis. Only in the higher realms of corporate planning is a necessary degree of abstraction possible. Unfortunately, such planning groups lack conceptual models for the kind of corporate freedom envisioned in global product mandating. This makes the task of the subsidiary president particularly difficult.

Finally, there are not many executives anywhere with the experience and energy needed to manage a product line globally. Those few who are managing global product mandates from Canada face a challenging and difficult set of tasks.

V
International Operations Management

C
Global Product Mandating

38
Branch Plants Bear New Fruit

Mark Witten

Mr. Witten is a Toronto-based business writer, who contributes frequently to such magazines as *Canadian Business*, *Quest*, *Maclean's*, *Toronto Life*, and *Saturday Night*.

The material in this chapter appeared originally in *Canadian Business*, November 1980. Reprinted by permission.

"The branch plant is dead." The speaker is Franz Tyaack, president and chief executive officer of Westinghouse Canada Ltd. Tyaack is not sensationalizing. He is not even gloomy. He is simply announcing the conclusion that he and many more managers of the Canadian subsidiaries of multinational companies have reached in the past few years: the branch-plant system that has so long dominated this country's business landscape is no longer economically viable. The evidence — a rash of production cutbacks, product pullouts, plant shut-downs and worker layoffs — is all around us. The country's branch plants are being swept up in an epidemic of corporate rationalization, which governments, federal or provincial, are seemingly powerless to do anything about. The only hope for the subsidiaries' survival, says Tyaack, is for them and their parent companies to begin playing by the fundamental rule of business in a free-trading world: export or perish. The subsidiaries that learn the game, he argues, are going to blossom anew.

Fresh from a remarkable company turnaround, Franz Tyaack is a vocal champion of world product mandates. That catch phrase refers to a strategy that has been around for a long time, but that is now being touted by both industry and government, with great enthusiasm and some desperation, as a one-shot solution to several problems. World product mandating is a corporate strategy that uses the international market power of a multinational to sell, on a worldwide basis, a specific product, product line or part of a product that is manufactured by a single subsidiary. When a subsidiary obtains exclusive world charter rights for a product — a mandate — it can then increase the scale of its production runs and lower its unit costs. Ultimately, if the product is a successful one, the benefits to the subsidiary can include increased production and R & D, greater profitability, and added jobs.

But global mandating does much more than reduce product costs. It also fundamentally changes the nature of the branch-plant operation by giving the subsidiary a far greater degree of autonomy. The focus of management shifts away from day-to-day operations and the domestic market and moves toward the effective exploitation of long-term and export opportunities. A world mandate usually means also that the subsidiary must not only set up the necessary engineering, design, and marketing capability to sell its product competitively around the world, but that it must be able to develop new or related products to keep abreast of fast-changing technologies.

World product mandating, say its proponents, ensures that foreign multinationals serve the national interest of subsidiaries' countries along with their own. Under the conventional branch-plant system, tough times for parent companies, as in the auto industry today, mean that host countries pay a very steep price for foreign ownership — in lost jobs, inability to adapt, balance-of-payments problems, lack of R & D or high-technology input, and so on. With tariff barriers crumbling all around us, economists, politicians, and Canadian subsidiary managers quite rightly worry that the future will be much worse. The bleakest scenarios would have most of our branch plants functioning a few short years from now as little more than sales offices that do virtually no production. Rather than pursuing the old Buy Back Canada option, governments are hoping that world product mandating will turn out to be an advantage for the nationalists and the multinationals alike.

The idea combines hard business appeal with potentially widespread political advantages. It is very different from the familiar straightforward rationalization of a subsidiary's operations to serve a North American market, which simply involves narrowing the product mix and increasing the production runs. Such subsidiaries are really truncated manufacturing operations that do no R & D, export only to the U.S., and import components on a scale that contributes to our huge balance-of-payments deficit. The Canadian subsidiary with successful world mandates is a far more entrepreneurial entity. And that, of course, entails some risk. "The business basics still apply," warns Franz Tyaack. "World mandates are academic if you can't be competitive once you've got them."

Case 1: Litton Systems Canada Ltd.

Ten years ago, Litton Systems Canada Ltd. of Toronto was an empty shell. When the demand for North American military hardware plummeted in the late 1960s, manufacturing at the Canadian subsidiary was severely curtailed; employment dropped from 3,000 in 1968 to 670 in 1970. "We were kind of desperate," recalls President Ron Keating. During the 1960s, the Guidance and Control Division of Litton Industries Inc. in the U.S. had developed world mandates on inertial navigation systems (INS) for military and commercial aircraft. But the U.S. division still had a large amount of military work, and it was also convinced that the commercial product lacked potential.

Canadian management had a different view. In 1967, it proposed an R & D project aimed at developing a second-generation commercial system that would cut production cost by one-third. The Canadian government agreed to finance 50 per cent, or $4.5 million, of the project. By 1970, Litton Canada had developed greater technical expertise in commercial INS than its parent. Guidance and Control agreed to transfer the charter, preferring to remain in the less risky and more profitable military avionics market. In 1971, Litton Canada introduced the finished product to the commercial market with phenomenal success. Sales that year were a scant $22 million; this year they will reach an estimated $100 million.

Today, commercial INS are the principal product line for Litton Canada, which now has more than 2,000 employees. The subsidiary controls 65 per cent of the world market. Inertial systems are a very accurate, independent form of "dead-reckoning" navigation and, unlike other systems, are not dependent upon contact with ground facilities. The prime customers are commercial aircraft on transoceanic routes, military transports, and maritime patrol aircraft.

Sales from commercial INS have provided Litton Canada with the solid product base and cash flow needed to support additional long-term R & D programs, which have led to the development of many new product lines. "We always had ideas but we didn't have a production base," says Keating. "Once you have a base you can do R & D, and you get a constant fall-out of technology." In addition to commercial INS, Litton Canada now designs, develops, manufactures, and markets air-traffic control, ground-controlled intercept and other special purpose simulators; automated test equipment for entire navigation systems; commercial marine systems and gyrocompasses; and air-borne search and tactical radar systems. It has the exclusive world product charters within Litton Industries for all these lines. Outside of avionics, it also does custom electronic systems work, such as designing and manufacturing prison security systems.

Without the original world product mandate, the Canadian subsidiary might not have survived the 1970-75 slump in the military avionics market. But it's not only the sales volume that's changed. During the 1960s, Litton's work force was mainly semi-skilled, blue-collar production labor. Today, the company employs many more engineers, managers, trained technicians, and skilled tradesmen. Exports, which represent 80 per cent of sales volume, have increased from $18 million in 1971 to a projected $81 million in 1980, when the company expected an overall trade surplus of $50 million. More than 90 per cent of its sales are generated by world-mandated products.

Why, then, are there not more Canadian subsidiaries aggressively pursuing world product mandates? "The biggest difficulty is getting the Canadian companies to move their asses and be prepared to challenge the parent corporation," says Litton's Keating. "You've got to tell your corporation that if you're going to survive in Canada, it's got to give you a world charter. And you have to prove that it's cost effective to do the work in Canada."

Case 2: Westinghouse Canada Ltd.

During its first seventy years here, Westinghouse Canada Ltd. of Hamilton was a typical branch plant manufacturing a wide range of products similar to those of its parent for the small Canadian electrical market. As a result of strong domestic demand and high tariff protection, sales grew rapidly until the mid-1960s. But as tariffs began dropping and foreign competition became severe, the company was forced to begin a process of drastic product rationalization, which has continued over the past twelve years. Since 1969, it has phased out its production of water-wheel generators, video tubes, television sets, radios, and other home entertainment equipment. Other product lines were rationalized, and in 1977 the subsidiary sold its $100 million appliance division.

Soon after the company began phasing out its uncompetitive products, it also began aggressively pursuing exports to replace the outmoded branch-plant approach. Says President Franz Tyaack, "The branch plant focusses you in on the domestic market. So long as that market is growing, there's no problem. When the growth stops, though, you must have a broader field to play in if the company is going to be viable. We had to do something or we'd have gone down the tubes."

In 1969, Westinghouse Canada began to emphasize turbine manufacturing, and over the next two years (after being awarded a large Ontario Hydro contract for nuclear pump motors), it expanded its production capability. At the same time, the parent, Westinghouse Electric Corp., was concentrating on newer, larger turbines, and in 1972 the Canadian subsidiary won a world product mandate for the smaller low-temperature gas turbines. This mandate and one for electronic systems, later obtained, are largely responsible for Westinghouse's turnaround. Over the past five years, the firm's return on sales and earnings per share have improved dramatically, from $15.4 million and $5.76 in 1975 to $26.5 million and $10 in 1979. By 1979, despite the sale of its appliance division, sales reached an all-time high of $500 million, compared to $442 million in 1975. The large trade deficits of the 1960s and early 1970s have turned into surpluses; in 1979, the surplus was more than $7.5 million. In 1979, the turbines accounted for 75 per cent of the company's exports and more than $80 million in sales. Exports are now approaching 20 per cent of sales, but Tyaack still isn't satisfied. "We are striving to reach a 50 per cent level by 1990. There has to be an influx of new products to sustain that goal."

On that score, Tyaack maintains that Westinghouse is only beginning to realize the potential for world product mandates. The first units of a second-generation line of gas turbines were delivered to customers in 1979, and sales are expected to expand rapidly over the next five years. Tyaack thinks worldwide sales potential could be $2 billion. The company has also since acquired world mandates for other technology-intensive product lines, including ultra-high-voltage (core form) power transformers, large wound-rotor induction motors, powered shipboard sonar equipment, electronic line-tracing equipment, airport lighting equipment, baseboard electric heating, and information display systems.

"It's absolutely a must that the initiative for a world product mandate come from Canada initially," says Tyaack. "And if you can develop a spinoff that adds to the parent's portfolio, you'll certainly get your charter." He continues, "One advantage we have is that our subsidiary is small and more flexible. It can play the entrepreneur more easily than the large entity can. It knows how to make money with small money at risk." One example is Westinghouse's small mandate in airport lighting, a line that was originally produced in the U.S. "The parent firm was disillusioned with its product and decided to get out. Our sales in Canada were good. Rather than get out, we said, 'Give it to us in Canada.' Our Canadian managers are good at spotting the orphans in the parent's production line."

Case 3: Garrett Manufacturing Ltd.

At Garrett Corp., a multinational aerospace company with 1979 sales of U.S. $1.3 billion, world product mandating is the central organizational strategy. Garrett's operations are distributed among eight major manufacturing divisions, each of which holds exclusive world charter rights for a broadly defined product area. Virtually every North American designed military and commercial aircraft in service today uses a Garrett product, as do many of the U.S. missiles and space systems. The Canadian division, Garrett Manufacturing Ltd. (GML) in Toronto, is responsible for the design, development, and manufacture of the aircraft temperature control systems that run an entire aircraft environmental control system. These controls constitute an

electronic brain that monitors the performance of the complete
system and sends messages to individual components when an adjustment is required. Since the overall environmental control system
for every aircraft model is unique, the electronic brain that GML
develops to drive each of these systems must be custom designed.
A typical system for a large commercial jet could cost up to $80,000
per plane. The Canadian firm has a world market share of more than
75 per cent for this product.

Until 1959, GML was little more than a Canadian distribution and
service outlet for other divisions of the corporation. That year, GML
was assigned by its parent the task of producing the air data computer for the Canadian Air Force's CF-104 fighter program. That
established its domestic manufacturing base. By 1961, the work was
finished and the subsidiary again became a sales and service depot
for Garrett aerospace products. At this point, the Canadian government asked the company to set up a Canadian assembly plant to
serve the domestic market and reduce U.S. imports. The company
objected, saying that the small Canadian aerospace market couldn't
justify a Canadian production operation. Instead, it suggested turning
GML into a full-fledged division, with its own world product charter.

In 1961, GML won total responsibility for the design, development,
and manufacture of Garrett temperature control systems. Since then,
the Canadian subsidiary's sales have increased at an average annual
rate of 20 per cent. By 1979, gross sales were more than $50 million
and the number of employees climbed to more than 1,000. What
would GML be today without those mandates? "You would see a
company being basically what the Canadian industry has been," says
Vice-President and General Manager Bill Tate. "Flat. Doing a couple
or maybe five million a year, employing 100 to 200 people."

World sales of aircraft temperature control systems have given
GML a stable production base and the necessary cash flow to make
large investments in R & D, not only to support the mandate but to
spin off new products. GML is now one of the most R & D intensive
firms (up to 12 per cent of annual sales) in either Canadian avionics
or electronics. It pays. The company has developed on a world
mandate basis several additional lines of technology-intensive products: airline survival beacons, personal locator beacons, and very
high frequency transmitters and receivers for airport-to-airport communication; electro-mechanical and custom electronic systems such
as test equipment for air data computers and other flight instruments, and alarm control units for nuclear reactor cores; and custom-
designed, hybrid micro-circuits that incorporate both thick and thin
film technology.

Since 1961, GML has created an overall trade surplus of more than $110 million in finished products trade. Before that year the subsidiary exported nothing and imported about 90 per cent of its total sales from the U.S. as finished products. In 1979, export sales accounted for more than 93 per cent (excluding ground transportation sales) of the firm's total output.

Says Bill Tate, "When Garrett gives us the charter they are pretty damn straightforward about it. They say, 'Go make money.' You don't make money, you're not around very long. A world product mandate is nothing without a great product, but it's also nothing without the technical, managerial, and facility capability to continue to keep the product at the state of the art." He adds, "For some firms, one of the major problems in obtaining a charter is that their parent companies are concerned about transferring jobs to a Canadian company as a world product mandate. I think that's short-sighted."

Case 4: Black & Decker Canada Inc.

Until 1968, Black & Decker Canada Inc. produced the full core line of the parent company's consumer and professional products — drills, jigsaws, sanders, and circular saws — in its Brockville, Ontario plant. The rest of the Black & Decker line was imported from the U.S. The selling price of the company's power tools in Canada was much higher than in the U.S. because of low-volume production and high tariffs on imported power tools. During the late 1960s, the consumer market for power tools in the U.S. was expanding rapidly, and Canadian management became convinced that the home market could also be greatly increased if they could get just one of the corporation's core line products put into the Brockville plant on a rationalized basis. They argued not only that this would decrease production costs, but that a lower selling price would stimulate an expansion of the Canadian market. When the U.S. division began to experience capacity problems in 1968, the Canadian sub was granted a North American charter in orbital sanders.

Orbital sanders were chosen because they had the least market penetration of any Black & Decker core product in North America, thereby removing the least amount of production from the U.S. division and offering the greatest untapped market potential for the Canadian firm. The strategy of lowering the Canadian division's unit production costs proved so successful that, by 1972, Black & Decker's Brockville operation had the lowest unit costs for orbital sanders of all its divisions in the world.

The increased sales volume and cash flow allowed the Canadian subsidiary to begin its own R & D in 1974. A U.K. designer had developed a portable work centre for home handymen called the Workmate, and the European branch was buying it in small quantities. There was talk of buying the design, but the U.S. division reacted coolly, feeling that high production costs would make the Workmate difficult to sell. Canadian management thought otherwise and set out to reduce production costs and improve on the original. It won a mandate for the product, and the Workmate turned out to be a terrific success. Annual output has increased from 250,000 units in 1974 to considerably more than a million units in 1979. The Canadian company has now developed two spinoff models, called the Workwheel, a power stripper and sander designed for work on irregular surfaces, and the Workhorse, which consists of a pair of adjustable platform brackets that form the basis of an easy-to-assemble scaffold for use in the home or on construction sites. The company has world mandates on both products.

"Now we essentially do our own mandating," says Vice-President Ralph Butt. "Instead of being a small northern subsidiary, we find we don't have to remind the U.S. company about Canada any more."

Black & Decker has grown faster than the world organization; since its shift from domestic to world markets, sales and profits have multiplied from $11.4 million and $337,000 in 1968 to $118.2 million and $13.3 million in 1979. Its work force has grown from 500 to 1,200 in the same period, and the Brockville plant has been expanded five times to increase production capacity almost sevenfold. The company's share of the domestic consumer market for power tools has also grown from 30 per cent in 1968 to more than 50 per cent in 1979. It exports about 50 per cent of its output, and export sales increased at an average annual rate of 25 per cent during the 1970s. It enjoys an increasing trade surplus each year. Before 1968, there was always a deficit. "I don't think the benefit of world product mandates is just to the company," says Butt. "Eighty per cent of our product cost is in materials, and we buy most of our materials in Canada. So the country also benefits."

One of the great penalties we have paid for heavy foreign ownership has been the general failure of Canadian subsidiaries under the branch-plant system to innovate and develop distinctive products geared to export markets. Hence Canada's dismal $17 billion trade deficit in goods. Multinational corporations do provide easy access to world markets. Yet, more often than not, Canadian subsidiaries have been unable to exploit that ready-made route. World product mandating can be an opportunity to turn the presence of the multinationals into a situation of mutual advantage.

A recent study conducted by the Science Council of Canada found that subsidiaries of foreign multinationals with full-scale world product mandates did far more research and development here than conventional branch plants and were far more sophisticated users and producers of technology. Not only that, but such companies also tended to be more innovative and contributed far greater long-term economic benefits to Canada, whether measured in terms of exports, sales, productivity, or employment.

Nevertheless, a global mandating strategy is no panacea and is not universally applicable. "The high-technology areas are more conducive to world product mandates because, if you can stay state-of-the-art, you can attract attention outside your own country," suggests Garrett's Bill Tate. "That is not normally true. If you go into a low-tech field, you'll probably find the other countries have the capability to do it. You don't have that much to offer." When a company plays the world mandate game, its product must be the best, or the only one of its kind, in the world. Such products are not, as a rule, offered to the Canadian subsidiary on a platter. Often the sub must fight or scheme against other divisions within its own parent corporation to get a mandate that looks like a winner or must develop its own winning products. The infighting can be bitter.

For subsidiary managers who've spent most of their working lives in the comfort and security of a protected domestic market, the more aggressive, outward-looking, and risky management style that world product mandates require seems foreign and perhaps intimidating. Westinghouse's Franz Tyaack sees that inward habit as the main problem preventing wide acceptance of the strategy. "It's risk aversion. If you've been in a product for a long time, you're defensive. When you're defensive, you're not going out into the world and are not competitively strong. You're crawling into the womb. I sometimes hear comments like, 'Well, I don't know if you should depend on world markets. Suppose there's a world recession?'." He adds, hopefully, "There's less and less of that, though."

Companies like Garrett, Litton, Black & Decker and, more recently, Westinghouse are still exceptional, however. Many other corporations that say they're actively pursuing mandates are in fact making only token efforts. And while government procurements and R & D grants can be effective ways of encouraging world product mandating, Litton Canada's Ron Keating warns that ultimately the ball must rest in the Canadian subsidiary's court. "I don't think government can initiate charters," he says. "Companies must do it themselves. They have to show the parent they can be competitive." Nevertheless, the national interest would seem to dictate that rather than ignore the multinationals altogether — or simply blow off steam with ineffectual criticism — the happiest solution may well be for government to support world product mandating as a necessary complement to any industrial strategy that seeks, at the same time, to build a strong base of Canadian-owned, export-oriented companies. One can hardly thrive without the other, particularly when you consider the advantages to the aggressive, Canadian-owned supplier of selling his wares to healthy and entrepreneurial customers with global reach.

It just may be the post-nationalist solution.

V
International Operations Management

D
International Financial Management

39
Managing Exchange Risks Under Floating Exchange Rates: The Canadian Experience

Talaat Abdel-Malek

Dr. Abdel-Malek is professor of international business at the University of Saskatchewan. He is the author of a book, *Managerial Export Orientation: A Canadian Study*, and of several articles in academic and professional journals. He recently served for two years as chief technical advisor for the United Nations International Labor Organisation in Zambia.

The material for this chapter appeared originally in *Columbia Journal of World Business*, Fall 1976. Reprinted by permission.

Recent discussions concerning the choice between fixed and floating exchange-rate systems have tended to focus on macro-aspects of the problem nationally and internationally. Little explicit attention is given to the micro or managerial implications of alternative choices. Yet floating rates are now a fact of life and are likely to remain so for the foreseeable future, notwithstanding the call by some monetary authorities for a return to a fixed-rate system. How has business been coping with its changed foreign exchange environment and what effect has the shift to floating rates had on managerial decisions and practices relating to the firm's exchange-risk policies?

The purpose of this chapter is to present the findings of a study of exchange-risk management in a sample of Canadian firms under floating rates. In particular, the following four questions are examined:

1. What changes in exchange-risk policies have floating rates induced?
2. To what extent do these policies vary among firms? And do policy differences appear to be associated with given characteristics of the firms concerned or of their international operations?
3. How do firms actually set and evaluate exchange-risk policies?
4. How serious are the problems posed by floating rates, as perceived by management?

Methodology

The study is based on a national sample of firms involved in international business. Of sixty-five firms selected, responses were obtained from sixty. Table 1 shows that of these, forty-four are in various manufacturing industries and sixteen are trading firms. All respondents except eight have export operations and all except nine have import operations, while seventeen firms have foreign manufacturing subsidiaries in addition to their export-import operations. About one-third are foreign-controlled subsidiaries operating in Canada and two-thirds are Canadian-owned firms. In terms of size, as measured by total sales in 1973-74, roughly one-third had sales under $30 million, another third had sales between $30 million and $300 million, and the remaining third had sales of over $300 million.

Table 1

A Profile of the Main Features of Sample Firms

Features	Manufacturing	Trading	Total
No. of Firms	44	16	60
Ownership			
Canadian	28	11	39
Foreign	16	5	21
International Operations			
Exports	44	8	52
Imports	37	14	51
Foreign Manufacturing	17	—	17
Annual Sales (1973-74) in millions			
Less than $30	13	7	20
$30 - $300	14	7	21
Over $300	17	2	19
Importance of International Operations			
a. For Firms with no foreign subsidiaries: Imports/Exports as % of total sales			
50% or less	20	—	20
Over 50%	7	16	23
b. For Firms with foreign subsidiaries also: Canadian exports and sales by subsidiaries as % of total corporate sales:			
50% or less	3	—	3
Over 50%	14	—	14

Sample firms also varied with regard to the relative weight of international business in their total operations. For the seventeen firms with foreign subsidiaries, the total value of exports from Canada and sales by subsidiaries accounted for over 50 per cent of total corporate sales in fourteen firms and were below 50 per cent in the other three firms. For the remaining forty-three firms, total export-import operations represented over 50 per cent of total sales in twenty-three firms and 50 per cent or less in twenty firms.

Data were collected by means of a personal interview conducted by the researcher with the treasurer of each participating firm. An interview guide, consisting mostly of open-ended questions, was used to ensure uniform coverage of questions for all firms.

Findings

Exchange-Risk Policies Before and After Floating

Because the Canadian dollar (C$) was floated in June, 1970, a distinction is made here between the impact of its floating and the effects of the more general floating which has become prevalent since the early months of 1973.

Tables 2 and 3 summarize exchange-risk policies before and after floating with respect to (a) the extent of exchange-risk coverage, and (b) the means of coverage exposure. Analysis of these results and of the explanations provided by respondents in relation to their firms' policies and actions has led to four main conclusions.[1]

First, the floating of the C$ appears to have had only a modest effect on exchange-risk policies. A few firms moved to adopt a partial coverage policy instead of leaving their exchange positions completely exposed. Over 40 per cent of sample firms, however, continued to be fully exposed. The reluctance of most firms to adopt more defensive policies was due to a number of reasons. The principal of these was a belief, or a hope, that instability resulting from the dollar's floating was temporary and that once the full adjustments in rates were effected, the C$ would soon regain stability (as its record had shown during the 1950-62 period in which it floated) either through the market mechanism or as a result of its being repegged. It should also be noted that a subtle but significant effect of C$ floating was that it seemed to cause management in many firms to pay more attention to foreign exchange developments and, in this way, helped to speed up policy adjustments.

Table 2

Exchange Risk Coverage Policies Before and After Floating

Extent of Coverage	Before C$ Floating		After C$ Floating		After More General Floating	
	No. of Firms	%	No. of Firms	%	No. of Firms	%
Full Coverage	8	13.3	9	15.0	10	16.7
Partial Coverage	22	36.7	26	43.3	42	70.0
No Coverage	30	50.0	25	41.7	8	13.3
Total	60	100.0	60	100.0	60	100.0

1. A detailed analysis of these policies and changes therein is provided elsewhere. See my "Some Aspects of Exchange Risk Policies Under Floating Rates", a paper presented at the Annual Meeting of the Academy of International Business in Dallas, Texas, December 1975. The summary in this section of the present article draws heavily upon the earlier paper.

Table 3

Means of Covering Exposure by Partially and Fully Covered Firms Before and After Floating

Means of Coverage	Before C$ Floating		After C$ Floating		After More General Floating	
	No. of Firms[a]	%	No. of Firms[a]	%	No. of Firms[a]	%
1. Hedging in Forward Market						
a. as the only means	16	53	15	43	13	25
b. as one of the means	8	27	14	40	28	54
Sub-total	24	80	29	83	41	79
2. Use of C$	9	30	13	37	32	62
3. Leads and Lags	5	17	5	14	11	21
4. Local Borrowing	7	23	11	31	10	19
5. Currency Clauses	—	—	—	—	7	13
6. Intercompany Transfers	4	13	7	20	10	19
Total[b]	30		35		52	

(a) Numbers refer to total of partially and fully covered firms in each period.
(b) These totals are smaller than the respective sums of categories since most firms used more than one means of coverage.

Second, the more general floating has — in contrast — had widespread and pronounced effects on sample firms' policies. It has led as many as two-thirds of them to pursue more protective policies, thus raising the percentage of firms under partial or full coverage to over 85 per cent of the total.

Third, selective coverage has become even more dominant — as a policy alternative — with the more general floating. Since 1973, it has been pursued by 70 per cent of all firms. Full coverage was rejected by the majority mainly because it was considered costly and unsound as a business practice. The few firms which adhered to a policy of full coverage defended it by arguing that to do otherwise would mean speculating in an unfamiliar market. On the other hand, the few which maintained full exposure either had small exposures or believed that foreign exchange gains and losses were likely to even out in the long run.

Fourth, as shown in Table 2, most firms have used forward hedging as a means of covering exchange exposure both before and after floating. Following the general float, companies showed a tendency to seek protection in other ways. These entail either lower-cost coverage or coverage in terms of currencies for which restricted or no forward market facilities existed. Notable among the other ways is the use of the C$ as a substitute for foreign currencies in settling export-import transactions. Although the bulk of their foreign trade was still financed in U.S. $ and Z, more than half the firms studied now use the C$ as a "costless" means of coverage. This was made possible largely by the sellers' market conditions which helped many Canadian exporters to establish the new practice despite resistance from their foreign customers. Such conditions have also enabled some firms to use currency clauses to shift exchange risk onto their customers. Although the figures indicate some increase in the use of still other means, most sample firms have yet to evaluate them in a systematic manner.

Policy Differences and Given Company Features

The forgoing results show that important differences exist among sample firms in their exchange-risk policies. To what extent do such

Table 4

Significance of Policy Differences Among Groups of Sample Firms Classified by Five Characteristics, for the Periods Before and After C$ Floating and after the More General Floating (Chi Square Values)[a]

Classification Criteria	Before C$ Floating	After C$ Floating	After More General Floating
A. Full or Partial Coverage vs. No Coverage of Exchange Risk			
1. Size (Sales Volume)	7.90[a]	5.99	0.15
2. Ownership (Canadian vs. Foreign)	x	x	0.06
3. Primary Activity (Manufacturing vs. Trading)	x	0.01	0.10
4. Type of International Operations (Foreign Subsidiaries vs. Foreign Trade Only)	x	0.85	0.42
5. Relative Size of Foreign Trade (Exports + Imports as % of Sales)	0.03	0.01	4.53[a]
B. Use vs. Non-Use of Forward Exchange Market			
1. Size (Sales Volume)	9.49[a]	6.05[a]	2.04
2. Ownership (Canadian vs. Foreign)	0.37	0.04	x
3. Primary Activity (Manufacturing vs. Trading)	x	0.02	0.97
4. Type of International Operations (Foreign Subsidiaries vs. Foreign Trade Only)	0.17	1.71	0.30
5. Relative Size of Foreign Trade (Exports + Imports as % of Sales)	x	0.29	5.12[a]

(a) Significant at the 5% level.
(x) Less than 0.01.

differences appear to be related to differences in characteristics of the firms concerned?

To shed some light on this question, sample firms were grouped according to five characteristics and were then tested — with the aid of chi square analysis — to determine whether significant policy differences appeared among various groups during any of the three periods considered; namely, prior to C$ floating, subsequent to C$ floating, and subsequent to the more general floating. Classifications of sample firms are given in Tables 5 and 6.

Table 5

Sample Firms Classified According to Given Company Characteristics and Exchange-Risk Coverage in Three Periods: Before C$ Floating, After C$ Floating, and After More General Floating

Company Characteristics	Before C$ Floating			After C$ Floating			After More General Floating		
	Full or Partial Coverage	No Coverage	Total	Full or Partial Coverage	No Coverage	Total	Full or Partial Coverage	No Coverage	Total
	No. of Firms			No. of Firms			No. of Firms		
1. Size (Total Sales) (in Millions)									
Up to $30	6	14	20	9	11	20	17	3	20
$31-$300	9	12	21	10	11	21	17	4	21
Over $300	15	4	19	16	3	19	18	1	19
Total	30	30	60	35	25	60	52	8	60
2. Ownership									
Canadian	19	20	39	23	16	39	33	6	39
Foreign	11	10	21	12	9	21	19	2	21
Total	30	30	60	35	25	60	52	8	60
3. Primary Activity									
Manufacturing	22	22	44	26	18	44	38	6	44
Trading	8	8	16	9	7	16	14	2	16
Total	30	30	60	35	25	60	52	8	60
4. International Operations Firms with Foreign Subsidiaries and Foreign Trade Operations	9	8	17	12	5	17	16	1	17
Firms with Foreign Trade Operations only	21	22	43	23	20	43	36	7	43
Total	30	30	60	35	25	60	52	8	60
5. Relative Importance of Foreign Trade Operations (as % of Total Sales)									
50% or less	10	10	20	10	10	20	12	6	20
Over 50%	11	12	23	13	10	23	24	1	23
Total	21	22	43	23	20	43	36	7	43

Table 6

Sample Firms Classified According to Given Company Characteristics and Use vs. Non-Use of the Forward Market in Three Periods: Before C$ Floating, After C$ Floating, and After More General Floating

	Before C$ Floating			After C$ Floating			After More General Floating		
	Users	Non-Users	Total	Users	Non-Users	Total	Users	Non-Users	Total
Company Characteristics	No. of Firms			No. of Firms			No. of Firms		
1. Size (Total Sales) (in millions)									
Up to $30	3	17	20	6	14	20	12	8	20
$31 $300	8	13	21	9	12	21	13	8	21
Over $300	13	6	19	14	5	19	16	3	19
Total	24	36	60	29	31	60	41	19	60
2. Ownership									
Canadian	14	25	39	18	21	39	26	13	39
Foreign	10	11	21	11	10	21	15	6	21
Total	24	36	60	29	31	60	41	19	60
3. Primary Activity									
Manufacturing	17	27	44	21	23	44	28	16	44
Trading	7	9	16	8	8	16	13	3	16
Total	24	36	60	29	31	60	41	19	60
4. International Operations									
Firms with Foreign Subsidiaries and Foreign Trade Operations	8	9	17	11	6	17	13	4	17
Firms with Foreign Trade Operations only	16	27	43	18	25	43	28	15	43
Total	24	36	60	29	31	60	41	19	60
5. Relative Importance of Foreign Trade Operations (as % of Total Sales)									
50% or less	7	13	20	7	13	20	9	11	20
Over 50%	9	14	23	11	12	23	19	4	23
Total	16	27	43	18	25	43	28	15	43

We focussed on two main types of policy differences. The first distinguishes between fully exposed firms on the one hand and partially or fully covered firms on the other. It was not possible to distinguish between differences in the extent of coverage among members of the latter group due to the inadequacy of the information obtained. The second type of differences distinguishes between users and non-users of the forward exchange market.

The five characteristics used are company size, ownership status (Canadian vs. foreign), primary activity (trading vs. manufacturing), and type and relative size of international operations. Most of the characteristics were selected in light of recent writings which attempted to identify the main factors likely to influence risk-exposure policies.

Watts groups risk exposure according to (1) type of enterprise (exporters, importers, foreign investors, etc.); (2) type of exchange transaction (trade, borrowing, etc.); and (3) nature of the markets for the product.[2] Katz dismisses the number of foreign currencies used by the firm as a factor, since some currencies are low risk while others are high risk, and stresses instead the nature of the firm's foreign operations.[3] Eastman suggests that the extent of coverage is affected by the structure of the firm's operations as reflected by such variables as the ratio of equity to total assets, the importance of exports or imports relative to total sales or costs, and so on. The lower the equity ratio or the relative importance of foreign operations, the less the danger to the survival of the firm and the less it hedges.[4] Young and Helliwell found a noticeable difference in the behavior of small and large firms in the foreign exchange market, with more use of the forward market by larger firms than by smaller ones and a higher proportion of the latter dealing in the spot market only.[5]

Each of these factors could have a bearing on the firm's exchange-risk policies. But in the absence of empirical data, it is not easy to confidently specify on an a priori basis the extent or sometimes even the direction of the impact on policy, since conflicting variables are often at work.

Although the five characteristics chosen do not encompass all the factors identified above, they do distinguish between firms in terms of apparently relevant factors.

The results of the analysis are summarized in Table 4. All except two of the chi square values relating to differences among groups in respect to alternative policies of coverage (full or partial) vs. no coverage of exchange risk were found not to be statistically significant. In other words, with two exceptions, the evidence examined does not suggest the existence of any significant relationship be-

2. J. H. Watts, "The Business View of Proposals for International Monetary Reform", ed., George N. Halm, *Approaches to Greater Flexibility of Exchange Rates* (Princeton: Princeton University Press, 1970), pp. 167-176.

3. Samuel I. Katz, *Exchange-Risk Under Fixed and Flexible Exchange Rates, The Bulletin* Nos. 83-84 (New York: Institute of Finance, Graduate School of Business Administration, New York University, June 1972), pp. 23-26.

4. See Harry C. Eastman, "The Hedging of Commercial Transactions Between U.S. and Canadian Residents: A Canadian View", *Canadian-United States Financial Relationships* (Proceedings of a conference sponsored by the Federal Reserve Bank of Boston, Conference Series No. 6, Boston, Mass., Federal Reserve Bank of Boston, 1971), pp. 162-163.

5. J. H. Young and J. F. Helliwell, *The Effects of Monetary Policy on Corporations* (Study prepared for the Royal Commission on Banking and Finance, Ottawa, Queen's Printer, 1964), pp. 419-420.

tween the characteristics tested and the firms' behavior in terms of this policy.

The two exceptions, however, are noteworthy. The first indicates that smaller firms tended to behave differently from larger firms *prior to the floating of the C$* when a relatively larger proportion of smaller firms assumed the risk of *full* exposure than did larger firms. This is in accord with the findings of Young and Helliwell. But this difference, according to our data, has ceased to be significant following the C$ floating and has largely disappeared subsequent to the more general floating when most firms took up either partial or full cover.

The second exception indicates the emergence, following the more general floating, of a significant difference in behavior between firms whose total export-import operations assumed different degrees of importance in relation to their overall businesses. Firms with greater dependence on foreign trade appear to have become relatively more sensitive to exchange fluctuations and hence to have adopted coverage measures more than those with lesser dependence. This result also lends support to one of Eastman's hypotheses.

When sample firms were classified by company size and relative size of foreign trade respectively, memberships of various groups under the two criteria were notably different. For example, of the twenty firms with relatively lesser dependence on foreign trade (50 per cent or less of total sales), seven, nine, and four were classified as small, medium, and large firms respectively. It, therefore, appears that while total company size may have had an important bearing on coverage policy in the past, the degree of dependence on international operations *regardless of firm size* seems more relevant now. Presumably, smaller (as well as larger) companies which depend materially on foreign trade operations but which used to be more or less indifferent to exchange-risk exposure under a (deceptively?) stable fixed-rate system have reconsidered their policies and are now under at least partial cover.

Differences between groups with regard to their use of the forward exchange market show very much the same pattern as those just discussed. The figures show no statistically significant relationship between the criteria applied and the use of forward hedging, with similar exceptions to those reported above. This method of covering exposure was used by a significantly lower proportion of smaller firms than was true for larger firms until the more general floating, when the difference in behavior became insignificant. Whether the previous lesser use of forward hedging by smaller firms was a cause or an effect of their relative indifference to exchange-risk exposure is uncertain.

The other significant difference in the usage of forward markets distinguishes, for the period of the more general floating, between firms with lesser dependence and those with greater dependence on foreign trade. The more prevalent use among the latter than among the former is consistent with the difference found between these two groups regarding their coverage policy and is probably the result of the same factors, since most firms pursuing partial or full coverage policies use forward hedging as a means of coverage.

In sum, *under the present floating rate system*, we found no significant association between company size, ownership, type of primary activity, or type of international operations on the one hand and the firm's behavior in terms of assuming full vs. partial or no exchange risk or of its usage of forward hedging on the other hand. There is evidence, however, that a larger proportion of firms which are more dependent on foreign trade cover their exposure and use forward hedging as a means of doing so than do those that are less dependent on foreign trade.

Setting and Assessing Exchange-Risk Policies

Judging or evaluating a firm's approach to exchange-risk management requires: (1) knowledge of the specific objectives of the policy pursued; (2) an analysis of the firm's performance record under that policy; and (3) an assessment of other feasible alternatives.

How do firms actually assess their exchange risk policies? Of the sixty sample firms, most lack a systematic approach to assessing policy decisions (with the exception of five or possibly six firms). Many respondents admitted that this is an area where much work needs to be done. Typically, either no explicit assessment is made once a policy direction (for instance, full coverage of exposure) has been decided on, or an assessment of one or two aspects of policy is attempted from time to time. The policy aspect most commonly evaluated is the firm's forward hedging transactions. Of the forty-one firms which were engaged in them at the time of the survey, twenty-one made estimates of "gains and losses" resulting from forward contracts. The other twenty firms made no estimates, mostly because they felt this information to be either irrelevant or the gains and losses to be relatively insignificant.

Gains and losses are calculated on the basis of comparing the forward contract rate with the spot rate on the maturity date. Such estimates give an incomplete basis of assessing exchange-risk policies not only because no evaluation is made of other means of coverage that are used or could be used, but also because they ignore the outcome of decisions not to cover exposure during some periods.

The absence of a systematic approach is also reflected in the fairly widespread tendency among firms to change existing policies more (in response to events in foreign exchange market) than as a result of critical evaluation. In some cases, the changes appear to have been, in the words of one treasurer, "rushed and more or less forced on us by the rapid pace of events and greater uncertainty and fluctuations in foreign exchange markets." He went on to explain, "These prompted us to take quick action in order to protect ourselves, but without really having the time to make a more adequate study of the company's needs and of available options."

One important reason contributing to the above shortcoming is the absence of well-defined policies and operating procedures in the large majority of firms. Since policy assessment cannot be made in a vacuum but must have specific goals and priorities as a frame of reference, it is not surprising that effective assessment has not been practised in most cases. Again, with the exception of five or six cases, statements of ojectives are typically put in fairly simplistic and broad terms such as, "protecting the company against losses", or "minimizing exchange losses and avoiding unnecessary and expensive coverage", "avoiding speculation and pursuing a policy of full coverage whenever possible", etc. A few firms have specified a "threshold level" of exposure beyond which a certain action would be taken, but these constituted a minority. In some cases, in fact, there was some difficulty in arriving at an estimate of the firm's exposure because records were not kept in a manner which could easily provide such information. Between the few extreme cases of highly developed systems on the one hand and almost non-existent systems on the other hand lie the majority of sample firms. It is clear from survey responses that a wide gap exists between current practices and normative behavior as advocated by many — the latter requires that policy deal with such judgmental matters as what exposure levels are acceptable, when hedging is prudent, and when the costs of hedging appear too great.[6]

In addition to causing difficulties in appraising policy results,

---

6. See Robert K. Ankrom, "Top-Level Approach to the Foreign Exchange Problem", *Harvard Business Review* (July-August, 1974), p. 88. On the same point, see also Max J. Wasserman *et al., International Money Management* (American Management Association, Inc., 1972), pp. 136-137; *Foreign Exchange Handbook for the Corporate Executive* (New York: Brown Brothers Harriman & Co., 1970), pp. 40-41; and John Watts III, "Strategies for Financial Risk in Multinational Operations", *Columbia Journal of World Business* (September-October, 1971), p. 21.

inadequately defined objectives and policies have also led to ad hoc decision making, to either expensive hedges or unwarranted risks on occasions, and to wasted executive time.

Policies as well as specific decisions about exchange risk in the majority of cases appear to be made almost exclusively by the treasurer with little or no effective participation by other members of senior management. In twenty-four cases, the treasurer seems to have final authority to set policy and to take actions on his own. In the remaining thirty-six cases, a higher authority sets policy guidelines or approves policies proposed by the treasurer. This higher authority consists of the president, executive vice-president, or financial vice-president in seventeen firms, the board of directors in nine, a management committee (with varied membership and responsibilities) in six, and the foreign parent in four. Due to the broadness and ambiguity of most existing objectives and policy statements, however, the degree of apparent participation in effective policy making reflected by these figures is probably exaggerated. In some firms, exchange-risk issues have now become a genuine concern of top management, but this is still the exception. Some, though not many, treasurers felt strongly that top management should become more involved. A treasurer of a medium-size manufacturing firm who had been trying to encourage such involvement reported that he was "disappointed by the lack of progress, due to the lack of expertise as well as interest on the part of most members of top management".

The dominant role of the treasury department, coupled with the limited participation by top management in exchange-risk policies, creates a bias which can have an unfavorable impact on non-financial aspects of the business, particularly on marketing and purchasing. It can also make more difficult the undertaking of a more objective review of existing policies and the introduction of desirable changes.

The role which parent companies play in shaping exchange-risk policies in their respective subsidiaries has varied widely. Of the twenty-one foreign subsidiaries in the sample, thirteen reported that they were "autonomous" from their parent firms in setting these policies; the other eight operated under specific instructions or policy guidelines set by the parents. In contrast, Canadian firms with subsidiaries abroad have tended to centralize policy making at the Canadian head office. Of the seventeen firms in question, only two granted their subsidiaries autonomy to handle exchange risk, and both were reviewing the situation to exercise some direction of subsidiaries' policies.

The rationale behind centralizing exchange-risk policies is that it ensures an accurate view of the company's worldwide exposure, assuming of course that the head office has ready access to the necessary financial information on a regular and prompt basis.[7] Consequently, the autonomy reported by the majority of foreign subsidiaries in our sample is somewhat surprising. This autonomy, however, tends to be exaggerated where the parent has a strong representation on the foreign subsidiary's board of directors, and where the board sets or approves exchange risk policy or decisions. This appears to be the situation in eight of the thirteen "autonomous" foreign subsidiaries.

The effects of the shortcomings in policy formulation and evaluation vary substantially from one firm to another, depending on how deficient the situation is, on the relative importance of international operations, and on the size of exposure. The foregoing findings describe the main patterns and practices and do not, of course, apply equally to all firms.

Five or six firms have developed well-reasoned and comprehensive policy statements and operating procedure for managing their exchange risk. All six are very large and four of them have multinational operations; the other two have a substantial volume of export business as well as some foreign manufacturing activities. At the other end of the scale are nineteen firms which lag behind quite noticeably by comparison. Some are small firms which are generally interested in improving exchange-risk management but wonder if the extra costs would be justified. Others are firms — some small and some large — which are minimally involved in international operations or which normally have a very limited net exposure. They are not dissatisfied with their present practices. To them, a more "sophisticated" system is unnecessary. In between the two extremes lie the remaining two-thirds of sample firms. The majority were planning, or had already started, to review policies, and some were in the process of implementing changes already decided.

The changes recently introduced by some firms or contemplated by others have mostly been initiated soon after the emergence of general floating in early 1973, although few could be traced back to the latter months of 1971. These changes are of two types: one type consists of refinements in the definition of exposure, in organizing the foreign exchange effort, and in the reporting system. The other type focusses on improving the process and quality of policy making.

---

7. See *Hedging Foreign Exchange Risks,* Management Monograph No. 49, (New York: Business International, 1971), p. 22. See also Irene W. Meister, *Managing the International Financial Function* (New York: National Industrial Conference Board, 1970), pp. 6-7.

The bulk of improvements reported by sample firms have so far been of the former type. In a few cases, however, issues such as developing more specific policy objectives, setting more explicit review procedures, and expanding the base of participation in policy making are under consideration. Many treasurers reported a definite increase in the last two years in the amount of consultation with other departments as well as with top management. Another recent trend has been the increased use of outside expertise in order to improve exchange-risk decisions.

It is likely that the next few years — especially if exchange rates continue to fluctuate significantly — will see an accelerating trend toward the development of more systematic and more refined policies and procedures of handling exchange risk. This will be further encouraged by the greater tendency among firms to cover exposure on a selective basis. Since selectivity requires a constant monitoring of exchange markets and a careful appraisal of alternative strategies and methods of covering risk, it will probably help speed up the policy reviews currently in progress.

Managing Risk Under a Floating System: A Perspective
Most earlier surveys of opinion about the floating-rate system show the majority of respondents expressing a serious concern about its potentially adverse effects on international business activities and therefore being in favor of a return to a fixed-rate system.[8]

How did respondents to this survey view the current system of floating rates in the light of their exposure to it for a period of fifteen to twenty months? We posed two questions to each respondent to obtain his reactions. First, he was asked to assess whether, in his opinion, exchange-risk problems under floating were becoming more or less manageable than they were during the first few months of floating. Forty-six respondents (or 77 per cent) said that these problems have become more manageable, while fourteen (or 23 per cent) expressed the opposite view. The reasons most frequently given by the first group are listed below:

	No. of
Reasons Given	Responses
1. Adaptation of financial reporting system and stream-lining of hedging procedures.	31

8. See, for example, "An International Banking Review", *The Economist* (November 27, 1971), pp. xi-xxxvii; John Hein, *Business Looks at the International Monetary System, Recent Experience and Prkposals for Reform* (New York: The Conference Board, 1973); and P. B. Rosendale, "The Short-Run Pricing Policies of Some British Engineering Exporters", *National Institute Economic Review* (August 1973), pp. 44-51.

2. Acquisition or re-inforcement of expertise to
    handle the situation.   26

3. Greater use of forward hedging and other means of
    coverage than before.   22

4. Greater stability of rates following their realign-
    ment.   8

In contrast, virtually all respondents in the second group stressed two factors: namely, increased uncertainty associated with floating rates and the need to give constant attention to exchange risk. A third factor mentioned by six respondents was the difficulty of forecasting rates for the medium to long term.

In the second question, respondents were asked to put the problems arising from floating rates in perspective by rating them in relation to other problems of doing business abroad. Thirty-nine respondents (or 65 per cent) rated the former problems among the less difficult problems of doing international business, and the remaining twenty-one (or 35 per cent) rated them among the more difficult ones.[9]

We found a very high degree of positive correlation between responses to the two questions. In fact, all except two of those who rated the problems of floating to be relatively less difficult also felt that these problems have become more manageable. Some respondents pointed out that the actions taken by their firms to deal effectively with exposure risk under a floating-rate system and the overcoming of earlier apprehensions about its likely negative effects, have made the problems more manageable. Consequently, these problems have also become easier to handle than others.

Some respondents volunteered the opinion that their earlier misgivings about floating rates have proved for the most part to be exaggerated, and that they no longer viewed the present system as a

9. The results of a 1974 Conference Board survey of the problems facing seventy-two international operations executives in the U.S. show that although foreign exchange instability was mentioned by some as an important problem, more frequently cited problems included such matters as growing nationalism, the multinational controversy, excessive taxation, and so on. See Michael G. Duerr, *The Problems Facing International Management* (New York: The Conference Board, 1974). It is also interesting to note that exchange-rate issues are not considered to be among the more worrisome problems currently facing chief financial officers, or likely to face them in the next few years, according to a survey by the Conference Board in Canada which covered approximately 150 Canadian firms. Other problems, including government involvement in private enterprise, inflation, and corporate tax changes are perceived to be relatively more serious. See G. T. Caldwell and J. R. Levesque, *The Chief Financial Officer and His Function in Canadian Business* (Ottawa: The Conference Board in Canada, 1973), pp. 7-12.

less desirable alternative to the fixed-rate system. The treasurer of a large trading firm commented, "I'm now indifferent to either system. Our company has developed policies and methods by which we can handle a wide range of exchange-rate situations and events without difficulty." Whether this view echoes the views of the majority is not clear. But what has clearly emerged from this study is that more and more firms are leaning how to live with floating rates by adapting — some at a slower pace than others — to their new foreign exchange environment.

Conclusions

Our analysis has shown that the floating of the C$ had only a limited effect on exchange-risk policies of sample firms, as compared with the pervasive and pronounced impact which the subsequent more general floating (1973) has had. The greater uncertainty and rate variability associated with the latter have induced the majority of firms with previously fully exposed positions to adopt at least partial coverage policies. Following the more general floating, there has also been a tendency among firms to use other means of coverage beside forward hedging. The most notable of these has been the use of the C$ as a substitute for foreign currencies in settling export-import transactions. But forward hedging remains the most dominant means of coverage. By and large, most sample firms have yet to evaluate alternative means in a systematic way in light of their needs.

The analysis of policy differences among firms has indicated that, with two exceptions, there is no evidence to suggest the presence of a significant relationship between certain aspects of the firm's risk-taking behavior (in terms of assuming full vs. partial or no exchange risks and of the use vs. non-use of forward hedging) and any one of five company characteristics including size, ownership, primary activity, type of international operations, and their relative importance to the firm. One of the two exceptions indicates that smaller firms used to assume the risks of full exposure more than larger firms did prior to the C$ float; since then, however, this difference has become insignificant. The other exception reflects the appearance since the more general floating of a significant difference in behavior between firms which are more heavily dependent on foreign trade and those that are less dependent on it. The former appear to have adopted protective policies and to have used forward hedging as a means of doing so, more than have the latter. It therefore seems that while company size may have had a bearing on coverage policies in the past, the degree of dependence on international operations is more relevant now.

The study has also revealed certain features which characterize the practices of setting and assessing exchange-risk policies in the majority of sample firms. The general lack of a systematic method of policy appraisal, the absence of well-defined policies and operating procedures, and the minimal participation by top management in formulating policy and the resulting dominance of the treasurer's role were — and still are — prevalent characteristics. These shortcomings have had varying effects on different firms, depending on the seriousness of the deficiencies, the relative importance of international operations, and the size of exposure. Only a few firms — mostly large and with multinational operations — have well-developed policies and procedures. Others have noticeably underdeveloped policies. The majority of sample firms were found in between these two extremes and were in the process of reviewing and improving existing policies and systems.

Many of these firms reported that present reviews were initiated in response to the more general floating of currencies. The bulk of changes recently introduced have attempted to focus on technical aspects such as defining exposure, designing an appropriate reporting system, and so on. Issues pertaining to the development of more explicit policies, clearer priorities, and more effective participation by top management have yet to be tackled effectively by most firms.

Finally, most respondents perceived exchange-risk problems to have become *more* manageable as a result of the protective measures taken and the greater ability to deal with them through experience. They also rated these problems to be among the *less* difficult problems of transacting international business. In contrast to earlier surveys, these responses indicate that managers in charge of exchange-risk policies are becoming less anxious than before to see a return to a fixed-rate system. In fact, the few who have instituted well-reasoned policies to handle various exchange-risk situations are more or less indifferent to either exchange-rate system.

V
International Operations Management

D
International Financial Management

40
Foreign Exchange Rates and the International Financial System

Paul Bishop
Jacques Prefontaine

Dr. Bishop is associate professor in the School of Business Administration, University of Western Ontario. He teaches in the areas of corporate finance, investments, and international finance. His research interests centre on currency risk and exchange rate movements, and he is active as a consultant in several areas of finance.

Dr. Prefontaine is assistant professor in the Faculty of Administration, University of Sherbrooke. His professional and research interests centre on domestic and international capital markets. He is co-author of *La Gestion Moderne des Co-opératives*.

This chapter was written expressly for this volume.

Foreign Exchange Rate Systems and Economic Policy

Any attempt to understand the nature of foreign exchange rate movements should be interwoven with the study of overall government economic policy. In Canada and abroad, there seems to be a general consensus that primary economic policy objectives are:

1. a high and stable level of employment ("full employment");
2. a reasonably stable or slowly rising level of prices ("price stability");
3. a high rate of economic growth; and
4. a sound balance-of-payment position ("external balance").[1]

Given this set of generally accepted economic goals, governments have through the years developed the necessary policy tools and institutions to "manage" the economy. The purpose of this management activity is to "optimize' the aggregate level of welfare, which is defined as the level of gross national product at which an economy achieves both external and internal balance. Internal balance is reached when the economy is producing goods and services at a level which assures full employment, price stability, and full utilization of productive capacity. External balance is reached when a country's transactions with the rest of the world are in equilibrium as reflected by the balance of payments. External balance is characterized by an equilibrium level of reserves and a stable currency value on the foreign exchange market.

The basic relationships required for internal and external balance can be better understood by looking at the appropriate variables in both the national and balance-of-payments accounts.[2]

$$Y_{FE} = C + I + G + X_N \tag{1}$$
$$S + T = G + I \tag{2}$$
$$S_N + T + X = G + I_N + M \tag{3}$$

where

Y_{FE}: Full-employment level of GNP

---

1. Lawrence H. Officer and Lawrence B. Smith, *Issues in Canadian Economics* (Toronto: McGraw-Hill Ryerson Ltd., 1974), Chapter 1.
2. Ibid., Section II, ch. 2.

C : Aggregate consumption expenditures

I : Aggregate investment expenditures: domestic

G : Aggregate government expenditures at all levels of government

X_N : Net value of exports (X) over imports (M): $X_N = X - M$

S : Aggregate domestic savings

T : Government taxes levied at all levels

S_N : Net value of domestic savings (S_D) over foreign savings (S_F): $S_N = S_D - S_F$

I_N : Net value of domestic investment (I_D) over foreign investment (I_F): $I_N = I_D - I_F$.

Equations (1) and (2) define the conditions necessary to achieve the optimal level of GNP at full employment, or internal balance. When equation (3) is added, the economy has reached equilibrium at both the national and international levels, or external balance.

Given this framework for policy analysis we can now examine the primary policy tools which governments use to attain both domestic and international economic equilibrium:

1. *Monetary Policy*
   Level of interest rates
   Growth of money supply (+ or −)

2. *Fiscal Policy*
   Level of government expenditures
   Level of government revenues as determined by the overall tax structure
   Budget management
   Debt management

3. *Labor*
   Labor market policies and laws

4. *Competition Policy*
   "Combines Investigation Act" for Canada

5. *Incomes Policy*
   Voluntary restraint
   Wage and price controls

6. *Foreign Ownership Policy*
   "Foreign Investment Review Act" for Canada

7. *Commercial Policy*
   Foreign exchange rate policy
   Tariff structures
   Import-export subsidies and quotas

Trade treaties
Foreign aid
Tax treaties
Government procurement policies

The preceding list clearly reflects the complexity of "managing" a modern economy. Our focus in this chapter will be on commercial policy and particularly on foreign exchange policy. Foreign exchange policy has been described by a senior economist at the Bank of Canada as a process designed to:

Maintain appropriate flows of goods, services and capital between a country and the rest of the world. This has been done in Canada by adopting a foreign exchange rate system and developing a mechanism for the orderly transfer of international payments on goods, service, and capital flows. In Canada these responsibilities[3] have been given to the Bank of Canada, which administers the Foreign Exchange Equalization Fund. As you know, Canada has a floating currency on the foreign exchange market and as a matter of policy the Bank of Canada only intervenes to maintain an orderly market for the Canadian dollar. Interventions are done through our foreign exchange desk which is in contact with the world's major foreign currency centers such as London and New York.

As indicated earlier we don't intervene in the Foreign Exchange market as a rule. However, where appropriate, some transactions are done in both the spot and forward markets by buying Canadian dollars with foreign exchange or selling Canadian dollars for foreign exchange. You might compare the role of the Exchange Equalization Fund to that of a "market maker" on the Stock Exchange. That is, the bank tries to maintain an orderly market for the Canadian dollar. At any given day the value of the Canadian currency versus the rest of the world obeys the law of supply and demand. Generally, exports of goods and services and capital inflows create a demand for the Canadian dollar. On the other hand, the supply of Canadian dollars will be provided by the level of imports of goods and services and capital outflows to the rest of the world.

Some observers maintain that the activities of the bank in the foreign exchange market have, in the last few years, sometimes gone beyond maintenance of an orderly market to include fairly strenuous efforts

---

3. In Canada, the minister of finance is responsible for the Bank of Canada and its operations.

to support the value of the Canadian dollar. Support can be generated by drawing down foreign exchange reserves and by arranging stand-by credits with commercial banks. However, in the longer term the currency must find its level. Figure 1 illustrates the market process.

Fixed or Floating Rate

One of the primary issues in commercial policy involves the choice between a fixed or flexible foreign exchange rate. A fixed-rate policy involves fixing or pegging the value of the currency to some external indicator of value such as another currency, an index of currencies, or gold. A flexible-rate policy is followed when there is no official conversion parity and the value of a currency is allowed to change in response to supply and demand on the international foreign exchange market. However, one can seldom find a pure exchange-rate policy because most so-called fixed rates are altered from time to time and are, thus, not only quite flexible but often quite unstable in the long run. Flexible rates, on the other hand, may in fact be relatively stable in the long run, and much of their stability may in fact be due to unobtrusive activity in the foreign exchange markets by the central monetary authority. As a practical guide, the classification in Table 1 is based on the scope of official management and on the limits set to the variability of the exchange rate.

Table 1

Classification of Exchange Rate Variability

	Unlimited Variability	Limited Variability	
		Around Parity ("Wider Band")	Of Parity ("Crawling Peg")
Unmanaged	Freely flexible (no interventions)	Interventions only at the edges of the band	
Managed	a) By discretion of national authorities b) By international agreement c) By discretion of international authority	Interventions also within the band	a) By discretion of national authorites b) By international co-operation c) By fixed formula

Source: Gottfried, Harberler, et al., *Readings in International Trade and Finance*, (Boston: Little, Brown and Company, 1974), p. 345.

Following the preceding framework, Canada's current official

Figure 1

The Supply and Demand of Canadian Dollars on the Foreign Exchange Market.

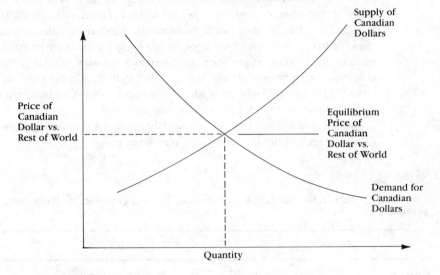

foreign exchange rate policy can be classified as one of unlimited variability which is managed according to both the (a) and (b) conditions. The currencies of most industrialized countries can be classified accordingly; however, the majority of the world's currencies fall into the "crawling peg" category. For example, in early 1978, forty-two countries pegged their currencies to the U.S. dollar, twenty-three to another single currency, and thirty-two to an index of currencies.

Countries choose a foreign exchange rate system to suit their needs and circumstances. Basically, strong open economies which trade widely abroad choose a floating rate. Under this system a change in the rate by market forces helps to restore equilibrium; for example, countries with a balance-of-payments deficit will find their currencies depreciating. The depreciation raises import prices and reduces export prices, thus helping to restore balance.

Countries with less robust economies find they must resort to exchange controls and trade barriers to protect domestic employment and conserve capital within the country. Under these circumstances, a fixed exchange rate will permit tighter control of the domestic supply of foreign exchange. In addition, some countries peg their currencies to that of their major trading partner to facilitate such trading activities. Under a fixed-rate system, a central authority such as the International Monetary Fund oversees the use of a country's reserve of foreign exchange, credit, or gold as a buffer to support that currency during a period of short-run national deficits. External credits are also available from the fund, from other countries, or from commercial sources. In the longer term, central bankers and the fund exert pressure on the deficit country to change the economic conditions giving rise to the deficit. Changes in the "fixed" rate should only be made (either up or down) when other remedies fail, and with authorization by the fund.

Table 2 summarizes the conventionally recognized advantages and disadvantages of flexible and fixed exchange rates.

Table 2

Advantages and Disadvantages of Floating Versus Fixed Exchange Rate Systems.

	Advantages	Disadvantages
Floating Exchange Rates	1. Allows much more flexibility in domestic monetary and fiscal policy.	1. May disrupt confidence in the stability of the domestic currency.
	2. Stabilizes domestic supplies of foreign exchange reserves.	2. May lead to wide fluctuations in short-term capital flows.
	3. Allows a domestic economy to perform better than its trading partners.	3. May discourage trade with and investment in a given country.
	4. Adjusts gradually the price of a currency.	4. May lead to competitive rounds of devaluation.
Fixed Exchange Rates	1. Promote confidence in a country's currency.	1. Emasculates domestic monetary policy.
	2. Has a built-in disciplinary effect on a country's internal policies.	2. May lead to large swings in a country's international reserves.
	3. Tends to favor worldwide harmony in fiscal and monetary policies	3. Leaves the burden of readjustment of external balance to deflationary or inflationary domestic policies.

Canada is an open economy in the sense that its foreign trade sector represents a large portion of gross national product, and there are no exchange or currency controls. Canada depends on the United States for roughly 70 per cent of its merchandise trade. The extent of U.S. direct investment in Canada also contributes to closer trading ties, since foreign-owned firms tend to trade with their foreign parents. Canada is one of the world's largest exporters of raw materials and grains. The value of export earnings thus varies with the level of economic activity in the world in general and with the volatility of commodity prices. Under these circumstances, maintaining a fixed exchange rate would throw a heavy adjustment burden on domestic fiscal and monetary policy. For these reasons and others a floating exchange rate is considered best for Canadian national interests.

Foreign Exchange Rates and Systems, 1875 to 1980

The Gold Standard
The world's monetary system was largely based on the gold standard during the forty years before the First World War. By the mid-1870s each major country had pegged its currency to gold, establishing a system of fixed exchange rates that was not altered until 1914. Under the pre-1914 gold mechanism, the monetary authorities of the member countries paid for their unalterably fixed parities by being forced to change another price of strategic importance, the short-term interest rate, to a greater extent than domestic considerations alone would have warranted. Through discount rate changes, the central bankers tried to induce equilibrating capital flows and produce just enough domestic price inflation or deflation to achieve external balance while maintaining fixed gold parities and gold convertibility. In the case of a deficit economy, deflation was required to reduce local prices and the demand for imports. The result was frequently a period of high unemployment. By the 1920s, the gold standard had evolved to a "new Gold-Exchange-Standards" as the central banks altered the composition of their reserves by adding foreign currencies such as American dollars and pounds sterling.

The Great Depression
The early 1930s gave birth to a new generation of trade controls. Struggling to prevent the spread of depression, country after country restricted imports, seeking to stimulate domestic production by protecting business against foreign competition. After a run on the Bank of England, Great Britain abandoned the new gold-exchange-standards in 1931 and devalued the pound. The United States followed in 1933 and pegged again to gold in 1934 at a lower parity. France and other European countries used import controls to defend their currencies. Foreign trade lagged far behind the resumption of industrial production in the slow recovery from the Great Depression.

In 1928, world imports totalled 60 billion dollars, while in 1938 they were a mere 25 billion dollars.

The Second World War

The Second World War was even more damaging to world trade than was the Great Depression. Most of the belligerents imposed strict exchange controls to prevent their citizens from spending foreign currency which was needed to purchase war supplies. They then carried controls into the post-war period in order to save scarce foreign currency for their reconstruction programs. Very early in the war, however, plans were drawn for the liberalization of foreign trade and payments in the post-war period. Even before the fighting stopped, the Allied governments established two new financial organizations, the International Monetary Fund (IMF) and the International Bank for Reconstruction and Development (IBRD, or World Bank). A new fixed exchange rate system was established by the Bretton Woods Agreement of 1944, which founded the IMF and erected the framework for post-war monetary co-operation. Participating governments agreed to peg their currencies to gold or to the U.S. dollar (which in turn, was pegged to gold). They agreed to make their currencies fully convertible as soon as possible, and to dismantle their exchange controls. And they agreed on rules to govern exchange rate changes. The Bretton Woods system, sometimes called the system of the adjustable peg, sought to assure maximum exchange rate stability, to facilitate orderly changes when needed, and to avoid competitive devaluations like those of the 1930s. Pursuant to the Bretton Woods agreement, Canada and most other industrial countries established initial par values (fixed exchange rates) for their currencies on December 18, 1946. The Canadian dollar was fixed at 100 U.S. cents (that is, at par with the U.S. dollar).

Post-War Monetary Co-operation

The Bretton Woods Agreement of 1944, by establishing the key currency role of the U.S. dollar, was to pave the way for the international monetary scene of the next twenty-five years. The United States would determine the price of gold and guarantee convertibility of the dollar into gold at that price. Other countries determined the exchange rates of the U.S. dollar by pegging their own currencies to it. Given that other countries had manoeuvrability in their exchange rates while the U.S. had not, it was clearly in the interest of the U.S. to try to limit freedom of exchange rate movement in general. With a strong tendency toward payments surplus during the early years of the agreement, the United States could not use controls or devaluation to achieve external balance. This concern was reflected in the determination of the U.S. authorities to limit the use that others could make of these instruments. The concern was justified, as Britan devalued the pound sterling from $4.80 U.S. to $2.80 U.S. in 1949. Many countries in Europe and the Commonwealth also devalued shortly thereafter. Canada followed Britain in devaluing and set the value of the Canadian dollar at 90¢ U.S., and on September 30, 1950, the Canadian dollar was allowed to float. The decision to do so caused controversy at the time as most other currencies remained pegged. However the Canadian currency was not repegged until 1962. The French franc was also devalued, going from 3.50 per dollar to 4.20; in 1958 it was again devalued from 4.20 to 4.94 per dollar; and a third devaluation finally brought the price to 5.55 per U.S. dollar.

A shift from international dollar shortage in the 1950s to dollar surplus in the 1960s did not change the basic situation. The United States continued to be limited in any attempt at exchange rate management. As the United States moved into payments deficits, foreign countries had to choose between very large U.S. dollar accumulation and being undersold by the U.S. in their own and foreign markets.

On May 1, 1962, the Canadian dollar was again pegged and assigned a value of 92.5¢ U.S., to cope with severe speculative pressures against the dollar. Finally on June 1, 1970, Canada returned to a floating exchange rate in order to halt increases in foreign exchange reserves. However, a limited degree of overt exchange rate management was practised from 1963 to 1968. Canada had agreed to maintain international reserves at less than $2.6 billion U.S. in return for an exemption from the "Interest Equalization Tax" imposed by the U.S. in 1963 in an effort to stop the flow of U.S. loans abroad and aid a deteriorating U.S. balance of payments. The effect of the tax was to increase borrowing costs for foreign borrowers in the U.S. markets to a level closer to what they would have to pay in their own countries. The reserve ceiling and the obligation to maintain parity with the U.S. dollar sharply reduced the effectiveness of Canadian monetary policy as a domestic policy alternative during this period. Canadian interest rates were dictated largely by the need to keep pressure, either up or down, off the exchange rate. The Bank of Canada was during that period sometimes referred to as the 13th Federal Reserve Bank.

At the end of the 1960s, the Bretton Woods system gave signs of breaking down. The pound sterling was devalued from $2.80 to $2.40 U.S. in November 1967 after a series of measures such as domestic deflation and heavy borrowing from the IMF and various central banks. Severe speculation, owing to chronic weakness of the U.S. balance of payments, developed against the gold-U.S. dollar link that had served so long as the cornerstone of the Bretton Woods system. On three separate occasions (November and December 1967, and March 1968) private interests speculated on a U.S. dollar devaluation, which of course would have meant a rise in the price of gold. The price of gold in the London market had been stabilized at $35.00 U.S. an ounce, by an arrangement under which eight governments jointly bought and sold gold on the private market to keep the price within a specified range. The speculative buying amounted to a private raid on official gold stocks, because the supporting governments had to supply gold to meet the demand at $35.00 an ounce. Some three billion U.S. dollars worth of gold flowed out of monetary stocks into private hands in the space of a few months. Central bankers, realizing they were unable to stabilize the market, returned to an earlier agreement. In March 1968, with the introduction of the "two-tier system", the price of gold in the free market was cut loose from the fixed exchange value of gold in official transactions among monetary authorities. The free market price of gold was left unregulated and the monetary authorities would deal among themselves at the "official gold price" of $35.00 an ounce. The decade came to an end after a speculative flurry between the French franc and the German Deutsche mark. The French payments position was seriously threatened by the increase in wages and prices which followed the May 1968 student riots. The speculators were also gambling on a large revaluation of the mark as large sums of money poured into Germany. Finally the franc was devalued by 12.5 per cent in August 1969; Germany allowed the mark to appreciate by 9.3 per cent in October 1969.

By May 1971, a crisis of confidence in the U.S. dollar had been building up for two years in response to historically high inflation and a general policy of neglect toward its balance of payments on the part of the U.S. The U.S. deficit rose in the first quarter of 1971 to a staggering 22 billion dollars in annual terms. The counterpart of this deficit, of course, was the need for tremendous U.S. dollar absorption by the central banks of all surplus countries in order to maintain their exchange rates against the dollar. These additional dollar balances alone were larger than the U.S. gold stock, which supposedly could redeem all dollar reserves. The German Federal Bank attempted to honor its IMF commitment to maintain the dollar/mark exchange rate by absorbing U.S. dollars from the foreign exchange market and distributing marks. However, on May 5, 1971 during the first forty minutes of trading, the bank absorbed 1 billion U.S. dollars and was forced to abandon its stabilization commitment and to allow the mark to float upward in value. The Dutch guilder was also allowed to float as Austria and Switzerland revalued their currencies and stabilized them at a new parity. On August 15, 1971, President Nixon shook the world by announcing his "New Economic Policy", which included the following measures:

1. a general freeze on domestic prices and wages;
2. a 10 per cent surcharge on all imports currently subject to tariffs;
3. an appeal for voluntary quotas on exports to the U.S.;
4. an "invitation" to other countries to float their currencies; and finally,
5. the announcement that the U.S. would no longer convert on demand U.S. dollars held by central banks into gold.

The linkage of the U.S. dollar to gold had been viewed as the cornerstone of the adjustable peg system, and such a widespread breaking of the system threatened financial chaos. Every major currency floated in relation to the dollar and to each other in the fall of 1971. The floats were so-called dirty floats, meaning central bank intervention was frequent and often substantial, but not predictable. A number of countries invoked complicated controls on capital movements and foreign exchange transactions.

A meeting of the "Group of Ten"[4] in December 1971 led to the Smithsonian Agreement; under which participants agreed to:

1. a general realignment of their exchange rates;
2. a return to the adjustable peg system and a pledge to support the new rates;
3. a widening of the range in which currencies could move without intervention from 2 per cent to 4.5 per cent from official parity; and
4. an increase in the "official price of gold" from $35.00 an ounce to $38.00.

Another crisis, however, was in the offing. In mid-1972, Britain's severe inflationary pressures caused the pound to weaken. After a week of stabilization efforts by Britain and several European central banks, Britain abandoned its Smithsonian Agreement parity and let the pound float. In early 1973, large balance-of-payments surpluses

---

4. "The Group of Ten" is often used to denote the ten richest and most industrialized nations in the Free World, and includes the United States, France, Germany, the United Kingdom, Japan, Belgium, the Netherlands, Italy, Canada, and Sweden.

for Japan and Germany convinced the world that the yen and the mark were once again undervalued. Furthermore, a tight monetary policy in Europe compared to the United States in late 1972 and the strong upturn of the U.S. economy relative to Europe's, produced unexpectedly large U.S. balance-of-payments deficits. The apparent easing of anti-inflationary measures in the U.S. coupled with new inflationary pressures made the foreign exchange market very edgy. In February 1973, the floating of the Swiss franc was forced by large capital inflows from Italy. These disturbances occurred as a result of Italy's adoption of a "dual-exchange-rate system"[5]. The floating of the Swiss franc and the partial floating of the Italian lira placed renewed speculative pressures on the Deutsche mark. The German central bank was forced to supply marks to the market and absorb U.S. dollars to keep the mark within the Smithsonian band. Six billion U.S. dollars were bought in seven days! At a mid-February meeting in 1973, the world's monetary authorities quickly agreed to the following measures:

1. The U.S. dollar would be devalued by 10 per cent in relation to gold and all other major currencies, raising the "official price of gold" from $38.00 to $42.22 U.S. dollars.
2. The Japanese yen would be floated. (The yen promptly gained 15 per cent at the reopening of the foreign exchange markets.)

The Deutsche mark also began to feel buying pressures, as it seemed undervalued by the February realignments from the U.S. dollar to European currencies. The Europeans consulted quickly and decided to implement a "Joint European Float", that is:

1. six out of nine members of the European Community (E.C.) agreed to maintain pegged exchange rates among themselves but to allow the value of their mutually pegged currencies to float relative to non-E.C. currencies.
2. Germany agreed to revalue the mark 3 per cent relative to E.C. partners before the "Joint European Float".

Three members of the E.C. abstained from the joint float, thus partially setting back the European move toward a common currency. Italy and Britain (with Ireland) maintained their universally floating currencies. Exchange rate flexibility had carried the day: central

---

5. A "dual-exchange-rate-system" is one in which the rate for a foreign-exchange transaction depends on the nature of the transaction. For example, trade in commodities and services (except tourism) may be directed to a pegged market, while capital-movement transactions may take place at a floating or free market rate.

banks would no longer attempt to offset all market-dictated movements in exchange rates. Currently, no explicit parities are being
maintained among the European bloc, the U.S., Japan, Canada, Italy,
Switzerland, and others.

The Oil War and Its Economic Consequences
Those who regretted the final breakdown of the fixed exchange rate
system in March 1973 did not suspect that generalized floating
would provide the international monetary system with much of the
required flexibility to cope with the forthcoming events. In October
1973, members of the Organization of Petroleum Exporting Countries (OPEC) raised posted prices of crude oil by 70 per cent, followed by a further rise of 130 per cent on January 1, 1974. Because
of embargoes and reductions in output, spot prices at times reached
levels almost twice as high as posted prices. Delivered prices of
crude oil for all of 1974 are estimated to have averaged about $10.00
a barrel, 150 per cent higher than the average 1973 prices.

Prices were relatively stable until late 1978; however, between
that time and May 1980 they moved up an additional 140 per cent.
Oil, which sold for an average producer price of $2 a barrel at the
beginning of the decade, cost $31 a barrel in May, 1980.

The oil price rises placed a heavy burden on the balance of
payments of most non-oil-producing countries, exacerbating the effects of price rises of many other essential imports, especially food
and fertilizers. As oil prices soared, so did OPEC export revenues
(from 42 billion U.S. dollars in 1973 to a forecast 306 billion dollars
in 1980), and OPEC current account surplus rose from 8 billion to a
forecast 114 billion dollars in the same period. Table 3 summarizes
these data, together with estimates of the disposition of OPEC cash
surpluses.

The extent of the disruption of international financial flows caused
by the oil price increases can be seen from the current account
balances of selected groups of countries. For example, the current
account balance of all OECD[6] countries was +10.5 billion U.S. dollars
in 1973. It fell to −26 billion in 1974 with the first oil price shock
and recovered to +0.5 billion in 1975. The oil price increase of
1979-80 again moved this balance from +10.5 in 1978 to an estimated −81 billion in 1980. The problems caused for the non-oil-
producing developing countries of the world, given their lower

---

6. OECD is an acronym for Organization for Economic Co-operation and Development, a group of twenty-four industrialized countries (1980), including Canada,
   the United States, and most of Europe.

Table 3

OPEC Revenues and Cash Surpluses, 1973-1980 ($ billion)

	1973	1974	1975	1976	1977	1978	1979[a]	1980[b]
Exports	42	116	107	132	145	146	212	306
Imports	21	39	58	68	84	104	102	138
Net Services and Transfers	−14	−17	−22	−28	−32	−37	−43	−54
Current Surplus	8	59	27	36	29	5	67	114
Cumulative Surplus		67	94	130	159	164	231	345
Estimated Cash Surplus Invested In:		57.0	35.2	37.2	33.5	13.4	53.8	
United States		11.6	9.5	12.0	9.1	1.3	8.9	
United Kingdom		21.0	4.3	4.5	3.8	−1.8	17.2	
Other Countries		20.9	17.4	18.7	20.3	13.8	28.1	
International Organizations		3.5	4.0	2.0	0.3	0.1	−0.4	

(a) Estimates
(b) Forecasts

Sources: Bank of England Quarterly Bulletin, Federal Reserve Bulletin.

borrowing capacity, are perhaps more severe. Aggregate current account balances for this group moved from −7.5 billion in 1973 to −49.5 billion in 1980 without an intervening recovery. All these deficits must be financed by short- and long-term financial flows in the international payments system, and it was to this end that the inherent flexibility of the floating rate structure proved very effective. Table 4 summarizes annual current account balance changes for selected groups of countries for the period 1973-1980.

All these events led to a slowing down of the world economy. As their oil imports bills soared, many countries had no choice but to curtail industrial production and adopt domestic stabilization policies to cope with inflation. The recession of 1973-75 was to be the worst since the Second World War in terms of length, decrease in real GNP, and unemployment. At the time of writing, it remains to be seen whether the second oil price shock in 1979-80 will produce an economic contraction of equal severity. Figure 2 summarizes economic trends for the period 1960-1979 for selected countries. The drop in output and high rates of inflation resulting from the first oil price are clear. Rates of inflation on a worldwide basis are shown in tabular form in Table 5.

Table 4

Summary of Balance of Payments on Current Account of the OECD Area and Other Major World Groupings*

	1973	1974	1975	1976	1977	1978	1979	1980
	$ billion							
Trade Balance								
OECD	8	−26	6	−18	−23½	6	−41½	−89½
OPEC	21½	77	49½	65	61½	42½	110	168
Non-Oil Developing Countries	−7	−23½	−29	−16	−12	−24	−31	−43
Other Non-OECD Countries	−4	−10½	−18½	−13	−8	−8	−6½	−9½
Total[a]	**18½**	**17**	**8**	**18**	**18**	**17**	**31**	**27**
Services and Private Transfers, net								
OECD	11	10½	7	11½	13½	23	25½	34
OPEC	−12½	−15	−19½	−26	−30	−36½	−40½	−51
Non-Oil Developing Countries	−4½	−8	−9	−9½	−7½	−9½	−14	−18½
Other Non-OECD Countries	½	1	½	0	−½	−1½	−2	−3
Total[a]	**−5½**	**−11½**	**−21**	**−24**	**−24½**	**−24½**	**−30½**	**−38**
Balance on Goods, Services, and Private Transfers								
OECD	19	−15½	13	−6½	−10	29	−16	−55½
OPEC	9	62	30	39	31½	6	69½	117
Non-Oil Developing Countries	−11½	−31½	−38	−25½	−19½	−33½	−45	−61½
Other Non-OECD Countries	−3½	−9½	−18	−13	−8½	−9½	−8½	−12½
Total[a]	**13**	**5½**	**−13**	**−6**	**−6½**	**−7½**	**0**	**−11**
Official Transfers, net								
OECD	−8½	−10½	−12½	−12½	−14½	−18½	−21½	−25½
OPEC	−1½	−2½	−3	−2½	−2½	−1½	−2½	−3
Non-Oil Developing Countries	4	5½	7	7	7	7½	10	11½
Other Non-OECD Countries	0	0	0	0	0	½	½	½
Total[a]	**−6**	**−7½**	**−8½**	**−8**	**−10**	**−12½**	**−14**	**−16½**
Current Balance								
OECD	10½	−26	½	−19	−24½	10½	−37½	−81
OPEC	7½	59½	27	26½	29	4½	67	114
Non-Oil Developing Countries	−7½	−26	−31	−19	−12½	−25½	−34½	−49½
Other Non-OECD Countries	−3½	−9½	−18	−13	−8½	−9½	−8	−12
Total[a]	**7**	**−2**	**−21½**	**−15**	**−16½**	**−20**	**−13**	**−28**

* Historical data for the OECD area are aggregates of balance of payments data reported by each individual country. For non-OECD groupings the data are estimated. In deriving data on trade and invisibles of these areas use is being made of data compiled by the IMF; they are completed by OECD estimates on official transfers for all areas and on all current transactions of non-IMF members.

(a) Reflects statistical errors and asymmetries. Given the very large gross flows of world balance of payments transactions, statistical errors and asymmetries easily give rise to world totals (balances) that are significantly different from zero.

Source: OECD, *Economic Outlook* 27 (July 1980).

Figure 2

Economic Trends 1960–79

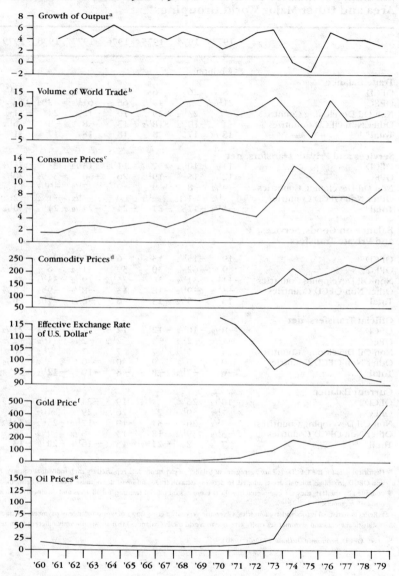

(a) GNP of industrial countries in real terms, percentage change from preceding year.
(b) Percentage change from preceding year, for Fund members and Switzerland.
(c) Index of industrial country prices; percentage change from preceding year.
(d) Index, excluding oil and in terms of U.S. dollars, 1970 = 100.
(e) Based on IMF multilateral exchange rate model (MERML 1975 = 100).
(f) London prices in U.S. dollars per fine ounce.
(g) Saudi Arabian Light, index of wholesale prices. 1976 = 100.

Source: *International Financial Statistics* and IMF Research Department.

Table 5

World Consumer Prices (average annual percentage increases)

	1950-54	1955-59	1960-64	1965-69	1970-74	1975-79
World	3.4	3.2	3.5	4.8	8.5	11.5
Industrial Countries	3.0	2.2	2.2	3.6	7.3	8.8
Oil Exporting Countries	. . .	3.1	2.0	2.5	8.5	14.2
Non-Oil-Developing Countries	5.2	9.4	11.9	12.0	15.9	26.4

Source: IMF, IFS Yearbook for 1980.

The international monetary system was required to recycle enormous amounts of funds from surplus to deficit countries. The OPEC surplus poured into the industrialized world in the form of increased imports or investments. The floating exchange rate system permitted substantial exchange rate adjustments in response to these financial flow pressures. Major currency exchange rate changes for the period 1970 through 1979 are shown in Figure 3. The extent of the currency revaluations reflects a very turbulent decade for the international financial system.

The International Institutions

There are several international financial institutions which play a key role in the international financial system. These organizations include the International Monetary Fund, the World Bank, and the Bank of International Settlements. It is also worthwhile noting several international trading blocs or groups of countries which tend to co-operate for common economic trade objectives.

The International Monetary Fund

Since its founding in 1944 concurrent with the Bretton Woods agreement, the International Monetary Fund has been instrumental in fostering international co-operation in financial matters such as exchange rate systems, trade and tariff policy harmonization, and reserve management and recycling. The fund is really a central bankers' bank in which members deposit a proportion of their domestic reserves in exchange for certain privileges. The individual contributions to the fund are called quotas, and are established in proportion with each country's level of international trade.

Until 1976, quotas were made up of 25 per cent gold and 75 per cent of the country's own currency. Since 1976 the 25 per cent gold portion can be contributed in currencies acceptable to the IMF or in

Figure 3

Rates of Change in Major Currencies Vis-à-vis the U.S. Dollar

(Percentage deviations with respect to dollar parities of the first quarter of 1970)

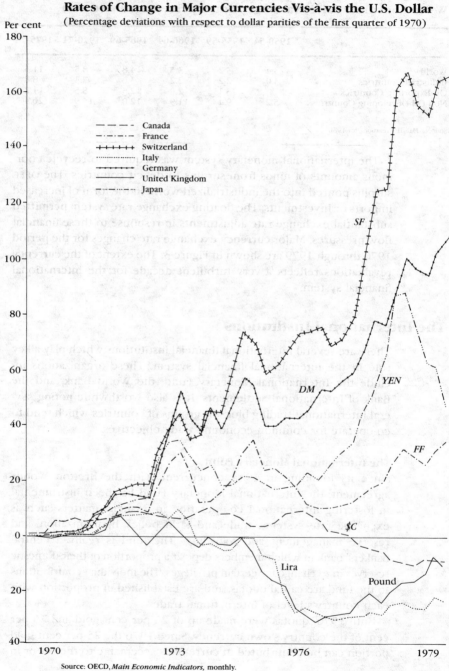

Source: OECD, *Main Economic Indicators,* monthly.

special drawing rights (SDRs). The 25 per cent in gold, hard currencies, or SDRs (the gold tranche) can be drawn upon at any time by the
member country, usually as a means of stabilizing the country's
currency value. Beyond this point a country can draw additional
credit (the credit tranche) only with the approval of the IMF, and
permission to draw down this credit is usually accompanied by
increasingly severe restrictions and conditions as the drawings increase. Thus the IMF has considerable influence with which to persuade the member country to alter the conditions giving rise to the
weakening of its currency.

Following a meeting in September 1967 of the fund's 104 members, the members agreed on the creation of a new international
reserve asset, the special drawing right. The members agreed that 9.5
billion SDR could be allocated in the 1970 to 1972 period. The SDR
was at first given a fixed value in relation to gold and in relation to
the American dollar (1 SDR = 1 U.S. dollar = .0888671 gram of fine
gold, January 1970). Since the U.S. dollar was soon devalued twice
relative to gold (from $35.00 to $38.00 to $42.22) the SDR ceased
being liquid, since borrowers could be obliged to repay their loans
in appreciated U.S. dollars (1 SDR = 1.25 U.S. dollar = .0888671
gram of fine gold, June 1975). To overcome this problem, it was
decided to base the value of the SDR on a trade weighted index of
sixteen currencies. It follows that an appreciation (depreciation) of
any currency in the basket in terms of all other currencies, raises
(lowers) the value of the SDR in terms of each other currency. Since
this reform the SDR has gained both liquidity and respect as a widely
held international reserve asset. In 1980, the currencies in the index
were to be reduced from sixteen to six.

There were 139 member countries in the IMF's SDR department in
January 1980. Total reserves (all member countries) of SDRs have
gone from about 3 billion SDRs in 1970 to 16 billion in 1980 with a
further allocation of 4 billion planned for January 1981. Growth of
gold as a reserve asset is limited by production of the metal and
individual countries have become reticent to hold too much of the
currency of another single country as a reserve. SDRs were conceived
as a means of increasing world supplies of foreign exchange reserves
and encouraging world trade. Although SDRs represent a world currency, they have not been used extensively to date by the private
sector; their prime use is still settling international accounts between
central banks.

The World Bank
The International Bank for Reconstruction and Development (the

World Bank) was established by allied governments concurrent with the formation of the IMF. Its purpose is to foster social and economic progress in the less developed nations. Its operations include financial and development assistance through loans and grants. During the 1970 to 1974 period 16 billion U.S. dollars were committed, and about three times that amount was committed during the 1975 to 1979 period. The World Bank is financed by contributions and loans primarily by the OECD countries. Membership is similar to that of the IMF, and includes virtually all independent nation states in the non-Communist bloc.

The Bank for International Settlements

The Bank for International Settlements, located in Basle, Switzerland, is financed by IMF members and acts as a clearing house for central bankers in international financial transactions. The bank also fosters monetary co-operation and education internationally.

GATT

The General Agreements on Tariffs and Trade (GATT) was established in 1948 as a parallel organization to the IMF in order to regulate and streamline trading rules between nations of the world. In a series of discussions since the end of the Second World War, for example the Kennedy Round (1960 to 1967) and the Tokyo Round (1974 to 1980), the industrialized and developing countries agreed on a set of rules to regulate international trade. These rules cover various restrictions to free trade, including tariffs, quotas, border tax adjustments, countervailing duties, dumping, voluntary restrictions, variable levies, exceptional custom valuation procedure, health regulations, import surcharges and deposit schemes, and finally the use of export-import banks as government subsidies to foreign trade.

OPEC

The Organization of Petroleum Exporting Countries (OPEC)[7] generally refers to the oil producers cartel which now regulates both the price and supply of almost 80 per cent of the oil used in the Free World.

The European Economic Community (EEC)

The Rome Treaty of 1957 formed a full customs union of six European countries: France, Germany, Italy, the Netherlands, Belgium,

---

7. OPEC membership in 1980 was Algeria, Ecuador, Gabon, Indonesia, Iran, Iraq, Kuwait, Libya, Nigeria, Qatar, Saudi Arabia, The United Arab Emirates, and Venezuela.

and Luxembourg. These countries agreed to work toward the elimination of all barriers to trade between them and to surround themselves with common external tariffs. The agreements led to a Common Agricultural Policy, and a series of discussions in order to achieve economic and political unification by the late 1980s. The United Kingdom, Denmark, and Ireland joined the group in 1973.

As a prelude to a European Monetary Union, the members agreed in April 1972 to reduce from 4.5 per cent to 2.25 per cent the official band between their currencies and the U.S. dollar. After the February and March events of 1973 occurred, most EEC countries adopted a joint float against the U.S. dollar but kept the narrow band concept to regulate the currency variation allowed within the EEC. The market variations of the different currencies in relation to the U.S. dollar and among themselves is often called the European snake. The narrow 2.25 per cent allowed variation band is called the tunnel. However when conflict between domestic economic goals and exchange stability occurs, the intensity of domestic pressure is frequently so great that attempts to maintain exchange parity of the currency are at least temporarily ceased. As of June 1978, only six currencies were still participating in the snake; three of the early strong proponents (the United Kingdom, France, and Italy) had allowed their currencies to move away from the group limits.

Outlook for the Canadian Dollar

In the long run, any currency value is dependent on the supply and demand for that currency in the international market place. In the short run governments can support a currency and hold it to a pegged position if necessary by buying up the currency in the foreign exchange markets, using supplies of reserve assets or borrowing abroad to do so. The supply and demand position of a currency is determined by the size and direction of both trade and capital flows, which in turn are determined by many factors, including relative incomes, interest rates, direct investment opportunities, and productivity levels. For example, high domestic interest rates will tend to encourage portfolio investment in a country by foreigners, and offshore borrowing by residents. The resultant capital flows will strengthen the currency because non-residents must purchase the local currency prior to investing, and offshore loans must be converted to local currency before they are patriated and spent. Relative incomes and productivity levels affect the trade balance, or the balance between imports and exports. Higher local incomes usually increase the demand for imports, while lower domestic productivity levels tend to reduce the competitiveness of exports on world markets. Both these conditions would of course tend to weaken the currency.

The balance-of-payments statement is designed to summarize all transactions which affect the purchasing power of the residents of a country, or, in other words, all the transactions (trade and capital flows) which affect the value of the country's currency. To anticipate future balances, however, it is necessary to look at the condition of the economy relative to the rest of the world. For example, Table 6 shows Canada's performance with respect to unit labor costs in manufacturing and export prices of manufactures. The former is a combination of productivity and wages, and the latter is a combination of domestic costs and foreign exchange rate.

Table 6

Competitive Positions (Indices based on calculations in a common currency, 1970 = 100)

	1975	1976	1977	1978	1979	1980	1978 II	1979 I	1979 II	1980 I	1980 II	1981 I
A. Relative Unit Labor Costs in Manufacturing												
United States	67	69	68	65	65		64	65	65			
Canada	94	104	96	81	80		78	79	80			
Japan	156	154	165	186	159		197	171	147			
France	106	103	99	99	101		101	103	99			
Germany	107	108	112	116	114		116	114	114			
Italy	104	91	92	90	98		90	92	105			
United Kingdom	97	90	89	97	110		98	104	116			
Belgium	102	102	105	103	104		102	104	104			
Netherlands	111	111	114	112	113		112	115	112			
Denmark	97	95	95	96	98		98	98	97			
Norway	125	134	140	130	124		128	125	123			
Sweden	102	117	117	105	98		102	99	98			
Austria	121	121	128	125	122		125	123	120			
Switzerland	127	131	121	146	144		154	146	143			
B. Relative Export Prices of Manufactures												
United States	87	90	89	84	87	87	84	88	87	86	87	88
Canada	92	95	90	81	77	77	79	77	76	78	77	76
Japan	107	102	105	117	107	102	120	110	104	102	101	100
France	104	102	100	99	100	103	99	99	100	102	103	104
Germany	112	114	114	117	114	109	117	114	113	110	108	106
Italy	97	90	96	94	96	98	94	95	97	98	98	100
United Kingdom	93	89	93	101	106	117	101	104	108	116	118	120
Belgium	97	96	97	98	102	102	98	101	102	102	102	102
Netherlands	99	100	101	99	101	100	98	99	102	101	99	99
Denmark	108	110	109	109	108	102	109	107	109	103	102	101
Norway	118	110	108	99	101	102	97	99	103	102	102	101
Sweden	112	117	114	108	109	108	110	110	108	108	108	108
Austria	110	106	110	107	105	106	107	104	107	106	106	106
Switzerland	116	119	115	133	128	125	138	129	127	125	125	124

Source: OECD, *Economic Outlook*, Number 27, July 1980.

For comparative purposes, it is useful to look at other common indicators of economic activity as well. Table 7 shows per cent change in GNP and consumer prices and per cent of the labor force unemployed for Canada and its major trading partners. Canadians enjoyed relatively low inflation, high unemployment, and very good growth, at least until the last three years. These data, however, mask a major threat to the future strength of the Canadian currency. Canadians collectively have imported a great deal of capital in the past, both as direct investment and debt. Net service payments, primarily interest and dividend payments, exceeded 9 billion dollars in 1979, up from 2 billion in 1970. The large service account deficit more than equals a positive trade balance, producing a net current account deficit of about 5 billion dollars. As indicated earlier, the current account deficit must be financed either by drawing down reserves or by borrowing. In Canada's case offshore borrowing has been substantial, which of course tends to make the service account deficit larger in the future. Figure 4 shows the relation between the Canadian

Figure 4

Balance of Payments Current Account

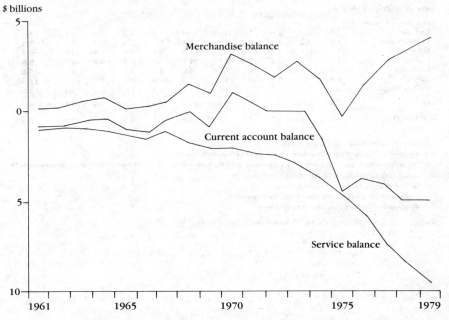

Source: Statistics Canada; *Quarterly Estimates of the Canadian Balance of International Payments,* quarterly cat. 67-001.

Table 7

Principal Indicators of International Economic Activity, 1970-1979

	1970	1971	1972	1973	1974	1975	1976	1977	1978	1979[a]	Average 1970-1979
Real GNP/GDP (Per cent change) Seven Major Countries											
Canada	2.5	6.9	6.1	7.5	3.6	1.2	5.4	2.4	3.4	2.9	**4.2**
United States	−0.3	3.0	5.7	5.5	−1.4	−1.3	5.9	5.3	4.4	2.3	**2.9**
Japan	11.8	5.2	9.4	9.9	−0.3	1.5	6.5	5.4	6.0	6.1	**6.1**
France	5.7	5.4	5.9	5.4	3.2	0.2	4.9	2.8	3.3	3.4	**4.0**
Germany	5.9	3.4	3.6	4.9	0.3	−1.8	5.3	3.5	4.3	4.4	**3.3**
Italy	5.0	1.6	3.1	6.9	4.2	4.7	5.9	2.0	2.6	4.5	**4.1**
United-Kingdom	2.3	2.8	2.4	8.0	−1.5	−1.0	3.7	1.3	3.3	0.8	**1.9**
Total[b]	2.7	3.8	5.6	6.3	−0.1	−0.5	5.4	4.0	4.2	3.4	**3.4**
Total OECD[b]	3.1	3.8	5.5	6.3	0.5	−0.4	5.2	3.7	3.9	3.4	**3.5**
Unemployment Rates[c] (Per cent) Seven Major Countries											
Canada	5.7	6.2	6.2	5.5	5.3	6.9	7.1	8.1	8.4	7.5	**6.7**
United States	5.0	6.0	5.6	4.9	5.6	8.5	7.7	7.0	6.0	5.8	**6.2**
Japan	1.2	1.2	1.4	1.3	1.4	1.9	2.0	2.0	2.2	2.1	**1.7**
France	2.4	2.6	2.7	2.6	2.8	4.1	4.4	4.9	5.2	5.9	**3.8**
Germany	0.6	0.7	0.9	1.0	2.2	4.1	4.1	3.9	3.8	3.4	**2.5**
Italy	5.4	5.4	6.3	6.3	5.3	5.8	6.6	7.1	7.2	7.8	**6.3**
United Kingdom	2.2	2.9	3.2	2.3	2.1	3.4	5.1	5.5	5.5	5.3	**3.8**
Total[d]	3.1	3.6	3.7	3.3	3.6	5.4	5.4	5.3	5.0	5.1	**4.4**
Total OECD[d+e]	3.0	3.5	3.6	3.2	3.5	5.2	5.3	5.3	5.1	5.1	**4.3**
Consumer Price Index (Per cent change) Seven Major Countries											
Canada	3.3	2.9	4.8	7.6	10.9	10.8	7.5	8.0	8.9	9.1	**7.4**
United States	5.9	4.2	3.3	6.2	11.0	9.1	5.7	6.5	7.7	11.3	**7.1**
Japan	7.7	6.1	4.5	11.8	24.5	11.8	9.3	8.0	3.8	3.6	**9.1**
France	5.1	5.5	6.2	7.4	13.7	11.7	9.6	9.4	9.1	10.7	**8.8**
Germany	3.3	5.4	5.5	6.9	7.0	5.9	4.5	3.7	2.7	4.1	**5.0**
Italy	4.8	5.0	5.7	10.8	19.1	17.0	16.8	18.4	12.1	14.8	**12.5**
United Kingdom	6.3	9.4	7.1	9.3	16.0	24.2	16.5	15.9	8.3	13.4	**12.6**
Total[f]	5.6	5.0	4.4	7.6	13.3	10.9	7.9	8.0	7.0	10.5	**8.0**
Total OECD[f]	5.6	5.3	4.7	7.8	13.2	11.4	8.5	9.1	8.3	10.0	**8.4**

(a) OECD estimates for all but Canada and the U.S.

(b) Weighted by a centred three-year moving-average of GDP in each country.

(c) The unemployment rates for Japan, France, Germany, Italy, the United Kingdom and the total OECD are adjusted according to international definitions by the OECD.

(d) Calculated by Department of Finance.

(e) Total represents about 90 per cent of the OECD countries.

(f) Weighted by consumer expenditure in each country.

Source: Department of Finance, Canada, *Economic Review*, April, 1980.

service, trade, and current balances from 1961 to 1979. Appendix I of the first chapter of this book shows the overall Canadian balance of payments, indicating how the current account deficit has been financed.

Turning to domestic fiscal policy, the Canadian federal government began in 1975 to run substantial deficits, particularly as a per cent of GNP. Deficits of this magnitude tend to create inflationary pressure and lower the confidence in the currency on the part of non-residents. Table 8 shows revenues and expenditures for Canada over the last decade. These deficits must be financed by borrowing. To the extent the required funds are borrowed from non-residents, the Canadian dollar is strengthened now and possibly weakened in the future by principal and interest payments.

On the positive side, it appears likely that resource development activities in Canada will require very large amounts of capital for the next decade and perhaps longer. Most of this money will very likely be raised in foreign capital markets. Financing abroad of the magnitude now being projected suggests considerable support for the Canadian dollar.

Table 8

Federal Government Revenue, Expenditure and Net Position — National Income and Expenditure Accounts Basis

	Revenue		Expenditure		Surplus or deficit(−)	
	($ m)	(Per cent)	($ m)	(Per cent)	($ m)	(Per cent of GNP)
1970	15,528	7.2	15,262	13.3	266	0.3
1971	17,241	11.0	17,386	13.9	−145	−0.2
1972	19,560	13.5	20,126	15.8	−566	−0.5
1973	22,809	16.6	22,422	11.4	387	0.3
1974	29,978	31.4	28,869	28.8	1,109	0.8
1975	31,703	5.8	35,508	23.0	−3,805	−2.3
1976	35,437	11.8	38,793	9.3	−3,356	−1.8
1977	36,146	2.0	43,839	13.0	−7,693	−3.7
1978	37,644	4.1	49,001	11.8	−11,357	−4.9
1979	43,269	14.9	52,438	7.0	−9,169	−3.5

Source: Statistics Canada, *National Income and Expenditure Accounts,* quarterly, cat. 13-001.

For Further Reference

The Bank of Canada Review.

The Bank of Canada Review. *Annual Report.*

Bond, D. and R. Shearer. *The Economics of the Canadian Financial System: Theory, Policy and Institutions.* Toronto: Prentice Hall, 1972.

Branson, W. "The Minimum Covered Interest Rate Charge Needed for International Arbitrage Activity". *The Journal of Political Economy* (November and December 1969): 1028-1035.

Baldwin, Robert E. and David J. Richardson. *Readings in International Trade and Finance.* Boston: Little, Brown and Company, 1974.

The Conference Board. *Canada's Quarterly Forecast* (March 1975).

Department of Finance, Canada. *Economic Review* (April 1980).

The Department of Commerce Survey of Current Business. *The United States Balance of Payments.*

Dunn, Jr., R. M. *Canada's Experience with Fixed and Flexible Exchange Rates in a North American Capital Market.* Montreal: Private Planning Association of Canada, 1971.

The Economic Council of Canada. *Annual Review.*

Eckstein, Otto. *Public Finance.* Englewood Cliffs, New Jersey: Prentice-Hall Inc., 1973.

Eiteman, D. K. and A. I. Stonehill. *Multinational Business Finance.* Don Mills, Ontario: Addison-Wesley, 1979.

The Federal Reserve Bank. *The Federal Reserve Bulletin.*

Gottfried, Harberler, et al. *Readings in International Trade and Finance.* Boston: Little, Brown and Company, 1974.

Holmes, Roome, and Schott. *The New York Foreign Exchange Market.* The Federal Reserve Bank of New York, 1965.

Holmes and Schott. "Foreign Exchange". *The Canadian Banker* (Autumn 1966).

The International Monetary Fund. *The Balance of Payments Yearbook.*

The International Monetary Fund. *Finance and Development.*

The International Monetary Fund. *International Financial Statistics.*

The International Monetary Fund. *The Monthly Direction of Trade and Annual Supplement.*

The International Monetary Fund. *Staff Papers.*

The International Monetary Fund. *The Survey.*

Kenen, Peter B. and Raymond Lubitz. *International Economics.* Englewood Cliffs, New Jersey: Prentice-Hall Inc., 1971.

OECD, *Economic Outlook 27,* July 1980.

Officer, Lawrence H. and Lawrence B. Smith. *Issues in Canadian Economics.* Toronto: McGraw-Hill Ryerson Limited, 1974.

The Quarterly Economist Review.

Rodriguez, R. N. and E. E. Carter, *International Financial Management.* Englewood Cliffs, New Jersey: Prentice-Hall, 1979.

Shearer, R. "The Foreign Currency Business of Canadian Chartered Banks", *The Canadian Journal of Economics and Political Science* (August 1965).

Shearer, R. "A Critical Note on Two Sectors of the Financial Flow Accounts". *The Canadian Journal of Economics and Political Science* (November 1972).

Statistics Canada. *Canada's National Accounts, Income, and Expenditure and the Canadian Balance of International Payments.*

Statistics Canada. *A Compendium of Statistics from 1964-1965.* Ottawa, 1967.

Statistics Canada. *The Canadian Balance of International Payments, 1965-1970.* Ottawa, 1972.

Wonnacott, Paul. *The Canadian Dollar 1948 to 1962.* Toronto: University of Toronto Press, 1965.

The World Bank. *Annual Report.*

The World Bank. *"World Debt Tables".*

The World Bank. *Borrowing in International Capital Markets.* EC-181/751.
The World Bank. *World Development Report,* 1980.
de Vries, Margaret G. *The International Monetary Fund, 1945 to 1965: Twenty Years of International Monetary Cooperation.* Washington, D.C.: The International Monetary Fund, 1973.

V
International Operations Management

D
International Financial Management

41
Financing Canadian Exports

K. C. Dhawan

Dr. Dhawan is associate professor of international business and marketing at Concordia University, Montreal. He has been an executive with and consultant for a number of major multinational firms and governments in Canada, U.S., Japan, the Middle East, and India. His current research includes international acquisition, diversification, and divestment strategies of MNCs, international political risk management, and Canadian national trading corporation alternatives.

This chapter was written expressly for this volume.

In Chapter 1, the importance of international trade in the Canadian economy was examined. International business transactions between Canada and the rest of the world are summarized in the merchandise trade and balance of payment tables (see Appendices I and II of Chapter 1).

Part III of this book discussed the marketing strategies of various sectors of Canadian business and the new marketing vehicles available to Canadian firms, which will enable them to meet the challenge of overseas markets. In Part V evolving forms of international operations management and aspects of contract procurement for turnkey projects were critically analysed.

The area which is perhaps most contentious involves export financing, covering credits which are made available to Canadian suppliers of goods and services (supplier credits) and foreign purchasers (buyer credits). It is generally recognized by Canadian business, financial, and government communities that even if the quality, price, delivery schedule, and after-sale services offered by Canadian firms are internationally competitive, a critical factor in the award/non-award of an export contract/project is the *internationally competitive* "financial packaging". In this chapter "financial packaging" means the type of financing available, time duration, repayment period, and effective cost of export credit. Also included are export credit terms covering such areas as official and private sector (such as a chartered bank) participation, Canadian content of goods and services exported, risk protection, and procedures for commitment/disbursement of export credit. Often a Canadian exporter is required to arrange or make an offer of credit to the buyer (usually a foreign government agency or a private entity), complementing the commercial contract.

There are usually three separate issues involved in Canadian export financing:

1. the type of support which is provided by the government to Canadian exporters;
2. the manner in which this support is channelled to exporters, and the role played by the banking system in this regard; and
3. the international competitiveness of the "financial package" offered by Canadian participants to the buyer.

In this chapter, each of these elements of financing of Canadian exports of goods, services, and capital projects is presented.[1] It is sufficient to generalize here that Canada has generally chosen different paths from those adopted by most other developed countries.

Type of Export Finance Support Available to Canadian Exporters.

Government financial assistance generally falls into two major categories: protection against trading risks (foreign credit risks, foreign exchange exposure, etc.) and concessionary financing (partial or complete funding at below-market interest rates). This sort of aid has been a matter for international competition for some time, as governments have acted to boost their industries' export sales for economic and political reasons. In the late 1970s, a "gentleman's agreement"[2] was reached among the OECD nations to limit this competition by setting minimum rates and maximum terms on concessionary financing, but the economic slowdown in Europe in 1980 put severe strains on the pact. Early in 1981 it appeared problematic as to whether the system would hold together.

Recognizing the need for "matching" export finance terms offered by other countries, Canada has significantly improved its financial package since 1969 when the Export Development Corporation (EDC) was established (replacing Export Credits Insurance Corporation) with an overall mandate to promote and facilitate export trade. A summary of EDC's export financing services provided in 1981 is presented in Table 1. Services provided for export trade financed by the Canadian banking system are also summarized in Section B of the Table.

1. A discussion of documentary credits (letters of credit) for export-import purposes, though important, is excluded here. Canadian chartered banks, as is the case with banks in just about every country in the world, are active in financing both imports and exports. On the most basic level, they carry out the actual transactions of international trade by remitting and receiving international payments between Canadian and foreign parties, by selling and purchasing foreign exchange, by offering documentary credits and collection facilities, and so on. Readers interested in examining these services offered by a Canadian chartered bank and various types of documentary credits should refer to the literature available from Canadian and foreign banks on the international banking services. Also see *Guide to Documentary Credit Operations* (Paris: International Chamber of Commerce, 1978).
2. The gentleman's agreement provides for consensus minimum interest rates for relatively rich countries (per capita income over $3,000), intermediate countries (per capita $1,000 − $3,000), and relatively poor countries (under $1,000). The respective rates in July 1980 for credits over five years were $8^3/_4$, $8^1/_2$, and $7^3/_4$ per cent respectively. However, in 1981 a credit war has broken out among the rich Western exporting countries. See "Rich Western Exporting Countries Tempt Importers with Loan Offers", *Globe & Mail* (March 9, 1981), p. B5.

Table 1

A Summary of Export Financing Services Provided by: (A) The Export Development Corporation and (B) The Canadian Banking System

A. Export Development Corporation

(1) Types of financing *Loans:* to foreign borrowers, normally for more than five years. A Disbursement Procedures Agreement (DPA) between foreign borrower/buyer and EDC, specifies how to disburse funds to the exporter on the borrower's behalf.
Allocations: under lines of credit to public agencies and private banks in many foreign countries.
Purchases of Notes: promissory notes issued to Canadian exporters by foreign buyers can be purchased by corporation (medium term financing).
Loan Guarantees: to a bank/financial institution which does not wish to assume credit risk with the export transaction.

(2) Duration Medium term (up to five years)
Long term (five years or more)

(3) Limit of financing Up to 85 per cent of the contract value of the export transaction. Financing of local costs incurred by the buyer may be available if competition warrants.

(4) Range of products covered Goods and equipment; pre-feasibility, feasibility, and engineering studies; complete projects of all sizes from design to completion.

(5) Interest charge/ other costs Generally effective costs of funds not internationally competitive. (see Table 2).

(6) Repayment period Services: generally five years.
Goods/projects: flexible

(7) Canadian content At an achievable level set by EDC.

(8) Risk of non-payment Loan pre-disbursement insurance available as a complement to export financing service.

(9) Commitment procedures EDC issues various types of commitment letters depending upon the level of interest and stage of contract negotiations. Some of these commitment letters are:
(a) Letter of General Interest (interest in the concept of export transaction);
(b) Letter of Interest (to consider offering the required financing);
(c) Letter of Offer in Principle (sets out the terms, in principle, which EDC would be willing to offer for the required financing); and
(d) Letter of Offer (a binding offer, usually expires after thirty days).

(10) "Credit-mixte" financing introduced in 1981.

(11) Other services offered such as: performance related insurance and guarantees of various types: foreign investment insurance; and specific transaction insurance where credit is granted by the exporter or his bank, risk of non-payment by the foreign buyer can be covered.

(12) Bank Participation   (a) Co-lending where banks and EDC are jointly involved;
                           (b) Participation where EDC invites a bank into a loan
                               which has already been negotiated; and
                           (c) Parallel lending where EDC and the bank make
                               separate loan agreements with the foreign borrower

B. Canadian Banking System

(1)   EDC-Canadian Banking System Interface: See (12) above and the discussion in
       this chapter.

(2)   Contract Guarantee. Bank guarantees available for bid and/or performance
       under a commercial contract. The "special documentary credits" may be issued
       in conjunction with EDC insurance.

(3)   Loans on a "supplier credit" basis provided through the exporter by purcha-
       sing promissory notes signed or drafts accepted by the foreign importer.

(3)   Loans directly to the foreign buyer of Canadian goods and/or services ("buyer
       credit"), usually for large export sales or major foreign projects, can form an
       integral part of the commercial package.

(4)   Other financial services:
       (a) Receivable financing against accounts receivable from foreign purchasers
           with assignment of EDC insurance as security;
       (b) Acceptance or discounting of trade bills;
       (c) Pre-export financing as interim financing to a manufacturer to cover material
           and other costs of producing an export order;
       (d) Import credits for purchase of foreign goods and services.

(5)   Documentary credits (Letter of Credit) for exports/imports; selling and
       purchasing foreign exchange.

Notes: (1) "Credit-mixte" ties foreign aid in the form of very low interest rates to
           the purchase of Canadian goods. Foreign aid is channelled through
           Canadian International Development Agency (CIDA) whereas commercial
           transactions for loan funds are administered by EDC.
       (2) For a breakdown of volume of EDC business transactions, see EDC Annual
           Reports.

Sources: Personal interviews by the author with business, financial, and government communities.
         Export Development Corporation, "Export financing services: What are they?"
         Information Circular No 81-82 (January 25, 1981); and
         Export Development Corporation, *Annual Report*, 1979.

Canadian Channels of Export Finance: EDC-Canadian Banking System Interface.

Perhaps secondary to the absolute level of export finance assistance,
but also important, is the ready availability of the benefits. The
British and French rely on their banking systems to provide export
finance directly to their country's producers of goods and services.
Most of Canada's other major competitors (for example, Japan) do
likewise (see Table 4). Canada has, however, taken the opposite
approach.

When EDC was established in 1969, the chartered banks welcomed this development. Recognizing that EDC represented a concrete commitment to Canadian exports by the government and that it filled a void which the banks themselves could not fill, the financial community responded by reorganizing their trade finance marketing groups, expanding and increasing the resources devoted to them and establishing the basis for joint co-operation.

In retrospect, however, the establishment of EDC was in fact the first step in reducing the relative importance of the banks in Canadian trade finance.[3] Canada has chosen not to work through the banking system to a large degree, and EDC has its own "delivery system" for export financing assistance to Canadian suppliers. This trend has been developing gradually over the past decade and, while banks still play a major role, particularly for smaller transactions, the government clearly sees EDC's responsibility to be paramount.

It is worthwhile to review the advantages and disadvantages of each approach. In working through their banking systems, the British, French, and others have both provided the incentive and made it easier for their indigenous institutions to take on the commitment to export financing. Their banks now use their worldwide networks to promote export activity and develop particular opportunities; they simultaneously use their extensive domestic branch coverage to publicize and deliver the various services locally. Volumes of business are such that specialized trade departments are economically justified, further improving the level of service to exporting customers.

Balanced against this are the high operating costs and the loss of hands-on control by the government agency or department involved. It is impossible to quantify the costs of utilizing the commercial banking system to deliver export financing services, since these are not separable from the subsidy provided to the exporters themselves (in the form of below-market interest rates and low insurance premiums). Nevertheless, it is clear that the incentives provided to the banks are substantial.

The Canadian approach, on the other hand, is administratively simpler and less costly. It also makes it a great deal easier to use the system for other than strictly export promotion purposes, for example, to encourage exports to specific areas on a selective basis without issuing a public announcement. However, it could be argued that the Canadian method is less effective in reaching existing and potential exporters and in using the leverage of the domestic banks to encourage export trade.

3. The author gratefully acknowledges assistance provided by the business and financial communities for compiling information in this article on comparative performance of foreign official support programs.

The chartered banks are actively involved in assisting Canadian exporters by providing both transactional and financial support. However, their role may have been constrained by government policy which emphasizes public sector control and tends to place the private sector on the periphery. This trend seems likely to continue, and it is still an open question as to whether this approach, which differs from that found elsewhere, will benefit or harm Canadian producers of goods and services. This is one of the main reasons given by Canadian exporters (familiar with the services provided by government, EDC, and chartered banks) for the conservative and non-innovative approach adopted by EDC and Canadian chartered banks in providing their "financial package" to meet the dynamic challenges of the international market place. A senior executive of a Canadian bank accepts the fact that the financing available to Canadian exporters through the chartered banks "is just not good enough" to compete effectively in world markets.[4]

Canadian International Competitiveness

In an extensive study by Dhawan and Kryzanowski[5] of Canadian experiences with foreign-based technological projects, it was evident that Canadian companies were not successful in procuring projects abroad, for the following main reasons:

1. Canadian interest rates and financial packaging of foreign projects were not competitive.
2. Export credit insurance and finance programs of Canada's competitors were superior.
3. Bid or performance guarantees were difficult to procure.
4. Successful foreign firms used "political marketing".
5. Canadian bids were not internationally competitive. The Export Promotion Review Committee (EPRC) analysed more than 170 briefs, mainly from Canadian business executives, and similarly concluded:

   If Canada is to move aggressively to increase her exports, it is essential that we realize how the competitive game is played by other nations. Export financing and insurance have become im-

---

4. "Greater Aid Said Needed for Exporters", *Globe and Mail* (March 11, 1981), p. B2.
5. For a comprehensive examination of official support programs for other competitors from OECD countries, see K. C. Dhawan and L. Kryzanowski, *Export Consortia: A Canadian Study*, (Montreal: Dekemco Ltd., 1978), pp. 100-115.

portant elements in the indirect export subsidy competition, and Canada must respond quickly to put her exporters on an equal footing with their foreign competitors.[6]

Evaluations of Canadian international financial competitiveness for two key characteristics [(1) effective cost of export credit; and (2) share of total exports receiving official support], are presented in Tables 2 and 3.

From these tables it is obvious that:

1. Effective cost of export credit (buyer credits over five years) has been the highest for Canada for the two time periods of March 1977 and September 1978 (Table 2).
2. Canadian share of total exports receiving official support for 1976, 1977, and 1978 is the lowest among Canada's competitor countries (Table 3).

Table 4 compares three major elements of the financial packaging — loans, insurance, and guarantees — for Canada and her two major competitors, the United Kingdom (its official agency dealing with export support programs is known as the Export Credits Guarantee Department — ECGD) and France (its official agency is the Compagnie Française du Commerce Exterieur — COFACE). While not an all-inclusive comparison among systems, Table 4 serves to highlight the relative types of assistance given to exporters of each country's goods.

Conclusion

One result of the move toward wide-open competition among Western countries' export promotion agencies has been increasing orientation towards innovative and competitive financial packaging being offered by Canada. This is reflected in the Canadian government's 1981 decision to offer "credit-mixte" financing, which ties foreign aid in the form of very low interest loans to the purchase of Canadian goods. The minister of trade, while announcing the Canadian capacity to match "credit-mixte", defined it as an "export financing device that mixes concessional financing with conventional export financing to produce low interest rates."[7] Loans using the new capa-

6. Export Promotion Review Committee, *Strengthening Canada Abroad* (Toronto: Export Promotion Review Committee, 1979), p. 31.
7. "Canada Establishes Capacity to Match 'Credit-Mixte'", *Export News Bulletin* (January 1981), p. 1.

Table 2

Export-Import Bank of the United States — Derivation of Export Credit Interest Rates — Buyer Credits Over Five Years; March 1977 (Per Cent per Annum)

Country	Official Participation	% Rate	Per Cent of Contract	Other Participation	% Rate	Per Cent of Contract	Blended Rate	Insurance (I)[a] and Fees (F)	Effective Cost of Export Credit	Effective Cost of Export Credit as at Sept. 1978
Canada	EDC	8.5	60	Commercial Bank	10.25[b] (Prime + 1.5)	25	9.0	0.2F	9.2	9.4
France	Bank of France/BFCE	—	60	Commercial Bank	—	25	7.5[c]	0.5I 0.2F	8.2	8.55
Germany	KfW	8.0	45	AKA: C-line Commercial Bank	7.25[b] 7.75[b] (Prime + 1.25)	10 30	7.8	0.7I 0.1F	8.6	8.4
Italy	Mediocredito	8.5	85	None	—	—	8.5	0.5I	9.0	9.85
Japan	Eximbank	7.5	50	Commercial Bank	9.2	30	8.1	0.3I 0.2F[d]	8.6	8.0
United Kingdom	ECGD	8.0	85	None	—	—	8.0	0.6I 0.3F	8.9	8.3[e]
United States	Eximbank	8.4	42	Commercial Bank	7.75[b] (Prime + 1.5)	43	8.1	0.2F	8.3	8.875[f] 8.325

(a) Insurance premiums and fees for good credit risks.

(b) Variable.

(c) Combined public and private rates for credits over five years always yield a blended export credit rate conforming to the interest rate minimums specified in the Consensus Understanding.

(d) No fees associated with supplier credits.

(e) US dollar credit. (The rate for sterling credits is twenty-five basis points higher).

(f) Standard and exceptional rates respectively.

Sources: Export-Import Bank of the United States, Report to the U.S. Congress on Export Credit Competition and the Export-Import Bank of the United States (Washington, D.C. July, 1977). Annex, p. 21; Report to the US Congress on Export Credit Competition and the Export Import Bank of the United States (Washington, D.C., March 1979). p. 20.

667   *Financing Canadian Exports/41*

Table 3

Share of Total Exports Receiving Official Support (%)

	1976	1977	1978	1980[b]
Canada	4	6	3	N.A.
France	36	30	29[a]	34
Germany	10	12	N.A.	14
Italy	9	7	12[a]	N.A.
Japan	49	42	35	39
United Kingdom	36	34	35[a]	35
United States	7	7	6	18

(a) Estimated on the basis of data through June 30, 1978.
(b) Figures for 1980 as reported in "Rich Western Exporting Countries Tempt Importers with Loan Offers," *Globe and Mail* (March 9, 1981), p. B2.

Source: Credit Competition and the Export-Import Bank, March 1979, pp. 52, 62, 73, 86, 96, and 111.

city, to a maximum of $900 million over the next three years, will be made available through the Export Development Corporation. Individual projects to be supported by "credit-mixte" will be subject to cabinet approval. In general, however, the Canadian export assistance programs are the least competitive in terms of financial benefits, placing this country's suppliers at a disadvantage against producers from other countries. This is attributable to two primary factors: the modelling of the Canadian system on that of the United States, which only grudgingly accepts the principle of export assistance; and the requirement that EDC not generate an operating deficit. Where other systems accept explicitly the need for export subsidies and act accordingly, the Canadian system is not only non-subsidizing, but it aims to make a profit for the government as well. The Export Promotion Review Committee reflected this concern in one of its recommendations (Recommendation 5: See Chapter 45 of this book).

Obviously, banks, EDC, the government of Canada, and the Canadian business community have a long way to go before Canadian financial packages in support of Canadian exports, particularly for short- and medium-term, become internationally competitive and are innovative enough to lead, rather than react to and match, the competitors' terms.

Table 4

Comparative Summary of Financial Support Programs

	UK (ECGD)[a]	France (COFACE)[b]	Canada (EDC)[c]
1. Loans Funding:	Private, banks	Majority by banks; longer term portion by BFCE[d]	EDC portion, government
Interest Rates:	Short-term credits at 5/8% over Base Rate; Medium-long-term credits at 7.5 – 8.75% (banks are guaranteed a 1% credit spread), rates may be reduced if dictated by foreign competition	Rediscount facility with concessionary rates; rediscount facility at Bank of France (4.5%); credit-mixte facilities	EDC portions fixed rates in line with OECD "gentleman's agreement", credit-mixte facilities
2. Insurance Risks:	Commercial risk Political risk	Commercial risk Political risk Trade fair insurance Market development insurance Catastrophy	Commercial risk Political risk
	Foreign exchange risk Inflation — Capital goods Export inventory Wrongful call of a performance guarantee	Foreign exchange risk Inflation — Capital goods	Wrongful call of performance guarantee
Minimum coverage:	Whole turnover or group of markets for short-medium-term Individual coverage for long-term transactions	Whole turnover or acceptable spread of risks for most transactions Individual coverage for long-term transactions	Whole turnover (ex. U.S.) for short-term transactions Individual coverage for medium-term transactions
Eligibility:	Manufacturers, merchants, banks, U.K. subsidiaries in third countries, foreign subcontractors; foreign content usually maximum of 40% — flexible	Exporters, banks; Foreign content usually maximum of 10% (30–40% EEC in case of capital goods)	Exporters with relatively high Canadian content
3. Guarantees	Comprehensive guarantees given to manufacturers, merchants, banks, etc.	Medium-long-term loans may be discounted at the BFCE, or they may have been guaranteed by the BFCE.	Reluctantly given to banks for medium- and long-term exports and performance guarantees.

(a) ECGD   = Export Credits Guarantee Department.
(b) COFACE = Compagnie Française du Commerce Exterieur.
(c) EDC   = Export Development Corporation.
(d) BFCE   = Banque Française du Commerce.

Sources: Personal interviews with Canadian executives.

For Further Reference

"Canada, U.S. Criticize 22-Country Export Credit Pact". *The Financial Post* (June 21, 1978): B5.

"EDC Starts Insurance Project to Help Builders Win Overseas Projects". *The Financial Post* (September 19, 1978): B3.

"Ex-Im Aid to Exports Goes Under the Knife". *Business Week* (February 23, 1981): 34-35.

Groenhart, N., ed. *Export Credit Guarantee Systems*. Bruxelles: Orgalime, September 1976.

Guide to Documentary Credit Operations. Paris: International Chambers of Commerce, 1978.

Halpin, J. G. and R. Van Eyk. "Financing Canadian Exports". *Canadian Business Review* (Spring 1975): 46-48.

Lloyd Bank International Ltd. *Guide to Selected Export Credit Systems*. London, July 1976.

V
International Operations Management

D
International Financial Management

42
Multinational Transfer Pricing: A Canadian Emphasis

Roger Y. W. Tang

Dr. Tang is associate professor of accounting in the Faculty of Management, University of Calgary. He is the author of *Transfer Pricing Practices in the United States and Japan* and of numerous articles in accounting and management journals.

This chapter was written expressly for this volume.

Transfer pricing is concerned with the pricing of goods and services transferred between divisions within a company. A division may be a unit of the parent company or it may be a wholly or partially owned subsidiary. These interdivisional transfers may include the flow of raw materials, intermediate goods, finished goods, and a wide range of services. Determining the prices for these transfers is among the thorniest of corporate problems of divisionalized firms.

The main purpose of this chapter is to provide a better understanding of the complexity and strategic implications of many issues involved in international transfer pricing. Another objective is to offer some general guidelines for managing a transfer pricing system. Specifically, the following subjects will be dealt with in the paper:

1. the nature of transfer pricing problems;
2. the importance of transfer pricing to the Canadian economy and other related issues in a Canadian context;
3. multinational comparisons of transfer pricing practices in Canada, Britain, the U.S., and Japan;
4. some broad guidelines for managing a transfer pricing system.

The Nature of Transfer Pricing Problems

Transfer pricing information may affect many critical decisions concerning the acquisition and allocation of corporate resources, just as prices in the entire economy influence decisions regarding the allocation of national resources. Even in a purely domestic context where all company activities are conducted in one country, transfer pricing is still vital to company profits and to the appraisal of divisional performance.

Transfer prices are necessary for almost all large companies unless there is no transfer of goods or services between divisions. The costs of doing away with a transfer pricing system may be substantial, as Joel Dean stated:

Abolition of transfer prices prevents meaningful measurement of the profits of individual operating units. . . . . It also prevents accurate estimates of the earnings on proposed capital projects. . . .

And there is no way to assure that the product will be directed where it will produce the highest dollar return, either as among alternative processes or as among alternative channels and levels of distribution.[1]

Similar comments have also been made by other writers who suggested that the responsibility centre concept and transfer pricing are necessary, and indeed desirable.[2]

In a multinational context, transfer pricing has often been viewed as an important means of transferring the funds and earnings of a multinational company (MNC) in pursuit of its various corporate objectives.[3] Carefully designed transfer prices may yield substantial tax savings or can be used to overcome import restrictions imposed by host countries. However, in recent years, tax and customs authorities in many countries as well as some international organizations, including the United Nations Conference on Trade and Development (UNCTAD), the European Economic Community (EEC), and the Andean Group, have intensified their surveillance and investigations of multinational transfer pricing practices.[4]

Since the mid-1950s, the issues on transfer pricing have been discussed extensively in business literature. Most of the studies, however, deal with the theoretical merits of various pricing methods. A summary of the proposals on proper transfer prices and their proponents (or discussants) can be seen in Table 1. These proposals range from the extreme of abolishing transfer prices under most circumstances to the opposite extreme of accepting all methods as long as they help accomplish corporate objectives. Unfortunately, the arguments supporting the various proposals are often inconsistent and sometimes contradictory.

1. Joel Dean, "Decentralization and Intracompany Pricing", *Harvard Business Review* **33** (July-August 1955), p. 66.
2. K. W. Lemke, "In Defence of the Profit Centre Concept", *Abacus* **6** (December 1970), pp. 182-88; and G. M. McNally, "Profit Centres and Transfer Prices — Are They Necessary?" *Accounting and Business Research* **4** (Winter 1973), pp. 13-22.
3. See James S. Shulman, "When the Price Is Wrong — By Design", *Columbia Journal of World Business* **2** (May-June 1967), pp. 69-76; and Michael Z. Brooke and H. Lee Remmers, *The Strategy of Multinational Enterprise* (London: Pitnan, 1978), pp. 172-76.
4. See, for example, "U.K. Tax Authorities Zero in on Multinationals' Intercorporate Transfer Pricing", *Business Europe* (June 18, 1976), pp. 193-94; Jane O. Burns, "How (the United States) IRS Applies the Intercompany Pricing Rules of Section 482: A corporate survey", *Journal of Taxation* **52** (May 1980), pp. 308-14; and United Nations Conference on Trade and Development, *Dominant Positions of Market Power of Transnational Corporations: Use of the Transfer Pricing Mechanism* (New York: United Nations, 1978).

Table 1

A Summary of the Proposals on Proper Transfer Price(s)

I. **Do away with transfer price under most circumstances:**
Wells (1968, 1971)

II. **Cost-oriented methods:**
A. Economic cost-oriented methods:

  1. Marginal cost: Hirshleifer (1956); McMurray (1961)
  2. Opportunity cost: Samuels (1965); Onsi (1970); Holstrum and Sauls (1973)

B. Accounting cost or cost-plus methods:

  1. Incremental cost: Goetz (1967)
  2. Standard variable cost plus the lost contribution margin:
  Benke and Edwards (1980)
  3. Cost plus some allowance for profit: Gordon (1970);
  Crompton (1972); Vendig (1973)

III. **Market-oriented methods:**
Market price: Cook (1955); also proposed by Hirshleifer (1956) under some circumstances

IV. **Negotiated price:**
Dean (1955); Li (1965); Haidinger (1970); Fremgen (1970); Shaub (1978)

V. **Contribution approach:**
Schwab (1975)

VI. **Dual pricing (the use of two transfer prices):**
Drebin (1959); Greer (1962); Edwards and Roemmich (1976)

VII. **Mathematical programming:**
A. The decomposition procedure: Dantzig and Wolfe (1963); Baumol and Fabian (1964); Charnes, Clower, and Kortenek (1967); Hass (1968)
B. Linear programming: Petty and Walker (1972), Murphy (1977)
C. Goal programming: Bailey and Boe (1976); Merville and Petty (1979)
D. Other method: Rutenberg (1970)

VIII. **Different prices for different purposes:**
Bierman (1959)

Note: The years in parentheses represent the years the writers' articles or books were published. Details of the references can be found in Roger Y. W. Tang, *Multinational Transfer Pricing: Canadian and British Perspectives* (Toronto: Butterworth, 1981).

There is rarely a single transfer price that will meet all the needs of an organization. The correct price will depend on the economic and legal circumstances and the decision at hand. This is equally true in multinational transfer pricing. Because no single system is best in all managerial environments, transfer pricing systems within large organizations differ among industrial nations.[5]

5. David Granick, "National Differences in the Use of Internal Transfer Prices", *California Management Review* 42 (Summer 1975), pp. 28-40.

Transfer Pricing in a Canadian Context

The Importance of Transfer Pricing to the Canadian Economy

The importance of transfer pricing to the Canadian economy and Canadian firms has been noted by J. Alex Milburn:

> The Canadian Economy may be more susceptible to international transfer pricing variability than that of any other country in the world. This is because much of Canadian industry is foreign-owned and also because there is a great deal of trade between Canadian companies and their foreign associates.[6]

As shown in Table 2, in 1978, the foreign-owned Canadian companies with assets of more than C$5 million reported that their exports

Table 2

Merchandise Trade with Parents and Affiliates Abroad of Major Foreign-Owned Canadian Corporations, 1964-78
(in millions of Canadian dollars)

	Exports		Imports	
Year	To Parents and Affiliates Abroad	As a Percentage of Total Canadian Merchandise Exports	From Parents and Affiliates Abroad	As a Percentage of Total Canadian Merchandise Imports
1964	1,335	16.2	1,628	21.6
1965	1,496	17.1	2,035	23.6
1966	2,292	22.2	2,422	23.9
1967	3,005	26.5	2,891	26.8
1968	3,763	27.8	3,722	30.6
1969	4,534	30.6	4,365	31.2
1970	4,549	27.2	4,090	29.5
1971	5,209	29.2	5,018	32.2
1972	5,747	28.5	5,916	31.7
1973	6,594	26.0	7,142	30.6
1974	7,684	23.7	9,417	29.7
1975	8,848	26.7	10,243	29.6
1976	10,613	27.6	12,152	32.5
1977	12,375	27.9	13,377	31.7
1978	14,609	27.5	15,150	30.2

Source: Department of Industry, Trade, and Commerce, *Foreign-Owned Subsidiaries in Canada* (Ottawa: Information Canada, 1974), and other information provided by the department.

Note: The information in this table is derived from the annual or quarterly surveys of the large foreign-owned subsidiary companies operating in Canada conducted regularly by the Canadian government. The participants taking part in the surveys are non-financial companies incorporated in Canada with assets of more than C$5 million and whose voting shares are more than 50 per cent owned by a non-resident corporation.

6. J. Alex Milburn, "International Transfer Transactions: What Price?" *CA Magazine* **109** (December 1976), pp. 22-27.

to and imports from related companies abroad were C$14,609 million
and C$15,150 million respectively. These amounts accounted for
27.5 per cent of the total Canadian exports and 30.2 per cent of the
total Canadian imports in 1978. While sufficient to demonstrate
significance, these statistics understated the proportion of intercompany
transactions in Canadian exports and imports because of two factors:
(1) trade between foreign-owned Canadian companies (with assets
of less than $5 million) and their foreign affiliates were excluded;
and (2) these statistics did not include intercompany transfers between
Canadian-owned parent companies and their foreign affiliates.

From Table 2, one can also see that the reporting company's
exports to and imports from parents and affiliates as percentages of
total Canadian exports and imports had increased almost steadily
during the 1960s. This was due mainly to the expanding U.S.-Canada
automotive trade as a result of the auto pact signed by the two
countries in 1965.[7] These percentages seemed to have stabilized
during the 1970s.

Table 3

**Proportion of Exports to Parents and Affiliates Abroad, and of Imports
from Parents and Affiliates Abroad for Major Foreign-Owned Canadian
Corporations, 1976-78** (in percentage)

	Exports to Parents and Affiliates as Percentages of Total Exports by the Corporations Studied %			Imports from Parents and Affiliates as Percentages of Total by the Corporations Studied %		
	1976	1977	1978	1976	1977	1978
Mining and Primary Metals	45.3	46.7	46.0	76.2	74.2	73.3
Gas and Oil	51.2	46.2	47.9	91.2	88.9	85.9
Machinery and Metal Fabricating	67.6	67.7	67.6	83.1	81.5	81.1
Transportation Equipment	93.8	95.2	94.4	79.1	79.0	78.9
Electrical Products	44.0	46.4	50.7	66.9	64.2	64.0
Chemical Products	68.6	66.2	66.0	67.2	69.6	70.7
Food and Beverage	40.8	40.9	30.5	30.1	30.9	36.1
Pulp and Paper	48.6	49.9	44.3	30.1	39.2	56.8
Other Manufacturing	63.4	52.3	55.6	70.7	71.7	72.7
Wholesale Trade	67.6	73.1	75.4	88.8	85.0	81.5
Other Non-Manufacturing	99.2	72.7	86.6	51.8	37.0	39.5
Total	**74.2**	**76.0**	**75.7**	**77.6**	**76.7**	**76.5**

Source: Canada, Department of Industry, Trade, and Commerce.

7. For a detailed discussion of the U.S.-Canada Automotive Agreement, See Carl E.
Beigie, *The Canada-U.S. Automotive Agreement: An Evaluation* (Montreal: The
C. D. Howe Research Institute, 1970).

Table 3 shows the proportion of exports to and of imports from parents and affiliates abroad for the major foreign-owned Canadian corporations by industries. On the average, about 75.7 per cent of their exports and 76.5 per cent of their imports in 1978 were intercompany transactions. Of course, in some industries like transportation equipment, the proportions of intercompany transactions in their exports or imports are even higher.

A large part of the intercompany transactions shown in Table 3 were conducted between the Canadian companies and their parents or affiliates in the United States. It is not surprising to see that even a small change in international transfer prices for these transactions could have a significant impact on both the tax revenue and customs duties collected by the U.S. and Canadian governments as well as on the balance of payments of the two countries.

Canadian Tax Provisions on Transfer Pricing
Many countries have developed rules to deal with situations involving transfer pricing for goods and services.[8] Canadian rules on intercompany transactions can be found in Section 69 of the 1972 Income Tax Act which contains general provisions relating to payments made or received in non-arm's length transactions. The relevant subsections are 69(1), 69(2), and 69(3).

Section 69(1) applies to the acquisition and disposition of goods. The requirement is that the goods be traded at "fair market value". Sections 69(2) and 69(3) cover the payments between residents (or persons carrying on business in Canada) and non-residents on such items as rent, royalty, or other payments for the use or reproduction of any property. The requirement is that payment be made at an amount which would have been "reasonable in the circumstances" if the taxpayer and the non-resident had been dealing at arm's length.

Unlike their counterparts in the U.S., Canadian tax authorities have not issued detailed regulations to implement the rules in Section 69. In the past, the attitude of the Canadian government to intercompany pricing adjustments and to border pricing issues generally has been much less searching and sophisticated than that of the U.S. authorities, with some possible consequent loss to the balance of Canadian tax revenues.[9] However, there are signs that greater atten-

---

8. For an extensive discussion of the existing rules in the U.S. and major countries in Europe, see Peat, Marwick, Mitchell & Co., *Taxation of Intercompany Transactions in Selected Countries in Europe and U.S.A.* (Deventer, the Netherlands: Kluwer, 1979).

9. R. D. Brown, "Canada-United States Tax Relations Problems", *Tax Executive* **28** (October 1975), pp. 1-19.

tion will be paid by Revenue Canada to intercompany pricing issues in the future. In recent years, several cases have been heard before the Canadian courts dealing with transactions between Canadian corporations and affiliates abroad. Most of these cases relate to transfer prices between Canadian parent companies and their foreign subsidiaries but the principles involved may also be applied to transactions between Canadian subsidiaries and their parent companies in foreign countries.

In September 1980, Canada and the United States signed a new tax treaty.[10] This treaty, if ratified by the Canadian Parliament and by the U.S. Congress, will replace the antiquated 1941 treaty. One provision in the new treaty is related to multinational transfer pricing in a U.S. - Canadian context. According to the treaty, if related party arrangements vary from those that would exist between unrelated parties, either Canada or the United States is permitted to adjust income, deductions, credits, or taxes to reflect arm's length arrangements. The treaty also permits simultaneous examinations of the income tax returns of multinational companies obliged to pay taxes in both Canada and the United States. Before each tax audit begins, officials from both countries will plan and co-ordinate the examination. Information is then exchanged in accord with the tax treaty provisions.

These changes may have far-reaching implications for international transfer pricing considering the volume of cross-border investment and business transactions between related companies in the two countries. For example, the exchange of information between the treaty partners ensures co-ordination in the tax treatment of business firms with activities in more than one country. It will substantially reduce the flexibilities multinational corporations have in adjusting their transfer prices.

Multinational Comparisons of Transfer Pricing Practices

In an effort to analyse the transfer pricing practices of large industrial corporations in developed countries, the author has undertaken a series of studies on transfer pricing practices in four nations: the United States, Japan, Canada, and Britain.[11] These countries were selected because they are among the leading nations in international

10. *Globe and Mail* (September 26, 1980).
11. Details of the two studies are reported in Roger Y. W. Tang, *Transfer Pricing Practices in the United States and Japan* (New York: Praeger, 1979), and *Multinational Transfer Pricing: Canadian and British Perspectives* (Toronto: Butterworth, 1981).

trade and therefore are the ones whose companies are facing mounting international transfer pricing problems.

Some important aspects of transfer pricing systems in the four countries are compared and discussed in the following sections. These comparisons are based on the data recently provided by 192 Canadian, 80 British, 145 American, and 102 Japanese firms. Altogether, the information represents the experience of 519 large industrial companies in the four nations. The discussion should contribute to a better understanding of the management approaches in these four nations.

The Use of Transfer Prices
As shown in Figure 1, the extent of usage of transfer prices varies somewhat from nation to nation. Ninety-two per cent of the U.S. companies had transfer prices; 85 per cent of Canadian and 79 per cent of British firms also reported using transfer prices; but only 73 per cent of the Japanese firms were users of transfer prices. A possible explanation for this phenomenon is that the degree of divisionalization in North America may be greater than that in either Britain or Japan.

Divisionalization is a process whereby a company is divided into many organization units responsible for both the manufacturing and the marketing of a product or a group of product lines. Although

Figure 1

The Extent of Usage of Transfer Prices — A Multinational Comparison

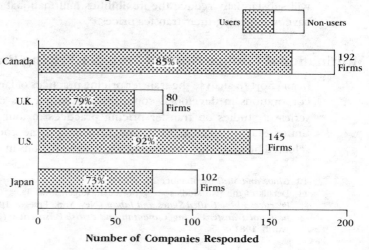

Number of Companies Responded

divisionalization and decentralization are not synonymous, division-alization should make greater decentralization possible. Both are often accompanied by the use of profit or investment centres. Recently, one study of 620 large U.S. firms discovered that 96 per cent of them were using profit centres or investment centres.[12] Since many large Canadian companies are controlled by U.S. multinational firms, these Canadian companies can be expected to follow, to a large extent, the divisional organizational structure of their parent companies in the U.S.

With divisionalization and decentralization, sound transfer pricing systems are needed to account for interdivisional transfers of goods and services. If the responsibility for a product line is divided among two or more divisions, a transfer pricing system also serves to fairly assign the profits to the divisions that have contributed to the development, production, and marketing of the product.

Pricing Methods for Domestic Transfers

The domestic transfer prices used by the respondents in the four national groups are compared in Table 4. There were no significant differences in the orientation (cost oriented or non-cost oriented) of pricing methods used by the respondents in the four nations. In Table 4, cost-oriented pricing methods are those derived mainly through cost information as opposed to using market price information of goods transferred. Non-cost-oriented pricing methods include market-oriented transfer prices and other transfer prices that are not formulated mainly from cost information on the products or services transferred.

The most popular domestic transfer pricing methods used by the four national groups included market prices, negotiated prices, full production cost plus, and standard full production cost. Neither marginal cost (variable cost) nor mathematical programming price was used by a large number of respondents, despite the fact that these methods have been advocated by many writers in the past.[13]

There were, however, some minor differences among the four groups in the use of domestic transfer prices. For example, market price less selling expenses was used by 16 per cent of Japanese respondents, but by only 3.3 per cent of the British firms. Negotiated

12. James S. Reece and William R. Cool, "Measuring Investment Center Performance", *Harvard Business Review* **56** (May-June 1978), p. 29.
13. See, for example, Jack Hirshleifer, "On the Economics of Transfer Pricing", *Journal of Business* **29** (July 1956), pp. 172-84; and J. William Petty II, and Ernest W. Walker, "Optional Transfer Pricing for the Multinational Firm", *Financial Management* **1** (Winter 1972), pp. 74-84.

Table 4

Transfer Pricing Methods for *Domestic* Transfers — A Cross-National Comparison

Pricing Methods	Canada (N=240)[a] %	Britain (N=91)[a] %	U.S. (N=232)[a] %	Japan (N=63)[a] %
Cost-Oriented Methods:				
Actual variable cost of production	2.9	0.0	0.0	0.0
Actual full production cost	8.7	9.9	9.0	9.2
Standard variable cost of production	1.3	2.2	3.0	0.8
Standard full production cost	12.5	13.2	16.9	15.1
Actual variable production cost plus a lump-sum subsidy	1.3	2.2	0.9	0.9
Full production cost (actual or standard) plus some allowance for profit	15.4	17.6	19.0	20.2
Other cost-oriented methods	2.9	2.2	1.7	0.0
Sub-Total for Cost-Oriented Methods	**45.0**	**47.3**	**50.4**	**46.2**
Non-Cost-Oriented Methods:				
Market price	25.8	22.0	21.6	17.7
Market price less selling expenses	8.3	3.3	8.2	16.0
Negotiated price	18.8	23.0	18.1	19.3
Mathematical programming price	0.0	0.0	0.0	0.8
Other non-cost-oriented methods	2.1	4.4	1.7	0.0
Sub-Total for Non-Cost-Oriented Methods	**55.0**	**52.7**	**49.6**	**53.8**
Total — All Methods	**100.0**	**100.0**	**100.0**	**100.0**

Note: The numbers of respondents in the four national groups are: Canada, 163; Britain, 63; the U.S., 133; and Japan, 73.

(a) = Number of times referred to by the respondents.

price was most widely used among the U.K. companies, while Canadian firms took the lead in using market prices.

International Transfer Pricing Methods

Table 5 shows the international transfer pricing methods used by the multinational companies in the four national groups. In terms of orientations, the methods used by the U.S. firms and the Japanese firms were more cost oriented than those used by either Canadian or British companies. Other major differences among the four groups can be seen in the use of full production cost plus and of negotiated price. Full production cost plus seems more popular among the U.S. and Japanese firms, while more Canadian and British companies like negotiated prices.

A comparison of Tables 4 and 5 shows that the domestic transfer pricing methods used by all four groups were more cost oriented than their international transfer pricing methods. The shift in pricing orientation from domestic to international transfers was most dramatic

Table 5

Transfer Pricing Methods for *International* Transfers — A Cross-National Comparison

Pricing Methods	Canada (N=108)[a] %	Britain (N=71)[a] %	U.S. (N=118)[a] %	Japan (N=63)[a] %
Cost-Oriented Methods:				
Actual variable cost of production	1.8	0.0	0.0	1.6
Actual full production cost	2.8	4.2	5.1	0.0
Standard variable cost of production	.9	0.0	0.8	0.0
Standard full production cost	3.7	2.8	5.1	4.8
Actual variable production cost plus a lump-sum subsidy	2.8	2.8	1.7	1.6
Full production cost (actual or standard plus some allowance for profit	19.4	22.6	32.2	33.3
Other cost-oriented methods	1.9	1.4	1.7	0.0
Sub-Total for Cost-Oriented Methods	**33.3**	**33.8**	**46.6**	**41.3**
Non-Cost-Oriented Methods:				
Market price	26.9	23.9	20.4	22.2
Market price less selling expenses	10.2	9.9	14.4	14.3
Negotiated price	25.9	26.8	13.6	22.2
Mathematical programming price	0.0	0.0	0.8	0.0
Other non-cost-oriented methods	3.7	5.6	4.2	0.0
Sub-Total for Non-Cost-Oriented Methods	**66.7**	**66.2**	**53.4**	**58.7**
Total — all methods	**100.0**	**100.0**	**100.0**	**100.0**

Note: The numbers of respondents in the four national groups are: Canada, 78; Britain, 48; the U.S., 85; and Japan, 42.

(a) = Number of times referred to by the respondents.

for British firms. While 47.3 per cent of the U.K. firms used cost-oriented methods for domestic transfers, only 33.8 per cent used cost-oriented methods for international transfers. Enforcement of the requirements for arm's length prices in Britain and in the EEC countries may have had some impact on the methods used by British firms.

Environmental Variables of International Transfer Pricing

In multinational transfer pricing a host of environmental variables including taxes, customs duties, and import restrictions need to be considered in formulating transfer pricing policies. Analysis of environmental variables in international transfer pricing can be found in several prior studies. For instance, Greene and Duerr found that tax and customs considerations and the desires of domestic divisional executives and local managers abroad have a profound influence on corporate policy in multinational transfer pricing.[14] One research

14. James Greene and Michael G. Duerr, *Intercompany Transactions in the Multinational Firm* (New York: The Conference Board, 1970).

report by the Business International Corporation also contains an extensive discussion of the external constraints for setting transfer pricing policies.[15] The list of twenty environmental variables in Table 6 was put together after extensive review of literature and tested with small samples.

Table 6

Rankings of Environmental Variables — A Cross-National Comparison

Variables	Canada (N=104)[a]	Britain (N=47)[a]	U.S. (N=88)[a]	Japan (N=57)[a]
Overall profit to the company	1	1	1	1
Rate of customs duties and customs legislation where the company has operations	2	11	6	9
The competitive position of subsidiaries in foreign countries	3	2	3	2
Restrictions imposed by foreign countries on repatriation of profits or dividends	4	4,5	2	4
Differentials in income tax rates and income tax legislation among countries	5	13	4	14
Maintaining good relationships with host governments	6	6	11	10
Performance evaluation of foreign subsidiaries	7	3	5	5
Anti-dumping legislation of foreign countries	8	12	15	13
The need to maintain adequate cash flows in foreign subsidiaries	9	4,5	9	6,7
Import restrictions imposed by foreign countries	10	9	7	11
Rules and requirements of financial reporting for foreign subsidiaries	11	10	10	15
Antitrust legislation of foreign countries	12	16	20	19
Devaluation and revaluation in countries where the company has operations	13	7	12	3
Restrictions imposed by foreign countries on the amount of royalty or management fees which can be charged against foreign subsidiaries	14	15	8	12
The need of subsidiaries in foreign countries to seek local funds	15	14	16	16
Volume of interdivisional transfers	16	18	14	18
The interests of local partners in foreign subsidiaries	17	8	17	6,7
Domestic government requirements on direct foreign investments	18	19	18	20
Rates of inflation in foreign countries	19	19	13	8
Risk of expropriation in foreign countries where the company has operations	20	20	19	17

(a) v Number of respondents.

15. *Setting Intercorporate Pricing* (New York: Business International Corporation, 1973).

Respondents from the four nations were asked to judge the importance of each variable on a five-point scale as follows:

Extremely Important	Very Important	Moderately Important	Not too Important	Not at all Important
5	4	3	2	1

The average importance of a particular variable was computed by summing the integer values assigned to the variable and then dividing the sum by the number of firms. Table 6 ranks the average importance placed on all twenty variables by four national groups. To facilitate the comparisons, the ordering of the variables follows the rankings by the Canadian firms.

Some interesting similarities and differences among the four national groups can be observed in Table 6. Predictably, "overall profit to the company" was considered as the single most important variable by all four national groups. Another variable considered very important by all four groups of firms is "the competitive position of subsidiaries in foreign countries". This is natural since the competitive positions of their subsidiaries (or affiliates) are vital to their survival. Other variables important to all four national groups include "restrictions imposed by foreign countries on repatriation of profits or dividends" and "performance evaluation of foreign subsidiaries".

Some variables were not important to the respondents in any of the four groups. One of them was "risk of expropriation in foreign countries". Another variable was "domestic government requirements on direct foreign investments". It was ranked eighteenth by both the Canadian and U.S. firms and was ranked as the least important variable by the British and Japanese firms.

There were some interesting differences among the four groups. For instance, "the interests of local partners in foreign subsidiaries" was ranked substantially higher by British and Japanese firms than by the Canadian and U.S. companies. Perhaps this can be explained by the differences in investment strategy and ownership policies of foreign joint ventures. The differences between Japanese and U.S. companies in these two respects were most pronounced as explained below.

Many foreign subsidiaries of Japanese firms are located in South Korea, Taiwan, and other developing countries. In fact, over 50 per cent of Japanese overseas investments are in the developing regions of the Far East, Middle East, and Africa.[16] In contrast, over 60 per cent

16. "Japan's Foreign Investments Continue to Soar as MITI Predicts Their Future Course", *Business International* (February 3, 1978).

of American direct foreign investments are in developed countries such as Canada, Australia, and Western Europe.[17] The governments of many developing countries require the local ownership of major portions of the subsidiaries of foreign companies. With regard to ownership policies, a study undertaken by Japan's Ministry of International Trade and Industry (MITI) reported that in over half of the 661 major manufacturing firms surveyed, the Japanese parent companies held only minority positions.[18] By contrast, nearly two-thirds of the subsidiaries of 177 leading U.S. multinational enterprises were majority or wholly owned.

The presence of local partners limits the flexibility of the parent company in determining transfer prices, because the local partners are anxious to obtain the lowest possible transfer prices (for intermediate goods transferred from the parent company) to ensure that the greatest profit accrues to the subsidiary. Yoshino found that transfer prices were a frequent source of conflict between Japanese parent companies and their joint venture partners in foreign subsidiaries.[19] This was especially so during the early stages when those joint ventures were heavily dependent on the Japanese parent companies for supplies of materials and components. This helps explain why the Japanese firms put more emphasis on the interest of local partners than do the U.S. firms.

Compared with the other national groups, Japanese companies placed significantly greater importance on the devaluation and revaluation of foreign currencies. The Japanese have had strong reasons to worry about this. The United States was her most important trading partner when the value of U.S. dollar fell sharply against the Japanese yen in 1977 and 1978. At that time, many Japanese industries saw their international competitiveness shaved away as the rising yen pushed their export prices higher. This problem may have eased somewhat in 1979 as the value of the Japanese yen declined substantially. This was caused mainly by the huge trade deficit (about U.S. $10.5 billion) experienced by Japan in 1979 as a result of skyrocketing oil prices.

Other aspects of transfer pricing systems for the four national groups were also investigated. It was found that systems authority was most centralized in the transfer pricing systems of U.S. firms. Japan had the most restrictive policies governing the outside purchase of raw materials and intermediate goods.

17. "U.S. Total Direct Foreign Investment and Rates of Return, 1971-1976", *Business International* (October 14, 1977).
18. Cited in M. Y. Yoshino, *Japan's Multinational Enterprises* (Cambridge, Mass.: Harvard University Press, 1976), pp. 142-43.
19. *Ibid.*, pp. 148-50.

The empirical evidence shown above supports the contention that the transfer pricing systems of large corporations differ across industrial nations. Nonetheless, the ultimate goals of these systems were strikingly similar from country to country. Profit maximization and performance evaluation were the dominant objectives given for most systems.

Some Guidelines for Managing a Transfer Pricing System

Up to this point, this chapter has been concerned primarily with historical developments and existing transfer pricing practices in the developed nations. In this section, a different perspective will be taken in discussing, from a normative point of view, some general guidelines that should be followed in managing a transfer pricing system.

Transfer pricing is not an end itself, but a means to achieve objectives. One of the most important issues in designing a transfer pricing system is to define the basic goals of the system. Without them, it is fruitless to argue about what transfer pricing methods a company should use. No one method can fill all the needs of a decentralized organization. Each company must select the pricing method or methods which most effectively satisfy the objectives it wishes to achieve through its transfer pricing system. Care must be taken to ensure that the objectives of any transfer pricing system, international or domestic, are compatible with those of the overall management control system of which it is a part.

After a company defines its objectives, a transfer pricing method or methods can be selected to meet those objectives. The system must ensure that actions taken by divisional managers to improve divisional profits also improve the overall company profits.

In international transfer pricing, besides studying the tax rules on transfer pricing, a multinational company should also examine the other aspects of government regulations and restrictions which may have an effect on transfer pricing. At a minimum, the following types of regulations and restrictions should be investigated for each country of interest:

1. Exchange control system — Most developing countries and even some developed nations still have exchange control systems which limit the free movements of funds to and from subsidiaries in these countries.
2. Restrictions on the repatriation of profits, dividends, interest, and royalties — These types of restrictions are still in effect in

some countries. Recent tax regulations in Columbia, for example, eliminate deductions for royalties, interest, and service fees paid to head offices and foreign affiliates.[20] In Guatemala, a deduction for royalties will be allowed up to the extent of 15 per cent of gross income but requires the prior approval of the Ministry of Economy.[21]

3. Antitrust legislation — Many countries have legislation controlling monopolies and restrictive business practices. The legislation may be applied in controlling abuses of a dominant market position occurring as a result of transfer price manipulations. When internal transfer prices are quite different from those charged to unrelated customers, they may be considered as discriminatory against suppliers and users outside of the company.

4. Customs and related legislation — Many governments, especially those in developing countries, are becoming increasingly concerned about transfer pricing manipulations by multinational companies. One way to control the adverse effects of these manipulations is to introduce special safeguards into their customs and related legislation. For example, in Argentina, a false declaration of the value of imported goods is punishable by a fine. Imports are also prohibited when such declarations might result in the improper transfer of foreign exchange abroad or when they entail an infringement of the foreign exchange, monetary, or credit regulations.[22]

Like many other financial control systems, the success of a transfer pricing system depends, to a large extent, upon proper planning and effective administration. A good transfer pricing system cannot be installed overnight. It must be installed gradually. Widen the coverage as experience is gained through implementation. Set initial pricing limits over which bargaining or negotiation can take place so as to prevent undue exploitation of inexperience at the outset.

After the initial testing period, a written policy statement and procedures must be prepared. A uniform and consistent policy not only reduces divisional disputes to a minimum, but also strengthens a company's position with tax and other government authorities. As a minimum, the statement of policy and procedures should cover the following:

20. Price Waterhouse & Co., *Corporate Taxes in 80 Countries* (New York: The Company, 1978), p. 44.
21. *Ibid.*, p. 104.
22. United Nations Conference on Trade and Development, *Dominant Positions of Market Power of Transnational Corporations: Use of the Transfer Pricing Mechanism* (New York: United Nations, 1978), p. 30.

1. objectives of the system;
2. list of products covered;
3. formulas for determining prices;
4. sources of information for determining market prices;
5. policy regarding purchases from outside sources;
6. procedures to be followed in the event of disputes;
7. the role of an arbitration committee or a price arbitrator;
8. review of policy and procedures.

These policies and procedures should be communicated to all divisional managers and to all other personnel affected. These policies should be reviewed and revised as circumstances change.

Summary and Conclusions

This chapter has attempted to explain the nature of transfer pricing problems and the importance of transfer pricing to the Canadian economy. Major findings from empirical studies on transfer pricing practices in the four industrial nations were presented. Some general principles and guidelines for managing a transfer pricing system were also described.

During the last two decades, the problems of transfer pricing have increased in magnitude and complexity, mainly because of the following factors which are still operative today:

1. Large multinational enterprises are expanding their foreign investment.
2. International trade, which consists of a large portion of transfers between related business entities, is increasing.
3. The tax and customs authorities of many countries are intensifying their surveillance of multinational transfer pricing practices.

Together, these developments mean that proper design and effective administration of a multinational transfer pricing system will be crucial for corporate success in a constantly changing international business environment. In addition to achieving the corporate objectives which the system is designed to accomplish, a transfer pricing system must be devised to lessen the firm's vulnerability to attacks by both national or supra-national governmental authorities.

V
International
Operations
Management

E
Recommendations for
the Future

43
Canada's Comparative Advantage: Implications for Industrial Strategy

D. J. Daly

Dr. Daly is professor of economics in the Faculty of Administrative Studies, York University. His areas of research and teaching include economic growth, the competitive position of Canadian manufacturing, and the productivity performance of Japanese manufacturing. His practical experience includes twenty years with the federal government and consulting with some of Canada's largest companies.

This chapter was written expressly for this volume.

This chapter will consider the implications of Canada's comparative advantage for industrial strategy. It is a companion to an earlier chapter (Chapter 3) in this volume, that summarized the means for analysing comparative advantage and the implications for Canada, with comparisons among the main countries of importance in Canada's international trade. It will outline the criteria used, point out that the problems are primarily related to the effective use of resources rather than to inappropriate or inadequate supplies of resources, and consider ways by which the environment for effective use of resources in the key broad industry sectors can be improved.

Criteria for Industrial Performance

The primary criterion that will be used is the level of real output per hour per person employed. These supply-oriented measures provide the basis for real incomes of Canadians, whether the output produced is consumed locally or exchanged in international markets for other goods at prices below the costs for which the items can be produced domestically. The emphasis is on the real incomes of Canadians.

Occasionally suggestions for economic policy are made, but there is no related evidence that the policies proposed are workable. One of the advantages of the approach emphasized here and in earlier chapters is that most of the policy options assessed are being used in one of the countries that has been studied, so the policies are all workable alternatives. In some cases, the environment for those industrial policies may be different, but the feasibility of modifying the elements that are affecting Canadian performance adversely has been considered.

In some cases, Canadian performance has been fairly satisfactory, but the longer-term changes in the world economy may make good performance more difficult in the future than it has been in the past. For example, the mining industry has been an important area of comparative advantage in the past (and this is expected to continue in the future), but mineral products have been a falling share of our world trade for decades, and this is expected to con-

tinue. Other product areas have become more important in world
trade, and some suggestions are proposed that would reduce the
comparative disadvantages that Canada has had in producing those
products profitably at internationally competitive prices.

Factor Supplies

Some indication of the relative importance of the main factors of
production in the Canadian economy can be provided by examining
their share of national income. Labor income, which amounts to 75
to 80 per cent of net national income, is the dominant income source
in net national income in Canada, as it is in the other countries
studied. Non-residential structures and equipment are much less
important, (about 14 per cent of national income during the post-war
period). Non-residential land (including mineral resources) is the least
important of the factors for Canada, (about 4 per cent of national
income).[1]

It is possible using this framework to compare the contributions
that the various factors of production make to the levels of real
national income per person employed in Canada, with corresponding figures for the United States. In an earlier study, only a small part
of the income differences then present were associated with the
differing availabilities of factor supplies per employed person. Larger
quantities of land, mineral resources, and non-residential capital
facilities were available in Canada per person employed than in the
United States. On the other hand, the average level of formal education in Canada was lower, and this has persisted in spite of the
increased expenditures on education of young persons that have
taken place since.

Limited further attention will be given in this chapter to the supply
of the factors of production chapter for several reasons. One reason
is that the quantity and quality of the various elements available to
the average member of the labor force can only be changed slowly in
the future. For example, most members of the labor force do not

1. Dorothy Walters, *Canadian Income Levels and Growth: An International Perspective* (Ottawa: Queen's Printer for the Economic Council of Canada, 1968),
   pp. 27-31 and Dorothy Walters, *Canadian Growth Revisited, 1950-1967* (Ottawa:
   Queen's Printer for the Economic Council of Canada, 1970), p. 59. For a fuller
   discussion of the rationale for using factor shares as weights see D. J. Daly,
   "Combining Inputs to Secure a Measure of Total Factor Input", *International
   Review of Income and Wealth* (March 1972), pp. 27-53. Some smaller income
   shares relating to income from housing, income on foreign investments, and
   inventories are not discussed as they are small and not too closely related to the
   themes being emphasized in this chapter.

continue further formal education after entering the labor force, so the education level of the average labor force participant only changes as older members retire, and the national average is increased by younger members coming in with higher levels of formal education. Change in education levels is a slow process extending over decades. This contributes to a widening or narrowing in intercountry real income differences as the rate of change in formal levels of education in the labor force diverges from the rate of change in the United States or other countries.

A second reason for giving limited further attention to the supplies of the factors of production per employed person is that the primary cause of the lower levels of real national income per person employed is a less effective use of the total resources available in Canada, rather than a difference in composition and level of resources available to the average employed person.[2]

Are Effective Demand Management Policies Sufficient?

The level at which government should try to influence economic decisions is a central issue in considering industrial strategies. One extreme would be for the government to limit its policies to demand management, using aggregate fiscal and monetary policies (and the related implications for balance of payments and exchange rate levels) and to leave the decisions on the industrial composition of employment, real income levels, prices, investment, and plant location to the price system. The other extreme would be to try to encourage product areas or even individual firms that were deemed to be in Canada's national interest and to give incentives and subsidies to encourage the developments regarded as desirable. A third option would be to identify an intermediate level of analysis where imperfections in the market or government policies have inhibited the emergence of internationally competitive and efficient produc-

2. See D. J. Daly and Dorothy Walters, "Factors in Canada — United States Real Income Differences", *International Review of Income and Wealth*, (December 1967), p. 285-309. This early work on the Denison model initiated by the Economic Council of Canada was not continued and no later intercountry comparisons have been made of the relative contribution of differing inputs and outputs in relation to total factor inputs. The real income differences have narrowed since the first estimates were made for 1960, partly because of statistical revisions for that year, but also because of a real narrowing that has taken place in the two decades since then. The developments are not likely to modify the point made in the text that the sources of the remaining real income differences come primarily from lower levels of output in relation to total factor inputs rather than from differences in the input side.

tion units.[3] Each of these options will be briefly considered to see which is the most promising for further investigation.

Aggregate demand policies have received a great deal of emphasis since the 1930s period of high unemployment and low rates of capacity utilization in many of the major industrialized countries. J. M. Keynes and later economists have put heavy emphasis on the current economic situation and short-term outlook as background for discretionary stabilization policies. One of the problems with demand management policies in Canada is that they have been more stimulative than in the United States. This is reflected in more rapid increases in wage rates, labor costs per unit of output, and the GNP deflator in Canada for most of the period from the late 1960s to about 1977. When this happens in a small open economy with a stable exchange rate, all the commodity-producing industries are squeezed by domestic costs that increase more rapidly than alternative sources of supply from abroad. During the above period, the profits in both the export-oriented resource industries and the import-competing sectors of manufacturing were put under even greater pressure by the appreciation of the Canadian dollar from a $7^1/2$ cent discount in the late 1960s to a slight premium in 1974.[4] This squeeze is reflected in lower profits and slower employment increases, and it will become apparent in both export oriented and import competing industries. There will be less of a problem in the domestically oriented industries of construction, trade, and personal services. Industries where the increases in costs originating from overall excess demand can be passed along to domestic buyers which are less open to international competition. This differential experience between internationally oriented commodity industries and domestically oriented trade, service, and construction industries will shift employment and investment from commodity producing industries that are on the margin of being competitive (such as parts of manufacturing and agriculture) into the domestically oriented industries.

It is clear from this example from the Canadian experience of the 1970s that inappropriate macro-policies can have differential impacts on individual industries. There should have been increases in

3. These distinctions are well-known, but Gilles Pacquet had emphasized their relevance for Canada at several recent conferences, the most recent being a presentation on "Adapting to a Changing Competitive Environment" at a Conference Board of Canada session on the medium-term outlook and issues, October 9, 1980 in Toronto.

4. For evidence on the three indicators for both the United States and Canada, see Donald J. Daly, "Weak Links in 'The Weakest Link'", *Canadian Public Policy* (Summer 1979), p. 310. The exchange rate changes are shown regularly in the *Bank of Canada Review.*

international competition from the Kennedy Round tariff reductions and from increased competition from developing countries. However, policies that led to greater domestic inflation plus exchange rate appreciation diminished these increases for some Canadian industries.

Another issue is whether macro-policies that are roughly adequate will be sufficient to ensure high levels of real incomes per person employed both in the aggregate and in some of the major industries. Relative freedom of entry into individual industries and production is a necessary condition for this to happen. This is generally the situation in most Canadian industries (the exceptions being regulated industries such as transportation and communications), although high costs of entry for new firms may be a further impediment for some industries. A further condition to ensure efficiency is a standard rate for tariffs and subsidies in different industries. The presence of higher tariffs or subsidies in particular industries can lead to plants of less efficient scale than prevail in new plants in large markets, and/or a tendency for high product diversity and the resultant high cost and low productivity. These considerations are emphasized in several empirical studies of Canadian manufacturing.[5] If there persists a number of important commodity-producing industries with high costs and low productivity levels, because of the differential impacts of tariff and non-tariff incentives, appropriate macro-policies will *not* eliminate problems either in theory or in practice.

The other extreme is to advocate highly selective policies which would identify particular firms or individual industries that the government should encourage. These policies can arise from a deep distrust of the market system which may be magnified if the major decision makers are in the head offices of parent firms, and if it is assumed that there are major differences between corporate goals and Canadian goals.[6]

There have been historical examples where governments have provided special subsidies or non-tariff barriers to assist individual

---

5. See the summaries referred to in footnote 18 of the earlier chapter by D. J. Daly in this volume.
6. The fullest statement illustrating this point of view is in John N. H. Brutton and James M. Gilmour, assisted by Mark G. Murphy, *The Weakest Link — A Technological Perspective on Canadian Industrial Underdevelopment* (Ottawa: Science Council of Canada, 1978). For detailed criticisms of this study see Daly, "Weak Links in 'The Weakest Link'", pp. 307-317; A. E. Safarian, "Foreign Ownership and Industrial Behavior: A Comment on 'The Weakest Link'",*Canadian Public Policy* (Summer 1979), pp. 318-335; and Kristian S. Palda, *The Science Council's Weakest Link: A Critique of the Science Council's Technocratic Industrial Strategy for Canada* (Vancouver: The Fraser Institute, 1979).

694   Part V International Operations Management

companies or industries. All too frequently, however, the net result is
to support high cost and inefficient production in areas of declining
demand, rather than to lead to world leadership through low-cost
production in innovative high-technology industries. Examples in
recent Canadian history are quotas on the import of clothing and
footwear, and the pricing and import limitation policies on chickens.
In practice, selective subsidies and tariff and non-tariff limits on
imports have been used to support ailing industries with high-cost
and low-productivity production, rather than to encourage efficient
industries.

Another serious practical problem is that there have been no
realistic proposals on how the government could "pick the winner".
It would require an unusual degree of knowledge about future
demand, long-term cost developments at the product and firm level,
managerial capabilities, and developments in world markets to correctly identify the growth firms of the future. This second option of
detailed planning at a precise level of disaggregation seems quite
unrealistic in practice, especially in a small open economy. In light of
the poor performance of the federal government in effective implementation of simpler macro-policies over the past decade, it would
be unwise to give the government increased powers in a more
difficult area. It would involve additional government discretionary
powers that would raise broader questions about the appropriate
role of government.

However, there is a need for some discussion of policies at an
intermediate level, between the broad macro-demand-policies and
the micro-level of the individual product and firm. To set a framework for such discussion, it is desirable to provide a further perspective through broad industry and country patterns on the medium-
term prospects.

Recent Trends and Medium-Term Prospects

Canadian comparative advantage in broad industry and country emphasis has a number of important characteristics. One important
pattern is the high geographic concentration of exports and imports
on the United States, a pattern that is also reflected in international
investment and indebtedness, capital flows, migration, tourist and
business travel, etc. A second important theme is the heavy emphasis
on exports of primary natural resource staple products. A third is the
quantity of imports of manufactured products, largely from the
United States, but also from other industrialized and developing
countries. These themes occur in the discussions of industrial strategies for Canada, and need some examination.

About 70 per cent of Canada's exports and imports take place with the United States, a higher share than in past decades. This market is physically near, and it has the largest total demand and the highest real income per capita in the world (excluding some of the oil exporting countries). It also has a relatively low level of tariffs (on both a nominal and effective tariff basis), limited non-tariff barriers, a largely common language, and many similarities in values and culture. These favorable factors are all aspects of the historical dominance of the United States in Canada's export markets, and are a part of our important advantage in that market.

Recently, trends have been emerging which have implications for the future. One development has been that many other regions and countries have grown more rapidly than the United States over the last three decades. Japan, for example, has already surpassed both Italy and the United Kingdom on per capita basis. Some slow down has taken place since 1973, but the rate of growth continues to be more rapid than the United States and the countries in the European Economic Community (EEC).[7] The economies in Northwest Europe have also grown more rapidly than the United States, and most of the developing countries have had faster growth rates in both population and real incomes. The United States has been experiencing a falling share of world GNP and world exports for some decades and this is expected to continue. The U.S. technological leadership is also being eroded with a slightly declining share of R & D and of scientists engaged in R & D. There is also a declining share of U.S. patents which are granted to domestic inventors and a growing share to foreign inventors.

These trends are important for Canada as the United States has been a major factor in Canadian options and developments. These developments have led to a heavy commitment to a market that has been shrinking in importance, and a limited involvement in other regional markets which are experiencing the most rapid growth and are changing dynamically in technology. However, at present Canadian exports to non-U.S. markets have been heavily oriented to primary products, with limited interest in manufactured products. The present structure of exports suggests that an emphasis on the third option would involve even more emphasis on primary products than at present.

Canada's most important comparative advantage is its endowment of natural resources. The data on the availability of agricultural

7. D. J. Daly, "Japanese Manufacturing: Recent Productivity and Cost Developments, (Mimeo, for the Economic Council of Canada, York University, Downsview, September 1980) and the Denison-Chung study referred to there.

land and mineral resources indicate that Canada has the most favorable endowment of any industrialized nation, a pattern consistent with general knowledge, and with the emphasis in Canadian economic history on the development and export of staples. The statistics for output per person in the Canadian mining industry put levels at more than fifty per cent above the U.S. levels a decade ago, although some narrowing in this difference has since taken place. Agriculture, on the other hand, has levels of output per man that are below the levels in such countries as the United States, Australia, New Zealand, and even Japan (which is regarded as inefficient in agriculture, partly because of the small size of farms and the limitation on imports of agricultural products).[8]

There have been some suggestions that Canada has an undesirably high dependence on natural resource industries and that it would be preferable to see a reduced emphasis in these industries and an increased emphasis on manufacturing. However, such a plan would imply a relative shift away from mining (an area of comparative advantage for Canada) and towards manufacturing (a clear area of comparative disadvantage thus far in the present century). This would cause an economic loss for Canadians as long as the current productivity differentials persist, with no economic gains to be expected.[9]

International trade in mineral, forest, and agricultural products has been a falling share of world trade for decades,[10] and this has been an element of vulnerability in our economy. Having a primary area of comparative advantage in an industrial sector of decreasing importance on a world scale can dampen the growth in real incomes in Canada and will begin to limit the range of options and opportunities. An area of strength can be eroded by the threat of limited further market growth.

The third major characteristic of the Canadian position is the serious comparative disadvantage in manufacturing (as reflected in

8. Saburo Yamada and Vernon W. Ruttan, "International Comparisons of Productivity in Agriculture", John W. Kendrick and Beatrice N. Varrara, ed. *New Developments in Productivity Measurement and Analysis* (Chicago: University of Chicago Press, 1980), pp. 530-531; and Ed Lincoln, "Japanese Agriculture: An Analysis" in *Japan Economic Survey* (Aug. 6, 1980), pp. 2 and 5.

9. For further discussions of the evidence on mining see D. J. Daly, "Mineral Resources in the Canadian Economy: Macro-Economic Implications", Carl E. Beigie and Alfred O. Hero, Jr., ed., *Natural Resources in U.S. Canadian Relations* (Boulder, Colorado: Westview Press, 1980), pp. 125-165; and Daly, "Weak Links on 'The Weakest Link'", pp. 307-317 and other references to the views of the Science Council on industrial strategy and footnote 6.

10. D. J. Daly, *Canada's Comparative Advantage* (Ottawa: Economic Council of Canada, 1979), pp. 71-75 and the analytical and statistical sources cited therein.

low-productivity levels and high-unit costs in a majority of the individual industries within manufacturing). Levels of output per man-hour in the majority of individual industries within manufacturing have remained below comparable levels in the United States for decades, although some narrowing in these disparities took place in the 1970s. However, the increases in total compensation per hour have been so much greater in Canada than in the United States that total costs per unit in domestic currencies have increased much more in Canada. An important easing in the competitive pressures on domestic manufacturers from foreign sources of supply has taken place with the decline in the relative value of Canadian currency. This exchange rate change has also led to a dramatic improvement in the profits of most natural resource exporters, as the receipts from sales are converted into Canadian dollars. The exchange rate changes have not led to any fundamental correction of the deep-seated and continuing comparative disadvantages in Canadian manufacturing.

World trade in manufactured products has had a growing share in domestic production and world exports for some decades. This is because of an increase in specialization within individual industries rather than an increase in world production and consumption of manufactured products. Some of these same tendencies have begun to emerge in individual Canadian manufacturing industries, but this process has not gone nearly as far as in the United States, the EEC, or Japan. Manufacturing has emerged as the most rapidly expanding area in international trade; but it is also the area in which Canada's comparative disadvantages are most pronounced.[11] Domestic manufacturing resulting from low productivity levels are bound to limit Canada's potential for export growth in the most dynamic areas of world trade.

Capital and Technological Change in Manufacturing

An important theme in this and the related earlier chapter in this volume has been the persistent lower levels of output per man-hour in domestic manufacturing than in comparable industries in the

---

11. For earlier discussions of Canadian manufacturing see D. J. Daly and S. Globerman, *Tariff and Science Policies: Applications of a Model of Nationalism* (Toronto: University of Toronto Press, 1976); D. J. Daly, "Remedies for Increasing Productivity Levels in Canada", Shlomo Maital and Noah M. Meltz, ed., *Lagging Productivity Growth Causes and Remedies* (Cambridge: Ballinger, 1980), pp. 223-245; D. J. Daly, "Further Improving Manufacturing Productivity in Canada", *Cost and Management* (July-August 1980), pp. 14-20 and additional references in footnotes 6 and 10 above.

United States. A clearer diagnosis of the reasons for this performance should precede any policy discussions or initiatives to correct the problems.

One influence on productivity levels and growth is the role of capital in that process. An increased degree of mechanization (capital deepening) has clearly been one of the sources of the increased productivity and the higher living standards that began with the industrial revolution in the United Kingdom some three centuries ago. An increase in the capital stock per person (measured in prices of some base year and reflecting the amount of net new investment over many years past) has been a part of the real income growth in the main industrialized countries since the Second World War. Although this is a significant element, its importance is frequently exaggerated by the business community. The modest size of the contribution of capital to economic growth reflects the low share of this aspect of capital in national income (10.9 per cent over the period).[12] From 1968 to 1975, profits before taxes were a modest 6.7 per cent of total assets in the non-financial corporate sector, below long-term corporate bond yields.

The same procedures to examine the sources of economic growth per person over time can be used to analyse the reasons for any differences in output per person between countries at a point in time. A comparison of the size of the capital stock per person in Canadian manufacturing with that in the United States shows an even *higher* level in Canada, and the degree of difference has increased since the 1960s. By the mid-1970s the quantity of machinery and equipment per employee was about one-third higher in Canadian manufacturing than in the United States.[13] Canada was the most capital-intensive country in the world, but the problems of low output per man-hour continued in spite of a large amount of capital per worker. The capital-intensive nature of the production process was due to past incentives to investment from the tariff, corporate tax incentives (such as fast write offs of capital assets through depreciation allowances), and tax encouragements to personal savings. The marked increase in capital stock per person employed has not caused a comparable increase in corporate profits. Net profits *before*

12. Edward F. Dension, *Accounting for Slower Economic Growth in the United States in the 1970's* (Washington: The Brookings Institution, 1979), pp. 49 and 94.
13. James G. Frank, *Assessing Trends on Canada's Competitive Position: The Case of Canada and the United States* (Ottawa: The Conference Board in Canada, 1977), p. 113 and additional discussion and alternative estimates for international capital stock comparisons in Daly, *Canada's Comparative Advantage* (see publication details in footnote 10), pp. 14-17.

taxes are lower (in relation to total assets in manufacturing) than corporations would have to pay on borrowings from banks or in the capital market. Valuation of depreciation allowances at replacement cost of the assets rather than historic cost would further reduce rates of return in manufacturing. As the private sector does not appear to be using the existing capital facilities very effectively (viewed both in relation to profits and productivity), it would seem quite inappropriate to propose additional incentives to encourage even more capital intensiveness.

It is important to consider the main sources of technological change, and assess Canadian performance in each of these main areas. The three main sources of technological change that have emerged in the quantitative studies of economic growth in the main industrialized countries are: the speed of introduction of new technology; the possible influence of the development location of new technology; and the influence of shifting labor and other resources from low paying industries to higher paying alternatives. Each of these potential growth sources will be outlined, followed by an assessment of the degree to which each has been a factor in Canada's performance.

New technology in the operation of both factories and offices (such as computers, data processing, and miniature transistors), and new approaches to organization, motivation, and morale have been developing throughout the world in recent decades. The numbers of articles, books, journals, and of scientific and professional people have been growing at rates well beyond previous historical experience (even after recognizing that some slowing down appears to have begun in a number of countries in the 1970s). Knowledge is now more quickly and widely diffused by faster and cheaper methods of transportation and communication. A higher level of education permits the fast assimilation and implementation of new knowledge. However, unless this new knowledge is implemented within organizations, it only provides intellectual satisfaction and has no impact on productivity and its associated benefits (lower prices to consumers and higher real incomes to the participants in the process of production).

One of the sources of concern about the implementation of new technology in Canada is the slowness of the diffusion process in domestic manufacturing. A number of studies indicated that new technology was adopted more slowly in Canada than in the United States. There are a number of possible reasons for this. There are costs and risks associated with implementing new technology, and these costs are less per unit of output if the initial overhead and implementation costs can be spread over a larger market than the smaller Canadian domestic market. The tariff reduces the competition from imports, and the lower value of the Canadian dollar dating from the latter part of the 1970s further moderated those pressures and encouraged some recovery in corporate profits. Furthermore, there seems to be some resistance to change on the part of Canadian management. A high proportion of top managers come from the existing elite. They tend to move into managerial positions later in their careers (at both middle and senior levels), and to have lower levels of university education (especially in fields related to business and science). These influences lead to less openness to change on the part of management.[14]

Thus far very little attention appears to have been paid to the implication of those findings. This is a very serious neglect in the light of the available evidence.

It is widely recognized that Canadian firms tend to spend relatively less on R & D, employ fewer scientific workers in relation to total employed, have produced very few significant innovations since 1945, receive limited receipts for patents, and have limited exports of research-intensive products. This partly reflects the high probability that it is cheaper to purchase the technology needed, than to produce it within Canada and have to recover these costs in a small market. Adaptation at the engineering and detailed design level and learning by doing can be just as important (if not more important) in improving productivity.

Canadian policy has placed heavy emphasis on encouraging the development of new technology within Canada. This is demonstrated by the establishment of the Ministry of State for Science and Technology, the creation of a variety of tax incentives (IRDIA, PAIT, DIP, IDAP), and the announced goal to encourage an increase to 1.5 per cent of GNP in research and development expenditures, significantly above recent levels, where this ratio has been declining for more than a decade. Studies of the effects of such government programs in Europe and Japan indicate no statistical significance in the proportion of successful and unsuccessful projects. It is also significant that an important number of new innovations arise quite accidentally as a by-product of attempting something quite different.[15]

14. Fuller documentation is provided in the references in footnotes 10 and 11 and D. J. Daly, "Canadian Management: Past Recruitment and Future Training Needs", (Downsview: York University).
15. T. J. Allen et al., "Government Influence on the Process of Innovation in Europe and Japan", *Research Policy* (1978), pp. 124-149 and additional references in footnote 6 above.

What is the point of encouraging the development of new technology in Canada with the use of both government and private funds, if there is no early implementation of any eventually commercially successful projects within Canada? The only real beneficiaries of any such incentives are the scientists who are involved in research and development, and their incomes are already above the national average.

Scientists, the universities, the government, and the Science Council of Canada need to deal with this issue more directly in the future. Their credibility among informed observers will continue to be eroded if they continue to ignore the accumulating evidence on Canadian performance and on technological diffusion.

A third important factor in productivity growth occurs when factors shift from low income earning industries and regions, to higher income alternatives. Such low incomes can arise if productivity levels are low, or if the demand for the output produced in those sectors is low or growing slowly. Low incomes during industrialization is, in many countries, associated with low incomes in agriculture. Productivity levels have frequently increased as rapidly in agriculture as in the non-agricultural sectors. However, expenditures on food per capita (as measured by calorie count for pounds of food) have not increased as rapidly as expenditures on non-agricultural products and services in response to higher real incomes. To use the terminology of economists, the income elasticity of the demand for agricultural products is low. This is reflected eventually in low incomes to agriculture that persist even with significant shifts to higher incomes elsewhere.

The shift out of agriculture was an important source of growth in Canada from the 1920s to early in the 1970s. As recently as 1946, agriculture included about one-fourth of the labor force. This had declined to about one-twenty-fifth three decades later. Since then, employment in agriculture has begun to increase for almost the first time in four decades. This partially reflects the effects of government measures, such as increased Canadian Dairy Commission payments, the effect of milk marketing boards, and increased trade barriers (such as that on imported poultry).

Government measures seem designed to delay or prevent the adjustment to change, rather than to facilitate the adjustment to new and more remunerative alternatives. Such measures are not limited to agriculture. Import quotas have been introduced in clothing, textiles, and shoes, and the government is being pressured to limit or prevent plant closures or support such ailing companies as Chrysler of Canada and Massey-Ferguson. These measures provide support and incentives for weak companies, industries, and regions. The policy choices are either to prop up the losers or to pick the winners. The Canadian government is choosing to support the losing and decaying industries. As *The Globe and Mail* editorialized: "This is the kind of daring Government industrial policy that will ensure that we continue to rise to the bottom of the heap."[16]

Policies have sometimes been proposed to identify industries as dynamic, solid, or mature (the latter including uncompetitive and slow-growth sectors). Government policies would concentrate on shifting resources into the high-growth, high-technology industries. There are two fundamental problems with this approach for Canada. For one thing, it would put Canadian firms into head-on competition with major firms already exporting from large domestic market bases. Secondly, it ignores the evidence that Canada has some important areas of comparative advantage on the natural resource side but has serious disadvantages in the areas of managerial and engineering skills and small market size. These factors suggest that there is limited scope for successfully exporting high-technology products on a widespread basis, although Canadian companies with enterprising management and the necessary technical expertise can find successful market niches for particular products.

Options for Commercial Policy

A recurrent theme in this chapter and the earlier one in this volume is the influence of a small market on productivity, costs, the speed of adoption of new technology, and management. This is particularly important for a small country like Canada. One of the important developments in industrial economies during the post-war period was the emergence of the European Common Market. It achieved complete free trade in industrial products for the initial six countries in 1968 and full membership for Britain, Denmark, and Ireland in 1973. Other Mediterranean countries were negotiating entry at the start of the 1980s. This would leave Canada as one of the few high-income industrialized countries that did not have access to a market of 100 million people or more on a free trade basis. The potential gains to Canada from free trade on just a Canada-U.S. basis are estimated at 8.2 per cent of real GNP in the mid-1970s.[17] Part of these gains will accrue during the 1980s, as the reductions negotiated under the Tokyo Round are gradually implemented.

16. *The Globe and Mail* (Oct. 13, 1980), p. 6, "Let's Back a Winner".
17. R. J. Wonnacott, *Canada's Trade Options* (Ottawa: Information Canada, 1975), p. 177.

A major part of the gains expected from the reductions negotiated will come about through increased specialization and longer runs in individual plants, and through increased purchases of materials from other suppliers (both domestically and in foreign markets). Such adjustments are relatively easy to accomplish on the production side, but little analysis has been done on the marketing implications especially the sale of increased output of selected products.

On the basis of statistical studies of tariff reduction for Canada and other countries, and from the experience of individual countries in Europe during the process of adjusting to free trade, we can expect that wide-scale closing of plants or companies, or the disappearance of individual industries, is not likely to occur. Companies are more likely to disappear from unwillingness to change on the part of management, persistence of low productivity, or slow market growth than from tariff reductions.

In any case, it would be preferable to facilitate the retraining of workers and assist their movement rather than to prevent such changes by retaining the tariffs or replacing them with non-tariff barriers as the tariffs are reduced.

Summary and Conclusions

The analysis above recognizes that macro-policies can help provide a stable environment within which more specific policies can be introduced. However, even these have not been too successful in the industrialized market economies. Most of them have experienced high unemployment, moderate price increases, and recurrent balance of payments problems (of either strength or weakness) during the 1970s.

On the other hand, highly disaggregated attempts to identify the more promising companies for the 1990s are unlikely to be successful. Picking the winner is very hard in a democracy. The risks are high that the government will provide support for the losers — who are much easier to identify. When the option in a marginal riding is productivity or jobs, the politician is tempted to maintain people in jobs with low productivity, low earnings, low profits, and management which is too old mentally to undertake new assignments.

At the industry level, many Canadian industries have higher levels of machinery and equipment and construction than in the United States. These large and growing capital facilities have not led to increases in output comparable to earlier periods since 1973. Corporate profits before taxes have been less than 7 per cent from 1968 to 1975 (less than what they could have been from investing in mortgages). The government and the private sector should give high priority to increasing output with existing labor and capital rather than trying to develop tax incentives to increase capital facilities.

There seems to be little justification to encourage more R & D in Canada. Both Canadian-owned and foreign-owned companies say that it is more profitable and economical to buy the latest technology abroad (where it is readily available) than trying to produce it internally. The government aspiration to have Canadian R & D up to 1.5 per cent of GNP by the middle of the 1980s is not likely to be achieved and does not seem that attractive as a goal.

In the short term, it is undesirable to try to encourage a shift of resources out of mining and into manufacturing, as it would involve a shift of resources away from an area of comparative advantage that helps finance the large deficit in trade in manufactured products.

There are, however, more promising avenues for Canadian policy. The recent tariff reductions on a multilateral basis were quite comprehensive. They will lead to further improvements in productivity in Canadian manufacturing through increased specialization. It is to be hoped that any small adjustments at the company and plant level will be facilitated rather than resisted, and that the tariff reductions are not replaced by non-tariff barriers in Canada and elsewhere.

Higher priority can be given by both companies and governments to the faster adoption of new technology. This topic has not had the attention it deserves, but it is of far more importance to the buyer, both in Canada and in the export market. Inertia and resistance to change have been important obstacles here, and Canadian management at all levels has a special responsibility to aim at faster adoption in the future.

It is also important to facilitate the shift of resources from low-income industries, firms, occupations, and regions to other areas with higher paying alternatives. This can be accomplished through adequate growth in the major industrialized countries and a more stable environment that encourages rather than inhibits growth domestically. Retraining policies, good information on the labor market, and paid moving expenses to new jobs will all help.

What are the chances that such policies will find active support from the Canadian government in the early 1980s? As a group, the new cabinet is reported to be the most nationalistic and most sympathetic to government intervention of any cabinet in history. Senior representatives of finance and business find communication with the government frustrating and difficult. Consultations on industrial strategies have had limited impact on decision making. The premier of a major province has been openly critical of the Japanese for not buying enough manufactured products, even though the Japanese have been asking for quality products at competitive prices and have been concerned about the confrontation style in both labor-management and federal-provincial negotiations in Canada.

There is a risk that the pressures of nationalism and protectionism in Canada and other countries could reverse the trends to increased specialization and productivity in Canadian manufacturing that have slowly been developing over the last two decades.

V
International Operations Management

E
Recommendations for the Future

44
Canada's Future Economic and Trading Relations

Randolph E. Ross
Peter M. Banting

Dr. Ross is associate professor of international business at McMaster University. He is the author of many articles, and he has served as a consultant to governmental agencies and private corporations.

Peter Banting is professor of marketing at McMaster University, and vice-president of the Academy of Marketing Science. The author of more than sixty articles and several books, including *Marketing in Canada* and *Canadian Marketing: A Case Approach*, he has broad experience advising Canadian and foreign governments and industries.

This chapter was written expressly for this volume.

What must Canada do as a nation if she wishes to change her current world position? Present concerns about the structure of Canadian interrelationships with the world economic community suggest that deeply rooted patterns must be changed if Canada is to improve her economic status. This chapter reports the results of a study undertaken to determine what types of research would be of greatest benefit to Canada's economic development.

A group of distinguished business executives, government officials, and academics participated in a year-long Delphi study, which was used to both generate and evaluate a large number of research projects of benefit to Canada's future economic and trading relations. The results reported here are presented not as individual research projects, but rather as a synthesis of the concepts underlying the proposed research projects that were generated by our study.

Broad Scale Considerations

Any consideration of Canada's future international trade position must first take into account the broad issues of her current position and limitations. This research study identified a number of macro-areas requiring study if future options are to be fully explored. These have been grouped under the categories: resources, resource-related industry, capability, market diversification, product competitiveness, liberalized trade, and rationalization of intergovernmental policies.

Resources
Rapid changes have taken place in worldwide supply and demand for Canada's traditional natural resource products. These changes have been initiated by increased exploration, foreign government development policies, offshore limits at sea, population changes, increased industrialization, exhaustion of foreign domestic-base supplies, and political disturbances, to name a few. As Canada makes investment plans for her resource industries, both industrialists and politicians must be aware of where the future global shortages and surpluses are likely to be. Two of the specific areas suggested by the panel are Canada's future forestry management and the impact of grain export

policies on the domestic livestock industry. In short, it requires careful planning not only to marshal resources to meet export demands, but also to provide long-term stability in both foreign sales and domestic needs.

Resource-Related Industry Development

The development of Canada's natural resource industries was such that the equipment, machinery, and certain infrastructure elements required in the early days had to be purchased from other countries. This pattern has not changed significantly, even though Canada has grown and acquired the domestic technical know-how to facilitate her resource industries. Capital equipment is still purchased from abroad, to a great extent, rather than being designed and manufactured by Canadian companies. The unfortunate result is that, in areas where our natural resource abundance should lead to the development of Hirschman linkages and their resultant contributions to Canada's trade in such equipment and services abroad, little development has taken place.

Canada could develop capital goods industries related to such areas as forestry, mining, exploration, fish and animal processing, grain milling, storage facilities, transportation and distribution systems, and so on. These, in turn, could gain relatively easy access to foreign markets by piggybacking their marketing efforts on the sales of the natural resource materials and thereby improving the value added component of our exports.

Capability

While the areas identified under Resources, above, may suggest opportunities for development, their rapid exploitation is likely to be hindered by a number of factors, most of which stem from domestic conditions. One project identified the following impeding conditions:

1. discrepancies between federal and provincial governments (mostly caused by politics);
2. an inadequate transportation and shipping system (rail, ports, merchant fleet);
3. a labor force plagued by frequent strikes, and comparatively overpriced in world labor markets;
4. a relatively small population and a relatively small proportion of highly-skilled labor;
5. export and import tariffs, quotas, and barriers imposed by Canadian or foreign sources;
6. lack of Canadian capital and/or guidelines regarding the integration of foreign capital and business management;

7. ecological constraints of the fragile environment of the Canadian North.

For example, a different project pointed out that there are indications that the Canadian reputation in meeting delivery quotas and dates is declining. Reliability has always been an important factor in expanding and maintaining markets. In this regard, yet another project indicated that, except for whole shiploads, Canadian exporters are still subject to space limitations, delays, trans-shipment surcharges, and other problems associated with inadequate shipping, especially to non-European destinations.

A possible approach to measuring the impact of these constraints might utilize such simulation models as Statistics Canada's CANDIDE or MIT — Forrester's DYNAMO. However, to overcome these constraints on our capabilities requires the development and implementation of new and aggressive national policies to be developed and implemented.

Diversification of Markets
For several years, an explicit policy objective of the federal government has been to achieve greater diversification of Canada's export markets, mainly by urging the business community to devote more effort to exploring and exploiting opportunities outside North America. While some firms have been quite successful in penetrating "new" markets, Canada's export statistics have yet to show any significant increase in market diversification, with the exception of British Columbia exports to Japan. Although this is a long-term goal, time alone is unlikely to produce the desired results. There are several possible reasons for delays in diversification. These include management's biased assessments of various market prospects, shortage of company resources required to explore other export opportunities adequately, lack of effective government support measures, etc. It is not until these reasons are identified more clearly and their significance is assessed that progress towards achieving greater diversification can be expected.

To understand the difficulties in diversification, the panel repeatedly recommended research studies of various areas of the world. These studies, however, were not focussed on government policy. Rather they illustrated the need for concrete, pragmatic studies of the day-to-day commercial requirements facing international marketers.

The federal government cannot prevent dependence on the U.S market. Pragmatic measures must be taken at the enterprise level. For example, to expand into markets in less developed countries requires a total change in management attitudes and cultural assumptions.

Other factors such as absence of foreign exchange coverage, lack of foreign language capability, inadequate capital to overcome non-tariff barriers, and other unrecognized obstacles must be identified before remedial programs and policies can be developed to foster diversification of Canada's foreign market.

Product Competitiveness

A frequently identified problem in Canada's export structure is its reliance on the sale abroad of raw materials. Major industrial nations of the world use these in processing and manufacturing, thereby capitalizing upon them in terms of value added. This raises two questions: Should Canada continue to export a high percentage of unprocessed items? Or is it feasible to increase the proportion of downstream processing and manufacturing of our natural resources?

There exist compelling — but not insurmountable — reasons for our lag in the export of secondary manufactured goods and consumer products generally. Relatively high production costs, extended transport distances within Canada as well as to distant foreign countries, unfavorable productivity levels in comparison to those of the United States and other industrialized countries, high import tariffs imposed on our merchandise, and lack of trading aggressiveness on the part of Canadian manufacturers all combine to restrict our economy and enshrine the cliché of our reputation as "hewers of wood and drawers of water".

One technique for effecting a shift, which was highly valued by business and government respondents, is a combination of export controls and a two-price system.

At present, Canadian raw materials are sold in the domestic market at world market prices, giving no margin of advantage to Canadian manufacturers. Other industrialized countries, purchasers of our raw materials, are often more competitive in third markets than Canadian manufacturers. A two-price system would offer Canadian manufacturers a cost improvement on Canadian raw materials vis-à-vis some of our world competitors, thereby permitting a more advantageous selling price for Canadian finished goods in the world market.

Beyond the basic question of this sector shift is the more fundamental issue of the competitiveness of Canadian products. To quote one panel member:

> To most foreigners, Canada is still very much a producer and exporter of raw materials, despite the significant changes in the structure of the Canadian economy and the gradual, though limit-

ed, increase in our manufactured exports in recent years. Diversifying the product base of our exports is essentially a slow process mainly because most newly established industries must first overcome the difficulties of achieving price competitiveness in world markets. In addition to these difficulties, however, there is also the resistance which "new" Canadian products are likely to encounter from foreign customers — industrial and consumer. This is especially significant for highly differentiated products where achieving price competitiveness alone will not automatically change foreigners' image of Canadian manufactures. Indeed, to the extent that foreign customers maintain an unfavorable image of a Canadian product, achieving price competitiveness becomes even more difficult.

One of the means by which Canadian manufacturers can improve the image of our products and differentiate them from global competition is through industrial design. Because of an abundance of natural resources, together with heavy foreign investment, Canadian industry has neglected to develop a strong orientation toward industrial design. Meanwhile, nations with sparse natural resources, such as Japan and the Scandinavian countries, have created global market opportunities through the development of unique industrial design niches.

Even with the advantage of better industrial design, continuation of low- and medium-technology manufacturing is seen by many respondents as the wrong approach. The argument is that the high growth and high profit industries in Canada belong to a small group of young, highly technological firms, which have been able to overcome material cost disadvantages, trade barriers, and unfavorable foreign exchange rates by offering extremely innovative and unique products and services in global markets. They argue that Canada's growth and future economic competitiveness will depend upon her ability to encourage the incorporation of more of these young, rapid growth, high-technology firms.

Rationalized Intergovernmental Policies

A unique aspect of Canada, as a major industrial trading nation, is the apparent disagreement between provincial and federal policies, objectives, and goals. This hampers our ability to present a consistent policy position relative to trading, investment, and industrial development. Thus, foreign businessmen and governments, when negotiating with political bodies in Canada, at times find the stated positions to be in conflict. Rather than becoming embroiled in domestic political issues, these foreign companies and government officials simply withdraw and do not engage in further negotiations. As our major trading partners increasingly approach the issue of international economic relations in terms of matters belonging to the central government rather than individual companies, Canada's ability to bargain is significantly weakened by a lack of public sector consensus.

Liberalized Trade

Canada has long been an advocate of freer trade and an ardent supporter of GATT. Canada has traditionally relied more on tariffs as protection for her industries than on the many, and more subtle, forms of non-tariff barriers favored by her principal trading partners. As tariffs are reduced, Canada is left increasingly vulnerable to crippling market disruptions from imports. These are accentuated in periods of surplus capacity and during times when Canada experiences balance-of-payment problems with her trading partners.

The small size of the Canadian market makes it particularly vulnerable. Such loss of the domestic market base has been, and will continue to be, an important deterrent to expansion in many Canadian industries. This, in turn, weakens her export capabilities as well.

There may be a need for Canada to develop safeguards against such market disruption. These safeguards should be:

* compatible with GATT rules;
* effective;
* capable of prompt activation;
* established prior to granting further tariff reductions.

It is noteworthy that U.S. trade legislation currently before Congress, while granting authority for substantial tariff reductions, also deals extensively with the strengthening of already comprehensive safeguard measures.

There was general agreement among panel respondents that Canada should fully understand the costs of unqualified support of "free trade" as it is practiced in today's world, and become more activist in her direct intervention with the free flow of goods in a way that is similar to the responses that other governments have made regarding such liberalization of trade.

Investment and Trade

The impact of capital on the trading position of Canada must be viewed in the context of both direct foreign investment in Canada and Canadian direct investment abroad.

On the capital importation side, the panel identified a number of issues which may limit Canada's exporting horizons. A common generalization is that foreign ownership of many large Canadian industries has impeded technological innovation in Canada in a number of ways, including:

1. Most research and development is performed at the "home office" with minor product adaptation the only R & D function resident in Canada.
2. Business planning, product design, plant layouts, etc., are performed partly or entirely outside Canadian borders.
3. These result in assembly-line-type, relatively low-skilled jobs together with restrictions on the development of upper level managerial skills.
4. Canadian plants are frequently restricted from exploiting export markets as this would conflict with the overall interests of the multinational company.
5. The process of technological transfer is both fostered (by the importation of know-how, products, and processes) and impeded (because a minimum of industrial R & D is performed here with the result that few products or processes originate in Canada).

In terms of capital exports, the experience of a number of advanced countries during the post-war years has shown that foreign direct investment is one of the most potent weapons that a country can use to protect its market position and to exploit more fully the opportunities available in foreign countries. Canada, itself a major recipient of foreign direct investment for several decades, has made some direct investment in foreign ventures through both Crown corporations and the private sector. But to the vast majority of Canadian firms, including many which conceivably can benefit from it, foreign direct investment appears to occupy a very low priority as a means of doing business outside Canada.

Many countries, particularly in the developing Third World, are becoming increasingly protective of domestic production and services at the same time as they are also circumscribing foreign investment in their countries. These factors make it increasingly difficult to break into and maintain, let alone enlarge, a position in many foreign markets at a time when Canada is trying to reduce dependence on traditional markets.

Improving Small Enterprise Trade

The majority of Canadian-owned companies (as opposed to subsidiaries of foreign parents) are relatively small and engaged almost exclusively in the domestic market. An old and continuing issue in Canada is how to encourage these firms to increase their participation in foreign markets. Many panelists suggested comparative studies of firms which have successfully exported in contrast to those which have not made such a commitment. Others have suggested that contrasting information be sought regarding firms which sell overseas versus those which restrict their exports to the United States. These studies would reveal enterprise profiles along such attributes as: resource commitment to export departments, willingness to customize products for export markets, geographic location, attitudes toward support from Canadian banks and other financial institutions, sensitivity to foreign culture characteristics, ability and willingness to explore overseas markets, definition of market scope, management perception of risks in selling abroad, and so on.

If these profiles show any clear delineation between exporters and others, such information could be of enormous value in directing areas of emphasis and, perhaps, reshaping the programs of the various government agencies which seek to improve Canadian export performance.

In addition to profile analysis, several other issues were suggested by the panel. It was felt that investigation of how well our products are promoted in trade shows, and by trade commissioners, would be a positive future direction. The ability of smaller firms to cope with such entry strategies as joint ventures, licensing agreements, etc. or to accept other forms of payment such as bartering, were felt to be potentially beneficial areas of investigation.

It is clear that if we wish Canadian-owned industry to increase its global presence, the constraints facing small enterprises must be addressed.

Grouping for Export

The respondents identified three fundamental modes of association for improving export performance. These are export consortia, trading companies, and producer cartels. Whatever form it may take, grouping for export was assigned leading importance of all the research issues suggested to improve Canada's future trading position.

As has already been mentioned, many Canadian companies, of all sizes, tend to be diffident about aggressively selling overseas — whether due to distances, difficulty of communication, language barriers, extra political and business risks, reluctance to cope with extra documentation and paper work, the slow initial returns on breaking into strange markets, costs of travel, or the shortage of experienced export managers. The limited initial prospects for sales also may discourage foreign agents from taking on new Canadian lines. Thus, Canadian firms tend to concentrate their sales efforts on the easier Canadian and U.S. markets. There may be a role for more Canadian foreign trading companies which could share these costs and risks, apply professional selling techniques, and present a common front for Canadian manufactured goods and engineering services in foreign markets. Canada seems to lag behind other industrial countries (for example, Japan) in this field, although a few Canadian groups such as Alcan Trading, Seaboard Lumber Sales, and Canatom are already active in the area.

When trading companies and export consortia are proposed for Canada, the assumption that they apply mainly to manufactured goods is too readily made. Nonetheless, Canada cannot afford to be without alternative strategies for the marketing of its raw materials in a world where prices are decreasingly set by open market negotiations. In very few commodities can Canadian producers or government take action without reference to other producers. In a situation where there is an apparent tendency towards increasing governmental intervention in price setting and trade directions, the Canadian government would benefit from having feasibility studies on the advantages and disadvantages of combining with other raw material exporting countries.

In short, where small companies with small domestic markets and limited resources wish to compete in the global arena against large economic concerns, such as the Eastern European State Trading Organizations, multinational enterprises, and Japanese Sogo Shosha, they must find a way to meet their opposition on a more equal ground through some form of association.

Conclusion

The beginning of this chapter asked the question: what must Canada do as a nation if she wishes to change her current world position? While we have attempted to synthesize the threads of our respondents' many and varied suggested research proposals, it is still apparent that the amalgam of concepts is somewhat fragmented. We believe that underlying all of the proposed approaches there is a fundamental need for Canada to introduce basic structural changes consistent with a newly established identity and mission for itself in the world economic community.

While these structural changes are as varied as rationalizing government policies, restructuring tax and competition legislation, the

education of future managers in trade affairs, and the designation
of favored industries despite political repercussions, they must be
arrived at through some form of national consensus — that is, an
agreed-upon national strategy. For example, if Canada were to undertake the development of energy-intensive industry, it would require
the support of energy-producing provinces to supply lower-priced
domestic energy (vis-à-vis world prices) and to encourage further
development of energy production.

Japan has shown the world that successful international competition
is as much a result of a common sense of national destiny as of economics. Canada appears to be facing the future with a fractional
approach. What Canada must do is "get her national act together".

V
International Operations Management

E
Recommendations for the Future

45
Strengthening Canada Abroad: Summary and Recommendations

Export Promotion Review Committee

The material in this chapter originally appeared in Export Promotion Review Committee, *Strengthening Canada Abroad*, 1979. Reprinted by permission of the minister of Supply and Services Canada.

If Canada's balance of trade is to improve significantly, a fundamental change is needed in the economic climate for Canadians doing business abroad. Export financing and taxation of export earnings in Canada are not competitive with those of other major trading nations; export promotion programs are impeded by regulatory procedures; and too few exportable products are designed and developed in Canada. The situation is aggravated by lack of co-ordination and consequent failure to ensure the sharper focus and more decisive thrust needed in foreign trade. Relative to other leading nations, not only is business-government co-ordination deficient, but also co-ordination between the various federal agencies that represent Canada abroad — and between federal and provincial governments.

These are some of the major problems that have surfaced from several months of field work carried out by the Export Promotion Review Committee. Submissions have been received from 170 firms and associations from Newfoundland to British Columbia. Interviews have been held with provincial governments, national associations, and key agencies of the federal government. The excellent co-operation of so many organizations in submitting briefs and otherwise assisting the work of the committee is evidence of a broad interest in improving Canada's export performance. If, therefore, the government acts quickly to improve the general framework for Canadian firms doing business abroad there is likely to be a swift and healthy response from Canadian managers.

It would come none too soon. Canada's international payments' position has been deteriorating throughout the 1970s, partly because of her economic growth which has exceeded that of many other countries, and partly because of her enormous reliance on technology from abroad and the consequent huge trade deficit in technology intensive manufactured goods. It seems we have coasted for years on our raw materials while imports of manufactured goods have climbed inexorably, reaching $30 billion in 1978 for a manufacturing deficit of $12 billion. The current account position began to get out of control in 1975 when the deficit jumped to $5 billion, a figure which has persisted each year since and which has been compensated by net external borrowing with annual interest commitments. The effect of this on the service account has been dramatic. By 1980, it is expected that a trade surplus of $10 billion will be needed to offset the ballooning service deficit if the current account is to be balanced.

What are the chances of so massive an increase in Canada's exports over the next five years or so? Not good at first glance. The medium-term outlook for the economies of our major trading partners is not encouraging. Such growth as there is appears to be in the Far East, the OPEC nations, and certain developing countries, and largely in the form of major turnkey capital projects. But, if the major economies are not growing and the arena of international trade is becoming more competitive, what are the chances of Canada increasing her exports by increasing her market share of world trade? Could Canadian exports grow at the expense of others? We believe so! In part because, for the last decade, others have been growing at our expense (Canada's share of the global export market for manufactured goods has slipped from 5.9 per cent in 1967 to 4.6 per cent in 1977). And also because the currency adjustments of the last two years have improved the international competitiveness of Canadian industry and made possible a reversal of this pattern.

The thrust of the committee's recommendations, therefore, is to go for growth in exports and to do it by improving the competitiveness of export services and the innovativeness of Canadian industry to the point that Canadian-based firms have positive incentives equal to or better than the incentives other nations offer to their firms. Because our international payments position has deteriorated so much, we recommend that serious consideration also be given to selective, low-key programs to encourage Canadian-based firms to manufacture in Canada certain products that are now heavily imported. For many firms, a significant share of the domestic market is a necessary prerequisite to export activity. As it is, Canada imports more manufactured goods per capita than any other industrialized nation, and in many areas lacks the in-house technology needed to manufacture them at home. Perhaps this is a luxury we can no longer afford. The committee endorses the efforts of the government to persuade other nations to reduce their non-tariff barriers to trade and open their markets more to competition from Canada. Pending success in this effort, Canada should reduce the openness of its own market, especially in the purchasing policies of its government and utilities.

The committee also recommends a more liberal policy toward direct investment in Canada with a view to reducing foreign borrowing with fixed interest obligations. Foreign direct investment needs to feel welcome in this country. There is concern, of course, about the sheer magnitude of it, but policies to redress that should, in the view of the committee, emphasize positive incentive for Canadian-owned firms to become internationally competitive, rather than negative measures to constrain the foreign multinationals. We touch on this subject because of the recently concluded Tokyo Round of GATT negotiations. Some United States firms are reportedly questioning whether the resulting tariff cuts remove the economic viability of their Canadian branch plants. Their answer may well be yes if the branch plants produce the same product lines as the parents, but otherwise, no. The committee notes that some subsidiaries have, in fact, developed unique products in Canada through which they have earned worldwide or regional marketing rights within their firms. This is a pattern which should be encouraged since it enables subsidiaries to contribute more actively to Canada's export effort.

At the same time Canadian-owned firms should be encouraged to innovate, and export support programs should favor those who do. It is the view of the committee that the Canadian market, with its vast energy related projects, has been the basis for many foreign firms to develop skills and technologies that they have exploited around the world. While foreign technology has often been necessary and beneficial for Canada, the effective transfer of it to Canadian-owned firms for downstream exploitation has been notably lacking. In future, opportunities in the Canadian market should be used to build the capability of Canadian-owned firms, where possible, through joint venture or licence agreements with key foreign firms.

The remainder of this summary deals with the committee's major policy recommendations to achieve export growth. The recommendations are influenced by widespread private sector support of the government's commitment to spending restraint, and a consequent rejection of adding new programs to old. They are also influenced by the dramatic changes in the world economic environment over the past few years and the consequent need for more active government-business co-ordination to keep Canada's export support services internationally competitive on an ongoing basis.

Recommendation 1 —
Fundamental Commitment to Exports

Canada needs a vigorous renewal of will on the part of corporate managements and labor to maintain international competitiveness and to get out and win export markets. That renewal of will needs a supportive federal government with co-ordinated and focussed export support services. The federal government should, therefore, make a high profile public commitment in support of Canadian exports. Active ministerial involvement is needed both in pursuit of contracts abroad and in emphasizing at home the enormous economic significance of international trade to the Canadian economy. Trade must become more important politically. Public statements by ministers of all departments must be examined more carefully for their potential impact on trade so that exports are not inadvertently harmed by political statements without due deliberation. In this connection, the appointment of a minister of state for international trade is viewed as a positive and favorable step.

For the past decade, Canada has been preoccupied with domestic issues. It is time to look outward. Public awareness of Canada's trade position with major nations must be sharply increased. With international trade close to 25 per cent of output, the need to maintain international competitiveness in our economy should be a pressing public priority. Renewed effort is needed in international education. Private sector firms active abroad should make sure their boards of directors contain some members with international skills or experience. And the overall public commitment for the long term must be to encourage more firms to invest in foreign markets and view them as an integral part of business activity.

Recommendation 2 — Formation of an Export Trade Development Board

As part of that fundamental commitment, Canada's export support services need to be co-ordinated on an ongoing basis, and private sector involvement in the framing of priorities needs to be established. The committee strongly recommends the formation of an export trade development board to supervise a more focussed and co-ordinated approach to export support services. The purpose of this recommendation is to provide an opportunity for responsible private sector participation in, (1) the development of international marketing strategies and priorities (including co-ordination of those activities of the Canadian Commercial Corporation (CCC), the Canadian International Development Agency (CIDA), the Export Development Corporation (EDC), Industry, Trade, and Commerce (ITC), External Affairs, and others which have an impact on export trade); (2) the design and implementation of government support programs (principally within ITC); and (3) the monitoring of performance based on the policies agreed by the board.

The majority of board members would be private sector executives, diverse both in terms of industry sector and geographic region;

others would be heads of the major governmental agencies, corporations, and departments involved in export trade. The board would be chaired by a private sector executive and would report to the minister of Industry, Trade, and Commerce through whom the funds for export services are voted. Provincial co-ordination would be achieved through the geographic diversity of private sector board members, selected with provincial government consultation, and through meetings of the Board with appropriate provincial government officers.

The need for improved co-ordination of Canada's activities abroad is urgent, and this recommendation has the vigorous support of the committee. The kinds of issues to which the board should address itself include:

1. determination of markets for concentration;
2. determination of marketing strategies for priority markets;
3. determination of allocation of ITC funds to the maximum benefit of the priorities agreed by the board;
4. examination of the programs of other countries to monitor the competitiveness of the Canadian export support package;
5. consideration of new means of support for exports.

Recommendation 3 —
Tax Incentives for Innovation and Exports

In the view of many respondents, Canadian exports could be stimulated enormously by tax incentives, not primarily to redress Canada's lack of international competitiveness, but to redress tax advantages other countries give to their firms. In this area Canada is lagging behind its major trading partners, and there seems ample room, in the light of what other nations are doing, for significant improvement in financial incentives for Canadian exporters. Exports have become a national priority, perhaps not so much by will as by economic circumstance and it is time, in the view of the committee, to recognize the related downstream economic and employment benefits through systematic tax incentive as other countries have done.

The kinds of incentives envisaged include measures to reduce or defer the payment of income tax on export earnings, better carry-forward and carry-back provisions, and more liberal tax treatment of Canadians working abroad in the interests of Canadian trade. Because of the complex nature of this specialized area, the committee recommends the formation of a government-industry task force to examine it further.

In one area, however, the evidence seems overwhelming. This has to do with the lack of innovation in Canadian secondary industry which reflects not only a lack of research and development in Canada but, more significantly, a lack of in-house product design and engineering capability in Canadian firms. The committee recommends that greater incentive be provided through the tax system for firms manufacturing in Canada to design, develop, and market their own unique products. The intent in so recommending is to promote the development of more exportable products on the one hand, and on the other to build the technology needed domestically for effective import displacement.

Recommendation 4 — Export Marketing

There is widespread praise for Canada's Trade Commissioner Service, and the view of the committee is that economic and trade considerations should be given greater weight in Canadian foreign policy and in the priorities of Canadian missions abroad. The Trade Commissioner Service has not grown appreciably over the past decade, and a greater proportion of government expenditures should be devoted to it. The committee does not feel that Canadian exports would benefit from subsuming trade commissioner activities under the jurisdiction of External Affairs. The committee endorses the development in recent years of greater trade and economic knowledge on the part of Canada's ambassadors. It urges that the process be encouraged further. One means to achieve this would be through greater exposure of officers of the Department of External Affairs to trade matters during their careers, perhaps through an enhanced interchange program. Ultimately, all ambassadors should be knowledgeable in Canadian trade policy and committed to trade support.

In the area of trade promotion, the committee would like to see foreign posts opened faster in areas of sudden commercial significance to Canadian firms, even though diplomatic links may have to be deferred. Trade commissioners should receive longer postings, should specialize in a particular region of the world, and should develop special knowledge of Canadian competence in the key industries of their regions during their recall periods. At home, simpler and faster procedures for frequent users of the PEMD program are strongly urged. Introduction of a "blanket authorization" for corporations with a well-defined and successful export strategy would eliminate the need for "case-by-case" application procedures. To assist less-experienced Canadian firms, all government support programs for export should be co-ordinated in single regional offices for "one-step shopping" by potential users.

Recommendation 5 — Export Financing and Insurance

Canadian firms voiced frequent concern about the lack of competitiveness of the Export Development Corporation, especially in relation to the shorter end of long-term financing (say five to twelve years). Meanwhile the EDC has been growing and making a profit while borrowing most of its capital abroad. As the committee examined this area, it became clear that EDC was competing best in the very long-term area (twelve to twenty years) by using the length of term to compensate for the interest rate, and that this approach was working best for large projects where adequate cash flow took many years to develop.

In order to compete in the five to twelve year area, EDC has been passing back part of the financing cost to the Canadian exporter, who has had to absorb it either through lower margins or through higher prices. This "cosmetic" charge is becoming more prevalent with twelve to twenty year loans also as Canadian interest rates continue to climb. Thus, while EDC has been fairly successful in its chosen area in the past, Canadian exports have been largely impeded. The committee's opinion is that the government should ensure that EDC has access to funds which permit the *effective* cost of its offers to finance to be internationally competitive, especially in five to twelve year term loans; and that when significant Canadian export business is at risk, EDC is able to match competitive financing by utilizing concessional rates. To make this possible, EDC should utilize its present profit margins and engage in linked parallel financing with CIDA. In addition, the committee believes it would be useful if consideration were to be given to the issue of tax-exempt bonds in Canada to raise loan funds for EDC at rates which would enable them to compete more effectively.

A number of additional financing services are needed by Canadian exporters, and the committee would like to see EDC offer them. These include: (1) one to five year term fixed-rate export financing (could be handled through Canadian commercial banks with EDC guarantees); (2) more flexible and broader insurance coverage, including partial cost escalation and currency fluctuation insurance; and (3) earlier entry by EDC into the negotiating process with foreign customers. If government subsidy of EDC is necessary to achieve and maintain international competitiveness in financing services, such subsidy should be given.

The committee also feels that business understanding of the activities of EDC would be improved if the board of EDC were composed in majority of private sector executives with a private sector chairman, and if EDC were represented on the proposed export trade development board.

Recommendation 6 — The Trade-Aid Interface

Canada's aid policy should be more closely related to what Canadian firms and institutions are able to deliver competitively. The committee sees a serious lack of co-ordination between the Canadian International Development Agency and the private sector. Too much aid money is going through multilateral agencies for funding of projects in which Canadians seldom participate. And bilateral aid is diffused over too many countries.

The committee strongly recommends a fundamental shift in the priorities of CIDA to do fewer things more thoroughly and with broader involvement of Canadian firms. The thrust of the present administration towards a better trade-aid interface is welcomed. Specifically, a smaller percentage of the aid budget should be multilateral and more Canadians should be placed in the multilateral agencies to insure Canada gets a reasonable share of the work. Bilateral aid should be more sharply focussed to fewer countries and should be tied to Canadian output using Canadian skills and technology wherever possible, or using the project to help develop them. CIDA staff should be deployed more extensively in the field (identifying projects) and in developing sectorial expertise in conjunction with ITC. This is not a recommendation for more staff.

The need for improved co-ordination is perhaps greatest between CIDA and EDC in the area of linked parallel financing. The committee feels there is a strong likelihood that this type of financing will become more common in the future. Canada needs to move swiftly to ensure that Canadian firms are in a competitive position when faced with credit-mixte financing from their competitors. To avoid possible delays, the lead role in negotiating parallel financing arrangements should be taken by EDC. The creation of the export trade development board recommended earlier should help to avoid the past divergence between Canada's aid policies and her commercial capability.

Recommendation 7 — Capital Projects Abroad

If Canada is to share in the growing proportion of world trade arising in the form of major turnkey capital projects, there is need for consistent high level ministerial support of Canadian efforts. Prime ministers, presidents, and monarchs of other countries have been used to support their firms. The stakes are high, and there is need for appropriate focus, but major turnkey projects have become politicized and Canadian political leaders must lend their weight too. The appointment of a minister responsible for international trade is seen as a very positive step in this connection.

The scale of some of these projects is so huge that often technically capable firms will not bid because of the possibility of unforeseen crippling risks for which insurance is difficult or impossible to obtain.

The committee, therefore, finds merit in the creation of a public-private facility, on a joint ownership basis, for risk evaluation and assumption of major risks in procurement and delivery of large capital projects for export markets. It is recommended that a contingent liability fund be established by the federal government for the recommended new facility, and that it operate on the principle of cost recovery rather than subsidy. The new facility would report through the export trade development board to the minister of Industry, Trade, and Commerce.

Recommendation 8 — Export and Small Business

Many Canadian firms that are active abroad are small firms with limited managerial and capital resources. Several of the foregoing recommendations are designed indirectly to help them via the financing of exports on one to five year terms, the streamlining of PEMD which is used heavily by small firms, the "one-stop shopping" concept for export support services, and taxation incentives on export earnings.

However, many small firms which could be exporting are not. Many of them are unaware of Canadian export services and many are intimidated by unknown documentation procedures and currency risks. It is recommended that government export support services be skewed toward small firms, that simpler export credit insurance procedures be offered, that help be given with documentation, and that trading houses be encouraged to operate in areas beyond the major cities.

In general, the committee feels that small Canadian firms that are internationally competitive should be given major economic incentive to overcome the cash flow impediments to growth and to exploit their competitiveness to Canada's advantage.

Conclusion

If Canada is to build on its strength as an exporter of raw products so as to include export of more differentiated manufactured goods, new skills must be learned and the climate for learning them must be made more attractive. It is the position of the Export Promotion Review Committee that a significant opportunity now exists to increase the volume and alter the mix of Canadian exports, and that the need to do so is pressing and urgent in terms of Canada's international payments. The recommendations put forth in this chapter are aimed to seize this opportunity and, in the national interest, help to resolve an increasingly intractable problem. Implicit throughout is the view that Canada must lead out in a more determined way to capture a greater share of world markets in the face of tougher competition and set aside the follower attitude that has characterized her international trade policies in the past.

VI
Cases

In this final section of the book, the concepts discussed earlier are illustrated and applied in a carefully selected set of specific case examples.

Protectionism (Case A) provides the basis for debate on the advantages and disadvantages of tariff protection, designed ostensibly to help maintain the real wage of domestic labor.

How I.T.T. Got Lost in a Big, Bad Forest (Case B) illustrates the impact of complex environmental variables in the foreign direct investment decision process. The long-range plans of a giant multinational company investing in Canada are thwarted by environmental complications such as government regulations, labor unions, raw materials supplies, and weather.

Asbestos Corporation Limited (Case C) provides a detailed analysis of nationalism and expropriation in Canada with an in-depth study of the Quebec government's attempt to expropriate Asbestos Corporation Limited. Information is presented on the background of the dispute, and on the views of both the Quebec government and the company, in a dispute which remains in the headlines today.

In *Modern Homes Limited* (Case D), a small Canadian manufacturer of prefabricated homes faces a complex set of international marketing decisions. Management must decide on the relative priority of developing exports versus expanding domestic market share; how to evaluate demand in different markets; whether to export directly or indirectly; the kinds of shipping and distribution arrangements to use; and related export marketing questions.

Farm Machinery Export Consortium (Case E) documents the efforts to put together a consortium of Canadian farm equipment producers to bid on an Algerian contract. The bid is successful, but the refusal of one of the producers to go along raises major questions as to the long-term viability of export consortia for a country such as Canada.

In *Canadian Machine Tool Company* (Case F), a Canadian-owned medium-size manufacturer of machine tools has developed a new, technologically advanced line. The company's managers visit Japan to investigate the possibility of entering the Japanese market via exports, licensing, or a joint venture.

Stewart Manufacturing Limited (Case G) involves a small Canadian producer of couplings and other automotive parts, facing the challenge of breaking into the European market. One of the company's overseas distributors proposes a licensing agreement, and the company's management has to decide if this is the best way to start into foreign markets, and if so, what the terms of the agreement should be.

Black & Decker Canada Inc. (Cases H and I) are related cases dealing with the introduction and implementation of the World Product Mandate in Canada by Black & Decker Company. The first case presents background on the company and on the jurisdictional relationships among its affiliated units. The second case discusses the attempt by the management of the Canadian subsidiary to win a global product mandate for the Workmate product.

The American Aluminum Corporation (Case J) deals with international transfer pricing. The problem concerns the appropriate intracorporate transfer price for petroleum coke purchased by an American aluminum company from its Canadian supply affiliate.

C. H. Masden Company Limited (Case K) provides the framework for a discussion of the effects of exchange rate changes. A Canadian-owned firm producing farm and garden machinery valves has a subsidiary in Argentina. Management must examine the consequences of an anticipated devaluation of the peso.

VI
Cases

A. Protectionism

B. How I.T.T. Got Lost in a Big, Bad Forest

C. Asbestos Corporation Limited

D. Modern Homes Limited

E. Farm Machinery Export Consortium

F. Canadian Machine Tool Company

G. Stewart Manufacturing Limited

H. Black & Decker Canada Inc. (A)

I. Black & Decker Canada Inc. (B)

J. The American Aluminum Corporation

K. C. H. Masden Company Limited

Case A
Protectionism*

The following statement was recently made by a Canadian labor union leader:

A high tariff on labor-intensive goods imported into Canada is essential if we are to preserve our high standard of living. Foreign labor, particularly in developing countries, often works for a fraction of the wages we do. This "pauper" foreign labor would undermine the existing wage structure of Canadian workers if imports of manufactured goods were allowed in without protection. If our workers had to compete without protection against the cheap labor in places like Hong Kong, then the real wage of our workers would necessarily decline, and our standard of living with it.

Discussion Question:

What is the usual effect of a tariff on wage levels?

Your response should distinguish (a) between short-term and long-term effects, (b) between money wages and real wages, and (c) between wage effects within the protected firm or industry and wage effects for the tariff-imposing nation as a whole.

---

*This case was written by Prof. R. W. Wright expressly for this volume.

Case B
How ITT Got Lost in a Big, Bad Forest*

"One day," reflected an ITT Rayonier line manager this fall, as he sat over coffee in the remote town of Port Cartier, Quebec, "I'm going to ask somebody in the know at ITT how a giant company gets into these things." The exhibit he had in mind was a very large, five-year-old Rayonier mill sitting three miles away on the banks of the Gulf of St. Lawrence. When open, the mill works at turning wood into chemical cellulose, also known as dissolving pulp, which is the raw material for such products as rayon, acetate, and cellophane. But the mill was not open as the manager talked, and, if it had been, it would surely have been pulping money a lot faster than wood. For the mill has been a total loser and absolute disaster — in brief, the latest corporate Edsel.

The reasons for the disaster have a diversity suggesting that familiar multiple-choice answer: "All of the above." The mill has been plagued by labor problems, some a matter of bad luck, some not. It lacks an economical supply of wood, and its engineering is deplorable. Intended originally to produce about 240,000 metric tons of chemical cellulose a year, the mill has in its five years of operation managed to produce only 378,000 tons of product in total, most of that not even chemical cellulose, but rather lower grades of pulp.

It may well have produced its last ton. On September 12, Rayonier announced, in substance, that it was biting the bullet — or more precisely, says a Wall Street analyst, the artillery shell — and would close this brand-new mill forever. Rayonier's parent, International Telephone & Telegraph, announced simultaneously that it would take, in its third quarter, a $320 million write off on the mill. To that wallop may be added other, very large losses that ITT had previously charged off on the mill and additional small losses that will be incurred as the plant is maintained in a moth-ball condition. Overall, the pre-tax damage to ITT can be thought of as about $600 million. Even after taxes, the bill comes to $475 million, enough to make an ITT stockholder suspect that he himself has been reduced to pulp.

The people he may blame indisputably include Harold S. Geneen, who is finally relinquishing the office of ITT chairman at year-end, and there are many ways in which he and others went wrong. The

* From *Fortune Magazine*, December 17, 1979. This case was written by Carol J. Loomis.

fundamental cause of their downfall, however, was an obsession with an immense stand of timber, so seductive in its size that ITT and Rayonier were driven to put on their rose-colored glasses and undertake a project that entailed an awesome collection of risks. The mill that Rayonier put at the timber's edge was the largest the company had ever built in one swoop, and it incorporated technology that was unproved. It was set in a foreign-speaking land and in a physically hostile climate with which Rayonier was unfamiliar. And, finally, the market for the mill's product, chemical cellulose, was uncertain. Any one of those risks might have been the undoing of the venture; as it was, they ganged up to bury it.

Today, it is not easy to find Rayonier or ITT executives, past or present, who will admit to having been wholeheartedly thrilled about Port Cartier's prospects. Geneen would not talk to *Fortune* about the subject. But it is clear from the accounts of many involved that Geneen was indeed an enthusiast — and at ITT, that's just about all the enthusiasm anyone ever needed.

The action in this affair began soon after ITT acquired Rayonier in 1968 for $293 million. The nation's largest manufacturer of chemical cellulose, Rayonier came aboard bearing a distinct corporate personality: it was conservative, technically very competent, and lean in management. At its head was Russell F. Erickson, fifty-seven, an engineer by background and a forceful manager in style.

Erickson and ITT wanted to see Rayonier grow, and they were encouraged by a good market for chemical cellulose that materialized in the late 1960s. There was much industry talk then also about a shrinking supply of woodlands. So, in 1969, Erickson sent Blanton W. "Buck" Haskell, Rayonier's forty-nine-year-old director of planning, to scout worldwide opportunities for tying up a large tract of timber, beside which Rayonier could put a mill. Haskell returned thinking there were possibilities on Quebec's "North Shore" (the north shore of the St. Lawrence), where there was a vast forest whose exploitation the province might be willing to help finance. But the consensus at Rayonier was that the immediate need was to expand in the U.S., by building a third production unit, with 175,000 tons of annual capacity, at an existing mill in Jesup, Georgia.

When the time came, in the fall of 1969, for Rayonier to present its annual business plan to Geneen and other ITT executives, it was this unit — "Jesup C", an $85 million project — that dominated the discussion and got a go-ahead. Quebec was not even on the formal agenda. But after the Jesup plans were settled, Geneen leaned back and said — as several people remember the gist of his words — *"Great!"* Pregnant pause. *"What else have you got?"*

Some Rayonier executives present were taken aback at this casual reaction to the demands of Jesup C, which was to choke Rayonier's balance sheet with debt, boost its pulp capacity by 15 per cent, and most likely require a lot of technical nursemaiding before it could be brought on stream. But the unmistakable message was "Think big", and Erickson rose to the challenge. "Okay," he is remembered as saying, a bit scornfully, as if dealing with a greedy kid, "if that's not good enough for you, here, listen to Haskell."

Haskell, a big Southerner, drawled out the findings of his trip, focussing on Quebec. Only one line he delivered seems to have really counted: a description of the provincial woodlands available there as "about the shape and size of Tennessee." Eyes bugged. One man present says Geneen "went gaga". Another: "The juices began to flow." The formal meeting was adjourned, and Geneen huddled with a small group to talk more about Quebec. "I remember thinking," says one man there, "this project is all but approved."

Nonetheless, a long round of study and negotiation followed, during which ITT and Rayonier began to get a kindergarten education (since expanded to a Ph.D.) about the North Shore. The area begins about 250 miles northeast of Montreal, and is largely wilderness, invaded in the last couple of decades by iron-ore companies. The inhabitants are few in number, implacably French Canadian — frontier variety — and, says a former Rayonier executive who lived among them, tend to be "hard drinking, hard smoking, and independent as hell". Possibly they took to drink because of the climate, which is fierce. The temperature sinks in the winter to perhaps minus 40 degrees, and a strong wind whips off the gulf year-round.

The trees that survive this punishment are mainly black spruce and, aside from possessing a dense fibre well-suited to the production of high-quality chemical cellulose, have few endearing qualities. They stand typically on rocky mountainous terrain and enjoy one of the world's shorter growing seasons — embracing, says one joker, "only July twentieth". In the milder parts of the North Shore, the trees inch to maturity in eighty years; in the really frigid zones, it takes 120 years. Even then, the growth will contain many small, unusable trees that impede logging operations.

Rayonier was not the first forester to do battle with these tigers: several Canadian companies had worked the area, and two had pulled out in the 1960s, unable to make money. The response of the property owner, the Province of Quebec, was to look for a new gladiator and to offer it economic help. One concession, in the deal eventually signed with Rayonier, was a rock-bottom price for the "stumpage", or cutting rights: a mere 50 cents a cord, with the amount scheduled to rise on an index basis with the price of Canadian bleached kraft pulp. (The rate earlier this year was 77 cents.) In sharp contrast, the cutting rights on a typical stand of southern pine in the early 1970s might have gone for about $18 a cord (and would today sell for about $40).

Even so, the key figure for Rayonier was total "wood costs", including the expenses — extra high in this case — of logging timber and getting it to a mill. Wood costs are usually stated in terms of "cunits" — 100 cubic feet of wood — and Rayonier was assuming a cut of 510,000 cunits a year. On that volume, a Quebec consultant, Omer Lussier & Associates, forecast initial wood costs of about $40 a cunit and assumed inflation in these of 4 per cent a year.

It takes about 2.2 cunits of wood — or $88 worth in this case — to make a ton of chemical cellulose, which was selling in 1970 for about $220 per ton. That $88 compared unfavorably with southeastern U.S. costs, which were more like $60. But Rayonier expected the south's costs to begin catching up on the north's (in part because the company anticipated that rise in southern stumpage charges). On this theory, Rayonier found the Quebec forecast tolerable.

Still another dicey judgment was required about the future market for chemical cellulose. While Rayonier was doing its feasibility studies in 1970 and 1971, U.S. sales of pulp buckled because of a recession. But hard questions were then also being asked about the longer-term demand for rayon and cellophane, two end products at which Rayonier felt a Quebec mill would have to aim. Rayon, perpetually in combat with cotton, was also feeling heightened competition from polyesters, which are petroleum-based. Cellophane's competition was polypropylene, then beginning to gobble up the market for such items as cigarette-package wrappers. One executive at another company, involved in the early 1970s with both rayon and cellophane, says his view of their prospects was so bearish that he was floored when he heard Rayonier was building the Quebec mill. "I just couldn't believe it."

Rayonier itself had doubts about cellophane, but the company viewed rayon as having good growth ahead (an opinion supported by Geneen personally and by an outside study done by Stanford Research). The supply of cotton, it was felt, could well be curtailed by a shortage of crop land; polyesters, the thinking continued, were likely to be hurt by rising oil prices, and besides, were no competition for rayon in comfort. Rayonier was also encouraged (though an opposite reaction might have seemed just as rational) by decisions being made in the chemical-cellulose industry to cut capacity. International Paper had just closed a losing mill in western Quebec, and the Scandinavians, major exporters, had announced they would begin using more of their pulp internally for paper production. Rayonier reasoned that the Scandinavians' pull back made the big, and still strong, European market even more attractive and so helped to justify a large mill. The thought was that this market could be wonderfully served from a site on the St. Lawrence.

The site by then in mind was Port Cartier (named after explorer Jacques, of course), with a population of 3,700 forty miles west of the North Shore's hub, Sept Iles (population today 33,000). Rayonier knew it would have to help build up Port Cartier's facilities and import labor. But the productivity of the Canadian worker was then quite good, and Rayonier foresaw no big labor troubles. Stanford Research did express some fears about the germinating Quebec separatist movement, but Rayonier dismissed these.

One financial hurdle was dealt with about as easily. Acknowledging the clogged state of Rayonier's balance sheet, ITT planned to finance the mill directly through a new subsidiary, Rayonier Quebec. Profit projections were a tougher hurdle. Several people who saw the numbers say the analysis indicated only a moderate return on equity — 10 to 13 per cent, one man recalls. Many financial experts would argue that to undertake a project promising so little in the presence of large risks is to invite serious trouble. But the planners clearly envisioned returns beyond those put on paper. Says one: "The feeling was that the timber's value was so great that ultimately we would have to make out."

Russell Erickson, now retired, says he himself believed in the timber, but retained doubts, as the feasibility studies wore on, about the ability of Rayonier to handle Jesup C and a Quebec mill all at once. He did not, however, press these opinions on his boss, of whom he says: "There's no point in saying no to Mr. Geneen."

ITT and Rayonier officially said yes on June 28, 1971 announcing that Rayonier Quebec would build a $120 million mill at Port Cartier, and that the Quebec and Canadian governments would chip in an additional $40 million (for woodlands equipment, and for roads and other support systems). In a *protocole d'accord*, Quebec said it was establishing a 52,200 square-mile Crown forest "as a source of supply for Rayonier", though initial cutting rights were granted on only about half of the area. The Crown forest is indeed shaped like Tennessee, but is actually 24 per cent bigger. The forest, in fact, is bigger than twenty-two of the fifty states, including such spreads as New York and Alabama.

In retrospect, the most remarkable thing about the protocol is that it spelled out Rayonier Quebec's plans to build not just the one large mill, but also two more by 1987. Mercifully for Rayonier and close kin, the company stopped short of legally committing itself to do so. The plans, in any case, gladdened Liberal Premier Robert Bourassa, who had come into office a year earlier promising to create 100,000 new jobs in Quebec and who thought he could see about 5,000 of them in Rayonier's three mills. Meanwhile, the opposition Parti Québecois (now in power under René Lévesque) denounced the whole deal as a "giveaway" of Quebec's natural resources.

Even had plunder been there, Rayonier would have had trouble gathering it in. Port Cartier was the company's first green field mill since 1953. The company was simultaneously building Jesup C and, in six mills, was beginning to engineer and install pollution-control equipment that to date has cost more than $250 million. And, says Buck Haskell, with anguish: *"We hadn't staffed up."* The stretched state of the management is indicated by the load hanging on Haskell by 1971: he had been promoted to senior vice-president for planning, research, and engineering, a big job; yet he was also head of Rayonier Quebec and directly responsible for planning and building Port Cartier.

On the side, Haskell handled a few odd jobs, and one of these, a 1971 sales trip to Europe with Rayonier's sales vice-president, Michael A. Brown, was a downer. Making the rounds of major customers, the two attempted to sell Port Cartier's planned output on long-term contracts. But the U.S. recession had created a world glut of pulp, and no customer was willing to tie himself up. One buyer, Akzo, in the Netherlands, spoke gloomily about the prospects for rayon. Over drinks on the plane coming home, Brown and Haskell talked unhappily for hours about where all this left Port Cartier, and even asked themselves whether they shouldn't try to "stop this thing". But they didn't try.

The ground-breaking party at Port Cartier, in October, 1971, was a bilingual bash, featuring 6,000 chicken dinners. The size of the hangover didn't become apparent until 1973, when the labor scene in Quebec degenerated into turmoil and strife. Part of the problem was a power struggle between two labor federations. Another part was the premier's drive to create jobs, an effort so successful it produced a shortage of skilled laborers and a feeling among them that they had the upper hand. A kind of anarchic fever gripped the building trades. Shoddy work, delays, and huge cost overruns became the norm, and violence flared at some sites.

There was no violence at Port Cartier, but there was everything else. ITT's political activities in Chile became an issue among the workers. Equipment was sabotaged and the pace of work crawled.

Says Haskell: "You could walk through the construction site during the last year, and if one man in three had a hand on a tool, you were lucky." Ironically, some of those otherwise unoccupied workers may have been busy making a movie: campaigning to recruit a permanent operating force, Rayonier produced an arty, prize-winning film, *The Ballad of Joe Caribou*, which included an in-plant ballet scene that employed construction workers as extras. Someone viewing the film today, and knowing the mill's fate, might be most struck by the fact that the movie begins and ends with the cry of a loon.

A special circumstance made the labor problems particularly insufferable: the complexity of the mill, which was designed to be highly automated, energy efficient, and non-polluting. That last goal, above all, was a corker, since Rayonier opted for a sulfite-process mill, a type that has traditionally generated large environmental waste problems.

The plot at Port Cartier was to bottle up these problems with an elaborate closed-loop system. The main pollutant, sulfur (a component of the acid that "cooks" the wood), would be recovered and reused. The procedure was on the frontier of technology and — in the words of an engineer close to the project — helped turn the mill into a mammoth "pilot plant". Building such an establishment might have been a horror show given the most congenial construction crew in the world — and that was not what Rayonier had.

In the end, the mill was not completed until late 1974, six months behind schedule. By then, Rayonier had also taken shortcuts to save money. But the savings hardly seemed to matter. E. & B. Cowan, Ltd., consulting engineers to Rayonier on the project, had thought that 3.2 million man-hours would be needed to build the plant; it took 6.2 million. Naturally, the $120 million budget became nothing more than an unpleasant reminder of all that had gone wrong. The actual cost was $250 million.

The Canadian Paperworkers were next on Rayonier's dance card and there was, at least, a certain symmetry in the relationship between the two parties. The union struck in 1974 — while most of its members were still in training — and it was again on strike (and had been for three months) when Rayonier announced, in September 1979, that the mill would be closed permanently. In the years between, there had been another two-month shut-down and assorted wildcat actions lasting up to twenty-seven days.

Furthermore, even when open, the mill experienced many days of ugly trouble. On one well-remembered occasion three workers, led by union leader Paul Babin, roughed up a supervisor they disliked, trucked him to the plant gate, and threw him out. Because the company was desperate to get labor peace, Babin and friends were not fired, only suspended for four months; the supervisor was transferred.

The atmosphere of conflict at Port Cartier can be traced to several sources. The workers who had responded to the siren song of *Joe Caribou* were relatively young and easily seduced by more militant refrains. They were happy, also, to take on ITT, which was still being excoriated last summer with "Remember Chile" graffiti. Many workers had left their families behind and were, in one union leader's description, "isolated and tired, lonely and angry". Turnover was extremely high, and extended even to union officials and the mill's managers, whom Rayonier kept changing as if they were pitchers for the New York Mets. This turbulence prevented the two sides, labor and management, from ever reaching a position of mutual trust.

Many of the union leaders, French Canadian to the core, also fumed about the paucity of French-speaking managers. Rayonier had originally hoped to hire experienced French Canadians as supervisors; but they were scarce, and, as interest in all things French grew in Quebec, they began to command pay that did not fit into ITT's salary framework. So Rayonier made do with English-speaking supervisors. Meanwhile, it kept trying unsuccessfully to find a French Canadian to run Port Cartier. Three of the four men who did hold the job were not at home in French, a fact that one of them, John Hartung, believes "did not matter at my level." It mattered to a provincial union leader named Serge Lord, who said recently, "People really hated that company. It was the only one in Quebec where we had to deal in English at that level."

Naturally, Rayonier never felt it deserved to be hated. The company paid the workers premium wages, and it subsidized their housing with $3 million worth of second mortgages, on which no interest was due for twenty-five years. Rayonier contributed $300,000 for a hockey rink and, of course, paid big taxes ($650,000 last year). The company even imported opera stars for a night of culture. There were some signs of easing tensions in 1978, a year of relative labor peace that was broken again by the strike in 1979.

One former Rayonier executive argues to this day that a solution to the labor problems would have been the salvation of the mill. "If there had been a way to motivate the people, make them as dedicated as those in the southeastern mills, we could have overcome our other problems. I really believe that."

It is hard to agree with him. He might as well argue that the *Titanic* would not have sunk had the deckhands put some real spirit into "Nearer My God to Thee". The labor troubles, plainly, were very severe, but were an independent, and probably surmountable, problem. There was no way to get over or around the inefficiency of the plant itself, or the cost of gathering its raw material.

Practically all pulp plants have start-up difficulties and certainly no one expected Port Cartier to be one of the lovely exceptions. But by early 1975, when no pulp to speak of had yet rolled out of the mill, those in charge were beginning to identify Port Cartier as a very special headache. Feeling the pain particularly were four top executives, two of them at Rayonier: Charles E. Anderson, a tall, good-looking man who had taken over as chief executive officer in 1973, and his Port Cartier lieutenant, Buck Haskell. The remaining two were at ITT: Richard E. Bennett, an executive vice-president who was in Geneen's office of the president, and J. Ronald Goode, a staff vice-president who was the liaison between ITT and Rayonier. Bennett and Goode (who escaped in 1976 to International Paper) share a common fascination: both have said they love "making things work".

So here they all were with a clunker. Haskell's response was to delegate most of his New York responsibilities and to move to Port Cartier, where he addressed an endless stream of manufacturing problems.

Their range cannot fully be described here. But it may be said that technical problems, like the labor relations, had a certain symmetry: they began with the first stage of wood handling (in which a machine called a Forano Slasher, of experimental design, would not slash wood properly) and ended in the finishing room (where a giant wrapping machine would not wrap rolls of pulp properly). A few scenic spots in between:

- Because the mill's de-barking drums had to deal in winter with ice-encrusted wood, they could not do a decent job of removing bark. The problem is intolerable in the manufacture of chemical cellulose, which requires very clean fibre. Eventually, de-barking in winter was curtailed and the mill began to use stockpiled wood chips, which are themselves a problem because they freeze together.
- The residue of the process that cooks the wood is "spent-sulfite" liquor (SSL), which must go through an evaporation process that reduces the liquor to a concentrate from which the sulfur can be recovered. Port Cartier's evaporators did not work properly. They corroded; they produced inadequate amounts of insufficiently concentrated SSL; and they leaked sulfur dioxide into the plant. Many workers were required to wear gas masks. The leaking gas also corroded large areas of the plant's walls.
- At most pulp mills, the "acid plant", in which the cooking brew is

prepared, is housed in a building all its own, since the process is apt to generate — again — sulfur dioxide leaks and also gives off oppressive heat. But because Rayonier wanted to conserve the heat, the company decided to locate its acid plant right in the mill. Sulfur dioxide has indeed leaked and corroded much heavy equipment, including the supports for the turbines that run the evaporators. New stainless-steel supports had to be put in.

All these problems, and the many others that surfaced, were particularly difficult to cope with because the plant was so large, so technologically unwieldy, and so rigid a closed-loop system. If the evaporators did not produce dense SSL, for example, the system could not recover the sulfur needed for use in the acid plant, which meant that too little acid was available for the cooking, and so on. Moreover, a lack of capacity for storing pulp at various stages of its manufacture meant that the pulp could not be "held" temporarily if some operating difficulty developed ahead of it. Basically, almost any hitch in the manufacturing process tended to shut down just about the whole mill.

That shortcoming was certainly apparent in 1975, when the mill, despite the ministrations of several Rayonier engineers called in from other locations, managed to produce only 30,000 tons of pulp (about one-eighth its rated capacity). Of that, just four tons — yes, four — was acceptable chemical cellulose, the remaining tonnage being off-grade pulps suitable, say, for photographic paper. The chagrin at Rayonier was enormous. Haskell says that he, Anderson, and Goode huddled together to discuss what could be done, going so far as to kick around the thought — almost unthinkable at that point — of closing the mill.

That option was not pursued; but its merits were being proclaimed also by dismal data coming in on wood costs, which had exceeded the forecast by a spectacular margin. Had the 4 per cent inflation rate built into Rayonier's forecast been accurate, and if the starting point may be considered 1973, the year Rayonier began cutting timber, the company's wood costs of $40 a cunit would since have risen to about $50. But actual inflation in Quebec — in woodland wages and other operating expenses — was more like 11 per cent, which would have raised the figure to $75.

That figure, however, bears no relation to reality at Rayonier: its costs this year were averaging about $115 a cunit. One explanation for this incredible overrun is that Rayonier never came close to cutting the 510,000 cunits annually that had been assumed in its forecast (the maximum cut was 300,000 cunits, in 1974); so the costs of a lot of expensive roads, camps, and logging equipment were spread over a reduced number of units. A second explanation is that the company ran into a shortage of loggers willing to work its northernmost camp (about one hundred miles above Port Cartier) and had to shift to highly automated, but very expensive, cutting methods.

In the years since Rayonier began to understand the disastrous implication of these costs, it has tried just about everything to get them down. With Quebec's permission, it even began to import wood chips from outside the Crown forest. (The irony of importing chips when you are sitting in a forest bigger than Tennessee will be apparent.) The effort helped; that $115 per cunit would have been even higher had not improvements been made. But it still takes 2.2 cunits of wood to make a ton of chemical cellulose, and though prices per ton have recently leaped to an all-time high of $500 and more, $253 is a very high wood cost per ton. That is ludicrously true at Port Cartier, whose 378,000 tons of pulp production over the years included 300,000 that was not up to quality specifications and that had to be sold for whatever it would bring. For the full 378,000 tons, the average realized price was $225.

It is an oddity of the Port Cartier situation that it mattered very little what was happening to the market for chemical cellulose; you can't sell pulp if you can't make it. It may be noted, however, that cellophane took it on the chin in the 1970s, losing out to polypropylene, and that rayon exhibited no growth between 1970 and 1978. The lack of growth was so conspicuous that Rayonier began, in 1973, to hold seminars around the world, at which the virtues of the fibre were extolled. It is possible, though unconfirmable, that the seminars were precipitated by Harold Geneen's inability to find a rayon shirt at his favorite clothing store. It is legend within Rayonier that Geneen suffered precisely that set back and was furthermore advised by a salesman that the store wouldn't think of carrying anything so tacky. Whereupon Geneen is supposed to have called Chuck Anderson and all but ordered him to do something about promoting the image of rayon.

Geneen is reported to have campaigned again for rayon a few years later, when a consultant's study forecast real growth for the product of only 1 per cent annually. Geneen declared that Rayonier just couldn't let it work out that way ("Harold Geneen at his best," says a former Rayonier insider). At Geneen's urging, Rayonier began an expensive advertising program for rayon (built around endorsements from such designers as Halston), which appears to have produced results. From a cyclical bottom in 1975, demand for the fibre has bounced back sharply.

Meanwhile, in 1976, Haskell got fired from his jobs. Rumors persist that Rich Bennett was also in danger of ouster because of Port Cartier. But he survived, perhaps because he was less exposed than Haskell, who, as one former Rayonier executive says, "had the rat in his pocket."

In the next couple of years, the rat passed in turn to three different men, each of whom achieved some gains in production, but basically fought a losing cause. The big news of these years was the arrival at the mill, in 1977, of the "RPMs" — the Rayonier Profit Makers — a group of twenty-nine supervisors and engineers assembled from every Rayonier plant in the country. They were certainly not the first skilled help to come, but their predecessors, says John Hartung, then running Rayonier Quebec, usually thought of themselves as serving time and "immediately hung up a calendar and marked off Day 1". The RPMs, in contrast, were recruited, told they were an elite corps, and promised bonus pay for staying in Port Cartier one to three years (with the bonuses to be one-third of their salaries). Their mission was "the systematic transfer of knowledge" to Quebecers, who would inherit the earth when the RPMs left. The Quebecers would in the meantime hear a few words of French, since the RPMs were required to study the language.

This extraordinary effort got production in 1977 to 90,000 tons and in 1978 to the peak of 129,000 (though Hartung by mid-1978 had left the company, having had differences with top management). But the bell had commenced to toll for the mill. As 1979 began, ITT and Rayonier were in deep discussion about its fate.

The reasons for discussion had piled up. The plant had by then incurred pre-tax losses of more than $200 million. It continued to have a very large "negative mill margin" — it was suffering operating losses on every ton produced — and it had no sure prospects of ever escaping these. Lyman C. Hamilton, then c.e.o. of ITT, was a bear about achieving a good return on assets, and he had to be asking himself whether the company should support the mill with more money. It is also quite likely that the company's auditors, Arthur Andersen & Co., were raising sticky questions, such as "Have you considered whether this plant — carried on the books as a large asset — might not be worthless?"

Hamilton's decision was to have outside consultants assess just what needed to be done to make the plant efficient and what it would cost. The consultants picked were Sandwell & Co., of Vancouver, experts in the forest products industry, and they delivered their opinions in the summer of 1979. In these, the firm had to all but ignore the existing investment in Port Cartier; if the carrying charges on that huge sum (more than $300 million) had been figured in, no plan could have been devised that would project a profit. It was hard enough just to conjure up a profit from here on in.

Sandwell's basic conclusion was that an infusion of about $125 million, spread over perhaps five years, was needed at Port Cartier, part of that to go for major fixes, part for more routine expenditures. That amount of money, Sandwell said, could raise production at the plant to near its rated capacity and reduce operating costs significantly. Then, assuming satisfactory prices for chemical cellulose — which another consultant thought were in the cards — the plant could begin showing a small operating profit that would grow as time went by.

However, there would, by that time, be a large new investment on the books, on which carrying charges would be heavy; these costs would, for many years (though not forever), more than offset the operating profit and keep the plant mired in the red. To sum it up: a large new investment, a decent market for pulp — and still a losing mill.

Hamilton was not around in September to present these findings to the ITT board; he had been forced out in July, as the result of a power struggle with Geneen that seems to have had no connection to Port Cartier. Rand V. Araskog, the new chief executive officer, was on stage, and it appears he could report that just about every executive concerned with the mill thought it should be closed; certainly Anderson says he felt that way, as did the head man at the mill, Joseph A. Krauth. The board's vote — Geneen's voice included — was unanimous: close it down.

The $320 million write off taken by ITT assumes some salvage value for equipment in the plant, and also reflects some capitalized start-up costs, termination payments to employees, losses expected on those second mortgages, and money due a Quebec provincial agency for woodlands equipment it financed. But the $320 million assumes no tax benefits, because ITT doesn't have enough Canadian profits, past and present, to offset the loss; its profits have apparently already been eaten up by the mill's *operating* losses. ITT obviously hopes to generate sufficient profits in the future (perhaps with the aid of Canadian acquisitions) to bring down the size of the after-tax loss.

It is hard to say what will happen to the mill. As Sandwell studied the plant, it investigated possibilities for converting it to a different kind of pulp production — say, to newsprint. But the investment required would again be enormous, and no plan looked good. Rayonier also talked to other companies and to the Quebec government to determine whether an outside investment could be encouraged; no one would bite. The mill could conceivably turn out to be another Labrador Linerboard, a plant built by promoter John C. Doyle and closed two years ago because it was a loser; it has recently been demothballed by a new owner and sent after today's good pulp prices. Then again, the Port Cartier mill may just sit there forever, catching the wind and silently keeping watch over its inefficiencies.

There is a weird reminder of Port Cartier in Rayonier's Stamford, Connecticut, offices. It is displayed, so to speak, on a large globe decorated with bright circles that identify Rayonier's plants, offices, and customers. But there is no circle in Quebec, no hint at all that the company has been locked there in battle with a dragon of a mill.

Rayonier executives say the globe is simply "out-of-date". But a person knowing Port Cartier's history might well fantasize a more dramatic explanation, embodying an emotional scene in which some Rayonier or ITT executive — perhaps even Geneen himself — descended upon the globe in rage and frustration and expunged from it every trace of the mill's existence. That is perhaps as far as imagination can go: nothing is likely to erase this affair from the hit parade of corporate disasters.

Case C
Asbestos Corporation Limited
Nationalization by Quebec
Government*

In October 1977, the Quebec government finally made public the
details of their policy on the Quebec asbestos industry. The announcement came after nearly a year of public speculation about the
fate of the industry under the new government which had come to
power on November 15, 1976 with strong sentiments for political
sovereignty for Quebec, strong ties to the labor movement, and a
"social democratic" platform.

Yves Bérubé, Quebec's minister of Natural Resources, outlined the
government's goals for the asbestos industry: 10 per cent of all
asbestos mined in Quebec to be transformed to end products within
Quebec within ten years; the proportion would grow to 20 per cent
eventually; improvement of environmental conditions in mills and
mines to reduce the threat of workers' health; an increase in the
participation in, and control of, management functions in the asbestos industry by French-speaking Quebecers. To achieve these goals,
the government would be acquiring control of Asbestos Corporation
Limited (ACL), the largest independent producer of asbestos in Quebec.

The government's reasons for choosing ACL were that it was
profitable, it had a strong market position, and it had substantial
reserves of asbestos. Also, it was not part of an integrated manufacturing firm. Nationalizing ACL was the most controversial part of
the policy on the asbestos industry and was seen by the government
as the key to successful implementation of their plan for the industry. They announced at the same time that Quebec would have a
new Crown corporation known as La Société Nationale de l'Amianta
(SNA) to engage in joint ventures with the private sector, to encourage research and to be a holding company for Quebec's ownership
of ACL.

Nationalization of ACL had been an important issue for the party in
power for a long time. The Parti Québecois (P.Q.) had been elected
with a strong majority in November 1976. One of the planks in their

* This case has been prepared by Prof. A. K. Jain, Prof. R. W. Wright and G. L. de
Villafranca of Faculty of Management, McGill University, as a basis for class discussion rather than to illustrate effectiveness of certain policies.

Copyright © 1981 by the authors.

* This case was written expressly for this volume.

election platform was a commitment to nationalize the asbestos industry. The reasons for this commitment and the policy declaration that followed in October 1977 have their roots deep in Quebec's political and industrial history, and the policy can only be analysed in that context.

History of ACL and the Industry

Asbestos was first discovered in Quebec's Eastern Townships region in 1876, by Joseph Fecteau of Thetford Township. Fecteau was walking to work in what is now St. Maurice Parish when he noticed an outcropping that seemed unusual. Fecteau showed his discovery to the owner of the land, Robert Grant Ward, who took samples to Quebec for identification. He was told it was asbestos but it had no commercial value, so Ward took the samples to Boston for a second opinion. The results of the second inquiry were far more promising.[1]

Soon there were numerous small companies mining asbestos in the area, many of them divisions of American or British companies. In 1881, the Jeffrey Mine was opened in Asbestos and it is still in operation by Canadian Johns-Manville, with the distinction of being the largest asbestos mine in the world. By 1885, a total of 350 men were employed in mining asbestos.[2]

In the period before the First World War, competition was fierce due to the number of companies. Capital requirements grew as the technology of mining asbestos improved, and prices, wages, employment, and financial structures were chronically unstable. There was an increasing tendency of manufacturers to integrate backward.

The Asbestos Corporation Limited of today finds its roots in the earliest days of asbestos mining. In 1878, the King brothers, timber merchants from Quebec City, began to mine asbestos on land they owned in the area. In 1909, the King Brothers Asbestos Company became part of Amalgamated Asbestos Corporation which was to develop the King Mine and the properties of the Beaver, British Canadian, and Fraser Companies. In fact, the mines of ACL today bear the names of the companies which originally owned them.

Another reorganization took place in 1912, reflecting the instability in the industry, when Amalgamated Asbestos Corporation became

1. George W. Smith, *Bell Asbestos Mines Ltd., 1878-1967*, (Bell Asbestos, 1968) (Limited Edition, no longer available). The discovery is often attributed to Andrew Johnson. The evidence does not seem better for Johnson's discovery than for Fecteau and Ward's, but in either case it was an accidental find.
2. *Annual Report* (Asbestos Corporation of Canada Limited, 1922).

Asbestos Corporation of Canada Limited. The instability was partly a result of the problems which would continue to plague the industry for many years: an inability to predict demand and manage supply, resulting in oversupply and very low prices. Manufacturers did not contract ahead for the supplies, buying instead "from hand to mouth at the lowest prices obtainable".[3]

Another factor contributing to industry instability was the level of capital investment required. Mining was becoming more mechanized and investment in steam shovels and other heavy equipment was necessary in order to compete. Those companies which could not manage the capital investment were absorbed by those which could, allowing further economies of scale.

In the period following the First World War, asbestos constituted 50 per cent of the total mining output of Quebec. This was due to new uses for the product and growing knowledge of it. Total world consumption of asbestos in 1918 was 155,000 tons of which 142,000 was from Canada,[4] with South Africa supplying the difference. Canada's high grades were among the world's best.

Uses of asbestos in this period were primarily for the longer fibres and included roofings and building materials, brake linings, as a replacement for rubber in high-grade packings, and as an insulation material in ships, factories, and homes. Asbestos had become a necessity, according to the *Scientific American* (July, 1920), and there was no substitute for it.

However, the post-war depression caused severe price wars. This made some mines marginally profitable and put others out of business. Despite some recovery in the economy, heavy competition prevented the asbestos industry from becoming very profitable with supply continuing to exceed demand. Finally in 1925, another large merger took place and Asbestos Corporation Limited was incorporated. It included seven other asbestos companies, many of which were the results of earlier mergers. The directors of the new company were largely the same as for the old Asbestos Corporation of Canada.

In 1931, the companies formed the Quebec Asbestos Mining Association (QAMA) for several reasons. Despite the intense competition between the mining companies it was necessary to combine forces to deal with a number of common problems. These included:

• constantly changing Canadian and provincial tax laws;

3. *Annual Report* (Amalgamated Asbestos Corporation, 1912).
4. *Annual Report* (Asbestos Corporation of Canada Ltd., 1919).

- growing environmental and health problems; and
- the need to develop uniform fibre grading standards.

In the late 1940s, 1950s, and early 1960s, the number of companies in the asbestos industry reported by the Dominion Bureau of Statistics (later Statistics Canada) grew substantially. By 1955, there were twenty-five, roughly half of which were engaged only in exploration and development work. Many disappeared within a year or two. However, this phenomenon is indicative of the importance of asbestos and the potential for profit from mining it.

By 1964, the industry had assumed the approximate dimensions seen at present. One further merger took place in 1964 when the Johnson's Company was sold to ACL. Lake Asbestos had come on the scene in 1958, and Carey Canadian was formed in 1955. There were eight companies in 1964, but by 1974, the field was down to five; the largest being Canadian Johns-Manville. The others were, in order of size: ACL, Lake, Bell, and Carey-Canadian.

All the asbestos mining companies with the exception of ACL were subsidiaries of British or American firms which were vertically integrated. The stock of ACL has been widely held by Canadians (and traded on both the Montreal and Toronto Stock Exchanges) for most of its history until recent years.

The purchase of Johnson's Company by ACL in 1964, however, held the seeds of future foreign ownership of a majority of shares of ACL. It put a large number of shares of ACL in the hands of the Johnson's Company. In 1968 the Johnson family sold its shares to Canadair, a Montreal aircraft firm, which also bought an additional 1,000,000 common shares after a public offer. They ended up with 54 per cent of the outstanding ACL shares. At the time Canadair was owned in turn by General Dynamics Corporation of the United States. The vice-president of General Dynamics soon became chairman of ACL and it joined the ranks of asbestos companies controlled by foreign firms. When Canadair was nationalized by the Canadian government in 1976, General Dynamics retained its shares of ACL. However, it was common knowledge the shares were for sale up until early 1976, probably because of ACL's poor dividend performance.

Since the Second World War, ACL has grown steadily. The old Vimy Ridge mine was closed in 1955 and replaced by the new Normandie mine and a modern mill. After the purchase of Johnson's in 1964, attention was turned to a prospector's report of a large orebody in Northern Quebec in the Ungava peninsula, 1100 miles north of Montreal. Consultants checked the site and a decision was made to develop it. After delays, resulting cost overruns, and revisions of the original plans, ACL brought Asbestos Hill into production in 1972. An ore concentrate is sent by ship from Asbestos Hill to the finishing mill at Nordenham, West Germany due to the harsh climatic conditions and resulting high costs of a full-scale operation in the north. This ore is of excellent quality and by 1976 Asbestos Hill produced 103,000 tons of asbestos.

ACL remained the only non-integrated company in the industry. All the others had a primary relationship with a parent company which used asbestos in one or more of its manufacturing processes. Even when control of ACL fell into foreign hands it was not for reasons of integration. M. E. Tashereau, president and chief executive officer of ACL, reaffirmed the company's decisions in mid-1977, saying that they are in the business of mining asbestos: they know how to do it well and feel they should confine their efforts to what they know and do well. They had no expertise in manufacturing, in his opinion, and it would not pay to try to learn. Thus, although majority-owned by a foreign company, ACL remained the only non-vertically integrated firm in the Quebec asbestos industry.

Unlike the other Quebec asbestos firms, ACL sells all its fibre on the open market. It gains market stability through negotiating long-term contracts and has maintained many customers for decades.

Because ACL sells most of its fibre on the open market, it has a great deal of market power and tends to be a price leader in the industry. However, ACL has found the basic demand for asbestos to be price elastic only within a fairly narrow range. In the past, market forces have operated on the asbestos market in an almost classic way: when customers perceived prices to be on the low side they built up inventories. Asbestos companies would see this as strong demand. As a result they would often take the opportunity to raise prices. Higher prices would cause customers to curtail their buying and rely instead on the accumulated inventories. This created a business cycle for the industry.

Superimposed on this business cycle are economic cycles of growth and recession. The asbestos industry is closely tied to the construction and automotive industries, both of which are often the first to be affected in a recession.

Asbestos manufacturing firms in Quebec have a mixed pattern of ownership. Johns-Manville, a wholly owned subsidiary of an American parent, has some manufacturing facilities in Quebec. Turner-Newall, a British firm, owns Bell Asbestos and a manufacturing company, Atlas Asbestos.[5] There are a number of small manufacturing opera-

5. Turner-Newall sold both companies to the Quebec government in early 1980.

tions in Quebec, about half of which are independent local firms. However, the total amount of manufacturing accounts for only about 3 per cent of Quebec's total output of asbestos fibre.

Asbestos: The Product and Its Uses

Asbestos is a unique mineral fibre with high tensile strength, high resistance to acids, and excellent insulating qualities. No man-made product has yet been able to imitate all these properties and yet be as inexpensive as asbestos.

The end use varies according to the length and quality of the fibre. Different orebodies have different characteristics and therefore different uses. These differences are significant enough to become a differential advantage for a company like ACL which has particularly high quality fibre.

The Quebec Asbestos Mining Association (QAMA) has worked to develop a standard grading system for use by the companies. The grades are 1 (the longest) also known as "crude", to 7 or 8 (the shortest) with subgroups to indicate other properties of a given grade. The mine of origin may also be indicated by the producer, as this has meaning to many long-term users of asbestos, who may actually order, for instance, a grade 4 from the British Canadian Mine. They may even request a location within the mine if their needs are that specific.

The general grading system gives the industry a common vocabulary. It has gained such acceptance and usefulness that it is being used by asbestos producers outside Quebec. Exhibit 1 shows the specifications and uses for various grades of asbestos.

ACL has a predominance of fibre in grades 4-5 which is particularly good for asbestos cement. Johns-Manville and Carey Canadian on the other hand have a significant share of the short fibre production in Canada. These differences of fibre grade give each company access to different uses and markets. Exhibit 2 gives a breakdown of different producers by various grades of asbestos.

Asbestos is considered to be a necessity for many uses such as strengthening and insulating. Plastic substitutes are available for some of asbestos's uses but there are problems with them:

- The costs of many plastics are related to the price of oil, making them far more expensive than asbestos.
- Many glass and plastic products appear to have the same health hazards associated with asbestos.

Asbestos has proven to be an important substance to industrializing countries. Asbestos cement is far cheaper for infrastructure than steel, and it is excellent for many construction purposes. As a result, ACL has invested in the development of markets in the Third World. Despite the fact that ACL's strongest markets are in the U.S., Western Europe, and Japan, ACL has high expectations of future growth in these Third World markets. This is especially true as certain uses of asbestos are banned for health reasons in industrialized countries. Exhibit 3 shows the geographical distribution of sales of ACL.

In the U.S., demand for various uses can be broken down as follows:

Table 1

Use	Per Cent of Total Use
Asbestos Cement Construction Products	37.4
Flooring Products	18.1
Friction Products	9.5
Roofing Products	9.0
Paper Products	7.4
Packing and Gaskets	3.4
Textiles	2.4
Insulation	1.8
Miscellaneous Others	11.1
	100.0

The total size of the world asbestos market is difficult to estimate. Along with USSR, Canada is one of the world's largest asbestos producers. The precise figures are not available because the production of USSR, which has a large market share can only be estimated. Canada accounts for about 50 per cent of the "Free World" production, but the USSR is posing a threat to this position as it increases its production capacity. Quebec produces 80 per cent of Canada's asbestos with the remainder coming from Newfoundland, Ontario, and British Columbia.

Almost 80 per cent of Canada's asbestos goes to ten countries, with the largest single share going to the United States. Exhibit 4 shows the destination of Canadian asbestos by major groups of countries and Exhibit 5 gives some projections of the demand.

The Mining Process

Chrysotile asbestos (the kind of asbestos found in Quebec) is found in serpentine rock in veins. The asbestos fibre lies across the vein, at right angles to the rock with the length of the fibre thus being determined by the width of the vein. Most asbestos is mined in open pits with a few exceptions. The King Mine of ACL is underground. Bell Asbestos's operations (on the same orebody as the Beaver Mine of ACL) is underground, and the Asbestos Hill operations are going underground at present (1980). The Jeffrey Mine of Johns-Manville is the largest open pit asbestos mine in the world. The mining process is approximately the same from mine to mine with variations in the size of trucks and modernity of milling facilities. Exhibit 6 shows the locations of major asbestos mining areas in Quebec.

Rock is blasted twice a day at ACLs British Canadian mine. It is then loaded onto trucks by mechanical shovels and driven to the primary crusher. ACL has jaw crushers at Thetford, while Johns-Manville has a single large ball crusher. Ore is usually wet as it comes from the ground so once crushing is done the ore fraction below $^3/_4$ inch which contains most of the fibre (and moisture) must be dried. Once dry, fibre and rock can be finally separated. The fibre then is ready to be milled. Milling is becoming more complex as the number of subgrades increases to meet market needs. Each company spends large amounts of time and money improving this part of their process. In general, a series of agitating screened boxes is used. The screens are devised to allow only a specific size and smaller fibre to fall through to the next box which in turn retains another size of fibre.

Once grading is complete, the fibre can be packed. Bags are packed under pressure in rectangular forms, making them efficient to transport.

The entire process is mechanized, and in some cases, controlled by computer. This mechanization plus the low yield-to-rock-mined ratio (about 5 per cent) means the asbestos industry has high capital costs relative to other mining operations.

Health Problems of Asbestos

Asbestos has been found to be a cause of several serious diseases. Asbestosis is a lung disease caused by asbestos fibres which are breathed in and lodge in the lung tissue. They are so durable that they can never be expelled by the body and eventually disease results. This disease is usually recognized after ten or more years of exposure, although some work is currently being done on the exposure threshold which leads to disease.

Mesothelioma, a type of lung cancer, is another disease which has been related to exposure to asbestos fibres. It is rare but more deadly than asbestosis. Asbestosis can sometimes develop into mesothelioma.

Asbestosis was first identified and named in 1931. The higher rate of mortality among asbestos workers was confirmed by a European researcher in 1951. In North America, however, experts did not come to an agreement on cancer-causing effects of asbestos until 1964.

The International Agency for Cancer Research now lists asbestos as one of the twenty-six most serious cancer-linked materials. The U.S. National Cancer Institute says 18 per cent of all future cancers may be asbestos-related. Legislation has followed in U.S., and in Canada in response to these and similar concerns. Exhibit 7 provides a summary of the health problems associated with asbestos and the reaction to these problems in the United States.

The health problems of asbestos became a public issue in Canada with the visit of Dr. Selikoff (whose work is described in Exhibit 7) to the mines in Quebec. Unions began to insist on better working conditions and the QAMA stepped up its research on health aspects of asbestos mining and products. Soon health officials became aware of the danger to the general public from high levels of asbestos in urban air, presumably from automobile brake linings wearing down. Asbestos was found to be flaking off the ceilings of older schools, and it was found to be getting into wine products from an asbestos filtration medium. Modelling clay for children was found to contain asbestos.

To protect the workers in asbestos industries, Canada followed suit when a maximum standard of five fibres of asbestos per cubic centimetre of air was set in the United States in 1972. In 1976, the limit was lowered to two fibres in the U.S. and in many provinces. In Quebec, the 1976 Beaudry report forced the government to set the limit at five fibres by 1978, and the limit has remained at that level.

Early in the 1970s, the federal government placed a ban on textiles containing asbestos fibre sold in or imported into Canada, except for use in special protective clothing. Children's toys containing asbestos were banned in 1977, and provincial legislation was enacted to prevent use of asbestos in wine filtration processes.

Asbestos exists in dozens of household appliances under federal or provincial regulations. Such devices are not now considered a hazard. There are current proposals in Ottawa to ban joint cement and patching compounds containing asbestos and decorative ash used in gas fireplaces. Manufacturers of these products have already dropped them.

Possible substitutes have been found to carry much the same health risks due to their durability. Fibreglass is dangerous and has been found to cause a disease similar to asbestosis. However, research is being done by many companies to try to find a substitute which is as good and affordable as asbestos.

Reasons for Public Resentment

After the Parti Québecois formed the provincial government in 1976, it began a study of the asbestos industry to outline a course of action for the industry. The new government was acutely aware of the growing resentment of the asbestos industry in the Eastern Townships mining region. Reasons for this resentment may be classified under three broad categories: processing of mined asbestos, English control of asbestos firms where the workers were mostly French, and health hazards associated with the industry.

Processing of Asbestos

Most asbestos firms in Quebec, at least the big ones, were foreign-owned. All but 3 per cent of the asbestos mined in the province was exported for processing outside Canada. Most of mined asbestos was shipped by subsidiaries in Quebec to their parents or affiliates abroad. Governments in Quebec, whether Liberal or P.Q., had long believed that further processing of asbestos would be in Quebec's interest.

Mining and shipping the ore elsewhere leaves Québecers feeling exploited and somewhat like the historical "hewers of wood and drawers of water" which had become so undesirable during the nationalism of the 1960s and 1970s. Quebec felt it was losing potential jobs associated with further processing. In addition, there was little or no research and development activity in Quebec, leaving the future of markets for asbestos in foreign hands. However, determining what is feasible and what methods may be used for implementing desired policies were and are matters of differing opinion.

English Control of Mining Operation

The second issue concerns the disproportionately low representation of French among the top management positions. Most of the managers in major asbestos firms were English speakers. The mines, however, are located in areas where the majority of the population is French. The workers in the mines were, thus, mostly French. The French-speaking workers resented the absence of Francophone managers and the French community in the mining region felt that it had little chance of acquiring management positions.

Health Issues and Labor Relations

The third major issue surrounding the asbestos industry had to do with the health problems associated with exposure to asbestos fibre, especially at the milling stage. The labor unions played an active role in bringing the health problems, especially the lung cancer caused by asbestos fibre, to the forefront and in demanding compensation for victims and stricter controls during the mining process.

The health problems as well as the issue of English control of mines played a very important role in the labor relations in the asbestos industry.

Labor relations in the industry were quite placid until 1949 when the workers struck at Johns-Manville in what was to become a bitter strike. The main issues of the strike were wages, the legitimacy of trade unionism itself, and the asbestos dust. That strike eventually spread to the rest of the industry. The 1949 strike, led by the Canadian and Catholic Confederation of Labor (CCCL), proved to be a symbolic one for the labor movement in Quebec. Although the strike was illegal under Quebec industrial relations laws, the CCCL asserted its independence and openly defied the conservative, pro-business government of Premier Maurice Duplessis. The union had the support of the trade unions, Le Devoir (a leading nationalist newspaper), and the sympathy of much of the Quebec public. Even the church, which traditionally had strong ties to the Duplessis government, supported the strikers. The strike was marked by considerable violence and although the union lost the strike, it was only the first in a series of bitter confrontations that pitted the labor movement against the combined forces of business and government. Furthermore, the strike accelerated the trend toward deconfessionalization within the church-affiliated segment of the labor movement. For these reasons, the Asbestos strike has been seen as the time when the Quebec labor movement "came of age".

Notwithstanding the broader connotations of the 1949 strike, ACL's labor relations were fairly routine afterwards. Between 1949 and 1975, a new contract was negotiated every two years, sometimes after arbitration. During this period, workers' wages rose steadily. The major conflict between the management and the workers was on the issue of health standards.

But another strike took place in 1975. Although higher wages were the main issue, working conditions played a very important role. The companies agreed to look into the issue, but the unions could win no more of a concession than that. The government of Premier Robert Bourassa commissioned the Beaudry Report soon afterward because of the bitterness of the strike and the growing militance of the unions, especially the Conseil des Syndicate Nationaux (CSN). The CSN represented the workers at ACL and two other companies. The Johns-Manville union, CSD (Conseil des Syndicats Democratiques), has been less militant and did not strike in 1975.

In response to the resentment of labor and community, the Parti Québecois first became involved with the asbestos industry in 1975 when at the party convention, the delegation from the Thetford Mines region managed to insert a plank in the party platform calling for the nationalization of the asbestos industry. After coming to power in 1976, however, a long time elapsed before the specific policy on the asbestos industry was announced in October 1977.

Government Responses

Provincial governments in Quebec had been concerned with the developments in the asbestos industry for a long time, at least since the 1949 strike. The Liberal government, led by Premier Robert Bourassa, commissioned the Alexandre Report. The report recommended in 1975 that the government acquire the control of ACL by purchasing 55 per cent of the shares which were then being offered by General Dynamics.

With an eye on increasing the volume of asbestos being processed in Quebec, the government hired Sores, Inc. in 1976 to look at the North American market for asbestos paper and textiles. These consultants, working in co-operation with Arthur D. Little of Boston, concluded that there were little or no growth prospects in those markets and felt that the only prospect for entry would be on a plant-replacement basis as U.S. plants became obsolete.

Jean Cournoyer, the Liberal minister of Natural Resources, claims that a White Paper would have been issued in January, 1977 on the asbestos industry had the Liberals not lost the election of November, 1976. The issue was not at the level of cabinet discussion, but it would have reached that level once the White Paper was presented. Cournoyer indicated in an interview since then that he had come to the conclusion that nationalization was *not* the best way to achieve some measure of control over an industry that was important politically and economically in Quebec. His goals were to develop new jobs in mining and manufacturing, and he felt that the best mechanism to accomplish these goals was a joint venture with private companies. He was especially interested in developing new mines in known deposits in northwest Quebec. His thinking was that the government should enter into contracts negotiated with the companies (rather than introduce legislation providing incentives), which would make the difference for the companies between an economically feasible and non-feasible project.

Cournoyer's deputy minister in charge of the asbestos policy emphasized the importance of taxation policy to regulate the industry; any change in taxation has a far greater effect on the industry than on government revenues. At the time the P.Q. was elected the industry was paying about $60 million annually in taxes compared to a total provincial budget of $10.5 billion in 1976-77. In fact, the deputy minister noted that the province made more on a 1¢ tax on cigarettes than the entire value of the taxes paid by the asbestos industry. A small change in taxes on the asbestos industry would not affect the government revenue very much, while such a small change in tax laws or regulations could have a major impact on each company. Therefore taxation or tax incentives could be a powerful tool of control for the government if it chose to use it.

Another concern of the Quebec government had been the prices at which the ore was transferred to parent companies. If these transfer prices were kept lower than market value of the ore by the parent companies, revenues of the Quebec-based subsidiary, and hence the taxes for the government, may be artificially low. Or, on the other hand, parent companies may have been charging artificially high prices for the transfer of equipment in order to show high costs and low taxable income. Despite a great deal of staff time invested in policing the companies on this issue, the government still seemed to feel they were not getting their rightful amount of taxes from the multinational asbestos companies.

The Liberals, however, lost power to the Parti Québecois in 1976. The P.Q. had risen to popularity in the province in a very short time as a social democratic party with strong ties to labor. Their election platform included a plank to nationalize the asbestos industry. Exhibit 7 briefly describes the social and political environment of Quebec prior to the election of the P.Q.

The P.Q. government wanted to control the asbestos industry to derive maximum benefits of the industry for Quebec. With this aim, the government studied various courses of action and felt that the acquisition of Asbestos Corporation Ltd. was essential to their policy.

ACL was one of the few companies selling its output in the open market rather than to its parent. The company had a diversified market for its output. ACL could be effectively used to increase mining and exploration as well as to give Quebec leverage in the market place. The grades of asbestos which ACL marketed are best-suited for asbestos cement, a product category that was forecast to be the sector with the bulk of the demand for asbestos in the coming years. Thus, to control ACL would be to control one of the largest and highest quality sources of the most important fibres for the future. An objective of the government's asbestos policy was to "play to the strengths" of each company, so it was unlikely ACL would have become an integrated manufacturing company under government ownership.

At the time the policy on the asbestos industry was being formulated, industry analysts felt that the government had the following alternatives to nationalization of ACL:

1. legislate and enforce health standards;
2. use taxation policy effectively — incentives and penalties regarding processing and opening of new mines;
3. joint ventures in new mines or manufacturing operations;
4. research into and development of new uses for asbestos. Taxation policy could be used to encourage companies like Johns-Manville to do their asbestos-related research and development in Quebec; and
5. set up a marketing board for the asbestos industry.[6]

One factor which weighed against nationalization of ACL was the risk of alienating U.S. business, especially lending institutions on Wall Street. Quebec borrowed frequently in U.S. market, both for government needs and for Hydro-Québec capital expenditures. U.S. financiers are traditionally conservative and could be expected to oppose any moves to nationalize private enterprise in Quebec.

Party leader and Premier Rene Lévesque, however, had sounded conciliatory notes toward Wall Street when in a speech to the Economic Club of New York in January 1977, he stressed that no industry would be nationalized in Quebec with the possible exception of the asbestos industry.

The government deliberated until October 1977 before announcing its policy on the industry: to take over the control of ACL with the objective of expanding the processing of asbestos in Quebec and increasing the provinces' share in the benefits arising from mining of asbestos.

---

6. The government has not pursued the idea of setting up a marketing board to control the supply and price of asbestos. The feeling has been that a marketing board would be unconstitutional under the British North American Act because a province has no authority over trade. However, the P.Q., while in opposition, had a plank in its 1975 platform calling for a marketing board. The constitutional issue may be less clear cut than was originally thought due to a recent Supreme Court ruling in favor of the Saskatchewan Government's pro-rationing scheme which allocated markets and set a floor price for sale of potash on international markets. However, ACL is the only one of the Québec companies which sells a significant amount of asbestos on the open market. Most other companies transfer a very high percentage of their output to their corporate affiliates, unlike the Saskatchewan situation.

Exhibit 1

Quebec Standard Grades (Simplified) of Asbestos

Grade	Length Specifications[a]	Uses
Long Fibre		
No. 1 crude	19 mm and longer	Textiles.
No. 2 crude	9.5 mm to 19 mm	Textiles and insulation materials.
No. 3	6mm to 9.6 mm	Fireproof textiles; packing; woven brake linings; clutch-facings; electrical, high-pressure and marine insulation.
Medium Fibre		
No. 4	3 mm to 6mm	Asbestos-cement products.
No. 5		Asbestos-cement products; low-pressure asbestos cement pipe; molded products; paper products; brake linings and gaskets.
No. 6	less than 3 mm	Asbetos-cement products; brake linings and gaskets; plaster; backing for vinyl sheets.
Short Fibre		
No. 7	less than 3 mm	Molded brake linings and clutch facings; plastics. Mostly "shorts".
No. 8	weight specifications apply	Used as a filler in vinyl and asphalt floor tiles, other asphalt compounds and caulking compounds; paints and drilling mud additives.
Very Short Fibre		
No. 9	weight specifications apply	Contains much rock and generally used for rock ballast, asphalt paving aggregate, and landfill.

(a) Converted from inches.

Source: Department of Energy, Mines, and Resources, Ottawa.

Exhibit 2

Canadian Asbestos Output by Producer & Grade (approx. % share) (QAMA Grade Equivalents)

	Group 3	Group 4	Group 5	Group 6	Group 7	% of Company Share In Canada's Output
Advocate (Nfld.)	—	13%	—	5%	—	5% - 6%
Asbestos Corp. (Quebec and West Germany)	24%	35%	25%	19%	3%	17% - 19%
Bell Asbestos (Quebec)	12%	2%	5%	3%	3%	3%
Carey-Canadian (Quebec)	—	1%	7%	4%	27%	12%
Cassiar Asbestos (B.C.)	42%	12%	7%	3%	—	6% - 7%
Johns-Manville (Quebec)	6%	27%	29%	51%	51%	38% - 40%
Lake Asbestos (Quebec)	15%	11%	24%	16%	16%	15%
	100%	100%	100%	100%	100%	100%

Note: We assumed production rates under ideal conditions at existing centres. We also included output from Nordenham operations of Asbestos Corp. Percentages are rounded to nearest decimal.

Source: Jones Heward & Company, Montreal.

Exhibit 3

Asbestos Corporation Limited Worldwide Sales of Fibre

	Percentage of Gross Sales	
	1978	1979
Western Europe	38.0	43.0
COMECON	20.0	20.0
Asia	15.0	14.5
Latin America	12.0	11.5
U.S.A.	5.0	3.0
Middle East	4.0	4.0
Africa	3.0	2.0
Oceania	2.5	1.5
Canada (Quebec)	0.5(0.3%)	0.5(0.4%)
	100.0	100.0

Source: ACL Annual Reports.

765   *Asbestos Corporation Limited/C*

Exhibit 4 (Part 1)

Canadian Group 3 Fibre Export Destinations and Fibre Value

	1970 Tons	%	1972 Tons	%	1974 Tons	%	1976 Tons	%	1978 Tons	%
W. Europe	10,530	34%	9,184	31.5%	12,026	35%	12,482	48%	6,956	28.5%
E. Europe	798	2.5	2,069	7	964	3	714	3	3,360	14
Middle East	211	0.5	111	0	540	1.5	215	1	140	0.5
Africa			110	0					6	0
Asia	4,089	13	3,013	10.5	4,755	14	2,973	11.5	2,910	12
Oceania	66	0	56	0	125	0.5	7	0	12	0
S. and C. America	769	2.5	891	3	3,440	10	2,012	8	2,369	10
U.S.A.	14,768	47.5	13,756	47	12,705	37	7,723	29.5	8,648	35.5
Total	**31,231**	**100%**	**29,190**	**100%**	**34,555**	**100%**	**26,126**	**100%**	**24,401**	**100%**
% of Total Fibre	2.0%		1.8%		1.9%		1.6%		1.6%	
Value of Per Ton	$458.71		$464.27		$620.69		$1,019.29		$1,046.23	
% of Total Value	6.3%		5.9%		6.4%		5.6%		4.5%	

Exhibit 4 (Part 2)

Canadian Group 4-5 (A-C) Fibre Export Destinations and Fibre Value

	1970		1972		1974		1976		1978	
	Tons	%	Tons	%	Tons	%	Tons	%	Tons	%
W. Europe	301,518	38%	277,216	37.5%	340,647	41%	329,953	44%	289,170	39%
E. Europe	22,875	3	21,793	3	17,808	2	13,244	2	37,323	5
Middle East	16,819	2	19,706	3	22,522	3	15,805	2	20,775	3
Africa	10,306	1	9,613	1	8,472	1	13,673	2	10,093	1
Asia	114,607	14	89,374	12	105,426	12	101,229	13.5	106,418	14.5
Oceania	53,296	7	48,213	6.5	42,943	5	52,919	7	35,231	5
S. and C. America	81,734	10	75,267	10	96,809	11	85,728	11.5	106,056	14.5
U.S.A	191,938	24	197,344	27	205,172	24	135,818	18	130,635	18
Total	793,093	100%	738,526	100%	839,799	100%	748,369	100%	735,701	100%
% of Total Fibre	50.8%		46.2%		47.4%		46.3%		47.7%	
Value per Ton	$198.62		$207.29		$268.88		$429.23		$550.48	
% of Total Value	69.3%		66.6%		67.2%		68.0%		71.3%	

Exhibit 4 (Part 3)

Canadian Group 6+ (Shorts) Fibre Export Destinations and Fibre Value

	1970		1972		1974		1976		1978	
	Tons	%	Tons	%	Tons	%	Tons	%	Tons	%
W. Europe	143,426	19.5%	156,078	19%	189,136	21%	170,480	20%	150,802	19%
E. Europe	3,690	0.5	1,068	0	4,519	0.5	3,277	0.5	2,056	0.5
Middle East	2,313	0.5	6,635	1	5,884	0.5	7,479	1	2,320	0.5
Africa	2,745	0.5	3,259	0.5	2,396	0.5	7,453	1	1,265	0
Asia	135,432	18.5	118,588	14.5	126,603	14	142,361	17	119,329	15
Oceania	16,257	2	11,033	1.5	13,662	1.5	6,653	1	2,308	0.5
S. and C. America	26,559	3.5	30,132	3.5	38,961	3.5	34,969	4	47,380	6
U.S.A.	407,585	55.0	503,522	60.5	517,273	55.5	469,852	56	455,408	58.5
Total	**738,007**	**100%**	**830,885**	**100%**	**898,454**	**100%**	**842,524**	**100%**	**780,868**	**100%**
% of Total Fibre	47.2%		52.0%		50.7%		52.1%		50.7%	
Value Per Ton	$74.94		$75.97		$98.61		$148.10		$176.43	
% of Total Value	24.3%		27.5%		26.4%		26.4%		24.2%	

Source: Jones Heward & Company Ltd.

Exhibit 5

Projected World Demand for Asbestos

(Selected years to 2000) (in thousands of tons)

Market	1980	1985	1990	2000
Canada	121	138	155	195
United States	826	946	1,085	1,428
E.E.C.	953	1,136	1,334	1,840
Other Western Europe	693	727	800	969
Japan	401	478	534	668
Rest of the World	2,174	2,490	2,796	3,526
Total	**5,168**	**5,915**	**6,704**	**8,626**

Source: Department of Energy, Mines, and Resources, Ottawa.

Exhibit 6

Quebec Asbestos Industry

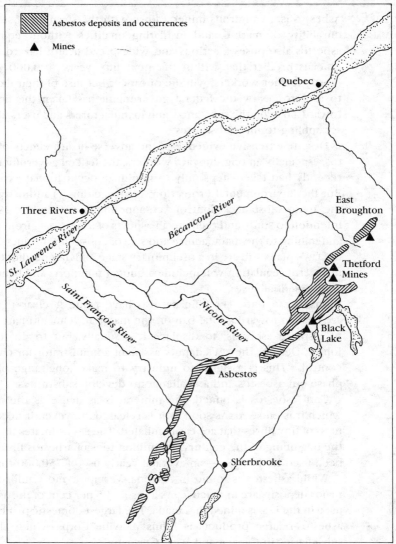

Source: *The Northern Miner*.

Exhibit 7

The Growing Need for Asbestos Substitutes*

Asbestos is a wondrous mineral fibre with the strength of steel, the durability of marble, and insulating qualities without equal. But asbestos also poses a serious and widespread health hazard. Health officials predict that within the next fifty years, 400,000 people, mostly former workers, will die of cancer because of their exposure to asbestos. Now the federal government has taken the first step toward a ban on the substance, and manufacturers and users alike are scrambling to find substitutes.

Despite extensive evidence of the adverse health effects of asbestos, especially among shipyard workers, the federal government until recently had taken steps only to minimize occupational exposures. But the Environmental Protection Agency, citing its authority under the Toxic Substances Control Act, announced in October, 1979, its intention to study and regulate all aspects of asbestos — from mining and milling to the manufacture and sale of consumer products. While the EPA's plans still are in a preliminary stage, officials predict that the near-term regulation will include a quota on imports and bans on all "non-essential" uses.

Plans for a ban. EPA officials also have made it clear that they are headed toward a total ban on the material. "Our ultimate goal is to displace asbestos, to displace it gradually, but to do it," says John P. Dekany, the EPA's deputy assistant administrator for chemical control. "This is a signal to industry to make long-range plans to phase out asbestos and a challenge to develop substitutes."

Until asbestos is mined, the mineral is as dense as the rock in which it is encased. As soon as it is released, however, it becomes a mass of tiny fibres that are easily inhaled. The EPA estimates that since the beginning of the century, 30 million tons of asbestos fibres have been used in the U.S. — an average yearly use of 750,000 tons.

While asbestos is found in Arizona, Vermont, and California, the major deposits are in Quebec. As a result, 95 per cent of the asbestos used in the U.S. is mined in Canada. The largest domestic producer of asbestos-related products is Johns-Manville Corp., which also has subsidiaries in Canada and West Germany.

The suggestion of a ban sends shivers through Canadian producers. The U.S. is far and away Canada's biggest customer. In 1978 American companies purchased 40 per cent of the asbestos produced in Canada, business worth more than $200 million. "We're greatly concerned about it, and we'll make every representation that we can," states J. Robert Hutcheson, chairman of Johns-Manville Canada Ltd. The

U.S. parent is working closely for now with the EPA, but company officials warn that if the agency's actions are unreasonable, they may test the Toxic Substances Control Act in court.

Many U.S. companies that manufacture products containing asbestos are worried, too. The single largest use of asbestos is in asbestos cement pipe. The asbestos serves as a reinforcing agent, resulting in pipes that are highly resistant to deterioration when used in sewers and water distribution systems. Roofing, sheathing materials, and vinyl floor tiles often contain asbestos because, in addition to its reinforcement qualities, it is fire-resistant. The substance's heat resistance also makes it important to auto and truck manufacturers for brake linings. "In my opinion, there is no substitute for asbestos in heavy-duty truck brakes," argues Edward J. Sydor, general manager of Kelsey-Hayes Co.'s National Friction Products Div.

Yet the EPA intends to target brake linings, along with asbestos paper products used in sheathing and roofing, in the agency's first regulation. EPA officials point out that there are more than 100 million motor vehicles in the U.S. today. Because most cars and trucks need a new set of brake linings every three or four years, agency officials believe that a considerable amount of material may be released into the environment during normal use, as well as during repairs, threatening both consumers and mechanics.

Phase out. U.S. auto makers are phasing in disc brake linings in which the asbestos content has been cut from 1 lb. to about 1 oz. GM decided last January to move away from asbestos brake linings after company officials discovered that the average repair person's response to a brake complaint is to sand the linings. "This puts all sorts of harmful fibres in the air," says Stanley B. Fowler, a staff engineer for GM's Buick Div., which spearheads brake design for the corporation. Both GM and Ford say that their suppliers now are seeking ways to eliminate asbestos totally in brakes.

In disc brake linings, asbestos is replaced by a semi-metallic friction material built around steel fibre and iron powder. However, this surface must be attached to the brake shoe with an asbestos backing material, which serves as a noise and heat shield while providing additional strength. "We are working very hard to come up with a material to replace this last bit of asbestos," says Charles M. Brunhofer, director of engineering for Bendix Corp.'s Friction Materials Div.

On drum brakes, there is a problem finding a suitable material that will hold the curved shape that such brake linings require. But Rockwell International Corp., which makes 60 per cent of the brakes used in heavy trucks, says it has a major development effort under way. "We will be in a position [to market non-asbestos brakes] in a reasonable amount of time," claims Leonard C. Buckland, director of engineering and product planning for Rockwell's Highway Brake Div.

Asbestos still is used in shingles and in roofing felt, a component of so-called built-up roofing for flat roofs. The National Roofing Contractors Assn. (NRCA) estimates that about 10 per cent of industrial and commercial flat roofs contain asbestos. But the trade group notes that such use of asbestos is declining. In 1978 asbestos felt was used as a fire-proofing agent in 16 per cent of roofs, a decline from the 24 per cent recorded the previous four years. There are a number of acceptable substitutes for asbestos in built-up roofing, including fibre glass and organic felt, which consists of treated rags and newspapers.

NRCA's general manager, William A. Good, admits that awareness of the environmental problems that may be created by asbestos in buildings is part of the reason its use is falling. A major use of asbestos from the Second World War through the early 1970s, insulation, has been almost completely eliminated. Asbestos has been almost completely replaced for that use by such substances as calcium silicate, cellular glass, mineral wool, fibre glass, and expanded perlite.

In addition, the EPA has prohibited since 1978 the spraying of asbestos on the walls or ceilings of buildings. The agency's original concern was the exposure of workers and others to the fibres during the spraying process, but the problem of sprayed asbestos, it turns out, is not that ephemeral. The Environmental Defense Fund recently sued the EPA to force it to take action to protect school children attending classes in aging buildings where asbestos insulation was flaking off the walls and ceilings. The EPA now intends to make mandatory its existing voluntary program, which requires school districts to seal in or replace asbestos in such structures. The agency estimates that 10 per cent to 15 per cent of all school buildings contain asbestos.

However, other construction users of asbestos insist that the substance is safe in their applications. Manufacturers of asbestos cement pipe, for instance, claim that their products do not pose a danger to the public because the asbestos is embedded in cement and the pipe is buried 4 ft. to 12 ft. underground. "We think our application of asbestos . . . is safe and that the government feels basically the same way," says William A. Krivsky, senior vice-president of piping products at CertainTeed Corp. But in fact, EPA officials are worried that the asbestos fibres may become loosened by years of rushing water.

Trying glass. While CertainTeed, with $100 million in asbestos cement pipe sales, appears optimistic that any EPA restrictions will not affect its operations, the company is busily studying possible substitutes. Glass fibres normally are attacked by the cement because of its alkalinity, but there is promise in fibre glass specially formulated to be alkali resistant. One such fibre, called Cemfil AR, was developed years ago under licence from Britain's National Research & Development Corp., a self-financing public corporation, and has been sold commercially worldwide since 1971 by Pilkington Bros Ltd. Both fatter and longer than asbestos fibres, Cemfil AR has proved to be a strong reinforcement. And it has not shown any of asbestos's harmful effects, although its inventor, A. J. Majumdar, reports "minor skin complaints".

Owens-Corning Fiberglass Corp., a U.S. licensee for the technology, is also working hard on glass as a substitute. "I don't think any one material will universally replace asbestos," says Robert C. Doban, senior vice-president for science and technology. But he is optimistic about glass's potential.

Part of the problem with glass is its tendency to soften at high temperatures; asbestos remains rigid until it reaches its melting point. Therefore, glass could not easily be substituted for the asbestos that is still used to reinforce the concrete sprayed on steel work in most buildings — a measure taken to prevent the steel from buckling from heat in case of fire.

Smaller companies also are vying for a corner of the asbestos-substitute market. Gentex Corp., of Carbondale, Pa., which manufactures metal-coated fabric for protective garments, recently introduced Preox, a heat-resistant fabric made of stabilized polyacrylonitrile. The fibre, called Celiox and developed by Celanese Corp., has a high carbon content that enables it to resist heat. Protective garments of this sort are worn by firemen and by iron and steel workers to protect them from the splash of molten metal. Eugene Alexandroff, general manager of the Gentex Textile Div., is interested in other applications, too. The company is exploring the possibility of entering the ship construction and maintenance markets, where asbestos is still used to wrap pipes.

Partial substitutes. In Bangor, Mich., American Filler & Abrasives Inc. has been marketing an asbestos substitute called Kay-O-Cel since April. It is made of cellulose and clay wastes and other materials and is being tested in brake linings. Company President Edwin F. Neckermann claims that the product is price-competitive with asbestos and should pose no health problems. "All the materials in Kay-O-Cel themselves are recognized as being safe," he says.

Earlier this year, 3M Co. moved to expand marketing of its substitute, Nextel — a cloth made of ceramic fibre that can withstand heat up to 2,600F. The company turned over substantial sales rights to equipment builder Babcock & Wilcox Co., which serves the steel, glass, and utility industries.

"We are seeing many companies, often with full-time corporate engineers working on the problem, coming to us asking if Nextel can be used as an asbestos substitute," says Arlen J. Rivard, sales and marketing manager in 3M's ceramic fibres project. Nextel can be used as high-temperature insulation in and around furnaces, but its relatively high price — $25 a lb. vs. $2 a lb. for fibre glass and less than $2 a lb. for asbestos — makes it an unlikely replacement for asbestos in that application.

Despite the surge in substitute development, it could be a long time before an effective alternative is found for asbestos in all uses. And Johns-Manville, the industry leader, is relying on that while the EPA begins its studies. "If the EPA ban on asbestos goes into effect, that would put us out of the asbestos business," says a JM source. "But there are enough essential uses of asbestos, and the scientific and medical research do not justify a ban."

Exhibit 8

Industrialism, Nationalism, Change in Quebec*

During the late nineteenth and early twentieth centuries, industrialism came gradually to Quebec. Here, as in neighboring Ontario, it responded to the general economic forces of the continent, assisted by the political structure of Confederation, the coming of railways, the advent of tariffs in 1879, and the abundant inflow of foreign capital and capitalists. The exploitation of Quebec's extensive wealth in forests, minerals, and water power gave the economy a special and lasting complexion.

In the nineteenth century the exploiters of the forests were concerned with cutting pine trees, shipping logs, and building ships on the St. Lawrence. But the growing importance of steam, steel, railways, and hydraulic power transformed this picture. As stocks of pine were depleted, the pulp and paper industries came to utilize timber in a different manner, aided by Quebec's other substantial asset, the power resources of Laurentian rivers.

In these abundant and turbulent waters, the province had a substitute for the absence of native coal. The central electric station became the chief instrument of industrial expansion, stimulated the economic life of a whole region rather than a restricted locality, and helped to sustain, not merely the production of pulp and paper, but widely scattered secondary industries in the satellite communities of Montreal: shoes, textiles, clothing products, foods and beverages, leather goods, electric apparatus, non-ferrous metals, and transportation equipment.

Industrialization and the social forces it generated brought rapid

* Reprinted from the *Banker and ICB Review*, January — February 1977.

urbanization. Factories multiplied, towns grew, and families deserted the lean life of marginal and northern farms for what seemed the superior amenities of town and city. In 1900 more than 60 per cent of Quebec's population was rural. But in almost every decade since then forces have tended to reverse this distribution of the people. Since the Second World War the urbanizing process has been so potent that three out of four French Canadians are now urban residents, and Metropolitan Montreal has a large proportion of them. Even by 1913 it accounted for half of the province's manufacturing and a quarter of its population. By the 1970s it contained almost a third of the provincial population.

Industrialism gradually sapped the foundations of Quebec's traditional culture, especially the commanding position and authority of the church. It brought ideas and values from the outside world, notably from the United States. The old image of a simple rural community insulated from external influences by barriers of language and guided by a small clerical and professional elite may have been adequate in 1900, but in the twentieth century it became increasingly irrelevant.

The church was obviously more influential in the rural parish than in the industrial town, where the tutelage of bishop and curé had to compete with numerous influences, especially the press, cinema, radio, and trade unions struggling to advance the material interests of labor. In the traditional rural society the parish priest was a supreme guide and counsellor who exerted a compelling personal influence on the lives of parishioners. But in the impoverished tenements of Montreal, he confronted problems of a more complex order, and his suasive power had less scope. Conflicts between large corporations and trade unions, both possessing intimate international bonds, posed difficult issues to resolve. The bishops distrusted the brusque intrusion of international unions, whose concepts of work, strategies of industrial strife, and ideas of education were alien to their own. They feared that such secular institutions would infect French Canadians with the virus of class warfare, threaten their religion, erode their traditions, and destroy their capacity to survive as a cohesive people.

This grim medley of fears convinced the hierarchy to sponsor unions confined strictly to French-speaking Catholics, advised by clerics, and dedicated to a system of industrial relations in harmony with the principles prescribed by papal encyclicals, especially Rerum Novarum of Leo III in 1891. These unions consolidated their forces into the Catholic Confederation of Labor founded in Hull in 1921. They had no counterpart elsewhere in Canada nor indeed in North America, and existed only because of Quebec's special environment and social circumstances. They were designed not merely to foster harmony between workers and employers but to help workers retain their French language and Catholic religion. They naturally operated best in areas subject to potent ecclesiastical influences. Quebec City, for example, favored them more than did Montreal, for in the larger heterogeneous metropolis Protestant, Jewish, and secular influences were conspicuous in business, newspapers, education, and international unions.

The emergence of Catholic syndicalism demonstrated the persuasive power of the Quebec church. Yet it was not long before the movement failed to retain its doctrines in the face of the relentless march of industrialism, secularism, and the fierce competition of other unions. Relaxing an earlier reliance on moral suasion, it was compelled to become more militant, more concerned with momentary expedients, and more disposed to employ the weapon of the strike. During and after the Second World War it increasingly came closer in character to rival unions, opened its ranks to other than French-speaking Catholics, and accepted co-operation between French-speaking and English-speaking organizations wherever common interests were involved.

In 1949, the changing temper of this syndical movement was dramatically reflected in the prolonged and bitter strike at Asbestos against an inflexible American corporation, supported by Premier Maurice Duplessis, who outlawed the strike and tried to crush it. Pierre E. Trudeau wrote a sympathetic assessment of the strike and its consequences in *La grève de l'amiante*, Montreal Cité Libre, 1956. (An English translation of this work was published by James Lewis and Samuel, Toronto, 1974.) The event was made specially significant by church leaders who despite the hostility of Duplessis strongly supported the workers.

In subsequent years the Catholic Confederation of unions grew in strength, radicalized, and politicized itself, and sought to make trade unionism and reform a more effective power in Quebec life. At the same time it realized that its industrial purposes were best-served by extending its outlook and enlarging its affiliations. In 1960 it eliminated its last links with the Roman Catholic Church and appeared as the Confederation of National Trade Unions (CNTU). It adopted measures to centralize its structure and enhance its strength in competing with its chief opponent, the Quebec Federation of Labor.

As a federation of unionists engaged in industrial struggle, the CNTU inherited from the Catholic Confederation one conspicuous feature: a confident ideological purpose, expressed in working for social betterment and the concrete reforms needed to achieve it. Some of its leaders now were likely to reflect less the ideas of Liberal Catholicism than the concepts of Karl Marx and his varied disciples. They became agents in helping to extend what was called the Quiet Revolution of the 1960s. But the chief instrument in effecting this event was the provincial Liberal party under Jean Lesage, which in 1960 acquired power a year after the death of Duplessis.

The Lesage Administration (1960-66) marked a special milestone in the province's social evolution. More than any previous group of politicians it made crucial decisions affecting modern Quebec. It enlarged the role of government in the society beyond anything attempted before, particularly in the management of schools, hospitals, and welfare programs. Hitherto these major services had developed under the church's fostering supervision. Religious orders established institutions to care for the orphans, the old, the sick, the insane, and the blind. They might request and receive funds from the province, but operated under clerical direction and staffing. Over the years an elaborate welfare structure emerged that respected the rights of family and church, and remained a distinguishing feature of Quebec's Catholicism without parallel in other provinces.

Specially important in this past era were the educational arrangements wherein the church's influence and guidance were dominant from primary school to university. At the same time the Protestant minority enjoyed almost a parallel independence, managing its own schools, hospitals, and welfare institutions. The Council of Public Instruction, established in 1869, was nominally the supreme agency for supervising provincial education but for some fifty years it seemed scarcely more than a formality, since it operated mainly through two committees, one for Catholic and one for Protestant schools. For all practical purposes two distinct public school systems existed, each in its separate arena dealing with problems of pedagogy, curriculum, and finance.

This framework of dualism in denominational schools reflected the type of practical accommodation reached before and after Confederation between English and French Quebecers. It rested on self-segregated institutions in education and welfare, conformed with the principle of live and let live for both cultures, and seemed appropriate in the circumstances of the period between Confederation and the Second World War.

But in the industrialized society after the war, Quebec no longer lived in relative isolation. Many French-speaking liberals, influenced partly by new winds of change from outside the country, became dissatisfied with the entrenched system and its attendant anomalies, confusions, and inefficiencies. They wanted to reshape it, render it more coherent, and make it conform to their newly-awakened nationalism and their sudden passion for modernization. They were anxious to employ education in developing within Quebec the mold of a liberal democratic society. Under Jean Lesage these reformers, including some clerics, were the architects of the Quiet Revolution. They did not create a revolution in any strict sense, but achieved a comprehensive and rapid acceleration in the pace of liberal reform.

The most significant result of these reforms was to diminish the ancient ascendancy of the church over education and transfer power to a provincial bureaucracy devoted to forms of instruction demanded by an industrial and commercial society. In 1964, amid furious controversy, a Ministry of Education was established and later a single Superior Council of Education acquired an advisory role. The appointment of a ministry was, for evident reasons, long opposed by the Catholic hierarchy. Being directly accountable to the legislature, a ministry was likely to favor a system of schooling at once more centralized, secular, and democratic. For these reasons its advocates believed that it would be better able to cope with some common deficiencies of Quebec schools: low per capita expenditure on the system, inferior pay, and qualifications of teachers compared with those in Ontario, a faulty pupil-teacher ratio, and a high drop-out rate.

The reformers of the Quiet Revolution were careful not to destroy a distinctive and cherished feature of Quebec's traditional school system: the presence of dual denominational public schools — Protestant and Catholic — sustained and financed both by local elected boards and by the provincial treasury. The Catholic schools differ from the Protestant in that they are guided by the Catholic principles of education, formulated by the rules of the church, and associated also with the church's age-long determination to foster in the St. Lawrence valley the French language and culture. The Protestant schools on the other hand resemble those in other parts of English-speaking Canada, with only a minimal amount of religion in the form of Bible readings. More conspicuous in them than religious creed is the secular and pragmatic outlook of English-speaking North America. In this dual school system the formal and verbal basis of division is denominational, but in turn this factor is intricately intertwined with language and culture.

Education was merely one of the important areas in Quebec in which the Lesage Liberals were anxious to achieve salutary changes. With a collectivist tinge, they were determined to pursue a far-reaching program of reform and development designed to augment the activities of government, carve out a large new public sector in the economy, accelerate the use of provincial natural resources, encourage new industries under French-Canadian control, increase and diversify employment, establish hospital insurance and welfare services, and generally quicken the rhythms of social change. Quebec more than Ontario had been accustomed to rely on industries with a low level of wages and a high level of protection. The government was resolved to change this situation, invigorate stagnant parts of the economy, quicken the mobility of labor, and diminish in the province the sharp regional disparities in income that had hitherto existed. Implementing these plans necessitated an emphasis on public bodies like Hydro-Québec, the General Investment Corporation, the Mining Exploration Corporation, and the recruitment of a new and vigorous civil service. The government was confident that its concern with economic accomplishment and progress would augment rather than diminish cultural survival.

The nationalization of Hydro-Québec in 1963 was intended to set an impressive example of state-planning, train French-Canadian executives and technicians in a key industry, and confirm the hope of Quebec nationalists that they could become effective masters in their own house. The venture involved financial risks that had long worried Lesage, but its importance in the reform movement was soon demonstrated. The far-ranging plans of the Liberals were dictated not merely by a voracious appetite for material progress similar to that in other provinces, but also by an upsurge of local Quebec nationalism. Leaders were confident that in their provincial stronghold French Canadians could reduce their former economic backwardness and assert their distinction as a people controlling their destiny. "We are not defending the autonomy of the provinces," said Mr. Lesage at the federal-provincial conference of 1963, "simply because it is a question of a principle, but rather because autonomy is to us the basic condition, not of our survival which is assured from now on, but of our assertion as a people."

The aspirations of the Lesage ministry had prompt and wide implications for Quebec's position in the federal system and its fiscal structure. Since a more copious flow of revenue was essential to implement their extensive schemes, Lesage and his colleagues early engaged in jousts with the national government over provincial tax rights and the necessity for their extension. They had little respect for many of the shared-cost programs that proliferated in Canadian federalism during the 1950s, for in their view they often failed to meet the special needs of the province's cultural and economic life and threatened its autonomy. On Quebec's behalf, they began a militant struggle to reduce the centralized economic and fiscal power fashioned in Ottawa since the Second World War. This is not the place to pursue a theme that also involves other provinces as well as Quebec and the technical issues of federalism in general.

In June 1966, the Lesage Government was rejected by the electors, especially by those in the countryside, villages, and small towns who feared that its reforms would destroy the old society and institutions they knew and instinctively respected. Despite this assertion of conservatism, the major innovations of the Lesage regime endured, and the nationalist ideas that it aroused continued to develop without interruption, although not always in the direction and manner that would have been acceptable to Mr. Lesage.

During the next decade (1966-76) Quebec's society evolved uneasily on lines determined in particular by two dominant influences: first, the industrial and urban forces growing ever more mature and pervasive and generating their accustomed tensions; and second the freshly awakened sense of French-Canadian nationalism now inspired a large number of Quebecers, especially the young and intellectual, with an ambition to achieve a new constitutional status appropriate for their nationality.

In industry, a conspicuous feature of these years was the emergence of powerful and militant labor unions, which utilized fully the free collective bargaining that the Lesage government had earlier established. The unions were grouped in two principal federations of relatively equal strength: the CNTU, which is almost exclusively confined to organizations in Quebec, and the QFL, which embraces the local units of international unions that extend across Canada and the United States. In this period both federations tended to reflect a militant outlook and temper. Public employees like other workers acquired the rights of collective bargaining including a right to strike, and in relentlessly pursuing their ends were not hesitant in closing schools, hospitals, and the operations of Hydro-Québec. Later their radicalism was emphatically demonstrated in their protest against the restrictive policies pursued by Robert Bourassa. In March 1972, more than 200 thousand public service employees staged a twenty-four hour general and illegal strike. The Bourassa administration pressed court charges against the two major federations and the union of teachers, and imprisoned their leaders for a limited interval.

The aggressive vision and language of labor leaders and their tactical employment of a general strike suggest a kinship with the revolutionary syndicalism of France and Europe rather than with North American trade unionism. In their tactics, the leaders were striving to exert a general proletarian pressure that would destroy the government and shake the economic system. Such was the unsettled mood of the time that a notable master of revolutionary rhetoric in the 1930s, Michel Chartrand, once more leaped to prominence as a leading figure in the CNTU and a hero of the local student power movement. He wanted a non-compromising socialism, sponsored by a close aggregation of blue and white collar workers, engineers, teachers, and students.

The trend to labor radicalism was intricately related to other circumstances in the economy and society, especially the unsettling speed of social change and the chronically high unemployment rate. Since the Second World War, employment has steadily risen, but the labor force has grown more rapidly. The number of farm jobs has dropped substantially as urban industrialism becomes more significant than cultivating the soil. Quebec's unemployment rate has consistently tended to be higher than that of Ontario, a fact rarely forgotten by local labor leaders. More general and important is the fact that since 1870 production in agriculture, mining, and manufacturing has grown at almost identical rates in both Ontario and Quebec, but per capita income and wages have always remained lower in Quebec. The Quebec unions are now more anxious than ever to change this situation.

In the years after the Quiet Revolution, Quebec's economic and labor developments have become intertwined with its nationalism. No longer is nationalism a sporadic movement of relatively small elite intellectual groups. It pervades the sentiments and attitudes of mind in the new and growing middle class that emerged with the advance of industrialization. It is the prevalent creed in one form or another in the first generation of Quebecers after the advent of compulsory education in 1943. The new middle class has been constantly exposed to the influence of the mass media in the French tongue. When in 1952 the Canadian Broadcasting Corporation started French language television in Quebec, it had to rely on its own local resources. Hence, in its Montreal studios, it proceeded to fashion a centre for producing and assembling the requisite plays, songs, and programs, and soon acquired a staff eminently skilled in appealing to the tastes and interests of Quebecers.

The results were impressive. The CBC French network succeeded in diminishing the cultural isolation of the province, reduced the former dominance of English-language American publications and films, and created an intellectual and artistic class with a vested interest in fostering a local culture distinct from the mass culture of English-speaking North America. Its main focus of interest was parochial, concerned with the life and aspirations of Quebec rather than with those of Canada as a whole. Not surprisingly the broadcasters engaged in these communication ventures felt a deep devotion to their own cultural inheritance, and politically leaned to an ultra nationalism or even separatism.

René Lévesque in his own career illustrated the link between broadcasting and politics. In 1960, he moved promptly from a distinguished position in the French network into the politics of the Quiet Revolution with a post in Lesage's cabinet, where he played a dynamic part in creating and defending the regime. A zealous minister, he was from the outset fired by the concept of Quebec as a political entity, carving out its own distinct future, and enlarging the opportunities of its people to realize themselves. From this position soon after the defeat of the Liberals in 1966, he reached the conviction that only through a separate state could the nationalist aspirations of Quebec be fulfilled. What followed was his creation of the *Parti Québécois*, dedicated to Quebec's ultimate independence. His building of the party is recent history, which needs no repetition here, other than to admit his superb skill and persistence as a propagandist for the cause.

The general provincial election of November 15, 1976, must be taken as a milestone in the history of Quebec. It marked the triumph of the P.Q., committed to secure the ultimate political independence of the province. Parties with separatist ambitions had existed before, but never were more than small revolutionary groups without substantial support. The P.Q. differs from its predecessors, not merely in the political backing it commands, but in its acceptance of the principle that secession from the rest of Canada must be approved by a majority of Quebecers in a referendum. This feature in its program was decisive in determining the choice of its electors. Many of these voted, not for separatism, but for an alternative democratic party that might improve on what the Bourassa Liberals attempted and failed to accomplish: effective rule and the extension of reforms begun in the Quiet Revolution of the 1960s. Indeed, during the electoral campaign the principal emphasis of the P.Q. leadership was focussed on remedying some of the many concrete ailments from which an industrial and urban Quebec had acutely suffered: high unemployment, social inequality, regional disparities, industrial strife, prolonged strikes, a harassed and depressed agriculture, and deficient housing.

In the election, the P.Q. had won a majority of seats with 41 per cent of the vote. Pollsters have tried to calculate the proportion of citizens in the province who actually favored separation. Early in November a poll that predicted a P.Q. victory also showed that only 18 per cent of those polled favored Quebec independence. Some 58 per cent were opposed. One post-election poll found only 11 per cent ready to vote for independence. These facts, however, failed to discourage ardent separatists, who are confident that through control over the machinery and resources of government they can potently influence opinions and foster separatist sentiments. Moreover they believe that Mr. Lévesque and his colleagues through honest and competent rule will demonstrate how well an independent Quebec could operate while at the same time they will illustrate the basic difficulty in reaching appropriate agreements with the administration in Ottawa. In the symbolism of politics the members of the P.Q. already behave as if they were separate from Canada, an attitude designed to encourage a separatist consciousness. Separatists in office are now clearly in a stronger position to enhance their appeal and make numerous converts.

Yet there is a reverse side to the medal. Although Mr. Lévesque assembled a talented and determined team, Quebec's major economic and social problems will not be resolved easily and quickly. In coping with them, the P.Q. is likely to encounter opposition from the right and the left, and may itself undergo severe internal strains. As a leader, Lévesque will doubtless strive to maintain a balance between extreme views. In the 1960s, he had shown considerable ministerial skill and resolution in resisting the pressure of extremists. He once reminded impatient radicals that they must shed "the illusion that everything can be changed by tomorrow morning". In the future, he is likely to have occasions for repeating this injunction and also reiterating his warning to trade unionists who make extravagant demands: "We are on the North American continent. We are a mouse, and if our ambitions carry us too far we will be squashed by the American elephant."

The efforts of Lévesque and his colleagues to establish a regime of realistic reform may so absorb them in the next three years that they will have insufficient time to conduct an effective campaign for independence. Consequently they may be disposed to defer the referendum, since ambitious politicians are usually unwilling to hold a vote that they may lose. For the country in general, postponement could be profoundly unsettling. But at least the delay can be utilized by federalists in and out of Quebec to examine afresh and at greater depth than ever before the substance and terms of their federal creed. They must begin with the fact that in the last hundred years the Canadian system has evolved from a highly centralized to a relatively decentralized federalism, and has done so in response to powerful forces, among them the constant quest of Quebec for the security of its culture.

Canada's constitution is not inflexible. It is capable of change, and indeed must change as the economic and social realities of the country demand. Whether federalists can effect change quickly enough to hold Quebecers within the union remains to be seen. They must at the same time ensure a better working unison between the other provinces and the national government, for all the federal difficulties have not been confined to Quebec. During the next three years, therefore, Canadians will witness a very critical era in the history of their country. They must require from their leaders a determination to study and cope boldly with the hard realities of their common plight. They must also require from them all the initiative, imagination, and patience that they can command.

Exhibit 9

Asbestos Corporation Limited and Subsidiary Companies
Consolidated Balance Sheet

Assets	December 31	
	1979	1978
Current Assets:		
Cash	**$ 176,507**	$ 1,140,737
Accounts and bills receivable	**39,923,582**	48,876,282
Inventories (Note 2)	**72,046,600**	63,830,524
Prepaid taxes, insurance, etc.	**4,476,647**	2,732,092
	116,623,336	116,579,635
Properties, at cost less depreciation and depletion (Notes 3 and 4)	**130,182,339**	121,725,851
Unamortized Exploration and Mine Development (Note 4)	**24,252,826**	20,056,706
Other Assets	**899,630**	971,496
	$271,958,131	$259,333,688

Liabilities		
Current Liabilities:		
Bank indebtedness	**$ 15,904,219**	$ 14,207,849
Accounts payable and accrued liabilities	**22,921,544**	26,926,978
Amounts due to affiliated companies	**124,840**	4,228,277
Income and other taxes	**3,465,602**	562,835
Instalments due within one year on long-term debt (Note 5)	**3,997,934**	1,917,573
	46,414,139	47,843,512
Long-Term Debt (Note 5)	**24,492,493**	23,553,524
Deferred Income Taxes	**43,744,000**	41,482,000
Shareholders' Equity:		
Capital stock —		
Preferred shares —		
Authorized and unissued — 500,000 shares par value $50 each issuable in series		
Common shares of no par value —		
Authorized — 3,600,000 shares		
Outstanding — 2,837,002 shares	**33,311,682**	33,311,682
Retained earnings (Note 6)	**123,995,817**	113,142,970
	157,307,499	146,454,652
	$271,958,131	$259,333,688

Approved by the Board:
G. W. Fiske, Director
M. E. Taschereau, Director

Exhibit 10

Asbestos Corporation Limited and Subsidiary Companies
Consolidated Statement of Income and Retained Earnings

		Year ended December 31	
		1979	1978
Sales		$171,787,934	$147,086,707
Cost of Sales, Selling, General and Administrative Expenses		146,451,360	127,607,191
Operating Profit (before taking into account the undernoted items)		25,336,574	19,479,516
Interest and Other Income		1,422,914	2,431,012
		26,759,488	21,910,528
Interest Expense —			
Long-term debt	$2,918,946		$2,542,549
Other	864,890	3,783,836	321,780 2,864,329
		22,975,652	19,046,199
Provision for Income Taxes		5,314,000	3,395,000
Net Income (per share: 1979 — $6.22; 1978 — $5.51)		17,661,652	15,651,199
Retained Earnings, January 1		113,142,970	104,300,576
		130,804,622	119,951,775
Dividends Paid (per share $2.40)		6,808,805	6,808,805
Retained Earnings, December 31		$123,995,817	$113,142,970

Exhibit 11

Asbestos Corporation Limited and Subsidiary Companies
10-Year Summary

	1979	1978	1977	1976	1975	1974	1973	1972	1971	1970
Sales	$171,787,934	$147,086,707	$145,344,178	$151,368,425	$84,834,412	$108,475,180	$66,209,138	$49,520,868	$52,320,410	$53,583,354
Income before Taxes	22,975,652	19,046,199	38,413,146	40,210,069	14,334,367	21,142,229	1,381,177	2,117,088	9,954,514	10,604,915
Provision for Taxes on Income	5,314,000	3,395,000	17,392,000	19,788,000	6,720,000	9,635,197	650,000	741,000	3,748,000	4,190,000
Income after Taxes and Extraordinary Items	17,661,652	15,651,199	21,021,146	20,422,069	14,239,332	11,850,032	1,706,177	1,376,088	6,156,514	6,414,915
Earnings per Common Share (assuming conversion of preferred stock)	6.22	5.51	7.40	7.19	5.01	4.17	0.60	0.48	2.17	2.26
Dividends Paid per Common Share	2.40	2.40	1.60	1.25	—	—	—	0.45	1.00	1.00
Paid to Shareholders as Dividends — common shares	6,808,805	6,808,805	4,539,203	3,546,253				1,276,651	2,837,002	2,837,002
Re-invested in the Business	10,852,847	8,842,394	16,481,943	17,585,067	13,530,081	11,850,032	1,706,177	99,437	3,319,512	3,577,913
Depreciation and Depletion	10,305,519	11,718,467	10,882,413	9,888,337	9,037,205	8,830,533	7,377,183	4,605,383	3,337,666	3,140,260
Total Assets	271,958,131	259,333,688	228,676,080	220,093,010	191,679,639	176,575,127	166,313,282	162,074,401	143,580,262	115,159,867
Paid to Employees During the Year	61,275,709	52,669,830	48,828,086	41,230,700	23,899,204	31,187,968	26,421,565	22,889,982	20,586,137	19,083,867
Number of Employees at Year-End	2,331	2,389	2,351	2,268	2,113	1,798	2,421	2,386	2,324	2,343
Number of Common Shareholders at Year-End	2,092	2,150	2,280	2,640	2,948	3,307	3,549	3,794	3,973	4,507

Case D
Modern Homes Limited*

Modern Homes is a Maritimes-based producer of factory-built homes. The company was formed in 1965 by the family that still owns and runs it, and it is located in Truro, Nova Scotia. The company was founded to capitalize on the growing market in Canada for relatively low-cost, factory-built homes. In the spring of 1978, Modern Homes filled its first export order in a number of years with the sale of four modular homes to an Iranian customer. Modern's operations had been focussed on the domestic market, but the Middle East sale alerted executive attention to overseas sales potential. The company became increasingly interested in export markets, both as a means of long-term growth, and to help alleviate manufacturing problems associated with underutilized capacity and seasonality in production.

The Factory-Built Homes Industry

The growth of a Canadian factory-built homes industry dates essentially from the post-Second World War period. Industrialized house production methods imply an increasing transfer of labor from the site to the factory.

The advantages of such a transfer are numerous:

1. Labor productivity in the shop is higher due to sheltered working conditions, better organization and supervision, and the breakdown of activities into smaller repetitive operations.
2. Apart from supervisors, machine setters, etc., only semi-skilled labor is required in the shop and is thus easier to train. Moreover, the greater the transfer of operations from site to factory, the lower the amount of skilled labor required for site erection.
3. Only low-cost wood-working machinery, hand tools, and simple jigs are necessary.
4. More rapid house completion; the speedy erection of the house shells enables services and finishes to be carried out under cover and completed more quickly.
5. Accelerated turnover of capital, conducive to higher profitability.

---

* This case was prepared by Professor Philip Rosson of Dalhousie University as a basis for class discussion rather than to illustrate effective or ineffective handling of an administrative situation.

Copyright © 1979 by Philip Rosson.

6. Reduction of waste, pilferage, and similar material losses.
7. Greater accuracy of finish can be obtained (through use of jigs and better work control).

These advantages in prefabrication are offset by a number of disadvantages:

1. The higher the degree of prefabrication and pre-finishing the more restricted the choice of end products, and the greater the difficulty in meeting varying local by-laws.
2. The capital required for investment in factory space and equipment, as well as for operation, grows in proportion to the extent of prefabrication.
3. Similarly, storage and transportation costs grow with production, and transport difficulties increase with size and degree of finish of the elements.
4. Factory overheads are much higher than on-site costs and can be justified economically only when there is a commensurate reduction of labor requirements for given operations. This generally means that beyond a certain point more sophisticated production equipment and techniques are needed if the operations are to be performed in the shop.
5. Large semi-finished panels and sectionalized houses require mechanized erection equipment, involving further capital investment and skills.
6. The socially desirable transfer of labor from the site to sheltered factory conditions is necessarily achieved at the cost of some labor redundancy. This may be acceptable only when an expanding building program can absorb this surplus labor or where there are alternative employment opportunities.

A number of different types of industrialized homes are produced: "panellized", "modular", and "pre-cut". "Panellized" construction is that type of construction made of panels which are completely pre-engineered and then factory built. This means that the individual wall panels are finished in every detail, including electrical wiring, fixtures, and outlets. On site, the panels are merely placed in position, fastened, and the various electrical connections between the various panels made. "Modular" construction is the type of construction involving the fitting together of pre-set modules. These modules can be assembled either on site or away from the site. "Pre-cut" construction implies that the various components, structure and frame as well as panels, are all pre-cut and then assembled on site.

Modern Homes currently produces modular homes in two or three sections which are shipped to the site, placed on the foundation, assembled, and finished. The production process is a straight-forward assembly line operation. All components are manufactured off the assembly line; that is, walls, floors, and ceilings.

These pre-built components are then brought together on the assembly line at various stages; for example, walls at one station, ceiling at another station, insulation at another station, wiring, exterior cladding and so on. Modern Homes are constructed of wood, providing an outlet for lumber firms in the area.

Michael Good, Marketing Manager, estimated that 90 per cent of low-rise construction in the metropolitan Halifax area in 1978 would be factory built in one way or another. The major factor accounting for this dominance of new construction is the 20-30 per cent price advantage over contractor built homes.

Modern Homes Ltd.

Although the company was very interested in export markets, the General Manager, Brian Harvey, was quick to stress that the company had to get the domestic operation under control first. Plant capacity was somewhere in the order of 700 units a year. In 1978, an upturn in orders had been experienced by the company, with current projections suggesting about 450 units sold. This was a good improvement over the previous year when 260 units had been sold. The growth in orders was attributed to a number of factors: better house designs and components, increased and improved advertising, new management and salesmen, and continued domestic price inflation.

The company structure is shown in Figure 1 below. There had been a good deal of movement within the company's management. For example, Ben Smith is the longest serving manager of the pres-

Figure 1

Modern Homes Ltd. — Organizational Structure

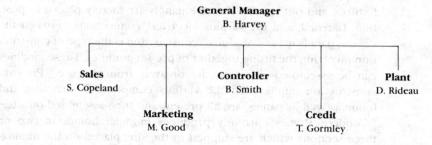

General Manager
B. Harvey

Sales	Controller	Plant
S. Copeland	B. Smith	D. Rideau

Marketing	Credit
M. Good	T. Gormley

ent group, having spent some four years as controller. Don Rideau has three years experience as plant manager. All other managers are recent arrivals. By July 1978 Stan Copeland, Brian Harvey, Ted Gormley, and Michael Good had been in post eight, five, five, and four months respectively.

The Iran Export Sale

For most of the Modern Homes executives, the Iran sale was their first engagement in exporting.[1] The sale had resulted from a family contact made in Iran. A Modern Homes salesman had been sent to negotiate with the potential buyer. The sale was made in one- and one-half hours despite the fact that the buyer had not seen the product, and the salesman had only been in the company's employ for two days.

The four houses had to be ready in one month, since the buyer had chartered a vessel which would be loading various consignments on the eastern American seaboard, and which could call in at Saint John, New Brunswick. The Iranians had decided to buy modular homes for a number of reasons. There is a lack of both building materials and skills in Iran and the purchase of an almost-completed house made a good deal of sense. Modern was happy to fill the contract since it had the houses the Iranians wanted sitting in their plant yard completed. However, some work had to be carried out to prepare the houses for export.

The plan had been for the homes to be loaded onto the deck of the chartered vessel, since at the time of the sale there was no cargo intended for this area. However, when the ship arrived one week early in Saint John the deck was not empty. A number of trucks and graders took up much of the deck space intended for the homes. Furthermore, some of the holds were not filled and would not be until a further voyage to Newfoundland had been completed. This complicated matters since one of the houses was to be loaded onto a hatch cover. Modern Homes management was bewildered at the lack of communication that had resulted in the dockside confusion at Saint John. Furthermore, Don Rideau, who was responsible for transporting and loading the houses, was amazed at the conduct of the ship's officers. He was in the hold of the ship, strapping a house in place when he discovered that the crew of the ship were dismantling the crane and preparing to sail. At this stage only one and a half homes

1. Limited sales of panellized homes had been made by Modern Homes in the late 1960s. However, little exporting expertise existed in the company in 1978.

were loaded. In order to prevent the ship sailing he was forced to negotiate with a number of agencies. First he called the Halifax agent, who had to consult with the New York agent he was representing, since the New York agent represented the Iranians. Eventually a satisfactory arrangement was worked out and the houses were loaded. The Modern loading crew crated everything very securely since they had seen considerable dockside pilfering at Saint John.

As well as loading the homes, Modern also included two home trailers, a complete set of erection gear, and metric measure small hand tools. These alone had been a problem. Modern management felt that the customer would need to be supplied with these, but had found it most difficult to verify this prior to shipping. Numerous telephone calls proved abortive until eventually it was discovered that the Persian New Year was celebrated between March 22 and April 3, and that during these thirteen days only one person manned the switchboard at the Iranian buying company. Finally a call was successful and Modern was asked to ship the erection tools along with the houses.

The whole deal was completed on a "good-faith" basis. The sale would not have taken place but for the family connections with the buying company. Because the chartered vessel arrived one week early, the necessary letter of credit was not finalized. This was contrary to accepted export practice, and the controller was aware that future export sales would have to be tightly controlled.

The Iranian-bound vessel was eventually unloaded at Bandar'Abbas, which is about one hundred miles from the planned erection point, Tehran. The ship was accepted for unloading at Bandar'Abbas after six weeks spent anchored offshore. This was not unusual in Iran where the ports were busy, poorly resourced, and fairly disorganized. Anything up to a six-month waiting period could be experienced. In August, the Modern executives were not sure where the four houses were. The plan was to set them up on blocks at an industrial exposition in Tehran. The customer was to display them as model homes, and hoped that sales would ensue. Modern management knew that the houses had not been erected, since the man they had agreed to fly to Tehran to supervise this activity had not been called upon.

Modern management were also mindful of the fact that certain changes would have to be made to make the Iran houses salable. For example, the Canadian plant had not had time to termite-proof the houses, which was vital in Iran. The electrical system also required some work since a 220-volt system is used in Iran, and a 110-volt system had been installed. Two choices were available here. A converter could be used to step down the power supply, or the electrical system could be replaced. The problem in the former case, however, was that existing electrical outlets probably would not be compatible with fixtures and appliances used in Iran. Basically the house met Iranian as well as Canadian specifications. The heavy insulation which kept out the cold Canadian winter, would also keep out the harsh heat of Iran.

Export Strategy

The Middle East had suggested itself as an area of potential to Modern executives. Looking at a number of export markets, the following criteria seemed important:

- The country must be relatively wealthy.
- A lack of building materials should exist.
- A lack of labor skills should exist.
- There should be a housing need.

Based on these criteria, Iran and Saudi Arabia were felt to present good opportunities. Summary data from a federal government survey of the Middle East Markets for manufactured homes is shown in Exhibit 1.

While some agreement has been reached within the company that the Middle East presents good opportunities, uncertainty exists concerning the type of home that Modern might export. While modular homes are reasonably priced in the Canadian domestic market, a major problem with exporting concerns transportation costs. Modular homes are essentially big empty boxes, and since shipping costs are based on volume, high costs are incurred. For example, the cost of shipping the four homes to Iran was approximately $80,000, and the homes themselves were valued at $100,000. Exporting panellized homes seemed more sensible in that the shipping costs were roughly one-quarter those for modular homes. This results from the possibility of knocking down the walls of the home and folding everything into a smaller "box".

However, depending on the type of home exported, different assembly skills were required in the export market. A panellized home could take about three-four weeks to erect whereas a modular home could be completed in four-five days. Given the relative wealth of some Middle East consumers since the OPEC oil embargo in 1973 it may well be that a modular Modern home will bear the high transportation rate. Don Rideau had been told that their house would sell in the range $80,000 to $100,000 in Iran. A typical Modern home with a c.i.f. value of $45,000 would offer quite a profit margin to a would-be Iranian intermediary.

Although there was agreement on the potential of export markets, contrasting points of view were expressed by individual executives. Brian Harvey recognized the potential of the Middle East, but was uncertain about how to proceed, what the operation would cost, and how exports could best be handled. On this latter point, there were three main alternatives:

- Modern to export directly and to handle the overseas sales operations;
- Modern to appoint overseas sales agents;
- Modern to seek out other interested parties and to go in on their coattails.

Don Rideau and Michael Good felt that an overseas trip should be made to investigate the markets more closely. As Rideau said, "No one in the company knows what is wanted in the various export markets." Rideau's feeling was that probably a strong relationship had to be developed between Modern and a local company once a market had been determined as suitable. Overall, he felt that there were good long-term prospects in the Middle East, but that the company should not rush into exporting since a lot of money had been won and *lost* by North American exporters in this area. Good thought along similar lines but when he asked the controller whether he would agree to recommend $50,000 front end money to investigate and develop Middle East markets, he was rebutted. Ben Smith's argument was that the company knew that a market existed, and what was required was for Modern to put together the right package, namely one that shipped easily. He pointed to the requests for sales literature as strong enough indication that Modern had a "hot" product.

By December 1978, the Modern management were involved in planning through to 1982. Part of the company plan could involve export marketing if some agreement could be reached on the matter. Materials gathered by the company included an Industry, Trade, and Commerce Export Survey completed in 1972 (Exhibits 1 and 2), and notes made at a recent seminar held in Halifax run by ITC (Exhibit 3). These notes in some degree updated the information contained in the 1972 Export Survey.

Exhibit 1

Summary Assessment of Middle East Markets for the Canadian Manufactured Homes Industry

Middle East

Although the Middle East is a relatively homogenous area from the point of view of this survey, there is the notable exception of Israel which is discussed separately.

The basic philosophy and culture is Arabic, which influences approaches to business and life. The climate and topography are also distinctive. The combination of these factors makes the area as different from North America as the oriental area. It is a reasonably solid bloc in terms of religion and language.

The politics of individual countries is an important consideration in doing business. It is useful to know whether a country has a fully managed economy where government agencies do all the purchasing according to present plans and priorities or whether it has an approach where businessmen deal with each other directly within national guidelines. Some countries are in between these positions or may be changing. Another important consideration is the source of national income, for example, is it an oil-based economy? There is a wide difference in ability to make foreign purchases which may be indicated by per capita income figures.

Although the whole area has a high defence budget, there is wide variation between countries as to the proportion of its income so allocated. Secondary priorities are education, health, agrarian reform, and housing. Opportunities for the sale of pre-built buildings exist in all these areas of concern but Canadians are prohibited from supplying any military-related materials or services.

Most men (very few women are involved) who hold senior levels of responsibility have received their higher education abroad. Some have English as a second language from U.S. and British experience, but others who have studied in France, Germany, and Russia do not. The European influence is strong and the metric system is generally used. Unless such people have had some North American experience, they have little understanding of wood-framed structures and their possible application to building needs.

Because of the relative lack of skilled construction labor and organization, building material production, and internal distribution systems, there is a desire to import whole buildings to be erected for turnkey turnover. This applies not only to housing but also to schools, clinics, farm buildings, warehouses, and light commercial buildings, many of which are to be situated remote from ports of entry. Wood-framed buildings can be modified to suit the climate and the life style and their transportability is much in their favor.

Recently, some Canadian businessmen responded to inquiries for substantial quantities of houses. One country is interested in vacation homes and motels for major resort developments as it seeks to add tourism to its sources of foreign exchange. In this instance, Finland is a prime competitor. Where U.S. companies are operating,

U.S. building sources may have a preferred but not necessarily exclusive position.

Countries that do not have formal building codes and materials standards are working toward them through foreign engineering consultants. This is a promising area for consulting, particularly in the fields of education, communications, agriculture, transportation, and construction.

Israel

Israel's urgent housing need is likely to continue because of the steady influx of immigrants and the chronic shortage of construction labor and materials. The Ministry of Housing is seeking new residential construction methods and systems internationally in an effort to provide housing without adding to the present pressures on the construction industry. Last year Canadian firms responded with proposals as did contractors from (thirty) other countries. In the negotiations other opportunities for the supply of turnkey houses (villas) and other buildings were identified.

The traditional residential construction materials are unit masonry and concrete with wooden roof structures and trim. In the cities, low walk-up apartments built with pre-cast concrete wall panels are common. These are slow to finish and are expensive to own or rent. There are many affluent new residents with North American experience who know and desire the amenities of wood-framed houses. A Canadian housing demonstration might prove the suitability and economy of our homes and lead to a substantial opening of the market in the private sector.

Source: Department of Industry, Trade, and Commerce, Resource Industries Branch, Manufactured Wood Products Division, *Export Opportunity Survey for the Products of the Canadian Manufactured Homes Industry*, Ottawa, 1972.

Exhibit 2

Information on Middle East Opportunities for the Canadian Manufactured Homes Industry

Country	Housing Needs[a]					Materials			Labor Supply	Opportunity for Supply of Whole Houses	Rating[b] (Feb./1972)
	Prestige 1	Ordinary 2	Vacation 3	Workers 4	Shelter 5	Traditional	Supply	Acceptance of Wood			
Syria	Fair	Fair	Low	Med.	Low	Stone Concrete	Good	Low	Good skilled	Low	-3
Lebanon	Low	Poor	Med.	Med.	Low	Concrete Masonry	Good	Poor	Good skilled	Low	-2
Israel	Med.	High	Low	High	Nil	Concrete	Good	Poor to date but improving	Very poor	High	2
Jordan	Low	Med.	Low	High	Nil	Concrete Masonry	Fair	Poor	Good skilled	Low	-4
Iraq	Med.	Med.	Low	High	Nil	Mud Brick Concrete	High	Poor	Good	Low	-3
Iran	Poor	Low	Med.	Good	Good	Stone Brick Plaster	Med.	Low	Good low skilled	Med.	-3
Kuwait	Low	Med.	Low	Med.	Nil	Concrete Masonry	Good	Poor	Moderate skilled	Low	-2
Saudi Arabia	Med.	Low	Low	Med.	Nil	Concrete	Good very cheap	Good	Skilled is scarce unskilled	Low	1
Trucial States	Low	Med.	Nil	Low	Nil	Concrete steel rod	Med.	Fair	Fair skilled Poor (imported)	Poor	-3

Notes to Exhibit 2:
(a) Housing needs
   a. Prestige — homes for dignitaries and influentials ($40,000 + Canadian equivalent — C.E.)
   b. Ordinary — middle-class homes ($25,000 – $40,000 C.E.)
   c. Vacation — individual chalet resort houses ($4,000 – $10,000 C.E.)
   d. Workers — low-income housing ($10,000 – $25,000 C.E.)
   e. Shelter — mass housing, minimum finish and equipment, no winterizing. No Canadian equivalent.

(b) Rating
This is a numerical expression to make the relative overall assessment of the opportunity readily visible. By using a scale of 10 from +5 to -5 with the better current probabilities being in the plus part, the opportunities average easily. The rating is based on an overview of information from all available sources and is related to the opportunity existing in the United States. The Canadian trade offices involved reviewed the final draft of this report in July and August 1972. Some new information was added and some data updated.

Readers will note that the majority of countries are not considered to be good potential markets at present. However, there are many where further investigation could be productive. It is suggested that the ratings not be taken as absolute because they may not hold under particular circumstances and they could change quickly. Rather, it should be useful to read the whole report to get a feel of conditions on an area basis and an appreciation of the criteria, proportion, and attitudes which apply.

Exhibit 3

Notes from an Industry, Trade, and Commerce Seminar on the Manufactured Homes Industry — December 1978

1. The oil crisis and its aftermath have changed the picture for Middle East as export markets for many goods, including manufactured homes.

   Revised Ratings:

Saudi Arabia	+3
Iran	+3
Iraq	+2
Kuwait/Trucial States	+2 (generally)
Syria	+1

   Israel's, and Lebanon's ratings have deteriorated such that both are rated negatively. However, the long-term prospects for both countries are good. Currently, there is an embargo on imports of house components in Israel, and income levels are being squeezed. In Lebanon, it was the opinion of ITC officials that it would be at least one year after peace before rebuilding would start.
2. Attitudes towards wood as a building material have improved since 1972, mainly because it is available and can be brought into the market quickly.
3. Two types of Canadian involvement have prevailed, mainly in Iran and Saudi Arabia:

   a. Demonstration homes — two-three units for individual buyers — testing consumer acceptability.

   b. Contractual erection of 100-300 units on planned development sites.
4. Sales have almost exclusively been of the panellized variety. Modular homes have been erected for camp use, but most modular designs are either too small or, if they are large enough, transportation costs make them costly.
5. Four Canadian companies are active in the area. Competition is stiff involving U.S., U.K., Rumanian, and Scandinavian companies.
6. Price is not the only important factor. Perhaps more critical are quality, reliability, and delivery.
7. ITC review of most would-be exporters reveals

   a. little experience;

   b. little assessment of company capabilities or goals;

   c. little knowledge of what is involved.

ITC suggest companies *first* review what units they want to sell, when they want to sell them, and what level of involvement they desire, and then review markets with the objective of making a compatible fit.

Case E
Farm Machinery Export Consortium*

In March of 1975, Bob Kelly, vice-president of Interimco, made a formal proposal to several Canadian farm machinery manufacturers that they form a permanent export consortium to exploit markets which none of them could reach individually. The firms approached were Versatile Manufacturing, Canadian Co-operative Implements Limited, and Ezee-On Manufacturing, each of which had been participating in a loose co-operative export program under the aegis of Interimco — a Canadian trading house in embryo. Due to a number of circumstances, Mr. Kelly's proposal was turned down by the manufacturers, but he was subsequently able to conclude three-year agreements with each company individually which allowed him to continue exporting Canadian farm equipment to the growing off-shore markets with which he had been working. This arrangement had the potential of greater financial rewards for Interimco than the proposed consortium had, while eliminating some of the uncertainties which had existed in the previous arrangement. However in September of that same year, Versatile announced that it was selling controlling interest to a U.S.-based farm equipment manufacturer whose product line complemented that of Versatile, and which had made rapid inroads into international markets during the last two years.[1] The reason cited for the sale, which was subject to approval by the Foreign Investment Review Agency, was that Versatile's founders were nearing the age where they did not want to take on the financial burden of a major expansion.

This case describes the circumstances which led up to Mr. Kelly's proposal for a farm machinery export consortium in an attempt to better understand the potential role of such organizations in Canada.

---

* This case was written by Mr. Will Redd under the direction of Associate Professor Harold Crookell for illustrative classroom purposes. It should not be reproduced without permission. Funds for the development of the case were provided by the Centre for International Business Studies.

1. Hesston Corporation, Hesston, Kansas. 1975 sales approximately $200 million. Products: Windrowers, cotton, potato, sugar beet equipment, forage harvesters, straw choppers, hay handling equipment, lawn and garden, waste handling, and office furniture.

Collective Marketing

The Honourable Jean-Luc Pépin, Minister of Industry, Trade, and Commerce from 1968 to 1972, was one of Canada's strongest proponents of co-operative export marketing. As minister, he received repeated complaints from many sectors of Canadian business about attractive opportunities to export Canadian goods which had been missed. These businessmen generally acknowledged that "collective marketing" of Canadian products may have helped to overcome the situation, but each found reasons not to get involved in such co-operative efforts.

Other countries were rapidly developing co-operative marketing organizations. Japan had over 5,000 trading houses. Mitsubishi, the largest of these, had annual revenues exceeding $18 billion in 1972, while Canada's total exports were less than $20 billion that year. Export consortia had been widely developed in Europe during the last several years, particularly in the smaller countries such as Denmark and Sweden, which did not have large enough domestic markets to support large manufacturing firms. Several smaller firms would band together to provide financial resources and a broad enough manufacturing base to support the international marketing arm which they set up.

Canada was experienced in certain areas of collective marketing. Marketing boards and co-operatives had existed within the domestic market for some time in the agricultural sector. Several other primary industries had also developed co-operative organizations for export purposes, such as Canpotex and Seaboard in potash and lumber products respectively. Tertiary areas such as engineering or consulting services were also being successfully organized into co-operative groups for non-domestic use, but the consortium idea was not working particularly well in the secondary manufacturing sector of Canadian industry. And this sector was not doing well in export markets. Of the $20 billion in exports in 1972, $12 billion were in raw and fabricated materials, $4.7 billion in auto part goods, and $2.3 billion in other manufactured goods to the U.S., leaving only one billion dollars worth of manufactured goods being sold offshore. About half of these exports were supported by government agencies. Total exports have climbed to $34 billion by 1974.

The Canadian government, in an attempt to stimulate exports among manufacturers, had provided several export incentives programs. Some of these programs are summarized in Exhibit 2. However, Canadian businessmen were not catching on, and Mr. Pépin saw the need for a "John the Baptist" to prepare the way for co-operative exporting. He felt that, until a change in the basic philosophy of

Canadian business was effected, the sizable deficit in manufactured goods trade ($6 billion in 1972) would continue to grow.

Organization of Interimco

In October 1972 Mr. Pépin was defeated in his Drummond riding by "the lack of co-operative support", as he put it later in a speech on collective marketing. This freed him to become his own "Jean the Baptist" and attempt to carry out the programs which he had been advocating as DITC minister. After discussing many extremely attractive job offers with various organizations, Pépin decided to branch out on his own to try to set up a national trading house. He met with over 150 businesses and universities in an attempt to determine the level of support that might be forthcoming. He then pulled together three of his former acquaintances who left their positions to undertake the new venture. All of these men had extensive experience in international marketing and shared the same ideas and frustrations that Mr. Pépin had as DITC minister. The other partners were A. B. Appel, C. R. D. (Bob) Kelly, and P. E. Labbe.

While many questions remained unanswered concerning the type of export organization which was best-suited to the Canadian economy, and indeed whether they could be successful at all in stimulating exports, they decided to undertake the task of promoting co-operative marketing among Canadian businesmen. Interimco was formed in April 1973, with the creation of a full-fledged trading house as its ultimate objective. Pending that development, efforts were concentrated on the following areas:

- direct international sales activity and contract negotiation on behalf of individual Canadian firms;
- organizing consortia among Canadian firms for the purpose of international marketing;
- trading on its own account;
- consulting Canadian firms regarding all aspects of international marketing;
- direct support of firms or consortia in their pursuit of turnkey projects;
- preparation and implementation of suitable training programs for purchasers of Canadian equipment and services; and
- acting as procurement agents on behalf of international buyers.

In its role as a catalyst in fostering international trade, Interimco intended to help companies achieve more economic use of the limited economic and human resources available for international marketing and to reduce destructive intra-Canadian competition in international markets. It was hoped that this would cause a dynamic improvement in Canada's international trade position, particularly in the secondary industry sector. A partial organizational chart of the company is provided in Exhibit 2.

Interimco began working with all sectors of the Canadian economy in an attempt to isolate those sectors which showed the strongest potential for exporting. These sectors were then set up as export groups under the direction of one of Interimco's officers. A number of consortia were formed to facilitate the sale of various products, but none of them seemed to achieve any lasting success. However, the agricultural sector, which showed strong export potential and had a long record of experience with co-operatives and marketing boards in commodities, seemed a natural target. An agricultural group was formed within Interimco, under Mr. Kelly's direction, for the purpose of co-ordinating exports of Canadian agricultural equipment and related services to countries trying to form agricultural development programs. Massey-Ferguson, one of the world's largest manufacturers of agricultural machinery, was approached about its involvement in this venture, but it did not show any interest in co-operating with the group.

The Algerian Sale

In May of 1973, Canada extended to Algeria a $100 million line of credit for the purchase of Canadian goods and services. This credit was in the form of a thirty-year, low-interest loan, consisting of $15 million put up by CIDA at 3 per cent, $50 million through the EDC at about 9 per cent, and the remainder from private Canadian banks bearing interest slightly above prime. Algeria was undergoing rapid industrial development (see Appendix A) and was receptive to Canadian exports for several reasons. Most important among these were Canada's familiarity with the French language and the North American image of advanced technology. Massey-Ferguson had been heavily involved in the country through its French facilities until the revolution, and the Canadian reputation was alive in the many M-F tractors still operating there after eleven years. In addition, Bob Kelly had visited Algeria on trade missions during his time as international sales manager of Dominion Road Machinery Company and was therefore familiar with local conditions and government purchasing procedures.

On a Thursday in October 1973, Mr. Kelly learned that Algeria planned to use $15 million of its credit to purchase agricultural equipment. Algerian representatives had already been to Canada to discuss with DITC officials their desires to purchase a line of machinery including tractors, cultivators, diskers, discs, press drills, swathers, and other equipment. Kelly knew from experience that the Algerians would prefer to deal with a long line manufacturer such as Massey-Ferguson. Small individual Canadian companies lacked the complete range of products desired. They had neither the capital nor the international marketing expertise to woo foreign buyers; and they lacked the credibility of the giant multinationals. However, their overhead was lower, and Kelly felt they could provide comparable or superior products at competitive prices, if only they could be organized to compete directly with the long line companies.

Mr. Kelly compiled a list of five western Canadian firms which together could provide the equipment Algeria wanted. These firms were: Versatile Manufacturing of Winnipeg which would supply a line of large horsepower, four-wheel-drive tractors; Co-op Implements of Winnipeg which would supply cultivators and diskers; Killbery Industries, also of Winnipeg, which manufactured swathers and manure spreaders; Agristeel, a source of press drills in Minnedosa, Manitoba; and Ezee-On Manufacturing in Vegreville, Alberta, which produced a heavy-duty disc.

Exhibit 3 shows the relative size of each of these companies and provides a summary of the organization and major products of each.

Friday morning, Mr. Kelly telephoned the top executives of each of these companies and invited them to discuss the possibility of a joint effort to win the Algerian contract. The following Monday morning found him in Winnipeg. He spent an hour and a half with the senior management of each company proposing that they participate in an export marketing consortium. His argument included four key points:

- The cyclical nature of Canadian agriculture could be circumvented via an export program;
- The Algerian deal represented incremental sales at a price above normal domestic retail;
- A minimum of effort would be required by the companies as Interimco would handle all details for a modest fee (expenses, half of its time, and a commission of 1.6 per cent); and
- The companies stood little or no chance of successfully concluding a worthwhile sale by operating as individual entities on the Algerian project.

At 10:30 that evening, representatives of the five firms met together with Kelly and four and a half hours later an agreement to co-operate in filling the Algerian contract as well as future prospects developed by Interimco was concluded.

Shortly thereafter, the Algerian buyer came to Canada to visit the plants of these five companies, as well as several other interested suppliers. At that time, Mr. Kelly was introduced as the Negotiator for each of the five companies. Then began a marathon series of visits to Algeria. After seven months of persuading and promoting, Algeria agreed to negotiate on 300 Versatile tractors. Four more months of wooing won contracts for 300 cultivators from Co-op Implements. The larger contracts for Co-op's diskers was lost because the Algerians changed their minds regarding the suitability of the product, as well as their own plans to build a similar product. The disc contract was also lost because of a claimed lack of suitability. The problem was compounded when a European Company bid $3,000 per unit compared to Ezee-On's $10,000. It was pointed out that the European product weighed 2,500 pounds compared to 10,000 for the Ezee-On. However another European company claimed that it would be able to produce an equivalent product for $8,000. Kelly, acting on behalf of Ezee-On, chose not to match the price for a non-existent product, so negotiations were terminated. Seven units of each of these products were later shipped as samples and subsequent orders for the full 300 discs as well as other equipment totalling $4.5 million were anticipated. Exhibit 4 shows the breakdown of the initial sale by product and supplier.

Mr. Kelly said that the key to his success was patience and tenacity. "You just have to keep hammering to convince them that you can provide the very best product and the very best service. You have to prove to them that you are not another "white slaver", that you really have their interest at heart. They won't deal with you unless they trust you."

Mr. Kelly explained that other small Canadian businessmen who were pursuing this contract on their own didn't have any idea what the costs and complications of exporting were. Had they been successful at their prices, they would have lost a lot of money because of the high miscellaneous costs involved in exporting. Such businessmen, in their scramble to recover whatever they could on their bad deals, inevitably gave Canadian exporters a bad name abroad and were turned off subsequent export possibilities themselves.

The Algerian contract, for example, included along with the equipment, training of operators in Algeria; technical instruction at the Canadian plants for two different groups of Algerians; follow-up of warranty parts, and services; and the establishment of four Canadian mechanics equipped with service trucks in Algeria for one year. All of these costs needed to be included in the selling price of the original equipment. Exhibit 5 gives a sample breakdown of the miscellaneous costs involved in the Algerian sale.

Subsequent Operations

By March 1975, Mr. Kelly had contacted a great many small- and medium-size Canadian manufacturers of farm machinery and related services. Working arrangements had been developed with many of these firms, and Interimco was able to offer a full line of goods and services to offshore buyers. Sales agreements had been reached with Morocco, Nigeria, Venezuela, the Ivory Coast, Australia, and France and contact had been made with a number of other potential markets. Agricultural sales through Interimco for the year ending April 1976 were projected at $18 million. In many cases sales prospects were developing faster than Interimco and the manufacturing companies could satisfy them. As an example, the Nigerian government wanted to develop up to 600,000 acres of farm land. Interimco's Agricultural Group proposed a $4.5 million contract to supply equipment, management, and special consulting to develop 25,000 acres as a pilot project. This allowed Interimco's suppliers more time to fill 600 units of power and equipment for the full 600,000 acres. Production scheduling and delivery became a major concern to Kelly in filling such orders from manufacturers like Ezee-On whose annual production of discs amounted to only 750 units in 1975.

Competition from the major companies was a continual threat to the agricultural group. Exhibit 6 shows the relative strengths of farm equipment manufacturers. Most of these long line companies had sales and service centres set up throughout the world. Their trademarks were internationally known, and they had little trouble filling orders such as the Nigerian proposal.

Interimco's Role

Interimco's role in marketing was basically that of the export branch of a trading house. Although Interimco seldom took title to the goods, it developed market contacts in foreign countries, followed up leads, and suggested bid prices to manufacturers. Interimco officers designed and negotiated contracts and had the authority to close on behalf of sellers. They co-ordinated production and shipping with manufacturers and handled packaging and export documentation. Finally, Interimco collected payment for the goods and co-ordinated follow-up programs such as operator training and supply of replacement parts. In return, Interimco received its expenses and time, as well as a small commission.

This system provided several advantages to Interimco. It granted them complete autonomy in developing markets and negotiating sales. They were able to select suppliers and put together packages of goods which matched the buyers' needs using the most profitable of these suppliers. An individual arrangement was made with each supplier and commission rates were established for each one depending on the level of service required. There were no by-laws or outside directors restricting Interimco in its pursuit of new foreign contracts.

However, there were also several disadvantages. Central buyers preferred to deal directly with manufacturers. Because of the reputation of Mr. Pépin, Interimco had an advantage over most intermediaries, but Kelly had to go so far as to reveal his modest commission rate to the Algerian buyer in order to convince him that he was not an ordinary middleman. Interimco lacked power to enforce policies or settle differences between exporters. The heavy front end costs involved in obtaining export sales were also creating a financial strain on the company. Its officers were unable to follow a co-ordinated and consistent approach in their marketing efforts because of lack of commitment of the exporters. The heavy dependence on Versatile, which was the only manufacturer of tractors in Canada, caused some concern. Because of the several equipment suppliers, it was impossible to develop a single brand image in export markets and thus create an impression of permanence. In fact, most of Interimco's suppliers were not so much interested in supplying offshore markets as they were in getting rid of excess production during slow periods in the domestic market.

Mr. Kelly felt that in order to maintain the commitment and co-operation of his major suppliers, it was necessary to set up a formal consortium with defined responsibilities and sufficient power to enforce its programs. Such an organization would also eliminate many of the difficulties Interimco had encountered in dealing with foreign buyers on behalf of manufacturing firms.

Mr. Kelly's Proposal

Two of the five original companies contacted by Mr. Kelly were no longer involved with Interimco in supplying the export market. Agristeel had experienced financial difficulties as the Canadian economy cooled down in late 1974. A vigorous expansion program aimed at doubling production from $4 to $8 million and beginning production of the disker-seeder for the first time, coupled with severe material and labor shortages, had exhausted the company's resources and it went into voluntary receivership followed by bankruptcy. In March 1975, under the temporary management of Clarkson Gordon and Co., Agristeel was manufacturing under contract for a major farm equipment company.

Killbery Industries which had experienced similar financial difficulties during the down swing in the farm equipment business from 1968 to 1970, was also producing under contract for the major farm equipment companies. Joe MacDonald, the former president of White Farm Equipment of Canada who had left that position to purchase Killbery from its founding brothers in 1970, had restored the firm to prosperity. Net sales rose from $2.6 million in 1971 to $6.4 million in 1974. Sales for the fiscal year ending in July 1975 were projected at $15 million, and orders worth $18 million had already been received from major customers for the 1976 season.

Killbery produced 70 per cent of the world's pull-type swathers as well as a large share of the self-propelled models. Contracts with long line companies included Massey-Ferguson, International Harvester, and White. Mr. MacDonald said he was very satisfied with his relationship with the long line producers and was not able to supply the export market even though the potential return on such a venture appeared to be very attractive. He was also unwilling to place the free sample equipment requested by the Algerians and therefore terminated his involvement in the export consortium. He questioned the morality of giving away Canadian taxpayers' money ($65 million of the Algerian line of credit was a thirty year low-interest loan funded by CIDA and EDC) to be later returned to the pockets of a few Canadian businessmen. He suggested that in the spirit of free enterprise as well as the interest of the purchaser and the Canadian taxpayer, there should be at least two competing export consortia in Canada.

Regarding Kelly's proposal to form a limited consortium to handle exports, he stated that he would prefer to sell through a well-established local distributor as he had been doing in South Africa. The distributor assumed the responsibility of selling and servicing the equipment, releasing Killbery from the after-sales commitments and the risk which the company was not large enough to assume.

In March, 1975, after considerable preparatory work, Mr. Kelly made a formal proposal to the remaining three companies inviting them to participate as shareholders in a limited company organized to promote export sales of farm equipment and services. A summary of the proposal sent to these companies is provided in Appendix B. Revenue and expenses to the manufacturing firms would have remained basically the same as depicted in Exhibit 5, but these firms would have a say in policy matters concerning its operations as well as sharing in profits generated by the export sales. The commission would be paid to the consortium instead of Interimco and would be sufficient to cover marketing expenses and executive salaries, etc. Marketing executives would have authority to act within guidelines provided by the directors, which would remove much of the uncertainty under which Mr. Kelly had been operating. A brief outline of the history and development of the three candidate firms now follows.

Ezee-On

Ezee-On was a private company located in Vegreville, Alberta, which derived its name from its quick-attaching tractor loader. Its president, Gene Demkiw, began as a retail implement dealer for Cockshutt (later called White Farm Equipment), but by 1967, the loader he had designed had become so successful that he sold his dealership and devoted all his time to manufacturing. His family, who operated a 2,500 acre farm nearby, became frustrated at the difficulty of finding large enough equipment to pull behind its large Versatile tractors so they asked him to design a heavy-duty disc. In 1975, these two products represented his complete product line.

Sales for 1974 exceeded $4 million with existing facilities operating at capacity. An addition was under consideration which would double capacity by 1976. Because of the uniqueness of its products, Ezee-On had enjoyed a strong market demand even during periods which were difficult for other manufacturers.

In spite of the strong domestic market for his products, Mr. Demkiw, with his eye to the future, was interested in the export market and was willing to supply Interimco with the discs required for the Algerian package. He would have won the contract if he had matched the European bid, but Mr. Kelly was unwilling to match a bid on a non-existent product. His normal price to his distributors was 40 per cent below retail but he would have received twice that amount on the Algerian contract before deducting all additional export related costs. Because of the heavy domestic demand for his products, he had only been able to place a few samples in the international market since that time.

When Mr. Kelly approached him about the formation of an exporting consortium in 1975, he was still interested and readily accepted the proposal. He hoped that by 1976 he would be able to provide a large volume of product for export purposes.

Co-op Implements

Co-op Implements was purported to be the only farm machinery manufacturing co-operative in the Western world. It was owned by over 84,000 farmer-members throughout the Canadian prairies. The members were divided into seven regions and sixty-eight depot districts, each with its own sales and service outlet. Farmers were elected from each region and district to serve as delegates and directors of the co-operative. The directors appointed the president and other executive officers and provided general operating policies for the company. Co-op distributed fourteen different types of agricultural implements. Exhibit 3 lists several of the most important of these. This line of equipment was continually expanding as the co-operative endeavored to provide "one-stop shopping" for its members.

Excess profits were distributed to the members in the form of purchase dividends which had ranged as high as 28 per cent of the price of equipment purchased during the year. Earnings distributed in this manner were not taxable to the co-operative. However, a large portion of the members exercised their option to accept additional shares in lieu of cash, allowing the company to retain funds to finance expansion. Exhibit 7 summarizes Co-op's financial position over the last fifteen years. It can be seen that Co-op's sales recovered rapidly from the severe drop caused by the 1968-70 slump in the agricultural industry. However, earnings did not keep pace with the recovery due to the high start-up cost of a new manufacturing plant and the sudden rise in material and labor costs not recovered because of advance sales at firm prices which the company had contracted with its members. The company was in a very tight cash position, with working capital down to $6 million and inventories accounting for over 90 per cent of current assets by October 31, 1974. Sales for the 1975 fiscal were projected at $80 million, including $4 million in export sales.

Co-op Implements became interested in the export market some time before Interimco approached it in 1973. Initial probes were made into Columbia, South Africa, Cuba, and the USSR. Co-op's reasons for expanding export sales included balancing out the cyclical nature of agricultural machinery sales in Canada, protecting members' investment by regulating and increasing volume, and reducing unit costs through more economical production. It was seeking markets with agricultural industries similar to that of western Canada so that its products could be exported without modification. Although Co-op did not manufacture tractors, it was able to supply a growing number of other Canadian-made products to the export market.

The potentially attractive prices on the Algerian deal, as well as the incremental nature of the sale appealed to Mr. Wilson Matthews, Co-op Implements' marketing director. He knew that the company did not have the international marketing expertise available through Interimco. He realized the importance of offering a full line of equipment to offshore buyers and saw the necessity of co-operating with Versatile in this venture.

When Co-op Implements was invited to participate in the limited export consortium it was at a most opportune time. The 1975 slow down was affecting company earnings and its management was anxious to broaden its marketing base. The co-operative spirit which had developed through the Algerian and subsequent sales was beneficial to the company, both in terms of export possibilities and savings on follow-up services, and the officers were anxious to consolidate this effort and build in a guarantee of longevity and dependability. The investment required was low enough to be acceptable to them, although they recognized that additional in-plant expenses would be incurred in supplying the consortium. They were also concerned about the effect that a long-term financial obligation might have on their operations, and the reaction of the members to their co-operating with a competitor. They were willing to accept a common brand name for export purposes, but were hesitant to accept that of a domestic competitor. They were also concerned about possible differences of opinion between the manufacturers, which derived their profits from sales to the consortium, and Interimco whose sole source of revenue would be from excess of commissions over expenses incurred by the consortium. The question of unanimity among the members of the board caused some obvious concern because of this possible conflict of interest. Nevertheless, they agreed to accept the proposal if Versatile gave its approval, because of the difficult financial position in which the company found itself at the time.

Versatile Manufacturing

Versatile had its beginning in the basement of a house in Toronto in 1946. Peter Pakosh, a former Saskatchewan farm boy who was working for Massey Harris (later Massey-Ferguson), began designing and building agricultural implements in his spare time. His implements were of such simple and economical design that they were immediately accepted by the farmers, who have been frustrated by high purchase and maintenance expenditures. Mr. Pakosh still insisted thirty years later that an implement should be built so that it could be repaired in the field "using baling wire and spit" if necessary. He was soon joined by his brother-in-law, Roy Robinson, who had grown up on a farm in Ontario. Mr. Robinson showed the same ingenuity as a business executive that Mr. Pakosh had developed in designing the company's equipment, and together, they built a reputation for simplicity, dependability, and low prices that were feared by small manufacturers and respected by the majors throughout the farm equipment industry. One of their major developments was the hydrostatically-driven, self-propelled swather which has been widely copied since its introduction in 1968. However, the most successful innovation was the articulated, four-wheel-drive tractor introduced in 1966 at a price competitive with much smaller conventional models.[2] The majors had previously tried to introduce four-wheel-drive tractors, but production costs had been prohibitive. By introducing the articulated (pivoted in the middle) steering system, Versatile was able to retail its early models below $10,000, while competitive models were priced between $15,000-$18,000. This tractor soon became Versatile's major product. In 1974, tractors accounted for 60 per cent of sales with three models ranging from 200 to 300 horsepower. Versatile did not produce conventional two-wheel-drive tractors, although there had been much thought given to introducing an articulated utility tractor in the 60-100 horsepower range — that of most standard farm tractors.

In 1963, Versatile was made a public company in order to protect the personal property of its founders who had been forced to mortgage everything they owned to raise the funds required in the early stages of the company's growth. The Pakosh and Robinson families retained just over 50 per cent of the voting shares in the company. This event was followed by a period of rapid growth, as can be seen in Exhibit 8. However, when the down turn in farm machinery sales came in 1968, Versatile was hard hit. The hydrostatic swather introduced that year was much larger and tougher than its competitors as well as having the revolutionary hydrostatic ground-drive. Yet, in order to make it competitive in price with other models, it was retailed at a very low margin. In 1970, the hydrostatic idea was extended to Versatile's self-propelled combine in an effort to stimulate its sales, which had been hardest hit by the recession, but the higher priced model was not well received by the recession-struck farmers and production was terminated that same year. The company had hopes of successfully re-entering that market at some future time.

In 1969, as profits continued to drop, the vice-president of finance announced his resignation and Jack Eckmire, a widely experienced

---

2. Four-wheel-drive tractors have been observed to pull their own weight in authorized field tests, while conventional tractors generally pull between two-thirds and three-quarters of their weight.

chartered accountant was brought in. Sound financial management together with a general recovery in the farm implement business returned Versatile to prosperity. Profits for each year were outstripped in the first six months of the succeeding year, and sales began an upswing of almost the same magnitude. This growth continued into 1975 despite a new leveling in farm business as well as the general economy. The reason for this was that Versatile tractors were positioned at the high end of the market where sales were traditionally less affected by economic fluctuations. These tractors had become so well-known in North America that price advantages were becoming less important. Therefore, Versatile had been able to keep its prices in line with costs of production and thus avoid the squeeze which was being put on other manufacturers. Yet, its prices still compared favorably with those of long line manufacturers who were virtually all producing four-wheel-drive tractors by 1975. Sales for the 1975 fiscal year were projected at $100 million and after-tax profits for the first six months had already exceeded $8 million on $56 million of sales.

As early as 1954, Mr. Robinson turned to the U.S. market when the farm implement business turned sour in Canada. He found dealers in North Dakota and Montana who were willing to buy his equipment. This kept the firm alive through a very difficult period for Canadian farm equipment manufacturers. Minnesota and South Dakota were subsequently added to the company's list of sales territories, but although U.S. sales grew steadily, they did not keep pace with those in Canada. By 1967, U.S. sales accounted for only 29 per cent of total business. However, the down turn in 1968 caused renewed interest in the U.S., and particularly the corn belt area which accounted for roughly 80 per cent of all farm equipment sold in that country. By 1970, U.S. sales accounted for 71 per cent of company sales, and in 1975, the U.S. market still absorbed twice the volume that was sold in Canada.

Company officers also became interested in offshore markets during the same period, and by October 1973, a few tractors had been shipped to Australia.

When Bob Kelly approached the Versatile management about the Algerian deal, it was generally felt that Versatile should expand offshore sales as a cushion against swings in the domestic business cycle. It was recognized that Versatile did not have the international marketing expertise in-house required to compete successfully with long line companies which had long been involved in exporting. Yet Versatile's products were of a quality and price sufficient to attract the interest of many foreign buyers. By accepting Kelly's proposal,

Versatile could benefit both from the experience and reputation of the Interimco staff as well as the advantages of providing a full line of products until its own line was filled out. An additional benefit was that even after deducting the many expenses involved in completing the offshore sale (see Exhibit 5), the revenue accruing to Versatile was 15 per cent above what it would have derived if it had sold the units in the home market at current domestic price.

Offshore sales jumped from $155,000 in the five months between October and March, 1974 to almost $7.5 million for the same period a year later as a result of Interimco's selling efforts. These sales had proven very profitable to the company and several officers were very committed to the export market when Mr. Kelly approached them about forming a co-operative exporting subsidiary. However, others, including Mr. Robinson, the president, were not so committed to supplying the offshore markets. Mr. Robinson maintained that the same profit could have been achieved through a slight price increment on all domestic sales.

Mr. Robinson resided in Mexico. He felt that top executives should not be involved in day-to-day matters, at the risk of blurring their long range vision. He was also very concerned about the effect that his eventual retirement or death might have on the company's operations as well as the investing public. He cited an article he had recently read which discussed the detrimental effect of the sudden withdrawl of founding officers from their companies. By moving to Mexico, he was concientiously grooming his second-line management for top management responsibilities. He was also disturbed about the high inheritance tax levied against the estates of Manitoba residents, and stated that it could effectively be greater than 100 per cent, if the investing public perceived that a company's fortunes were too closely tied to the efforts and charisma of its founder. Nevertheless, he kept in close touch with the company, and the many trips he made each year — often overland towing a thirty-six-foot trailer — to discuss and give directives on matters of major importance such as company policy and pricing, indicated that at fifty-six, he was far from slowing down. Mr. Pakosh, who was chairman of the board of directors, worked daily in the Winnipeg plant but his time was spent in design and product improvement, and he left managerial decisions entirely in the hands of Mr. Robinson and his staff. Mr. Robinson was not involved in the Algerian sale and did not meet Mr. Kelly until after the negotiations had been concluded.

Through the years, Mr. Robinson had shown an exceptional ability to make far-sighted and correct decisions. He had the reputation of penetrating quickly to the heart of a problem, and the speed with which he solved complicated calculations in his head created a healthy respect for him among his employees. He was also very independent and was reluctant to co-operate with other suppliers. He was particularly unhappy about becoming involved with Co-op Implements, Versatile's direct competitor in the domestic market. He felt that co-operatives enjoyed an unfair business advantage because of the special tax treatment on distributed earnings. He stated that corporate taxes kept inefficient companies in business and made prices higher for all Canadians. Special tax concessions such as that extended to co-operatives not only further aggravated that situation, but were a threat to the entire free enterprise system in his opinion. He felt that the only equitable way for the government to extract revenue from corporations would be through a sales tax. Becoming involved with Co-op Implements in an export consortium was not only morally wrong in Mr. Robinson's view, but it would strengthen Co-op's competitiveness in the domestic market as well, which he did not wish to do.

Mr. Robinson, therefore, turned down Mr. Kelly's proposal to form a limited consortium. He felt that the company's identity would be lost by selling through another organization. This would be particularly so if another brand name or color was used. On the other hand, he had reservations about putting the Versatile logo on equipment manufactured by someone else. Versatile had a deliberate policy of selling directly to 600 dealers throughout western Canada and twenty-five states in the U.S. in order to maintain the close contact with the farmers which it needed to stay innovative. He felt that a consortium would tend to isolate his people from offshore users whose special needs might easily be overlooked. Furthermore, he was not anxious to build an organization which would add to his administrative costs until a successful track record had been established. When asked what his main reason for rejecting the proposal was, he turned to Mr. Kelly's projected first year expenses and said that he felt that they couldn't possibly be less than two to three times that amount. He added that expenses such as that were terribly hard to cut off, once the project had been undertaken. He said that he preferred to pay more to avoid a contractual outflow which might outlive Versatile's need for it. Also, there was a risk that Kelly's sales projection might not be reached. It was his style to keep things clear-cut and simple and he felt that it would be extremely difficult to lay out specific details to ensure successful co-operation of members under all possible conditions. Not doing so, however, would be to invite problems. He added that Interimco's officers would do a better marketing job if their own money was involved. He also pointed out that

Versatile's plants were not well located for exporting and that they were operating to capacity to satisfy domestic orders.

Mr. Kelly was very concerned by Mr. Robinson's rejection of his proposal to set up a formal export consortium. Almost every attempt to set up a consortium in the secondary sector of Canadian manufacturing had shown disappointing results, and he had hoped that this one would prove to be different. He wondered what specific factors had caused his efforts to fail. He wanted to determine a set of criteria which would ensure the successful operation of a consortium in Canada. Also, in assessing the progress of Interimco over its first two years, he felt that the time might have arrived to redefine the company's basic strategy with regard to promoting exports among Canadian manufacturers.

Exhibit 1

Government Export Promotion Programs

Organization	Functions
Canadian Commercial Corporation (CCC)	—Engage in government (including CIDA) procurement. —Assist in developing trade between Canada and other nations. —Assist individuals in Canada to obtain or dispose of goods and commodities outside Canada. —Import goods or commodities into Canada. —Export Canadian goods or commodities.
Export Development Corporation (EDC)	—Insure Canadian exporters against non-payment for a wide range of reasons when they grant credit to foreign buyers. —Make long-term loans to foreign purchasers of Canadian capital equipment and services. Also guarantee private loans to such borrowers. —Insure Canadian investors against certain political risks of loss of their investments abroad.

Program For Export Market Development (PEMD)	—Incentives for participation in capital projects abroad.
	—Incentives for market identification and adjustment.
	—Support to participation in trade fairs in which Canada does not officially participate.
	—Support to incoming foreign buyers.
	—Originally planned by former DITC minister:
	    Support for consortia formation
	    Support to trading houses

Exhibit 2

Interimco Organizational Chart

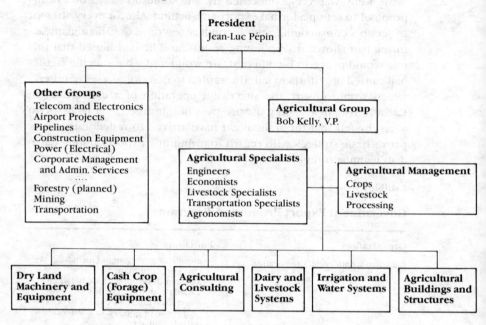

Exhibit 3

Profile of Original Consortium Member Companies

Company	Company Sales[a]	Estimated Retail Equivalant	Description	Employment	Products	Retail Value
Versatile	67,627,000	90,100,000	public family-controlled manufacturer sells direct to 600 dealers	1,150	Tractors —4-wheel-drive Swathers —self-propelled —pull-type Cultivators Sprayers Grain Augers Harrowers	23,000 - 32,000 6,700 2,300 3,700 1,000 1,300 2,300
Co-op Implements	41,100,000	41,100,000	co-operative farmer-owned integrated — manufacturer to 68 retail outlets	800 plus 500 in retail system	Tractors —4-wheel-drive[b] —2-wheel-drive[b] Swathers —self-propelled —pull-type Combines —pull-type Cultivators Diskers (dual) Harrowers	34,000 - 45,000 10,000 - 18,000 5,200 2,500 13,000 4,000 7,800 1,000
Ezee-On	5,000,000	8,300,000	private sells through distributors	100	Discs Loaders	6,700
Killbery	6,400,000	12,500,000	private manufactures for long line companies	350	Swathers —self-propelled —pull-type Manure Spreaders	7,000 2,300 1,300
Agristeel	4,600,000	9,000,000	private — manufactures for long line companies	250	Cultivators Press Drills Diskers	4,000 3,300 3,300

(a) 1974.
(b) Distributed for other manufacturers.

Exhibit 4

Breakdown of Algerian Sale by Product and Supplier

	85.0%	14.0%	0.5%	0.5%
67%	300 Tractors (Versatile) $9,000,000 Equipment	300 Cultivators (Co-op) $1,500,000	7 Diskers (Co-op) $65,000	7 Discs (Ezee-On) $70,000
23%	Export Related Services			
10%	Replacement Parts			

Note: Chart not drawn to scale.

Exhibit 5

Breakdown of Exporting Costs for Sample Item*

FAS Port		$26,912
Export Packaging	60	
Inland Freight	500	
Port Charges (et al)	350	
Ocean Freight	—	
Marine Insurance	—	
Consignment Replacement Parts (2%)	540	
Warranty (release of obligation 2%)	540	
Dealer Commission (A.S.S. — 7%)	1880	
After Sales Service (our reps.)	700	
Training: Canada	100	
Abroad	25	
Marketing Cost	150	
Transportation (local)	150	
Miscellaneous (5%)	1350	
Interimco (1.6% of FOB Factory)	430	6,775
Net Revenue to Manufacturer		$20,137

* Based on sale of 300 Versatile model 700s with obligations to provide all items listed above.

Exhibit 6

Major Manufacturers of Agricultural Power (1973-millions $ U.S.)

Manufacturer	Corporate Sales	Corporate Profit	Agricultural Sales	% Ag Sales	Product Line
Allis Chalmers	1,166	16	265	23	long line
Case	919	65	370	40	long line
Deere & Co.	2,002	168	1,498	75	full line
Ford Motor Co.	23,015	906	650[a]	3[b]	long line
International Harvester	4,193	114	1,355[b]	32[b]	full line
Massey-Ferguson	1,506	58	930	62	full line
Steiger	20	.9	20	100	tractors only
Versatile Manufacturing	38	3	38	100	short line
White Motor Corp.	1,179	41	203	17	long line

(a) Estimated.
(b) Includes industrial tractors.

Exhibit 7

Canadian Co-operative Implements Limited — Sales, Dividends, and Members' Equity

Year	Sales	Surplus	Dividend Allotted	Rate	Member Equity
60	6,485,566	609,941	426,171	12.0	3,787,309
61	7,717,069	583,146	528,315	9.8	4,196,729
62	8,739,293	853,335	534,884	8.0	4,488,844
63	13,217,847	1,958,349	744,838	9.0	4,798,228
64	19,191,220	2,059,743	1,840,782	14.1	5,873,647
65	20,336,388	1,899,138	1,947,568	10.3	6,914,386
66	19,994,351	2,529,125	1,804,181	9.0	8,142,764
67	19,778,736	1,310,377	2,399,797	12.2	9,920,606
68	17,482,031	800,029	1,218,525	6.2	10,680,703
69	14,167,947	(412,615)	746,465	4.3	11,075,938
70	9,438,603	(436,480)	—	NIL	10,995,312
71	15,722,482	156,061	—	NIL	10,727,476
72	22,091,472	319,614	—	NIL	10,229,013
73	37,076,372	(36,455)	—	NIL	10,222,375
74	41,100,764	(96,597)	—	NIL	10,224,674

Exhibit 8

Versatile Manufacturing
Ten-Year Summary of Financial Highlights ('000 dollars except when per share)

	1974	1973	1972	1971	1970	1969[a]	1968	1967	1966	1965
Sales	$67,627	$38,044	$25,513	$19,688	$24,533	33,787	$22,757	$22,506	$16,816	$11,376
Income (Loss) Before Taxes	$13,287	$ 4,479	$ 2,869	$ 1,810	$(1,390)	$ 1,138	$ 3,299	$ 5,691	$ 4,621	$ 2,789
Net Income (Loss)	$ 7,549	$ 2,506	$ 1,457	$ 885	$(678)	$ 551	$ 1,600	$ 2,809	$ 2,252	$ 1,378
Total Shares Outstanding[b]	2,911	2,900	2,812	2,812	2,809	2,808	2,804	2,773	2,766	2,760
Net Income (Loss) per Share	$2.59	87¢	52¢	31¢	(24¢)	19¢	57¢	$1.01	81¢	50¢
Total Dividends	$ 582	—	—	—	—	$ 673	$ 671	$ 554	$ 368	$ 276
Dividends per share	20¢	—	—	—	—	24¢	24¢	20¢	13¢	10¢
Shareholders' Equity per Share	$7.38	$4.99	$4.10	$3.58	$3.26	$3.50	$3.55	$3.18	$2.37	$1.69
Additional Investment in Plant, Property, and Equipment	$ 2,380	$ 2,526	$ 649	$ 208	$ 482	$ 452	$ 491	$ 623	$ 838	$ 241
Income on Shareholders' Equity at Beginning of year —%	52.1	21.7	14.4	9.7	—	5.5	18.1	42.8	48.4	38.8
Working Capital	$19,711	$14,888	$13,264	$ 8,787	$8,263	$10,833	$12,236	$ 6,542	$4,529	$3,129
Number of Employees	1,166	801	631	534	545	582	459	800	675	575

(a) 14-month Period.
(b) Adjusted for 3-for-1 stock split in 1968.

Appendix A

Algeria*

The Algerian government will have invested more than $17 billion in its economy between 1970 and 1977, about 45 per cent of it for industrial development. The economic system can best be described as one of "state capitalism" in which government and industrial leaders make decisions based principally on efficiency and economy of resources. Economic development plans call for imports of vast quantities of capital goods which, in 1971, were valued at $1.6 billion and made up approximately 72 per cent of total imports. The value of imports rises considerably each year, and potential foreign suppliers are flocking to Algeria — hotel rooms must be booked weeks in advance.

The key to success is a personal visit. And if you speak French, the working language in Algeria, you will have a distinct advantage over your competitors.

The Democratic and Popular Algerian Republic won its independence from France in 1962 after a particularly bloody seven-year war. With independence, the new regime decided to create a viable autonomous country based on Algerian needs and realities. To achieve economic development, foreign-controlled industry and agriculture was nationalized. During the past several years, economic policy has been marked by the firm commitment to establish a strong industrial base and to centralize decision-making powers. State control has been extended to such fields as foreign and domestic trade, credit, and pricing.

The backbone of Algeria's economy is the oil and gas industry which provides more than 70 per cent of all foreign exchange earnings. Algerian natural gas reserves, which are just starting to be developed, include over 10 per cent of known world supplies. Although agriculture accounted for only 9 per cent of the Algerian GDP in 1972, it employs over half of the nation's 14 million inhabitants. Large quantities of cereals (wheat, barley, and oats) are produced, although the country remains a major importer of wheat as well as other food products. In order to achieve the projected annual growth of 8 per cent, doubling GDP by 1980 with per capita income reaching $600, the country will have to become self-sufficient in many products including food. Modernization of the agriculture industry is a priority in the current four-year plan. Export opportuni-

* From: *Canada Commerce* (October 1973).

ties are available to Canadians for both equipment and services in this and most other industries except consumer products.

Doing business in Algeria is not difficult, and rewarding personal relationships can be developed with warm and hospitable decision makers.

Visits are absolutely essential if exporters wish to penetrate the expanding Algerian market. Confidence in the supplier plays a far greater role in selling than in most other countries.

There are no two companies which do the same thing in Algeria. If you are selling agricultural equipment, there is only one client who buys for the whole country. He is severely overworked and cannot always devote sufficient time to each project. He therefore welcomes face-to-face discussions with potential suppliers to decide who can be counted on to provide suggestions, guidance if required, and support in the event of difficulties. Importers often do not know exactly what sort of equipment or services they need, and the degree of confidence in a supplier can be crucial in the final purchase decision.

Technical documents describing a given requirement are often intentionally vague in order to provide suppliers with maximum latitude in suggesting various alternate possibilities. After a first study of these documents, suppliers should come to Algeria to discuss the requirements and obtain a precise idea of what is needed and why. Algerian buyers are prepared to accept proposals which differ from those initially requested and have done so on several occasions. They are pragmatic and look only for the best solution at the best price. Bidders who don't visit the market are limiting their chances of success.

Competition for Algerian export orders is considerable, and to be successful a supplier should invite decision makers to Canada. The resulting benefits of such an initiative are obvious: one of the most important being the opportunity of impressing the Algerian visitor with the competence, technological ability, and reliability of your firm. Algerian buyers don't have time to make mistakes and can't afford to take chances with suppliers unknown to them.

Contracts signed with Algerian firms are usually broader in scope than those signed in many other countries. Apart from technical clauses, there are several other areas which must be covered.

Technical Assistance. Whenever equipment is involved, suppliers are expected to send technicians to Algeria to train local service personnel in all aspects of after-sales service. Their stay can vary from a week to several months, depending upon the complexity of the equipment. Fully trained Algerian technicians are in short supply and the importance of technical assistance cannot be overemphasized.

Training in Canada. In addition to offering technical assistance in Algeria it is often a good idea to offer local technicians a training period in the supplier's plant.

Servicing. After-sales servicing is, as always, most important. Potential suppliers must ensure that the buyer is provided with maximum assistance to permit the rapid and efficient servicing of his equipment.

Pricing and Payment. Having read so far, you are probably saying "all this is fine, but it costs money". The Algerians will be the first to agree. They prefer to pay more to be sure they are getting quality equipment and excellent training for their technicians who, in turn, will be capable of training others. Algerians fully realize suppliers are building costs into their proposals, but they accept the fact, provided exporters don't become greedy.

Down payments of 10 per cent and progress payments can be obtained. Letters of credit are rarely extended and the common technique is cash against documents for smaller contracts. All proposals for larger transactions must include financing, which may vary from two to ten years. Large loans are increasingly being signed on a government-to-government basis and with foreign banking consortia.

Calls for Tender. Algerian law specifies that all foreign purchases must be preceded by a call for tender giving a minimum of three weeks to submit bids. Calls for tender can be public or restricted. Restricted calls, when only suppliers known to Algerians receive tender documents, are numerous and Canadian suppliers should send as much information as possible on their products and firm.

The Algerian economy is booming and imports are rising to impressive levels. The Algerian market can serve as a door to the whole French-speaking market in Africa. Algeria sees itself, and rightfully so, as one of the leaders of the Third World. It offers a very important market, and numerous requirements for equipment and services could be satisfied by Canadian firms.

Appendix B

Proposal for Creation of Canadian Farm Machinery Trading Company

Interimco Ltd., Versatile Manufacturing Ltd., Canadian Co-operative Implements Ltd., and Ezee-On Manufacturing have worked closely together over the last eighteen months in marketing Canadian agricultural equipment abroad. The experience gained in the markets approached thus far confirms the existence of a sizable demand for such equipment. Export orders of over $13 million have already been concluded, all at excellent profit margins, and several million dollars of additional sales are expected in the near future.

It is obvious that no one Canadian farm machinery manufacturer can, on its own, match the export efforts of the main line companies. However, Interimco, Versatile, CCIL, and Ezee-On, in a combined endeavor, can assemble the material, human, and financial resources required to organize a Canadian farm machinery trading company which could compete effectively with the established majors, at a much lower cost.

This document proposes the creation of such a "Farm Machinery Trading Company" and puts forward some basic suggestions with which we hope you will agree with regard to its powers, structure, financial organization, and methods of operation.

A number of factors which would affect the decision on whether or not to proceed are taken for granted since they have been tacitly accepted by all three firms and repeatedly confirmed over the last eighteen months' experience. Among these factors are:

- the need to offer a wider range of products than those currently produced separately by Versatile, CCIL, or Ezee-On;
- the need for supplying, in addition to the equipment concerned, a broad range of services such as training in equipment handling and maintenance, technical advice on seeding and harvesting, plus, on occasion, the services of agronomists;
- the need to approach the various markets of the world in a selective, regular, and systematic fashion;
- the need for close liaison between the participating companies in market development, sales, and production scheduling.

All these are standard advantages of group marketing as successfully practiced today in many countries of the world — in Scandinavia for example, and even in Canada, in primary and semi-processed exports.

The proposed company would have sole marketing responsibility

outside Canada and the United States for all of the equipment manufactured by Versatile, CCIL, and Ezee-On. It would also market and sell
agricultural equipment and services supplied by third companies
where necessary, to fill out the "long line" capability as desired.

Proposed Structure
The company would be incorporated under a federal charter. It
would comprise only four shareholders (the three manufacturers
and Interimco Ltd.) with the following suggested holdings and positions on the board:

Shareholders	%	Board of Directors
Interimco	45	2 — the president of Interimco and one other.
Versatile	35	
CCIL	15	4 — the presidents of each of the three other companies
Ezee-On	5	and one other.

All policies will require *unanimous agreement* by the board of
directors of the new Farm Machinery Trading Company. Directors'
fees are projected at $1,200 or $200 for each director per year.

Proposed Officers of the Company
One President   C. R. D. Kelly (Proposed)
Two Vice-Presidents   One nominee each of CCIL and Interimco
One Secretary-Treasurer   One nominee of Versatile

Proposed Initial Permanent Staff
A President,
a Sales Representative,
a Technical Representative, and
a Secretary-Typist.

Additional forwarding/sales administration services and clerical
support functions will be arranged as required.

Technical support will be provided for by the manufacturers;
continuing spare parts requirements and necessary inventory levels
will be maintained by the manufacturers in co-ordination with the
company.

Revenues
Sales during the first year of operation are estimated at approximately $15 million. It is proposed that the trading company collect a
commission on export sales. The amount of commission will be
approved by the board.

We believe that positive benefits will flow to your organization through participation in the proposed Farm Machinery Trading Corporation for the following reasons:

1. The long line of equipment offered will promote the sale of your equipment more easily.
2. The better profit margins achieved on export sales will improve your company's profitability.
3. The commission will probably be less than your normal domestic selling costs.
4. The additional income opportunities available through offshore sale of non-shareholder suppliers' equipment.
5. The modest investment in the proposed company in the form of loans and redeemable preferred stock should be returned within a reasonable time. The investment in non-par value common stock would be minimal from a monetary stand point.
6. The "unanimous agreement" requirement of the directors would assure that the trading company took no actions which in your opinion would be undesirable.

It is very probable that the resolution of questions as to an appropriate name and paint color for the proposed farm machinery equipment company lean very much in favor of including the name "Versatile" and use of your red and yellow colors.

In addition, we have discussed the matter of supplementary equipment with potential suppliers and received an excellent response from them.

We would deem it a special favor to be able to talk to you personally about this proposal at your earliest convenience.

Yours very truly,

Exhibit 9

Projected Expenses for First Year Operations

Directors (6 at $200)	$ 1,200
Communications	14,000
Supplies	3,500
Office	5,000
Insurance and Business Taxes	1,000
Legal Audit	2,000
Salaries — Executive	30,000
Salary — Office	9,000
Salary — Sales Representative	20,000
Salary — Technical Representative	20,000
Expenses — Travel	50,000
Miscellaneous expense	20,000
Total	$175,700

Case F
Canadian Machine Tool Company*

As Jim Adams rode on the bus from Narita Airport to Tokyo he stared at the lush green countryside dotted with small rice paddies and truck gardens. So this was the Japanese industrial miracle. CMT's Japanese agent, Yoshi Imura, explained that the airport was eighty kilometres outside Tokyo and soon they would be enveloped by the urban sprawl of Tokyo's 10 million inhabitants. The fact that they were in a bus and not a company car or taxi had surprised and disappointed Jim: it might be indicative of the Japanese assessment of CMT's importance and the chances of success of his trip.

CMT was a medium-size, Canadian-owned manufacturer of precision drill presses and milling machines. Its sales in 1978 were $41 million, up 25 per cent over 1977. CMT produced a narrow line of high-precision presses and lathes that were particularly suited for the low tolerances and exotic metals increasingly being used by industry. Over 65 per cent of CMT's products were sold to aircraft manufacturers in the U.S. and their Canadian subcontractors. The expansion of the aircraft industry in 1978-79 combined with the falling Canadian dollar had pushed CMT to capacity and led to a substantial order backlog. This market, however, was unstable and could easily fall off dramatically if the forecasted worldwide depression was severe or protracted or if air fare hikes precipitated by the price of OPEC oil reduced air travel. Jim Adams, president of CMT, hoped that his trip to Japan would lead to both a geographical and industrial diversification of CMT's sales. To be sure CMT had sold slightly over $1 million to Japan in 1978, but these sales had been sporadic and, Jim suspected, motivated more by the "look-see" propensity of Japanese firms and their desire to diversify their sources, than by any long-term commitment of CMT's products.

At least on paper, the Japanese market presented a huge potential for CMT, and also substantial risks. In fact, any increase in sales to Japan would necessitate an expansion of the plant in Canada, a direct investment in Japan, or in a third country. Alternatively CMT could continue with its present policy of ignoring the Japanese market and continue to produce for Canada and the United States or try to cash in by licensing its technology to a Japanese firm.

---

* Case material of the Western School of Business Administration is prepared as a basis for classroom discussion. This case was prepared by Professor D. Lecraw.

Copyright © 1980. The University of Western Ontario.

CMT was founded in 1910 to produce drills and metal-working tools for the automobile industry which was just beginning in Canada, fostered by high tariffs under Canada's "National Plan". Initially the firm had flourished but had fallen on hard times during the depression. During the Second World War, demand for CMT's products from the armaments industry had soared, with demand far exceeding supply. With re-conversion of the economy following the war, several factors influenced CMT to gradually shift out of its former product lines. (1) Mr. Johnson, then president of CMT, had noticed a trend toward the use of ever-larger, more sophisticated machinery. (2) For the older, more standard items in CMT's line, price competition became fierce, and economies of scale became important in determining relative competitive strength. Since CMT was quite a small firm in its industry, particularly when compared to some U.S. firms, it could not compete on a basis of price. (3) In the late 1940s and early 1950s the locus of production and, more importantly, the sourcing decisions of the auto industry shifted from Canada to the U.S. Auto plants in Canada became mere assemblers of parts and knocked-down bodies produced in the U.S., with a consequent decline in the Canadian industry's demand for CMT's products. The Canadian-U.S. auto pact in 1964 had partially offset this trend, but by 1970, the auto industry accounted for only 20 per cent of CMT's sales.

To meet these challenges CMT pursued two main product policies:

1. With its older, more standardized products, it pursued a quality image and produced generally short runs to meet specific customer demands in the Canadian market. It developed a strong network of sales agents who kept in close contact with manufacturers and who gave CMT good information about industry needs in terms of delivery time and minor product modifications which made its goods attractive to Canadian buyers in spite of their generally higher prices.

2. CMT used the high cash flow coming from the war and early postwar years to invest heavily in R & D and product design in order to constantly upgrade the quality and performance of its existing products and develop a series of new ones. CMT used its five full-time salaried salesmen to gather market information and maintain close contacts with its customers both in the U.S. and Canada. Its designers and engineers then developed new products to meet the individual specifications of its customers while at the same time planning the overall upgrading of its lines. Its latest line featured computer-controlled milling machines and drill presses which could be pre-set for both the shape of the final product and for the technique used in the process, for example, drilling speed,

bit angle, and pressure. The computer monitored the process and automatically made adjustments for bit wear and changing characteristics of the piece being drilled due to changes in temperature or composition. To produce this line, CMT had brought in a small Canadian computer firm, whose products matched any available on the market.

Mr. Adams had noticed several disturbing trends in CMT's competitive position, however. Its older products were coming under increased price competition from the more advanced of the "low-wage" countries. After a certain point, its quality image and strong dealer network were no longer enough to offset the significantly lower prices of some items produced in low-wage countries. The quality and market response time of these products were also improving over time. At home, CMT was having increasing difficulty in hiring the machinists, lathe operators, mechanics, etc., necessary to produce a quality product. On the engineering and design side, however, CMT was holding its own, yet even here, the Japanese were beginning to sell increasingly competitive products in Canada.

The recent decline in the Canadian dollar had given CMT a new competitive edge in many of its products, but Mr. Adams was concerned that this success would be only temporary and masked potential underlying problems for some of CMT's products, problems that might necessitate a rethinking of CMT's long-run competitive strategy. One area which CMT had largely neglected was the international market, both as potential competitors and as a market for CMT's products. Mr. Adams felt that any substantial move into either production or sales outside North America would have to be on a long-term basis and would require considerable capital and management time. One possible use of CMT's current high cash flow would be to support just such a venture. Yet CMT had no expertise in overseas operations and virtually none in overseas sales. In the past, CMT had "let the products sell themselves" abroad. Put another way, abroad its customers bought CMT's products, CMT didn't sell them. Sales to Japan averaged about 2 per cent of sales, but varied considerably from year to year. Following the Second World War, sales of a new product line to Japan increased for five to eight years and then fell off. More recently, the new line sold very well at about 5 per cent of sales, but within three years fell off sharply. Mr. Adams believed that this reflected the increased sophistication of Japanese manufacturers both in their demand for increasingly sophisticated production machinery and the increased ability of Japanese drill press and milling machine producers to bring out a comparable product in a short time.

However, Mr. Adams believed that the new line was more sophisticated, flexible, and easier to use than anything on the market in Japan. This competitive edge was due not so much to the machinery itself, but to the computer back up and programming software. Consequently when the initial orders had been slow, he had first queried Mr. Imura by Telex and later by phone. Mr. Imura's explanations of a "depression" in Japan, a "decline in manufacturing", and "fierce competition" didn't make any sense to Mr. Adams. As best he could understand, Japan's economy was growing faster than that of the U.S. In addition, Japan's current high labor costs (10 per cent higher than in the U.S. and 15 per cent higher in Canada) should have made the new line all the more attractive.

Finally after several meetings with Ralph Lawson, the president of Computex, the manufacturer of the computer that was incorporated in the new line, Mr. Adams decided to go out and see what the situation was for himself. As the bus approached Tokyo, the magnitude and potential of the Japanese market were dramatically brought home to Jim: mile after mile of factories stretching as far as the eye could see under a gray-brown sky. Since the weather coming into Narita had been bright and clear, this must be Tokyo's famed pollution. Jim had expected the heavy industrial concentration and resultant pollution; what he had not expected were the large number of small factories, each with a different sign on top. Mr. Imura explained that the manufacturing sector in Japan had many small companies that were each loosely affiliated with one of the giant trading companies. These huge conglomerates controlled much of the Japanese economy and its international trade. Mr. Imura said, "Over the past five year's depression thousands of these small firms have failed and tens of thousands of workers have been fired. This has given us great trouble, even the big trading companies." Jim found this hard to believe after all he'd heard about the Japanese industrial juggernaut.

The next several days proved frustrating and perplexing. Representatives from several major Japanese companies that had previously bought CMT machines were very complimentary about the product and enthusiastic about the new line but "not at this time, maybe later". Mr. Imura also introduced Jim to two manufacturers of competing Japanese products. They also were very complimentary and expressed a definite interest in licensing CMT's technology or (more vaguely) some form of joint venture arrangement. They were especially interested in the computer hardware and support software packages. Mr. Imura explained that although in the past the Japanese government had encouraged firms to license technology only, recently under intense pressure from the United States, the powerful

Ministry of International Trade and Industry (MITI) had started to liberalize the procedures for direct investment in Japan. As yet, however, most Japanese firms were uncertain about how to react to this new environment and were taking a very cautious approach. Most of their time was devoted to meeting the challenge of foreign imports in their traditional internal market and by investment opportunities in the low-wage countries. Mr. Imura was not enthusiastic about CMT's chances of setting up a joint venture in Japan (possibly because his firm of sales representatives would be squeezed out by such an arrangement). Such an arrangement would take at least three years and half a million dollars in salaries and expenses, not to mention almost continuous supervision by the top management of CMT.

On the basis of these talks with Japanese companies, MITI, and Mr. Imura, Jim had a much better understanding of Japan, its economy, and CMT's opportunities and problems in the Japanese market. He was still uncertain of what strategy CMT should follow or where Computex fit into the picture. Whatever course they decided upon, Jim felt that the Japanese market would be a tough nut to crack and the cracking would be a long and expensive process.

The next stop on Jim's trip was the Philippines and then Singapore to investigate sales and possible production in these countries.

Exhibit 1

Income Statement

(Figures have been disguised)

Sales	40,000,000
Cost of Goods Sold	17,000,000
Administration	500,000
Interest	200,000
R & D	3,000,000
Selling Expense	2,000,000
Depreciation	5,000,000
Profit Before Tax	12,300,000
Taxes	6,000,000
	6,300,000

Balance Sheet

Assets		Liabilities	
Cash	200,000	Accounts Payable	1,500,000
Inventory	1,500,000	Short-Term Debt	500,000
Accounts Receiv.	3,100,000	Long-Term Debt	1,500,000
Plant and Equip.	23,700,000	Retained Earnings	15,000,000
(Net)		Capital Stock	10,000,000
	28,500,000		28,500,000

Note: CMT is a privately owned company whose stock is closely held.

Case G
Stewart Manufacturing Limited*

Alex Stewart had inherited his father's business in 1965 at a time when the auto trade agreement between Canada and the United States presented particularly attractive opportunities for rapid growth. The business, founded in 1947, manufactured small engine parts (bearings, couplings, etc.) for automobiles which were sold to original equipment manufacturers, and a number of items for the automotive after-market (oil and air filters, fan belts, wiper blades, etc.). The after-market replacement parts were sold through distributors to garages and automotive retail outlets in Canada; they were not subject to duty remission under the auto pact and sales had not therefore penetrated the U.S. market. The engine parts, however, were sold to the four major auto producers in both Canada and the United States.

When Alex took over the business, sales had reached $5.8 million (of which OEM parts accounted for $3 million) and profits were $350,000. Two years later, in 1967, sales had almost doubled to the $10 million mark with most of the growth coming from OEM sales. Profits were $600,000. Alex, a graduate of a leading Canadian business school, spent his first two years coping with two major issues. The first was to secure the funds and expand the plant to support the rapid sales growth. The second was to go public in order to alleviate some impending estate and inheritance problems.

By 1967, both of these goals had been accomplished. The company had a 350,000 square foot modern factory located on a twenty-acre site near St. Catharines. Seven hundred and fifty thousand shares had been issued, with 250,000 held by the Stewart family[1] and close relatives, and 500,000 widely held by the public. The shares traded on the Toronto Stock Exchange in 1967 within a range from $3.50 to $5.25. Alex then turned his attention to the development of longer-term strategic matters and in particular to ways of alleviating the company's growing dependence on the Big Four auto producers; by 1967, OEM sales accounted for 70 per cent of total sales.

Diversification Strategy

The high level of automation in the auto industry resulted in the use

* Copyright © 1975, The University of Western Ontario.

1. Of these 100,000 were held by Alex, and 100,000 by his retired father.

of much special-purpose equipment and extensive standardization of parts requirements. What this often meant was that Stewart couplings and bearings were manufactured to precise auto industry specifications and did not find a ready market outside the industry. It was clear that without some major product innovation, dependence on the Big Four was likely to continue. An even more poignant realization was that the company had developed no "in-house" technological strength from which to launch an attempt at new product development. In the past, product specifications had come down from the auto makers and Stewart's job had been to produce to specification at the lowest possible cost. The need for product development engineers had never arisen, with the result the company had never hired any.

Developing In-house Technology

Once the decision to diversify had been made by the executive team at Stewart, the question of direction arose. Alex took the position that the company should avoid building a research base and should opt instead for the developing of products related to the existing line but with a wider, "non-automotive" market appeal. The decision was made to commit $150,000 to the building of a four-man team of engineers whose sole task would be to work on new product adaptations. At the end of a disappointing first year, little positive progress had been made, and the question of whether to fund the team (two had quit and been replaced) for another year came to the management group:

Alex: "Maybe we just expected too much in the first year. They did come up with the flexible coupling idea, but you didn't seem to encourage them, Andy (production manager)."

Andy McIntyre: "That's right! They had no idea at all how to produce such a thing in our facilities. Just a lot of ideas about how it could be used. When I told them an American outfit was already producing them, the team sort of lost interest."

John Ellis (finance): "We might as well face the fact that we made a mistake, and cut it off before we sink any more money into it."

Alex: "Why don't we shorten the whole process by getting a production licence from the U.S. firm? We could start out that way and then build up our own technology over time."

Andy: "The team looked into that, but it turned out the Americans already have a subsidiary operating in Canada — not too well from what I can gather — and they are not anxious to license anyone to compete with it."

Alex: "Is the product patented?"
Andy: "Yes, but apparently it doesn't have long to run."

At this point a set of ideas began to form in Alex's mind, and in a matter of months he had lured away a key engineer from the U.S. firm with a $40,000 salary offer and put him in charge of the product development team. By mid-1968 the company had developed its own line of flexible couplings with an advanced design and an efficient production process using the latest in production equipment. Looking back, Alex commented, "We were very fortunate in the speed with which we got things done. Even then the project as a whole had cost us close to $300,000 in salaries and related costs, and another $80,000 for preliminary equipment and tooling."

Marketing the New Product

Alex continued, "We then faced a very difficult set of problems, because of uncertainties in the market place. We knew there was a good market for the flexible type coupling because of its wide application across so many different industries, but we didn't know how big the market was nor how much of it we could secure. This meant we weren't sure what volume to tool up for, what kind of size of equipment to purchase, or how to go about the marketing job. We were tempted to start small and grow as our share of market grew, but this could be costly too and could allow too much time for competitive response. Our U.S. engineer was very helpful here. He had a lot of confidence in our product and had seen it marketed in the States. At his suggestion we tooled up for a sales estimate of $5 million — which was pretty daring. In addition we hired five field salesmen to back up the nation-wide distributor and soon afterwards hired three U.S.-based salesmen to cover major markets there. We found that our key U.S. competitor was pricing rather high and had not cultivated very friendly customer relations. We were able to pay U.S. tariffs and still come in at or slightly below his prices. We were surprised how quickly we were able to secure significant penetration into the U.S. market. It just wasn't being well serviced."

During 1967 and 1968, the company actually spent a total of $1.4 million on the project, including expenditures on equipment. In addition, a fixed commitment of $600,000 a year in marketing expenditures on flexible couplings arose from the hiring of salesmen. A small amount of trade advertising was included in this sum. The total

commitment represented a significant part of the company's resources and threatened serious damage to the company's financial
position if the sales failed to materialize.

"It was quite a gamble at the time," Alex added. "We actually spent
even more on additional administrative programs and ways of maintaining high morale amongst the sales force. One unexpected benefit
of these efforts was an improvement in our sales of after-market auto
parts. By the end of 1969, it was clear that the gamble was paying off
as sales in all sectors began to expand." (See Table 1)

Table 1
Sales by Market Sector ($ millions)

	OEM Parts	Replacement Parts	Flexible Couplings	Total	
	Sales	Sales	Sales	Sales	Profits (a.t.)
1965	3.0	2.8	Nil	5.8	.350
1966	4.8	2.8	Nil	7.6	.450
1967	7.0	3.0	Nil	10.0	.600
1968	8.9	3.8	1.4	14.1	.650
1969	10.5	5.5	4.2	20.2	1.750

Stewart's approach to competition was to stress product quality
service and speed of delivery, but not price. Certain sizes of couplings were priced slightly below competition but others were not.
In the words of one Stewart salesman, "Our job is really a technical
function. Certainly we help predispose the customer to buy and we'll
even take orders, but we put them through our distributors. Flexible
couplings can be used in almost all areas of secondary industry, by
both large and small firms. This is why we need a large distributor
with wide reach in the market. What we do is give our product the
kind of emphasis a distributor can't give. We develop relationships
with key buyers in most major industries, and we work with them
to keep abreast of new potential uses for our product, or of changes
in size requirements or other performance characteristics. Then we
feed this kind of information back to our design group. We meet with
the design group quite often to find out what new types of couplings
are being developed and what the intended uses are, etc. Sometimes
they help us solve a customer's problem even when it doesn't
involve a new sale for us. Of course, these 'solutions' are usually built
around the use of one of our existing products."

Production

Stewart's production operations were all located in its St. Catharines plant. By 1970, the plant was nearing capacity and the company was considering an expansion of 40 per cent to 500,000 square feet. The outlook for sales in all three product sectors was most encouraging. Some thought was being given to separating the production of flexible couplings from the auto parts production. According to the production manager, "There are two problems pressing us to put flexible couplings under a different roof. The first is internal: we are making more and more types and sizes, and sales have grown to such a point that we may be able to produce more efficiently in a separate facility. The second is external: the Big Four like to tour our plant regularly and tell us how to make auto parts cheaper — that's usually a prelude to lowering their price. Having these flexible couplings all over the place seems to upset them, because they have trouble determining how much of our costs belong to auto parts. If it were left to me I'd just let them be upset, but Alex feels differently. He's afraid of losing orders. Sometimes I wonder if he's right. Maybe we should lose a few orders to the Big Four and fill up the plant with our own product instead of expanding."

Flexible couplings were produced on a batch basis and there were considerable savings involved as batches got larger. Thus as sales grew, and inventory requirements made large batches possible, unit production costs decreased, sometimes substantially. Mr. McIntyre gave an example in relation to one popular coupling (product J-5X) which he regarded as typical. More detailed information on this product is given in Exhibit 2.

"There's a learning curve at work in the production process. Take the J-5X, for example. Produced in lots of 150, our unit cost for labor is about $12.00. With lots of 300 the average unit cost drops to $9.00, and with 400 to $8.00. The main reason for this, of course, is that speed improves as workers concentrate on a particular size and type of coupling. Our variable overheads are similarly affected."

Some cost savings, however, were more a function of the type of equipment used. The production process as a whole consisted of three major steps. First was the cutting and forging of steel bars; second, the machining to very close tolerances; and third, the assembly process. There were virtually no scale economies to be derived from the first and last processes. In the machining department, however, economies could be derived both from more efficient labor and from the use of special purpose equipment as lot sizes increased. The special purpose equipment was faster and more automated but required longer set-up time and was more costly to maintain.

Foreign Markets

As the company's market position in North America began to improve and its financial position along with it, Alex began to wonder about foreign markets. The company had always been a major exporter to the United States, but it had never had to market there. The auto producers placed their orders often a year or two in advance, and Stewart just supplied them. As Alex put it, "It was different with the flexible coupling. We had to find our own way into the market. The U.S. engineer was useful in this regard in that he knew personally a lot of key U.S. customers and was able to help us choose some good U.S. salesmen."

"One unexpected benefit of entering the U.S. market was that we started getting orders from Europe and South America, at first from the subsidiaries of our U.S. customers and then from a few other firms as word got around. We got $40,000 in orders during 1969 and the same amount during the first six months of 1970. This was a time when we were frantically busy and hopelessly understaffed in the management area, so all we did was fill the orders on an FOB, St. Catharines basis. The customers had to pay import duties of 20 per cent into most European countries and 30-50 per cent into South America on top of the freight and insurance, and still orders came in."

A Licensing Opportunity

In the late summer of 1970, Alex made a vacation trip to Scotland and decided while he was there to drop in on one of the company's few foreign customers, McTaggart Supplies Ltd. Stewart Manufacturing had received unsolicited orders from overseas amounting to $40,000 in the first six months of 1970, and over 10 per cent of these had come from McTaggart. Alex was pleasantly surprised at the reception given to him by Sandy McTaggart, the sixty-year-old head of the company.

Sandy: "Come in! Talk of the devil. We were just saying what a shame it is you don't make those flexible couplings in this part of the world. There's a very good market for them. Why, my men can even sell them to the English."

Alex: "Well, we're delighted to supply your needs. I think we've always shipped your orders promptly, and I don't see why we can't continue. . . ."

Sandy: "That's not the point, laddie! That's not the point! Those orders are already sold before we place them. The point is we can't really build the market here on the basis of shipments from Canada. There's a 20 per cent tariff coming in, freight and insurance cost us another 10 per cent on top of your price, then there's the matter of currency values. I get my orders in pounds $(\pounds)^2$ but I have to pay you in dollars. And on top of all that I never know how long the goods will take to get here, especially with all the dock strikes we have to put up with. Listen, why don't you license us to produce flexible couplings here?"

After a lengthy bargaining session, during which Alex secured the information shown in Exhibit 4, he came round to the view that a licence agreement with McTaggart might be a good way of achieving swift penetration of the U.K. market via McTaggart's sales force. McTaggart's production skills were not all that impressive, but the firm seemed committed enough to invest in some new equipment and to put a major effort into developing the U.K. market. At this point the two executives began to discuss specific terms of the licence arrangement.

Alex: "Let's talk about price. I think a figure around 3 per cent of your sales of flexible couplings would be about right."

Sandy: "That's a bit high for an industrial licence of this kind. I think 1.5 per cent is more normal."

Alex: "That may be but we're going to be providing more than just blueprints. We'll have to help you choose equipment and train your operators as well."

Sandy: "Aye, so you will. But we'll pay you for that separately. It's going to cost us £50,000 in special equipment as it is, plus, let's say, a $10,000 fee to you to help set things up. Now you have to give us a chance to price competitively in the market, or neither of us will benefit. With a royalty of 1.5 per cent I reckon we could reach sales of £50,000 in our first year and £100,000 in our second."

Alex: "The equipment will let you produce up to £400,000 of annual output. Surely you can sell more than £100,000. Our sales to U.K. customers should reach $30,000 this year without even trying."

Sandy: "With the right kind of incentive, we might do a lot better. Why don't we agree to a royalty of 2.5 per cent on the first £100,000 sales and 1.5 per cent on the rest. Now mind you, we're

---

2. One pound was equivalent to Canadian $2.61 in 1970.

to become exclusive agents for the U.K. market. We'll supply your present customers from our own plant."

Alex: "But just in the U.K.! Now 2 per cent is as low as I'm prepared to go. You make those figures 3 per cent and 2 per cent and you have a deal. But it has to include a free technology flow-back clause in the event you make any improvements or adaptations to our product."

Sandy: "You drive a hard bargain! But it's your product, and we do want it. I'll have our lawyers draw up a contract accordingly."

Alex signed the contract the same week and then headed back to Canada to break the news. He travelled with mixed feelings, however. On the one hand, he felt he had got the better of Sandy McTaggart in the bargaining, while on the other, he felt he had no objective yardstick against which to evaluate the royalty rate he had agreed on. This was pretty much the way he presented the situation to his executive group when he got home.

Alex: ". . . so I think it's a good contract, and I have a cheque here for $10,000 to cover our costs in helping McTaggart get set up."

John (finance): "We can certainly use the cash right now. And there doesn't seem to be any risk involved. I like the idea, Alex."

Andy: (production): "Well I don't and Chuck (head of the Stewart design team) won't either when he hears about it. I think you've sold out the whole U.K. market for a pittance."

Alex: "But Andy, we just don't have the resources to capture it ourselves. We might as well get what we can through licensing, now that we've patented our process."

Andy: "Well, maybe. But I don't like it. It's the thin edge of the wedge if you ask me. Our know-how on the production of this product is pretty special, and it's getting better all the time. I hate to hand it over to old McTaggart on a silver platter. I reckon we're going to sell over $3 million in flexible couplings in Canada by the end of 1970."

Questions

1. What seems to be the critical requirements for success in the market place with flexible couplings?
2. Can these critical requirements be replicated abroad through a licence agreement?

3. Is the royalty rate adequate?
4. Can Stewart afford to expand to meet foreign market demand?

Exhibit I

Stewart Manufacturing Ltd.
Income Statement
for Year Ended December 31, 1969
($000)

	1969	1968
Net Sales	$20,250	$14,120
Cost of Goods Sold		
Direct materials	2,400	1,650
Direct labour	5,200	3,800
Variable overheads	3,500	2,500
Fixed overheads	3,200	3,000
Total	14,300	10,950
Gross Profit	5,950	3,170
Expenses		
Selling	1,700	1,050
Admin. (includes design team)	650	620
Other	70	180
Total	2,420	1,850
Net Profit before Tax	3,530	1,320
Income Tax	1,780	670
Net Profit after Tax	$ 1,750	$ 650
Shares Outstanding	750,000	750,000
Earnings per Share	$ 2.33	0.87
Share Price at December 31	$ 13½	$ 6¼
Price-earnings Ratio	6	7

**Stewart Manufacturing Ltd.
Balance Sheet
as at December 31, 1969
($000)**

	1969	1968
Assets		
Cash	$ 300	$ 700
Accounts receivable	2,150	1,625
Inventories	5,000	3,750
Total Current Assets	7,450	6,075
Property, plant, and equipment (net)	4,750	4,100
Total Assets	$12,200	$10,175
Liabilities		
Accounts payable	620	510
Dividends payable	375	150
Accrued items (incl. taxes)	1,405	890
Instalments on long-term debt	400	200
Total Current Liabilities	2,800	1,750
Long-term debt (15 year, 9%)	1,800	2,000
Government loans	1,000	1,200
Common Stock (750,000 shares, $5 par)	3,750	3,750
Retained earnings and surplus	2,850	1,475
Total Equity	6,600	5,225
Total Liabilities	$12,200	$10,175

Exhibit 2

**Stewart Manufacturing Ltd.
Production Cost Breakdown on Product J-5X**

	Labor costs per unit		
	Lots of 150	Lots of 300	Lots of 400
Operation			
I Cutting and Forging	$1.80	$1.75	$1.75
II Machining			
Boring and Turning	3.50	1.95	1.75
Facing	1.80	1.30	.80
Drilling	1.80	1.10	.80
Finishing	1.50	1.40	1.40
III Assembly	1.60	1.50	1.50
Total	**$12.00**	**$9.00**	**$8.00**

Exhibit 3

Stewart Manufacturing Ltd. Breakdown of Sales and Profits by Major Product Area, 1969 ($ millions)

	Flexible Couplings	OEM Auto Parts	After-market Replacement Parts	Total
Sales in Canada	2.21	4.80	5.50	12.51
Sales in U.S.	2.00	5.70	—	7.70
Sales elsewhere	.04	—	—	0.04
Total Sales	4.25	10.50	5.50	20.25
Variable Costs	1.50	6.70	2.90	11.10
Contribution	2.75	3.80	2.60	9.15
%	65%	36%	47%	45%
Indirect Costs[a]				5.62
Profit				3.53

(a) Indirect costs included

fixed manufacturing overhead	$3.20 mln
selling expense	1.70 mln
admin. overhead, etc.	.72 mln
	$5.62 mln

Exhibit 4

Data on McTaggart Supplies Ltd.

1969 Sales
£4.2 million (down from £5.6 million in 1967).

Total Assets
£1.6 million: Equity £800,000.

Net profit after tax
± £30,000.

Control
McTaggart Family.

Market coverage
15 salesmen in U.K., 2 in Europe, 1 in Australia, 1 in New Zealand, 1 in India.

Average factory wage rate
£.80 per hour (versus $4.75 in Canada).

Factory
Old and larger than necessary.

Reputation
Excellent credit record, business now 130 years old, good market contacts (high-calibre sales force).

Other
Company sales took a beating during 1966-67 as one of the company's staple products was badly hurt by a U.S. product of superior technology. Company filled out its line by distributing products obtained from other manufacturers. Currently about one-half of company sales are purchased from others.

Pricing	Index
Stewart's price to McTaggart	100
(distributor price in Canada)	
Import duty	20
Freight and insurance	10
Total cost to McTaggart	130
Price charged by McTaggart	165
Price charged by Canadian distributor	125

Case H
Black & Decker Canada Inc. (A)*
The Power Tool Industry

For thirty years power tool manufacturers have systematically improved their productivity by constant attention to product design and manufacturing process. This has allowed a steady drop in market price (adjusted for inflation) of power tools such as electric drills, sanders, and saws. As prices dropped, the market base expanded rapidly,[1] justifying yet more investment in productive designs and processes. Black & Decker now spends, worldwide, over $19 million per year on R & D, and 40 per cent of 1978's sales was from products that did not exist five years before.[2] Faced with this relentless competition, companies who could not keep improving design and production dropped out. In this austere environment, Black & Decker has systematically improved its products and productivity and now claims over 60 per cent of global market share for consumer power tools,[3] though it is less entrenched in professional and industrial tools.

For the past two decades, Black & Decker has maintained an average annual growth of 16.7 per cent in net sales[4]: sales have doubled every five years. Global sales in 1968 were U.S. $189 million with $14 million net income; in 1978 sales had risen to U.S. $960 million with $66 million net income.[5] The prices of most Black & Decker power tools have dropped significantly. For example, the 1978 real dollar price of a 1/4″ drill (economy model) is 30 per cent of the 1958 price.[6] Thus the sales figures need not be adjusted for inflation.

B & D's growth has not only been fast, it has been consistent. Sales have risen in each of the past twenty years; net earnings have increased in nineteen of these twenty years.[7] Since moving into the international field forty-eight years ago, Black & Decker has also

---

* This case was prepared by Professor David Rutenberg, assisted by Clayton V. Jaeger, and with the co-operation of the management of Black & Decker Canada Inc. Copyright © 1979 by Queen's University, Canada.

1. *Business Week* (November 28, 1970), p. 79.
2. *Globe and Mail* (May 7, 1979), p. B7.
3. *Ibid.*
4. *Black & Decker Annual Report* (1978), p. 2.
5. *Ibid.*, p. 16.
6. *Ibid.*, p. 13.
7. *Ibid.*, p. 12.

been successful, with almost every foreign subsidiary profitable within its first year.[8] Foreign subsidiaries are virtually 100 per cent owned.[9] On capital investments, Black & Decker uses a pay back limit of one to three years, depending on the subsidiary.

Black and Decker tools are marketed in forty-five countries at over 100,000 retail outlets. The national marketing managers source tools from thirty plants in sixteen nations, striving for the most economical pattern. In order to achieve productivity gains from economies of scale and accumulated experience, the decision to rationalize some of its products into one plant was made by Black & Decker around 1966.[10] Implementation began in 1968 and the process continues. Although United States headquarters and 40 per cent of Black & Decker's market is in the United States, these designated plants are not necessarily in the United States. Locations are examined at the local level by the most immediate subsidiary. Because raw materials costs for Black & Decker are essentially the same around the world, government incentives, market accessibility, and the price of labor (if labor content is high) constitute the primary determinants of a plant location.

Black & Decker Canada has grown even faster than the corporate whole. Sales of $12.5 million in 1969 rose to approximately $115 million in 1979,[11] almost a tenfold rise. About 40 per cent of Canadian profits go to the parent company, and the balance is retained for expansion and other investment.[12] Due to rationalization, substantial capital expenditures, and focussed management, productivity rose from $15,000 sales/employee in 1968[13] to $25,000 sales/employee in 1969, to $50,000 per employee in 1978, and finally to $95,800 sales/employee in 1979. Employment rose from 450 to 1,200 over the same decade.

Bob Tivy, president of Black & Decker Canada in 1976, described the situation in Canada prior to rationalization,[14] "For many years Canadian manufacturing plants were plagued with producing a wide variety of goods but at a low volume. They were trying to make the full production range as in the United States, but the low volume beats the hell out of costs." Describing the present situation in Canada, Tivy said, "Our pay rates and benefits are among the highest

---

8. *Business Week* (November 28, 1970), p. 78.
9. *Ibid.*, p. 78.
10. *Brockville Recorder and Times* (March 11, 1976).
11. *Brockville Recorder and Times* (July 25, 1978).
12. *Globe and Mail* (March 1, 1972), p. B5.
13. *Black & Decker Annual Report* (1978), p. 13.
14. *Brockville Recorder and Times* (November 24, 1977).

of any power tool plant in the world, and unless we offset these with high productivity, we would not only lose our exports but also allow imports to gain a share in the Canadian market."[15] In 1979, after visiting China, Tivy noted that although in China labor is paid only 17¢/hr., they take over twelve hours to produce the same electric drill which Canadians can produce in ten minutes, where average labor cost is almost $7/hr.

The Black & Decker plant at Brockville, Ontario was given the global product mandate for B & D orbital sanders to supply all B & D's forty-five national markets. To achieve economies of scale and accumulated experience, global sander production could be concentrated at one factory. Because of B & D's market share, the Brockville plant now produces more sanders than any other single power tool plant in the world.[16] Of all the possible locations, Canada was selected, according to Mr. G. Hale, president of B & D Canada in 1968, because of the proximity to the American market; the potential of the domestic market; Canada's status as a respected nation throughout the world; Canada's position in the Commonwealth; and the country's favorable tariff position, following the Kennedy Round negotiations.[17] Brockville also fit Black & Decker's preference for a rural community which is near the large cities of Montreal, Toronto, and Ottawa.

Because many power tools contain common sub-assemblies, rationalization also cuts production costs for local markets. For example, sanders use the same electric motor components as drills and jigsaws. Hence the export volume of sanders allows B & D Canada to lower its motor manufacturing cost, and in turn the assembled cost and price of drills and jigsaws for the Canadian market.

Competition and Co-operation

There is interplant rivalry within any multinational corporation. Within Black & Decker great care has been taken to channel that rivalry into productive channels using five integrated methods.

First, Black & Decker internationalizes its executives by freely moving them between subsidiaries. This breeds familiarity with other operations as well as a strong tendency towards co-operating with former and future postings. A primary consideration in the promotion of an executive is his ability to work with an intersubsidiary team.

15. *Ibid.*
16. *Brockville Recorder and Times* (March 11, 1976).
17. *Industrial Canada* (1968), p. 39.

Second, although Black & Decker uses a responsibility accounting system which compares subsidiary performances, managers are nevertheless reminded of the effect of their efforts on the entire company. Jack Beckering, vice-president of product development at Brockville, pointed out that the stock price is affected by all aspects of the business in all global locations. However, he added that it is sometimes not easy to reconcile local goals with global strategy.

Third, over the years the more mature subsidiaries have developed a system of co-ordinating objectives. B & D Canada does this at an annual three-day "Management Seminar" held outside the plant, where the managers outline their respective goals for the following year. These goals are then published in a reference book, and a summary of each book is sent to B & D headquarters in Towson, Maryland. The objectives of each country collectively make the global objectives of Black & Decker. This provides a frame of reference within the subsidiaries and between countries; the more contact between subsidiaries, the more they are aware of each other's goals.

Fourth, there is a belief that disagreement should be solved by an analysis of data, not through interplant politics. Capital investment decisions are prepared in detail at the local level in a manner suitable for headquarters. Every manufacturing and marketing step is justified by a make/buy analysis, not only of present costs but also of forecast costs based on accumulated experience. Black & Decker headquarters in Maryland employs only eighteen people, including clerical staff, and does not often interfere with local operations, except when superimposing a particular global strategy. However, headquarters is buttressed by outside consultants, chosen to combine objectivity with analytical prowess. In several instances subsidiary B & D companies have independently used these same consultants for local market evaluation and strategic planning.

Fifth, each plant has specified market territories for each product. The boundaries can be shifted with headquarter's permission, but surreptitious poaching is not allowed. The Canadian plant manufactures drills for the Canadian market only. The Canadian plant manufactures sanders for the world. Any other subsidiary could propose to manufacture sanders, and headquarters would grant it permission if the shift in production would adequately increase Black & Decker's total profitability. To forestall this, Canada designs and assembles sanders into forty-seven different end versions. Members of the Canadian executive appear to have a higher sensitivity to protecting and satisfying their export business than their U.S. counterparts, as B & D Canada's exports are 40 per cent of production, while exports are less than 20 per cent of U.S. output.

In Canada, drills are produced only for Canadian consumption. On the other hand, sanders are for global marketing. Either extreme is relatively easy to manage. This case explores the dynamics of an intermediate situation, exemplified in the product called Workmate.

Canada and Ireland, the two leaders in Workmate manufacture, consciously decided to actively exchange design and production improvements. Now the United States is to become the third manufacturing leader and the same technical exchange is expected. Canada is now assisting the fledgling Workmate operations in Mexico and Brazil, loaning them managers and hosting visits. This paternal relationship was initiated when Brockville was headquarters for South American and Pacific operations; it continues because of Canada's acknowledged competence with Workmate as well as its power tool manufacturing expertise. No fees other than normal salary are paid to motivate the individual Canadian managers to give their time to help their Mexican and Brazilian counterparts.

Within Black & Decker, worldwide technology is shared. The willful withholding of information so as to cause a sister subsidiary to be less profitable is a temptation which the Black & Decker executive culture has not tolerated.

Black & Decker headquarter's control is guided by three principles: strong market share, tight fiscal rein, and decentralized managerial control. Referring to market share, Chairman Alonzo Decker said, "We increase our level of presence as fast as we can, (while) we let the local managers make their own destiny."[18] Black & Decker has captured over 90 per cent of the British market, and claims over 50 per cent of the market in many other countries.[19]

Black & Decker budgets are rigid, for their executives believe that a flexible budget is meaningless.[20] Budgets originate at the foreman level and are eventually consolidated at the subsidiary level, at which point they are submitted to headquarters. Failure to meet a budget is scrutinized at all levels.

Decentralized managerial control is held by Black & Decker to be the key to their success. According to Robert Appleby, previously managing director of the U.K. subsidiary while simultaneously deputy chairman of the parent corporation, "Black & Decker's organization succeeds because if forces a complete commitment in people who know they are responsible. While their results are carefully watched, they are free to solve their own problems their way."[21]

18. *Business Week* (November 28, 1970), p. 78.
19. *Ibid.*, p. 79.
20. *Financial Times* (January 26, 1972).
21. *Business Week* (November 28, 1970), p. 79.

Black & Decker feeds lower level managers detailed corporate information that most top managements keep a closely guarded secret.[22]

Boundaries and Flexibility

Think of a child playing in the back yard of his home. If the yard has a good fence and gate, the parent has no need to interfere with the child; both find the boundary valuable. Black & Decker managers work to clearly establish boundaries. Within the boundary the employee can exercise initiative and see how well she/he is doing. If an assembly line has made quota for the day, its workers are allowed to leave up to half an hour before normal quitting time. In management, the standard cost of each item is known and forecast with precision. At the executive level for each product, each plant supplies a clearly bounded market territory.

Fluctuations in demand strain this focussed system. In the past, Black & Decker attempted to smooth seasonal fluctuations by using dating incentives; customers who took early delivery could defer payment. An increasing reluctance of customers to hold inventory had led to a reduction in the dating programs offered. There are now increased fluctuations in orders. In the months prior to Christmas and Father's Day, the Workmate production manager (who knows each of his workers, not just his foremen) asks each if she/he would mind increasing output to catch the peak. In exchange, the workers can be more flexible in arranging their schedules at other times — such as four ten-hour days in the week prior to a Monday holiday so as to create a very long weekend. The marketing group provides a market forecast to the production planner, who in turn arranges orders with the parts vendors. In early 1979, a recession was forecast in the United States, so the Workmate forecast was revised down. Brockville ran one shift and curbed hiring. By June 1979, actual Workmate demand had continued to climb, stores were back-ordered, shipments had to be allocated, and Brockville was running two shifts, then even three shifts in August 1979.

Accounting's standard cost of a Workmate remains unchanged during these adjustments. In fact, the spurt of effort will show up as a negative variance on labor, so that pre-Christmas Workmates will appear to be less expensive to produce. Obviously the real cost of a Workmate will be higher. Under the present product mandate this peculiarity poses no difficulty.

22. *Ibid.*

Within the Brockville plant a few workers may be asked to transfer to products which are selling better. While some workers like the continuity of knowing exactly what they will do each day, other workers prefer variety, and it is they who switch. In other words, the flexibility of the Brockville plant can accommodate demand fluctuations. Only two weeks of finished product inventory is on hand. Managers talked of matching production to demand, and avoiding "a 1975" when they misread a demand reduction, continued full production on low-demand products too long, and then had to lay off abruptly.

One of the difficulties of having each plant produce unique products arises when there is a down turn for the products of one plant while demand grows for products of another plant. In the short run, it is most difficult to adjust the global Black & Decker system. Export markets cannot be transferred from the overtime plant to the layoff plant because each plant produces unique product designs. (An easy adjustment would be possible if just one item was produced to an identical design in both plants. A cost system different than standard cost would be required to guide the mutual adjustments.) In the long run of over a year, the global system is adjusted by assigning new products to the lowest-cost plants. Thus the Canadian plant now assembles McCulloch chain saws, and the German plant no longer produces Workmates. Firm boundaries in the short run allow clear data that facilitate flexibility in the long run.

Black & Decker Canada

Black & Decker Canada is controlled by its own seven-man board of directors, six of whom are Canadian.[23] Mr. Decker, who serves as a director emeritus in Canada, has attributed large part of the success of B & D Canada to the company's autonomy from the parent American company, as well as the "esprit de corps" of the employees.[24]

This emphasis on individual responsibility extends down to the assembly line employees. For example, all employees at Brockville are paid on a weekly salary for filling an assigned quota. Responsibility for production and costs is outlined in the management seminar book, having been drawn up from employee and managerial suggestions. Employee turnover is low and B & D Canada had layoffs only in 1975 and 1977, both followed by rehirings. The result is a non-

23. *Brockville Recorder and Times* (July 25, 1978).
24. *Ibid.*

unionized plant with high morale. Attempts to unionize the plant have met with failure. The most recent union organizer, Robert Stewart of the Canadian Chemical Workers, after meeting at the local Masonic Hall in 1977 with "several" Black & Decker employees, left Brockville frustrated.[25] Ideas and recommendations on "product improvements" are encouraged from workers and foremen informally and through a special employee participation cost education/cost avoidance program called FOCUS. In mid-March each year thirteen teams of five to eight workers begin a ten-week cost reduction/cost avoidance exploration. The individuals have access to accounting, marketing, and engineering data. Every effort is made to implement their ideas within the ten-week period. Fresh teams of workers volunteer each year. When possible, if a job is eliminated as a result of an improvement in productivity, the employee is transferred rather than fired.

The physical space of the Brockville plant has been expanded from 150,000 square feet in 1969 to 387,000 square feet in 1979.[26] The number of employees has grown from 330 in 1968 to 600 in 1972 and finally 1,200 in 1979. This growth has been due to the global rationalization of the sander and several sub-assemblies, which took place around 1968-69; the 15 per cent per annum growth in sales; the addition of the Workmate to the product line in 1974; and the merging with McCulloch in 1978, allowing substantial savings of import costs by manufacturing chain saws domestically. The plant now produces over 2.5 million power tools[27] and over 1 million Workmates per annum.

In 1969 and 1971, Black & Decker Canada received grants of $221,000 and $233,000 (actually forgivable, interest-free loans) from the Ontario Development Corporation to help finance plant expansions.[28] Since then Black & Decker Canada has become less receptive to government aid and in 1978 Bob Tivy, then president and chief executive officer of Black & Decker Canada, made a point of stating that the $1.2 million expansion program of 1978 had received "no government funding whatsoever" and was funded entirely by the company.[29] Tivy attributed the most recent expansion to the very high productivity of the Brockville workers, calling them "the very best Black & Decker has in the world."[30]

25. *Brockville Recorder and Times* June 16, 1977).
26. *Brockville Recorder and Times* (July 25, 1978).
27. *Ibid.*
28. *Black & Decker Manufacturing Company, Limited; Financial Statements* (September 29, 1974)
29. *Brockville Recorder and Times* (July 25, 1978).
30. *Ibid.*

Exhibit 1

Black & Decker Sales Data (000,000)

Year	U.S. (U.S. $)	Canada (Can. $)
1972	345.6	26.1
1973	427.0	34.9
1974	641.9	43.5
1975	653.8	53.8
1976	748.1	69.2
1977	811.6	80.0
1978	959.9	102[a]

(a) Including McCulloch product line volume merged during 1978.

Case I
Black & Decker Canada Inc. (B)*
Workmate

The Workmate, focus of this case, is similar in distribution to other Black & Decker products, but quite different in manufacture. The Workmate can be used as a sawhorse, a workbench, a vise, or a power tool support. The Workmate is about the size of a trestle sewing machine stand, and was ingeniously designed to function as "a third hand", hence the name.

The designer of the English Lotus car, Ron Hickman, conceived what has become the Workmate and developed its design in the late 1960s. His effort to license the design to established tool companies such as Stanley, Black & Decker, etc., was thwarted by their guestimates that only dozens, not hundreds, would sell. Hickman went into business for himself in August 1968 selling Workmates door to door and by mail order at the rate of one hundred per month.[1]

Four years later, in 1972, Hickman licensed Workmate to Black & Decker. Several factors occurring simultaneously led to this decision. In 1971, Hickman had redesigned the product to add a foot stabilizer so that the Workmate could function at the height of a sawhorse or of a workbench. Redesign, retooling, new marketing techniques, and rapid sales growth meant negative cash flow for Hickman. Mail order sales had been significant; then in 1972 the United Kingdom suffered a prolonged mail strike. One might wonder how Hickman's banker evaluated his prospects at that time. The Black & Decker re-evaluation was made by Walter Goldsmith, Managing Director of B & D's U.K. subsidiary. The U.K. subsidiary had no tradition of innovation, its product development group was new, and Goldsmith had rejected the Workmate in 1968. Nevertheless the phenomenal actual sales data on the Workmate appealed to him. When he made the decision to license the Workmate, Goldsmith had been working with Black & Decker for ten years.

Workmate *appears* no more useful than two chairs and a door. Yet its vises and utility have to be used to be believed. It was a natural for T.V. advertising, then newly legal in the United Kingdom. In addition to television, Black & Decker's normal distribution channels pushed the new product. In 1972 Workmates sold well.

---

* This case was prepared by Professor David Rutenberg, assisted by Clayton V. Jaeger, and with the co-operation of the management of Black & Decker Canada Inc.

1. *Financial Times* (December 29, 1977).

The Italian subsidiary of B & D adopted the Workmate almost immediately, cutting production cost by replacing the die cast aluminum legs with stamped steel.

However, the U.S. marketing manager, Dick Campbell at that time, wrote a market evaluation white paper in which he concluded that the price/value relationship of the Workmate would not be apparent to U.S. consumers, especially if priced at $100/unit. Ironically, Campbell is now president of Black & Decker Canada.

Canadian Adoption of Workmate

In 1973, the Canadian president sent his vice-president of sales to Britain to evaluate the product. Workmate fit the established channels of distribution that Black & Decker Canada had used, and his report was positive. Importing from England would not have been economical; the shipping cost would have totalled $8/unit, partly because of the bulk and partly because Canada Customs classified the Workmate as a vise, subject to 10 per cent import duty (reduced from 17.5 per cent because of Commonwealth preference). If the Workmate were to sell in Canada, its cost had to be reduced. The product would have to be redesigned, and an assembly line would need enough volume to take advantage of economies of scale.

The 1972 sales guestimate for Canada was 20,000 Workmates per year at some time in the future. The U.S. market is about ten times that of Canada, so a North American market of 200,000/yr. could be envisioned. This was a speculative forecast.

Preliminary production process designs indicated that there would be substantial economies of scale up to about 100,000 units per year. So unless actual Canadian sales would exceed their estimate by five times, the U.S. market was necessary. Unfortunately the U.S. marketing manager was still unconvinced about the volume of sales.

In early 1973, the Canadian executives approached Sears, Roebuck & Co. of Chicago. The Sears product testing labs were sent several English Workmates. Interestingly, Sears had long been regarded as a principal rival, competing against Black & Decker with their Craftsman tools manufactured by Singer Co. (Recently however, Black & Decker has become a supplier to Sears for non-core products, although they still compete with Craftsman tools.) After testing the Workmate for several months, Sears gave some indication of interest but no purchasing estimates. Sears normally markets only accepted products, and rarely pioneers products such as the Workmate. However, the Sears lab did recommend design changes. In the United States in 1973, consumer safety had become a litigious issue; the

Consumer Products Safety Commission had been created and there was anxiety as to where the spreading law would stop. In this milieu, the Sears labs noted that if an individual stood on a Workmate and jumped, the resultant force might overload the Workmate legs. The possible snapping of die cast aluminum legs was referred to in the legal phrase, catastrophic failure. Sears also noted that the unit could tip if users stood at the extreme front of the Workmate step. So the legs would have to be redesigned in a material subject to plastic deformation, and at a more spread-out angle.

The management of Black & Decker Canada turned the redesign over to a local Brockville inventor, who met the Sears suggestions by using bent steel, and simultaneously redesigned other parts to cut the manufacturing cost. By this time Black & Decker Canada had grown enough to support its own product development group. Headquarter's permission was granted, and an experienced development engineer, Jack Beckering, was transferred from Maryland to Brockville in April 1974 with a development budget of $70,000.[2] (Within three years the group totalled twenty-two[3] with a budget of $610,000 per annum[4] and growth has continued.)

Meanwhile the Canadian management committed themselves to build a manufacturing line capable of 100,000 Workmates per year. The operation opened in August 1974. Although this volume would achieve many of the economies of scale in assembly, it would be too small for stand-alone steel stamping, aluminum die casting, or vise screw turning. The steel stamping contract was let to F & K Manufacturing, an established, medium-size Toronto company. Black & Decker's purchase contract was sufficiently irrevocable to be used as collateral for a bank loan which the Toronto company needed for equipment purchases. By 1979, F & K had accumulated experience making Workmate parts so their bids were persistently lowest. Between 60 per cent and 70 per cent of F & K's production was going to Black & Decker Canada.

Black & Decker U.S. committed itself to take a token number of Workmates for one year only, to be used for a market test on the west coast. They viewed their down-side risk as low because U.K. sales were continuing to climb, and Workmates, unsold in the U.S., could be shipped to Britain. To meet this commitment, in the fall of 1974 the Workmate was launched in California, Oregon, and Washington.

2. Black & Decker Manufacturing Company, Limited; *Financial Statements* (September 29, 1974).
3. *Design in the Corporation* (1976), p. 10.
4. Black & Decker Canada Inc.; *Financial Statement* (September 24, 1978).

Sales were excellent with more orders than shipments.[5] It was launched nationally in March 1975 so as to be available for Father's Day in June, again with rapid sales growth.[6]

Black & Decker Canada uses four methods to monitor sales data. First, records of shipments are stored in the plant computer. Second, a customer who buys a B & D product is encouraged to mail the warranty card back to the plant. In the case of Workmates about 20 per cent of the customers return the warranty cards. The number of days of inventory in the distribution channel can be inferred from the delay between the date when the warranty card left the factory with a Workmate, and the date it returned by mail. Third, selected stores are monitored for inventory levels and product movements. Fourth, a representative group of wholesalers are monitored monthly for product movement and inventory levels. These four data sources are summarized and provide quite accurate daily, weekly, monthly, and yearly predictions of orders, which avoid inventory back ups between customer's warehouses and retail stores.

When the Workmate was launched in Canada, shipments from the factory proceeded on target for six months, but the flow of warranty cards was high, indicating a minimal inventory of Workmate in the channels of distribution. In the monitored stores, customers were back-ordered, yet the store buyers were still cautious lest the Workmate prove to be a fad. On the basis of three months flow of warranty cards, Black & Decker Canada decided in late 1974 to expand its manufacturing capability from 100,000/yr. to 250,000/yr. at the cost of $1.5 million.[7] For that expansion, the production capability of one Workmate per year cost $10.

Continued expansion of U.K. and European sales necessitated that a new plant be built to supplement the English Spennymoor facility. The U.K. and European management chose Ireland, and the plant opened in 1974 in Kildare, a 64,000-person county south of Dublin. The Irish plant was designed to produce 500,000 units/year and cost $15 million.[8] In other words, their production capability of one Workmate per year cost $30 (from which Irish government grants should be subtracted).

Ireland was chosen for several reasons. First, because Ireland is a member of the EEC, no tariffs are imposed on Irish products sold within the EEC. Second, Ireland offers a long tax-free period, and

5. *Black & Decker Workmate Review*, p. 1.
6. *Ibid.*
7. *Brockville Recorder and Times* (July 20, 1974).
8. *Financial Times* (December 29, 1974).

income earned in Ireland is free of U.S. taxes until it is brought home. Third, cash grants and other financial assistance are available from the Irish government. The disadvantages to manufacturing in Ireland are that all materials must be imported and most finished products must be exported. There is neither a solid manufacturing base nor much of a domestic market.

The Canadian and Irish plants are different. The Canadians subcontracted out their metal stamping. The Irish had to make instead of buy, so their on-the-book capital investment of $30 per Workmate/year and their plant area per Workmate/year appear less efficient than the Canadian plant, notwithstanding the differences between initial investment and expansion.

Increasing the Canadian production from 100,000/yr. to 250,000/yr. justified redesigning the Workmate. Black & Decker Canada now had their own design staff. Assembly bottlenecks had been uncovered, and could be designed out of the product. Workmate had been envisioned for apartment dwellers, yet the prime market turned out to be established do-it-yourselfers;[9] the secondary market was gifts-for-father. In April 1975, there was a world meeting in Ireland at which the Black & Decker subsidiaries pooled their ideas for Workmate redesign. The Canadians brought detail improvements, such as nylon handles for the vises, an innovation that Black & Decker Japan adopted. The Italians brought a simplified single height variant, a design now used in Mexico and Brazil. The English brought a thorough cost-cutting redesign. The merging of ideas which occurred in 1975 led to thirteen versions of Workmate within a year.

In the last four years, the Workmate capacity of the Canadian plant has been expanded fourfold, and an executive decision has been made to stabilize it at 1.2 million units/year. Only 15 per cent of this output is sold in Canada where marketing executives estimate that 6 per cent of households now own a Workmate. Black & Decker predicts that the market will be saturated when approximately 24 per cent of all the households in Canada own a Workmate. In 1974, it was felt that economies of scale precluded a plant of less than 100,000 units/year. In 1979, it was felt that incremental economies of scale were small beyond one million units/year.

Manufacturing Process

The deluxe dual height model Workmate now consists of sixty parts, fifty-seven of which are purchased; all parts are made in Canada. The

9. *Black & Decker Workmate Review*, p. 11.

Workmate operation has been separated almost completely from the other sections of the plant. The only common links are financial, executive, and some general overhead. Workmate has its own production, delivery, and shipping areas. Three types of Workmates are produced in Brockville; the standard, deluxe, and bench-top models. The standard and deluxe models both fold, but the deluxe model has two heights (sawing and worktable).

Steel stampings and tubes for all models are delivered rough and unpainted to Workmate's own loading dock from F & K Manufacturing of Toronto. Most of the wooden tops are purchased finished from Weldwood of Vancouver. The three internally sourced parts (all plastic) are for the vise assembly (handle and swivel grips) and are moved from the Brockville plastic department in large boxes. The Workmate manager thus has clear control of his raw material. He is accountable, and has a computer system to help him keep track of details.

U.S. Joins Ireland and Canada, Boundaries Alter

In mid-1979 a second North American production line for Workmates opened in Easton, Maryland. Both U.S. and Canadian executives had become dissatisfied, even anxious, about sourcing Workmates exclusively from the Brockville plant.

As the United States bought an increasing percentage of their output, the Canadians became more dependent on the whims of the U.S. marketing and product managers. They were losing their independence. This created a fear that Brockville could develop into a branch plant of U.S. operations, a distasteful thought to the semi-autonomous members of the Canadian and the Pacific International Group executives. The results have been a one million unit ceiling placed on Workmate export production, the decision not to produce a new Workmate model, and the decision to increase product development effort on other more indigenous products. This ceiling was to help to avoid two trends. First, the product development group would not become an extension of the U.S. plants, for as the Canadian executive stated in 1976, "We are not in the business of exporting engineering."[10] Second, Brockville will not lose its entrepreneurial capacity and suffer from a "not invented here" syndrome.

From the U.S. point of view, domestic Workmate product would utilize unused capacity in the Easton plant, and would increase U.S.

10. *Design in the Corporation* (1976), p. 10.

profits and control while decreasing the risk of a break in supply from Brockville.

For three years after the U.S. national introduction of the Workmate, much of the manufacturing and marketing direction came from Brockville. This situation persisted because there was still some U.S. scepticism about the Workmate's rapid growth in sales.[11] Not only were there the normal fears of a short product life cycle, but the U.S. corporate headquarters looked on the Workmate through the prejudiced eyes of a "power tool company". Because a workbench vise is not a power tool, it was regarded as another of the many small fringe products which every subsidiary produces to satisfy local demands. In 1977, after three years of excellent sales, Black & Decker U.S. began to devote higher marketing priority to the Workmate line. Prime-time television exposure was doubled from forty-nine spots in 1975 and 1976 to eighty-three in 1977, compared with seventy-nine spots on other key products. The Workmate now has the largest national T.V. exposure of any single product in the hardware industry.[12] A staff was created to handle the Workmate and related products exclusively.

The U.S. will continue to rely on Brockville for the original dual-height model; however the Easton plant, site of the new management of the U.S. Workmate, produces a less expensive tabletop model with an injection-molded top, and will soon be producing a large Italian design with a horizontal/vertical vise. The Italian design model will be exported to Canada, while a Canadian designed bench-top unit is being manufactured in Canada.

The concentration of other North American Workmate models in Easton somewhat reduces transportation and duty costs, but primarily it gives the U.S. management a greater degree of control over the Workmate and an extended line for more segmented distribution channels. They perceive the U.S. market to be much more complex than the Canadian, and although most Workmate patents have been upheld in court (notably against the Sears "workbuddy", produced by Emerson Electric), the U.S. is more competitive at the retail level. Easton's market management team will strive to keep the distribution gaps filled with different models, packages, and price points.

The decision to locate the Workmate plant in Easton was part of an overall plan to divisionalize the separate product groups. Workmate is located in Easton along with house and garden tools; the consumer power tools will be headquartered in Raleigh, N.C.; and all consumer

11. *Black & Decker Workmate Review.*

product divisions will be within twenty-four-hour trucking distance from each other. The world headquarters at Towson will be much leaner as a result, for the product management groups have moved to their respective plants.

Case J
The American Aluminum Corporation*

By the end of July 1974, Charles M. Hall, a recent MBA graduate from a leading U.S. business school, had been on his first assignment with American Aluminum Corporation (AMAL) for only two weeks and he found himself facing the first important problem of his very brief career. Hall's boss had assigned him the responsibility for the petroleum coke aspects of the primary aluminum production process and with this responsibility came two related problems with important long-run consequences. The first problem was whether or not to accept an offer from British Columbia Aluminum, Ltd., a Canadian company, to supply 50,000 tons of petroleum coke at a delivered price of 10 per cent less than the delivered price of the best alternative source of petroleum coke from U.S. sources. America used large quantities of petroleum coke and needed to purchase 50,000 tons in order to tide it over for the next six months. The second problem was to establish and justify a price at which a new long-run source of petroleum coke should be transferred from a newly formed Canadian subsidiary to AMAL's U.S. smelting operation. But before deciding what to do about these two problems, Hall reviewed what he knew about AMAL operations.

The Company Structure

American Aluminum Corporation, a U.S. corporation located on the west coast of the Pacific northwest, refines high-quality aluminum ingot from aluminum oxide (alumina) which is transported in bulk ocean carriers from bauxite mines in western Australia to AMAL's smelter. The aluminum smelting process combines a few basic raw materials, (alumina, cryolite, aluminum fluoride, pitch, and petroleum coke), with large quantities of electric power to produce aluminum ingot (see Exhibit 1). AMAL's smelter is located so that it has access to a deep-water harbor for unloading the alumina, as well

---

* Prepared by J. Frederick Truitt, Associate Professor of International Business, with the assistance of Rex Loesby, MBA student, of the Graduate School of Business Administration, University of Washington. This material was prepared as the basis for classroom discussion rather than as an illustration of an effective or ineffective handling of an administrative situation.

Exhibit 1

The Aluminum Refining Process: Raw Materials Required

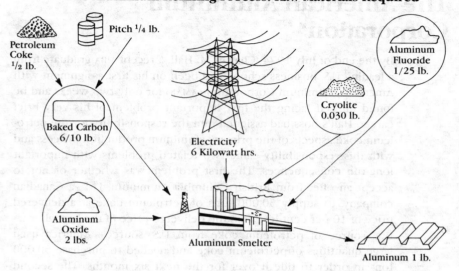

as convenient rail service and relatively inexpensive hydroelectric power.

AMAL is owned by two U.S. corporations, Eastern Metals Corporation and North American Metals Corporation. Each owns 50 per cent of AMAL. Eastern Metals Corporation is in turn 40 per cent owned by European Resources, Ltd., a French corporation (see Exhibit 2).

The Petroleum Coke Suply Problem

During the two years immediately preceding Hall's assignment, AMAL had been experiencing problems securing dependable supplies of petroleum coke[1] at a stable and reasonable price. AMAL used a maximum of 110,000 tons of petroleum coke per year, and between late 1973 and December 1974 the delivered price of petroleum coke had increased from $45 to $90 per ton. This dramatic increase in price along with interruptions in supply and decrease in the quality of petroleum coke available from U.S. West Coast refineries led AMAL to

---

1. Petroleum coke is the last product resulting from the petroleum refining process after all the higher-grade fuels and chemicals are taken off. Before the coke is suitable for use in the aluminum smelting process, it must go through a calcining process which removes the impurities in the coke.

seek an alternative source of supply for a substantial portion of its petroleum coke requirements.

Canada Coke, Ltd.

AMAL management decided in late 1973 to procure their petroleum coke from Canada and had entered into a venture with British Columbia Aluminum, Ltd. (BCA, Ltd.) to construct a petroleum coke processing facility near the petroleum refineries in Edmonton, Alberta. Canada Coke, Ltd. was formed as a wholly owned Canadian subsidiary to carry out the details of the venture with BCA, Ltd. Canada Coke was a corporate façade or "non-firm" in the sense that no management personnel were employed by Canada Coke, Ltd. in Canada. All

Exhibit 2

Corporate Ownership Structure: American Aluminum Corporation

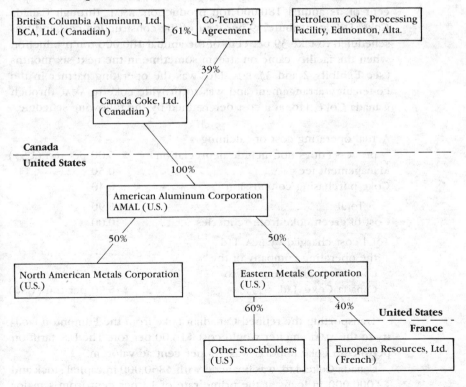

managerial decisions involving Canada Coke, Ltd. were made by AMAL personnel in the United States.

Hall found the nature of the agreement between AMAL's Canada Coke, Ltd. and BCA, Ltd. interesting because it did not seem to fit into any of the familiar categories (wholly owned subsidiary, joint venture, licensing arrangement, etc.) he had studied in his MBA program. AMAL (through Canada Coke, Ltd.) and BCA, Ltd. shared the output of the newly constructed petroleum coke processing facility proportional to the contribution each partner made to financing the construction of the facility. The arrangement was in many ways similar to a joint venture between AMAL and BCA, Ltd., but was in fact called a "co-tenancy" agreement. The petroleum coke producing facility had no separate legal identity and the co-tenancy form allowed each of the participating companies to write down their respective shares in the assets at different depreciation schedules. AMAL had decided to write down its share in the new facility using the straight-line method of depreciation over a twenty-year period.

BCA, Ltd. contributed 61 per cent of the cost of constructing the petroleum coke processing facility and was scheduled to take 61 per cent of its annual 180,000 ton production. AMAL, through Canada Coke, Ltd., contribute 39 per cent of the construction cost and was scheduled to take 39 per cent of the annual 180,000 ton production when the facility came on-stream sometime in the next six months (see Exhibits 2 and 3). BCA, Ltd. was the operating partner in the co-tenancy arrangement and was to provide coke to AMAL through Canada Coke, Ltd. at a cost determined by the following schedule:

Actual operating cost of calcining process (does not include depreciation) .	$ 5.00 per ton (US$)
Management fee	0.50
Coke purchasing commission	0.40
Total	5.90
Cost of green coke from refineries	40.00
Total cost charged by BCA, Ltd., the operating company of the co-tenancy arrangement, to Canada Coke, Ltd.	$45.90 per ton (US$)

Transporting the refined Canadian coke from the Edmonton facility to the AMAL smelter would cost $13.00 per ton. The U.S. tariff on petroleum coke imports was 7.5 per cent ad valorem.

Canada Coke, Ltd. was financed with $850,000 in capital stock and $2,000,000 in loans at the prime rate of 12 per cent from a major

Exhibit 3

Flow of Petroleum Coke from Edmonton

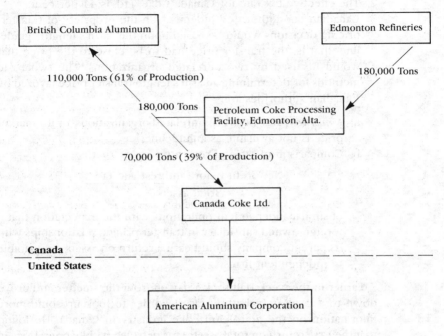

Canadian bank; that is, AMAL's 39 per cent participation in the Edmonton coke facility was through Canada Coke, Ltd. in the amount of $2,850,000.

The Transfer-Pricing Decision

The decision to go to Canada in this particular arrangement had been put into motion before Hall had joined AMAL. What remained for Hall to decide was the price at which Canada Coke, Ltd. sold its 39 per cent share of the petroleum coke output from the calcining facility to AMAL. Since Canada Coke, Ltd.'s profits, and hence Canadian income tax liability, were dependent almost entirely on this transfer price, Hall saw the need to proceed carefully, lest AMAL run afoul of Canadian (let alone U.S.) income tax authorities. Therefore he sought the assistance of tax lawyers on the corporate staff. Summarized, this assistance told Hall the following:

1. Since AMAL is a subsidiary of two large, complex U.S. corporations, the tax rates of the parent corporations must be taken into ac-

count when calculating AMAL's effective tax rate. The effective
rate of U.S. income tax turns out to be in the 30-35 per cent range.

2. The effective tax rate for Canada Coke, Ltd. is 41 per cent.

3. Canadian tax authorities' judgment on the propriety of transfer-
pricing decisions would be based upon the "arm's length" guideline, that is, the transfer price had to be close to the price that
would be used by two unrelated organizations. The two basic
methods for determining an arm's length transfer price favored by
Canadian authorities are:

a. A *market* price between unrelated organizations, or if a market
price is not available as a guideline;

b. Comparison of rates of return on assets, that is,

$$RTA = \frac{\text{Net profit before interest and tax}}{\text{Total assets}}$$

of similar independent operations with the expectation that a
foreign-owned subsidiary in transfer-pricing relationships with
its parent company should earn a return on assets comparable
to independent firms.

Earlier in the week Hall took a day off from the smelter and drove
down to a large university library in order to look up some more
information on the petroleum coke industry in Canada. He found
that the RTA (return on total assets) for petroleum coke operations in
Canada averaged a surprisingly low 5-6 per cent. Later he verified
this figure by telephone with the Canadian consulate nearest AMAL's
smelter. He also found that to the best of his and the consulate's
knowledge there was no market price for petroleum coke in western
Canada, because there were no sales of petroleum coke between
independent companies in western Canada.

It was Friday morning, the weather was promising, and Hall was
looking forward to a good relaxing weekend. But the weekend
would be all the more relaxing if in the next couple of hours he
could make the decisions on the BCA, Ltd. offer and Canada Coke, Ltd.
transfer price, write the two-page justification for his decisions, and
wrap up these two problems before leaving for the weekend.

Case K
C. H. Masden Company Limited*

C. H. Masden Company Ltd. is a large Canadian multinational company specializing in the manufacture of farm machinery and motorized domestic gardening implements. In addition to its Canadian operations, the company has wholly owned manufacturing subsidiaries in the United States, the United Kingdom, West Germany, France, Spain, Zambia, South Africa, Argentina, Mexico, Japan, and Australia. Worldwide sales in 1980 totalled nearly $1 billion. Fifty-five per cent of the company's sales and 61 per cent of its profits were derived from its international operations.

The subsidiaries operate with a considerable amount of autonomy, within broad guidelines set by the parent company. The subsidiaries were created mainly to serve the markets in which they are located. They are, however, free to compete elsewhere, and most have substantial export sales to neighbouring countries. There is also an active trade in sub-assemblies and parts between sister subsidiaries of the Masden group. Materials used in the manufacturing process are purchased from a variety of domestic and imported sources, including the Canadian parent and sister affiliates.

Subsidiaries are financed initially by equity investment from the parent company, combined with long-term local currency borrowing. Corporate guidelines prescribe that subsequent growth be financed from retained earnings. However, when local credit conditions are restrictive or unstable, or when a subsidiary has extraordinary financing needs, it is not uncommon for the Canadian parent to extend U.S.-dollar loans or for other subsidiaries to lengthen their payment terms on intercompany accounts. The corporate-wide policy is for each subsidiary to remit 50 per cent of its net earnings annually in dividends to the parent company.

Madeleine Charbonneau, who recently joined the company after receiving an MBA in finance from a leading Canadian business school, will soon be sent to Buenos Aires for a three-year assignment as financial controller for Masden's Argentine subsidiary. The subsidiary has grown rapidly in recent years, selling Masden products both in Argentina and in other member countries of the Latin American Free Trade Area (LAFTA). But Mlle. Charbonneau is aware that Argentina has, for several years, been experiencing 30-40 per cent domestic price inflation, accompanied by several abrupt devaluations in the exchange rate of the Argentinian peso relative to the

* This case was written by Prof. R. W. Wright expressly for this volume.

dollar and other currencies. Although the Argentinian government was struggling to contain inflation and to maintain an orderly exchange rate, rumors were rampant in business and financial circles that further major devaluations of the peso were almost certain to occur.

As she prepared to assume her new responsibilities, Madeleine Charbonneau was preoccupied with some fundamental questions:

1. In the event that another major devaluation of the peso were to occur, what would be the possible effects on the operations and profitability of Masden's Argentinian subsidiary?

2. What possible relevance or consequences could a peso devaluation have for the management and shareholders of the parent company in Canada?